Psychology
A Concise Introduction

2nd Edition

O.J. BEAr

Terry F. Pettijohn, the author of *Psychology: A Concise Introduction, 2nd Edition*, is an associate professor in the Department of Psychology at Ohio State University where he has taught introductory psychology for over a decade. He has twice been a recipient of the University Alumni Award for Distinguished Teaching. He received his Ph.D. in experimental psychology from Bowling Green State University in 1974. His current research interests include the study of social behavior in gerbils and computer-assisted learning. He is a member of the Psychonomic Society, the Animal Behavior Society, the Computers in Psychology Society and the American Psychological Association where he is affiliated with the Division of the Teaching of Psychology.

Psychology
A Concise Introduction

2nd Edition

Terry F. Pettijohn

Ohio State University

DPG

The Dushkin Publishing Group, Inc.

Credits & Acknowledgments

Cover: *Future Therapies*, collage by Frederick Otnes, *Pfizer Annual Report 1984*, reprinted with the kind permission of Pfizer, Inc. p. 5 Arthur Tress—Photo Researchers, Inc. p. 7 Ken Robert Buck–The Picture Cube; Pamela Carley Petersen—DPG. p. 8 Brown Brothers. p. 9 The Bettmann Archive. p. 10 Harvard University Archives; UPI/Bettman Newsphotos. p. 11 The Bettmann Archive; Culver Pictures. p. 14 UPI/Bettmann Newsphotos. p. 16 Baron Hugo Van Lawick (c) National Geographic Society. p. 17 Hays—Monkmeyer Press Photo Service. p. 35 AP/Wide World. p. 36 *The Integrated Mind* by M. S. Gazzaniga and J. E. LeDoux, 1978, New York: Picnum. p. 37 Professor José M. R. Delgado. p. 38 Buchsbaum et. al., University of California, Irvine, CA. p. 39 David Powers—Stock, Boston. p. 45 Enrico Ferorelli/DOT. p. 50 Per Sundstrom—Gamma Liaison. p. 52 "Origin of Form Perception," by R. L. Frantz, 1961, *Scientific American*, *204*, 66–72. p. 53 Jason Laure, 1978—Woodfin Camp & Associates. p. 55 Mr. & Mrs. Daniel Petit; Mr. & Mrs. Richard Yarien. p. 56 Pamela Carley Petersen—DPG. p. 57 (c) Erika Stone, 1985. p. 58 University of Wisconsin Primate Laboratory. p. 59 Leonard Freed (c) Magnum Photo. p. 61 Yves de Braine—Black Star. p. 62 Zimbel—Monkmeyer Press Photo Service. p. 63 Bob Fitch—Black Star. p. 68 UN photo by John Isacc. p. 69 Courtesy A.T.& T. Co. Photo Center. p. 70 UN photo by John Isaac. p. 71 UN photo by F. B. Grunzweig. p. 86 Cheryl Kinne—DPG. p. 88 David H. Wells—The Image Works. p. 89 New School for Social Research, N.Y.; UPI/Bettmann Newsphotos; The Granger Collection. p. 90 Greater Boston Convention & Tourist Bureau. p. 91 State of Minnesota, Department of Economic Development. p. 93 Topham—The Image Works. p. 94 Museum of Modern Art, New York. p. 96 (c) Paul Hughes—Photophile. p. 99 Pamela Carley Petersen—DPG. p. 101 "Pain Mechanisms: A New Theory," by Melzack and Wall, Nov. 1985, *The Journal of Science*, *150*(3699), 975. p. 102 Owen Franken—Stock, Boston. p. 103 Don Hogan Charles—NYT Pictures. p. 107 The New York Times Pictures. p. 108 Florida News Bureau, Department of Commerce, by James Gaines. p. 110 *Biological Psychology*, by D. P. Kimble, 1988, New York: Holt, Rhinehart, and Winston. p. 111 Stanford Sleep Disorder Center. p. 112 *Biological Psychology*, by D. P. Kimble, 1988, New York: Holt, Rhinehart, and Winston. p. 115 Courtesy Detroit Institute of Arts. p. 116 UN photo by Jane Schreibman. p. 117 (c) Frank Siteman—The Picture Cube. p. 118 EPA Documerica. p. 121 Dr. H. W. Leeman and R. W. Frei, 1955, Triangle, *Sandoz Journal of Medical Science*, Vol. II, pp. 119–123. p. 123 Ray Ellis—Photo Researchers. p. 129 Courtesy Dr. B. F. Skinner. p. 131 The Bettmann Archive. p. 132 Pamela Carley Petersen—DPG. p. 133 Elaine Ward. p. 137 George N. Peet—The Picture Cube. p. 138 Teachers College, Columbia University. p. 139 Marineland, Rancho Palos Verdes, CA. p. 140 Will Rapport. p. 141 William S. Sahakian, Ph.D. p. 142 "Pigeon Response Curves," by B. F. Skinner, 1961, *Scientific American*, *205*(5), 96. p. 143 Las Vegas News Bureau. p. 145 John Walter—Miami Herald; David Powers—Stock, Boston. p. 146 UN photo by John Isaac. p. 147 (c) George W. Gardner—The Image Works. p. 149 (c) Three Lions. p. 150 Tom Ballard—EKM-Nepenthe. p. 151 Thomas

continued on page 455

Psychology: A Concise Introduction, 2nd Edition

Printed in the United States of America

Library of Congress Catalog Card Number: 88–51700

International Standard Book Number (ISBN) 0–87967–751–1

First Printing

The Dushkin Publishing Group, Inc., Sluice Dock, Guilford, Connecticut 06437

Preface

"Vigorus writing is concise," counselled William Strunk, Jr. in *The Elements of Style.* "This requires," he went on, "not that the writer make all his sentences short, or that he avoid all detail and treat his subjects only in outline, but that every word tell."

I have strived to maintain the basic conciseness of the first edition and to expand judiciously some topics such as AIDS and human sexuality. In an attempt to provide an even clearer visual organization than before I have added more topic headings. In addition, I have included a significant number of new references and have updated many others.

I have reorganized some topics within chapters as well as chapters within the textbook. For example, chapter 4, "Sensation and Perception" is a combination of two previously separate chapters and has been moved closer to the beginning of the book in response to requests from users of the first edition. I have also combined the "Intelligence" and "Language and Thought" chapters of the first edition into chapter 8 "Language and Intelligence." The total number of chapters is, therefore, now 16 rather than 18. Besides adding a significant unit on human sexuality to chapter 10, "Emotion," I have expanded the coverage of adolescence and adulthood in chapter 3, "Development." In chapter 8, "Language and Intelligence," I have added a discussion of Sternberg's triarchic theory of intelligence. I have included the five factor personality model and the theories of Horney and Eysenck in chapter 11, "Personality." I have added a new section on health psychology to chapter 12, "Stress and Adjustment," including the latest information on Type A behavior pattern. I have moved the topics of social cognition and aggression to chapter 15, "Social Psychology" and I have added a discussion of sports psychology and educational psychology to chapter 16, "Applied Psychology." All references to abnormal behavior are based on the new DSM-III-R.

I believe that psychology is a delicate blend of rigorous science and humanistic perspective. I have tried to balance an intellectual approach to the subject matter with personal anecdotes and examples that I hope will give students an understanding and appreciation of the science of psychology.

As before I have included a number of features in the textbook to help make it an effective learning tool.

CHAPTER OUTLINE   At the beginning of each chapter I provide a brief outline consisting of the major headings in the chapter as a preview for students and to let them know what to expect in the chapter. The Chapter Outline is related to the Chapter Objectives and the Chapter Review, for a complete learning program.

CHAPTER OBJECTIVES The Chapter Objectives provide a guidepost for students to begin their learning of the chapter material. The objectives are always found on the second page of the chapter so students can easily find them and refer to them as they study. The major topics in each chapter are included in the objectives. *Each objective is directly keyed to an item in the chapter review at the end of the chapter.*

INTRODUCTORY PARAGRAPH Each chapter begins with a short paragraph set in italics that provides a glimpse of what the chapter covers. This should be especially useful when students first skim the chapter.

OPENING STORY Each chapter begins with a story of an important research study in psychology. The stories are nontechnical, and read easily. They often raise issues which are discussed in the chapter, and present interesting and useful information for the student which is integrated with the chapter material. One of the goals of the opening story is to motivate the student to understand the topics covered in the chapter.

INTRODUCTORY DEFINITIONAL SECTIONS Following the opining story, each chapter contains a WHAT IS? section. Here the general chapter topics are introduced, and the main concepts are defined. After reading "What is Therapy?" in chapter 14, "Therapy," for example, students know that there are two major forms of therapy for psychological disorders, and learn the names of the major types of each form of therapy. Of course, they then have to read the rest of the chapter to discover the details of the therapies mentioned.

APPLICATION HIGHLIGHTS Most chapters have one or two boxed inserts, which demonstrate how psychological theory can be applied to everyday situations. Applications include topics such as eating disorders, eyewitness testimony, stages of parenthood, television and aggression, jury selection, memory improvement, computers and programmed learning, education and learning disabilities, and stress and performance. Each application ends with several questions that require students to think about the issues raised.

BIOGRAPHICAL HIGHLIGHTS Most chapters have a biographical highlight which presents in-depth information on a psychologist who was instrumental in shaping psychology as we know it today. These biographies make psychology more personal for students, and provide them with knowledge of the important figures in the field such as the historically important psychologists Sigmund Freud, William James, John Watson, and Abraham Maslow and the more contemporary psychologists Elizabeth Loftus, Stanley Milgram, Anne Anastasi, and William Dement.

CHAPTER REVIEW   At the end of each chapter is a review, consisting of a brief summary of the main points in the chapter. Each summary paragraph is keyed to a Chapter Objective found at the beginning of the chapter. For example, in chapter 2, "Biology of Behavior," Objective 2 asks students to identify the parts of a neuron, and in the Chapter Review, number 2 describes the neuron as having a soma, dendrites, and an axon. I regard this a key feature of the text in effectively helping students learn the material by providing immediate specific feedback. One suggestion for effective studying is for students to write out answers to the Chapter Objectives and then check their answers in the Chapter Review.

FIGURES   A purposeful program of illustration was included in making this book. Many of the figures extend the text material by presenting details of research studies, or illustrating theories. This edition has more charts that help summarize key points. The photographs help make the concepts clear to students by presenting examples. Figures are expressly referred to when they contain research data that is important in understanding a concept, and otherwise appear on the same page as the text material. The captions in most cases provide detailed information that expands or supports the text and can be used by students as a quick review.

CROSS REFERENCES   An important feature is the extensive system of cross references used throughout the text to emphasize the importance of the inter-relatedness of principles in psychology.

GLOSSARY   Important terms and concepts are underlined in the text and defined in the glossary at the end of the text. Other important concepts are in italics. In addition, the glossary items for each chapter are included in the corresponding chapter of the *Study Guide* so students have ready access to the definitions when they study.

SUPPLEMENTS   The textbook is the core of a teaching/learning program. Unlike many other text programs, I have written all the supplements in conjunction with the textbook. There is a *Student Study Guide*, which includes both learning and self-testing activities designed to reinforce and extend the material in the textbook. A *Teaching Resource Manual* is available, and contains a variety of aids for teaching including discussion suggestions, classroom activities, audio-visual information and an array of practical tips to improve teaching. The *Testbank* contains a wide array of test items for measuring student accomplishments in learning concepts and principles of psychology. A *Microcomputer Test Program, E-Z Test*, can help teachers prepare tests for students. *Transparency masters* are available to help show the important concepts in the classroom. All these supplements have been carefully coordinated for maximum effectiveness.

FLEXIBILITY

Because this book is concise, teachers of psychology will be able to expand important topics, and assign entire chapters to students. The use of frequent cross-references to other chapters where topics are also discussed makes it easy for students to find related material. Teachers will also be able to use outside readings or short books for discussions of specific topics. One choice might be *Annual Editions: Psychology*, an anthology of current readings in psychology issued in a new edition each spring. Many of the readings parallel discussions in the text, and provide students additional insight into psychology. *Taking Sides: Clashing Views on Controversial Psychological Issues* is another option for those who wish to use a more structured tool to involve students in issues of concern in psychology today. Because of the low price of this textbook, students are able to purchase a supplemental reader along with the textbook for less expense than the typical text alone costs.

ACCURACY, CURRENCY, and RESEARCH

Psychology is an evolving science, and it is important to make sure that students have accurate and current information about the research findings in the field. I have checked and rechecked all of the sources in *Psychology: A Concise Introduction*, 2nd Edition. Many of the references in the book are from the recent decade but the classic theories and historical research are also included for a full picture of psychology. The findings and theories that are discussed in the book have all been derived from important research studies and are documented according to standard practice. Students can easily find a particular citation in the References section.

APPLICATION

Memorizing numerous theories and definitions helps students little unless they can use the theories and definitions to better understand people and their behavior. I have tried to help students appreciate the importance of the information gained from psychological research by showing them how it is applied to everyday situations by use of the application inserts in each chapter. But in many other places in the book I have included sections on practical applications. For example, in chapter 6, "Learning," special in-text sections explain applications of operant and classical conditioning. Time and stress management techniques are discussed in chapter 12, "Stress and Adjustment." Procedures for applying for a position in business are discussed in chapter 16, "Applied Psychology." Each chapter presents the basic theoretical background of the important topics in psychology, and also shows how these principles are applied to everyday life.

RELEVANCE and CHALLENGE   Students do better when they can relate topics they are studying to their personal lives. I have attempted to help students feel that the information presented is personal and relevant to each of them. Thus I have provided a variety of situations in which students are challenged to think about the issues. The application inserts in each chapter have explicit questions, and throughout the text, issues are raised in which students evaluate their own beliefs and feelings.

ORGANIZATION   The organization of *Psychology: A Concise Introduction*, 2nd Edition is traditional. Part 1, Foundations, presents the basic foundations for studying psychology, including history and methods, and the topics of biology and human development. In Part 2 Perceptual Processes, the areas of sensation, perception, and consciousness are reviewed. In part 3, Learning and Cognitive Processes, students learn about learning, memory, language, thinking and intelligence. In Part 4, Motivation and Emotion, students are presented with the theories and research findings of motivation and emotion. In Part 5, Personality and Adjustment, personality assessment and theories are presented, along with material on stress and adjustment. Part 6, Abnormal Disorders and Therapy, covers the area of abnormal psychology and therapy. And Part 7, Social Processes, examines social psychology and applied psychology.

Writing a textbook takes much more of just about everything than I ever imagined. Two years ago the first edition was published. Now, I have completed the second edition, which I believe is much improved over the first edition, and combines all of the elements of a successful teaching program for the instructor. I am very proud of the finished product, and hope that you find it extremely useful, relevant, challenging, exciting, and informative. I love teaching psychology and have attempted to convey my enthusiasm for the subject here.

ACKNOWLEDGMENTS   Although only one name appears on the cover, many individuals have contributed in countless ways to the text. A number of psychologists and teachers reviewed the book at various stages in the writing process. I am particularly fortunate to have colleagues around the nation who spent hours reading parts of chapters or the entire book at various times during the project.

I wish to thank the following psychologists and instructors whose ideas and suggestions were extremely valuable in guiding my writing and revising efforts: John Broida, University of Southern Maine; Robert Bruel, Kean College of New Jersey; Edward Caldwell, West Virginia University; Ernest Chavez, Colorado State University; Dan Christie, Ohio State University; Michael Compton, University of Hawaii; Christopher Cozby, California State University-Fullerton; Gary Dunbar, Central Michigan University; Thomas Eckle, Modesto Junior College;

Robert Gordon, Ohio State University; Marge Hazelett, Ohio State University; W. Richard Krall, South Central Community College; James Lamiell, Georgetown University; Richard McCrady, New Mexico State University; Marilyn Milligan, Santa Rosa Junior College; Alicia O'Neill, Monterey Peninsula College; Chris Paterson, University of Miami; Mary Helen Spear, Prince George's Community College; Sara Staats, Ohio State University; Larry Vandervert, Spokane Falls Community College; Gary Verett, Richland College; and David Wolfe, Ocean County College.

Students, of course, are extremely important in the final evaluation of a textbook, and during the writing and revising of this book, many students helped review, critique, and proofread sections. Over 300 students provided in-depth critiques of each chapter of the book. Those who contributed significantly to the project include Mary Trimner, Craig Philips, Susie Sobas, Juli Swartz, Roger Wren, Linda Banks, Meg Hiss, Joan Jernigan, Gretch Walker, Ed Shirley, Pat Ellefson, Tina Thompson, Kathy Barkley, Ray Coleman, Debbie Monroe, Glenn Mc-Cleese, John Matthews, and Susan Matthews.

The people at Dushkin Publishing Group have been outstanding, and I want to thank them all for their support and guidance. Their advice always turned out to be sound, and greatly enhanced the effectiveness of the book. Especially important in ensuring an excellent product are publisher Rick Connelly and managing editor John Holland.

In the first edition I acknowledged the sterling efforts of Michael Werthman in preparing my manuscript. In this edition I wish to give special credit to Marcuss Oslander for her valuable criticism and excellent editing skills. She went out of her way to ensure a quality text, and her effort is greatly appreciated. I would like to thank my family, whose patience, support, help, feedback, and understanding have all been extremely valuable through the entire process. Now I can finally tell them that I am doing something other than "revising my book."

Terry F. Pettijohn

Contents in Brief

Table of Contents

Contents

PART VI Abnormal Disorders and Therapy   **300**

PART VII Social Processes   **342**

Applications and Biographical Highlights

To the Student

AN INVITATION TO PSYCHOLOGY

Psychology is an exciting field that will contribute much to your life. This book serves as an integral part of your course in psychology. It will help you in numerous ways during the course and afterwards. A little effort on your part in noting the format and goals of the textbook, and the suggested study procedures will pay off in an increased understanding of psychology (and in a better course grade).

As you read the textbook, you will learn about many facts, theories, and applications of psychological information that will give you a working knowledge of what psychology is all about. Many of these concepts are interrelated and you will learn to identify the principles of psychology every day of your life.

You will also gain a better understanding of your own behavior and the behavior of those around you. You will better understand the motives, personality, social interactions, and biological forces on behavior. This will help you make better decisions concerning what *you* want to do and why other people behave as they do. Ultimately this should result in increased happiness and successful adjustment for you.

I think psychology is the most exciting discipline, in part because it is an ongoing activity. We don't have all of the answers, and current research continuously provides new information, as evidenced by the large number of references from the 1980s. I really hope you enjoy the book, and that it helps you better understand psychologists, psychological research, and of course, yourself.

HOW TO STUDY FROM *PSYCHOLOGY: A CONCISE INTRODUCTION*

Learning is a complex adventure that involves a variety of approaches. You will learn much in the classroom as well as from reading and studying the book. There are some procedures that help enhance your learning from your book.

In chapter 7, "Human Memory," we discuss the SQ3R study technique. This procedure requires that you survey a chapter, ask questions, read carefully, recite to ensure understanding, and then review what you have learned. This is an excellent study procedure, and is explained in more detail in the *Study Guide*.

Psychology: A Concise Introduction, 2nd Edition has been designed so you can effectively learn from it. It has a number of important characteristics that help guide you through the learning process. For every chapter you study, there are several steps you should take to enhance your learning:

1. SURVEY the chapter. Examine the brief outline at the beginning of the chapter, read the introductory paragraph, quickly read the introductory story, and then skim the rest of the chapter, noting the major headings and points of interest. This skimming is designed not to provide details, but rather to give you an overall picture or preview of what you will be covering.

2. QUESTION what you will be learning. A unique feature of the book is the incorporation of the Chapter Objectives at the beginning of the chapter. Use these to develop questions about important material in the chapter. You will notice that each objective corresponds to a major section of the textbook, usually identified with a heading. In addition, the book has been constructed so that each Chapter Objective is discussed in the Chapter Review at the end of the chapter. Take the objectives and turn them into questions as you read the chapter.

3. READ the entire chapter carefully, trying to identify the main ideas and important details in each section. Note that there are usually 3 to 5 main sections, with several detailed sections under each main section. You might want to read only one section before you stop and review what you have learned. But carefully read each section, as well as the special boxed inserts that provide insight into how psychology is applied to everday life. Take time to think about how you feel about the issues raised in the chapter. The important point in reading is that you learn and understand the information being presented.

4. RECITE What you have learned by returning to the Chapter Objectives and writing a very brief response to each objective, then check your responses with the corresponding items in the Chapter

Review. You might orally give your responses, but only if you really write them, can you be absolutely sure you actually have learned the material. If you have problems, you can at this time go back to the section in the book and study the material again until you do learn. Also, using the *Study Guide* at this time will help ensure that you master the main ideas and important details. You should also look at the underlined terms in each chapter and see if you can briefly write definitions, which can be checked for accuracy with the glossary.

5. REVIEW what you have learned by quickly going back over the outline, Chapter Objectives, and Chapter Review. Check to make sure everything makes sense to you, and you have no questions. Review is a step that you should do periodically to make sure you don't forget anything. Again the *Study Guide* will help you review the important information, and should be used on a regular basis.

The *Study Guide* is an integral part of your study program, and should be incorporated into the process as much as possible. After you read the textbook is the ideal time to recite and review with the *Study Guide*. This will alow you to review the major concepts presented in the chapter, study the relevant theories of psychology, and evaluate your knowledge of the material through practice tests.

For each chapter in the textbook, the *Study Guide* has a number of important features. There is a CHAPTER PRETEST to allow you to discover whether there are any overall weaknesses in your understanding of the material. The REVIEW ACTIVITIES are designed to help you master the concepts, and include working with the special features, such as the Applications and Biographical Highlights, as well as a Programmed Review of the main ideas in the chapter. As you are studying the textbook, you should use the glossary included in the *Study Guide*. The CHAPTER OBJECTIVES REVIEW provides an opportunity to check your general understanding of the key concepts in the chapter. The CHAPTER OBJECTIVE EXERCISES are designed to generate critical thinking of the applications and implications of the principles of psychology. The CHAPTER POSTTEST gives you one last chance to assess your readiness for a test. And for those who wish to go beyond the normal expectations, the USEFUL READINGS provide suggestions for studying topics in more depth. The CHALLENGE ACTIVITIES provide enriching experiences that should help you critically evaluate general psychological concepts. I designed and wrote the *Study Guide* to make sure it enhanced your learning experience. If you follow the study procedure outlined above you should have no difficulty learning the material of introductory psychology.

AFTER FINISHING THIS COURSE YOU SHOULD BE ABLE TO:

Discuss psychology as a science that approaches the study of human behavior in a systematic manner.

Describe how growth and development affect attitudes and personality.

List the bodily senses and show how they affect perception.

Identify the processes by which we learn skills and information.

Describe the importance of memory in attaining both short-term and long-term goals.

Define the various drives and needs that motivate us to behave.

Discuss the theories of personality that help us understand who we are.

Identify the causes of stress and learn how to adjust to them.

Outline the nature and causes of abnormal behavior.

Describe the various methods of treating psychological problems.

List how psychological research and principles can be applied in everyday life.

Finally, I hope you will share my enthusiasm for and enjoyment of the study of behavior and cognition. Good luck in your exciting learning adventure.

Terry F. Pettijohn

Psychology
A Concise Introduction

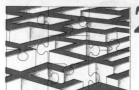

2nd
Edition

FOUNDATIONS

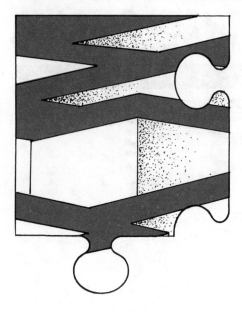

Part I provides the groundwork for understanding the science of behavior and cognition. In this section, the research methods used by psychologists, biological influences on behavior, and life-span human development are discussed.

After reading Part I you should be able to:

Define the science of psychology

Describe the different methods of psychological research

Compare different methods of statistical measurement

Describe the anatomy and functioning of the nervous system

Understand the influence of heredity on behavior

Describe the stages of human development

Identify the important theories of development

Chapter 1   The Study of Psychology

Although barely a century old as a formal discipline, the study of psychology has revolutionized how we look at ourselves. While psychologists are involved in a broad range of specialties, they share the common goal of understanding behavior. To accomplish this, psychologists use a variety of scientific research methods and measurement techniques.

Chapter 2   Biology of Behavior

In order to fully understand human behavior, we need to know something about the biological influences on people. Biological psychologists study the endocrine system and the nervous system and pay special attention to the functioning of the brain. Also of great interest to psychologists is how heredity and environment interact to produce the development of behavior.

Chapter 3   Development

The study of human development covers the entire lifespan from conception through infancy, childhood, adolescence, and adulthood, ultimately ending with death. Developmental psychologists are interested in changes in the physical, cognitive, and social aspects of behavior over time.

THE STUDY OF PSYCHOLOGY

Although barely a century old as a formal discipline, the study of psychology has revolutionized how we look at ourselves. While psychologists are involved in a broad range of specialties, they share the common goal of understanding behavior. To accomplish this, psychologists use a variety of scientific research methods and measurement techniques.

What would you do if you heard screams while walking to class? Would your first inclination be to stop and help or to keep going? Social psychologist Bibb Latané noted that people don't always help in emergency situations. He and his colleagues conducted scientific studies of the conditions under which people do not help others. *The Unresponsive Bystander* (1970) describes his experiments on helping behavior.

Subjects for one experiment conducted by Latané and Judith Rodin were 120 male students from Columbia University who were told they were participating in a survey on adult games and puzzles for a consumer testing bureau. When a subject arrived for the experiment, he was met by an attractive young woman who took him to a testing room. She explained the questionnaire and then went to her office, which was connected to the testing room by an unlocked sliding door.

Four minutes after the young woman left the testing room, the subject heard what sounded like an accident. The subject heard her climb up on a chair to reach a book on the top shelf. Then she apparently fell off, the chair crashing on top of her. "Oh, my foot. I can't move it. I can't get this off me," she screamed. Then she moaned a bit before becoming quiet.

Clearly, this appeared to be an emergency situation. Latané staged the "accident" and used a scientific approach to study helping behavior. He recorded whether or not the subject tried to help the victim and, if he did, how long it took the subject to take action. The sounds of the accident were prerecorded, so each subject would hear exactly the same thing. The subject's response and the length of time it took him to make the response were behaviors that could be easily observed and recorded.

There were four experimental conditions in the study. Some subjects were tested when they were alone, while others were tested with one other person. The other person was either a friend or a stranger (either a naive stranger, that is, someone who knew nothing about the experiment, or one who was actually working with Latané). Thus the four conditions were: the subject alone, the subject with a friend, the subject with a stranger, or the subject with a confederate of the experimenter.

Would you help out if you were in this situation? Latané found that it would likely depend on whether you were alone or with others. Of those subjects who were tested alone, 70% helped. When two friends were tested together, at least one person helped 70% of the time. When two strangers were tested together, at least one person helped in 40% of the pairs. But when paired with a confederate of the experimenter, who passively ignored the accident, only 7% of the subjects offered assistance.

What would your exact response be if you wanted to help? Latané found overall that 61% of the subjects who helped opened the sliding door and went into the office. In addition, of those who helped, 24% called out to get someone's attention, and 14% went around to the main door of the office. The vast majority of subjects (90%) who actually did help did so within the first minute.

From this and other experiments like it, psychologists have concluded that a bystander is more likely to help in an emergency when no other bystanders are present. The more bystanders there are, the less likely is each

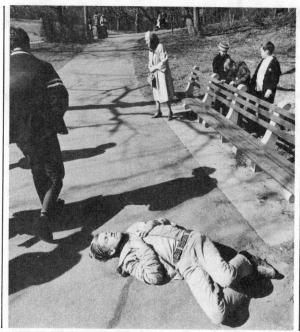

Figure 1.1. Helping Behavior
While many people are quick to help others in an emergency situation, others are not. Social psychologists such as Bibb Latané study the factors that explain when people are likely to help. These include the ability of the bystander to determine a real emergency and the likelihood of responding if that bystander is alone or with someone else.

person to help. This finding, called the *diffusion of responsibility*, provides some clues that might be used to increase helping behavior in people. Bibb Latané has researched helping behavior extensively. Diffusion of responsibility is discussed further in chapter 15, "Social Psychology."

CHAPTER OBJECTIVES
What You'll Learn About the Study of Psychology

After studying this chapter, you should be able to:

1. Define psychology.
2. Identify the four basic goals of psychology.
3. Outline the five major schools of thought which developed into modern psychology.
4. List five major subfields of psychology (what psychologists do).
5. Outline the scientific method used by psychology researchers.
6. Describe the naturalistic observation research method.
7. Describe the interview research method.
8. Describe the survey research method.
9. Describe the test research method.
10. Describe the case study research method.
11. Describe the experimental research method and identify research designs used to control potential sources of error.
12. Describe the correlation research technique.
13. Identify the code of ethics to which psychologists adhere when using research subjects.
14. Define the measurement concepts of validity and reliability.
15. Describe the procedures used in descriptive statistics (central tendency, variability).
16. Identify the concepts in inferential statistics (generalization, probability, and significance).

WHAT IS PSYCHOLOGY?

Latané's experiment described in the introductory story typifies the scientific approach in psychology. Rather than just casually noting that helping seems to be inhibited when others are present, he investigated the problem in a series of scientific experiments that spanned a decade. The scientific approach in the study of behavior is an important characteristic of psychology.

Psychology is the science of behavior and cognition. Behavior is generally defined as anything you do, especially if it is observable to others. Psychologists emphasize the study of behavior because it can be observed and recorded. Many behaviors, such as eating, talking, writing, running, or fighting, are easily observable.

Cognition includes mental processes like dreaming, thinking, remembering, or solving problems. These cognitive activities are usually not directly observable, and are often studied through self-reports provided by research subjects. Cognitive behavior is now usually included in the general concept of behavior.

Another area of scientific study is the biological, or physiological processes that often accompany both behavior and cognition. Brain wave activity during dreaming or thinking, heart rate during strong emotion or fighting, or blood chemistry changes during eating are examples of physiological processes.

While some psychologists may focus on one area, many study psychology from all three perspectives. Since the behavioral, cognitive, and physiological processes are usually interconnected, many psychologists include all three when they discuss the concept of behavior. Here behavior includes observable actions, cognitive activities, and their physiological processes.

Psychology is a fascinating discipline that touches every aspect of our life. Over the last century it has evolved from a fairly narrow field that emphasized immediate experience into a diverse discipline with a variety of goals and procedures. As you explore the science of behavior, you should develop a better understanding of why people do the things they do.

THE GOALS OF PSYCHOLOGY

As stated earlier, psychology is defined as the science of behavior and cognition. As a science, psychology shares goals and scientific methods with other sciences, such as biology, chemistry, sociology, and anthropology. Scientists begin with a body of knowledge and then proceed systematically to investigate a topic to add to that body of knowledge. Scientists use a variety of research methods, including observation, survey, test and experiment. These research methods allow scientists to reach the goals of description, prediction, control and explanation. The ultimate aim for psychologists is to understand behavior and help people.

As an example of this aim, many clinical and counseling psychologists are involved in helping people with personal and emotional problems. Others, called experimental psychologists, are engaged in research to discover the basic principles of behavior, using a wide variety of subjects: monkeys, rats, children, and very often students. Still other psychologists are busy applying research findings to people's everyday problems. Consumer psychologists study purchasing behavior, including what type of advertisements influence people most. Educational psychologists help make teaching in the classroom more effective. And social psychologists are involved in reducing prejudice and aggression.

Most psychologists try to understand and help people. Yet some experimental psychologists (called comparative psychologists) study and often compare the behavior of animals, including fruit flies, rats and monkeys. Why? Animal research can suggest new techniques for helping people. For example, behavior modification techniques which are discussed in chapter 6, "Learning," are currently used in schools and mental hospitals but were first developed in animal studies. And producing what looks like helplessness in dogs, discussed in chapter 12, "Stress and Adjustment," has led to recent therapies for relieving depression in humans. Often animals are substituted for humans in dangerous experiments, such as testing a new drug or depriving a subject of sensory stimulation. While some psychologists hope the results of animal behavior research will directly generalize to human experience, others study animals solely to provide additional information about the behavior of animals.

Psychology seeks to understand behavior through meeting four basic goals: *description, prediction, control,* and *explanation.*

Description is important in any science. It helps psychologists understand basic patterns of behavior. Description of behavior allows them to develop theories, or assumptions, about the behavior. It also helps to fill in the gaps of what we know about behavior. Child development, discussed in chapter 3, "Development," is an area of psychology that describes the stages of motor development in babies and has enabled psychologists to formulate a theory of normal motor development. This helps people identify possible problems in babies who do not develop in the normal sequence.

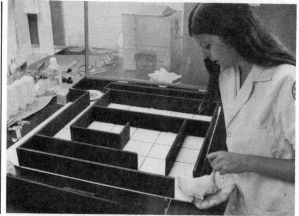

Figure 1.2. Animals in Behavioral Research
Comparative psychologists study the behavior of animals to learn more about basic psychological processes such as learning, perception, and motivation. The study of animal behavior helps us better understand the general principles of human behavior and may suggest practical solutions to problems where they exist.

Psychologists often make predictions about behavior; these are based on the descriptions they have obtained. For example, psychologists have described many situations where people exhibit certain behaviors in order to have something pleasant occur. These pleasant occurrences can be called rewards or reinforcements (and are discussed in chapter 6, "Learning"). After observing that reinforcements encourage people to modify their behavior, you might develop a theory predicting that people will increase a particular behavior if rewarded. Then you could test this prediction by making further observations. As an example, you might find that when you smile, people are nice to you. You could then predict that if you smiled more, more people would be nicer. You could easily test your prediction by keeping a record of your observations.

After psychologists verify predictions, to a certain extent, they can control behavior. Once you conclude that the frequency of a given behavior increases after a reward, you are in a position to control (modify) behavior by giving or withholding rewards. For example, you could control the frequency with which your dog sits up and begs by offering dog biscuits as a reward. When you stop giving biscuits, the dog will probably decrease begging behavior.

People sometimes have a difficult time understanding the issue of control. They mistakenly think that psychologists want to control millions of people with secret "mind-bending" techniques. Actually, you are controlled by others and you control others all the time, each and every day. Remember the person who smiled at you yesterday? What did you do in return? Very likely, you smiled back. That was control. When you place an order in a restaurant, you are controlling another person. Psychologists are interested in learning about control so that they can help people gain control over their own actions. For instance, psychology may be able to help you overcome your shyness (discussed in chapter 14, "Stress and Adjustment") so you will gain enough confidence to be in control of a situation.

The fourth goal of psychology is explanation. By describing, predicting, and controlling behavior, we gain insight into the forces that motivate people. Then we can begin to explain why people engage in various behaviors. For example, hunger has been explained as motivated behavior in some studies that are discussed in chapter 9, "Motivation." The conditions that cause and alleviate hunger are described as well as the behaviors that control it. You feel hungry both because your body needs food for energy and because you have learned to eat at certain times of the day.

Figure 1.3. Goals of Psychology
Psychologists are interested in describing, predicting, controlling, and explaining behavior. A familiar social activity is sitting down to dinner with one's family. This common ritual raises many questions of interest to the psychologist. For example: What motivates people to eat? Does eating with others cause people to eat faster than eating alone? How can parents encourage children to eat properly? Will people act more politely if they have more time to eat?

THE DEVELOPMENT OF PSYCHOLOGY AS A SCIENCE

People have always been interested in the behavior of other people. We can trace some of the philosophical ideas in psychology back to the early Greeks. For example, Aristotle and Plato debated whether human ideas are *innate* or need to be experienced. Philosophers have always been interested in the nature of people. In the seventeenth century, the British philosopher John Locke described the human mind as a blank slate (*tabula rasa*) upon which could be written all of life's experiences.

Other influences on early psychology came from biology and physics. Charles Darwin was a naturalist whose observations while on a worldwide voyage were published in his 1859 book, *The Origin of Species*, which also outlines his theory of evolution. Darwin's influence on psychology included both his method of naturalistic observation of behavior and his theory of evolution. In his theory of evolution, Darwin suggested that animals and people show behavior that is adaptive to the environment and that helps them to survive.

A year after Darwin's book, Gustav Fechner published *Elements of Psychophysics*, in which he outlined his experimental method of measuring sensory experience. Fechner would produce a tone on a metronome and determine if his subject could hear it. By manipulating the conditions of the situation, he was able to examine the relationship between the physical stimulus and sensory experience. His experimental approach was important for the new science of behavior.

These early developments finally led to what is now known as psychology. The formal history of psychology can be best described by the "schools of thought" which guided psychologists in their actions. There are five major historical schools that we discuss: structuralism, functionalism, behaviorism, Gestalt psychology, and psychoanalysis.

Structuralism

The science of psychology had its formal beginning in 1879 when Wilhelm Wundt, a German physiologist, set up a laboratory at the University of Leipzig to study consciousness.

The school of thought associated with Wundt and his student E. B. Titchener is called structuralism or the science of the structure of the mind. He studied the

Figure 1.4. E. B. Titchener
Edward Titchener (1867–1927), a British psychologist who studied under Wilhelm Wundt, came to the United States in 1892 to help promote structuralism. Titchener defined psychology as the study of the human normal, adult mind. His empirical approach to psychology was important to the new science.

conscious experience of the mind through introspection. Introspection was a method in which specially trained subjects reflected on their immediate experience of some stimulus. First they would be shown an apple. What would come to mind? Red, round, shiny, slender green rod on top, brown spot, small. Next the subjects might be shown a peach or a pear, and the procedure would be repeated.

Through careful recording of immediate conscious experience, Wundt believed he could discover the structure of the elements of mental life. While his definition of psychology did not survive, Wundt's important contribution to the field was his strict reliance on a systematic method of research in his efforts to determine the structure of the mind.

An American, G. Stanley Hall (1884–1924) also studied under Wundt. Hall was an active psychologist, and among his many accomplishments were establishing the American Psychological Association in 1892 and the first American psychology journal, *The American Journal of Psychology*, in 1915. He was especially interested in psychological development, and published research on childhood, adolescence, and aging.

Functionalism

If you think structuralism doesn't sound much like modern psychology, you're right. Many people didn't see the relevance of studying the elements of the mind.

One of these people was William James. In 1890 he published *Principles of Psychology*, in which he expressed his ideas of what psychology should be.

William James was the first American-born psychologist. He was greatly influenced by Darwin's work on evolution and believed that psychology should explain the function of consciousness as it influences behavior.

The ideas of William James paved the way for the school of <u>functionalism</u>, which described psychology as the study of the adaptive properties of consciousness and behavior. Important functionalists included John Dewey (1859–1952) and James Angell (1869–1949) from the University of Chicago, and Edward Thorndike (1874–1949) and Robert Woodworth (1869–1962) from Columbia University. Dewey's 1896 paper on the reflex arc is often considered to be the formal beginning of the functional school of psychology. The concept of the reflex arc was also considered a unifying principle of psychology because as the complete nervous path that is involved in a reflex, it unified the mind and body. Thorndike's 1898 book, *Animal Intelligence*, is also considered a major work in this approach.

Functionalists not only used introspection to study behavior, but also used tests, surveys, and experimental techniques (Benjamin, 1988). In studying children and animals as well as adults, the key question they asked was, "What function does the specific behavior have?" The school of functionalism studied topics such as thinking, memory, consciousness, animal intelligence, learning, and motivation.

Figure 1.5. John Dewey
John Dewey (1859–1952) greatly influenced American thinking as an educator, philosopher, and psychologist. While at the University of Chicago, he argued that psychology needed a unifying principle. Dewey believed that behavior and consciousness could not be studied as separate entities, but should be understood in terms of the individual's adaptation to the environment. This approach to psychology became known as functionalism. Dewey later made significant contributions to education.

BIOGRAPHICAL ☆ HIGHLIGHT ☆

WILHELM WUNDT

Wilhelm Wundt, the son of a Lutheran clergyman, was born in 1832 in a small German village called Nekarau. He was a solitary child who shunned the games of children in favor of books and study.

At 19, Wundt decided to study medicine, most likely as a means of entering a scientific career. His attention shifted to physiology, the field in which he lectured widely and published a number of articles during the years following his graduation. Psychology was just beginning to emerge as a distinct science, and much of Wundt's work anticipated the value of physiological methodology in dealing with psychological problems.

In 1879, at the University of Leipzig, Wundt established the first psychology laboratory. Here, he concentrated almost exclusively on psychological research, particularly on the study of human sensory experience—research that had previously belonged to the realm of physiology and philosophy. Wundt's use of a systematic methodological approach in tackling psychological problems was a landmark in establishing psychology as a science.

Wundt pursued his work with the boundless energy and enthusiasm of a man half his age up until the time of his death near Leipzig, two weeks after his 88th birthday in 1920.

Figure 1.6. William James
While he believed that a goal of psychology was the study of consciousness, William James (1842–1910) rejected the notion that this could be accomplished by structuralism's attempts to reduce the mind to elements. He regarded consciousness as an ongoing process in continuous interaction with the environment. In addition to consciousness, his numerous interests included the learning of habits, the development of emotions, the awareness of self, and religion. James was the first to set up a laboratory in 1875 at Harvard University to demonstrate psychological principles to his students.

Figure 1.7. Important Dates in Psychology

1859	Darwin publishes *Origin of Species*
1860	Fechner publishes *Elements of Psychophysics*
1879	Wundt sets up psychology lab; structuralism
1885	Ebbinghaus publishes *On Memory*
1890	James publishes *Principles of Psychology*
1892	Hall founds American Psychological Association
1896	Dewey publishes paper on reflex arc concept; functionalism
1898	Thorndike publishes *Animal Intelligence*
1900	Freud publishes *The Interpretation of Dreams*; psychoanalysis
1905	Binet and Simon publish first intelligence test
1912	Wertheimer publishes paper on Gestalt ideas; Gestalt psychology
1913	Watson publishes paper on behaviorism; behaviorism

Behaviorism

Some psychologists felt that functionalism did not go far enough in getting away from the structural study of the mind. In 1913 another American psychologist, John B. Watson, became the founder of the school of thought called behaviorism. Watson believed that psychology should be the science of overt behavior. He rejected the ideas of introspection and mental processes. Behaviorists concentrated on the objective measurement of observable behavior. They believed that psychology should be a "hard" science, like physics or chemistry.

The early behaviorists went to an extreme with their ideas. They limited psychology to the study of the observable behavioral response given by an organism to a stimulus. For example, a sudden loud noise causes a person to respond by startling—giving a little involuntary jump. The behaviorists believed all behavior was determined by stimuli in the environment.

Psychology is still considered the science of behavior. Of course, the concept of behavior has been broadened to include the unseen cognitive processes, such as thinking, which lead to observable behavior. All psychologists study behavior, not just behaviorists. Since its formation by Watson, the school of behaviorism has been extremely influential in psychology. But other schools of thought helped to broaden its outlook.

Gestalt Psychology

At about the same time that behaviorism was becoming the dominant force in American psychology, another movement was taking place in Germany. The Gestalt school of thought moved away from the analysis of individual elements or parts. It did not accept structural-

Figure 1.8. Max Wertheimer
A founder of Gestalt psychology, Max Wertheimer (1880–1943) began his research in perceptual studies in Germany. He and his colleagues, Wolfgang Köhler and Kurt Koffka, believed that the whole person has to be studied rather than just individual parts in order to gain a complete understanding of human behavior. Wertheimer was also interested in creative thinking and problem solving, especially in educational settings.

ism's goal of studying the parts of the mind or behaviorism's goal of studying parts of behavior.

Max Wertheimer is usually regarded as the leader of the Gestalt school along with Wolfgang Köhler and Kurt Koffka. They believed that people are more than the sum of their parts and that we cannot understand the whole by studying only the parts. The German word gestalt means "whole," and Gestalt psychology's goal was to study the whole person.

The Gestalt school has had its greatest influence in the area of perception. Stop reading for a moment and think about someone you know. Do you think about his or her nose, eyes, each strand of hair, the ears, each separate tooth? Or do you have a complete image of the whole person? The Gestalt psychologists argue that we perceive the entire person and not just parts of the person.

Psychoanalysis

The last major historical influence on psychology was psychoanalysis. At approximately the same time that the behaviorism and Gestalt schools of thought were being formulated, a young Austrian physician named Sigmund Freud was beginning to use hypnosis as a method of treating people with emotional problems.

Freud found that people who were hypnotized were able to recall hidden feelings about others, especially sexual feelings and hostility toward their parents. This led him to formulate his psychoanalytic theory, which

Figure 1.9. Sigmund Freud
An Austrian physician, Sigmund Freud (1856–1939), developed the theory of psychoanalysis to explain personality and to treat people with psychological problems. Although his important book on dreams was published in 1900, he did not make an impact on psychology until the 1930s. Freud wrote on many topics, including personality development, human sexuality, therapy techniques, and adjustment.

concentrates on the unconscious motivations often expressed in dreams or "slips of the tongue" (accidently saying something you don't want to). In other words, Freud believed that past experiences of which a person is unaware significantly influence current behavior.

BIOGRAPHICAL ☆ HIGHLIGHT ☆

JOHN B. WATSON

John B. Watson was born in 1878 in a rural community outside Greenville, South Carolina, where he attended the local country schools near his parents' farm. At 16, he entered Furman University where he earned an M.A. degree.

Watson received his Ph.D. in experimental psychology at the University of Chicago in 1903. His research was on the sensory cues used by rats in learning to run through a maze. He married and remained at Chicago for several years.

In 1908 he began teaching at Johns Hopkins University, where he remained until 1920 when a highly publicized divorce forced him to resign. Watson was the driving force for the school of behaviorism, and his approach can be seen in a popular quote: "Give me a dozen healthy infants, well-formed, and my own specified world to bring them up in and I'll guarantee to take any one at random and train him to become any type of specialist I might select—doctor, lawyer, artist, merchant-chief, and yes, even beggarman and thief, regardless of his talents, penchants, tendencies, abilities, vocations, and race of his ancestors." In 1921 Watson entered the business world and soon became vice president of an advertising agency. He married his former laboratory assistant and continued to write popular articles on psychology for some time. He died in 1958 at the age of 80.

Psychoanalytic theory had its major impact on concepts of personality and on therapy techniques in psychology. It helped broaden the behavioristic notion of psychology to include unconscious motivations as well as observable behavior.

Current Approaches to the Study of Psychology

Today, psychology does not have one strict school of thought. As previously discussed, it has been influenced by a variety of viewpoints and approaches. Psychologists now are most likely to have an eclectic approach to the study of behavior, combining theories and methods from a variety of sources. The current major approaches to the study of psychology include the biological, humanistic, psychoanalytic, cognitive, and behavioral.

The Biological Approach.   Understanding the biological processes that underlie behavior is an important objective in today's psychology. The past several decades have seen an increased emphasis on understanding the function of behavior, as evidenced by behavior genetics studies. The nervous system helps us interpret perceptions, coordinate actions, and store information. There are biological explanations of motivation, personality, social behavior, memory, and abnormal behavior.

The Humanistic Approach.   Some of the ideas of the Gestalt psychologists have come to be represented in what is known as humanistic psychology. These psychologists stress that people are unique and complex organisms and emphasize that each individual person has a capacity to reach his or her maximum potential. Humanistic theories are especially important in the fields of personality, motivation, and psychotherapy.

The Psychoanalytic Approach.   Freud's theory of psychoanalysis has continued to influence the way we think of ourselves. Psychoanalytic theory emphasizes unconscious motivation and the influence of sexual and aggressive drives on behavior. It has its major impact on the areas of personality and abnormal behavior.

The Cognitive Approach.   Cognitive psychology is a rapidly growing approach that includes the study of mental processes, such as thinking, perception, memory, and problem solving. Because of their emphasis on consciousness, the schools of structuralism and psychoanalysis strongly influenced cognitive psychology. Today, cognitive theories are important in virtually every area of psychology.

The Behavioral Approach.   Many of the ideas from the schools of behaviorism and functionalism are evident in the current behavioral approach to understanding why we act as we do. Although many psychologists utilize behavioral theories, today behavior is defined very differently from the way it was originally; it now

Figure 1.10.   Approaches to Psychology

Approach	Goal Is to Understand:
Biological	Biological processes that underlie behavior
Humanistic	Human potential
Psychoanalytic	Unconscious motivation
Cognitive	Mental processes
Behavioral	Fundamental causes of behavior

encompasses cognitive processes like thinking and feeling as well as directly observable behavior.

As we study the findings and applications of today's diverse psychology, keep in mind how psychology as a science has developed from a great variety of methods and approaches.

SUBFIELDS OF PSYCHOLOGY

The question of what psychology is today can also be answered by describing some of the different areas, or *subfields,* of psychology. They best illustrate the diversity that exists within psychology today. The American Psychological Association, the major organization of psychologists in the United States, has 45 divisions, each of which represents a different interest area in psychology.

Clinical Psychology.   "What do you do?" is a commonly asked question. When I respond, "I'm a psychologist," the other person often says, "Oh, I'd better watch what I say or you'll analyze me." This attitude reflects the fact that the largest single group of psychologists (over 40%) is in clinical psychology (Stapp, Tucker, and Vander Bos, 1985). Many clinical psychologists work in institutions that care for and treat people who need help—mental hospitals, homes for the retarded, prisons, mental health clinics, juvenile courts, university health centers, and child guidance clinics. Like medical doctors, some clinicians have private practices and treat persons with abnormal behavior problems. Others may teach in schools and universities. Clinical psychologists evaluate mental and emotional problems, administer and assess personality tests, and treat patients who have behavior problems, using psychological techniques such as psychotherapy. We discuss behavior problems in chapter 13, "Abnormal Behavior," and psychotherapy in chapter 14, "Therapy."

Figure 1.11. Divisions of the APA

1. Division of General Psychology
2. Division of the Teaching of Psychology
3. Division of Experimental Psychology
5. Division on Evaluation and Measurement
6. Division on Physiological and Comparative Psychology
7. Division on Developmental Psychology
8. Division of Personality and Social Psychology
9. The Society for the Psychological Study of Social Issues
10. Division of Psychology and the Arts
12. Division of Clinical Psychology
13. Division of Consulting Psychology
14. Society for Industrial and Organizational Psychology
15. Division of Educational Psychology
16. Division of School Psychology
17. Division of Counseling Psychology
18. Division of Psychologists in Public Service
19. Division of Military Psychology
20. Division of Adult Development and Aging
21. The Society of Engineering and Applied Psychologists
22. Division of Rehabilitation Psychology
23. Division of Consumer Psychology
24. Division of Theoretical and Philosophical Psychology
25. Division for the Experimental Analysis of Behavior
26. Division of the History of Psychology
27. Division of Community Psychology
28. Division of Psychopharmacology
29. Division of Psychotherapy
30. Division of Psychological Hypnosis
31. Division of State Psychological Association Affairs
32. Division of Humanistic Psychology
33. Division of Mental Retardation
34. Division of Population and Environmental Psychology
35. Division of the Psychology of Women
36. Psychologists Interested in Religious Issues
37. Division of Child, Youth, and Family Services
38. Division of Health Psychology
39. Division of Psychoanalysis
40. Division of Clinical Neuropsychology
41. Division of American Psychology—Law Psychology
42. Division of Psychologists in Independent Practice
43. Division of Family Psychology
44. Society for the Psychological Study of Lesbian and Gay Issues
45. Society for the Psychological Study of Ethnic Minority Issues
46. Media Psychology
47. Exercise and Sport Psychology

Note: There is no Division 4 or Division 11.

The American Psychological Association is the major professional organization of psychologists in the United States; its subdivisions indicate the diverse interests of its members.

It is important to distinguish between the clinical psychologist and the psychiatrist. The clinical psychologist obtains a bachelor's degree in psychology, and then goes on to graduate school. After about two years, he or she receives a master's degree in clinical psychology, and after approximately another two or three years of study, is awarded the Ph.D. (doctor of philosophy) degree, the customary degree for psychologists. The clinical psychologist will then spend a year in an internship, working under the supervision of other psychologists, before beginning to evaluate or treat people independently.

The psychiatrist is quite different. Psychiatrists are physicians, like your family medical doctor, and as such can prescribe medication which a psychologist cannot do. Psychiatrists go to medical school and obtain an M.D. (doctor of medicine) degree. They then specialize in the treatment of abnormal behavior. Psychiatrists often see the patient's behavior problems as stemming from medical causes and thus often use medical treatments, like drug therapy, along with psychological therapy. Psychiatry, then, is a branch of medicine and is not a subfield of psychology.

Counseling Psychology. Counseling psychologists help people to adjust to emotional or personal problems that are less severe than those treated by the clinical psychologist. Counseling psychologists may help high school students choose a career, prisoners reform, or a wife and husband discuss their marriage. Like clinical psychologists, counseling psychologists assess and treat people with behavior problems, but will refer them to clinicians or psychiatrists if the problems seem too severe. We will discuss the topic of adjustment in chapter 12, "Stress and Adjustment."

School Psychology. Some psychologists help students. These school psychologists are responsible for administering and interpreting intelligence or aptitude tests. They also consult with teachers and students about academic and emotional needs. And they place students in appropriate educational programs.

Educational Psychology. Other psychologists who work in schools are called educational psychologists. School systems and colleges hire them to study and test the effectiveness of textbooks, classroom organization, methods of teaching, and the design of tests. Some educational psychologists conduct research on learning and methods of education while also teaching at colleges or universities.

Social Psychology. Have you ever noticed that you perform some tasks better in front of an audience than when you are by yourself or with close friends? This phenomenon, called *social facilitation*, is one of the many topics that social psychologists are studying. Social psychologists are interested in how people influence other people in areas such as attitudes, aggression, liking and loving, helping, and prejudice. For example, Kenneth Clark, a social psychologist, studied how prejudice is learned in children. In a 1947 study with his wife Mamie, he found that black children preferred light-skinned dolls over dark-skinned ones. Clark concluded that prejudice is learned by minority as well as majority children through the process of socialization. Another example of the type of research conducted by social psychologists was illustrated in our opening story.

An area closely related to social psychology is environmental psychology, a subfield in which psychologists are interested in discovering how the environment influences human behavior. They study topics such as the effects of personal space, crowding, and noise on behavior. For example, as we discuss in chapter 16, "Applied Psychology," environmental psychologists have found

Figure 1.12. Kenneth Clark
Kenneth B. Clark (b. 1914), an influential social psychologist, served as president of the American Psychological Association. He was interested in how racial prejudice is learned. In 1987 he was given the American Psychological Association gold medal award for contributions by a psychologist in the public interest.

that people are less likely to help others in a noisy environment.

Industrial Psychology. Improving working conditions is an important concern of industrial/organizational psychologists. They engage in a variety of tasks including increasing communication within an organization, consulting with management to improve employee satisfaction, developing employee training programs, and counseling workers on career choices. We explore industrial psychology further in chapter 16, "Applied Psychology."

When cooking on your stove, do you have any trouble turning the correct burner on? If not, it could be because of engineering psychology, a field in which psychologists help design machines and equipment for efficient use by people. They work with visual displays of information, location of dials on airplane control panels, as well as environmental factors in the workplace, such as temperature, light, and color.

Developmental Psychology. Behavioral changes that occur in individuals over time are the concern of developmental psychologists. Since the greatest changes in humans occur most rapidly during childhood, many developmental psychologists specialize in child development. They study the development of the person—his or her likes, fears, and abilities. Development doesn't stop at adolescence, and there has been a trend to study development from a life span approach. We cover developmental psychology in chapter 3, "Development."

Experimental Psychology. The last group of psychologists we describe here falls into the broad area of experimental psychology. Experimental psychologists research the fundamental causes of behavior. They investigate questions such as: Why do people dream? Why do we forget? Why do people go on roller coasters? How can animals identify one another? What is the effect of alcohol on aggression in dogs? Why do people experience optical illusions? Experimental psychologists provide much of the information that is used by other psychologists who apply the research findings to practical situations.

Currently, experimental psychologists can be divided into cognitive psychologists, who study cognitive processes in humans and psychobiologists, who study biological processes in animals. Cognitive psychologists are interested in topics such as perception, memory, thinking, problem solving, language, and intelligence. Physiological psychologists are psychobiologists who study the physiological processes involved in animal behavior. They might study how the nervous system and brain are involved in motivation, learning, perception, or social behavior in animals. Comparative psychologists are psychobiologists who study the behavior of animals in a variety of situations. They might be interested in how heredity influences social behavior, or how behaviors of different species of animals function to help the animals survive.

This brief overview of the subfields should help you understand the great diversity that exists in psychology today. Even within a field of specialization, not all psychologists spend their time doing just one thing. For example, academic psychologists often divide their time among teaching, research, and service activities. Psychologists are thus flexible enough to meet the demands placed upon them by students, the community, and their profession. It is their professional research to which we turn next.

METHODS OF RESEARCH

Research methodology is an important part of psychology. You may be wondering, "Why should I study research methods if I'm not going to major in psychology?" Actually, there are a number of good reasons for learning about research methods. Robert and Barbara Sommer (1986) point out that almost all occupations are concerned with information about human behavior. Schools want to attract students. Businesses want to increase profits. Parents want to help children. Manufacturers want to sell products. Studying research methods will help you understand how psychologists obtain information.

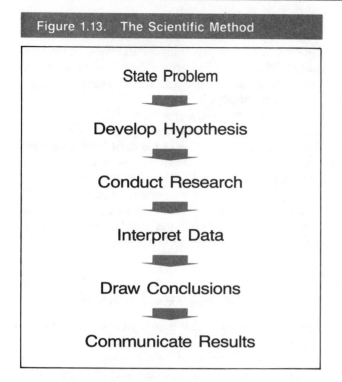

Figure 1.13. The Scientific Method

State Problem

Develop Hypothesis

Conduct Research

Interpret Data

Draw Conclusions

Communicate Results

You can also gain the skills necessary to evaluate claims made by others. For example, when an advertisement claims "no other product is better than ours," does it also mean that all products are the same? It might, but this fact is not always obvious to the consumer. And you will find that scientific research can be fun. You might also be surprised to learn that you already use some of the research methods employed by psychologists.

Psychology researchers utilize the scientific method. Research basically organizes into a series of broad steps, which collectively are often called the scientific method. First, you start with a problem. Let's assume you are interested in the effects of color on emotional expression. Next, you develop a hypothesis, or prediction about observable events. You might predict that students taking a test of emotions which is printed on yellow paper would score higher on positive emotions than students taking the same test printed on blue paper. Then, you conduct a research study by arranging to have the same test printed on both blue and yellow paper and having students actually take the test.

After you collect the information (*data*), you interpret it. In the color test example, you would record the scores for students with yellow and blue tests. Finally, you draw your conclusions. You might find the test scores of students with yellow tests showed they were happier and more enthusiastic, while students with the blue tests rated sadder and more apathetic. If so, you have some new evidence supporting your hypothesis.

Psychologists, like all scientists, need to communicate the results of their research to others. One useful way is to publish the research in scientific journals. The four main sections of the research paper correspond fairly closely to the steps in the scientific method. The introduction section gives background information and states the hypothesis being tested. The methods section describes how the research was conducted and includes information on subjects, materials, and procedures. The results section presents the information obtained, and the discussion section draws conclusions and discusses the relevance and implications of the research evidence.

Research is sometimes divided into basic and applied categories. Basic research is research conducted to obtain information for its own sake. Many experimental psychologists research topics that may provide valuable information for future problems but do not solve immediate problems. Applied research is conducted to solve a practical problem or pressing question. The industrial psychologist who wants to determine the best approach for a TV advertisement is conducting applied research.

Although there is great diversity in the subject matter of psychology, there are a limited number of research methods used in most subfields. The major research methods reviewed here include: naturalistic observation, interview, survey, test, case study, and experiment.

Naturalistic Observation

How many times have you attended a social event with other people? A party, dance, or picnic? A circus, zoo, or school event? While you were there, did you observe what people were doing? Some people were quiet, while others were very talkative. Couples were holding hands. People were yelling, fighting or comforting one another. If you noticed the behavior of people or animals in any of these settings, you were using the research technique of observation. Naturalistic observation is simply the objective recording of what you see and hear when watching people or animals in their natural environment.

The library is a fascinating place to conduct naturalistic observation research. In their 1975 study, Fisher and Byrne observed students sitting alone at a library table. In an earlier research study, it was reported that males prefer to sit *across* from people they like, while females prefer to sit *next* to those they like. Fisher and Byrne reasoned that if people have a preference for sitting with friends, they might be upset if strangers were in their preferred space. They were testing the idea that males are more vulnerable to an invasion by strangers from the front and females are more vulnerable from the side. In their study, they found that males built barricades out of their books and placed them in front of themselves to protect their privacy and keep intruders away. Females, however, placed book barricades to the side of themselves. The next time you are in the library, conduct an

Figure 1.14. Naturalistic Observation
Psychologists use the research technique of naturalistic observation to obtain information on animal and human behavior. As Jane van Lawick-Goodall observed, chimps can and do use tools to obtain food.

observation of your own and see if you come up with the same results.

Comparative psychologists (or animal behaviorists) make extensive use of observation in their studies. A classic study was published in 1971 by Jane van Lawick-Goodall, who spent years in Tanzania observing chimpanzees. Through her research, she discovered that chimpanzees used simple tools in getting food. Before her findings, it was believed that only humans used tools for food getting. This sort of observation allows psychologists to understand better the behavior patterns of different animals.

Naturalistic observation involves recording information about subjects in their normal environment. In one such observation, several psychologists studying obesity went into restaurants and observed the eating habits of normal and overweight patrons (LeBow, Goldberg, & Collins, 1977). They found that overweight people tend to eat faster and take larger bites. This information is now being used to help people lose weight. Robert Plutchik (1983) pointed out that an accurate description of naturalistic behavior is extremely important because it provides a true picture of life outside the laboratory.

The Interview Method

In an interview, the subject interacts with the psychologist by responding to verbal questions. The interview is designed to obtain information about a person from the exhibited behavior as well as the responses to the questions. Some interviews are *structured,* in which standardized questions are asked. Other interviews are *unstructured,* in which the person just talks about general topics with the interviewer.

Interviews are used by a variety of psychologists.

Clinical psychologists may use an interview to assess the personality of a client so they can select the proper treatment. School psychologists interview students to obtain information concerning their interests and attitudes. Industrial psychologists use the interview to select or evaluate employees.

The interview takes a great deal of time. However, it allows the trained interviewer to obtain extensive information about a topic. One of the most famous research programs employing in-depth interviews was the sexual behavior research conducted in the 1930s and 1940s by Alfred Kinsey and his co-workers. They successfully interviewed hundreds of people on their sexual attitudes and practices, and used the detailed information to develop a profile of sexual behavior in America.

The Survey Method

Many times psychologists need a great deal of information in a relatively short period of time. The survey, or questionnaire, is designed for this need. A survey has written questions that the respondent can usually answer briefly. If proper sampling techniques are used, a researcher can often get a true picture of how people feel about an issue.

Imagine you need to survey the students in your school on their opinions concerning the athletic program. How could you make sure you really had a true school opinion? One way, of course, would be to survey the entire school. But this may be impractical, so you could survey a sample of students by selecting every third or fourth name on the school registration list. This will help assure that there is no bias in your procedure, and will cut down on time.

What do surveys measure? Just about everything. The Gallup Poll is famous for surveying people's presidential preferences. It is especially publicized during election campaigns. The Nielsen Ratings measure people's opinions on TV show preferences. Other surveys may have questions on eating habits, sexual preferences, religion, income, career goals, television favorites, educational background, recreational activities or ideas for tax reform. Consumer psychologists use surveys to determine which products will succeed. Social psychologists use surveys to obtain information on attitudes and beliefs. A major survey that is conducted once every ten years is the U.S. census.

Research with a survey, or questionnaire, obtains written answers very quickly. However, one weakness of surveys is that you must rely on impersonal answers that might not be totally honest. For example, if anonymous, a subject may give an answer to please or upset the person giving the survey. Still, a survey is a popular research tool in the social and behavioral sciences.

The Testing Method

The testing method can also be used to collect and compare information about people's behavior. However, it also has the weakness of having to rely on the honesty of the test taker for accurate information. You are certainly familiar with tests given in school. In addition to the regular academic tests of ability, you undoubtedly have taken achievement tests, such as the Metropolitan Achievement Test or the Stanford Achievement Test. You might also have been given the Strong-Campbell Interest Inventory by your school counselor. Tests often used for admission to college are the SAT and ACT.

Figure 1.15. Testing Method
Clinical psychologists, developmental psychologists, and social psychologists all use tests to measure a person's abilities, interests, personality, and intelligence. Here a student is taking an intelligence test.

Psychologists use many types of tests to measure people's abilities, interests, personality, and intelligence. School psychologists may use an intelligence test to help place a student at the correct class level. Clinical psychologists give personality tests to help assess a person's emotional problems. A test of anxiety may give some insight into why you are having trouble when you take academic tests. Developmental psychologists use motor skills tests as indicators of a child's developmental readiness to enter school. If used correctly, tests can be very useful tools. They can help predict the best alternative for future action. We review the requirements for a good test in chapter 8, "Language and Intelligence."

The Case Study ✶

Often psychologists want to know what led to a particular behavior or event. The case study, or scientific biography, is a reconstruction of a person's life to discover the background leading to the current situation. For instance, a person who is showing signs of severe depression may have a case study conducted to help discover where the problem began and why it developed.

Case studies are especially useful to clinical psychologists who need to evaluate a client's problem and then decide upon an appropriate treatment. It's much easier if the psychologist knows the specific experiences the client has had in his or her lifetime that may have led up to the problem. Information on childhood, school, employment, and relationships with his or her parents and friends is valuable in gaining insight into the current situation.

Abraham Maslow developed a theory of personality called *self-actualization*, which he based partially on intensively researched case studies of individuals he considered to be self-actualized. Self-actualization, which is the state of having reached your full potential, is discussed in chapter 11, "Personality."

Although the case study provides a great deal of information about a particular person, one of its weaknesses is that the information is usually only pertinent to this one person and often cannot be used to help others. Another weakness is often the difficulty of recalling and retracing a person's life.

Unlike the case study and many of the other methods, the next method, the experiment, tends to have more general application, permits researchers to exercise a great deal of control over the objects of their study, and allows replication (duplication) of any experimenter's successful procedures by other experimenters.

The Experiment

Psychologists often want to know specifically what causes a particular behavior. They may conduct an experiment in which conditions can be carefully manipulated and controlled. The experiment allows psychologists and other scientists to infer cause-and-effect relationships among conditions, or *variables*, of interest. Many experiments are conducted in a laboratory so that extraneous, irrelevant conditions can be carefully controlled, and the variables can be precisely measured.

There are many variables that are taken into consideration when designing an experiment. Environmental variables include such things as temperature, lighting, color of walls, amount of space available, and time of day. Subject variables include age, sex, background, experience, intelligence, personality, and ability. Many times, most of these variables are not of prime interest, and the psychologist tries to control them so that they will not influence measurement of the condition of interest. At other times, some of these conditions are what the experiment is all about, and the psychologist carefully manipulates them so that their effects on some particular behavior can be measured.

Figure 1.16. Psychological Experiment

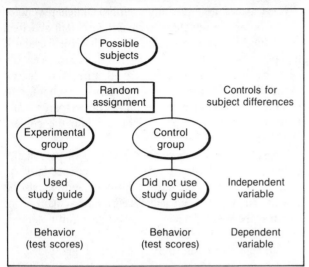

Controlled conditions of an experiment allow psychologists to infer cause-and-effect relationships among variables. In a typical experiment, subjects are randomly assigned to the experimental group or to the control group. Independent variable treatment is given to the experimental group such as the use of a study guide to prepare for tests. No specific treatment (study guide) is given to the control group. The behavior, or dependent variable, exhibited by the two groups is then measured. Finally a comparison, usually expressed statistically, is made between the behavior of each group.

Independent and Dependent Variables. In an experiment, a psychologist is usually interested in the relationship of two specific variables. The independent variable is the condition that is manipulated by the experimenter. It is a stimulus that will cause a response. The dependent variable is the behavior or response outcome that is measured. The behavior depends upon the independent variable. These two variables form the basis of an experiment, so it is essential that you understand them. In our opening story, Latané conducted an experiment on helping behavior. The independent variable was the social condition (alone or with another person) and the dependent variable was the helping response.

A few other examples might help you grasp the concept of independent and dependent variables. A social psychologist predicts that alcohol will decrease aggression. Alcohol is the independent variable and aggression is the dependent variable. A child psychologist wants to know whether a reward of candy will affect the time required to toilet train a toddler. The independent variable is reward and the dependent variable is toilet training. An experimental psychologist hypothesizes that the amount of space available will affect social contact time in gerbils. The independent variable is space and the dependent variable is contact time.

Experimental and Control Groups. In many experiments, there are two groups of subjects. Subjects who receive the independent variable are in the experimental group, while subjects who do not receive the independent variable are in the control group. Notice that the only difference between the two groups is the presence or absence of the independent variable. They are treated identically in every other way. And the dependent variable is measured exactly the same way in both groups.

Control of Extraneous Variables. In an experiment, a psychologist usually manipulates one independent variable. But sometimes, other variables also influence the dependent variable, a condition called confounding. For example, in an experiment to determine how lack of dream sleep affects anxiety, the experimenter would wake up the subjects whenever they would enter dream sleep. The control comparison group of subjects would be allowed to sleep through the night. When it was determined that the group with less dream sleep had more anxiety, the conclusion might be obvious, but two independent variables were confounding the results. The amount of dream sleep the subjects had and the number of times they were awakened could both be factors in determining their subsequent anxiety. Psychologists must also control the extraneous variables, the conditions that are not of interest in a particular experiment. Often a matched group design is used, in which the experimental and control groups are "matched" on as many variables as possible. For example, both groups might be given a pretest to make sure they each contain subjects with similar IQs, personalities, or ability levels. In many situations it is not possible to match all variables for the experimental and control groups. Experimenters may then use random assignment to assign subjects to groups, and assume that differences in individual subjects will cancel out with a large sample size. The design of this experiment is called a between-subject experiment. Another way to control extraneous variables is to have each subject serve as his or her own control. In this situation, when the same subjects serve in both the experimental and control groups, it is a within-subject experiment design.

Let's assume that I am interested in whether or not the size of the classroom influences student performance on tests. I could test one class of students in a large room and another class in a small room. But I am not sure that the ability level of both groups is similar. Perhaps a better alternative would be to use a procedure called counterbalancing. In counterbalancing (a within-subject design), subjects are exposed to both the experimental and control conditions, but half receive the experimental condition first, and the rest receive the control condition first. When using counterbalancing, the experimental group scores are compared to the control group scores to determine whether significant differences exist. But everyone has been exposed to both conditions and order effects can be examined to determine whether receiving the independent variable first or second makes a difference.

Control of Bias. One other source of potential error exists in an experiment: bias of the experimenter or subjects. Robert Rosenthal and Lenore Jacobson (1968) conducted an experiment that demonstrated the possibility of experimenter bias in the classroom. Briefly stated, the researchers went into an elementary school in the fall and gave the students an intelligence test (which they disguised as a test that could identify those who would do exceptionally well during the school year).

They actually picked certain students at random and told the teachers that these students would "bloom." Rosenthal and Jacobson then returned in the spring and readministered the intelligence test. They found that those students that the teachers had been told would do the best actually made the highest gain in intelligence scores. This phenomenon has been called expectancy. This effect may not always be present in experiments, but experimenters should be aware of the possibility.

Subject bias can also affect the outcome of an experiment. When subjects believe the experiment requires or demands a certain way of behaving, they may react according to the demand characteristics of the experiment. Assume you were a subject in an experiment to assess the effects of caffeine (independent variable) on reading speed (dependent variable). If you were given a dose of caffeine (experimental group), would you have a tendency to expect that you would read faster? If so, it is because of the demand characteristics of the experiment. Probably both you and the experimenter would expect this result. One way to avoid expected behavior is to use the blinding technique, in which the assignment of a subject to the experimental or control group is unknown to the subject (resulting in a single-blind experiment) or to both the subject and experimenter (resulting in a double-blind experiment).

When the experiment involves giving a drug, the group assignment can be hidden from the subject by giving him or her a placebo. A placebo is an inert substance, usually a sugar pill, that has no effect on behavior, but because subjects may think that a placebo is real and should have an effect, expectancy and demand characteristics lead to biased behavior. In the caffeine experiment, for example, half of the subjects (the experimental group) would receive caffeine and the other half (the control group) would receive a placebo.

The experiment is one of the most powerful methods that psychologists can use to infer cause-and-effect relationships. Some experiments can become quite complex, with several independent and dependent variables being tested simultaneously. The basic purpose of the psychology experiment, however, is to gain a better understanding of behavior by exerting control over stimuli that lead to responses.

The Quasi-Experimental Method. Sometimes there are situations in which a true experiment cannot be conducted. Many times studies of naturally occurring events prevent random assignment of subjects to experimental or control groups, and a quasi-experiment can be used (Ray & Ravizza, 1988). For example, you might wish to know whether students in wealthy or poor school districts can solve problems faster. The variable of school district wealth cannot be manipulated for individual subjects. The quasi-experimental method provides answers to real life questions, but loses some of the control usually associated with an experiment.

Correlation Research

Some researchers are interested in the relationship between two variables. For example, you might want to know whether a person with high grades in high school will also do well in college. Or you might be interested in the relationship between watching violence on television and aggressive behavior. As we discuss in chapter 2, "Biology of Behavior," psychologists are often interested in the relationship between genetically related people for characteristics such as intelligence, personality, and abnormal behaviors. The technique of correlation can be used to determine the degree of relationship that exists between two variables.

The correlation coefficient is a statistical measure of relationship ranging from −1.00, a perfect negative relationship (correlation), to 0.00, no relationship, to +1.00, a perfect positive relationship. The closer the correlation coefficient is to 1 (either positive or negative), the stronger the relationship is. For example, a correlation coefficient of +.89 indicates a very strong positive relationship between two variables, whereas −.17 suggests a very weak negative relationship between two variables. Think of measurements of two variables and plot them on the vertical and horizontal axes of a graph, making a scatterplot. If one variable increases as the other one does, a positive relationship exists. There is likely to be a positive correlation between high school and college grades, thus the higher your high school grade average, the higher your college grades will be. There is also likely to be a positive correlation between amount of time spent studying and test scores.

If one variable decreases as the other one increases, a negative correlation exists. There is probably a negative correlation between grade average and school dropout rate. As grade average increases the dropout rate decreases. There should be a negative correlation between the loudness of a sound and the distance to the source of the sound. As the sound increases, the distance decreases. If absolutely no correlation exists, the two

Figure 1.17. Correlations

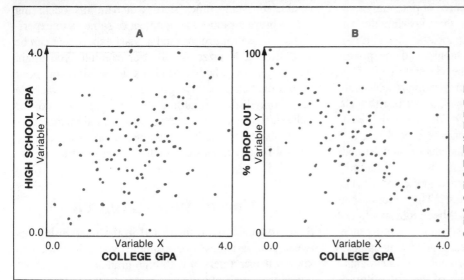

Researchers use the correlation technique to determine the degree of relationship between two variables. In graph **A**, the scatter plot demonstrates a positive correlation between the high school and grade point averages (GPA) of college students; as their high school GPAs increase, their college GPAs also increase. Graph **B** shows a negative correlation that indicates a decrease in the dropout rate of college students as their GPAs increase.

variables are completely independent. We would expect there to be no correlation between a person's height and grade average. Likewise, no correlation should exist between a person's age and his or her IQ.

The research and statistical method of correlation helps psychologists make predictions. For instance, if all we knew about a student was that he or she had an extremely high grade point average in high school, we could predict fairly accurately that the student could be successful in college. Since there is a positive correlation between height and weight, if all I knew was that a person was tall, I would predict that the person also weighed more than another person who was short.

Correlation does not, however, imply a cause and effect relationship. It only tells us that as one measure changes, the other one will also. For example, as the number of churches in a town increases, the number of criminals also increases. Does this statement mean that churches turn people into criminals? Of course not. In this case, the number of both churches and criminals probably increases as the population increases. Correlation allows psychologists to gain insight into how different behaviors are related.

Ethical Considerations in Research

Psychologists have a very strict code of <u>ethics</u> when dealing with human or animal subjects. Researchers typically must submit a proposal of their planned research study with humans to a "human subjects committee," which reviews the methodology to ensure it is ethically sound. The human subjects committee is concerned that the research does not embarrass or cause pain in unsuspecting subjects.

When human subjects are used, they are usually asked to sign a consent form which explains the general purpose of the experiment and informs them of the possibility of any stress or pain. The researcher has the ethical responsibility of protecting subjects from mental and physical harm. Unless agreed to beforehand, the responses of subjects are strictly confidential, and the researchers may not disclose names or the scores of individual subjects.

The American Psychological Association has published a set of ethical principles for research. The ultimate responsibility rests with the individual investigator. Sometimes *deception* must be used in a specific experiment, in which case the researcher must take extra precautions to ensure the welfare of the subjects. If deception is necessary, the subject must be debriefed when the study is over. The experimenter then carefully explains the true purpose of the study and answers any questions.

Several ethical issues have recently been raised about research with animals. Scientists argue that many standards and mechanisms exist for the humane treatment of animals such as the Federal Animal Welfare Act passed in 1966, and amended by Congress in 1970, 1976, and 1979. Animal rights advocates, on the other hand, argue that much cruelty does exist in the name of science and is largely undetected and unreported. Many animals, such as rats for example, are not protected by the Federal Animal Welfare Act.

Scientists indicate that animal research is necessary to achieve benefits for humankind. Medical advances include vaccines against infectious diseases, surgical ap-

Publication of Psychological Research

How can we find out about the research psychologists conduct? The research results are communicated to others in a variety of ways, including discussions with colleagues, interviews with the media, presentations at psychological conventions, and publication in professional journals and books.

Psychologists are able to keep current by attending conventions and learning about the latest research findings. In the United States, the American Psychological Association's annual convention is the largest. In addition there are several regional conventions.

The communication method that reaches the widest audience and provides a permanent record is publication in scientific journals. Many journals, including several by The American Psychological Association, publish psychological research. You might want to browse through some psychology journals to become familiar with the style of writing and the research in which psychologists are currently engaged.

A research article is organized so that its four major sections correspond fairly closely to the steps of the scientific method.

The introduction section provides background information on the problem and includes a statement of the hypothesis being tested. The literature review included in the introduction is a good place to find detailed information on a topic. All of the articles described in the introduction are included in the reference section at the end of the article.

The methods section includes information on the subjects, apparatus, and procedures. A description of the subjects used in the research is included in enough detail so that the reader is aware of any unique characteristics. The specifics of materials and any experimental apparatus used are given so that the study may be replicated. The actual procedures followed are carefully enumerated.

The results section is where the actual data is summarized, often in graphs or tables indicating the outcomes of the statistical tests.

The last major section is the discussion, in which the conclusions of the study are explained as well as its relevance and implications.

Although research articles in scientific journals are usually written for other scientists, students can obtain a great deal of information on current research trends by reading them. If you can't find psychology journals in your library, ask your instructor about finding them.

THOUGHT QUESTIONS

1. What are the major sections of a research article?
2. Why is publication in scientific journals important for psychologists?
3. How is the organization of a research article like the scientific method?

proaches to eye disorders, and the discovery of insulin. Psychological benefits are less well known but include biofeedback for the control of high blood pressure and tension, conditioned taste aversion to help cancer patients who have lost their appetite, and behavior modification to help people control alcohol, drug, and tobacco abuse. Despite these benefits, advocates for animal rights are quick to point out the fallacy of extending research from one species to another and use the thalidomide scandal as an example. Thalidomide, an ingredient in some sleeping pills, was tested and found safe in animals, but when taken by pregnant women resulted in horribly deformed babies.

Perhaps the most difficult issue to resolve involves the concept of animals as distinctly different lower forms of life than humans incapable of language, self-consciousness, or suffering versus the concept of humans and animals as different but equal species on the evolutionary scale.

These issues have yet to be resolved and thus, for now, psychologists are involved in making sure animal rights are maintained and that research is conducted in an ethical manner.

MEASUREMENT IN PSYCHOLOGICAL RESEARCH

Psychologists use a variety of measurement techniques in collecting and analyzing research data. Two measurement terms are so important that they are described here and referred to throughout the textbook. We want our measurements always to be *valid* and *reliable*.

I might tell you that I have just invented a new test to measure intelligence. It's very simple. Just write down your height. According to this test, you are assigned 2.5 intelligence points for every inch of height. So anyone 6 feet 6 inches tall would have an intelligence score of 195. This "pretend" test would not be valid, but it would be reliable.

Validity refers to the degree that you actually measure what you intend to measure. A valid intelligence test would actually measure intelligence. A valid personality test would actually measure personality. My "intelligence test" is not valid because it measures height rather than intelligence.

Reliability is the consistency of a measurement. It is the degree to which a person's score at one time is the same as when the measurement is repeated. A reliable intelligence test would yield consistent scores from one test time to the next. Therefore, my "intelligence test" would be reliable because your height would not change significantly from one time to the next. We want our measurements to be *both* valid and reliable. It is important to note that although a measurement could be reliable without being valid, it could not be valid without also being reliable.

Measurement techniques help psychologists efficiently collect and analyze data on behavior. There are two classes of analysis techniques that you should be familiar with: *descriptive statistics* and *inferential statistics*.

Descriptive Statistics

Descriptive statistics are techniques that help summarize large amounts of information (Gravetter & Wallnau, 1988). A teacher might wish to tell a colleague about the recent test scores in her class. She might start out, "On the last test, students received scores of 95, 63, 90, 78, 82, 77, 85, 91, 72, 85, 92, 81, 85 . . ." I strongly suspect that before she had the opportunity to list all of the scores from the class, her colleague would be gone. This is not a very efficient method of communicating information. Descriptive statistics could help her summarize the scores for a meaningful conversation.

Frequency Distribution. Developing a frequency distribution allows the researcher to graphically represent the information he or she has collected and to organize the scores into a frequency distribution that shows the number of times each score occurs so that they can be interpreted. If the teacher had 100 test scores, she would take each possible score and count how many times it occurred.

Next she would show the scores in a frequency distribution on a graph called a *frequency polygon*. All of the possible scores would be arranged in ascending order on the horizontal axis (the abscissa) and the frequency of each score indicated on the vertical axis (the ordinate). A point would be placed on the graph for each score's frequency and a line drawn to connect the points. A graph allows people to quickly understand a great deal of numerical information.

Often when a large number of scores are plotted on a graph, scores begin to fall into a bell-shaped distribution called a normal curve. A normal curve has about as many low scores as high scores, with the highest frequency of scores occurring in the middle range. A

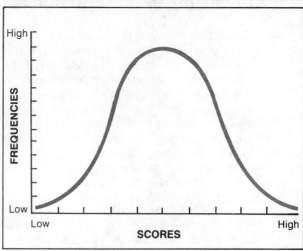

Figure 1.18. Normal Curve Distribution

A normal curve has about as many low scores as high scores, with the highest frequency of scores occurring in the middle range. Many measurements tend to fall into a normal distribution, including intelligence scores, height, and weight. Measures of central tendency, such as the mean, provide a number that represents the entire sample.

variety of measurements tend to fall into a normal curve, including height, weight, and intelligence scores (see also Figure 8.16).

To summarize a set of data using descriptive statistics, we need to calculate measures of *central tendency* and *variability*.

Central Tendency. Measures of central tendency give a number that represents the entire group or sample. Instead of repeating all of the scores that her students earned on their test, the teacher could state one number that represents all of the scores in the distribution. Since distributions of scores tend to be grouped toward the middle, a number that represents this middle range will likely be representative of the majority of scores. The statement "men are about 69 inches tall" suggests that 69 inches represents all of the heights of men. This may be interpreted in several different ways using three commonly used measures of central tendency: the *mean*, *median*, and *mode*.

The most commonly used measure of central tendency is the mean. The mean is simply the arithmetic average. All scores are added and the total is divided by the number of scores. For example, the mean for the 13 test scores provided above would be 82.8. To obtain the mean, you need to first find the sum of the scores, which is 1076. Then divide 1076 by 13, the number of scores, to obtain the mean of 82.8. Usually, when people talk about an average score, they are referring to the mean.

The median is the middle score when the scores are arranged from the lowest to the highest with 50% of the scores falling below the median and 50% above it. The median of the above test scores is 85. There are 6 scores below and 6 scores above the middle score of 85. If there are an even number of scores, the median is determined by adding the two scores in the middle and dividing by two.

The mode is the most frequent score in a distribution. In the test score example above, the score of 85 occurs three times and thus is the mode. The mode is most useful when the number of scores is high.

In distributions such as the test score example, where one mode clearly exists, it is called a unimodal distribution. In some distributions, two modes are present and the distribution is referred to as a bimodal distribution. For example, if a teacher gives a test and many students do well and many others do poorly, the bimodal distribution will have two modes, one high and one low. In this case the mode is a better measure to use than the mean, which would suggest everyone did average.

Variability. Measures of variability communicate how dispersed or spread out the scores are in the data. A measure of central tendency, such as the mean, is important because it is a number that is representative of the entire group. But this is only part of the picture. For instance, the mean of the test score distribution above is 82.8. However, the mean by itself does not tell you how much the scores varied. Did everyone score in the low 80s? Or were some scores in the 40s and others in the 90s? A measure of variability will show how spread out the scores are. The commonly used measures of variability are the range and the standard deviation.

The range is the simplest measure of variability to calculate. It is merely the highest score minus the lowest score. For the above test scores, the range is 32 (95 minus 63). This tells us how far apart the scores are. A small range indicates that everyone scored similarly. A large range indicates dissimilar scores. If in the above test score data, the mean was 83 and the range 5, you would know that everyone scored in the low 80s. However, if the mean was 83 and the range 32, you would know some scored in the high 90s while others scored in the 60s.

The range conveys a great deal of information about a group of scores. But its weakness is that it is based on only two scores (the highest and the lowest) and can easily be influenced by one extreme score. Perhaps in the above example, all of the scores were in the low 80s except one score which was 50, producing a range of 32. One deviant score produced a range which was really not representative of the majority of the scores. A more complex, but often more informative measure of variability is the standard deviation.

The standard deviation is a measure of variability that describes how scores are distributed around the mean (Couch, 1987). The standard deviation is calculated from all of the scores, not just the two most extreme ones. To calculate the standard deviation, first the mean

Figure 1.19. Calculation of Standard Deviation

Raw Data

Scores (n)	d	d²
95	12.2	148.8
63	−19.8	392.0
90	7.2	51.8
78	−4.8	23.0
82	−0.8	0.6
77	−5.8	33.6
85	2.2	4.8
91	8.2	67.2
72	−10.8	116.6
85	2.2	4.8
92	9.2	84.6
81	−1.8	3.2
85	2.2	4.8

Formula for Calculating Standard Deviation

$$SD = \frac{\text{sum of } d^2}{n - 1}$$

d = deviation scores; the subject's score minus the mean
n = the number of scores in the distribution
SD = standard deviation

Results

Mean of scores = 82.8
Sum of d² = 935.8
Standard deviation (SD) = 8.8

of the distribution is obtained. Then the difference between each score and the mean is determined. These difference scores are squared and the squared difference scores are added together. This number is then divided by the number of scores minus 1. And finally, the square root of this result is obtained. This is the standard deviation. A distribution with a large standard deviation consists of scores that are spread out, whereas a small standard deviation describes a distribution with scores more similar to one another.

The concept of the standard deviation helps us understand the properties of the normal curve. In a true normal curve, about 68% of the scores lie within a standard deviation above or below the mean (34.13% above and 34.13% below). Over 95% of scores lie within two standard deviations of the mean, and over 99% lie within three standard deviations.

As we learn in chapter 8, "Language and Intelligence," scores from the general population approximate the normal curve. With a mean score of 100 and a standard deviation of 15, 68% of the IQ scores lie between 85 and 115, and 95% lie between 70 and 130 (two standard deviations). The Scholastic Aptitude Test (SAT) has been constructed so that it has a mean of 500 and a standard deviation of 100. Thus 68% of the SAT scores lie between 400 and 600, and 95% of the scores on the SAT lie between 300 and 700 (two standard deviations).

Sometimes there are more scores at the high or low end of a distribution. When this happens, we say the distribution of scores is skewed. Let us hope that when your instructor gives a test, the scores are skewed toward the high end of the distribution.

Inferential Statistics

Psychologists employing the experimental method want to draw proper conclusions from their research. A problem with research methods like the experiment is that they deal with a limited number of subjects. Psychologists want to be sure that their results can be generalized to a much larger number of subjects. Inferential statistics are techniques that help researchers make generalizations about a finding based on a limited number of subjects (Gravetter & Wallnau, 1988).

All of the individuals from the large experimental group that the subjects were selected from is called the population. The actual subjects make up the sample. Let's look at an experiment that examines the effects of using a study guide (the independent variable) on student test scores (the dependent variable). Is the experimenter only interested in the sample of students who were actually involved in the experiment? No, the experimenter wants to generalize from the sample to the population of all students in a similar situation. But since all students cannot be tested, the researcher needs to rely on inferential statistical techniques to provide the answers.

Although the actual calculation procedures are techni-

cal, what is important for you to know is that tests of significance are inferential statistical techniques for determining whether the difference in scores between the experimental and control groups is really due to the effects of the independent variable or just due to random chance. Some tests that psychologists use include the chi-square test, the t-test, and analysis of variance.

The concept of probability is important in inferential statistics. A test of significance that shows $p < .05$ indicates that the outcome (the difference between experimental and control groups) has a probability (p) of occurring by random chance less than five times per hundred and researchers arbitrarily conclude that the effect of the independent variable is significant (real). This means that the probability that the outcome is due to a real effect of the independent variable is 95%. When a statistically significant effect is found, it is concluded that the independent variable made a real difference between the experimental group and the control group. Psychologists then have confidence that research has helped in understanding human behavior. ■

We have seen in this chapter that psychology is a diverse field of study. As shown in the opening story on helping behavior, the common denominator in all of psychology is the fact that psychologists study behavior scientifically. Latané approached the problem of understanding helping by systematically studying the variables that lead to helping behavior. In a relatively brief period of time, psychology has developed into a relevant discipline that touches many areas of everyday life. We turn next to the area of psychobiology to discover how biology influences our behavior.

© by the United Feature Syndicate, Inc.

CHAPTER REVIEW
What You've Learned About the Study of Psychology

1. Psychology is the science of behavior and cognition. Psychologists study easily observable behaviors, mental processes, and physiological reactions in humans and animals.

2. The ultimate aim of psychology is to understand behavior. Psychologists seek to understand behavior through four basic goals: description, prediction, control and explanation.

3. Five major schools of thought help trace psychology's formal history. The first psychology laboratory was set up in 1879 by Wilhelm Wundt at the University of Leipzig to analyze the elements of mental life through introspection in the school called structuralism. William James of Harvard University influenced functionalism, which included the study of overt behavior as well as conscious experience. In 1913, John Watson excluded everything except overt behavior, in the school of behaviorism. Gestalt psychologists studied whole or complete perceptions rather than individual elements. Psychoanalysis, under the leadership of Sigmund Freud, broadened the viewpoint of psychology to include consciousness once more. Today's approaches to the study of psychology include the biological, humanistic, psychoanalytic, cognitive, and behavior perspectives.

4. The American Psychological Association has numerous divisions which represent the different subfields and interest areas in psychology. Some of the subfields include: clinical, counseling, school, educational, social, industrial, developmental, and experimental psychology.

5. Psychologists utilize the scientific method of research, in which hypotheses are tested, data are interpreted, and results are published. Basic research is conducted to obtain information for its own sake, whereas applied research is conducted to help solve a practical problem.

6. The research method of naturalistic observation involves the objective recording of what you see and hear when watching people or animals in their natural environment.

7. In the interview research method, the subject interacts with the psychologist by responding to questions being asked. Interviews can be structured or unstructured.

8. In the survey research method, written questions are presented to the respondent. Research with a survey, or questionnaire, allows psychologists to obtain a great deal of information in a brief time.

9. Psychologists use many types of tests to measure people's abilities, interests, personality, and intelligence.

10. The case study is a reconstruction of a person's life to discover the background leading to the current situation.

11. The experiment allows us to infer cause-effect relationships among variables of interest. The independent variable is the condition that is manipulated by the experimenter. The dependent variable is the behavior or response measured. Subjects who receive the independent variable form the experimental group, while those who don't are in the control group. In order to control extraneous variables, psychologists can match groups or use random assignment of subjects. When different subjects are used, the design is between-subject, while when the same subjects serve in experimental and control groups, the design is within-subject. Bias and demand characteristics can be controlled through the double blind technique and the use of a placebo.

12. The research technique of correlation can be used to determine the degree of relationship that exists between two variables.

13. Psychologists have a strict code of ethics when dealing with human or animal subjects. The researcher has the responsibility of protecting subjects from mental and physical harm.

14. Validity refers to the degree that you actually measure what you intended to measure. Reliability is the degree to which a person's score at one time is the same at different times.

15. Descriptive statistics are techniques that help summarize large amounts of information. Measures of central tendency (such as the mean, mode and median) give a number that represents the entire group or sample. Measures of variability (such as the range and the standard deviation) communicate how dispersed the scores are.

16. Inferential statistics are techniques that help researchers make generalizations about a research finding based on a limited number of subjects. If a statistical test shows that the outcome (difference between experimental and control groups) has a probability of occurring by random chance less than five times per hundred, the effect of the independent variable is said to be significant.

BIOLOGY OF BEHAVIOR

In order to fully understand human behavior, we need to know something about the biological influences on people. Biological psychologists study the endocrine system and the nervous system and pay special attention to the functioning of the brain. Also of great interest to psychologists is how heredity and environment interact to produce the development of behavior.

In order to determine what each part of the brain does, a neurosurgeon may use a procedure called brain mapping. The surgeon carefully places tiny electrodes, or thin pieces of insulated wire, into the outer layer of the brain while the patient is awake. Then the surgeon gives the patient a very tiny amount of electrical stimulation through the electrode and observes the reaction.

Wilder Penfield used the brain mapping technique to learn about the sensory and motor areas of the cortex. When he electrically stimulated certain places on the cortex, patients reported sensations in various parts of their bodies (the sensory cortex areas) or moved various parts of their bodies (the motor cortex areas). The number of neurons associated with movement of a particular part of the body increases as the body is more able to move (Penfield & Rasmussen, 1950). For instance, the fingers and mouth areas of the brain have a large number of neurons, whereas the legs and back areas have few neurons.

Penfield was studying epileptic patients at the Montreal Neurological Institute in the 1950s. While he was stimulating a certain part of the brain one day, he discovered that electrical stimulation sometimes evoked vivid auditory and visual memories in patients. Imagine you are in Penfield's surgical amphitheater witnessing an operation on the brain of a person who has epilepsy. You observe that in order to avoid removing crucial brain tissue, Penfield electrically stimulates areas around the damaged part while the patient is under local anesthesia. The patient is awake and can respond to the stimulations, talking about what is being felt and enabling Penfield to make a map of the brain. At one point during

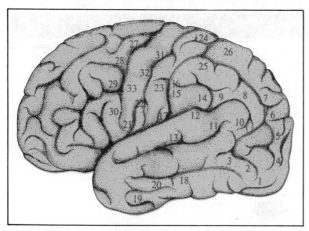

Figure 2.1. Electrical Stimulation of the Brain
Wilder Penfield discovered that when specific locations of the brain were stimulated, indicated by the numbers, patients sometimes responded with recollections of events in their lives. For example, when number 20 is stimulated, a patient might recall hearing a symphony playing, or when number 5 is stimulated, memories of childhood might be revived. Each patient is unique and produces different memories.

this brain-mapping procedure, the patient vividly recalls experiences in his childhood home, talking with his young cousins. It is as if the tiny electric current started a filmstrip which included the details of a past event experienced by the patient.

Another patient, a 26-year-old woman named M. M., reports an epileptic seizure that begins with a feeling of fear and a dream-like experience. When Penfield stimulates the right hemisphere, she experiences tingling in her thumb and movement of her tongue. Stimulation of the temporal lobe part of the brain causes the patient to recall an early memory of her old neighborhood. Other placements of the electrode elicit memories of voices at a river, a scene in an office, and various other sensations.

Many of Penfield's patients were able to recall fragments of different memories such as certain types of music, conversations with particular people, or specific scenes or events. Every time a particular spot was stimulated, the exact same memory was evoked, as if a very specific memory was stored at a very specific location in the brain.

What does this tell us about the biology of memory? While these findings suggest many future possibilities, it is important to remember that science is a slow and exacting business. In his 1975 book, *Mystery of the Mind*, Penfield discussed the limitations of his research. Over the course of his career, he explored the brains of 1,132 patients under local anesthesia. Of these, 520 had the temporal lobe part of the brain explored where their memories were evoked by electrical stimulation. But Penfield found only 40 out of the 520 patients (7.7%) showed these vivid auditory and visual experiences.

There are a number of questions that have been raised about the memory experiences produced by stimulation (Loftus & Loftus, 1980). First, the research was done on epileptic patients rather than normal individuals. The findings have not been replicated in normal people. Second, the fact that Penfield obtained these memories in only 40 patients suggests that further research is needed before we can draw general conclusions about the location of memory in the brain. But the most serious problem is that the reports have not been verified. It is not known whether these memories were indeed memories of past experiences or created thoughts about probable past events. In some cases, it was found that the patient could not have had the experience indicated by the elicited memory.

Penfield's research on mapping which areas of the cortex elicit a specific response greatly advanced our knowledge of how the brain functions. So far we have not been able to unravel the complete mystery of the brain but we have made great strides in understanding how human behavior is biologically influenced.

CHAPTER OBJECTIVES
What You'll Learn About Biology of Behavior

After studying this chapter, you should be able to:

1. Define biological psychology.
2. Identify the parts of a neuron.
3. Describe how a neuron functions (the neural impulse and the synapse).
4. Identify the major functions of the central nervous system (spinal cord and brain).
5. Describe the major structures of the brain.
6. Describe the research findings on cerebral hemisphere functioning.
7. List three research methods used to study the brain.
8. Compare the functions of the somatic nervous system and the autonomic nervous system.
9. Identify the functions of the hormones produced by four important endocrine glands.
10. Describe the basic principles of genetics.
11. Explain how heredity influences behavior.
12. Outline three research methods used in behavior genetic research.

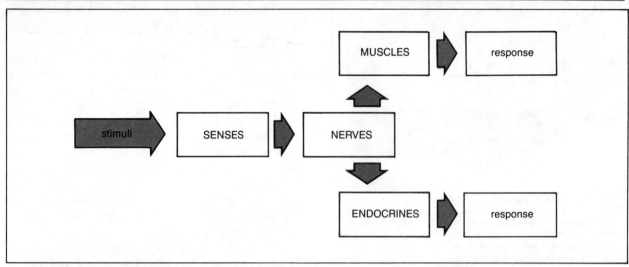

Figure 2.2. Biological Response Systems

The biological response systems are the parts of the body that gather information, process it, make decisions on the information, and then act on them. A stimulus enters through the sense organs and is carried by the nervous system to the brain, where it is interpreted. The brain then directs the muscles and endocrine glands to respond.

WHAT IS BIOLOGICAL PSYCHOLOGY?

Penfield's dramatic demonstration of the brain's role in memory is a good illustration of the biological basis of behavior. However, it isn't necessary to don surgical robes in order to demonstrate that biology influences behavior.

Think about the last time you went to class. Perhaps you were a bit late and your heart was racing as you took your seat. Then the teacher called on you and as you responded you noticed your hands were sweating. Your behavior depended on your being able to hear the teacher, see your environment, speak, move, recall information, and recognize signs of emotional nervousness. To behave appropriately, you relied on various biological response systems. By biological response systems, we mean the parts of your body that gather information, process it, make decisions based on the assimilated information, and act on these decisions.

The biological response systems include your sense organs, nervous system, muscles, and endocrine glands. It was the interplay between your eyes, ears, brain, and muscles that allowed you to respond in the classroom. And your endocrine system was partly responsible for your sweaty hands and racing heart.

Our biological response systems play a major role in our behavior. In fact, along with the genes, they form the biological basis of human behavior and constitute a subfield of experimental psychology called biological psychology, psychobiology, or physiological psychology. It is in this part of psychology that we study the sense organs, nervous system, muscles, endocrine gland system and genetics—all of which influence our behavioral responses to the world around us.

It is important to study biological psychology at this point in the textbook because an understanding of how biology influences behavior will promote better understanding of many other complex topics later. For instance, knowing how the nervous system works helps us understand how thinking develops in a child or how a person remembers learned information. Similarly, genetics teaches us how our biological heritage influences our behavior.

THE NEURON

The human nervous system helps us respond with appropriate behavior to stimuli in the environment. It communicates information throughout the body. Specifically, the human nervous system carries messages about the environment from our sense organs to our brain where the messages are analyzed and decisions made. Then the nervous system carries messages about these decisions to our muscles and glands, so we can respond with the appropriate behavior. The human nervous system is made up of billions of tiny nerve cells called neurons.

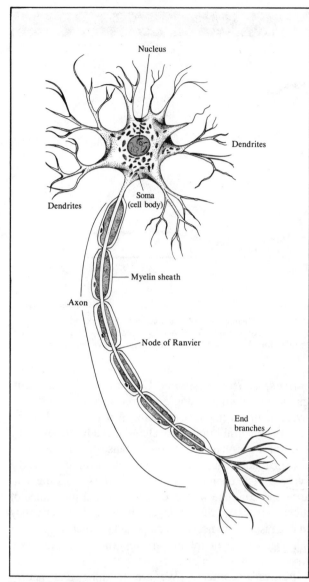

Figure 2.3. Neuron
A neuron is a specialized cell that carries messages throughout the body. Its major parts include dendrites, a cell body, and an axon. Sometimes the axon is covered with a myelin sheath so information can be carried more quickly over long distances.

Structure of the Neuron. The neuron is the basic unit of the nervous system. It is a specialized type of cell that conducts messages throughout the body. Like all cells, the neuron has a soma, or cell body, that contains the nucleus and cytoplasm. The genetic material is contained in the nucleus and the normal cellular metabolism occurs in the cytoplasm. The cell membrane encloses the entire cell. The neuron has short, finger-like projections extending from the soma called dendrites. These receive incoming information from other neurons.

Each neuron has one axon, a tail-like fiber projection along which messages are conducted. The place at which the axon meets the cell body is called the axon hillock. Axons may project up to several feet. For example, an axon from an individual neuron may travel down the length of a giraffe's neck, a distance of 3 meters. The axon is often covered by a protective substance called a myelin sheath. The fatty myelin helps insulate long axons so information can travel through them quickly and will not be interfered with by neighboring axons. The myelin sheath is not a continuous covering, but consists of segments with small gaps, called nodes of Ranvier. The lack of myelination, such as occurs in multiple sclerosis, results in severe disruptions in sensory and muscle functioning. At the end of the axon are the terminal buttons, or end branches.

Types of Neurons. The body has three types of neurons: sensory neurons, interneurons, and motor neurons. When you hear your teacher ask you a question in class, sensory neurons, or afferent neurons, carry the information from your ears to your brain. Interneurons, or association neurons, carry the information throughout your brain so you can interpret the sensory information and think about what action to take. When you decide how to respond, motor neurons, or efferent neurons, carry the information to your muscles so you can talk.

The axons of neurons outside of the brain and spinal cord run together in bundles called nerves. Thus sensory neurons form sensory nerves and motor neurons form motor nerves. These form the peripheral nervous system, which will be discussed later. Next we focus on how neurons function.

The Neural Impulse

Neurons are able to receive and carry messages throughout the body because these cells have two unique properties—irritability and conduction. Irritability is the characteristic that allows a neuron to change in response to stimulation. Conduction is the ability to carry a message—actually an electrical impulse—along the length of a neuron. When a stimulus irritates the dendrites of a neuron, the dendrites conduct the information to the cell body, and then the impulse travels down the axon. This process, conduction of a neural impulse, is basically electrical in nature.

The neuron might be compared to an electrical battery containing positive and negative particles called ions. The normal electrical charge of a passive neuron is called a resting potential. In this state of polarization, there are more negative ions (such as chloride) inside the neuron and more positive ions (such as sodium and potassium) outside. The resting potential (electrical charge) of a neuron is −70 millivolts (mV).

When a stimulus irritates the dendrites of a neuron, the cell membrane becomes permeable and lets the

Figure 2.4 Neural Impulse

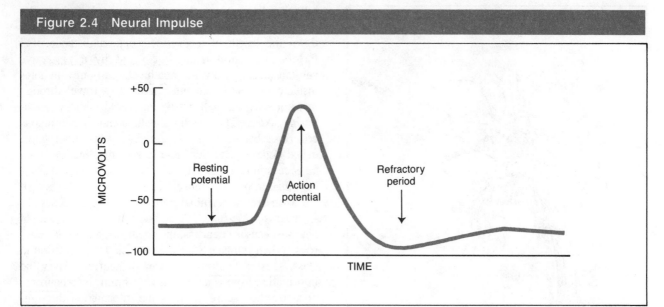

Conduction of a neural impulse along a neuron is an electrical process. The normal electrical charge of a neuron in resting potential is −70mV. When the dendrites are stimulated, the cell membrane allows positive ions to enter. As soon as the electrical charge reaches −50mV, the neuron fires and creates a condition called an action potential. During an action potential, the charge briefly goes to +40mV before dropping back to −90mV during the refractory period, and then to −70mV, the resting potential.

positively charged particles pass through to the inside of the neuron to meet the negative ions stored there. Any change in which the internal electrical charge becomes more positive is called depolarization. As soon as the electrical charge reaches about −50 mV, the neuron *fires* and an electrical charge called the action potential is created, which travels down the length of the axon. During an action potential, the electrical charge briefly goes to about +40 mV before becoming negative again.

According to a principle called the all-or-none law, a neuron only fires when the stimulus is above a certain minimum strength, called the threshold, and when it fires it always fires at full strength. This is similar to the way a smoke alarm operates: a small amount of smoke won't set off the alarm, but when a sufficient amount does set it off, there is no increase in the alarm's duration or loudness even if there is a lot more smoke. After firing, there is a brief period of time, called the refractory period, during which the neuron cannot fire again. During the refractory period the electrical charge drops to nearly −90 mV before returning to −70 mV, the resting potential.

✳ The Synapse ✳

For information to get from one neuron to the next, it must cross the synapse, the space between the axon of one neuron (called the presynaptic neuron) and the dendrites of the next (called the postsynaptic neuron). The synapse is typically very tiny, about .03 microns wide or a millionth of an inch.

Synaptic Transmission. Unlike the electrical communication within a single neuron, communication between neurons involves a chemical reaction. When the electrical neural impulse reaches the end branches of the axon of a presynaptic neuron, it causes the release of a chemical substance, called a neurotransmitter, into the synapse. The chemical neurotransmitters cross the synapse and combine with receptor chemical molecules of the dendrites of the postsynaptic neuron, where they may cause a new neural impulse to be either initiated or inhibited. Without inhibition every nerve in our body would be turned on at once.

Neurotransmitters. We are learning that neurotransmitters play a key role in controlling behavior, and understanding how they work has become a vital part of physiological psychology. Currently over three dozen neurotransmitters have been identified (Panksepp, 1986). Four neurotransmitters have been studied fairly thoroughly: acetylcholine, serotonin, dopamine, and norepinephrine. One of the first neurotransmitters to be identified was acetylcholine, which is involved in activation of muscle movement as well as arousal, memory, and motivation. Recent research suggests that the severe memory disruption in persons with Alzheimer's disease is due to degeneration of brain neurons that use acetylcholine.

The neurotransmitter serotonin is produced in the raphe nuclei in the brain stem, and is involved in sleep and sensory experiences. As many folk remedies have long suggested, drinking a glass of milk may indeed help induce sleep, since milk contains serotonin.

The neuromuscular breakdown symptomatic of Par-

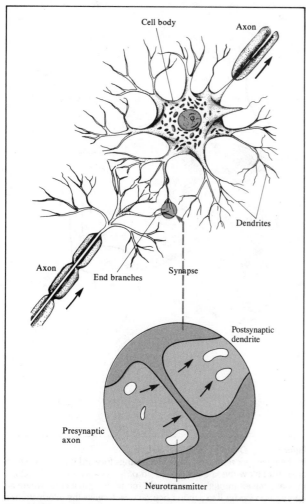

Figure 2.5. Synapse
The synapse is the space between the axon of one neuron and the dendrites of the next. When the electrical neural impulse reaches the end of the axon, it releases a chemical neurotransmitter into the synapse. This crosses the synapse and causes the dendrites of the next neuron to fire.

neuropeptides include cholecystokinin (food regulation), vasopressin (learning), substance P (pain, reinforcement, and memory) and the endorphins (pain, reinforcement, and memory). The term "endorphin" comes from "endogenous morphine," or morphine produced by the body. Two of the endorphins, the enkephalins, are produced throughout the brain and spinal cord, while the others are primarily found in the hypothalamus (Bolles and Faneslow, 1982). The endorphins appear to be a major discovery in understanding behavior because they are involved in such fundamental processes as reinforcement, learning, memory, and pain. In later chapters, we will further discuss the role of endorphins in pain (chapter 4, "Sensation and Perception"), reinforcement (chapter 6, "Learning"), and memory (chapter 7, "Human Memory").

① regulate nerve so yo do not feel pain
②

CENTRAL NERVOUS SYSTEM

Imagine that you're sitting in class trying to concentrate on a discussion. You remember how pleasant it was to run into the person you date. You suddenly snap to attention as you hear your name called; you've been asked to define a term written on the board. Fortunately, you remember the definition. Next, the lights are turned off to show a slide. When the lights come back on, you blink and cover your eyes to protect them from the bright light. After class, while walking toward the door, you decide to ask your friend to go to the big soccer game with you. In order to understand what's happening in these scenes, we need to understand some of the basic functionings of our nervous system.

Our nervous system is divided into two parts: the peripheral nervous system, which receives messages from the sense organs and carries messages to the muscles and glands, and the central nervous system, which interprets and stores messages from the sense organs, decides what behaviors to exhibit, and sends appropriate messages for responding to the muscles and glands. Most of the behaviors involved in the above scenes are accomplished through the working of the central nervous system, which is composed of the brain and the spinal cord.

Thanks to the part of your brain that controls muscle coordination, the *cerebellum,* you are able to sit in class. You remembered a pleasant event from the past because that memory was stored in the *cerebral cortex* of your brain. You were also able to think about future events because of the cortex. You became alert when your teacher called your name because of a network of neurons in your brain, called the *reticular formation,*

kinson's disease is associated with low levels of the neurotransmitter dopamine in the brain; high levels of dopamine have been implicated in the severe abnormal behavior disorder called schizophrenia.

Levels of norepinephrine in the brain are associated with learning, wakefulness, and emotion. Low levels of norepinephrine are associated with depression; thus, antidepressant drugs are used to raise its level.

Many of the other neurotransmitters are not well understood yet. Two additional groups of neurotransmitters include the amino acids and neuropeptides. Two amino acids, glutamate and aspartate, are excitatory neurotransmitters; two others, glycine and GABA (gamma-aminobutyric acid) are inhibitory neurotransmitters (Roberts, 1986).

A number of neuropeptides, short chains of amino acids, are currently believed to function as neurotransmitters (Bloom, 1983). Some of the prominent

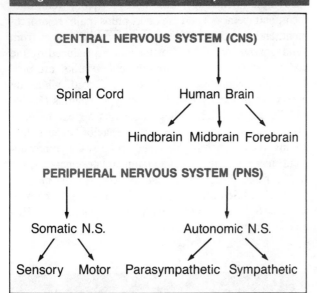

Figure 2.6 Human Nervous System

CENTRAL NERVOUS SYSTEM (CNS)

Spinal Cord   Human Brain

Hindbrain Midbrain Forebrain

PERIPHERAL NERVOUS SYSTEM (PNS)

Somatic N.S.   Autonomic N.S.

Sensory Motor   Parasympathetic Sympathetic

The human nervous system can be divided into the central nervous system (brain and spinal cord) and the peripheral nervous system (autonomic nervous system and somatic nervous system). The peripheral nervous system receives messages from the sense organs and carries information to the muscles and glands. The central nervous system interprets and stores information from the sense organs and sends messages via the peripheral nervous system to the muscles and glands.

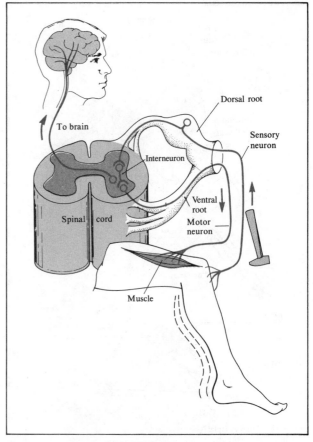

Figure 2.7. Diagram of Spinal Reflex
In the knee jerk reflex, the lower leg swings forward quickly when an area just below the knee is tapped. In order for this reflex to occur, a message travels through a sensory neuron to the spinal cord, where an interneuron carries it to a motor neuron which sends the information to the leg muscle, and causes the movement.

that controls arousal. You were able to understand what you saw on the board because the occipital lobe of your brain analyzes visual information. And you could plan to ask someone for a date because of a part of your brain called the *hypothalamus,* which controls motivation. We will begin our discussion of the central nervous system by reviewing the functions of the spinal cord.

The Spinal Cord

The spinal cord, housed in the spinal backbone, consists of bundles of nerves that form a communication link between the brain and the peripheral nervous system. One important function of the spinal cord is to serve as the pathway along which neural impulses from the sense organs travel up to the brain and other neural impulses from the brain travel down to the muscles and glands. Most of the peripheral nerves connect with the central nervous system through the spinal cord, and thus are called spinal nerves.

Besides serving as a pathway for neural impulses, the spinal cord controls certain types of reflexes. A reflex is an automatic movement that occurs in direct response to a stimulus. Spinal reflexes need not involve the brain, but rather rely on the neural pathways in the spinal cord for their activation. You are probably familiar with a number of reflexes. In the classroom scene above, you

blinked your eyes when the lights were turned on because the pupil of the eye automatically contracts when exposed to bright light. Another reflex you are probably familiar with is the "knee jerk," in which the lower leg swings forward quickly when an area just below the knee is tapped. Reflexes enable people to respond quickly to potentially painful or dangerous situations.

The Brain

The brain has always attracted the attention of psychologists because its physiological activity governs most behaviors. Made up of billions of neurons, the human brain is more intricate than any computer. Most of the behaviors described earlier in the classroom scene were controlled by the brain. It is the center for "higher" mental functions such as thinking and memory. It processes the messages carried to it by the peripheral nervous system and the spinal cord, makes decisions about what responses are necessary, and sends orders to

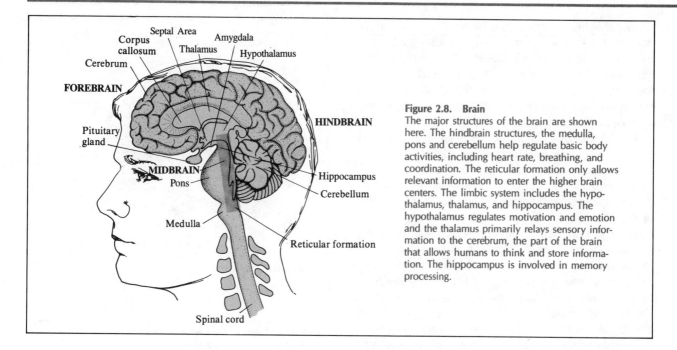

Figure 2.8. Brain
The major structures of the brain are shown here. The hindbrain structures, the medulla, pons and cerebellum help regulate basic body activities, including heart rate, breathing, and coordination. The reticular formation only allows relevant information to enter the higher brain centers. The limbic system includes the hypothalamus, thalamus, and hippocampus. The hypothalamus regulates motivation and emotion and the thalamus primarily relays sensory information to the cerebrum, the part of the brain that allows humans to think and store information. The hippocampus is involved in memory processing.

the muscles to carry out the appropriate behavior. The brain can best be understood by examining its three major divisions: the hindbrain, the midbrain, and the forebrain. Keep in mind, however, that it is the interactions of many brain structures that control behavior.

The Hindbrain. The hindbrain connects the spinal cord with the rest of the brain. It controls the basic life-support functions of the body, such as breathing and heart rate. The hindbrain consists of the medulla, pons, cerebellum, and reticular formation.

The medulla, the part of the hindbrain that directly connects the spinal cord with the brain, helps regulate basic bodily functions, such as breathing and heart rate. The medulla is where a number of peripheral nervous system cranial nerves, which include sensory and motor nerves, enter the central nervous system. Lying just above the medulla is the pons which, through the cranial nerves, plays a role in controlling such behaviors as eating and facial movement. Next to the medulla is a convoluted structure known as the cerebellum, which controls body balance, movement, and muscle coordination, allowing us to walk and run without tripping.

The reticular formation is a network of neurons extending from the medulla up to the higher brain centers found in the forebrain. This structure, sometimes called the *reticular activating system (RAS)*, acts as a gate, allowing relevant sensory information such as that involved in arousal and sleep to enter the brain. When your instructor calls your name, your reticular formation stimulates the higher brain centers that allow you to become alert. When you are sleeping, your reticular formation prevents most environmental stimuli from entering your brain. All of the structures in the

hindbrain work together and are influenced by other parts of the brain.

The Midbrain. The midbrain is a relatively small region that connects the hindbrain with the forebrain. Although the midbrain appears to function mainly as a relay station for messages coming into the brain, it also contains structures that play a role in seeing, hearing, and movement.

The Forebrain. The forebrain is the largest and most complex part of the brain. It not only influences many of the basic life-support functions controlled by the midbrain and hindbrain, but also is responsible for the uniquely human higher-level behaviors such as thinking and speaking. The major structures of the forebrain include the thalamus, hypothalamus, and cerebrum.

The Limbic System. James Papez (1937) proposed the theory that the hypothalamus and related structures formed a circuit for emotional behavior. Paul MacLean (1949) later revised the theory and named the circuit the limbic system. Located in the most primitive part of the forebrain, called the rhinencephalon, it is a collection of structures that influences motivation and emotional behaviors such as sex, aggression, fear, pleasure, and pain. The structures usually included in the limbic system are the thalamus, hypothalamus, amygdala, mammillary bodies, fornix, and septal area.

The function of the limbic system was discovered accidently in 1954 by James Olds and Peter Milner who were testing the effects of electrical stimulation on the reticular formation in rats and placed an *electrode* in the septal area by mistake. When the rats learned that they could control the electrical stimulation and thus the pleasure by pressing a lever, they pressed it thousands of times per hour. Electrical stimulation of the brain (ESB) has a potent reinforcing effect, which means the individual will repeat whatever behavior led to the pleasurable sensation. The reinforcing effects of ESB have been found in a variety of animals, including humans. Some recent research suggests that ESB involves endorphin synapses (Wise and Bozarth, 1984).

The Thalamus. The thalamus is an important relay station for sensory information, including visual, auditory, tactile (touch), pain, and temperature stimuli. Messages from these sense organs are channeled into the thalamus, and from there are carried into a specific part of the forebrain for interpretation and action.

The Hypothalamus. An important part of the limbic system is the small structure called the hypothalamus. It is involved in the motivation of such behaviors as eating, drinking, having sex, sleeping, and regulating temperature, and influences the pituitary gland which regulates biochemical reactions in the body. The hypothalamus also influences the part of the peripheral nervous system that regulates the internal body organs. We discuss some of the specific motivated behaviors influenced by the hypothalamus in chapter 9, "Motivation."

Other areas in the limbic system are also important in a wide variety of behaviors. The hippocampus is important in learning and memory. The amygdala and septal area are involved in fear, aggression, and other social behaviors. Research has shown that reward sites for ESB are located throughout the brain, but are especially concentrated around the medial forebrain bundle, a tract that runs through the limbic system.

The Cerebrum. The cerebrum, the largest part of the forebrain, consists of two distinct structures called hemispheres. The two hemispheres are connected by the corpus callosum, a bundle of nerves that keeps each hemisphere informed about what is happening in the other. Basically, the left hemisphere controls the right side of the body and the right hemisphere controls the left side. For proper motor coordination, each hemisphere must know what the other is doing. An activity involving both sides of the body, such as crossing our hands or tying our shoes, would be difficult if our two cerebral hemispheres were not connected.

The outermost layer of the cerebrum, the cerebral cortex, is the part of the brain that renders humans truly unique. Here is where messages from our sense organs are interpreted and stored, and where decisions about behavior are made. The cortex has distinct sections, or lobes, that control different activities. When you are in the classroom remembering past events or giving the answer to a question, you are using the frontal lobes of your cortex. Your occipital lobes allow you to interpret what you see in the environment. When you hear your teacher talking, your temporal lobes are operating. And your parietal lobes are responsible for interpreting so-

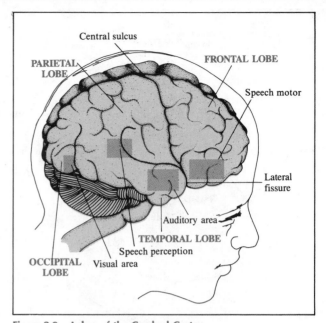

Figure 2.9. Lobes of the Cerebral Cortex
The cerebral cortex is divided into four distinct sections, or lobes. The frontal lobe controls thinking and motor coordination. The occipital lobe interprets visual information. The temporal lobe perceives speech and hearing. The parietal lobe receives sensory information.

matosensory senses such as touch, pain, and temperature.

Although each lobe of the brain is primarily responsible for one main function (frontal lobes, movement and memory; occipital lobes, vision; temporal lobes, hearing; and parietal lobes, somatosensory senses), much of the area of the cerebral cortex is involved in multiple sensory or motor functions. These association areas of the brain help integrate information for successful adaptation. For example, when you think about a dog, you utilize a variety of association areas. You remember the sound of the dog's bark, the feel of her fur, the sight of her body, the image of her running, and the features of her face.

Cerebral Hemisphere Functioning. In general, each hemisphere of the cerebrum controls the opposite side of the body: the left half controls the right side of the body and the right controls the left side. But the two hemispheres are not totally redundant in function. The left hemisphere is usually considered to be the more logical, analytical, and verbal half, exerting greater control over manual dexterity, reading, language, and understanding speech. The right hemisphere tends to process nonverbal information and is more concerned with emotion, imagination, and artistic information (Levy, 1985). For most people, the left hemisphere is the more dominant. Levy pointed out, however, that both hemispheres receive information simultaneously and both hemispheres can function independently.

When the corpus callosum, the nerve bundle connecting the two hemispheres, is cut, people appear to

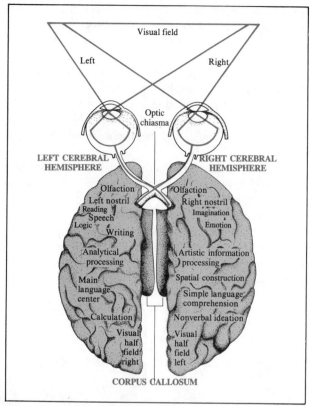

Figure 2.10. Cerebral Hemisphere
The cerebrum consists of two distinct hemispheres connected by the corpus callosum. The corpus callosum is a bundle of nerves that keeps each hemisphere informed about what is happening in the other one. Each hemisphere controls different functions but the exact location of those functions is not known.

function pretty much as they did previously, but in fact there are subtle dysfunctions. The classic research in this area was done by Roger Sperry (1968), who studied epileptic patients whose corpus callosum had been severed in order to reduce the frequency of seizures. Sperry received a Nobel Prize in 1981 for his work on what he termed the syndrome of hemisphere deconnection, popularly known as split-brain research. Our eyes are connected to our brains in such a way that the left field of vision is received initially only by the right hemisphere of the brain and the right field of vision only by the left hemisphere. With a normal corpus callosum the information is quickly transmitted to both hemispheres, and the left hemisphere will name it. Sperry devised a way to present different information to each hemisphere in split-brain patients and found that normal functioning broke down under such conditions. If you place an object like a pencil in the right hand, the information is received by the left hemisphere which also names it. But when the object is presented to the left side of the visual field or placed in the left hand, the patient can't say what it is. This is because the right hemisphere has received the information and can't transmit it to the center for the production of language in the left or dominant hemisphere. Although the right hemisphere does not control speech, it can recognize words. If a word is shown only to the left visual field, the patients cannot say what the word is. However, they can write the word with the left hand. If asked what they just did, patients cannot tell you, because the language

ROGER SPERRY

Roger Sperry was born August 20, 1913, in Hartford, Connecticut. He was rewarded with a Nobel Prize in physiology and medicine in 1981 for his more than 40 years of research on the brain. The prize was given specifically for his work on the "split-brain," in which he discovered that the two cerebral hemispheres of the brain had distinct functions. The left, usually the dominant side, is involved in reasoning, language, writing, and reading, while the right, or less dominant side, is more involved in nonverbal processes, such as art, music, and creative behavior.

Sperry received his Ph.D. from the University of Chicago in 1941. He did his early research at Harvard University and the Yerkes Primate Laboratory before joining the staff of the California Institute of Technology in 1954 as Hixon Professor of Psychobiology. He studied cats, and found that the corpus callosum, or nerve bundle connecting the two cerebral hemispheres, was necessary for the transfer of information from one side of the brain to the other.

Sperry next began to study epileptic patients whose corpus callosum had been severed to prevent seizures. His technique, which he termed "hemisphere deconnection," has contributed valuable information to the treatment of various brain disorders.

center, located in the left hemisphere, has not received the information from the right hemisphere (Gazzaniga, 1983).

It appears that sometimes different types of memory are stored best in different hemispheres. Results of research performed by Brenda Milner and L. Taylor (1972) suggest that the right hemisphere stores nonverbal information better than the left, whereas the left is more efficient at storing verbal information. Milner and Taylor reported that subjects with damage to the left side of the brain have trouble remembering new verbal information, such as a series of instructions or a list of words. Subjects with damage to the right side of the brain have more trouble remembering new nonverbal information, such as a face or a picture.

Under most conditions in the person without a split brain, information about the environment is sent from the sense organs through the peripheral nervous system to both hemispheres of the brain, so that the brain can make a decision and send the appropriate response message through the peripheral nervous system to the muscles and glands.

Therefore, it is incorrect to say that a normal functioning person is totally "left-brained" or "right-brained." Similarly, caution is urged in signing up for programs that try to teach "right-brain" skills (McKean, 1985). In most cases, both hemispheres work together, irrespective of the task.

Methods of Studying the Brain. Psychologists have developed a variety of techniques to study the brain so that they can better predict, control, and explain behavior. One early method was proposed by Franz Gall, who in the early 1800s measured the bumps on people's skulls and tried to relate them to various behavior characteristics. While this method, called phrenology, never produced significant results, it did set the stage for later

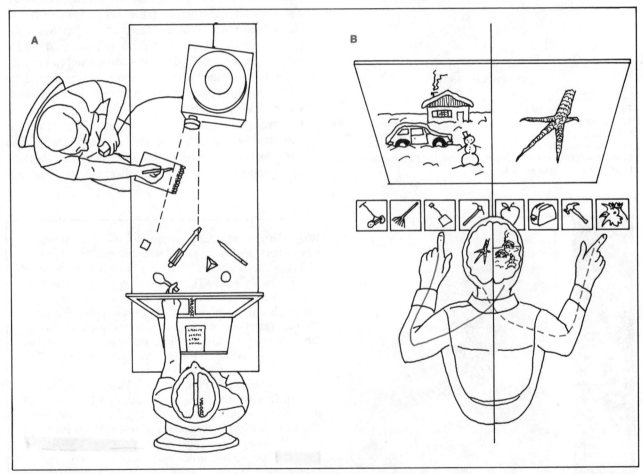

Figure 2.11. Testing Split-Brain Subjects
This figure illustrates the difficulty a split-brain subject has in integrating information between the two hemispheres of his brain. The subject with normal hemisphere function, **(B)**, points to the object that would be related to the visual information received in the opposite hemisphere of his brain. The subject with a split brain, **(A)**, sits in front of a divided visual display screen. In the first step of the test, the image of the spoon is shown on the left side of the screen, and on the right side, the image of a fork. The subject will respond that he has seen a fork, since the left, verbal hemisphere has received that image and can also name it. In the next step of the test, when asked to pick up that object with his left hand, the subject will choose a spoon since the left hand is controlled by the right hemisphere and that hemisphere saw a spoon. But when asked to name the object, he will respond "a fork" since the visual, tactile, information received in the right hemisphere cannot cross the corpus callosum into the left, verbal hemisphere.

methods of identifying the functions of particular parts of the brain.

In the 1930s, it was discovered that if the frontal lobes were disconnected from the rest of the brain, violent or extremely emotional mental patients became calm. This procedure, called prefrontal lobotomy, was for a time popular in treating severe behavior problems. However, studies showed that prefrontal lobotomy had negative side effects: lobotomy patients show little emotion, have no social inhibitions, and have trouble solving problems. Because of these behavioral side effects, and because of the ethical implications in cutting out part of a brain, lobotomies are no longer performed to treat mental disorders. Currently, the most common biological method for treating mental disorders is drug therapy. (See chapter 14, "Therapy.")

An important technique used presently for studying the brain involves the *electrical stimulation* of specific areas. In our discussion of the limbic system, we mentioned the discovery of pleasure centers in the brain by Olds and Milner. Using ESB with rats, they found that when an electrode, which is an extremely thin insulated wire, was inserted into the brain and a very weak electrical current was sent through the electrode, the rats increased whatever behavior had preceded the ESB.

Another demonstration of the effects of brain stimulation on behavior was described by José Delgado (1969). Delgado implanted an electrode in the brain of a bull, and then entered the bull ring armed only with a radio transmitter. When the bull charged toward him, Delgado pressed a button, causing the bull to stop and turn away. Less exciting, perhaps, than dodging around with a red cape, but an apt demonstration of the brain's direct control over behavior.

Electrical stimulation of the human brain can be used to help people with behavior problems, as demonstrated by the research of Wilder Penfield presented in the opening story. Penfield used brain stimulation to locate malfunctioning areas of the brain. His purpose was to find the areas of the brain causing a type of epilepsy in which a number of neurons begin to fire wildly. When the area was located, the malfunctioning part was removed. In the course of such brain surgery, Penfield discovered that stimulating areas of the cortex could produce vivid memories, as described at the beginning of this chapter.

Some people believe that electrical stimulation of the brain may someday be used to control complex behavior in people. While science-fiction writers love to speculate on the grim possibilities this suggests for an unethical control of people, most psychologists agree with Elliot Valenstein who pointed out in his 1973 book, *Brain Control*, that such fears are greatly exaggerated and the complex social behaviors of humans will never be controlled.

In addition to stimulating the brain electrically, psychologists also can record the brain's electrical activity. In this technique, called electroencephalography (EEG), electrodes are attached to the scalp to record general

Figure 2.12. Electrical Brain Stimulation
José Delgado implanted an electrode in the brain of a bull and stopped the bull from charging by giving him an electrical signal.

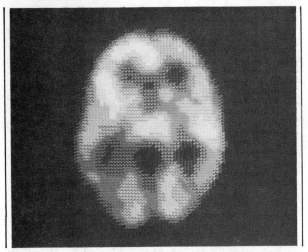

Figure 2.13. PET Scan Technique
In position emission tomography (PET) scanning, the location of injected radioactive sugar molecules in the brain are mapped. As neurons in any part of the brain fire, they require energy that is provided by the radioactive sugar. The brain patterns are then recorded and used by scientists to detect areas of specific activity.

brain-wave patterns. An extension of the EEG technique is the EEG imaging procedure. In EEG imaging, electrodes are placed on the scalp and the wires are connected to a computer. Then the activity of the brain as the person is responding can be measured (Fishman, 1985).

Recently, a method known as PET scan, or Positron Emission Tomography, has been developed to examine brain activity during particular behaviors or mental activities (Raichle, 1983). The patient is given an injection of radioactive glucose. Then the PET scan records the gamma rays produced by the radioactive glucose as it is used by the brain cells. Another approach to studying brain activity is NMR (Nuclear Magnetic Resonance) imaging that uses magnetic fields to study chemical activity of brain cells. Recording the electrical activity of the brain allows scientists to locate parts of the brain involved in specific behaviors, detect neural damage, and study states of consciousness such as sleep and dreaming.

If a recording indicates that a certain area of the brain is malfunctioning, ablation may be used to correct the problem. Ablation, the surgical removal of a part of the brain, falls within the general category of psychosurgery, which is brain surgery for the treatment of psychological problems.

Technology is quickly advancing our ability to study the functioning of the brain. With the newer methods of brain study, scientists are beginning to understand what the brain is doing when a person is in different states of consciousness, is solving problems, or is remembering previously learned experiences.

PERIPHERAL NERVOUS SYSTEM

On your way home from school, you are confronted by a large, snarling dog with its teeth bared. Immediately you feel "butterflies" in your stomach, you begin to breathe faster, and your heart speeds up. You can almost feel the blood flowing away from your inner organs toward your muscles, preparing you for what is called a "fight or flight" response. You begin to feel more energy as blood sugar is released. Then you breathe a sigh of relief as you see the dog's owner take it away. When you sit down to rest, your breathing begins to slow down and your heart rate decreases. After you feel relaxed, you get up and proceed home, thinking about what you will be eating for dinner.

While you were having your encounter with the snarling dog, your whole nervous system was active. Up to this point, we've concentrated only on the central nervous system—the part that allows us to interpret sensory information, think, remember things, and make decisions. Another branch of the human nervous system, the peripheral nervous system, carries messages from the sense organs to the central nervous system, and from the central nervous system to the muscles and glands. It includes all of the nerves outside the brain and spinal cord. The nerves that connect to the spinal cord are called spinal nerves; those that connect to the brain are cranial nerves. The peripheral nervous system consists of two major divisions—the somatic nervous system and the autonomic nervous system.

Somatic Nervous System

The somatic nervous system might be regarded as "external," since it involves the sense organs and the skeletal muscles, both located close to the outside surface of the body. The sensory division of the somatic nervous system carries messages from the sense organs, whereas the motor division relays information that directs primarily the voluntary movements of the skeletal muscles. When you first encountered the snarling dog, it was the somatic division of your peripheral nervous system that carried the information from your eyes and ears to your central nervous system. Also, it was your somatic nervous system that carried the directions to the skeletal muscles of your legs, enabling you to turn around and walk the other way. Without your somatic nervous system, you would not be aware of your external environment and you could not respond to changes in it.

Biofeedback

The autonomic nervous system is usually associated with emotions, stress, and emergencies. We measure responses such as heart rate, breathing, blood pressure, skin electrical activity (how well the skin conducts a weak electric current), and temperature (especially on the forehead and fingertips) to understand autonomic nervous system activity. All of these measures are controlled by both the sympathetic (arousal) and parasympathetic (maintenance) parts of the autonomic nervous system.

As discussed in chapter 12, "Stress and Adjustment," stress can lead to a variety of physical problems, including headaches, ulcers, heart attacks, rashes, and high blood pressure. It was long believed that the autonomic nervous system produced involuntary responses. Thus, if you were under stress and your sympathetic nervous system was active, you were doomed to suffer the consequences of ulcers and heart attacks. Now, thanks to the pioneering efforts of psychologists such as Neal Miller, people are learning to decrease or increase their heart rate, blood pressure, temperature, and other bodily functions through the technique of biofeedback.

In a typical biofeedback session, a person is taught to recognize the effects of the autonomic nervous system on bodily functions. For example, the subject might monitor his or her own blood pressure by listening to a machine that buzzes when blood pressure increases, then beeps when blood pressure decreases. The subject tries to become aware of the bodily feelings that accompany the higher and lower blood pressure. With practice, the subject can raise or lower blood pressure at will, even without the monitoring device. This is accomplished by learning to control the tension in the skeletal muscles (McGuigan, 1984).

Another form of biofeedback is electromyographic, or EMG relaxation. In one procedure, the subject focuses on the muscles in the forehead and attempts to reduce the tension activity in these muscles (Fridlend, Fowler, & Pritchard, 1980). A number of studies have shown that EMG biofeedback is about as effective as relaxation training for relieving headaches.

Figure 2.14. Biofeedback
In a biofeedback session, a subject is taught to recognize the effects of the autonomic nervous system on bodily functions.

Biofeedback is helping people cope with stress and is preventing some of the undesirable effects of long-term exposure to stress. As we learn more about the autonomic nervous system and its effects on bodily processes, we will be able to help more people effectively deal with stress.

THOUGHT QUESTIONS

1. How can understanding the activity of the autonomic nervous system improve the effectiveness of biofeedback?
2. What are some other applications of biofeedback?
3. What are the implications of gaining control of our autonomic nervous system activity? Could we then at will control our emotional expressions? Is this desirable?

Autonomic Nervous System

The autonomic nervous system is more of an internal system, connecting the central nervous system to the endocrine glands, the muscles controlling the heart, and the primarily involuntary smooth muscles controlling the other internal organs, such as the stomach, intestines, liver, and lungs. The autonomic nervous system is very important in emotion, and we'll be referring to it in chapter 10, "Emotion."

The autonomic nervous system is further divided into two branches: the sympathetic nervous system, which is more active in emergencies, and the parasympathetic nervous system, which is more active under normal circumstances. When you are calm and quiet, the parasympathetic nervous system causes your heart rate to slow down, your blood pressure to be lowered, and breathing to become normal. It also activates the stomach and intestines so that normal digestion can occur. The primary neurotransmitter found in the parasympathetic nervous system is acetylcholine, whose effects mainly inhibit muscle action. The parasympathetic system can be thought of as the maintenance system that is in control during relaxation. Your parasympathetic nervous system was dominant as you began to walk home from school and were not yet in any danger from the dog.

When you suddenly saw the snarling dog in your path, your sympathetic nervous system caused the increase in heart rate, blood pressure, and breathing. Your eyes dilated to take in more information, blood was redirected from your stomach to your limbs so you could fight or flee, and your adrenal glands secreted a chemical called adrenaline to provide you with extra energy. The sympathetic system utilizes norepinephrine as its main neurotransmitter, which helps to explain its excitatory effects on the muscles and glands. Often activated in emergency situations, the sympathetic nervous system is especially important when you are under stress.

Although our description implies a simple division of labor, we must remember that neither part of the autonomic nervous system acts in isolation. The sympathetic and parasympathetic divisions continuously act in opposition to each other, the sympathetic arousing and parasympathetic relaxing the body. Behavior is the end result of the interaction of both parts, along with the other biological response systems.

THE ENDOCRINE SYSTEM

The autonomic nervous system works closely with the endocrine (or ductless) glands to maintain homeostasis, or biochemical stability inside the body. Endocrine glands help provide you with the extra energy you require when faced with an emergency, and regulate the energy usage when you're relaxed. Although the endocrine glands are also a communication system, unlike the nervous system they secrete hormones directly into the blood stream to produce a slower but more generalized control over internal physiological processes, and ultimately, behavior. Hormones help regulate the body's biochemical activity, enabling us to make appropriate responses to environmental situations.

The Pituitary Gland. The pituitary gland, located near the hypothalamus at the base of the brain, is called the "master gland" because some of its hormones stimulate other endocrine glands into action. The pituitary gland secretes the growth hormone, which helps regulate growth, and the antidiuretic hormone (ADH), which causes the kidneys to retain water.

The Thyroid Gland. The thyroid gland secretes thyroxin, a hormone that helps determine the rate of

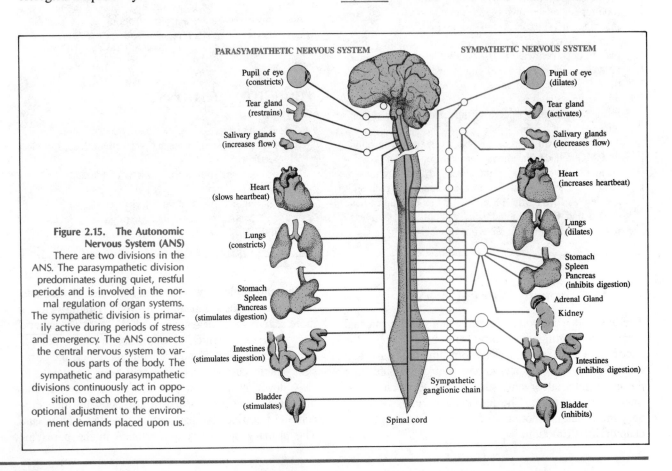

Figure 2.15. The Autonomic Nervous System (ANS)
There are two divisions in the ANS. The parasympathetic division predominates during quiet, restful periods and is involved in the normal regulation of organ systems. The sympathetic division is primarily active during periods of stress and emergency. The ANS connects the central nervous system to various parts of the body. The sympathetic and parasympathetic divisions continuously act in opposition to each other, producing optional adjustment to the environment demands placed upon us.

PARASYMPATHETIC NERVOUS SYSTEM

Pupil of eye (constricts)
Tear gland (restrains)
Salivary glands (increases flow)
Heart (slows heartbeat)
Lungs (constricts)
Stomach Spleen Pancreas (stimulates digestion)
Intestines (stimulates digestion)
Bladder (stimulates)

SYMPATHETIC NERVOUS SYSTEM

Pupil of eye (dilates)
Tear gland (activates)
Salivary glands (decreases flow)
Heart (increases heartbeat)
Lungs (dilates)
Stomach Spleen Pancreas (inhibits digestion)
Adrenal Gland
Kidney
Intestines (inhibits digestion)
Bladder (inhibits)

Sympathetic ganglionic chain
Spinal cord

metabolism, which is the biochemical process that produces energy for the body's maintenance. The condition resulting from an underactive thyroid, called hypothyroidism, results in sluggishness, sleepiness, and weight gain. On the other hand, if the thyroid gland produces too much thyroxin, a person will become easily excitable, have excess energy, and lose weight.

The Adrenal Glands. Located over the kidneys, your adrenal glands help the body react to stress by regulating short-term energy use. The inner part, or adrenal medulla, secretes adrenaline, a hormone that works with the sympathetic nervous system to bring about the arousal necessary to produce the "fight or flight" response required in an emergency, as when you encountered the snarling dog. The outer part, known as the adrenal cortex, produces steroid hormones that help regulate salt balance and provide energy. The adrenal cortex of each gland also secretes sex hormones.

The Gonads. The reproductive glands, or gonads, are ovaries in the female (secrete estrogen) and testes in the male (secrete androgen). They are involved in sex determination and development, secondary sexual characteristics, and sexual motivation. Each individual has hormones of both sexes, but females have a predominance of estrogen, and males of androgen. Estrogens produce female characteristics, such as breasts and wide hips, while androgens produce male characteristics, such as facial hair and low-pitched voices.

In the male, secretion of sex hormones is fairly constant, thus producing a fairly stable state of sexual motivation. In the female, hormonal secretion varies with the fertility cycle. Early in the cycle, large amounts of estrogen are produced, resulting in increased sexual motivation at that time. Other factors, such as learning and social customs, however, play a role in regulating the sex drive. (See chapter 9, "Motivation," for discussion of human sexual motivation.)

In summary, hormones secreted by the endocrine glands play an important role in behavioral responses. Hormones produce a readiness in the body for responding appropriately to environmental stimuli. Some hormones produce short-term changes, but most produce long-term physiological reactions in the body.

HEREDITY AND BEHAVIOR

The biological response systems, including the sense organs, nervous system, endocrine system, and muscles, permit us to respond appropriately and immediately to environmental stimuli. For example, we see a

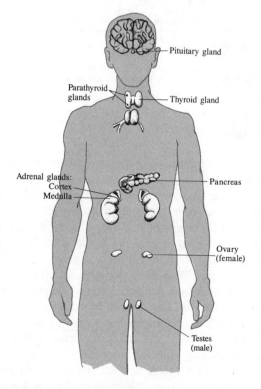

Gland	Hormone	Function
Pituitary	Growth	Growth regulation
	Antidiuretic	Water regulation
	Oxytocin	Smooth muscle control (child birth, milk releaser)
Thyroid	Thyroxin	Energy metabolism
Parathyroid	Parahormone	Calcium metabolism
Adrenals	Epinephrine	Stress reactions Emotion
	Glucocorticoids	Carbohydrate metabolism
Pancreas	Insulin	Sugar metabolism
Gonads Testes—male Ovaries—female	Androgen Estrogen	Secondary sex characteristics, sex determination, and sexual motivation

Figure 2.16. Endocrine System
The endocrine glands secrete hormones directly into the bloodstream to control physiological processes. This figure shows the major endocrine glands and some of the activities regulated by them.

friend and wave in response. However, it is our heredity that determines the ultimate structure of our biological response systems, as well as their functioning ability. Heredity is the natural capability of individuals to develop the characteristics possessed by their ancestors.

In the study of heredity, called genetics, scientists study the laws that determine how traits are passed along from parents to offspring. Psychologists study genetics in order to understand better how behavior is influenced by heredity and the environment.

Basic Genetic Principles

The gene is the basic unit of heredity. The complete set of genes inherited by an individual from parents is called the genotype. The genotype interacts with the environment to produce the phenotype, which is the sum of observable characteristics of the individual: the phenotype includes sex, eye and hair color, height, weight, and intelligence, as well as personality characteristics such as shyness, aggressiveness, and strength—in fact, all the attributes that determine the unique individual.

Genes control the development of chemicals called proteins and enzymes, which in turn are involved in the biochemical reactions that ultimately produce the organs and biological response systems that make up an individual. Genes control maturation, or the physical growth of the individual. However, all the effects of genes are achieved through an interaction with the environment. We discuss maturation in chapter 3, "Development."

Genes are composed of organic molecules called deoxyribonucleic acid (DNA). It was only in 1953 that Watson and Crick found DNA had a double helix pattern (like a spiral staircase) that allows the gene to transcribe its message and direct the formation of biochemicals that can be utilized to ultimately produce the characteristics of the individual. Genes can be thought of as locations along chromosomes (from the Greek word for "colored bodies"). Chromosomes are slender bodies found in the nucleus of every cell.

Normally, every cell in the human body (except the sex cells) has 23 pairs of chromosomes, for a total of 46 chromosomes. However, the sex cells only have 23 chromosomes. At the time of conception, the 23 chromosomes from the egg combine with the 23 chromosomes from the sperm to produce a zygote, or fertilized egg, which then has 46 chromosomes. Thus, with an equal number of chromosomes from our mother and father, we maintain the stable number of 46 chromosomes in every body cell.

Twenty-two of the pairs of chromosomes are called autosomes, which carry genes that regulate various bodily processes and characteristics, such as eye color, intelligence, and height.

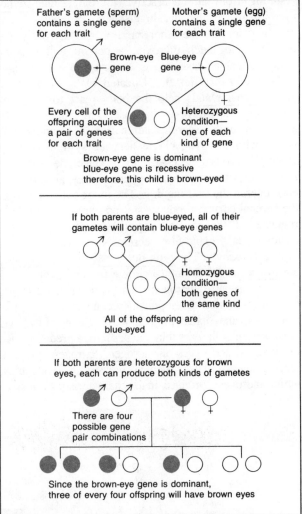

Figure 2.17. Heredity

Heredity is the tendency of individuals to develop some of the same characteristics as their ancestors. This figure demonstrates how eye color is likely to be inherited.

Since each chromosome of a given pair comes from a different parent, two forms of a particular gene are possible. Using eye color as a simplified example, one form of the gene (*B*) might result in brown eyes, whereas another form (*b*) results in blue eyes. If a child received a *B* gene from each parent, she would probably have brown eyes, and if she received a *b* gene from each parent, she would likely have blue eyes. But if the child received a *B* gene from one parent and a *b* gene from the other one, she would end up with brown eyes. Geneticists say the *B* form of the gene is dominant, whereas the *b* form is recessive. It takes only one dominant gene for the phenotype to be reflected but it takes both recessive genes to produce a recessive trait. An individual with both genes identical is said to be homozygous for the gene, whereas the individual with two different genes is called heterogeneous. Even though the phenotype of a

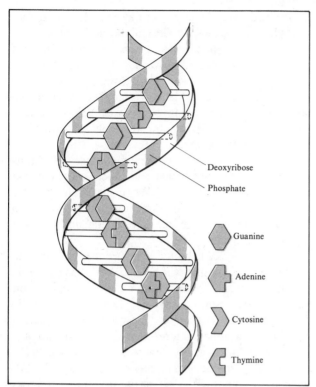

Figure 2.18. The DNA Molecule
Genes are made of organic molecules called deoxyribonucleic acid (DNA). Watson and Crick discovered that DNA has a double helix pattern that determines the code that directs the formation of biochemicals. They in turn will ultimately produce the characteristics of the individual.

Labels on figure: Deoxyribose, Phosphate, Guanine, Adenine, Cytosine, Thymine

Figure 2.19. Sex Determination

A

1 2 3 4 5
6 7 8 9 10 11 12
13 14 15 16 17 18
19 20 21 22 23 Male XY 23 Female XX

B

Female XX — Male XY — Parents
X X X Y — Eggs / Sperm
XX Female — XY Male — Offspring

At the time of conception, the 23 chromosomes from the egg combine with the 23 chromosomes from the sperm to produce a zygote, or fertilized egg cell which then has 46 chromosomes. **(A)** Two of these chromosomes determine sex. **(B)** If an X chromosome is inherited from both parents, the offspring will be a female. If an X is inherited from the mother and a Y is inherited from the father, the offspring will be a male.

heterogeneous person reflects the dominant gene, he or she still carries the recessive gene which could be passed along to offspring.

One pair of chromosomes is called the sex chromosomes, because the genes located on this pair are responsible for determining the sex of the person. If you are a female, you have two X chromosomes; if you are a male, you have one X chromosome and one Y chromosome. When the sex cells are formed, in a process called meiosis, eggs always carry an X chromosome, whereas sperm can carry an X or a Y chromosome. Therefore, at conception it is the sperm that genetically determines the sex of the offspring. If an X chromosome from a sperm combines with the X chromosome from the egg, the offspring will be a female. On the other hand, if a Y chromosome from a sperm combines with the X chromosome from the egg, the offspring will be a male. The sex chromosome also contains many other genes that control processes other than the determination of sex.

Behavior Genetics

Behavior genetics is the study of how heredity influences behavior. The term behavior genetics might suggest to you that behavior is inherited directly from parents.

Actually, the only things biologically passed on from parents to offspring are the nuclei of the egg and sperm containing the genes. Thus, it is technically incorrect to say "You inherited your father's eyes" or "You inherited your intelligence from your mother." What you really inherited were the genes which influenced the physiological reactions necessary for you to ultimately develop eye color or intelligence.

The interaction of hereditary and environmental influences is necessary for any physical trait or behavioral characteristic to occur. For example, an individual who inherited the genes for the physical trait of brown eyes will probably develop brown eyes because of the various physiological reactions directed by the genes. But the person might also have the gene for albinism, which results in a lack of coloration, including a lack of eye color. Therefore, the person may not have brown eyes, even if the genes for brown eyes are present. This example illustrates that the development of a physical trait such as eye color depends upon the interaction of heredity and the physiological pathways of the internal body environment. Obviously, the development of behavioral traits can be even more complex as the external environment interacts with the body's physiological pathways.

How do genes influence behavior? Exactly the same way they influence physical characteristics—through the biological response systems. Genes influence behavior indirectly through the biochemical pathways that ultimately result in the functioning of muscles, endocrine glands, nerves, and sense organs.

Because each person has a unique set of genes, or a unique genotype, and we each have experiences that are different from other people's, the variability among people is the result of both genetic and environmental influences. To illustrate these influences, let's look at the sensation of taste. My wife prefers six spoonfuls of sugar in her tea, while I prefer no sugar in mine. What could have caused this behavior difference? It is very likely that learning played an important role in my wife's preference for sweetened tea, as her early experience included many more sweet foods than mine. Research has also shown, however, that there are genetic differences in the distribution of taste buds on the tongue and in the ability to perceive tastes. Genes affect the production of the hormones that help regulate the utilization of food energy sources such as sugar. This helps to explain why my wife is much slimmer than I am, even though she loves sweets.

Genes also influence behavior through their control of the development of the nervous system. This may be better understood by reference to an abnormality in the body's chemistry that can produce mental retardation. Phenylketonuria (PKU) occurs when the body is not able to convert a chemical found in some food proteins into harmless by-products. The chemical, phenylalanine, instead builds into a brain poison that results in severe mental retardation. PKU is caused by a single recessive gene that prevents the normal biochemical reactions in the body.

Researchers have discovered that when the condition is detected early enough and the child is placed on a phenylaline-free diet, intellectual development will proceed normally. For instance, phenylketonurics (individuals who have PKU) are warned not to eat any food which is sweetened with NutraSweet, as it contains phenylalanine. Note the label warning the next time you see a product containing NutraSweet. Fortunately, a simple test for PKU is now routinely performed on newborns in the hospital.

The point here is that the gene that causes PKU must interact with the nutritional and biochemical environment to produce its effect. When the environment is changed (in this case, the diet), the behavior resulting from the interaction (in this case, intellectual functioning) can be changed.

The influence of heredity on behavior is an extremely important concept that will be discussed throughout the textbook. Some relevant topics include biological constraints on learning (chapter 6, "Learning"), heredity and intelligence (chapter 8, "Cognition"), instinct, sociobiology, and motivation (chapter 9, "Motivation"), heredity and personality (chapter 11, "Personality"), and heredity and abnormal behavior (chapter 13, "Abnormal Psychology"). This partial list should convince you that behavior genetics is an important part of today's psychology.

Animal Studies. Psychologists believe that by understanding how heredity and the environment affect behavior, they will be better able to help people with behavior problems. However, basic research is often performed using animals. Two important research methods used in animal behavior genetics are inbred strain comparisons and selective breeding (Plomin, DeFries, & McClearn, 1980).

Researchers produce inbred strains by mating animals that are closely related genetically (such as brother-sister) over a number of generations. Eventually the animals become identical to one another genetically, and are then said to belong to an inbred strain. The inbred strains can be used to test whether genetic differences affect behavior. For example, if two genetically different groups of inbred strains of mice (inbred group A and inbred group B) are reared in identical environments, any differences in behavior should be due to the genetic differences of the strains.

Inbred strains can also be used to test the influence of the environment on behavior. If groups of animals from an inbred strain are reared in different environments, any behavior differences in the groups should be due to environmental influences (or more precisely, to the interaction of heredity with the environment).

Another important animal research technique is selective breeding, in which similar animals are mated over many generations. Because they have similar genes, if you continue to mate the most similar animals, eventu-

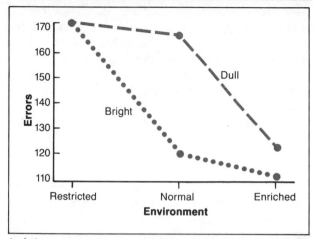

Figure 2.20. Genetic/Environmental Interaction

In their experiment Cooper and Zubek (1958) found that the behavior of selectively bred bright and dull rats was modified when the animals were raised in either an enriched or restricted environment. This demonstrates that behavior is the result of the interaction of both genetic and environmental influences.

ally you will obtain strains of animals that are different from the original population. In their 1965 book, Scott and Fuller explain that dogs have been selectively bred for ten thousand years, resulting in the wide variety of specialized breeds we have today. Wimer and Wimer (1985) review the types of animal behaviors that have been selectively bred, including activity, learning, emotionality, and even alcohol preference.

In a classic selective breeding study, Robert Tryon (1940) selected rats for their maze learning ability. He mated the animals that made the fewest errors (maze bright) together and the ones that made the most errors (maze dull) together. Then he mated the most similar offspring for 21 generations. After seven generations, Tryon had developed two genetically different lines of rats.

Another important behavior genetic study was conducted by Cooper and Zubek (1958). For their experiment, they used selectively bred rats which were maze bright and maze dull. Since the maze bright and dull rats were reared in identical environments, the difference could only be attributed to heredity. Cooper and Zubek placed rats from both groups in either a restricted environment (grey wall and empty cage) or an enriched environment (designs on wall and cage containing objects such as ramps, mirrors, swings, balls, slides, and tunnels).

When raised in restricted environments, the dull rats made many errors as usual, but the bright rats also made many errors. And when raised in the enriched environment, both groups made few errors. Since the genotypes did not change, it seems clear that the remarkable changes in behavior were caused by the changes in

environment. Cooper and Zubek argued that heredity and environment always interact to produce the final resulting behavior. (See Figure 2.20.)

Human Studies. Although in animals, selective breeding and inbred strain comparisons may be used to estimate genetic and environmental influences on behavior, it is more difficult to conduct behavior genetic research in humans. Because of obvious ethical considerations, researchers cannot produce people from specified matings, but rather must find subjects already living in the population. Experimental control can not be as rigid, since we cannot isolate people to ensure a uniform environment. Psychologists are able to study the effects of heredity and environment on behavior in twin studies, adoption studies, and family studies (Plomin, DeFries, and McClearn, 1980).

There is one natural population of people that allows behavior geneticists to control heredity and check some effects of environment—twins. Nonidentical (fraternal) twins, called <u>dizygotic twins,</u> are the result of two separate eggs fertilized by two sperm at about the same time, and are no more genetically related than any two siblings. Identical twins, called <u>monozygotic twins,</u> result from one fertilized egg that splits into two shortly after fertilization. Therefore, monozygotic twins are genetically identical.

Since monozygotic twins have identical genotypes, any differences between them should be due to environmental influences (more accurately, to interactions between genotype and environment). Results of research with twins are especially informative when the twins are

Figure 2.21. Twin Studies
Human twins provide a unique opportunity for psychologists to study the effects of heredity and environment on behavior. Monozygotic twins, having inherited identical genes, will demonstrate the influence of environment on behavior as shown in these benches built by these twins independently. Monozygotic twins are significantly more similar than dizygotic twins.

reared in different environments. Occasionally, each of a pair of twins is adopted and raised by a different family. Twin studies indicate that characteristics that make up intelligence, personality, and some behavior disorders are more similar in monozygotic twins than dizygotic twins, suggesting a significant genetic contribution to these behaviors.

A review of twin studies of intelligence (Loehlin & Nichols, 1976) concludes that monozygotic twins are significantly more similar than dizygotic twins. Data from over 6,000 pairs of twins indicated that the degree of relationship, or correlation, for all dizygotic twins was .62. (Remember from chapter 1, "The Study of Psychology," that correlation is a statistical measure of relationship ranging from 0, no relationship, to 1.00, identical as measured.) Since dizygotic twins have half of their genes in common, this figure (.62) might have been expected. The correlation for the monozygotic twins was .86, which is less than the expected 1.00 for a perfect relationship. Because monozygotic twins are genetically identical, the less-than-perfect correlation is due in part to environmental influences on intelligence. This study shows again that heredity and environment interact to produce behavior. We discuss heredity and intelligence further in chapter 8, "Cognition." In family studies the degree of similarity for particular behavioral characteristics is obtained for family members of known genetic relationship. Goldsmith (1983) concludes that a number of studies have shown a definite genetic basis for personality.

Genetic influences have been discovered in many behavior disorders, such as depression, alcoholism, schizophrenia, and antisocial personality (Henderson, 1982). In each case, the genotype predisposes the individual to react in a way that will vary according to environmental influences. For example, a person with a genetic predisposition to alcoholism could not become an alcoholic if alcohol were unavailable to her or him.

In adoption studies, comparisons can be made between children and their adoptive parents as well as between children and their biological parents. As we discuss in chapter 8, "Cognition," there have been a number of important adoption studies that show a genetic influence on behavior. For example, the Texas Adoption Project found that for 300 adopted children, their IQs were more similar to their biological mothers (.28 correlation) than to their adoptive mothers (.15 correlation) who reared them from birth (Horn, 1983). There are some problems with some adoption studies (for example, selective placement, in which adoptive children are placed in homes that are similar to their biological parents' homes), and more research needs to be conducted. But adoption studies do emphasize the importance of heredity in behavior development.

Behavior genetics is receiving more attention from psychologists because the biochemical pathways controlled by genes are now conclusively known to have an effect on human behavior. Genes always interact with the environment to produce the biological systems necessary for behavior. Genes influence the muscles, endocrine glands, nervous system, and sense organs. And these biological response systems all work together to allow us to successfully adapt to the changing demands of our environment. ■

Currently, great strides are being made in the field of biological psychology. From Penfield's pioneering efforts on studying the brain to today's research on understanding the role of the brain in memory and thinking, researchers have always been fascinated with human potential. This chapter has described the fundamentals of the biological affects on behavior. As you will see throughout the textbook, heredity, the nervous system, the endocrine glands, and the sense organs play a major role in what we do and think. In the next chapter, we continue to apply the biological approach to psychology when we examine the development of the person from birth through death.

Drawing by Chas. Addams; © 1981 The New Yorker Magazine, Inc.

Separated at birth,
the Mallifert twins meet accidentally.

CHAPTER REVIEW
What You've Learned About Biology of Behavior

1. Biological psychology, or psychobiology, is the field that studies the biological basis of behavior. The biological response systems include the senses, nerves, muscles, and endocrine glands.

2. The neuron is a specialized cell that functions to conduct messages (neural impulses) throughout the body. The neuron has a soma (cell body), dendrites (which receive messages from neurons), and an axon (which carries messages to the next neuron).

3. The neural impulse, the process of conducting electrical information along the length of the neuron from the dendrites to the axon, is possible because of the neuron's properties of irritability and conduction. The space between neurons is called the synapse. Neurotransmitters are chemicals released from the axon that travel across the synapse to stimulate the dendrites of the next neuron.

4. The central nervous system (CNS) consists of the spinal cord and the brain. The spinal cord consists of nerve bundles which serve as the pathway along which neural impulses from the sense organs travel to the brain and neural impulses from the brain travel to the muscles and glands. The spinal cord also controls certain reflexes. The brain processes and stores information, makes decisions about what responses are necessary, and sends orders to the muscles and glands to carry out the behavior.

5. The hindbrain controls the basic life-support functions of the body, such as breathing (medulla), eating (pons), muscle coordination (cerebellum), and arousal (reticular formation). The midbrain is a relay station for sensory information going to the higher brain centers. The forebrain receives sensory information (thalamus), regulates motivation and emotion (hypothalamus, a part of the limbic system), and is responsible for the higher level mental processes (cerebrum).

6. The largest part of the forebrain consists of two cerebral hemispheres connected by the corpus callosum. In general, each hemisphere controls the opposite side of the body. Research on hemisphere deconnection shows that the left, usually dominant, side is logical, analytical, and verbal, and exerts greater control over manual dexterity, reading, language, and understanding speech. The right hemisphere processes nonverbal information and is concerned with emotion, imagination, and artistic information. The outermost layer of the cerebrum, the cerebral cortex, is where sensory information is interpreted and stored.

7. Psychologists use a variety of methods to study the functions of the brain, including electrical stimulation of the brain (ESB), EEG brain-wave recordings, PET scan records, and NMR imaging.

8. The peripheral nervous system includes all the nerves outside the brain and spinal cord. The somatic nervous system carries messages from the sense organs to the central nervous system and relays information from the central nervous system that directs the voluntary movements of the skeletal muscles. The autonomic nervous system connects the central nervous system with the endocrines and internal organ muscles. It is divided into the sympathetic nervous system, more active in emergencies, and parasympathetic nervous system, which functions more in normal circumstances.

9. The endocrine glands work to maintain homeostasis, or biochemical stability within the body, by secreting hormones directly into the bloodstream. Hormones help regulate a variety of processes, including growth (pituitary gland), metabolism (thyroid gland), reaction to stress (adrenal glands), and sexual motivation (regulated by gonads).

10. Heredity is the natural capability of individuals to develop the characteristics possessed by their ancestors. The study of heredity is called genetics. The gene is the basic unit of heredity. Genes lie along chromosomes, which are slender bodies found in the cell nucleus. Human cells have 46 chromosomes, 22 pairs of autosomes and one pair of sex chromosomes. The complete set of genes for an individual is called the genotype. It interacts with the environment to produce the phenotype, the observable characteristics of an individual.

11. Behavior genetics is the study of how heredity influences behavior. Genes influence behavior indirectly through the biochemical reactions that ultimately result in the functioning of muscles, endocrine glands, nerves, and sense organs (the biological response systems). Behavior is the result of the interaction of heredity and the environment.

12. Behavior genetic research methods used with animals include selective breeding and comparison of inbred strains (genetically identical animals). Human behavior genetic research methods include studies of monozygotic (identical) or dizygotic (nonidentical) twins, adoption, and family relationships.

DEVELOPMENT

The study of human development covers the entire life-span from conception through infancy, childhood, adolescence, and adulthood, ultimately ending with death. Developmental psychologists are interested in changes in the physical, cognitive, and social aspects of behavior over time.

Children think in different ways than adults. This is sometimes difficult to grasp if you do not spend a great deal of time with children. For example, if you show a child in kindergarten four pennies and ask whether four pennies which are arranged close together make more or less than four pennies that are spread apart, chances are good that the child will tell you the ones that are spread apart are more. By the second grade, however, a student usually has no trouble seeing that the number of pennies is the same in each case. This is the type of observation that Swiss psychologist Jean Piaget spent over 60 years of his life exploring.

Trained as a zoologist, Piaget became interested in the behavior of children as they solved problems in their environment. He began by observing his own children and questioning them about their thoughts and behaviors. Piaget believed that cognitive (or intellectual) development occurred in children because their developing mental structures were challenged by events they observed in the environment. In order to overcome the problem, children have to develop more complex cognitive structures.

One of the best-known studies of Piaget is on conservation, the ability to recognize that properties of objects do not change even though their appearance might. For example, the kindergarten child who is about five years old does not understand conservation, he or she focuses on one feature of an object and excludes all other characteristics. As in the example above, if a child has four pennies grouped close together, he or she thinks there are more pennies than when they are spread out. But by the second grade (about seven years old), the child begins to show conservation and realizes that four pennies are equal to four pennies whether they are spaced out or close together.

Figure 3.1. Conservation of Volume
In a classic experiment conducted by Piaget, children were asked to judge the volume of liquid contained in beakers of varying shapes and sizes. When the liquid from one short beaker was poured into a tall beaker, children in the preoperational period judged there was an increase in the volume of liquid. Only children who had reached the period of concrete operations, and therefore understood the principles of conservation, realized that the volume of liquid in the tall beaker was the same as that in the original beaker.

A typical conservation study focuses on the child's ability to conserve liquids in glass containers. The child is shown two identical glass cylinder jars that have been filled to the same level with juice (or other liquid). The child is told that one of the jars is the child's and the other one belongs to the experimenter. When asked if they both have an equal amount of juice, the child responds positively. Next the experimenter pours the juice from one of the jars into a third jar which is short and wide, and the juice from the other original jar into a fourth jar which is tall and thin. The child is then asked who has more to drink. If the child responds that they both have the same amount, he or she shows

conservation. If the child says that the person with the tall thin jar has more, he or she has not yet learned how to conserve.

Piaget tested different types of conservation, such as the conservation of number, volume, mass, and length. Although each child develops conservation at a different time, in all cases it is due to development of cognitive skills. Especially important in elementary school are the experiences that help students think. For example, counting, sorting, explaining, observing, and manipulating are necessary for cognitive development. Conservation is just one of the many cognitive abilities that Piaget studied in children.

CHAPTER OBJECTIVES
What You'll Learn About Development

After studying this chapter, you should be able to:

1. Define development.
2. Describe the changes that occur during prenatal development.
3. Outline the sensory capabilities of the newborn infant.
4. Identify the variables that influence the development of motor behavior during infancy (reflexes, maturation, and readiness to learn).
5. Outline personality development during infancy.
6. Describe the sequence of attachment and explain how attachment develops.
7. Describe the development of social behavior in childhood.
8. Identify the concepts presented in Piaget's theory of cognitive development and describe the periods in the theory.
9. Outline Kohlberg's theory of moral development.
10. Outline physical development in adolescence.
11. Identify major areas of personality and social development in adolescence.
12. Describe Erikson's psychosocial theory of development.
13. Outline physical development in adulthood.
14. Identify the major milestones of adult personality and social development.
15. Outline cognitive development in adulthood.
16. Outline the psychological stages of dying.

WHAT IS DEVELOPMENT?

Piaget's research on conservation is important since it demonstrates the child's developing ability to reason or to think logically rather than to be "fooled" by his or her senses.

Development includes the changes in the physical, cognitive, and personality-social characteristics of the individual over time. Physical development includes the changes of the bodily features such as weight and height, refinement of motor behavior, and the physiological changes that accompany processes such as puberty and aging. Cognitive development refers to the changes in thinking, memory, language, and problem solving. Personality and social development includes the changes that occur in an individual's personality, social functioning and emotions. Changes in development can be described as quantitative (or growth) in which easily measured changes such as height occur, or qualitative in which the characteristics become more complex. For example, vocabulary growth is evidenced by a larger number of words being used by a child (quantitative), whereas language development is seen in the complexity of understanding the rules of language usage (qualitative).

Developmental psychology is the study of physical and mental growth and behavioral changes in individuals from conception to death. The approach to the study of development, which we use in this book, is usually referred to as life-span development.

Developmental psychologists haven't yet determined exactly in what proportion heredity and environment are involved in the development of human behavior. Maturation is the genetically controlled process of growth that results in orderly changes in behavior; it triggers changes in the capacity to function, rather than just quantitative changes (for example, the physical development of the sexual organs takes place before sexual reproduction becomes possible). Learning, the relatively permanent change in behavior that results from experience, is a factor that is presumed by some psychologists to have the most influence on development. This is the familiar nature-nurture argument. For some traits, such as height, it would appear that the genetic influence is stronger than the external environment. For traits such as shyness it would appear that learning would have the greater influence. Most scientists agree that maturation and experience interact to focus and shape development.

The study of development touches almost every other area of psychology, and will help you better understand topics discussed later. We begin our survey of development by examining prenatal development.

PRENATAL DEVELOPMENT AND BIRTH

Development begins at conception, when a sperm fertilizes an egg cell to produce a *zygote*, a fertilized egg cell. Prenatal development is the growth of an individual from conception until birth. Psychologists are interested in prenatal development because during the months before birth the various components of the biological response systems (the senses, muscles, nerves, and endocrines) are beginning to grow and develop.

As soon as the egg cell is fertilized, it begins to divide. This zygote stage lasts about two weeks. As the zygote divides, it travels down the fallopian tube to become attached to the wall of the uterus.

The embryonic stage lasts from the time the zygote becomes attached to the uterus to about eight weeks after conception. During this time, three distinct layers of cells form. The *ectoderm*, or outer layer, eventually will form the sensory system, nervous system, and skin. The *mesoderm*, or middle layer, will form the muscles, blood, and bones. And the *endoderm*, or inner layer, will become the digestive tract, many internal organs, and the endocrine system. It should be obvious that if anything should go wrong at this point in prenatal development, it could have severe consequences.

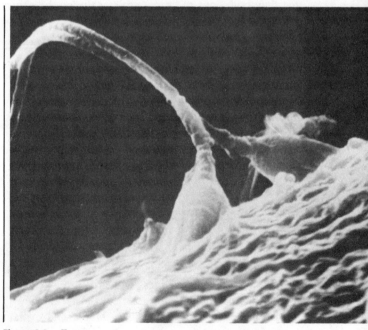

Figure 3.2. Zygote
Development begins at the moment of conception, when a sperm, seen here with its oval head and long tail, fertilizes an egg cell to produce a zygote. The zygote then moves to the uterus where it implants and begins its long development.

Figure 3.3. Summary of Prenatal Development

FIRST MONTH:
Fertilization occurs
Zygote implants itself in the lining of the uterus
Rapid cell division occurs
Embryonic stage lasts from 2 weeks to 8 weeks
Cells differentiate into three distinct layers:
    the ectoderm, the mesoderm, and the endoderm
Nervous system begins to develop
Embryo is ½ inch long

SECOND MONTH:
Heart and blood vessels form
Head area develops rapidly
Eyes begin to form detail
Internal organs grow, especially the digestive system
Arms and legs form and grow
Heart begins to beat faintly
Embryo is 1 inch long and weighs ¹⁄₁₀ ounce

THIRD MONTH:
Head growth occurs rapidly
Bone formation begins to form rapidly
The digestive organs begin to function
Sex organs develop rapidly and sex is distinguished
Arms, legs, and fingers make spontaneous movements
Fetus is 3 inches long and weighs 1 ounce

FOURTH MONTH:
Lower parts of the body show rapid growth
Bones are distinct in X-rays
Reflex movement becomes more active
Heartbeat detected by physician
Sex organs are fully formed
Fetus is 7 inches long and weighs 5 ounces

FIFTH MONTH:
Mother begins to feel reflex movements
A fine, downy fuzz covers the entire body
Vernix (a waxy coating) collects over the body
Ears and nose begin to develop cartilage
Fingernails and toenails begin to appear
Fetus shows hiccups, thumb sucking, and kicking
Fetus is 12 inches long and weighs 14 ounces

SIXTH MONTH:
Eyes and eyelids fully formed
Fat is developing under the skin
Fetus is 14 inches long and weighs 2 pounds

SEVENTH MONTH:
Cerebral cortex of brain develops rapidly
Fetus is 16 inches long and weighs 3 pounds

EIGHTH MONTH:
Subcutaneous fat is deposited for later use
Fingernails reach beyond the fingertips
Fetus is 17 inches long and weighs 5 pounds

NINTH MONTH:
Hair covering the entire body is shed
Organ systems function actively
Vernix is present over the entire body
Fetus settles into position for birth
Neonate is 21 inches long and weighs 7 pounds

The first three months of pregnancy, called the first trimester, are considered a "critical period" because during this period external stimuli can affect the pregnancy drastically. The mother must be especially careful not to contract contagious diseases such as German measles, take drugs other than those prescribed by her doctor, or have excessive X rays taken, for any of these outside stimuli could disrupt normal development. For instance, recent research has shown that cigarette smoking during pregnancy can result in premature birth of the baby. Infants born to alcoholic women may have fetal alcohol syndrome (FAS). FAS infants often have brain defects and retardation, and are usually underweight at birth. Heroin may cause retarded growth and produce withdrawal symptoms. The antibiotic drug Streptomycin may produce hearing loss. Even high doses of certain vitamins can cause problems (Stechler & Halton, 1982). The AIDS virus has recently been found to infect the unborn child.

Sexual differentiation occurs during the seventh week of gestation. Up to this time, all embryos have identical reproductive structures. If the XY chromosomes are present, at this time the undifferentiating gonads become testes which produce the male hormone testosterone. Testosterone causes the male reproductive system to develop; without it the female reproductive system develops (Wachtel, 1983). Developmental psychologists are interested in the biology of sexual differentiation because of the possibility that a variety of social behaviors are influenced by hormone levels in prenatal development (Money & Ehrhardt, 1972).

The fetal stage lasts from about eight weeks until birth. During the fetal stage the various structures develop and become refined. The fetus can suck its thumb, kick its arms and legs, and even hiccup. During this stage the fetus grows tremendously both in length and weight. (See Fig 3.3)

Ordinarily, miscarriages due to abnormality of the uterus or some genetic disorder are possible between conception and about 13 weeks. Women who are concerned about the possibility of genetic abnormalities can undergo amniocentesis, a procedure in which cells in the *amniotic fluid* are examined for chromosomal damage. A new prenatal test, called chorionic villi sampling (CVS), analyzes a sample of embryonic tissue for defects. This procedure can be used during the first trimester of pregnancy (Kolata, 1983). A more common testing procedure currently used is ultrasound, in which extremely high pitched sound waves are bounced off the embryo or fetus to produce a picture. Ultrasound can help determine the position of the fetus, identify structures, and monitor heartbeat when a problem exists.

During the last months of prenatal development, the fetus normally turns upside down in the uterus so that it is born head first. Because of the risks to the baby involved in the use of many pain-reducing drugs, many women prefer to have natural childbirth, in which drugs are used only if necessary. At approximately nine months after conception, birth occurs, and the fetus becomes a newborn baby, or neonate. At birth, most neonates weigh about seven pounds.

INFANCY

Infancy is usually defined as the first two years of life. During this period the neonate develops from a tiny and seemingly helpless being into a small, achieving child. In this section, we examine sensory development, motor behavior development, personality development, and attachment.

Sensory Development

Do you remember much about your experiences when you were born? Of course not, and because babies can't talk, psychologists find it difficult to understand what it's like to be a newborn baby. Until fairly recently, people thought that the senses were not well developed in babies. William James once remarked that the infant's world is full of "booming, buzzing confusion."

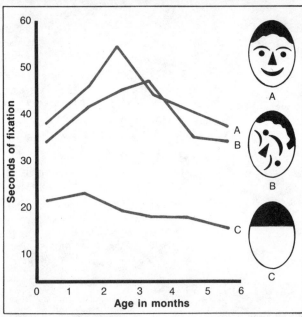

Figure 3.4. Infant Visual Preference

Fantz demonstrated that very young infants prefer complex visual stimuli, especially when the stimuli resemble the human face. After 3 months, infants spend more time looking at the face (after Fantz, 1961).

Actually, the infant's senses appear to be much more developed than was once thought. Right after birth, the ear canals are filled with amniotic fluid, but within a few days hearing is fairly normal. Neonates will turn their heads toward sounds very early in life. Decasper and Fifer (1980) found that 3-day-old infants preferred their own mother's voices to the voices of unfamiliar women, suggesting that even young infants perceive meaningful sounds.

It had been assumed that the senses of taste and smell were poorly developed in the neonate. Evidence has shown, however, that infants only a few days old can discriminate different tastes and different odors. Steiner (1979) found that neonates responded to sweet solutions by smiling and sucking, whereas they produced spitting reactions to bitter solutions. Ganchrow, Steiner, and Daher (1983) reported that neonates wrinkled their noses and stuck out their tongues when a cotton swab containing the odor of rotten eggs was placed under their noses. However, the subjects smiled and licked their lips when the odor was of strawberry or bananas.

Some research has focused on odor recognition in infants that may be biologically relevant. Aidan Mac-Farlane (1977) found that 1-week-old infants preferred the smell of their own mother's breast milk over the smell of another mother's milk. Researchers have found that breast-fed (but not bottle-fed) infants preferred their mother's underarm odor to the underarm odor of other mothers, suggesting that odors might be involved in attachment formation (Cernoch & Porter, 1985). And recent research also indicates that mothers can recognize their own newborn infants through odor cues alone (Kaitz, Good, Rokem, & Eidelman, 1987).

The visual sense is also more developed than you might expect. Neonates are nearsighted and can focus best at objects that are about 9 inches in front of them (Banks & Salapatek, 1983). Kellman, Gleitman, and Spelke (1987) recently reported that infants can perceive object motion while they are moving, suggesting their visual perception is better than previously believed. A classic study by Fantz in 1961 demonstrated that young infants showed a strong preference for complex visual stimuli, especially when they resembled the human face. Recently, Kleiner and Banks (1987) argued that the strong preference for faces in 2-month-old infants was due to a biological predisposition.

While the infant's brain cells are fully formed at birth, the neural networks connecting these cells that enable it to walk, talk, and remember are immature and undeveloped. In 1972 Mark Rosenzweig and his colleagues at the University of California conducted a study in which they observed caged rats, some in solitary confinement and some in a group environment enriched with numerous objects and toys. The researchers found that in almost every case the rats in the complex environment

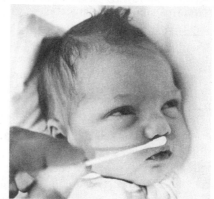

Figure 3.5. Sensory Development in Neonates
Newborn infants have much better sensory systems than was previously assumed. Infants only a few days old prefer a sweet smell to a sour smell. They turn away from unpleasant odors.

developed significantly more brain tissue and neural connections than those in the simple one. These studies suggest that the infant is much more prepared to attend to information in the environment than was often assumed. The practical implication of this information is that infants can begin learning immediately after birth, and that more learning can occur if the infant is given more stimulation.

Motor Behavior Development

When we brought our first baby home from the hospital, Terry looked very small and fragile. I soon found out, however, that he was anything but completely helpless. Although he definitely needed the care of adults, he was genetically programmed to show certain reflexes, use his senses, and mature and grow in a systematic fashion.

Reflexes. Babies are born with a number of reflexes that help them adapt to their environment. As described in chapter 2, "Biology of Behavior," a reflex is an automatic response to a stimulus that does not necessarily involve direct higher brain functioning.

The rooting reflex occurs when you touch a baby's cheek and he turns his head to search for the source. This is extremely adaptive for survival, since it prepares the baby for nursing. By turning his head toward the source, he is more likely to find the nipple.

If anything touches the baby's lips, he immediately begins to show the sucking reflex. This is a reflex that is readily apparent to anyone who has watched a baby eat. The swallowing reflex occurs automatically when something is in the baby's mouth.

The Moro reflex, or startle reflex, occurs when something in the environment changes quickly. When a loud noise, for example, is heard, the baby quickly extends both arms and brings the feet close to the body. And the Babinski reflex occurs when the bottom of the baby's foot is stroked. The baby first spreads out the toes and then curls them in. Since it is known when in the infant's development these reflexes normally disappear, they can be used to test for neurological development.

Motor Development. As defined earlier, maturation is the genetically controlled process of growth that results in orderly changes in behavior. The sequence, timing, and patterning of these changes are largely independent of experience and training. For instance, human babies vary greatly in the rate at which they mature, but they all go through pretty much the same sequence of stages. The development of the muscular and neural structures necessary for these successive stages are dependent upon maturation. Thus babies usually turn over before they sit, sit before they crawl, and pull themselves up before they walk.

The various steps that lead to the human baby actually walking generally follow this description from Frankenburg and Dodds (1967). During the first month, babies begin to lift their head and by 2 months, they can easily lift their head high. By about 3 months they can roll over. At about 4 months, babies can sit with a support, and by 6 months they can sit by themselves. At 6 months, they can stand when helped, and by about 9 months, they can walk with help. Around 11 months they can stand alone well, and at about 12 months, they can walk alone.

The sequence of motor development follows a fairly predictable pattern. This allows psychologists to devise developmental norms which describe the developmental rate for a typical person. While norms are useful for diagnosing possible problems of development, they are not rigid rules that every child must follow.

Readiness to Learn. In some cases, maturation appears to be largely responsible for the development of particular behaviors. For example, walking develops at a predictable rate regardless of environmental factors. Hopi Indian babies, for instance, develop motor skills as quickly as other children even though Hopi infants are carried on their mothers' backs and have less opportunity to practice such skills as turning over, sitting, and pulling themselves up (Dennis & Dennis, 1940).

In other cases, maturation provides only the readiness to learn, and the environment plays a more crucial role in behavioral development. Readiness to learn refers to the fact that babies cannot learn until their muscles and neural structures are developed enough. Infants cannot walk at 2 months of age because their muscles and nervous systems are not yet ready. But, without the proper environmental experiences, children will not develop the ability to speak and use language no matter how far their neural and muscular development advances.

At what age do you toilet train children? The correct answer is "When they are ready." You cannot teach children something until they are mature enough, physically and mentally. Maturation determines the readiness to learn. For toilet training, the muscles and the brain must be mature enough for children to learn to physically control their sphincter muscles. For many children, this is around 2 years old.

But what happens when the environmental experiences do not occur once maturation produces readiness to learn? There is evidence that for some animals critical periods exist, during which particular behaviors should ideally be learned. If learning does not occur at that time, the individual has great difficulty learning and may never be able to master the behavior. Critical periods have been noted in the social development of animals such as birds, sheep, and dogs. For example, if a dog has not been house trained by 6 months of age chances are it will never make a good pet (Scott, 1968). To date, no conclusive evidence for critical periods exists for humans. However, critical periods have been suggested for human behaviors such as attachment and language acquisition. Additional research is necessary to determine the exact nature of these periods.

Figure 3.6. Motor Development

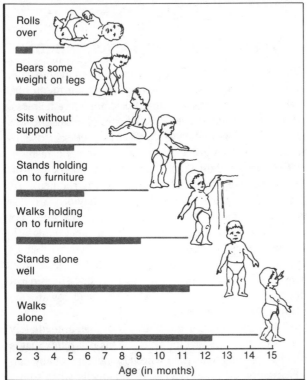

Rolls over

Bears some weight on legs

Sits without support

Stands holding on to furniture

Walks holding on to furniture

Stands alone well

Walks alone

2 3 4 5 6 7 8 9 10 11 12 13 14 15
Age (in months)

Infants follow a fairly predictable pattern of motor development. The various stages leading to walking begin with the infant lifting its head, and then continue with rolling over, sitting, and standing. When the infant is little over a year of age, he or she is usually able to walk alone.

Personality Development

Each individual's personality is unique. A person's distinctive temperament usually begins to become apparent soon after birth, and influences such as birth order and sex roles contribute to personality development.

Temperament. Newborn infants are not all the same. Different tendencies in temperament or ways of responding to the environment may begin to appear as early as the first days of life. Alexander Thomas and Stella Chess (1980) identified some of the basic categories of temperament, including activity level, rhythmicity, distractibility, approach, adaptability, intensity, attention span, quality of mood, and threshold of responsiveness. Some research has suggested that sex and ethnic differences may exist in neonatal temperament (Korner et al., 1985). Although the importance of these tendencies for later personality development is unknown, it is clear that individual differences are present at birth.

At one time it was believed that young infants could only show undifferentiated excitement. Recent research by Izard and his colleagues has begun to explain the range of emotional expressions present in very young infants. In one study (Izard et al., 1980) facial expressions of infants from 5 to 9 months old were recorded and played back for college students. The students were able to identify emotions such as joy, fear, sadness, anger, and surprise. Although we cannot be absolutely sure that the infants experienced these emotions, they were able to show the same expressions as adults. Termine and Izard (1988) found that 9-month-old infants looked at their mothers more when the mothers showed joy than when the mothers showed sadness, suggesting that infants can perceive different emotions at an early

age. We discuss emotion further in chapter 12, "Emotion."

Some evidence does suggest that early temperaments are influential later in life. Adam Matheny and his colleagues (1985) reported that emotional activity of neonates remained stable for at least the first 9 months of life. Jerome Kagan (1982) found infants who were shy at 21 months of age were still shy 10 months later. Thomas and Chess (1977) argued that an infant's temperament influences the way others will act toward him or her. It might be easier to show affection to an infant who enjoys being cuddled than to one who is upset upon contact with adults. Reid, Loeber, and Patterson (1982) showed that children who were more likely to be abused were ones who made extra demands on their parents. For example, premature, retarded, or hyperactive infants were more likely to suffer from child abuse.

Birth Order. Psychologists have looked at the relationship of birth order to personality characteristics. Firstborn children tend to be high achievers and more intelligent than later born children. In one study, Toni Falbo (1981) examined college students who were born first, middle, last, or were only children. He found firstborns to be more competitive and have higher self-esteem than those born last. Falbo also found that only children had more of a sense of control and more of a self-orientation than children with siblings.

Other psychologists have found that firstborn children tend to be more cooperative and helpful, especially when relating to adults. Children born later tend to be more friendly, social, and outgoing, which helps to increase their popularity among peers. Some of the differences among first- and later-born children are due to parental behaviors. Firstborn children (and only children) have more time to interact with parents, even if only for a year or two (Dunn, Plomin, & Daniels, 1986).

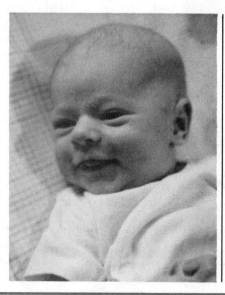

Figure 3.7. Temperament
Infants differ in a wide variety of characteristics, including their level of activity, irritability, adaptability, and their social preference. Their individual temperaments are apparent at birth.

Sex Roles. Among the personality differences that appear very early in life are characteristics associated with sex roles, or masculinity and femininity. From birth on, we are "labeled" according to our sex. In fact, often the first thing the doctor says is "It's a boy" or "It's a girl."

Many parents treat boys and girls differently, even as infants. Girls are often handled gently, while boys are played with more actively (Hoffman, 1977). Parents may not be fully aware of the subtle ways in which they encourage or discourage particular patterns of behavior. They may show approval of a male infant's boisterousness, while expressing disapproval of the same high spirits in a female, perhaps by withholding affection or some reward. An interesting study by Parke and Savin (1980) found that fathers tend to be more affectionate toward infant daughters, and mothers toward their infant sons. The implication is that sex-role development begins very early in life.

Parents also tend to give their children culturally defined "sex appropriate" toys, such as cars and trucks for their sons and dolls for their daughters. And parents

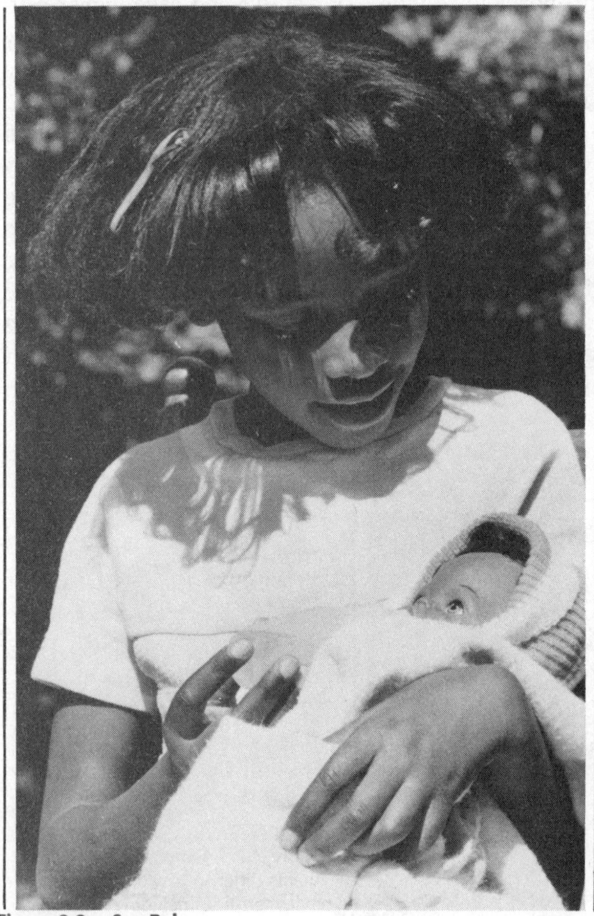

Figure 3.8. Sex Roles
From birth on, we are labeled according to our sex. Children often learn their sex roles by imitating their parents. This little girl is playing mommy, behaving just like her own mother.

serve as models for their children's behavior, often perpetuating traditional sex-role behavior. These early influences, although often unconscious, continue to reinforce society's traditional sex-role behaviors. Children develop gender identity, or the inner sense of being male or female, from their early experiences with their parents (Huston, 1983).

Usually by the age of 18 months, infants are faced with their first clearly defined social demands, and must learn to cope with an increasing number of these over the next few years. There are things they should do and things they should not do. For example, they must not handle certain objects. They must eat without making a mess. They must use a fork instead of their fingers. They must use a toilet instead of soiling their pants. And they must put their toys away. These social demands will contribute to later personality and social behaviors as the children grow older.

Attachment

Perhaps you have been the first baby-sitter that an 8-month-old baby has had. You know the parents and have seen the baby on several occasions. She is happy and seems very contented while sleeping in her mother's arms. But as soon as the parents leave, she wakes up, and upon seeing you, screams for hours until they return. The baby has obviously not yet become attached to you.

Attachment is the process in which the individual shows behaviors that promote proximity or contact with a specific person (Ainsworth, 1979). According to British psychiatrist John Bowlby (1980), the primary function of attachment behaviors is to help maintain an association with the attached person and prevent separation from that individual.

What behaviors are shown by babies that might produce interaction with the mother? They cry, which usually brings the mother to see what is wrong. They smile, and mothers "have" to smile back, creating more intense interactions between mother and baby. Babies vocalize when they get a little older. The cooing of little babies is fascinating to adults, who again often vocalize back. Babies also show sucking and clinging behavior, which tends to keep the mother in close contact. Bowlby points out that these behaviors all seem well adapted to promote the formation of attachment.

Schaffer and Emerson (1964) studied attachment in babies and identified four phases in attachment development. When first born, the neonate is in what might be called the asocial phase. Social stimuli are not distinguished from nonsocial ones. The neonate responds to people or mobiles or pictures that are interesting. This phase is actually the period before attachments are formed.

Figure 3.9. Attachment and Separation Anxiety
At about 6 or 7 months of age, infants become attached to one specific person, usually the mother. Whenever the mother is absent they show separation distress by crying and exhibiting great anxiety, even in the presence of other familiar persons.

Within a few weeks after birth the baby begins to prefer humans to objects. This is the beginning of the indiscriminate attachment phase. Babies like people to hold and rock them, but usually are not too particular about who the people are.

At about 6 or 7 months, infants become attached to one specific person, usually the mother. This is the specific attachment phase. They become distressed when the mother leaves them alone or even just leaves the room. About a month later, babies begin to show fear of strangers, called stranger anxiety. They demonstrate this by crying when someone unfamiliar approaches them.

The multiple attachment phase usually occurs by about 10 or 11 months of age. Here the baby begins to form attachments to people other than the primary caretaker (often the mother), such as the father, brothers or sisters, and others regularly seen by the baby. By 18 months attachment is fairly strong to a variety of people. The process of forming attachments continues throughout life.

A frequently used measure of attachment is Mary Ainsworth's (1978) *strange situation procedure*. It consists of eight phases during which the infant is increasingly stressed. It begins with an introduction to the unfamiliar room, followed by periods in which a stranger enters the room and tries to interact with the infant, while the mother leaves the room and later returns. These separations and reunions provide opportunities to measure attachment. A recent study (Bridges, Connell, & Belsky, 1988) of data from year-old infants indicated that their attachment to mothers and fathers are different, with the reaction to the fathers predicting how the infants will respond to strangers. The researchers suggest that fathers teach children social skills for

dealing with nonfamily individuals. Although the *strange situation procedure* has become the standard measure of attachment in infants, it is not without its critics. Field (1987) summarized research that suggests a more complex testing procedure, which measures meaningful attachment situations, is needed.

Mary Ainsworth (1978) has identified three types of infant-parent attachment. The first type (group A) is avoidant attachment, in which infants avoid their mothers when reunited in the *strange situation procedure*. The majority of infants (65%) fall into the second type (group B), called secure attachment, in which infants actively seek contact with their mothers. The third type (group C) is called ambivalent attachment, and is characterized by infants who seek contact but resist once the contact is made. These attachment types may be used to explain later social behavior. For example, if the infant shows anxiety in avoidant attachment, he or she may have problems forming social relationships later in life.

Does the mother's behavior affect the attachment of the baby? A number of studies suggest that the behavior of the mother is indeed important in the infant's development of attachment. Russell Tracy and Mary Ainsworth (1981) showed that mothers of babies who were "anxious" in an unfamiliar situation tended to kiss their babies, while mothers of babies who were "secure" tended to hug and cuddle them. Ainsworth has also shown that secure infants are more competent and well adjusted when older.

For a long time, it was assumed that babies form an attachment to their mothers because the mothers most often feed them. Food is rewarding, and since the mother usually gives the food, she becomes associated with the reward. While at the University of Wisconsin, Harry Harlow noticed that isolated baby rhesus mon-

Figure 3.10. Contact Comfort in Monkeys
Harlow found that infant Rhesis monkeys preferred the cloth-covered surrogate mothers to the wire ones, even when the infants were fed only by the wire mothers. Harlow called this preference contact comfort.

keys spent a great deal of time clinging to pieces of cloth in their cages, suggesting the importance of contact comfort in attachment formation.

Harlow (1958) designed an experiment in which an isolated baby monkey had two surrogate (substitute) "mothers": a wire mother and a cloth mother. These mothers consisted of a wire cylinder with a wooden head on top. In addition, the cloth mother had a soft terrycloth cover wrapped around it. Either "mother" could feed the baby via a milk bottle inserted in a hole in the body. And Harlow was able to vary which surrogate mother fed each baby monkey. Harlow found that the baby monkeys spent most of their time on the cloth mother, even when they were fed by the wire mother! Thus it appears that contact comfort is more important in attachment formation than is feeding, at least in baby monkeys.

Until fairly recently, attachment to fathers has not received much attention (Feldman, Nash, & Aschenbrenner, 1983). Fathers have been assumed to be the primary provider for the family, whereas mothers have been seen as the primary caretaker of the children. Research has shown that fathers do spend less time interacting with infants than mothers do. However, as Ross Parke (1981) pointed out, infants do develop attachment to both parents. It appears that the quality of the father's interaction with the infant is more important than the number of hours.

One force that keeps the infant trying to maintain contact with its parent is the distress experienced when separated (Scott, 1971). During the course of a normal day, the infant experiences numerous separations, and with each reunion after being separated, the attachment grows stronger. If separation distress does not occur, attachment may not develop normally. This may help to explain the childhood disorder called autism, characterized by severe withdrawal in which the child does not differentiate between social and nonsocial stimuli.

Studies such as these demonstrate that attachment is vitally important in the development of a child's self-concept and his or her ability to interact with others. For example, children raised in institutions where there is little contact comfort tend to become withdrawn, frightened, and despairing. Children raised in abusive or neglectful environments have a tendency to become abusive themselves. On the other hand, children who form secure attachments to their parents usually are more mature than others their same age, are outgoing and responsive with other children, and approach life with a sense of trust.

CHILDHOOD

Childhood is usually considered to be the period of development roughly between 2 and 11 years. Socially, the child becomes less dependent on his or her parents and more responsive to peers. Cognitive development proceeds rapidly as the child nears the end of the childhood period. In this section, we discuss social, cognitive, and moral development.

Social Development

During childhood the infant's sheltered environment and relatively narrow circle of human contacts gives way to a wider world in which ever-increasing numbers of people influence the growing child in various ways. Each child's social development is shaped by factors such as identification with his or her parents, the playing of social roles, peer pressure, and friendships.

Identification.   Overcoming their earlier self-centeredness, children of four or five begin to identify with their parents. They see themselves as being like their parents and begin to imitate the parents' characteristic ways of behaving. Through this process of identification, children adopt the attitudes, values, and behaviors of their parents. The child begins to carefully imitate his or

Figure 3.11. Identification in Childhood
Through the process of identification, children learn the attitudes, values, and behaviors of their parents. As shown in this photo, the child begins to imitate carefully his or her same-sex parent.

her same-sex parent. It is at this age that you see boys acting like "daddy" or girls dressing up like "mommy." Jerome Kagan (1971) suggested four processes that result in identification in children: children want to be like their parents, believe they are similar to their parents, experience emotions similar to their parents, and behave like their parents.

It is in this way that the development of self-concept begins. It moves from more external traits and behaviors to more internal personality characteristics in childhood. Eleanor Maccoby (1980) found that young children focus on the external characteristics of their name, age, home, family, friends, and favorite activities. Older children begin to emphasize the internal qualities of emotions, cognitive abilities, and personality. Eventually, as we will see later in this chapter, the question of self-identity becomes a central theme during adolescence.

Early Social Influences. From the ages of 6 to 10, the influences upon children's personality and social development expand to a wide range of sources beyond the immediate family. Schools, churches, clubs, and the mass media all exert influences. Children in elementary school learn to play social roles. They may become leaders, followers, bullies, cowards, peacemakers, mis-

chief-makers, or clowns. Children in this age group tend to show increasing signs of independence and even rebellion in their relationship with parents, teachers, and other adults.

However, during this period children come under the strong influence, and even pressure, of other children their own age. They become especially sensitive to the behavior of peers toward them, and carefully observe how these peers judge their behavior. They might feel that they have to take an electronic game to school to play during recess because "all" the other children have similar games. Or they feel that if they don't have a certain brand name athletic shoe, no one will like them at school. If children feel accepted by their peers, they will become confident and engage in more positive, social behavior. On the other hand, if they feel rejected, they may become aggressive and disruptive (Dodge, 1983). A recent review by Parker and Asher (1987) found that children who have low acceptance by peers and exhibit aggressiveness tend to have difficulties later in life, including the tendency to drop out of school and to criminal behavior.

Friendships. From early infancy on, it is very evident that people are social beings. Even young infants appear interested in other people. Friendships tend to first develop when children are 3 to 4 years old. Selman and Selman (1979) interviewed people from 3 to 45 years old to describe the development of friendships. Very young children tend to view friendship as a convenience and label any other children they play with as friends. Around 9 years of age, children define friends as children who do what they want them to. Finally, older children develop friendships that tend to be mutually satisfying.

Freud's Theory of Personality Development

Freud theorized that from birth to adolescence children go through five developmental periods called psychosexual stages. Each stage focuses on an area of the body that is of prominent concern to the individual at that particular time. During the first, or oral stage, the baby gets pleasure mainly from sucking. During his second and third years, the baby goes through an anal stage, in which the first restrictions on impulses are experienced during the process of toilet training. Around the age of 4, the phallic stage begins and the child starts to find pleasure in stimulating the genitals. From the age of 6 to puberty, there is a latency stage during which the child appears to have little need for erotic satisfaction. As sexual maturity is reached, the genital stage begins, in which the individual can begin to relate in a positive sexual way toward other people.

Figure 3.12. Developmental Theories

Ages	Freud	Piaget	Kohlberg	Erikson
Old age				Integrity vs. Despair
Middle Adulthood				Generativity vs. Self-Absorption
Early adulthood				Intimacy vs. Isolation
18				
17				
16				
15	Genital	Formal operations	Post-conventional morality	Identity vs. Role confusion
14				
13				
12				
11				
10		Concrete operations	Conventional morality	
9	Latency			Industry vs. Inferiority
8				
7				
6				
5				
4	Phallic	Preconceptual thought	Pre-conventional morality	Initiative vs. Guilt
3				Autonomy vs. Doubt
2	Anal			
1	Oral	Sensorimotor		Trust vs. Mistrust

Freud, Piaget, Kohlberg, and Erikson all have developmental theories that propose an orderly sequence to some aspect of human behavior. Freud's psychosexual development theory focuses on areas of the body important at different ages. Piaget's cognitive development deals with the thinking abilities of the individual. Kohlberg's theory of moral development outlines various stages in the awareness of ethical values. Erikson's psychosocial theory relates to the social development of the individual from birth through old age.

Freud considered these stages crucial in the development of a healthy personality. The child's experiences during these stages form the foundation for the development of many personality traits that continue into adulthood. For instance, according to Freud, such traits as disorderliness, cruelty, and destructiveness may develop as an expression of anger in reacting to punitive and repressive toilet-training tactics during the anal stage. Irregularities and difficulties in passing from one stage to the next, can, according to Freud, result in prolonged and serious emotional disorders. We discuss Freud's personality theories further in chapter 13, "Personality."

Piaget's Theory of Cognitive Development

As we discussed in our opening story, children do not think the same way adults do. Long before children develop a measurable intelligence score, before they can read or write and take intelligence tests, they have already begun to show the ability to think and handle ideas. This cognitive activity was intensively studied for over 60 years by Jean Piaget.

Piaget believed that cognitive development occurred in a child because the developing mental structures were challenged by events that the child observed in the environment. In order to overcome a problem, the child has to develop more complex cognitive structures or schemes. A scheme may be thought of as a unit of knowledge that the person possesses, or a mental picture of the world. At the simplest level, a newborn has reflexive schemes for grasping, sucking, and swallowing. Eventually, the child coordinates these schemes so that he or she can think through a series of actions and imagine the consequences of those actions. For example, your schemes allow you to realize that when you open the refrigerator, you will find food.

Piaget studied the ways in which children acquire certain concepts and organize ideas, and he outlined the predictable and orderly periods of intellectual development. The progress of these periods depends upon the child's constantly increasing adaptability to new situations. For Piaget, motor development and exploration of the environment are the foundations for later logical thought.

Two processes are fundamental to cognitive development: assimilation and accommodation. Assimilation is the process by which the child integrates new stimulus events into already existing schemes. For example, the child might assimilate a new breed of dog into the existing scheme of dog.

Children try to incorporate any new stimulus into their already existing schemes of the world. However, sometimes the child cannot assimilate a new stimulus into existing schemes and must instead use accommodation. Accommodation is the process of creating a new scheme or changing an existing scheme to make room for a new stimulus event or experience. The child accommodates a cat by creating the new scheme of cat. According to Piaget, the interaction and balance of the processes of assimilation and accommodation, called equilibration, are responsible for moving the child through the periods in the child's intellectual development (Piaget, 1960).

Sensorimotor Period. During the first two years of life infants learn to differentiate themselves from their environment. In this sensorimotor period they spend a great deal of time learning to coordinate sensory experiences with motor activities. They learn to coordinate looking, tasting, touching, and hearing with sucking, reaching, and grasping. Newborn infants spend much of their time looking around. As they grow older, they explore their world, touching everything they can. This exploration is important, since the only way they can learn to coordinate their senses and their muscles is to try things out. During this period infants go from trial and error reflexes to more deliberate manipulation of the environment.

During the sensorimotor period infants also learn object permanence. Until about 8 months old, infants will not look for an object if it is removed from sight. They act as if it ceases to exist. Once they have developed object permanence, the ability to realize that objects continue to exist even though they can no longer see them, they will search for the missing object. When you place a pillow over their rattle, infants with object permanence will simply lift the pillow and find the rattle. Piaget considers this to be an important step for infants; this is why they enjoy peekaboo. This tells us the infants are beginning to use images.

Preoperational Thought Period. From roughly 2 to 7 years of age, children pass through the preoperational thought period when they acquire language and learn to represent their environment with objects and symbols (Wadsworth, 1984). In the early part of the preoperational stage, children are learning to use symbols and mental representations of the world. They enjoy playing with stuffed animals or dolls because they can believe the playthings are real animals or friends, a concept called animism. An example of animism occurs when children say that the sun is sleeping for the night.

Children have vivid imaginations at this age. Given a few Star Wars figures and a place to play, children can become heroes and villains from outer space. This is also the age when children sometimes develop imaginary playmates. They will play and talk to their imaginary friends and sometimes even bring them to dinner.

Children in the preoperational thought period are egocentric. This means that they see themselves as the center of their universe. They focus on their own pleasures, pains, and desires, and are unaware of those of other people. They see the world from one perspective—theirs. This is the reason that children at this age might point to your left hand and say it is your right, especially if you are facing them when you ask the question.

In the latter part of the preoperational thought stage, children can group objects into classes according to their similarities. However, they cannot yet give a clear account of the features common to a class of objects. Although they show intuitive thought and can work out problems in a fairly orderly fashion, they have trouble reversing their reasoning and tracing their thinking back to its starting point. Eventually, however, they proceed to the next period.

Concrete Operations Period. From about 7 to 11 years, children's ability to solve problems with reasoning, as well as their ability to think symbolically with words and numbers, greatly increases. They can now solve problems of classification, in which objects are

BIOGRAPHICAL ☆ HIGHLIGHT ☆

JEAN PIAGET

Jean Piaget was born in Neuchâtel, Switzerland, in 1896. His father was a professor of medieval literature. As a child, he became absorbed in philosophy and zoology, and wrote his first scientific article, on the albino sparrow, at the age of 10. After graduating from the University of Neuchâtel in 1918 with a degree in zoology, he turned to psychology, going to Zurich to pursue his studies. There he met Theodore Simon, who invited him to work on the development of intelligence in a grade school in Paris.

Trained as a zoologist, Piaget had the skills necessary to begin observing children. He found that children make certain types of errors when solving problems, depending upon their age. He concluded that their thinking is qualitatively different than adults', and thus it was important to understand children from their own viewpoint.

Because of his extensive work studying the development of intelligence he has had an important impact on developmental psychology. He believed that cognitive development occurred because of the child's unsatisfactory experiences in solving problems. His observations led him to develop his famous theory of cognitive development.

Piaget was a prolific writer and produced numerous books and articles. He continued to teach and write until his death at 84 in 1980.

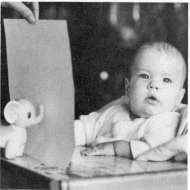

Figure 3.13. Object Permanence
During the sensorimotor period infants learn that an object continues to exist even when they can no longer see it. If an infant, such as the one shown in the photo, has not yet developed object permanence, he or she quickly loses interest in an object that has been hidden from view.

ordered into hierarchies of different classes. For example, they understand that 10 pennies equal a dime, that 10 dimes equal a dollar, and that a dollar is equal to 100 pennies. They can also order objects in a series, using increasing size or some other simple property as a criterion.

If you place two same-sized balls of clay in front of a child in the preoperational period (before about 7 years old) and ask which is bigger, he or she will say they are the same. Now, if you roll one out into a long snakelike form and ask again, the child will probably say that the snake is bigger than the ball. This demonstrates that a child in the preoperational thought period does not show conservation (Piaget, 1967). Conservation is the ability to recognize that properties of objects do not change even though their appearance does. Its emergence marks the beginning of logical thought. Probably the most famous conservation experiment (discussed in our opening story) focuses on the amount of water in two jars (conservation of volume).

Children in the concrete operations period develop conservation. They are now able to see that the mass of clay is the same in both the ball and the "snake" forms. They can also attend to both height and weight and thus realize the volume of liquid stays the same when placed in jars of different sizes. Also children can conserve numbers, and realize that the number of items stays the same whether the items are grouped together or spread apart.

Children at this age are able to decenter, or realize that their way of looking at the world is only one perspective. They can understand other people's point of view. They also show reversal, the ability to work a problem backwards. If asked to make the snake into a ball, they will have no trouble reversing the process and rolling it back into a ball. Despite these cognitive abilities, children in the concrete operations period still rely on what they see. They cannot yet effectively deal with abstract reasoning. If, for example, you ask them, "If A is greater than B, and B is greater than C, is A

greater than C?" they will not be able to solve the problem. This ability appears in Piaget's last period.

Formal Operations Period. At about age 11, adolescents begin to understand how abstract scientific, moral, religious, and political ideas work, and to see their logical implications. They also begin to understand hypothetical relationships (if X were to happen, then Y would follow) and the logic of systematic experimentation and hypothesis testing. Although people are in the formal operations period throughout the rest of their

Figure 3.14. Conservation

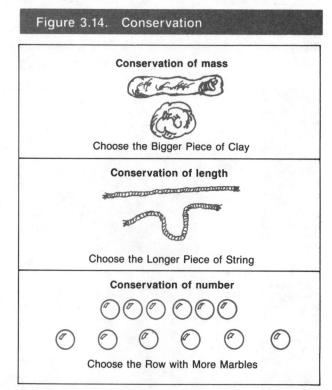

Conservation of mass

Choose the Bigger Piece of Clay

Conservation of length

Choose the Longer Piece of String

Conservation of number

Choose the Row with More Marbles

Conservation is the ability to recognize that properties of objects do not change even though their appearance might. Piaget and other researchers have demonstrated conservation of mass, length, and number, as well as volume. Children in the concrete operations period of development, from about 7 to 11 years of age, begin to demonstrate an understanding of conservation.

lives, Piaget considered that the basics of formal operations are mastered by about age 15.

Instead of starting with only the information available to their senses, like children in the concrete operations period, adolescents in the formal operations period begin with possible hypotheses, or guesses, which can be tried out in the head rather than worked out with objects in the environment (Phillips, 1981). Adolescents and adults in the formal operations stage are able to approach a problem by thinking through several possible solutions and discarding unworkable ideas until they arrive at a workable one.

Piaget's work on cognitive development has taught us that children and adults think differently—a fact that adults engaged in educating or rearing young children should not forget. Children are now viewed as developing individuals and not simply as "miniature adults" as they historically once had been. With a knowledge of Piaget's periods, the teacher or parent has a better grasp of the intellectual capabilities of children.

Criticism of Piaget. Piaget's work has greatly contributed to our understanding of children. However, the theory has been criticized by a number of researchers. John Flavel (1982) argued that cognitive development is more gradual than discontinuous. The ages indicated in Piaget's periods may be higher than they should be. For example, Gelman and Gallistel (1978) found that nursery school children were capable of demonstrating some degree of number conservation. Flavel (1985) found that $2^1/_2$- to 4-year-old children may be able to decenter under some conditions. Future research will continue to refine our knowledge of how children think.

Figure 3.15. Examples of Postconventional Morality
Martin Luther King, Jr. and his idol, Mahatma Gandhi, both demonstrated the level of moral thinking and behavior that Kohlberg described as postconventional. In stage 5 of this level the individual is concerned with democratically determined laws and in stage 6 with his or her own conscience determining universal ethical values.

Kohlberg's Theory of Moral Development

Cognitive development is also involved in moral reasoning. Lawrence Kohlberg (1969, 1985) studied the development of the awareness of ethical behavior, or moral development. Kohlberg, who based his theory on Piaget's early research, proposed that the way a child reasons about right and wrong develops according to a specific pattern. Kohlberg's theory consists of six stages arranged on three levels of moral reasoning.

Kohlberg's Level I, preconventional morality, is a period in which moral reasoning is based largely on expectation of rewards or punishments. Level I has two stages. In stage 1, the child obeys rules in order to avoid being punished. In stage 2, the individual conforms to society's rules in order to receive rewards. At Level I, behavior is guided largely by the tendency to seek pleasure. Children under the age of ten are generally in Level I.

Kohlberg's Level II, conventional morality, is a period in which moral reasoning is based largely on conformity and social standards. In stage 3, the individual behaves morally in order to gain approval from other people. Stage 4 is characterized by conformity to authority to avoid censure and guilt. By the time a person is 13 years old, he or she is likely to be at Level II.

Kohlberg's Level III, postconventional morality, is the highest level of moral thinking and is based largely on personal standards and beliefs. In stage 5, the individual is concerned with individual rights and democratically decided laws. In stage 6, the individual is entirely guided by his or her own conscience. According to Kohlberg, many people never reach Level III in their moral development.

There is considerable evidence that supports Kohlberg's theory of moral reasoning. It appears that the stages develop in the order suggested by him. Indeed, research on a variety of cultures supports the basic theory. There is controversy, however, in the link between moral reasoning and moral behavior (Blasi, 1980). Just because

Figure 3.16. Kohlberg's Moral Development

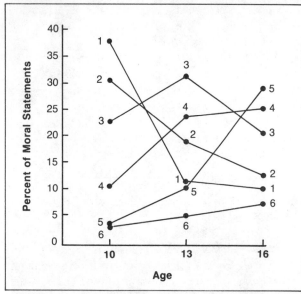

Moral development in American boys was examined by Kohlberg (1968). Statements from boys 10, 13, and 16 years of age were analyzed to determine which stage of moral development they represented. At age 10, the subjects were motivated to avoid punishment or gain concrete rewards (stage 1 and 2), whereas by age 13, most subjects were interested in either gaining approval or maintaining conventional social order (stage 3 and 4). At age 16 most boys remained at stage 4 or progressed to stage 5, a concern for democratically determined laws.

an individual is at the postconventional morality level does not automatically mean that he or she will behave in a particular manner. As you might imagine, many variables influence the actual behavior of a person.

Nancy Eisenberg and her colleagues (1987) examined moral judgment that related to social situations in which one person's wants conflicted with another's wants. They studied groups of children for 7 years to determine how prosocial moral judgment developed. She agreed with Kohlberg that reasoning became more sophisticated with age. Adolescent girls were more sympathetic and other-oriented than boys in their moral reasoning and empathy tended to lead to sharing behavior in older children. This prosocial research extends Kohlberg's emphasis on cognition by demonstrating the importance of emotion in moral reasoning and social behavior.

ADOLESCENCE

Most psychologists agree that adolescence begins at puberty. For males, that is approximately age 13; for females, about age 11. Psychologists don't agree on when adolescence ends and adulthood begins, but it is

usually sometime between 18 and 21. Adolescence is, in a very real sense, a transition from dependence to independence and ends when the individual achieves adult status. We will review briefly some of the significant developmental changes that occur in adolescence. Then we view a life-span psychosocial theory by Erikson that helps us understand how this transition period fits into the development of human behavior in general.

Physical Development and Puberty

Although there is a great deal of individual variation among individuals, adolescence is closely associated with the onset of puberty or the maturation of the sexual and reproductive systems and the development of secondary sex characteristics. During adolescence many other physical changes also occur, such as the growth spurt.

Adolescent Growth. Both boys and girls experience a growth spurt during adolescence which significantly increases their height and weight (Katchadourian, 1985). For girls, the growth spurt begins between 8 and 10 years old and peaks at about age 13 (Tanner, 1981). Boys begin their growth spurt between 10 and 12 years old, with a peak at about age 14. Both sexes may gain about 12 pounds during this period. Height increases during adolescence with females reaching adult height by about age 17, and males reaching adult height by about age 20.

Female Sexual Development. Girls typically become sexually mature a year or two before boys. Menarche, or the onset of menstruation, is an obvious sign of puberty. Many North American girls experience menarche when they are between 12 and 14 years of age, with the range being from 10 to 18 years old. The development of secondary sex characteristics, such as breasts, pubic hair, and broadened hips, occurs about this time. Breast development begins about age 11, and pubic hair appears at about age 12.

Male Sexual Development. In boys, the testes and penis begin to grow at about 12 to 13 years of age. Pubic hair appears shortly thereafter. By the time he is 15, a male can usually produce sperm. Secondary sex characteristics for males include development of beards, lower voices, broadened shoulders, and pubic hair.

In general, boys who become sexually mature early seem to have fewer problems than those who mature later. They are more popular, often because of their superior athletic ability, and they tend to have higher self-respect than later maturing boys. Other studies show that these earlier maturing boys continue to have higher self-respect (Jones, 1965). Early maturing boys tend to become leaders and have positive self-images. The findings are less clear for girls. For example, in some cases early maturation means that girls are looked down upon, or even teased, by peers (Brooks-Gunn & Peterson, 1983). But later, in high school, the early maturing girls are often more popular.

Personality and Social Development

Stanley Hall (1916) conceived of adolescence as a time of "storm and stress." Although adolescence usually is accompanied by some problems, Conger and Peterson (1984) point out that it is not necessarily as stressful a period as has been suggested in the past. Practically everyone in our culture encounters some problems during adolescence, whether related to sex, self-consciousness, parental controls, morality codes, or conformity to social norms. Adolescents also have to begin thinking about adulthood, of who they are, and of the need to make decisions about the future.

Cultural standards play a large part in the life of the adolescent. Some cultures have elaborate "rites of passage" ceremonies that may bring adolescents immediate and complete adult status, both in their own eyes and those of their society. Other cultures (such as ours) leave the adolescents more or less on their own, and they achieve adult status only gradually. In fact, in American society, full maturity can be defined only vaguely in terms of age, leaving home, earning a living, marriage, and bearing children.

Identity Development. According to Erik Erikson, the successful adolescent is one who has answered the question, "Who am I?" Identity is a major goal in adolescence. Onyehalu (1981) believes that much of the identity crisis in our youths today is the result of conflicting demands made upon them by society. Adolescents are in a transition period between childhood and adulthood. They are sexually mature but are expected to refrain from sexual encounters. They are intelligent thinkers, but are not allowed to make important decisions concerning future careers and families.

James Marcia (1980) defines identity as the internal organization of drives, abilities, and beliefs of an individual. Like Erikson, Marcia believes crisis and commitment are important in identity formation. During crisis, the individual considers the alternatives, whereas during commitment the individual decides to take a particular action. Marcia classified identity status as identity achievement (commitment by accepting other people's ideas), identity diffusion (not making a commitment), and moratorium (in crisis and moving toward commitment).

Carol Gilligan (1983) has studied sex differences in identity formation. She suggested that males form their identities as separate individuals whereas females are more likely to develop their identities based on social responsibilities and relationships rather than individual achievement. These sex differences in identity formation may help explain some of the difficulties men and women have when interacting.

Family Relationships. As adolescents develop a sense of identity they also strive for more independence. The reaction of parents to this independence often determines the relationships within the family. Parents and adolescents must learn to deal with concerns about communication, control, autonomy, responsibilities, authority, and styles of interaction (Knox, 1985). Some conflict within the family appears to be inevitable. For instance, Steinberg (1988) reported that puberty is associated with increased adolescent autonomy and parent-adolescent conflict.

Friendships. Individuals who have similar interests, personalities and temperaments are likely to become friends. Hays (1985) investigated the development of friendships in college students and found that over the course of time, the amount of time spent and the intimacy level of friends increased. Hays suggested that male friendships may develop from shared behavioral activities, whereas female friendships may develop from more verbal communication.

Adolescent Sexual Relationships. During adolescence, the practice of dating helps individuals develop interpersonal skills and facilitates mate selection in anticipation of marriage or cohabitation. For a variety of reasons, premarital heterosexual activity has increased in recent years. Jessor and colleagues (1983) reported that over 50% of females and 70% of males have engaged in premarital sex before the age of 20. Along with increased sexual activity has come increased teenage pregnancy. Recent reports indicate approximately 10% of adolescent girls become pregnant by age 18.

Serious Adolescent Problems. Although all adolescents experience problems, some are affected by extreme stress and have severe problems. We discuss some of these problems in more detail in later chapters, but mention them here because of their impact on adolescents. One serious problem, which is increasing significantly, is adolescent suicide. Over 5,000 teenagers commit suicide each year. Although there are a variety of reasons for suicide, many victims feel depressed and worthless (Colt, 1983). Drug abuse is a dangerous problem in adolescence. Although alcohol and marijuana are the most common drugs, cocaine and other illegal drugs are also being used. Adolescent females may experience anorexia nervosa, a disorder in which a normal person starves herself because she believes she is overweight. And delinquency and crime have increased in recent years. Still, as mentioned earlier, most individuals are able to deal successfully with adolescence and become healthy adults.

Erikson's Psychosocial Life-Span Approach

An important theory in developmental psychology was proposed by Erik Erikson (1963). Erikson took a life-span approach to development, in which he described eight stages that take a person from birth to death. In each stage, the person faces a crisis, and if it is successfully met, the person then progresses to the next stage. If at any of the stages the individual does not develop the required capacity, there will be problems of varying degrees of severity later on.

Erikson's Stage 1 is *trust versus mistrust*. During the first year of life, infants should develop a sense of trust. They are completely dependent on others, and it is hoped that they will learn that others will help them and will do them no harm. If infants are loved, they will develop trust for the future. But if their life is uncertain, they will develop fear and suspicion of others.

Erikson's Stage 2 is *autonomy versus doubt*. During the second year of life, children have the potential to develop a sense of autonomy, a knowledge that they have the freedom and capability to take certain actions quite independent of those around them. How children respond to and take responsibility for toilet training can be an important aspect of developing autonomy. If others are critical, they may develop doubts about their independence.

Erikson's Stage 3 is *initiative versus guilt*. At the "play stage," the third through fifth years, children should develop a sense of initiative. They should develop the power to begin projects on their own, and to do so guided by their developing conscience. They often imitate the actions of their parents in this stage. If parents punish initiatives, the child may develop guilt feelings and loss of self-confidence.

Erikson's Stage 4 is *industry versus inferiority*. In school children have to learn industry, competence, and persistence at activities which they master. During this period, which runs roughly from 6 to 11 years, they must learn that they are members of society, who must cooperate with others and channel aggression in accept-able ways (such as in sports). They must develop confidence in their own abilities. If they do not master the tasks given them, or if they are too severely criticized, they will experience a sense of failure and feelings of inferiority.

Erikson's Stage 5 is *identity versus role confusion*. This stage encompasses adolescence, from around age 11 to 18. As noted above, according to Erikson adolescents face the problem of personal identity, the question of "Who am I?" They may imitate other people, including parents, friends, or even teachers. If the behaviors they imitate are conflicting or contradictory, they may face an "identity crisis," and then they must modify or discard their imitations. In this stage, adolescents must begin to decide what they want to do in life.

Erikson's Stage 6 is *intimacy versus isolation*. The theme of young adulthood is intimacy, the challenge of integrating one's whole life with that of someone else. The most common occasion for sharing deeply in someone else's life is marriage. If a person does not learn to relate intimately with someone else, he or she may face isolation and loneliness throughout life.

Erikson's Stage 7 is *generativity versus self-absorption*. In middle adulthood, the challenge is one of establishing goals, commitments, and lasting attachments that permit reasonable productivity. The adult is concerned for his or her family and with contributing to the world at large. The alternative is self-absorption and stagnation, where the person feels that his or her own life is the only thing that matters.

Erikson's Stage 8 is *integrity versus despair*. In later adulthood and old age, individuals must learn to accept life as it was lived, with its disappointments as well as its joys, and thereby face death bravely in this final stage. If unable to do this, they face the despair of believing they are no longer useful and may have indeed missed life altogether.

While it is important to remember that Erikson's "psychosocial" theory of development is only one way to think about development, it allows a view of the entire life span. In recent years, psychologists have become more interested in the lifespan approach to development.

Figure 3.17. Erikson's Stages of Psychosocial Development

Age	Stage	Developmental Task	Resolution
0–1 year	Trust vs. Mistrust	Feel secure	Hope
2–3 years	Autonomy vs. Shame & doubt	Gain independence	Will
4–5 years	Initiative vs. Guilt	Explore environment	Purpose
6–11 years	Industry vs. Inferiority	Manipulate objects	Competence
Adolescence	Identity vs. Role confusion	Form positive self-concept	Fidelity
Young adulthood	Intimacy vs. Isolation	Form social relationships	Love
Middle adulthood	Generativity vs. Self-absorption	Develop concern about world	Care
Old age	Integrity vs. Despair	Achieve personal fulfillment	Wisdom

ADULTHOOD

Development does not stop when we become physically mature. During adolescence, we complete our education and plan what we want to do with our lives. Then during adulthood we are able to carry out our adolescent plans. One way to view adulthood is to divide it into early (ages 18–45), middle (ages 46–65), and late (ages 65–death) stages (Levinson, 1978). In this section we will survey physical, social, and cognitive development, and review the psychological stages of dying.

Physical Development

Early Adulthood. Early adulthood might be characterized as the "prime of life." The body is at its physical peak during the early twenties. Muscle strength is maximum, and the sense organs are functioning well. The current trend for adults to exercise and maintain proper nutrition is an excellent means of prolonging this youthful fitness. Some research suggests that physical activity and proper nutrition are important in longevity (Fries & Crapo, 1981).

Middle Adulthood. Physical aging becomes noticeable during middle adulthood. During the 40s, the hairline begins to recede and by 50 many people have grey hair. The skin is not as flexible as it once was and wrinkles begin to appear. The cardiovascular system becomes less efficient at pumping blood. By 50, the breathing capacity is 75% of what it was in early adulthood (Skalka, 1984). The sense organs begin to decline in efficiency during this period. The leading causes of death in middle adulthood are cardiovascular diseases and cancer. Menopause, or the end of menstruation, occurs in women who are about 50 years old.

Late Adulthood. During late adulthood, the aging process accelerates, and people experience a variety of physical deteriorations. Wrinkling of the skin continues, and hair loss is accelerated. Many people lose their teeth and require dentures in old age. There is general deterioration of the cardiovascular, respiratory, and muscular systems. And the senses gradually become less effective.

Theories of Aging. The study of late adulthood and

Developmental Stages of Parenthood

Erikson pointed out that raising children can serve as an important function of adulthood. Generativity involves helping the next generation, and this can be done through parenthood. Some research has focused on the developmental stages of parenting. In her book, *Between Generations: The Six Stages of Parenthood* (1981), psychologist Ellen Galinsky described how adults develop through the interaction with their children. She based her theory on interviews with over 200 parents.

Husband and wife become father and mother at the birth of their first baby. This is the beginning of the first stage, the *parental image stage*, during which the mother and father form their image of themselves as parents. They have a desire to be perfect, but often experience heavy demands that were unexpected.

The *nurturing stage* occurs during infancy, when attachment occurs and relationships with spouse, infant, and other people are challenged and determined. Often heavy demands are made upon parents at this time, as they establish their roles.

During the *authority stage*, between 2 and 4 years of age, adults face questions of their effectiveness as parents. The young child is beginning to develop independence and more demands are made on a parent's time. Often a second child is born, adding to the stress of the family.

The *integrative stage* extends from preschool through middle childhood. As children develop more autonomy and social skills, parents are required to set realistic goals, motivate their children, develop effective communication skills, and establish authority.

The fifth stage, the *independent teenage stage*, is the time that adolescents wrestle with identification, responsibility, and maturity. Parents must provide support for their adolescents, while maintaining authority and responsibility.

Finally, the *departure stage* occurs when the adolescent leaves home. At this time, parents evaluate their past performance and prepare for the future relationship with their offspring.

The important point of Galinsky's theory is that parenthood develops as the children grow and that the adult's self-concepts are shaped through interactions with children at each stage. When parents are aware of and can achieve their goals, they will be happy and satisfied. If not, they will be frustrated, stressed, and depressed. Therefore, it is critical that more people understand and prepare for the developmental stages of parenthood.

THOUGHT QUESTIONS

1. What are the stages of parenthood?
2. Why is it important to be aware of the demands and role expectations of each stage?
3. How can new parents become more aware of their parental roles?

aging is called <u>gerontology</u>. There are many theories of aging. Some theories suggest that the body just wears out over a period of time. The immunity theory focuses on stress and the accumulated effects of illness and contaminants in our environment. Eventually, the body loses its ability to protect itself from stress and disease. Some of the most promising research has concentrated on cellular aging.

One finding by a prominent researcher is that human body cells are programmed to reproduce themselves a finite number of times (Hayflick, 1980). He took cells and let them reproduce until they eventually died. He found that most human cells die after about 50 doublings under ideal conditions. But Hayflick believes that most cells probably never reach their maximum because of physiological changes that take place in the cell. Perhaps we will be able to extend the human life span by discovering how cellular aging occurs.

Adult Personality and Social Development

Personality is not "set" by the time the individual attains full physical maturity at adulthood. Stevens and Truss (1985) found that between ages 20 and 40, people increase their need of achievement, autonomy, and dominance, and decrease their need of affiliation and abasement. However, the need for order and endurance remained stable. As an adult, the individual must face and learn to cope with many situations that are likely to influence his or her personality, such as marriage, career, rearing children, retirement, and the prospect of old age and dying.

Levinson's Theory. Daniel Levinson (1978) studied 40 adult males between 35 and 45 years of age. From his interviews, he proposed a theory based on a series of stages that adults go through as they develop. Although he limited his observations to men, he suggested that women develop in a similar fashion. Early adulthood is entered when men begin careers and families. After an evaluation of themselves about age 30, men settle down and work toward career advancement. Then another transition occurs at about age 40, as men realize some of their ambitions will not be met. During middle adulthood, men deal with their particular individuality and work toward cultivating their skills and assets. Finally, the transition to late adulthood is a time to reflect upon successes and failures and enjoy the rest of life.

Gould's Theory. Psychiatrist Roger Gould (1978) surveyed 524 people between 16 and 50 years of age to help him formulate his theory of adult personality development. Gould argued that in order for normal development to occur, adults must eliminate irrational childhood ideas that restrict their lives. For example,

Figure 3.18. Family
With the joy of parenthood come added responsibilities—both emotional and financial.

Gould stated that some irrational ideas include believing one will always belong with one's parents, that only one's parents can guarantee one's security, and that one's parent's way of doing things is always right. In early adulthood (from 16 to 34), people must deal with assumptions that parents are always available to solve their problems. During the "mid-life decade" (ages 35 to 45), adults must establish priorities and most probably deal with the death of loved ones. Then they can move into a more stable middle adulthood stage. More research will undoubtedly provide additional insights into personality development in adulthood.

Marriage and Family. Much of our adult life centers around family and work. As Erikson pointed out, the main theme of young adulthood is intimacy, in which the individual finds another person to share life with, often through marriage. According to the U.S. Bureau of the Census (1982), 95% of Americans get married. Although marriage is chosen by the vast majority of individuals, it is important to remember that there are alternative life styles, including remaining single, cohabitation, and homosexuality.

There are many reasons for marrying, including commitment, intimacy, companionship, love, happiness, sex, and children (Stinnett, Walters, & Kaye, 1984). The first several years of marriage are spent in the practical pursuits of getting established and getting to know one another. Children are a major responsibility of married couples. The birth of a first child turns a husband and wife into a mother and father. And with each additional child, the social structure of the family becomes increasingly complex. As the children grow, the financial burden becomes greater. When the children leave the home, it is often a major transition for parents, but it usually eases the financial burden, and they find they have time to pursue other interests.

For many couples, this later period is the happiest time of their lives (Mudd & Taubin, 1982). However, some couples may find that they have drifted apart over the years and without the children to focus on may elect to divorce rather than to stay married. Divorce can, of course, occur at any time, and the causes are extremely varied. It often produces a major disruption of family life and requires a great deal of effort to adjust to it. Nearly half of the marriages in the United States and Canada end in divorce today (Glick, 1984).

Work. An occupation is extremely important in adulthood. Most people go through several stages in selecting a career (Tiedeman & O'Hara, 1963). In the exploration stage, young adults think about various work options. In the crystallization stage career choices are narrowed down in preparation for the actual career choice. In the induction stage, workers enter the new job.

Whatever the job—homemaker, accountant, secretary, teacher, mother, or laborer—people need to be engaged in some worthwhile activity as adults. As Erikson suggested, a major task of adulthood is generativity, or being productive. Being satisfied in one's work is very important. Positive evaluation and promotion will help people feel that they are leading useful, productive lives.

A topic of increasing interest to psychologists is women in the workplace. Currently about 65% of women over 16 work in jobs outside of the home. However, what some consider the less prestigious clerical jobs are held by women whereas the traditionally more prestigious jobs are still held by men. Occupations such as nurse, school teacher, secretary, and librarian are dominated by women, while professions such as lawyers, physicians, and corporate presidents are dominated by men. And statistics show that women typically receive less pay than men in comparable jobs. These inequities, both in the attitude and behavior of society, should be changed.

Retirement. A major transition period occurs when a person retires. Retirement reminds us once again that we are getting older and will die eventually. It often signals a drastically different financial picture for the family. And it usually means a major reorganization of the person's time and activities.

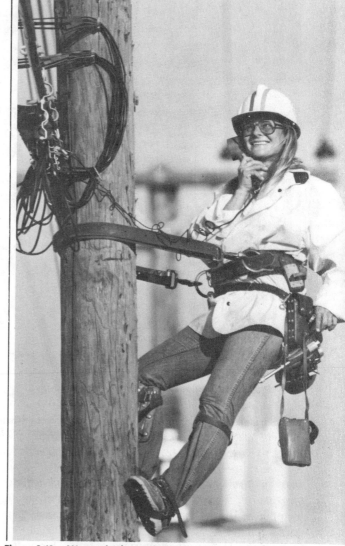

Figure 3.19. Women in the Workplace
Erikson indicated that a major task of adulthood is generativity, or productivity. Some women have found satisfying work in what traditionally have been considered masculine fields.

Cox (1984) described several factors important in adjustment to retirement. Personality and life-style will influence how easily a person can make the transition to retirement. A person dependent upon others for motivation may experience difficulty in managing his or her time in retirement. The person who adapts quickly to changes should enjoy the challenge of retirement. People who have hobbies and family interests outside of the workplace generally enjoy the excess time on their hands more than people who have devoted all of their energy to their job.

Robert Atchley (1985) has proposed a model of retirement that includes six phases. In the *preretirement phase*, the worker becomes aware that retirement is approaching. The *honeymoon phase* occurs immediately after the actual event and is normally characterized by

Figure 3.20. Retirement
A major transition period in someone's life occurs when he or she retires. Proper preparation ensures that a retired person will continue to lead a productive, although different, life. Many retirees have hobbies and family interests to which they can devote their time and energy.

enjoyment of one's free time. During the *disenchant-ment phase*, the retiree begins to feel depressed about life and the lack of things to do. Often the person then goes through a *reorientation phase* of developing a more realistic attitude toward effective use of time. During the *stability phase*, the retirement routine is established and enjoyed. The *terminal phase* occurs when illness or disability prevents the retiree from actively caring for himself or herself.

Cognitive Development in Older Persons

Are most old people wise or senile? Many cultures respect their elders for having the wisdom to solve important problems. Other cultures sometimes tend to portray old people as forgetful, incompetent, and feeble-minded. Recent evidence suggests that intellectual capacity does not automatically decline once you're past the age of 50 (Schaie, 1983). Intelligence is a complex concept. Some areas appear to remain stable with age (vocabulary and general information), while other areas decline somewhat (short-term memory and problem solving).

There are problems with the testing methods used to measure intelligence in adults. For example, it is difficult to compare people born and reared at different times in history. Also older people are at a disadvantage on subtests of intelligence that require quick reactions. Cattell (1965) suggested that biological processes result in a gradual decline in fluid intelligence (ability to solve novel problems), but have little if any effect on crystalized intelligence (verbal reasoning and comprehension of cultural concepts). It is also important to remember that people often act the way they think they should. According to one view, it is possible that some decline in cognitive ability may be due to older people's belief that they are expected to be less intelligent or it may be due to their lack of motivation to perform well on tests (McKenzie, 1980). At any rate, there are many very capable older people in our society, and with the influence of medical science extending life expectancy, this trend is likely to continue. We will discuss the concept of intelligence further in chapter 7, "Intelligence."

A problem of growing concern for older individuals is *Alzheimer's disease*, a degenerative disorder of the brain that results in irreversible memory loss. Along with the memory loss are other symptoms, such as intellectual and personality deterioration. Many patients lose the

Figure 3.21. Cognitive Activities in Older Persons
Many older people stay intellectually alert in old age by continuing to seek new information and participating in programs designed to challenge their knowledge and problem solving skills.

ability to do more than simple body functions (Reisberg, 1983). Alzheimer's disease often occurs in the elderly (sometimes called senility), but may occur in people as young as 40. The exact cause of Alzheimer's disease is not known but it appears that a decrease in the neurotransmitter acetylcholine plays a role. To date, treatment has been ineffective in preventing the inevitable intellectual decline in Alzheimer's disease patients.

Psychological Stages of Dying

Ultimately, the final stage of life is the process of dying. Erikson's last psychosocial stage is integrity, where the person learns to accept life and feel satisfied with its accomplishments. Recent research has shown that fear of death decreases with age. Dorothy Rogers reported in 1980 that almost 20% of young adults were afraid of death, compared to less than 2% of those over 65.

Psychiatrist Elizabeth Kübler-Ross (1969, 1981) pro-

posed a theory that describes the stages terminally ill people usually go through as they prepare to die. While all the stages are not experienced by everyone, they do provide a basis for thinking about this last stage of life.

The first stage is *denial*. The person believes the doctor made a mistake and that it is not possible that he or she could actually be dying. The second stage is *anger*. When people realize they are dying, they become angry and resentful of all those around them. The anger is replaced by the third stage, *bargaining*. The person tries to buy time by bargaining with doctors, family and God. Typically, those who are dying say that if they survive, they will work harder, go to church, be faithful, and so on. Finally, they recognize the inevitable fact that they are going to die and go into the fourth stage, *depression*. Eventually the dying person may reach the last stage, *acceptance*. He or she accepts death as part of life, and then is able to make the necessary preparations for death, quietly.

E. Mansell Pattison (1977) argued that there are so many individual differences in dying that it is not possible to identify specific emotional stages. He suggested three phases that the terminally ill go through. The *acute phase* occurs when an individual realizes that he or she will die. The *chronic living-dying phase* involves a host of emotions, including fear, loneliness, pain, and sorrow. Eventually the *terminal phase* is reached when the individual withdraws from people and life.

The hospice movement provides an alternative for the terminally ill to spend their last days in the loving company of their family (Holden, 1980). A hospice is an organization that helps the person and the family with social needs, as well as medical attention. Psychologists

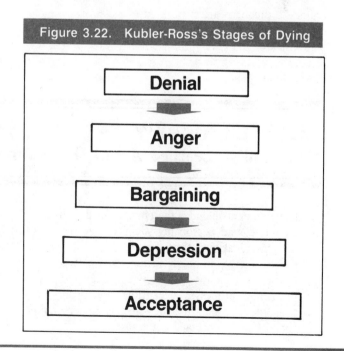

Figure 3.22. Kubler-Ross's Stages of Dying

Denial

Anger

Bargaining

Depression

Acceptance

are becoming involved in learning more about dying so that they can help others successfully meet the challenges of this last stage in life.

Originally developed in England, a hospice is a center established for the care of dying patients and their families. The program provides supportive services, including physical, psychological, social, and spiritual aid for people who are dying.

According to Holden (1976), hospices serve several important functions. Medical personnel help make patients physically comfortable by providing pain medication. Psychological personnel provide support for patients by helping them feel secure. This support might be in the form of talking to patients or helping them get

their legal and social affairs in order. Finally, hospices provide support for the bereaved through counseling or pastoral care. ■

This final stage of life marks the end of our brief survey of developmental psychology. As indicated in our opening story on cognitive development in children, development changes over time and is due to the interaction of heredity and the environment. We have spanned the human life cycle from prenatal development through adulthood. As you read through the rest of the textbook, keep in mind the developmental stages that people go through in life. We turn next to how people know about the outside world, sensation and perception.

"Why did you cut my squash in half, Mommy? Now I have TWICE as much to eat."

CHAPTER REVIEW
What You've Learned About Development

1. Development includes the changes in the physical, cognitive, and personality-social characteristics of the individual over time. Physical development includes changes in bodily features and physiological processes. Cognitive development refers to changes in mental processes over time. Personality and social development includes changes in personality, social functioning, and emotions.

2. Prenatal development includes the growth of an individual from conception until birth. Stages in prenatal development include the zygote stage (first two weeks), the embryonic stage (two to eight weeks, during which ectoderm, mesoderm, and endoderm develop), and fetal stage. At nine months, birth occurs and the fetus becomes a neonate or newborn.

3. The first two years of life is defined as infancy. Overall, the infant's senses appear to be much more developed than was once thought. Within a few days of birth, the neonate's hearing is normal. Young infants can discriminate different tastes and smells. Infants prefer complex visual stimuli, especially when they resemble the human face.

4. Infants are born with a number of reflexes, or automatic responses to stimuli, including the rooting reflex, Moro reflex and Babinski reflex. The sequence of motor development follows a fairly predictable pattern in infancy. Readiness to learn states that children cannot learn until they are mature enough to be able to use their muscles.

5. Temperament tendencies, or ways of responding to the environment, may begin to appear as early as the first days of life and influence later behavior. Sex-role differences (masculinity and feminity) also appear early in life. Gender identity develops from early experiences with parents. Usually by the age of 18 months, the infant is faced with social demands made by other people.

6. Attachment, the process in which the individual shows behaviors that promote contact with a specific person, begins to develop during infancy. Infants go through the phases of asocial, indiscriminant, specific, and multiple attachments. Ainsworth identified avoidant, secure, and ambivalent types of infant-parent attachment. Approaches to attachment focus on separation distress and contact comfort.

7. Childhood is the period roughly between the ages of two and eleven years. At about four years, children begin to identify with their same-sex parents. From about six years, children begin to be influenced by their peers, schools, churches, and the mass media. Friendships begin to develop when children are about three or four. Freud's psychosexual stage theory of personality includes the oral, anal, phallic, latency, and genital stages.

8. Piaget's theory of cognitive development emphasizes the processes of assimilation (integrating new information into existing schemes) and accommodation (creating or changing schemes for new information). In the sensorimotor period, the infant coordinates sensory experiences with motor activities. In the preoperational thought period, the child acquires language, is egocentric, and learns to represent the environment with objects and symbols. In the concrete operations period, the child develops conservation, decentration, reversal, and the ability to solve problems with logical thought. In the formal operations period, the adolescent is capable of abstract logical thinking.

9. Kohlberg studied moral development, or the development of the awareness of ethical behavior. In Level I, preconventional morality, moral reasoning is based on expectations of rewards or punishments. In Level II, conventional morality, moral reasoning is based on conformity. In Level III, postconventional morality, moral reasoning is based on personal standards.

10. Adolescence is the period of development between the onset of puberty and about 18 to 21 years. Both boys and girls experience a growth spurt during adolescence. At puberty (about age 11 in girls, age 13 in boys), adolescents are capable of reproducing. Secondary sex characteristics also develop at puberty.

11. A major goal in adolescence is the development of a personal identity. Parents and adolescents must learn to deal with concerns about communication, autonomy, and authority. Adolescents develop friendships and date members of the opposite sex as they develop interpersonal skills.

12. Erikson's psychosocial theory of development, in which eight major stages (taking a person from birth to death) are described, is a life-span theory. In infancy, we develop a sense of trust. In early childhood, we develop autonomy. In middle childhood, we develop initiative. In later childhood, we develop industry. In adolescence, we develop identity. In early adulthood, we develop intimacy. In middle adulthood, we develop generativity. In later adulthood, we develop integrity.

13. The body is at its peak physically during early adulthood. Physical aging becomes noticeable during middle adulthood. There are several theories that focus on the aging process.

14. Our society does not have a rigid definition of adulthood. You become an adult when you leave home, get a job, get married, or have children. Much of our adult life centers around family and occupation. Major transitions occur when a person becomes married, works at an occupation, has children, and retires.

15. By the end of adolescence, a person has mastered all of the basic cognitive operations that will be used for the rest of life. From then on, cognitive development may continue indefinitely, but it will consist of elaborations on themes already developed. Intellectual capacity does not decline automatically in later adulthood. Alzheimer's disease is a degenerative disorder of the brain which results in irreversible memory loss.

16. Ultimately, the last stage of life is the process of dying. Kübler-Ross described five stages that people usually go through in the process of dying. These stages are denial, anger, bargaining, depression, and acceptance.

PERCEPTUAL PROCESSES

Part II provides an overview of the role perception plays in our lives. The areas covered include sensation, perception, and altered states of consciousness.

After reading Part II you should be able to:

Define sensation and perception

Describe the basis of visual illusions

Describe the functions of the senses

Define consciousness

Describe the function of sleep

Recognize types of drugs and their effects on consciousness

Chapter 4   Sensation and Perception

Everything we experience in our environment comes to us through our senses. Psychologists study how the sense organs receive sensory input, which is carried through the nervous system to the brain, for perception, the interpretation of sensation, to occur. Much attention has focused on the sense of vision, but psychologists are also interested in the perceptual systems of hearing, smell, taste, and the skin and body senses.

Chapter 5   Sleep and Consciousness

Consciousness has long been an area of concern for psychologists. Much of the research has been conducted on altered states of consciousness, including sleep, hypnosis, and meditation. The information learned about sleep and dreaming has practical consequences. An area of current interest is the effects of drugs on behavior.

SENSATION AND PERCEPTION

Everything we experience in our environment comes to us through our senses. Psychologists study how the sense organs receive sensory input, which is carried through the nervous system to the brain, for perception, the interpretation of sensation, to occur. Much attention has focused on the sense of vision, but psychologists are also interested in the perceptual systems of hearing, smell, taste, and the skin and body senses.

W hen we are deprived of the normal stimulus information from our environment, does our brain rest or does it make up for the lack of stimulation by creating its own? This basic question has been studied through research on sensory deprivation in which the normal environmental sensory stimuli available to an individual are reduced drastically.

In 1951 a group of researchers headed by Donald Hebb began experimenting with sensory deprivation at McGill University in Montreal. The original intent of the research was to learn more about the brainwashing techniques used on prisoners in some countries. The researchers were interested in the effects of deprivation on perception, memory, thinking, emotion, attitudes, social interactions, and physical reactions. Woodburn Heron (1957) described the McGill University research project.

McGill University male college students volunteered for experiments in which all they had to do was remain in a room until they decided to withdraw from the study. For this, they were paid $20 per day, during which they were required to lie quietly on a bed for all 24 hours. The deprivation was lifted only for meals (which subjects ate while sitting on the edge of the bed) and for using the restroom.

Their sensory inputs were severely restricted. They wore special goggles through which only diffused light could penetrate. Cardboard cuffs and cotton gloves restricted their sense of touch. A special pillow and the steady hum of an air conditioner in the background impaired their hearing. Essentially, the normal and varied sensory input was cut off for the subjects.

The students had great difficulty concentrating during

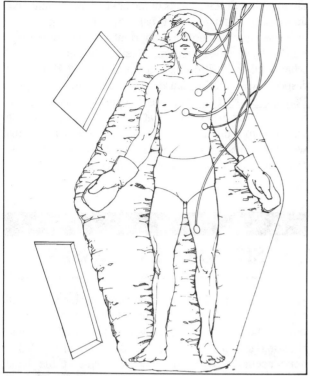

Figure 4.1. Sensory Deprivation Experiment
In studies of sensory deprivation, volunteers have sensory stimuli reduced or eliminated through a variety of techniques.

As time went on, many subjects showed extreme mood swings. Much of the time they were irritable, but sometimes they were very happy. After longer periods of isolation, some subjects reported seeing images as though they were dreaming while they were awake. Occasionally subjects also reported hearing sounds, such as music or singing. Most subjects were restless while they lay on the bed with nothing to do and were able to remain in isolation for only 2 or 3 days.

The McGill University students were given a variety of tests at various times in the experiment including before the isolation began, at 12, 24, and 48 hours during the isolation, and 3 days after the isolation ended. Some of the tests included arithmetic problems, anagrams, word associations, copying paragraphs, substituting symbols, and identifying incorrect details in pictures. During the isolation, the researchers played a tape about ghosts and supernatural phenomena and tested the subject's attitudes in this area before and after the sensory deprivation experience.

On most of the tests, the subjects' performance was affected by the sensory deprivation experience. They did poorly on tasks that required them to concentrate or think abstractly. The subjects could remember things, but some had trouble with reaction time or tasks that required the use of perception. It appears, then, that sensory deprivation disrupts complex thinking.

This research is particularly relevant for understanding a situation in which people must engage in a monotonous task for long periods of time. Truck drivers and airplane pilots on long trips have reported some of the symptoms shown by the college students. Heron (1957) concluded that a varied sensory input is essential for human beings, and that without it, the brain produces its own stimulation.

the experiment. In the beginning, they tended to think about school, the experiment, and their own lives. Then they started thinking about their families and earlier personal incidents. Eventually, their thoughts seemed to become scrambled, and they could only think about something for a brief period of time. Some subjects reported drifting from one thought to another, and others said they could not think of anything at times.

CHAPTER OBJECTIVES
What You'll Learn About Sensation and Perception

After studying this chapter, you should be able to:

1. Define sensation and perception.
2. Describe transduction and sensory adaptation.
3. Differentiate between absolute and difference thresholds.
4. List the major structures and function of the eye.
5. Compare the two major theories of color vision.
6. Define perceptual constancy and identify four types.
7. Describe Gestalt perceptual organization.
8. Identify monocular and binocular cues used in depth perception.
9. Describe the perception of motion.
10. Define visual illusion and list six examples.
11. Outline the functioning of the ear.
12. Compare the two major theories of hearing.
13. Outline the process of sound localization.
14. Describe the sense of smell.
15. Describe the sense of taste.
16. Describe the skin sense of pressure.
17. Outline the gate-control theory of pain and the role of endorphins in controlling pain.
18. Describe the skin sense of temperature.
19. Describe kinesthesis and the vestibular sense.

WHAT ARE SENSATION AND PERCEPTION?

In our daily lives, most of us do not experience sensory deprivation. Our world is filled with a wide variety of environmental stimuli which we are aware of through the processes of sensation and perception. Although difficult to distinguish, psychologists tend to view sensation as a physiological attribute and perception as a cognitive one.

Douglas Bloomquist (1985) stated that <u>sensation</u> is the passive process through which stimuli are received by sense receptors and transformed into neural impulses that can be carried through the nervous system. It is the first stage in becoming aware of the environment. <u>Sense receptors</u> are physical structures at the end of the nervous system directly affected by environmental stimuli. Everything we experience in the environment comes to us through our sense receptors, or senses.

<u>Perception</u> is a more active process in which the sensory information is carried through the nervous system to the brain and is organized and interpreted (Matlin, 1988). Perception involves other cognitive processes, such as memory and thinking and an ability to form meaning through the sense processes. One distinction that we will use in this chapter is that the study of sensation focuses on sense activity whereas the study of perception emphasizes what we actually experience.

At any one moment we experience a vast array of sensory stimuli. Since we cannot attend to all of the stimuli in our environment simultaneously, we must select and pay attention to only a limited number, screening out all the rest. Through experience, we have learned to attend to the sensory data relevant to our purposes. As drivers, for instance, we pay close attention to other cars, bends in the road, street signs, and stoplights, but as passengers, we probably don't. This process, called <u>selective attention</u>, is extremely important to our survival, since it allows us to concentrate on the most important aspects of the environment. Selective attention is determined, in part, by motivation.

Expectancy is another important variable in perception. If I were to say to you, "Get ready, get set . . . ," what would you fill in the blank space with? You would respond with "go" because you expected to see it there. <u>Perceptual expectancy</u> can be thought of as the culmination of all our experiences that directs us to perceive the world from a unique perspective. How we perceive the world depends upon our previous learning experiences, our culture, and our biological makeup.

SENSORY PROCESSES

A basketball game is a sensational experience—for all our senses. Even before we enter the court, we hear the noise. The sounds of the crowd laughing, talking, and shouting contend with the sounds of bouncing balls, announcements over the loudspeaker, and the band playing. As we enter, we see people everywhere—spectators making their way to their seats, and the teams practicing their shooting. If we take the time to sort them out, we may detect several distinct odors: cigarette smoke, popcorn, and the overall smell of people in a gymnasium. At a basketball game, not even our sense of touch is spared as you bump into people on the way to the bleachers. Our sense of taste is tested by drinks, popcorn, hot dogs, gum, and candy. And after a while, we may begin to feel warm as the game gets exciting and we jump up and down.

Overview of the Senses

Each of our senses is designed to receive a particular type of information. Before we review each of the senses in detail, a brief overview of the human senses may help you understand the general processes of sensation and

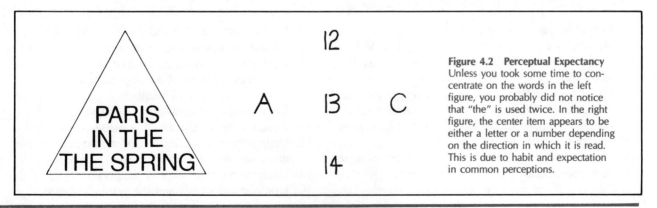

Figure 4.2 Perceptual Expectancy Unless you took some time to concentrate on the words in the left figure, you probably did not notice that "the" is used twice. In the right figure, the center item appears to be either a letter or a number depending on the direction in which it is read. This is due to habit and expectation in common perceptions.

Figure 4.3. The Human Senses

Sense	Stimulus	Sense Organ	Receptor	Perception
Vision	Light waves	Eye	Rods and cones	Sights
Hearing	Sound waves	Ear	Organ of corti	Sounds
Smell	Volatile substances	Nose	Olfactory epithelium	Odors
Taste	Soluble substances	Tongue	Taste buds	Tastes
Pressure	Light pressure	Skin	Nerve endings	Pressure
Pain	Deep pressure	Skin	Nerve endings	Pain
Warm	Temperature	Skin	Nerve endings	Warmth
Cold	Temperature	Skin	Nerve endings	Cold
Kinesthesis	Muscle movement	Tendons, joints	Golgi tendon organs	Movement
Vestibular	Gravity	Inner ear	Semicircular canals	Balance

The senses provide us with critical information about internal and external events. The study of sensation is a search for the lawful and consistent correlations between physical events acting on living organisms and the behavior or experiences that they evoke.

perception. The 10 senses discussed in this chapter include vision, hearing, smell, taste, pressure, pain, warmth, cold, kinesthesis, and the vestibular sense.

Vision is probably one of the most important senses in humans. The stimulus for vision is light, and the sense organs are the eyes. Hearing, or audition, depends on sound, and the sense organs are the ears. Smell and taste are called the chemical senses because the sensory stimulation of the receptors involves contact with chemical substances. The sense organs for smell are located in the nasal passages, and the taste receptors, the taste buds, are found in the tongue.

The somatic, or body senses include the skin senses of pressure, pain, cold, and warmth and the proprioceptive senses: kinesthesis and vestibular. The skin senses are sensitive to stimuli on the body surface. Pressure receptors are located just below the surface of the skin, and respond to a slight touch. Pain receptors are located more deeply under the skin and are stimulated by stronger pressure. The skin senses of warmth and cold are sensitive to changes in temperature. The proprioceptive receptors are located within the body and allow us to respond to changes in body movement and position. Kinesthesis is the sense of bodily movement, whereas the vestibular sense helps us maintain our balance.

Transduction and Sensory Adaptation

As we saw in the basketball game example, people have a variety of senses that help them perceive the environment so they can respond appropriately. Sensation is the first step in the sequence. As we saw in chapter 2, "Biology of Behavior," the senses are the biological response systems that must originally receive stimuli. Sensation is the process in which stimuli are received by the sense receptors and transformed into neural impulses that can be carried through the nervous system. The

sensory stimulus is some form of physical energy that excites the sense receptor.

Transduction. The process of changing the stimulus energy from the environment into neural impulses that travel through the nervous system is called transduction. The receptors in each of the sense organs are specialized structures that are sensitive to a particular type of physical energy, such as light waves, sound waves, pressure, temperature, or chemical reactions. The receptor is a biological transducer. Once the sense receptors are stimulated, they transform the energy into electrical neural impulses. All neural impulses are the same and follow specific nervous system routes to the areas of the brain where the electrochemical information is perceived and acted upon.

The "doctrine of specific nerve energy" states that nerves carry the message the sense organ is programmed to send, regardless of the source of stimulation to the sense organ. For example, the eyes are sensitive to light energy and the process of transduction in the sensory receptors of the eye takes light energy and converts it into electrochemical energy for the nervous system to use. But what happens when you close your eyes and gently press them with your fingers? The perception of light is created (can you see the little stars?) even though the environmental stimulus energy was pressure. Most of the time, of course, our senses respond to the specific form of energy for which they were made and we correctly perceive the information.

Sensory Adaptation. Imagine that you have just come home from a vacation and your house smells musty from being closed up. You start to open a window to air out the house, but stop first to look over the mail which has accumulated during your absence. After reading a couple of letters, you suddenly realize the house no longer smells musty even though you haven't yet opened the windows. But when you go out to the car to bring in the rest of your luggage and come in again, you notice the musty smell once more. You've just discovered the phenomenon of sensory adaptation.

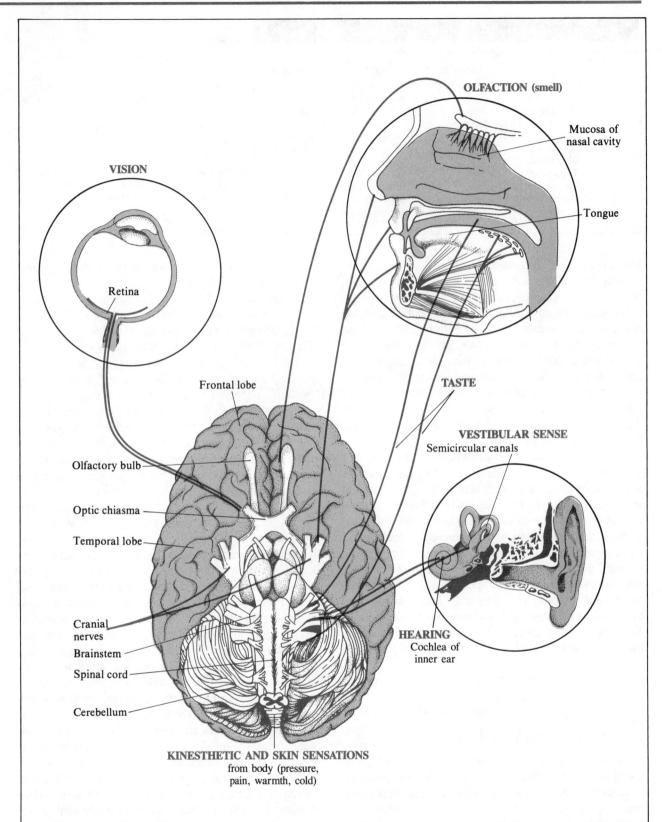

Figure 4.4. Sensory Pathways to the Brain
The sensory receptor, such as the eye, ear, or a simple nerve ending, stimulates a discharge in the nerve fiber to the brain. Sensations from the nose, eyes, face, ears, and tongue travel via the cranial nerves directly to the brain. Kinesthetic and skin sensations enter the brain via the spinal cord.

Sensory adaptation is the tendency of the sense organs to adjust to continuous, unchanging stimulation by reducing their functioning. In other words, a stimulus that once caused a sensation may become less effective. Your different senses vary quite a bit in their capacity to adapt. The smell receptors adapt to a new odor within a few minutes, often so completely that the odor is no longer detectable (as in our musty house example). The sense of hearing shows less adaptation; we are all familiar with the experience of shouting to be heard well after the noise of a passing train or plane has died down. Visual adaptation is a very slow process, but if we stare at a stimulus long enough, the stimulus will eventually disappear (Moushon & Lennie, 1979).

Sensory adaptation is important for our survival. If we paid total attention to every stimulus in our environment, we would not be able to concentrate on important tasks. For example, you might be in a classroom that has a fluorescent bulb flickering, a closed-in odor, or a ventilator fan humming. Sensory adaptation lets you ignore all of these ambient stimuli so that you can do the most important task—concentrate on the class discussion.

Measurement of Sensation

Psychophysics is the area of psychology that compares the physical energy of a stimulus with the sensation reported by a subject. A stimulus must have a certain minimum energy before it can be detected by a sensory receptor. Some of our senses seem to have extremely low thresholds. For example, Galanter (1962) reported that we are capable of perceiving the wing of a bee falling on our cheek. And we can detect one drop of perfume diffused throughout an average-size apartment.

Absolute Threshold. When we ask the question, what is the minimum light intensity we can see, or the minimum sound pressure we can hear, we are asking about the absolute threshold of these senses. The absolute threshold is the minimum amount of physical energy required to produce a sensation. In the method of constant stimuli, the experimenter determines the absolute threshold by presenting stimuli of various intensities and the subject has to report their presence or absence.

In an actual experiment to determine absolute threshold for hearing, a subject would be in a soundproof room, and the experimenter might present sounds of different intensities, from so soft that the subject could not possibly hear them to so loud that there could be no doubt that they would be heard. In between these extremes lies the absolute threshold. It is usually accepted that the absolute threshold is the level that produces a response sensation 50% of the time.

We use absolute thresholds all the time. We might use

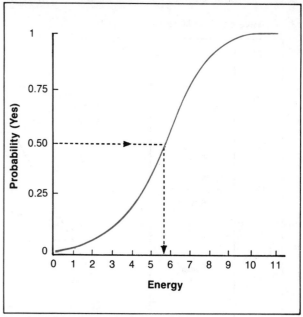

Figure 4.5. Absolute Threshold

In order to determine an absolute threshold, the experimenter presents a stimulus at a variety of intensity levels, and asks the subject whether the stimulus was presented. The point at which the subject responds 50% of the time is the absolute threshold, and can be shown by this hypothetical graph.

a detectable amount of perfume or after-shave, but not enough to upset those around us. When talking to someone in the library, we whisper in order to keep the sound below the absolute threshold of the other students but above the absolute threshold of the person we are talking to.

Difference Threshold. When we ask, what is the minimal change in sound pressure or in brightness that we can detect, we are asking about the difference threshold of these senses, or their discriminative capacity. The difference threshold is the minimum amount of physical energy change required to produce a difference in sensation. It is a discrimination threshold identifying a difference between two stimuli. The difference threshold is often called the just noticeable difference (JND). In the method of limits, the experimenter determines the difference threshold by presenting stimuli of greater or lesser intensity than the original. The subject has to report whether the test stimulus is greater than or less than the original stimulus.

When someone asks you to turn down the volume on the television, you go up to the set and turn the knob, but before you get back to your seat, the other person complains that you didn't reduce the volume. Of course you did, but from where the other person is sitting the adjustment was not enough to reach the difference threshold.

In 1834 Ernst Weber noticed that the difference

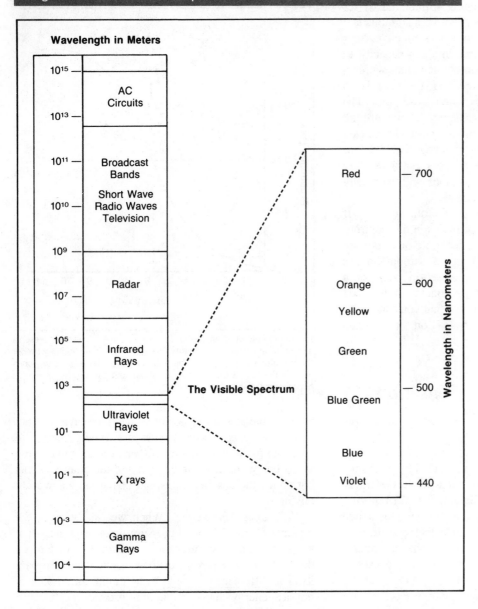

Figure 4.6.   The Visible Spectrum

Wavelength in Meters

- 10^{15}
- 10^{13} — AC Circuits
- 10^{11} — Broadcast Bands
- 10^{10} — Short Wave Radio Waves Television
- 10^{9}
- 10^{7} — Radar
- 10^{5} — Infrared Rays
- 10^{3}
- 10^{1} — Ultraviolet Rays
- 10^{-1} — X rays
- 10^{-3}
- 10^{-4} — Gamma Rays

The Visible Spectrum

- Red — 700
- Orange — 600
- Yellow
- Green
- Blue Green — 500
- Blue
- Violet — 440

Wavelength in Nanometers

Visible light is only a small part of the electromagnetic spectrum. The human eye only responds to wavelengths of between 380 and 760 nanometers, but a wider range exists, including X rays and radio waves. The colors of the visible spectrum range from violet to red.

threshold depends upon the intensity of the stimulus. He found that for a strong stimulus a larger change is necessary for a difference to be noticed than for a weak stimulus. For example, if the television volume is loud, it will take a greater change to reach the just noticeable difference than if the volume is very soft to begin with. Weber's Law states that the difference threshold depends on the *ratio* of the intensity of one stimulus to another rather than on an absolute difference.

Signal Detection. Psychophysics depends exclusively on subjective reporting of sensation. To help overcome the problem of guessing in subjects, the signal detection theory was developed (Green & Swets, 1966). Signal detection theory approaches the subject's behav-

ior in detecting a threshold as a form of decision making.

In each trial of a signal detection test, two sets of two probabilities are possible: the sensory stimulus can be presented or withheld, and the subject can report perceiving the stimulus or not. If a stimulus is presented and the subject says yes, the trial is a "hit." If no stimulus is presented but the subject still says yes, it is a "false alarm" and might indicate that the subject is motivated to guess. If a stimulus is actually presented and the subject says no, it is a "miss" and gives information on the subject's ability to detect the stimulus. Finally, if no stimulus is presented and the subject says no, it is a correct rejection. From this data, it is possible to plot a

Figure 4.7. Common Difference Thresholds

ITEM	QUALITY	PERCENTAGE
solutions	saltiness	8%
lights	brightness	8%
sounds	intensity	5%
objects	weight	2%
sounds	frequency	0.3%

A noticeable difference will normally be detected by someone if the qualities of the items vary by the given percentages.

subject's responses when the intensity of the stimulus is varied. The resulting curve is called the receiver operating characteristic (ROC), and provides additional information on the detection of sensory thresholds. By including the subject's psychological characteristics as well as the subjective reporting of sensation, signal detection theory has helped psychologists learn more about how sensation and perception operate.

VISION

Most people rely more on vision than on any of the other senses. A larger portion of the brain is devoted to vision relative to the other senses, and we often trust visual information more than other types of sensory information (seeing is believing). The dominance of vision over the other senses is called visual capture, and is one reason psychologists have studied vision so thoroughly.

The stimuli that affect vision are light waves, a type of electromagnetic wave energy. Visible light is only a small part of a spectrum of electromagnetic energy. The human eye is capable of responding to electromagnetic energy with a wave length of between about 380 and 760 nanometers (nm). (A nanometer is one billionth of a meter.) The electromagnetic spectrum also includes energy with wavelengths shorter than 380 nm (such as ultraviolet rays, X rays, and gamma rays) and energy with wavelengths longer than 760 nm (such as infrared rays, radar, television and radio waves).

Wavelength and wave amplitude of visible light determine what we see. The wavelength of light waves is the distance between any point in a wave and the corresponding point on the next cycle. Wavelength determines our experience of hue, which is the color we actually perceive. Psychologists refer to the purity of a hue as its saturation. A hue from a single wavelength is high in saturation, whereas one that results from the mixing of several wavelengths is low in saturation. The shortest wavelength produces the color of violet. As wavelengths get longer, the hue changes to indigo, blue, green, yellow, orange, and at the longest wavelength, red. (You might have memorized the mnemonic Roy G. Biv to remember the colors of the visible spectrum.) The wave amplitude is the height of a wave. Wave amplitude primarily determines our experience of brightness. Essentially, the higher the amplitude, the brighter the light.

The Eye

The human eye is sometimes compared to a magnificent living camera. It has a fine lens that can focus images viewed from as close as a few inches to a distance of many miles. It has a mechanism (the pupil) that automat-

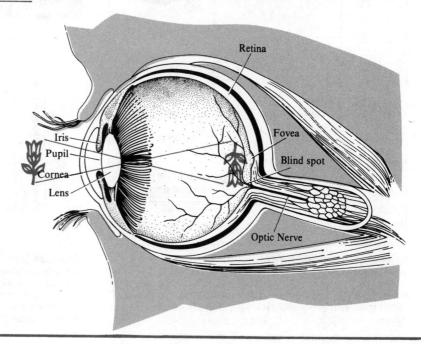

Figure 4.8. The Human Eye
The eye contains complex structures which convert light waves into neural impulses that are carried by the optic nerve to the occipital lobes of the brain where they are interpreted as vision. The image enters the eye through the cornea and then passes through the pupil opening in the iris. The lens focuses the images on the retina where the sense receptors, rods and cones, are located. The image is reversed and upside-down because light rays travel in a straight line and are striking the curved surface of the retina. Images are most sharply seen when they fall on the fovea and not seen at all when they fall on the blind spot.

Labels: Retina, Fovea, Blind spot, Optic Nerve, Iris, Pupil, Cornea, Lens

ically adjusts to changing light intensities, and a remarkably sensitive and constantly available "film" (the retina).

Light rays enter the eye through the cornea, the tough outer membrane that covers the eyeball and holds it in shape. The rays then pass through the opening in the iris (the colored part of the eye). This opening is the pupil, which contracts or expands automatically, controlling the amount of light getting through. The rays are focused by the lens, which flattens out for more distant objects and thickens for those closer. The focused images fall on the retina at the back of the eyeball. In the retina lie the sense receptors for vision: the rods and cones.

Rods and Cones. The rods and cones are so named because of their shapes (Sterling, 1983). Rods respond to differences in brightness, so they are most important for seeing in dim light. The rods are most sensitive to light waves in the 500 nm range, or to blue and green light. They contain a chemical pigment called rhodopsin that breaks down into substances that stimulate the neurons

sending visual messages to the brain. Vitamin A is involved in the chemical process of rebuilding rhodopsin, lending support to the notion that, within limits, consuming foods like carrots is good for vision.

The cones respond to hue, or color variations, so they are most important for color vision in bright light. Unlike the rods, which are primarily distributed around the outside edge of the retina, the cones are clustered more in its middle, particularly in an area called the fovea. Images are seen most sharply when they fall on the fovea, and this is the area we try to aim at an object when we focus on it. Although the cones respond to all color variations, they are most sensitive to wavelengths in the 550 nm range, or to green and yellow light. Fire departments are beginning to paint their fire engines lime yellow so people can more easily see them.

Have you noticed what happens when light intensity changes rapidly as when you go from a dimly lighted room into a brightly lighted one? You are dazzled by the light at first, but your eyes soon adapt. Your pupils contract, letting less light into the eyes, and in a short while the cones begin functioning efficiently again. Upon reentering the dimly lighted room, it then takes a while for dark adaptation to occur. Dark adaptation takes place in two stages. Cones adapt as much as they can (remember cones are for color vision) in about 10 minutes, while rods reach dark adaptation in about half an hour (Hecht & Shaler, 1938). In dark adaptation, the eye receptors adjust to the dimmer levels of light for optimum vision.

Optic Nerve. The retina also contains several other types of cells: bipolar, ganglion, horizontal, and am-

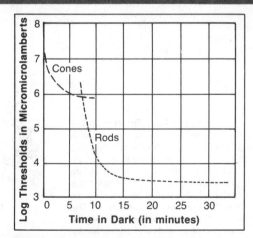

Figure 4.10. Dark Adaptation

Subjects are placed in total darkness after being in bright light. They are then asked to identify the weakest light they can. The longer they stay in the darkness, the weaker the light they can see. The typical curve for the threshold drops rapidly, flattens out, then drops again. The first curve represents cone adaptation, and the second curve represents rod adaptation (after Hecht & Shaler, 1938).

Figure 4.9. The Human Retina
In the retina lie the rod and cone sense receptors for vision. The cones of the fovea, the area of greatest visual sensitivity, have their own direct paths through bipolar cells with single endings. Outside the fovea, larger bipolar cells with multiple endings collect signals from a number of sensors.

Figure 4.11.   Blind Spot Demonstration
Close your right eye and look at the spot on the right. Move the book slowly up to your face. The symbol on the left will disappear because it is focused on your blind spot.

acrine cells (Dowling & Dubin, 1984). Light causes the rods and cones to send electrical energy to the bipolar cells, which then pass on neural impulses to the ganglion cells. The horizontal cells and amacrine cells interconnect the neurons in the retina (Linberg & Fisher, 1986). The axons of the ganglion cells come together at the eye's blind spot to form the optic nerve. You cannot see objects focused on the blind spot. There are about 120 million rods and six million cones, which converge on about one million optic nerve fibers. This means that many rods or cones send information to the same neurons. An exception is the 100,000 or so cones directly at the fovea which are connected one-to-one with optic nerve fibers (which helps explain why vision is best here).

Information from each side of the visual field ultimately reaches the opposite hemisphere of the brain, but first it follows a rather complicated pathway. Stimuli from the right visual field travels through the lens to the retina on the left half of each eye, and information from the left visual field goes to the right half of each eye. The optic nerve from each eye consists of two nerve fibers carrying information from each half of the retina. The nerves from the retina on the same side of each eye join at the optic chiasma. Then the optic nerve tracts travel to the brain and eventually reach the occipital lobes, where the sensation of vision is interpreted. Images from the left half of each eye go to the left hemisphere of the brain, and images from the right half of each eye go to the right hemisphere. But ultimately the visual information from the right visual field ends up in the left hemisphere and information from the left visual field ends up in the right hemisphere.

Visual Processes

The ability to discriminate fine details when looking at something is visual acuity. One of the most popular ways of measuring visual acuity is with the Snellen eye

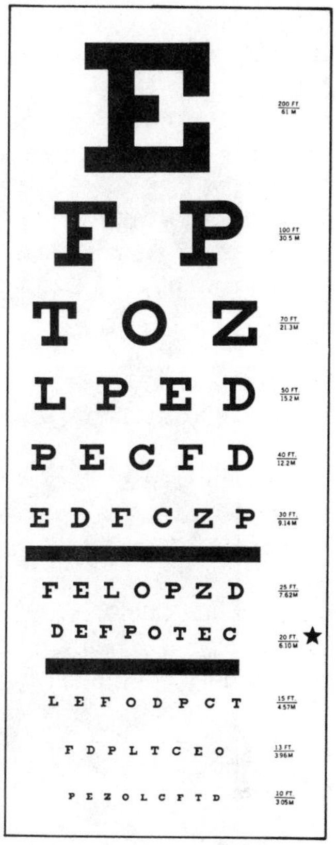

Figure 4.12.   Snellen Eye Chart
Visual acuity is typically measured with the Snellen eye chart. A person with normal vision can read the row of letters marked with a star at a distance of 20 feet. This sample is reduced for illustration purposes.

chart. This measurement is often called the 20/20 test because a person with normal vision can stand 20 feet from the chart and easily identify the row of letters fourth up from the bottom (starred in Figure 4.12.). A person whose eyes cannot be corrected with glasses to 20/200 is considered legally blind.

In the visual impairment of myopia (nearsightedness) the eyeball is unusually long, so the image is focused in front of the retina. Glasses can be used to see normal to long-range stimuli in the environment. In hyperopia (farsightedness) the eyeball is unusually short and the image is focused beyond the retina. Glasses permit close-up work, such as reading. Another common visual problem is astigmatism, in which the cornea of the eye has an irregular shape that distorts vision. Eyeglasses can usually correct this problem.

Theories of Color Vision

Our world is filled with a richness in all the color variations. How are we able to see the many colors in our environment? There are various theories of color vision, and they all agree on the importance of the cones in producing all the colors we see. The disagreement among theories of color vision is on the nature of the complex processing that allows the cones to send correct messages to the brain.

Figure 4.13. Color Blindness
Someone with red-green color blindness would be able to identify traffic signal lights because of the color's position on the traffic signal and differences in its brightness.

There are three types of cones, each of which is most sensitive to a particular wavelength producing either red, green, or blue colors. But if there are only three different receptors how is it we see so many colors? In 1807 an English physicist, Thomas Young, proposed that the eye sees color because of a combination of these three colors. He showed how mixing red, green, and blue lights in different amounts could produce all colors in the spectrum.

Later, the German physiologist, Hermann von Helmholtz, extended the theory by suggesting that three different types of receptors are responsible for the colors red, green, and blue, and when different combinations of receptors are stimulated, different colors are produced. The Young-Helmholtz theory is called the tri-chromatic theory of color vision, since it depends on three basic color receptors.

Shortly after Helmholtz, physiologist Ewald Hering proposed the opponent-process theory of color vision. Hering believed that yellow is also a basic color. He argued that while there are three types of color receptors, rather than being only sensitive to one color, each

type of color receptor responds to opposing pairs of colors: blue-yellow, red-green, and black-white. Each receptor can respond to one color at a time, but can combine with the other receptors to produce the colors in the visual spectrum.

Which theory is correct? The debate is still going on, but it appears that both theories may be partially correct. Researchers have identified three types of cones in the human retina. MacNichol (1964) showed that one type is most sensitive at about 450 nm (blue), one is most sensitive at about 540 nm (green), and the third somewhere around 577 nm (red). This information supports the trichromatic theory.

Other evidence supports the opponent-process theory. If you were to look at an American flag that is yellow instead of blue, black instead of white, and green instead of red, for about a minute, and then stare at a white space, you would see a great red, white, and blue American flag. This is known as a negative afterimage, because it is the reverse of the original colors, as suggested in the opponent-process theory. Other studies have suggested that the higher visual centers may operate in an opponent-process manner. And Hering's theory does a better job of explaining color blindness.

Color Blindness. While most of us can see the wide variety of colors in the world, some people see only shades of gray. If you have normal color vision, you are a trichromat, and if you can see only light and dark, you are totally color-blind, or a monochromat.

It is more common to be partially color-blind, or a dichromat. Color blindness is determined genetically, is sex-linked, and occurs mostly in males (10% of men are color-blind, while only about 1% of women are). The dichromat lacks one of the three types of cones. For example, if the red-green complement of cones is missing, he will be unable to distinguish red and green and will see all colors as yellow or blue. Among men, about 7% of the population suffers from red-green color blindness. A few individuals have blue-yellow blindness and see all colors as red or green. Throughout the animal world, many animals, including dogs, are monochromats. These animals do not seem to have any trouble adjusting to a world of gray. There are very few cases of total color blindness in humans.

VISUAL PERCEPTION

As we discussed earlier, most people rely more on vision than on any other sense. Because vision is so important for humans, and so much work has been done in this area, in this section we review visual perception in great detail. Many of the principles that apply to visual perception also hold true for the other senses.

The sensory properties of objects differ from moment to moment depending on such factors as the amount of light reflected by them and the distance and angle at which we view them. We are not slaves to such variations in sensory stimulation, however. Regardless of momentary change, the perceptions we experience seem pretty much the same to us from one moment to the next.

Perceptual Constancy

Perceptual constancy is the tendency to perceive objects in a consistent manner despite the changing sensations that are received by our senses. Visual constancy plays an important role in helping us adapt to our environment successfully. Can you imagine the chaos that would result if you could not identify your friends because they wore different clothes each time you saw them? Visual constancy allows us to focus on the permanent features of objects rather than the changing retinal images.

Brightness Constancy. A sheet of white paper seen in the bright sunlight reflects a very different amount of light than the same sheet of paper seen later that night in a softly lighted room. Yet we perceive the paper as having the same whiteness in each case. This is an example of brightness constancy, our ability to see objects as continuing to have the same brightness even though light may change their immediate sensory prop-

erties. Psychologists have determined that an object will exhibit brightness constancy as long as both the object and its surroundings are in light of the same intensity.

Color Constancy. Although you probably do not notice, the illumination of the environment determines what color you perceive. For example, if you took a color photograph (without flash or filters) of an outdoor scene, it would be more red at daybreak and more blue at midday. Photos taken under fluorescent lights are greenish, while photos taken with tungsten light (in your home) are yellowish. The different colors result from the different wavelengths of the illuminating source. However, we do not normally notice the subtle changes in color. Color constancy is the perceptual tendency to see familiar objects as the same color consistently, regardless of the illumination. This is why we tend to see our blue shirt as blue, irrespective of the circumstances.

Shape Constancy. Do you eat from round dinner plates? Do they look round while you are eating? Unless you sit directly above it, chances are good that more often your plate appears elliptical rather than round, because of the angle from which you view it. Yet we see dinner plates as round, and doors as rectangular. Shape constancy allows us to perceive familiar objects as having a permanent shape, even if we look at the objects from different angles. In a movie theater, if we are forced to sit very close to the screen or far off to one side, the actors and objects we see at first may look distorted. After a short time, however, we partially make up for this distortion and see the scenes in normal perspective.

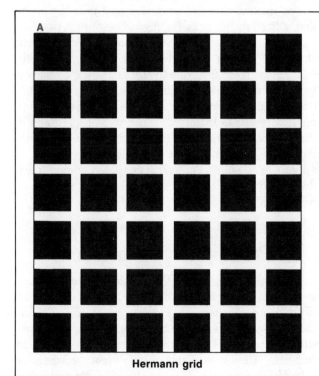

Hermann grid

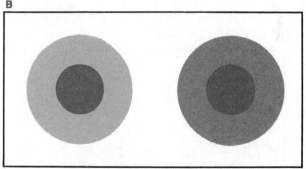

Figure 4.14. Brightness Perception
The brightness of an object depends on the light reflected from itself and its background. Its brightness relative to other objects appears the same in bright light or dark. The Hermann grid (**A**) is an example of the perceived brightness depending on the surrounding area. The gray spots at the intersection of the white strips do not exist but are a perceptual effect of the surrounding black. The two inner circles (**B**) are of equal intensity yet may appear different because of their backgrounds.

Figure 4.15. Shape Constancy
Even when we look at an object from different angles, we perceive it to have the same shape, due to shape constancy.

Size Constancy. Generally, we perceive a familiar object as remaining the same size even though the image it casts on the retina may vary. As a person walks away from us, the retinal image of that person becomes smaller and smaller, yet in reality he or she is not perceived to be any smaller. Here again, cues other than the retinal size of the image determine how objects appear to us.

Research has shown that young children are more likely than are adults to judge the size of distant objects on the basis of the size of the retinal image. According to Zeigler and Leibowitz (1957), the younger child takes fewer cues into account, and, of course, has had fewer perceptual experiences. Even in adults, however, size constancy can be violated in two-dimensional pictures, in which objects actually the same size appear to be different.

An anthropologist, Colin Turnbull, nicely demon-

Figure 4.16. Size Constancy
As the distance of an object from us increases, its retinal image becomes smaller. We tend to correctly perceive it as being farther away, rather than it changing size. Sometimes our perceptions can be fooled, as in this figure, where the light posts are really the same size but because of the changing background, we interpret the one on the right to be taller.

Figure 4.17. The Ames Room
The Ames room is specially constructed to appear normal even though one corner is much closer to the viewer than the other. This results in the perception of the people in the corners as disproportionate in size relative to their age.

strates the importance of experience in size perception in a 1961 anecdote about a pygmy who had lived his entire life in a forest. People in the forest culture never looked at any distant object because the trees blocked the view. When Turnbull took Kenge, the pygmy, into an open plains area for the first time, they saw a herd of buffalo several miles away. Kenge wanted to know what sort of insect they were. He could not believe they were buffalo because he had never before experienced size constancy in his forest life.

You may have visited an amusement park fun house that utilized the research findings of perception psychologists: Balls appear to roll uphill and people appear to shrink before your eyes. The Ames room is a specially constructed room that, due to size and shape constancy, looks normal. Actually, the walls and windows are trapezoidal and one corner is much farther away from the observer than the other. When two people stand in the corners, one person looks small while the other appears a giant and when a ball is rolled straight, it appears to go uphill. Perceptual constancy demonstrates that the brain is actively involved in the process of perception.

Perceptual Organization

In chapter 1, "The Study of Psychology," we described the Gestalt school of psychology. A number of German psychologists, including Max Wertheimer, Kurt Koffka, and Wolfgang Köhler, were disturbed with the way structuralism and behaviorism broke things down into elements. They argued that people view the whole or complete picture, not merely parts. The greatest influence of Gestalt psychology has been in the field of perception. The rules of perceptual organization discovered by the Gestaltists earlier in this century and published by Koffka in 1935 are still valid today.

Read the following sentence quickly and count the number of *f*s in it. "The field of psychology is full of fascinating facts." How many *f*s did you find? Most people will say four. Try counting them again. Gestalt psychologists would argue that the reason you did not count six *f*s is because you were looking at the sentence as a whole and were not breaking it down into individual units. Therefore, the *of*s were not of major consideration, and you probably didn't count their *f*s. In a sense, the *of*s were part of the background of the sentence.

Figure and Ground.   An important rule of perceptual organization is the figure-ground relationship. When we look at a scene, we tend to separate a main figure from a background. Familiar shapes and objects are usually seen as figure and the surrounding space is seen as ground. Often the figure is distinctive and solid, while the ground is vague and formless. And often the figure is seen as being in front of the ground.

Sometimes it is difficult to identify the figure-ground

4.18.   Figure-Ground Relationship
Do you see a vase or two profiles? Normally there is one figure which stands out from the background, but here the figure and ground are reversible.

relationship. In a reversible figure scene, the figure and ground appear to reverse themselves. One of the most famous ambiguous reversible figures is the Rubin vase (vase-profile), in which the figure can either be a vase in the middle or two profiles on either side.

While many figure-ground relationships are visual, we also tend to perceive figure-ground with our other senses. In hearing, for example, when we are at a noisy party talking with someone, that person's voice becomes the figure and all the rest of the talking becomes the

BIOGRAPHICAL ☆ HIGHLIGHT ☆

MAX WERTHEIMER   **WOLFGANG KÖHLER**   **KURT KOFFKA**

Gestalt psychologists were interested in studying the whole rather than the fragments suggested by structuralism and behaviorism. In 1910 the three founders of Gestalt psychology met in Frankfurt, Germany, where they started their study of perception.

Max Wertheimer was born in Prague, Germany, in 1880. His parents wanted him to become a musician, but he chose psychology. He obtained his Ph.D. from the University of Würzburg in 1904. He taught at several universities in Germany until Hitler came into power. Then he fled to the United States and became a professor at the New School for Social Research in New York, where he remained until his death in 1943.

Wolfgang Köhler was born in Revel, Estonia, in 1887 and grew up in Germany. He obtained his Ph.D. from the University of Berlin in 1909 and then went to the University of Frankfurt, where he met Wertheimer and Koffka. In 1913 he went to the Canary Islands, where he was the director of a research station on ape behavior. Köhler applied the Gestalt principles to study insight learning by chimpanzees. In 1921, he went to the University of Berlin. In the 1930s he fled to the United States and became a professor at Swarthmore College. Köhler died in 1967.

Kurt Koffka was born in Berlin in 1886. He earned his Ph.D. from the University of Berlin in 1908, and then went to the University of Frankfurt, where he met the other Gestalt founders in 1910. In 1927 he became a professor at Smith College in the United States. Koffka was especially interested in studying the laws that govern our perceptions of the environment. He was the chief spokesman for the Gestalt movement. Koffka died in 1941.

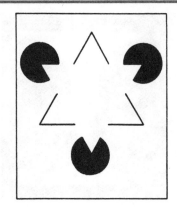

Figure 4.19. Closure Through the process of closure, we are able to close the gaps in an image and see a triangle resting on top of three circles rather than three circles with notches in them.

background. In olfaction this might occur when we visit a friend in the hospital and smell a fresh bouquet of roses; the other odors fade into the background.

Closure. The Gestalt psychologists discovered that people have a tendency to group stimuli according to certain rules or principles. This grouping, or association, of separate sensory stimuli into a whole—a complete pattern—provides structure for our perceptions.

What would you call a circular form made out of dashed lines? A circle, of course. Why? You filled in the gaps and provided the missing spaces for yourself. Closure is the principle of filling in the gaps to perceive a complete form. Closure allows us to see a whole stimulus even when part of it is out of view. For example, you recognize a house as a house, even if bushes and trees block your view partially.

Continuity. Continuity is the principle of perceiving a line as continuing on its course. The lovable alien in *E.T.* wanted to help the boy with the fake arrow in his head because continuity made the arrow appear to go through the boy's head. Continuity helps to explain the success of camouflage. We see the objects in a scene continuing, even if something foreign is blocking part of our view.

Similarity. We tend to perceive similar stimuli as being together. Thus, in rows of black and white circles,

the black ones are perceived as one line and the white ones are perceived as another. Similarity is the principle of organization in which similar stimuli are perceived as a unit.

Proximity. Stimuli close to one another are perceived as belonging together. Proximity is the principle in which stimuli next to one another are included together. For example, lines that are nearer are perceived as a unit. People standing close together are perceived as a group.

Common Fate. The principle that groups together stimuli or objects that are moving together is common fate. Thus, we see a flock of birds, a group of marathon runners, or a collection of lines converging together as units.

Depth Perception

Think for a minute about walking down a street. It's relatively easy to judge the distance between buildings, even though the path might not be straight. This is partially possible because of depth perception which is the ability to judge the distance to an object. We can

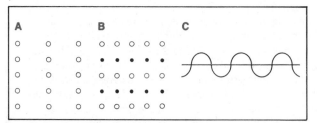

Figure 4.20. Perceptions According to Gestalt Principles
  A. Proximity. Spacing influences whether we see rows or columns. Here we perceive columns rather than rows because the stimuli in the columns are closer together.
  B. Similarity. When all of the stimuli are equally spaced we group similar ones together. Here we perceive distinct rows of circles and rows of dots.
  C. Continuity. When one shape is interrupted by another, we perceive the original form as continuing and complete the whole image in our minds.

Figure 4.21. Interposition
When one object partially blocks the view of another, we perceive the blocking object as being closer.

even perceive depth in two-dimensional pictures. What are the cues we use to judge depth? Is depth perception innate or do we learn to perceive it correctly? Some of the cues work when we use only one eye, and are called *monocular* cues; others need both eyes, and are called *binocular* cues. Both types require the brain to interpret the images received on the eye retina.

Monocular Depth Cues. Monocular depth cues only require one eye to detect distance. There are a number of monocular depth cues that help us turn two-dimensional retinal sensations into three-dimensional visual perceptions. Some of these include interposition, size perspective, linear perspective, texture gradient, aerial perspective, and motion parallax.

When one object partially blocks our view of another, we assume that this overlap is due to the first one being closer. Interposition helps us realize that a tree in front of the library is closer to us than the library itself. Yonas (1984) found that infants as young as 7 months can judge distance on the basis of interposition.

Perspective refers to changes in the appearance of objects or surfaces as the distance from the perceiver increases. The monocular depth cue of size perspective helps us recognize that the smaller an object becomes the farther away it is perceived to be. We normally interpret distance by the relative size of one object to another. In the school's parking lot, for example, the closest cars appear larger, so we perceive the smaller cars as being farther away. We also use the cue of familiar size, in which our past experience and knowledge about an object helps us to judge its distance (Fitzpatrick, Pasnak, & Tyer, 1982).

Parallel lines, as they become more distant from the observer, appear to converge. The convergence of rail-

Camouflage

Many animals blend in with the background of their environment to hide them from predators. This is called camouflage, and is often an effective tool to aid in survival. Camouflage is effective because of the Gestalt laws of perceptual organization.

If coloration and patterns are very similar, it might be difficult to separate figure from ground. Thus, we tend not to be able to see the animal in its natural habitat, and focus instead on other objects in the environment. Many animals are colored in such a way as to make them easily blend into the background. If the animal were significantly different than the background of its habitat, then we could easily spot it. But the spotted fawn in the forest, the fish in the water, or the polar bear in the snow all blend in so well that it is difficult to detect them.

The principle of continuity is an important part of camouflage because it encourages us to perceive lines as continuing in a natural progression. When an animal blends into the background, continuity helps us see the background lines and shapes as continuing, often through the animal. A walking stick or an inch worm on a tree branch illustrate this. Expectancy is also important, and when we expect to see a forest or prairie, we tend to do so, often ignoring the animals that might also be contained there.

Color is often very important in helping the animal hide in an environment. Color helps the animal blend in, and combined with expectancy, continuity and figure-ground effects, results in effective camouflage. Some animals can even change colors to blend in better with the environment. One example of this is the chameleon that can change from brown to green, depending on its surroundings. If people practice and become more observant, they can improve their detection of camouflage.

THOUGHT QUESTIONS

1. Why is camouflage effective?
2. Think of some everyday situations in which the concept of camouflage is used.
3. Why might color-blind individuals be immune to some forms of camouflage?

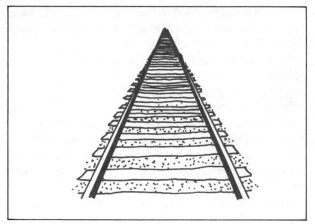

Figure 4.22. Linear Perspective
The railroad tracks converge, suggesting a farther distance at the top of the figure.

road tracks in the distance is an example of <u>linear perspective</u> often used in drawings to illustrate distance. We interpret the converging lines as being farther away from us, a three-dimensional perception even though the drawing is two-dimensional.

As we stand on grass, we might notice that the individual blades of grass near our feet can be identified, but as we look farther away, the texture becomes blurred and we just see green. <u>Texture gradient</u> is an important depth cue because many surfaces, such as buildings, sidewalks, and floors have texture. <u>Aerial perspective</u> is a monocular cue in which we use brightness, color, and detail to determine distance. On a hazy day, buildings appear to be farther away than on a bright sunny day. Also, objects close to us appear bright and clear, objects that are farther away often have shadows.

As we walk down the street, notice that people and objects close to us appear to move by faster than objects farther away. Buildings in the distance do not seem to move within our field of vision at all. <u>Motion parallax</u> causes us to perceive that telephone poles at the side of the road are flying by when we're riding in a car, while the distant scenery or the moon appears to be standing still relative to us. It is one of the important monocular cues.

Binocular Depth Cues. While we have many cues for judging depth that depend on only one eye, for even greater accuracy at judging depth, we have <u>binocular depth cues</u> that depend on both eyes working together. The principal binocular depth cues are retinal disparity and convergence.

A very important binocular cue for depth is <u>retinal disparity</u>. Our eyes are about five *cm* apart. This means that each eye (retina) receives slightly different (disparate) sensations, which must be combined by the brain for normal vision. Look at an object in your room with only your left eye. Then close your left eye and look at

the object with your right eye. The object will appear to move to the right, especially if you hold your index finger out at arm's length while you are looking at the object.

How does retinal disparity help in depth perception? Try the demonstration above outdoors, while looking at a distant object. What happens now? Distant objects will be seen as more similar in each eye. Therefore, the less retinal disparity we have, the greater the distance of the object we are looking at.

Retinal disparity has been used to create the feeling of depth in 3-D movies. If a scene is photographed simultaneously by two cameras close together, and the viewer wears special glasses which permit the image from each camera to go to one eye only, a three-dimensional effect is obtained. Retinal disparity has also been suggested as one of the problems in some children with learning disabilities. It is possible that some children have difficulty interpreting the disparate images presented by the eyes. Until the brain matures to a point where it can correctly interpret these images, the child may be confused by them.

When we look at objects in our immediate environment, our eyes have to converge, or move inward toward one another, to focus on the objects. The kinesthetic sensations produced by the muscles of the eyeballs send this information to the brain. The brain interprets the amount of <u>convergence</u> as a cue to depth. The farther away an object is, the less convergence we experience. Distant objects do not create any convergence at all. Putting all of these monocular and binocular depth cues together allows us to be fairly precise in judging the distance between us and objects in our environment.

Development of Depth Perception. Depth perception has been studied in infants with the use of the <u>visual cliff</u>, developed by Gibson and Walk in 1960. The <u>visual cliff</u> is a device that appears to have a solid support on one (shallow) side and a cliff drop-off on the (deep) other. Actually, a large sheet of heavy glass is on top of both halves so the subject cannot fall. A variety of infant animals have been tested on it, including chickens, goats, kittens, pigs, and puppies. Newborn animals stayed on the shallow side, indicating that depth perception is innate in these infants.

Human infants as young as 6 months of age have been tested on the visual cliff. Even at this age, most of the babies appear to have depth perception, as they stay on the shallow side. Does this prove depth perception is innate in humans? Not completely, since the infants could have acquired it in the first 6 months of life before they were tested. But it does strongly suggest that depth perception is important in humans, and is developed at an early age. Infants younger than about 6 months cannot crawl and therefore cannot effectively be tested on the visual cliff.

Figure 4.23. Visual Cliff
Depth perception in animals and human infants is tested using a visual cliff. One side of the table top is clear glass with the checkered cloth running down the side and across the floor several feet below it so that a cliff is simulated. Both humans and animals hesitate to cross this end of the table even when encouraged to do so. Experimenters use this information as evidence of innate depth perception.

Perception of Motion

As we look out of our window, we see people and cars moving by. How do we know that the people are moving? The perception of movement is a complex process that involves the visual receptors in the retina, the eye muscles, and the interpretation by the brain of the visual sensations provided by the environmental stimuli.

Although occasionally we may misinterpret the object that is moving, generally we are fairly adept at detecting real motion, or movement that is actually created by objects in motion. Sometimes, however, we perceive movement when in fact there is none. Apparent motion has interested psychologists since the Gestalt psychologists first studied it. Let's look at several types of apparent motion.

Induced Motion. Have you ever seen the sun go behind a cloud? If so, you experienced induced motion. Actually, the sun is relatively stationary and the clouds move through the sky. But we see the sun as the central figure and the clouds as background, so we often incorrectly perceive that the sun is doing the moving. The tendency to see the figure move against the background is so strong that sometimes we misinterpret what is happening. Another example of induced motion occurs when we are waiting at a stoplight and the car next to us begins to move forward. We will likely try to put on our brakes as we feel our car moving backward. Because our car is the figure, we induce movement to it, rather than the car next to us.

Phi Phenomenon. One type of apparent motion occurs when we look at a neon sign with arrows that seem to move. This is an application of the phi phenomenon. If we are in a darkened laboratory room and see two lights alternately turning on and off, we will perceive a single source of light that seems to jump between the two points. Of course, the lights have to be a certain distance apart, and the second one has to be turned on at the right time to achieve the effect. The phi phenomenon is an example of an illusion, or misinterpreted sensation. (We discuss illusions later in this chapter.)

Stroboscopic Motion. We all are familiar with the movement produced in stroboscopic motion. This is the basis for movement that occurs in motion pictures. What we see is a series of still pictures, each one just slightly different from the previous one. The pictures are presented in rapid succession, and we perceive smooth,

Figure 4.24. Induced Movement
How many times have you said that the sun went behind the clouds on a sunny day? Actually, the clouds went in front of the sun, but we tend to induce movement in the figure (the sun) rather than the ground (the clouds).

Figure 4.25. Stroboscopic Motion
Motion can be perceived even though none actually has occurred. When viewed in rapid sequence, figures on the frames of this 1885 series from the Museum of Modern Art (New York) appear to move.

coordinated movement. Part of the explanation for stroboscopic motion (as well as for the phi phenomenon) is the afterimage that remains briefly after the stimulus is gone. Thus, the last image is still in the nervous system and brain as the next one is received. The Gestalt principle of closure helps us fill in the gap and produces a smooth motion from individual still pictures.

Autokinetic Motion. If we stare at a small spot of light in a dark room for a few minutes, it will appear to begin to move around. Although the light is stationary, we see it move randomly back and forth in the darkness. While we don't know the reason for this positively, the autokinetic effect may be caused by the eye muscles moving to keep the eyes moist.

Visual Illusions

An illusion is an incorrect perception that occurs when sensation is distorted. Although many of our illusions are visual, they are not limited strictly to the sense of

sight. The study of illusions helps psychologists understand better how we process perceptions.

In our discussion of depth perception we have, in effect, already discussed many illusions in this chapter. Constancy can create powerful illusions. For example, in monster movies, a small "monster" close to the camera gives the false perception of bigness. The Ames room is sometimes called the distorted-room illusion. Monocular depth cues are used to create an illusion of depth in a two-dimensional painting or photograph. Likewise, the apparent motions of the autokinetic effect and stroboscopic motion are illusions of movement, as is the movement we see in a motion picture. Certain patterns, such as a moiré pattern, make lines in a figure appear to move. There are many illusions that have been studied extensively in psychology; here we sample only some of the more interesting and familiar ones.

Impossible Figures. Our brain is able to take sensation that is two-dimensional and produce perception that is three-dimensional. Sometimes, a figure can be drawn that contains information that is incompatible with the processing system. Impossible figures demonstrate the complexity of perception; they are figures that logically cannot exist. One of the best known is the three-pronged figure that has only two sides at the opposite end.

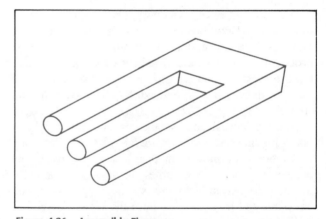

Figure 4.26. Impossible Figure
As shown here, sometimes a figure can be drawn that contains information that is incompatible with the visual processing system. This three-pronged figure only has two sides at the opposite end.

Reversible Figures. Closely related to impossible figures are reversible figures. Reversible figures present ambiguous information that can be interpreted in more than one way. One well-known reversible figure is the Rubin vase figure mentioned earlier. Most of us alternate between making the vase the dominant foreground (with the profile in the background) and vice versa. We lack the cues to confirm which perception is correct.

Another example of a reversible figure is a drawing of a person's face which can be either a beautiful young woman or an ugly old woman. The young woman is looking to the side, whereas the old woman is looking

Figure 4.27. Reversible Figure
Do you see a beautiful young woman or an ugly old woman in this figure? The young girl is looking to the side, whereas the old woman is looking forward. We tend to organize complex stimuli into meaningful relationships.

forward. The nose of the old woman is the chin of the young woman, and the eye of the old woman is the ear of the young woman. The drawing is ambiguous enough that we again alternate between the two perceptions. The Necker cube is a drawing of a cube designed so that it is difficult to determine which side is toward the observer. One side is shaded and as we look at it the shaded side appears to shift from the front to the back of the cube. Usually, the more we look at reversible figures, the more ambiguous they appear.

Müller-Lyer Illusion. One of the most popular illusions is the Müller-Lyer. In this illusion, two horizontal lines of equal length appear to be different lengths due to the wings or arrows at the ends of each line. When the end lines point back toward the line, the line appears shorter than when the end lines point out away from the line. Because the end lines going away from the horizontal tend to produce an illusion of depth, we perceive this line as longer.

Gregory (1978) pointed out that one application of the Müller-Lyer illusion occurs when looking at the corner of a room. When viewing it from within the room, the ceiling and floor lines appear to flair out forming a "v" shape, giving the illusion of a taller wall. When viewing the corner from outside the room, the ceiling and floor lines appear to form the shape of arrowheads, giving the illusion of a shorter wall.

Ponzo Illusion. Another well-known illusion is the Ponzo illusion. Here the two converging vertical lines are likely to be interpreted as two parallel lines receding into the distance, much as railroad tracks might. The two horizontal lines are of equal length, but because of linear perspective, we tend to perceive the top line as longer since the background (the converging lines) makes it appear farther away from us.

Poggendorff Illusion. The Poggendorff illusion involves both physical and cognitive factors. Look at the straw in the glass of water in Figure 4.28. As it emerges from the water, it looks as if it is bent. Actually, it is a straight line. The Poggendorff illusion is found in a variety of everyday situations. For example, if the middle part of a pencil is covered by an index card, one end of the pencil will look bent, or if the vertical architectural lines of a building are partially blocked from view by its pillars or columns, one end of the architectual lines will appear bent.

The Moon Illusion. When we look at the moon on the horizon, it looks larger than it does when it is high in the sky. Although many explanations have been suggested for the moon illusion, probably the best is the 1962 theory by Kaufman and Rock. They propose that when we view the moon on the horizon, we compare it to the objects on the terrain, such as houses, trees, and telephone poles. Next to these, it is large. But in the sky,

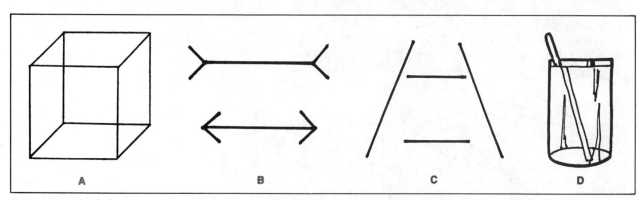

Figure 4.28. Visual Illusions
  A. In the Necker Cube illusion, one side appears to shift from the front to the back of the cube.
  B. In the Müller-Lyer illusion, the two horizontal lines of equal length appear to be different lengths due to the wings at the ends of each line.
  C. In the Ponzo illusion, the two horizontal lines of equal length appear to be different lengths due to the linear perspective of the converging lines.
  D. In the Poggendorff illusion, the straw appears to jump to one side as it emerges from the liquid due to differences in diffraction of light.

what do we compare it to? Since there are no familiar objects in the sky to compare to the moon, it appears smaller. The moon is actually the same size in both cases. Try this: in a sheet of paper, cut a hole just large enough through which to see the moon on the horizon. Later on, when the moon is higher in the sky, look at it through the same hole. The view of both the moon on the horizon and the moon in the sky will fit the same-sized hole.

HEARING

The stimuli that affect our sense of hearing are sound waves. These are rapid changes in air pressure caused by a vibrating object, such as vocal cords or a guitar string, in contact with the air. Sound waves in the air are similar to ripples on the water caused by a pebble dropped into a still pond. One cycle of a sound wave includes a *peak* of highest pressure and a *valley* of lowest pressure.

Sound waves vary in three ways, each with a distinct sensory effect: frequency, amplitude, timbre. They vary in frequency, that is, the number of cycles of sound pressure per second measured in hertz (Hz), which determines their pitch. The young healthy ear can hear sounds from 20 Hz to 20,000 Hz. High-pitched sounds are the result of a rapid frequency of vibration, while low frequency produces low-pitched sounds.

Sound waves also differ in amplitude, or intensity, which determines a sound's loudness. Amplitude is the height of the sound wave peak. High amplitude creates loud sounds, while low amplitude produces soft sounds. Loudness is usually measured in decibels (dB). As shown in Figure 4.29., normal conversation is about 60 dB, while a rock band can be about 110 dB. Sound above 130 dB is usually painful. You are probably aware that deafness may be caused by listening to very loud music for too long.

The complexity of the mixture of sound waves determines a sound's distinctive timbre. Two people talking at the same level of amplitude and frequency sound different because each voice has its characteristic timbre. The most complex pattern of sound waves we hear is *white noise*, such as the roar of the surf or the hum of an air conditioner, where all the frequencies are jumbled together. The simplest sound is a single pure tone, like that produced by a tuning fork.

The Ear

Sound waves are first received by the pinna of the outer ear, which "collects" them and directs them into the auditory canal. The waves then hit the eardrum or tympanic membrane, stretched across the inner end of the auditory canal, and cause it to vibrate. The three bones of the middle ear (called the *hammer*, the *anvil*, and the *stirrup*), carry these vibrations to the cochlea, a spiraled organ in the inner ear that looks something like a snail. Sound vibrations entering the cochlea create

Figure 4.29. Rock Band
Sounds as high as 110 dB are often generated by rock bands. Exposure to a loud sound like this over a long period of time can result in deafness.

waves in the fluid it contains. These waves cause a delicate partition, the basilar membrane, to change its shape. Low frequencies cause an indentation in the basilar membrane near the base of the cochlea, and high frequencies an indentation near the other end at the top of the spiraled cochlea.

When the basilar membrane is deformed by a traveling sound wave, the organ of Corti is also displaced. This organ contains the auditory receptors, a collection of hair cells. Above it is the tectorial membrane. The fluid in the cochlea pushes the basilar membrane up so that the hair cells brush against the tectorial membrane. This action triggers neural impulses in the auditory nerve which carries messages up to the temporal lobes of the brain.

Hearing Processes

The process of audition is nearly as remarkable as the process of vision. We can determine sounds as faint as the gentle wind rustling the branches of a blue spruce or as loud as a rock band in concert. We can recognize the individual voices of our friends and acquaintances. The physics of sound waves, namely frequency, amplitude, and timbre, and the biological structure of the ear are well understood. However, the process of transmitting and understanding sound impulses has not yet been completely explained.

Theories of Hearing.   The two basic theories of the process of hearing are the frequency and place theories.

The frequency theory of hearing (first proposed by Rutherford in 1886) states that the frequency of vibrations at the basilar membrane determines the frequency of firing of neurons that carry impulses to the brain. The problem with this theory is that nerves cannot fire as fast and continuously as the frequency of many sound waves. Therefore, the volley principle was proposed by Wever (1949). This states that individual neurons fire in sequence, thus increasing the total frequency of impulses it is possible to send to the brain.

Hermann von Helmholtz (the same person who developed the trichromatic theory of vision) proposed the place theory of hearing in 1863. Helmholtz suggested that the sensation of pitch is determined by the place on the basilar membrane that is stimulated. The nerves attached to the basilar membrane are sensitive to differ-

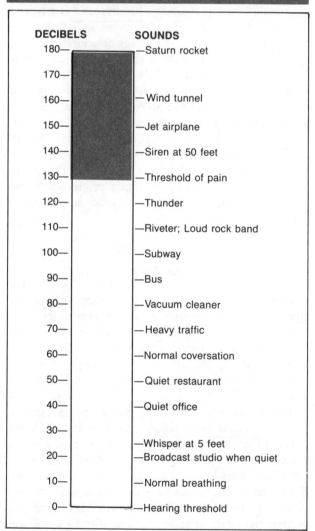

Figure 4.30.   Sound Decibel Scale

DECIBELS	SOUNDS
180	Saturn rocket
170	
160	Wind tunnel
150	Jet airplane
140	Siren at 50 feet
130	Threshold of pain
120	Thunder
110	Riveter; Loud rock band
100	Subway
90	Bus
80	Vacuum cleaner
70	Heavy traffic
60	Normal coversation
50	Quiet restaurant
40	Quiet office
30	
20	Whisper at 5 feet / Broadcast studio when quiet
10	Normal breathing
0	Hearing threshold

Loudness of a sound is measured in decibels. The threshold of hearing is defined as zero decibels. Some common sounds have intensities above the threshold of pain. Perceived loudness increases geometrically with decibels; for a 10 decibel increase, the perceived loudness doubles.

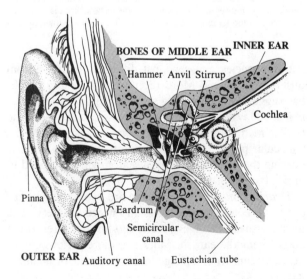

Figure 4.31.   The Human Ear
The ear is divided into three major components, the outer ear, middle ear, and the inner ear. The outer ear collects sound waves and transmits them to the bones of the middle ear. There they are amplified and received by the cochlea in the inner ear which vibrates and moves sound waves from the organ of Corti through the auditory nerve to the temporal lobes of the brain. The utricle and saccule in the inner ear contribute to the vestibular sense.

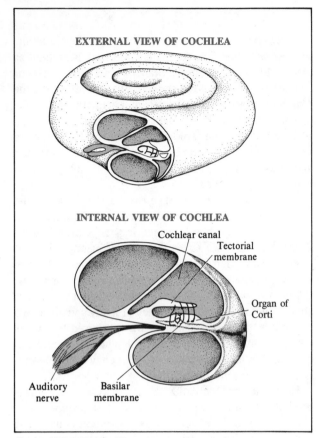

EXTERNAL VIEW OF COCHLEA

INTERNAL VIEW OF COCHLEA

Cochlear canal

Tectorial membrane

Organ of Corti

Auditory nerve

Basilar membrane

Figure 4.32. Hearing Receptors
The illustration at the top is a close-up of the external view of the cochlea. The illustration at the bottom shows a cross section of the cochlea. The true auditory receptors lie in the organ of Corti, which rests on the basilar membrane. Deflection of the basilar membrane activates the hair cells which brush against the tectorial membrane producing impulses in the auditory nerve. These impulses transmit messages to the temporal lobes of the brain which are interpreted as sound.

ent frequencies and send out different impulses from different locations. More recently, von Békésy (1960) has suggested the traveling wave principle, which states that sound waves traveling through the cochlea move the basilar membrane at a location that corresponds to the particular pitch. There are problems with both of these hearing theories, and future research will be needed to unravel some of these questions.

Hearing Impairment. There are two basic types of deafness: conduction deafness and nerve deafness. The former usually involves problems with structures in the outer or middle ear; the latter is a more serious condition resulting from damage to the inner ear or auditory nerve.

How many times have you been told not to put anything smaller than your elbow into your ear? My grandmother would always tell us that, and I found it pretty funny until I discovered that a ruptured eardrum can cause a loss of hearing called conduction deafness. Conduction deafness results from a structure in the outer

or middle ear not functioning properly. This type of deafness can be congenital (from birth), or it may be caused by damage to the ear from an injury or infection. Temporary conduction deafness could result from a head cold or a buildup of wax. Fortunately, many people with conduction deafness can be helped with a hearing device that helps conduct sounds to the inner ear, where they can be transformed into nerve impulses and sent to the brain.

A more severe problem occurs when the inner or auditory nerve is damaged or missing. Nerve deafness could result in the loss of high-frequency sounds, or in the total loss of hearing. Often nothing can be done when nerve deafness occurs, since a hearing aid cannot make a nonexistent neuron fire. Prolonged exposure to extremely loud noises, such as factory noise or very loud rock music, can cause nerve deafness. Excessive reliance on certain drugs or the aging process may also be responsible for this disability. Presbyacusia is a type of nerve deafness that normally occurs as people grow older. Our auditory nerve endings deteriorate, starting with those at the top of the cochlea and working down. McBurney and Collings (1984) argue that is why the older you become, the more difficulty you have in hearing high-pitched tones and the higher frequencies in speech, especially when they are of a low amplitude. Zimbardo and his colleagues (1981) suggested that hearing loss could lead to paranoid behavior, especially if the person were unaware of the loss. If you cannot hear what others are saying, you might think they are whispering behind your back and thus become suspicious of everyone.

Auditory Perception

Earlier we learned that auditory information is carried from the ears through the auditory nerves to the brain where it is interpreted. Each ear is connected with the brain through a separate auditory nerve. Thus, sound received only by the left ear is carried only to the left side of the brain. Sound delivered only to one ear is referred to as monaural.

The higher brain auditory centers are designed to process binaural information from both ears. We use binaural cues to help us judge the location of a sound source. Sound that reaches one ear slightly before the other ear serves as a cue for the location of the sound. For instance, if a friend who is standing to your left calls your name, you will hear it first in your left ear and then in your right ear. In addition, your friend's voice will appear slightly louder in your left ear, providing another binaural cue for localization. Often we are unaware that there is a difference, but we respond appropriately by turning toward the sound source.

Auditory information travels from the cochlea through the auditory nerve to the thalamus before reaching the auditory cortex in the temporal lobes of the brain. Next to the auditory cortex is a part of the temporal lobe known as the Wernicke's area, which is important in speech perception. Damage to the Wernicke's area leads to aphasia, a disorder in which a person loses the ability to understand speech. In most right-handed people, the Wernicke's area is located in the left hemisphere.

THE CHEMICAL SENSES

The senses of smell and taste are sometimes called the chemical senses because the sensory stimulation of the receptors involves contact with chemical substances in liquid or gaseous form. We know less about these senses than we do about vision or hearing, although the general processes for all of these senses are similar: a stimulus excites a receptor cell, and the energy is transformed into neural impulses and sent to the brain.

Smell

The sense receptors for smell, or olfaction, are located high in the nasal passages leading from the nose to the throat. Vapors interact chemically with the cilia of the olfactory epithelium to produce the neural impulses that go to the olfactory bulbs of the brain to be interpreted and acted upon. Olfaction is dissimilar to the other senses in that the qualities smelled cannot clearly be broken down into distinct physical properties. Research indicates that there may be seven basic forms of molecules that produce seven basic smells, which then combine to form various complex smells. The description of basic smells has not been definitely established, but according to Amoore (1970), it includes: camphoraceous, musky, floral, pepperminty, ethereal, pungent, and putrid odors.

One theory of smell is that the odor receptors have "holes" the same shape as the odor molecules. The odor molecules fit into the "holes" like a key fits a lock. This theory is called the stereochemical theory of olfactory coding (Amoore, Johnston, & Rubin, 1964). More recent research by Susan Schiffman and her colleagues (1981) does not support the key-and-lock explanation of smell. She tested molecular shapes of various substances and found no relationship between the shape and the odors produced. At present, psychologists do not have a theory that fully explains the perception of smell.

As we discuss in chapter 10, "Emotion," chemical signals, called pheromones, are used by some animals to communicate by olfaction. Very little research has been done on olfaction and social behavior in humans, but a study by Baron in 1981 suggests that perfume does have an effect on the perceptions of males toward the attractiveness of females. Research by Richard Doty and his colleagues (1982) has shown that both males and females can identify the gender of a person breathing through a hole in a wall (although females are better at it).

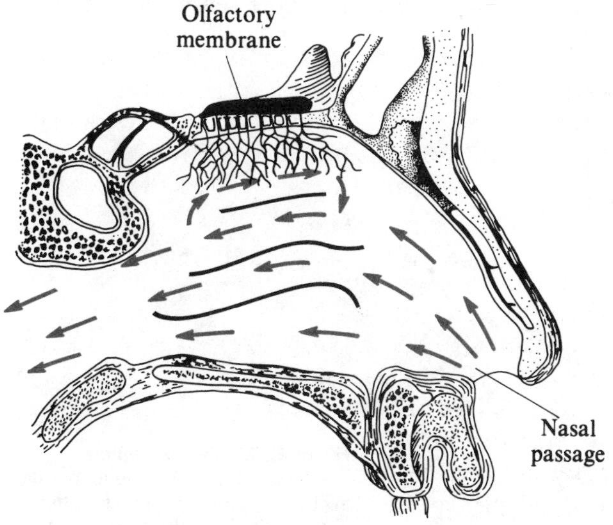

Figure 4.33. Cross section of a Nasal Passage
Odors enter the nasal passage and stimulate nerve endings in the olfactory membrane, the receptors for smell. The messages then travel to the olfactory bulbs of the brain.

Figure 4.34. Identifying Odors
People are able to easily identify a wide variety of odors. Researchers are attempting to discover seven basic molecules that produce basic smells. This basic list, however, has yet to be scientifically verified.

Although humans have the potential to utilize odors in social interactions, it is not known to what extent they actually do.

Taste

The sense receptors for taste, or <u>gustation,</u> are located in our tongues. The surface of the tongue is covered with little bumps, called <u>papillae.</u> The walls of the papilla contain the <u>taste buds,</u> the actual taste receptors. Substances tasted must be <u>soluble,</u> so that they can penetrate the taste pores or spaces between papillae to get through to the taste buds. Anything that is absolutely dry and solid is tasteless, although our own saliva contributes to making certain "dry" foods tasty.

Although there is some debate, some researchers agree with Virginia Collings (1974) who pointed out that we are sensitive to four distinct tastes: sweet, sour, salty, and bitter. We are the most sensitive to bitter, next to sour, then salty, and the least sensitive to sweet tastes. The cross fiber theory of taste (Erikson, 1984) proposes that taste quality is coded neurally by the firing pattern of receptor cells. The sensory information of taste is interpreted in the parietal cortex of the brain.

New taste buds quickly replace those killed by scalding hot cups of coffee or red-hot chili. In fact, they renew themselves completely about every ten days. Infants have few taste buds, but the number increases to about 10,000 by the time we are adults (Cowart, 1981). As we grow older, we gradually lose taste buds, which explains why older people are generally less sensitive to tastes than are young children (Schiffman, 1983).

The <u>flavor</u> of particular foods we eat or the way we taste them is due to their smell, appearance, texture, and temperature as well as our sensitivity to taste. With the nostrils pinched tight, we often cannot tell the difference between mashed squash and mashed potatoes or between strawberry and vanilla ice cream. When we have a congested nose, food often does not taste right to us, again because we don't smell it. Appearance and temperature affect our sense of taste. Would we eat green eggs or pink mashed potatoes? Do we enjoy cold french fries as much as sizzling hot ones? Taste is an important biological function in fueling the body since it makes eating a pleasurable experience.

THE SKIN AND BODY SENSES

We have six additional senses that provide us with valuable information. The four <u>skin senses</u> include pressure, pain, cold, and warmth. These sense receptors are located throughout the body under the skin, and provide information about the environment. We have two <u>proprioceptive senses:</u> kinesthesis, which is the sense of bodily movement, keeps us informed of the movement of various parts of the body, and the vestibular sense, which helps us maintain body balance.

Pressure

<u>Pressure,</u> or touch, is detected by receptors located throughout the body just under the surface of the skin. Some parts of the body are more sensitive to pressure

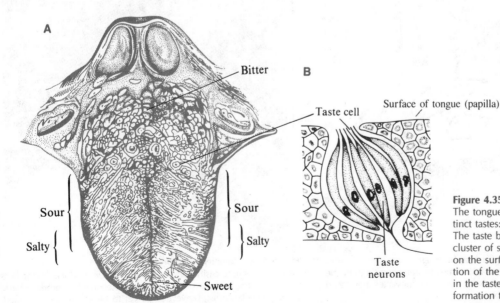

A
Bitter
Sour
Salty
Sour
Salty
Sweet

B
Taste cell
Surface of tongue (papilla)
Taste neurons

Figure 4.35. Taste Receptors
The tongue (**A**) is sensitive to four distinct tastes: sweet, sour, salty, bitter. The taste bud cell (**B**) consists of a cluster of sensory taste cells located on the surface of the tongue. Stimulation of the taste cells causes impulses in the taste neurons that carry the information to the brain.

than others. For example, the belly, back, and face are very sensitive to light pressure, whereas the feet, lower legs, thighs, and fingers are much less sensitive (Weinstein, 1968).

A number of different kinds of receptors have been identified in the skin, including *free nerve endings, Pacinian corpuscles, Ruffini endings, Meissner's corpuscles, Merkel's discs*, and *hair nerve endings*. At one time it was thought that each of the skin senses had its own type of receptor. For instance, the Pacinian corpuscle is designed to detect pressure and the hair nerve endings can detect hair movement caused by light pressure. However, there is not a one-to-one correspondence for all of the receptors or the various skin receptors.

Our sense of touch, or our haptic sense, is important in helping us keep aware of stimuli in the environment. Warren (1982) stated that we use the haptic sense to help us perceive the shape, size, texture, and location of objects in our environment. Ginsburg and Pringle (1988) found that both blind and blindfolded sighted subjects were able to estimate the number of cardboard disks glued on a surface. When the arrangement pattern was regular, the estimates were 10% higher than when the arrangement of disks was random, suggesting that touch perception is subject to illusions in a manner similar to vision.

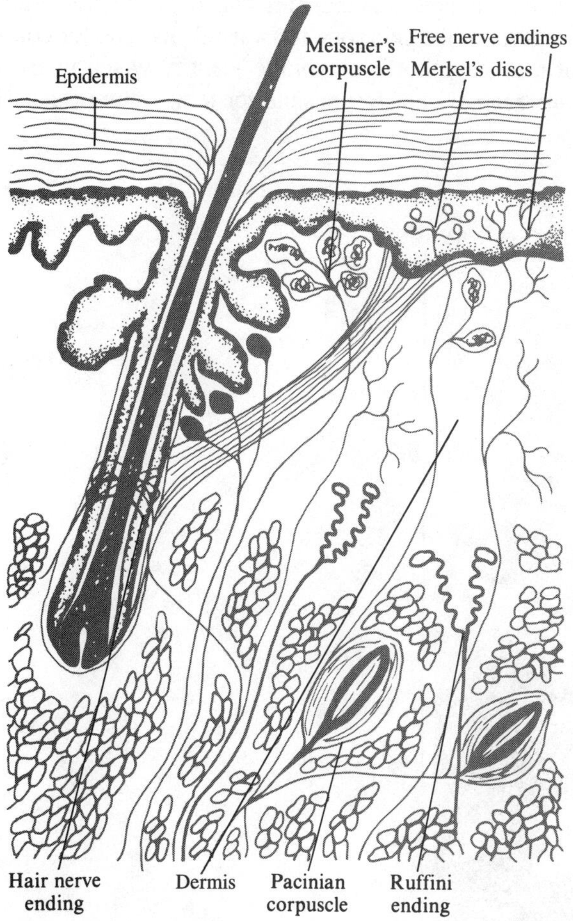

Pain

Pain has always been of particular interest to both psychologists and medical scientists. The free nerve endings mentioned above are believed to be the receptors for pain. It is possible that the pain receptors utilize histamine as their neurotransmitter. (Histamine is the substance responsible for the misery of allergy sufferers.)

Gate-Control Theory. The current theory of how pain sensations operate is the gate-control theory of pain first proposed by Melzack and Wall in 1965. An area of the spinal cord called the substantia gelatinosa acts as a gate that regulates the level of nerve impulse transmission from the free nerve endings to transmission cells in the spinal cord. There are two types of nerve fibers that interact at the substantia gelatinosa—large fast ones and small slow ones. When the neural impulses in the fast fibers reach the "gate," they tend to close it and prevent the slower pain signals from reaching the brain. As slower fiber impulses are transmitted, they open the gate

Figure 4.36. Skin Senses
A graphic representation of a section of skin showing the various structures involved with the sensations of pressure, pain, warmth and cold. The free nerve endings are sensitive to pressure. Meissner's corpuscles detect texture and movement on the skin. Merkel's discs keep us aware of objects. Ruffini endings and Pacinian corpuscles are located deeper in the skin and are sensitive to heavy pressure.

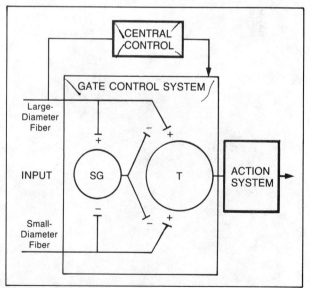

Figure 4.37. Gate-control Theory of Pain
Melzack's gate-control theory argues that the fast large diameter fibers in the substantia gelatinosa (SG) regulate the level of nerve transmission (T) in the spinal cord like a gate by preventing the slow small diameter fibers that open the gate from sending pain messages to the brain (after Melzack & Wall, 1965).

and allow more pain signals to reach the thalamus in the brain.

This would explain how the body is able to distinguish between minor discomforts and major pain. It could also dispel the mystery in the perplexing cases of phantom-limb pain, in which people who have lost an arm or a leg still feel pain in the missing limb. The theory demonstrates that what the neurons of the spinal cord allow to be transmitted to the brain is more significant than the actual sensations at the site of pain reception.

Endorphins and Pain. By identifying the mechanism of pain transmission, the spinal gate-control theory gives promise of new therapies for pain reduction. During the past decade, great advances have been made in our understanding of the endorphins, peptides produced in the brain that have a morphine-like effect on the reduction of pain. There are several types of endorphins, including leu-enkephalin and met-enkephalin (Bloom, 1983). Frederickson and Geary (1982) proposed a theory in which the periaqueductal gray (PAG) area of the brainstem produces endorphins which then inhibit the neurons in the spinal cord from transmitting the pain. Recent research also suggests that intense stress (such as an emergency) can cause the release of beta-endorphin,

a hormone that travels through the cerebrospinal fluid and could inhibit pain through the PAG circuit. This could be the mechanism that allows an injured person to conduct heroic acts without feeling pain at the time of injury.

Acupuncture. The gate-control theory may provide possible insights into the ancient Oriental art of acupuncture and why it may be successful in controlling pain. Through centuries of practice and tradition, practitioners of acupuncture may have discovered the areas of the body where needles can be inserted and somehow cause the pain control gates to close. It is currently believed that acupuncture can stimulate the production of endorphins in the brain, which in turn inhibit the pain-carrying neurons of the spinal cord (Han & Ternius, 1982).

Temperature

Scientists believe that there are two kinds of temperature receptors in the skin (one for warmth and one for cold), but they have not been able to identify which types of skin receptors are responsible for temperature (Hensel,

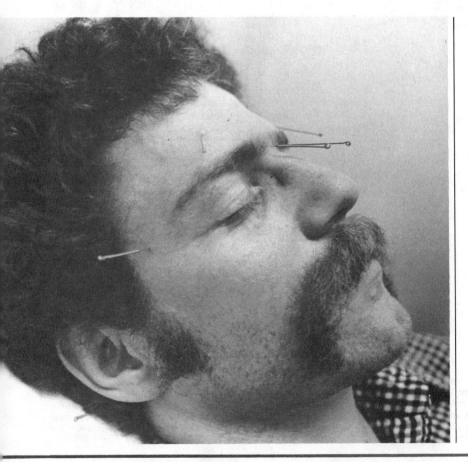

Figure 4.38. Acupuncture
The ancient Oriental art of acupuncture stimulates the body's natural pain killing substances, the endorphins. The insertion of needles in particular areas of the body may work to block pain by using the gate-control theory.

1982). The skin has spots about 1 mm in diameter that respond to either warm or cold stimuli. Warmth receptors are maximally sensitive to temperatures slightly above normal skin temperature whereas cold receptors respond maximally to temperatures just below normal skin temperature.

An intriguing finding is that there apparently are no specific receptors that respond only to hot temperatures. Sherrick and Cholewiak (1986) pointed out that when stimuli have temperatures of about 45° C (112° F), they sometimes feel cold, a phenomenon called paradoxical cold. For example, you might turn on a hot shower and at first touch it appears cold. After a couple of seconds, however, it feels hot. Bennett (1982) suggested that the warmth receptors stop functioning at about 45° C and the cold receptors, along with the receptors for pain, begin to function. Thus the sensation of hot might be due to the simultaneous firing of cold and pain receptors. Remember this the next time you get into a hot shower.

Skin sensitivity to temperature varies throughout the body (Stevens, 1979). The forehead is most sensitive to warmth, followed by the chest, stomach, shoulder, and arms. The chest is most sensitive to cold, followed by the arms, legs, and foreheads. People usually find an air temperature of about 22° C (72° F) as most comfortable. Hancock (1986) found that performance on a variety of tasks decreased significantly at temperatures above 29° C (85° F). Temperature can affect the way you feel and act.

Your body has the ability to maintain a normal skin temperature of 33° C which keeps the normal internal body temperature at 37° C (98.6° F). When you begin to get cold, you shiver and the skin's blood vessels constrict so you lose less heat. Likewise, when you become too warm you sweat and the skin's blood vessels dilate to release body heat. The ability to regulate temperature is important to survival, since without maintaining normal body temperature we could not effectively function.

Kinesthesis

The sense of bodily movement, or kinesthesis, tells us what various parts of our bodies are doing. The kinesthetic sense enables us to know whether our foot is pointed, our stomach full, our fist clenched, or our neck tense. We use information from our kinesthetic senses to coordinate our movements. The receptors (Golgi tendon organs) are located in the tendons connecting muscles to bones, and in the linings of the joints. They are activated when muscles are stretched or contracted (Clark & Horch, 1986). These receptors are generally slow to adapt and continue to provide information over long periods of time. The sense of kinesthesis is obviously

Figure 4.39. Vestibular System
The semicircular canals in the inner ear help us maintain a sense of balance both in everyday life and in specialized circumstances such as ice skating, tightrope walking and space flight.

extremely valuable in everyday behaviors, such as walking, reaching, and sitting.

The Vestibular Sense

The other important proprioceptive sense is that of equilibrium or the vestibular sense, which helps us keep our balance, orient properly to gravity, and tell when we are being moved. For example, without seeing motion we know when an elevator starts and stops. Without this sense, we would not know when we are thrown off balance or how to "right" ourselves to get back on balance. When we are constantly in motion, such as on a boat or in a car, the vestibular sense is upset and we may experience motion sickness. The sense of equilibrium is different from all the others, for most of its operations are not accompanied by our awareness.

Hair cells in the semicircular canals of the inner ear are the receptors for the vestibular sense (see Figure 4.?). The canals are filled with a fluid that moves when the head moves, and causes the hairs projecting from the receptors to bend, triggering nerve impulses to the brain signaling the need for reflex adjustment of the eyes and body (Benson, 1982).

Additional receptors for the vestibular sense are located in the utricle and saccule inside the inner ear. Here the hair cells form a mass and contain small solid crystals that exert gravitational pressure on these cells. Any change in this pressure "tells" the brain that we are not upright. In a weightless condition, like that of the astronauts in space, the lack of gravity affects the shape of these hairs. ■

As illustrated in our opening story, sensory awareness is essential for survival. Without sensation, we would have no idea of what the internal or external environments are like. The sensations that are received by the sense organs and sent to the brain are interpreted by a nervous system that is actively involved in the process of perception. An understanding of the processes of sensation and perception will help us understand other areas of psychology. Learning, memory, motivation, and social interaction all require that we receive and interpret environmental information. In the next chapter, we review consciousness, the awareness of the perceptions we experience.

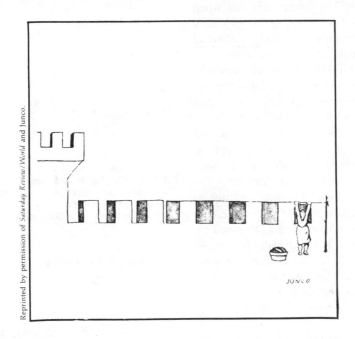

Reprinted by permission of *Saturday Review/World* and Junco.

CHAPTER REVIEW
What You've Learned About Sensation and Perception

1. Sensation is the process through which stimuli are received by sense receptors and transformed into neural impulses that can be carried through the nervous system. Perception is the process in which the sensory information is organized and interpreted in the brain. The 10 human senses include vision, hearing, smell, taste, pressure, pain, cold, warmth, kinethesis, and the vestibular sense.

2. Transduction is the process of changing the stimulus energy from the environment into neural impulses that travel through the nervous system. Sensory adaptation is the tendency of the sense organs to adjust to continuous unchanging stimulation by reducing their functioning.

3. The absolute threshold is the minimum amount of physical energy required to produce a sensation.

The difference threshold (or JND) is the minimum amount of physical energy change required to produce a difference in sensation.

4. The stimulus for vision is light waves, a type of electromagnetic wave energy. The eye includes a cornea, pupil, lens, and retina. The rods in the retina are for dim light vision, whereas color vision is made possible by the cones. People have the clearest vision at the fovea and have a blind spot where the optic nerve leaves the eye.

5. The trichromatic theory of color vision proposes that cones are most sensitive to one of three different colors: red, green, or blue. The opponent-process theory states that there are complementary colors most received by a type of cone: red-green, blue-yellow, and black-white. Both theories are par-

tially correct and help explain negative afterimages and color blindness.

6. Perceptual constancy is the tendency to perceive objects in a consistent manner, despite the changing sensations that are received by our sense organs. Four types of visual constancy include brightness constancy, color constancy, shape constancy, and size constancy.

7. We tend to organize our perceptions by following certain principles developed by the Gestalt psychologists. In the figure-ground relationship, we tend to identify a dominant figure and an ambiguous background. Closure is the organization principle of filling in the gaps to perceive a complete form. Continuity is the principle of perceiving a line as continuing. Similarity is the principle in which similar stimuli are perceived as a unit. Proximity is the principle in which stimuli next to one another are included together. Common fate is the principle that groups together stimuli that are moving together.

8. Depth perception is the ability to judge the distance to an object. We use monocular, or one-eye, cues such as interposition, size perspective, linear perspective, texture gradient, aerial perspective, and motion parallax to help determine depth. We also use binocular, or two-eye, cues in determining depth perception. Retinal disparity helps us perceive depth by noticing the disparate sensations received by each retina. Convergence operates when we interpret the kinesthetic sensations produced by the muscles of the eyeballs as we look at close objects in the environment.

9. We are fairly good about detecting real motion, or movement that is actually created by objects in motion. Sometimes we perceive movement when in fact there is none, a phenomenon called apparent motion. Induced motion occurs when we attribute movement to a figure rather than the ground. The phi phenomenon occurs when two lights are alternately turned on and off in a dark room and we see a single light jump back and forth. Stroboscopic motion occurs when a series of still pictures are shown in rapid succession, creating smooth motion. The autokinetic effect occurs when we look at a single spot of light in a dark room and see it move around.

10. An illusion is an incorrect perception that occurs when sensation is distorted. There are many illusions in everyday life. Some of the better known visual illusions include: impossible figures, reversible figures, the Müller-Lyer illusion, the Ponzo illusion, the Poggendorff illusion, and the moon illusion.

11. The stimuli that affect our sense of hearing are sound waves. Sound waves cause the eardrum to vibrate. The vibrations are carried to the cochlea, where they cause the basilar membrane to change shape. This stimulates the organ of Corti, which contains the auditory receptors that carry neural impulses to the brain.

12. The frequency theory proposes that the neuronal firing frequency determines sound. The place theory of hearing states that the sensation of sound is possible because of the particular place the sound waves hit in the ear.

13. Sound delivered to one ear is called monaural, whereas sound delivered to both ears is called binaural. Binaural sound that reaches one ear slightly before the other serves as a cue for the location of the sound.

14. The senses of smell and taste are called the chemical senses. The receptors for smell, or olfaction, are located high in the nasal passages leading from the nose to the throat. Vapors interact chemically with the nerve endings to produce nerve impulses that go to the brain. There are at least seven distinct odors. The stereochemical theory argues that odor receptors have holes that odor molecules fit into, producing the sensation of smell.

15. The taste receptors in our tongues are sensitive to four qualities: sweet, sour, salty, and bitter. It is suspected that taste qualities are coded neurally by the firing pattern of the receptor cells.

16. The somesthetic, or skin senses, include pressure, pain, cold, and warmth. Pressure, or touch, is detected by at least six types of receptors located throughout the body in the skin.

17. Pain is thought to be mediated through the free nerve end receptors. The gate-control theory of pain states that fast fibers inhibit and slow fibers facilitate a gate that allows pain to be transmitted through the spinal cord. Endorphins are brain peptides that have a morphine-like effect on the reduction of pain. Acupuncture consists of inserting needles in specific parts of the body and rotating them in order to block pain.

18. Cold receptors are responsible for the sensation of cold, whereas warm receptors are responsible for the sensation of warmth. The sensation of hot may be due to the simultaneous responding of the cold and pain receptors.

19. The sense of bodily movement, or kinesthesis, tells us what various parts of our body are doing, and we use this information to coordinate our movements. The sense of equilibrium, or the vestibular sense, helps us keep our balance, causes us to be properly oriented to gravity, and tells us when we are being moved.

SLEEP AND CONSCIOUSNESS

Consciousness has long been an area of concern for psychologists. Much of the research has been conducted on altered states of consciousness, including sleep, hypnosis, and meditation. The information learned about sleep and dreaming has practical consequences. An area of current interest is the effects of drugs on behavior.

Why do we sleep? Poets and philosophers have pondered this question for centuries, and recently psychologists and other sleep researchers have provided partial answers. In 1975 Wilse Webb reported the results of a study he conducted in which people were deprived of normal sleep. He was trying to determine the effects of sleep loss on physiological processes, mental activities, and behavior contrasted with energy loss during sleep loss. The different ways that people react to being deprived of sleep give us clues to the role sleep normally plays in everyday life.

The subjects in Webb's study were required to stay awake continuously for 51 hours from 8 A.M. the first day until 11 P.M. the third day. There were two "nights" in the experiment, and during one of these, subjects were to lie in bed but remain awake. During the other "night" the subjects remained active by using an exercise bicycle at regular intervals.

The experimenters monitored a variety of physiological measurements, including body temperature, heart rate, and brain-wave patterns. During the normal waking hours, the subjects were given a variety of tasks to complete, such as listening to a tone signal, taking tests, and playing card games.

During the first "night," everyone was able to stay awake easily. Some subjects became sleepy in the early hours of morning, but were able to fight off the urge to sleep. They all remained cheerful and appeared to enjoy the experience.

By the second "night," however, their moods began to change. They had trouble staying awake and, as soon as the experimenter left the room, they would try to doze off; the experimenter had to shake them to keep them awake. They became irritable and emotionally apathetic. They had trouble focusing attention on a task; they acted almost mechanically. Staying awake became a chore.

On the third "day," most subjects were overcome with an urge to sleep. Many fell asleep during an activity in which they had to monitor a tone signal for a brief period of time; their mood was serious and their behavior very apathetic. When they did not have a specific activity, they would fall asleep and then deny it when waked up by the experimenters.

Webb reported that there were many individual variations among the subjects, but most reacted in a similar fashion. They preferred the scheduled exercise program and had real problems during the "night" that they were required to stay awake while lying in bed.

Webb points out that while the need for sleep was very strong, he did not observe any "strange" behaviors in these subjects. They did not have long attention spans and became extremely irritable, but they were still able to function fairly normally.

In his report, Webb also described some of the typical reactions in other sleep deprivation studies. In some cases, subjects have shown delusions about the experiment, such as thinking the experimenters were plotting against them or that the experiment was a joke. Many subjects typically have shown confusion, problems in attention, irritability and apathy.

Sleep deprivation has some effect on performance, although less than what might be expected. Complex tasks that require constant attention tend to give subjects the most difficulty. On the other hand, short-term tasks are not greatly affected by sleep loss, especially if the subjects are motivated to do their best. Short-term memory tasks are sometimes adversely affected.

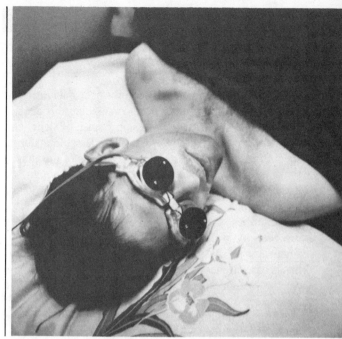

Figure 5.1.   Dream Research
This subject is participating in dream research in a sleep laboratory at Stanford University. The goggles indicate when a subject's eye movements suggest that he is dreaming and at that moment flash a red light in an effort to make him conscious of his dreams even when sleeping.

Webb also pointed out some physiological changes associated with prolonged sleep deprivation. Subjects tend to develop hand tremors, have difficulty focusing, and have an increased sensitivity to pain. Overall, autonomic nervous system activity is not greatly affected by sleep deprivation until the sleep loss is extended for more than five days. After reviewing the results of his own study as well as other studies of sleep deprivation, Webb concluded that while sleep is necessary for human survival, people are able to live without it for several days.

CHAPTER OBJECTIVES
What You'll Learn About Sleep and Consciousness

After studying this chapter, you should be able to:

1. Define consciousness.
2. Describe the two basic types of sleep (REM and NREM).
3. Outline the theories of the physiology and function of sleep.
4. Review the topics that people dream about.
5. Identify four sleep disorders.
6. Define the concept of psychoactive drugs.
7. Describe the depressant drugs.
8. Identify the opiate drugs.
9. Describe the stimulant drugs.
10. Describe the psychedelic drugs.
11. Describe the techniques and uses of hypnosis.
12. Describe the effects of meditation.
13. Describe the technique of biofeedback.

WHAT IS CONSCIOUSNESS?

Webb's study of sleep deprivation is important because it demonstrates an approach to understanding this area of psychology. We all realize the importance of sleep, and yet there are many things we don't understand about its specific functions. Sleep is considered one of the altered states of consciousness we experience. Although we know what it is like to be conscious of events, ideas, time, feelings, and the world around us, trying to define consciousness is surprisingly difficult. One definition provided by Wallace and Fisher (1987) states that consciousness is the processing of information at various levels of awareness. Most definitions stress an awareness of the sensations, thoughts, and feelings that we experience.

Although philosophers have debated the nature of consciousness for hundreds of years, the modern study of the psychology of consciousness can be traced to William James who defined consciousness as the capacity to be aware of experience and knowledge (James, 1904). In his 1890 book, James described four major characteristics of consciousness. First, every thought is part of an individual's personal consciousness. Second, consciousness is always changing. Third, consciousness is a continuous process that cannot be broken down into segments. And fourth, consciousness selects from its environment what it will be aware of. Thus, according to James, who compared consciousness to a flowing river, our "stream of consciousness" is private, changing, continuous, and selective.

As we discuss in chapter 11, "Personality," Sigmund Freud (1900) suggested that the structure of personality includes three levels of conscious awareness. The conscious mind is what we are aware of in everyday life. The preconscious mind is where we store information we have learned. And the unconscious mind is where material is kept that is not readily available to us (such as fears and unpleasant memories).

Most introductory psychology textbooks around the turn of the century defined psychology as the study of consciousness. But then in 1919, John Watson, the founder of the school of behaviorism, effectively eliminated the study of consciousness from psychology by saying he didn't know what it meant and could get along without it. It has been only with the past few decades that psychologists have begun again to study seriously the different states of consciousness (Webb, 1981).

There are currently various theories on the function of consciousness, all of which focus on awareness. Kihlstrom (1984) suggested that consciousness allows us to selectively pay attention to certain aspects of our-

Figure 5.2. Altered State of Consciousness
People may have a need for altering their state of consciousness through deliberately exciting activities such as hang gliding, marathon running, or amusement park rides.

selves and our environment so we can effectively think and carry out our actions. Marcel (1983) stated that consciousness allows us to pull specific ideas and events into our awareness so that we can analyze them and make decisions about our behavior. Ornstein (1986) argued that because of consciousness we have the ability to think, remember and reason. Consciousness is one of the important contributions to our survival as the human race.

Psychologists tend to divide the study of consciousness into two types, waking consciousness and altered state of consciousness. The awareness of sensations and thoughts while we are awake and alert is often called waking consciousness (or conscious awareness). Much of psychology studies such aspects of behavior and cognition of the individual in waking consciousness as memory, language, thinking, problem solving, and perception.

This chapter focuses on the altered state of consciousness (ASC). In an altered state of consciousness, there is a redirection of attention, in which different aspects of the world occupy our thoughts, and different stimuli cause us to respond.

Charles Tart (1969) stated that an altered state of consciousness occurs when there is a qualitative shift (differentness) in the mental processes rather than just a quantitative shift (alertness). For example, during sleep, except for intense stimuli (the buzz of an alarm), we lose the ability to attend to much of what is going on around us.

Many of our altered states of consciousness are completely normal and occur effortlessly, such as day-dreaming, sleep, and dreaming. Andrew Weil (1973) argued that people have an inborn urge to actively alter their states of consciousness occasionally. He pointed out that children around the world spin themselves to become dizzy. And of course many of us love those thrilling wild rides at amusement parks.

Other altered states of consciousness are obtained by more deliberate efforts. Hypnosis, meditation, and drug-induced states are more voluntary altered states of consciousness that are fairly common experiences around the world. Some researchers refer to them as extended states of consciousness. We review the topics of sleep, drugs, hypnosis, meditation, and biofeedback in this chapter.

SLEEP

At about the same time every night, you look at the clock, yawn, and prepare to go to sleep. You lie in bed with the lights off and your eyes closed, waiting for that drowsy feeling to take hold and carry you off into the state in which you will spend the next eight or so hours.

You spend approximately a third of your life sleeping. For many people, that means about 25 years. Since you sleep more or less regularly every day, you simply take sleeping for granted. Scientists are just now learning some of the many mysteries of sleep and dreaming.

In our opening story, we mentioned some of the tests used to measure sleep. If we look at sleep deprivation, we may be able to get some clues as to the functions of sleep in daily life. Let's begin with some of the measurement techniques used in sleep research.

Research on sleep often is conducted in university sleep laboratories, where variables can be monitored carefully and controlled. The subject lies in a comfortable bed while the experimenter prepares to record electrophysiological measures. Electrodes (recording devices) to measure brain waves are taped to the scalp. The record of brain-wave activity is called an electroencephalogram (EEG). Electrodes are connected also to the face and body to measure variables such as heart rate (EKG), blood pressure, temperature, eye movement (EOG), skeletal muscle activity (EMG), and respiration (Hassett, 1978). Then the subject is told to relax and go to sleep. (This, of course, may take a little practice.)

During the waking state, the EEG shows two basic brain-wave patterns: alpha activity and beta activity. Alpha activity has a frequency of 8-12 Hz and is produced when a person is relaxed and resting quietly with eyes closed. Beta activity has a frequency of 13-30 Hz, and is produced when a person is alert. Resting will produce an alpha EEG, while reading this textbook should produce a beta EEG.

The Two Types of Sleep

The two types of sleep were first labeled in 1953. This was the year that Eugene Aserinsky and Nathaniel Kleitman of the University of Chicago reported that periodically during sleep the eyes moved very rapidly back and forth under the eyelids. This activity, called REM (rapid eye movement), indicated a type of sleep that was very active compared to the other more passive stages of sleep, called NREM (non REM) sleep. Up to this time, most researchers had considered sleep a totally passive phenomenon.

Stages of NREM Sleep. The EEGs of the brain show that there are four distinct stages of NREM sleep. Sometimes these stages are collectively referred to as slow-wave or classical sleep, since this is the classical idea of what sleep is like. When we go to bed each night, we pass through each of the four stages of NREM sleep before going into REM sleep. We then pass through several cycles of these sleep stages before waking in the morning. The NREM stages of sleep are called Stages 1, 2, 3, and 4.

Stage 1 is the transition from relaxation to sound sleep. The EEG is characterized by theta activity having a frequency of 4-6 Hz. The sleeper is drowsy and may have visual images that are more like hallucinations than daydreams. He or she can be easily awakened, and can be influenced by outside stimuli such as a ringing telephone. The EEG of Stage 2 also contains theta activity and is characterized by *sleep spindles*, which are brief bursts of 12-14 Hz waves. Stage 2 also contains *K-complexes* that are sharp rises and drops in the EEG. We spend about 50% of our sleep in Stage 2. Stage 3 is a transition stage from Stage 2 to Stage 4 in which we spend about 10% of our sleep. The EEG of Stage 3 may still contain sleep spindles, but also begins to show delta activity, which has a frequency of 1-3 Hz. The EEG of Stage 4, often called deep sleep, consists of over 50% delta activity. We spend approximately 15% of our sleep in Stage 4. It is extremely difficult to wake someone from Stage 4, and when we do, the person tends to be groggy and does not function fully. As we discuss later, sleep talking, sleepwalking, night terrors, and bedwetting all occur mostly in Stage 4 sleep.

Certain characteristics are common in NREM sleep. The eyes may move slowly from side to side. The heart

Figure 5.3. EEG Sleep Patterns

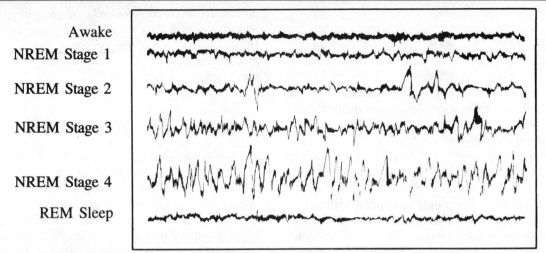

Awake
NREM Stage 1
NREM Stage 2
NREM Stage 3
NREM Stage 4
REM Sleep

Each stage of sleep can be identified by its distinctive EEG pattern. The *alpha* waves of the awake, relaxed state are quite different from the large rhythmic *delta* waves of stage 4. The REM patterns of sleep more nearly resemble the awake patterns, thus REM sleep may be known as paradoxical sleep.

rate slows down and blood pressure falls slightly. Breathing is slow and regular (this is when snoring occurs). In general, muscular tension is absent and the sleeper is immobile. Watching the sleeper in NREM sleep, we would conclude that he or she is resting peacefully.

REM Sleep. Rapid-eye-movement sleep is often called dream sleep, active sleep, or paradoxical sleep, because dreaming occurs here and the characteristics of REM sleep are similar to those in the waking state. The eyes move quickly back and forth. The heart rate accelerates, blood pressure rises, breathing becomes variable, and sexual arousal occurs in both sexes (Kiester, 1980). There is peripheral twitching of the face and fingers, but the large muscles of the body are completely paralyzed by the nervous system, so that no overall body movement can take place. In general, the EEG activity is similar to the alert waking state but contains the characteristic "saw-tooth" waves of the EEG sleep patterns. Reviewing these characteristics, we conclude that REM sleep is indeed an active state of sleeping.

REM sleep is regarded as dream sleep, since most dreaming occurs in this stage. Dement compiled the results of a number of studies in 1976 and reported that when subjects were awakened from REM sleep, they could recall dreams up to 83% of the time. However, when subjects were awakened from NREM sleep, they reported dreaming only about 14% of the time. Dreams in the REM stage are often vividly recalled, while the few occurring in the NREM stages are often vague and ambiguous.

Time Patterns of Sleep. When we fall asleep, we progress through the various NREM stages to deeper and deeper sleep (Dement, 1976). Stage 1 lasts for a few

Figure 5.4. Sequence of Sleep Stages

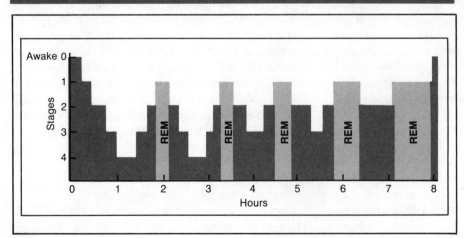

This figure shows the sequence of sleep stages for a typical night. Note that early in the night, more time is spent in stage 4, whereas later in the night more time is spent in REM sleep. We wake naturally from this stage of sleep (after Dement, 1976).

minutes, followed by several minutes of Stage 2. We are in Stage 3 for about 10 minutes before we enter Stage 4. Forty minutes or so after sleep begins, we go through the stages of NREM sleep in reverse order (Stages 4, 3, and 2).

Approximately an hour-and-a-half after first falling to sleep, we go from Stage 2 to Stage REM (or Stage 1-REM, which now takes the place of Stage 1). The first REM period might last about 10 minutes. This cycle is repeated throughout the night. During the first part of the night, we spend more time in NREM sleep, especially in Stages 3 and 4, but during the last part of the night, we spend much more time in REM sleep, with brief alternations with Stage 2. At the end of the sleep period, we might spend 60 minutes in a final REM sleep period. We usually wake from REM sleep (unless the alarm wakes us first).

Although there are wide variations, sleep researchers have found that most people show a common pattern of sleeping over their lifetimes (Roffwarg, Muzio, & Dement, 1966). The neonate sleeps up to 16 hours a day, usually in relatively short sessions distributed across the 24 hours. In the first year, nighttime sleep with several day naps becomes the norm. Between the ages of 2 and 5, children sleep about 11 hours per day, including an hour of daytime napping. Between 6 and 16 years old, the total sleep time goes from an average of 11 to about 8 hours per night and remains at about 8 hours during most of adulthood.

As people age, they tend to have more difficulty sleeping. Webb (1975) reported that in a group of 60-year-olds the number of awakenings during the night increased significantly over a group of 30-year-olds. The older group took longer to fall to sleep, woke spontaneously more often at night, and had less overall "quality" sleep. The majority of the older people also took naps during the day. The women tended to be more resistant to age changes than the men.

In general, adults have about five REM periods each night and spend up to 2 hours in REM sleep. This represents about 25% of their total sleep time. Newborn infants spend approximately 50% of their sleep time in REM. This drops to about 30% by age 2, and levels out at about 25% by about age 10. The level of REM sleep remains fairly constant until old age, when it declines very slightly.

Stage 4 constitutes about 18% of a 10-year-old's sleep, and this remains constant until the early thirties, when it begins to decline. Individuals over the age of 50 may have very little Stage 4 sleep (Kelly, 1981). This helps to explain the increase in spontaneous wakings in older individuals who often become light sleepers. Stage 2 sleep remains fairly constant across the lifespan.

Theories of Sleep

Acquiring knowledge of how the brain controls sleep and developing theories about the functions of sleep has been a very slow process. Partially this is because it is difficult to study the brain while it is functioning. The mechanisms involved are much more complicated than early researchers believed. Although we now have an idea of sleep's functions and of how the brain influences some aspects of sleep, there are many gaps that need to be filled in by future sleep researchers.

WILLIAM C. DEMENT

William C. Dement was born in 1928 in Wenatchee, Washington. He decided on a career in medicine and, as a second year medical student, was working in Nathaniel Kleitman's sleep research laboratory at the University of Chicago in 1953, when rapid eye movements were discovered. Dement first used the term REM, which is now standard nomenclature in sleep research.

William Dement earned his M.D. degree from the University of Chicago in 1955, and his Ph.D. degree in physiology in 1957. In 1963 he established the sleep laboratory at Stanford University, and in 1970 he established the Stanford University Sleep Disorders Clinic. Dement started the publication *Sleep Reviews*, and has written hundreds of scientific papers on sleep and dreaming.

Currently, Dement is professor of psychiatry at the Stanford University Medical School. As director of the sleep laboratory, he is busy researching the problems that plague millions of people when they sleep. He has contributed significantly to our knowledge of the altered state of consciousness in which we spend a third of our lives.

Figure 5.5. Changes in REM/NREM Sleep Needs Through the Life Cycle

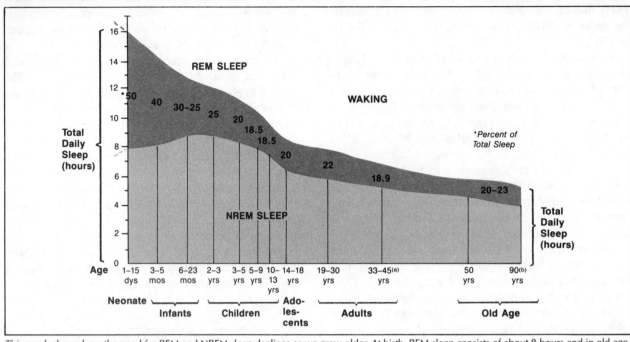

This graph shows how the need for REM and NREM sleep declines as we grow older. At birth, REM sleep consists of about 8 hours and in old age declines to about 1 hour. NREM sleep needs decline less radically from about 8 hours at birth to about 5 hours in old age. This chart also graphically portrays the percentage of REM sleep to total sleep time in 24 hours (after Kimble, 1988).

Physiology. Michel Jouvet has been a leading researcher in the field of neural sleep control. In 1967 Jouvet reported that NREM sleep seemed to be influenced by an area in the brain stem known as the raphe nucleus. Electrical stimulation of this area usually causes sleep, while lesions tend to eliminate sleep. Jouvet proposed that the raphe nucleus influences NREM sleep by producing the neurotransmitter serotonin (see chapter 2, "Biology of Behavior"), which inhibits the activity of the reticular activating system and in waking periods normally causes alertness. While other brain systems are also involved in neural sleep control, Jouvet's theory appears useful in directing future sleep research.

The research on the brain areas influencing REM sleep is much less clear. Jouvet found that the pons area of the brain stem called the locus coeruleus is involved in REM sleep. This area inhibits muscle tone during REM sleep, as shown by Jones, Harper, and Halaris (1977), essentially paralyzing you and preventing you from acting out your dreams. Hobson and his colleagues (1974) proposed that the pontine reticular formation's gigantocellular tegmental field and the locus coeruleus connect with the higher brain structures to produce cortical arousal during REM sleep. The pons and the neurotransmitters norepinephrine and acetylcholine also appear to be involved in REM sleep. Currently there is a great deal of research being conducted in this area, and it is too early to conclude anything specific yet.

Functions of Sleep. What are the functions of sleep? One way to learn about these functions is to deprive a subject of sleep and then note changes that occur. Webb's 1975 study discussed in the opening story totally deprived subjects of sleep for several days. He concluded that his subjects wanted to sleep and had some trouble paying attention to required tasks, but otherwise didn't show any bizarre or unusual behaviors. Because the EEG record indicates precisely which stage of sleep a subject is in, it is possible to deprive a subject selectively of one type of sleep at a time. A few studies have done this.

An early report by William Dement (1960) suggested that lack of REM sleep results in personality changes, increased anxiety, and irritability. Later studies failed to find any decrease in psychological functioning when subjects were deprived of REM sleep for long periods of time. In later research, Dement did, however, find a need for REM sleep, and after REM deprivation, a subject often shows a rebound effect, spending much more time than usual in REM sleep.

Some studies suggest that REM sleep is involved in learning and memory. For instance, Greiser, Greenberg, and Harrison (1972) reported that REM sleep deprivation produced deficits in recall of emotionally related words. And a study by Lucero (1970) found that REM sleep increased immediately after rats learned a new maze.

Hartmann (1973) proposed that REM sleep is important in memory consolidation, especially when stress is involved. He compared people who slept 6 hours or less a night with people who slept 9 hours or more. In general, the "short sleepers" were happier and more energetic, while the "long sleepers" were more thoughtful and anxious. Hartmann found that both groups spent about the same time in NREM sleep, but the people who slept 9 hours or more spent much more time in REM sleep. Apparently, we need more REM sleep when we are stressed or have a need for more fantasy in our lives.

A recent theory of REM sleep by Francis Crick, the codiscoverer of the structure of DNA, runs in the opposite direction. Crick and Mitchison (1983) proposed that the function of REM sleep is to clear the brain of memories which might interfere with normal thought and memory. This is why we don't remember many of our dreams. Currently, we cannot draw any definite conclusions from these hypotheses except to say that it does appear that REM sleep is important enough to require us to dream every night.

Most studies of NREM sleep deprivation focus on Stage 4 sleep, since it is the farthest from REM, and shows a distinctive EEG pattern. People deprived of Stage 4 sleep also tend to show a rebound effect by doing more of it when allowed to sleep normally, as shown in a study by Agnew, Webb, and Williams in 1964.

Some research suggests that Stage 4 sleep is important in the physical restoration of the body. Moldofsky and Scarisbrick (1976) that subjects deprived of Stage 4 sleep complained of muscle and joint pain. Shapiro and his colleagues (1981) reported that after strenuous physical activity such as running a marathon, NREM sleep increases while REM sleep decreases for several nights. There is some evidence that our sleep habits may be genetically determined (Webb & Campbell, 1983). Other evidence concerned with tissue growth and repair comes from a study by Sassin and colleagues (1969) that indicated that human growth hormones were released during Stages 3 and 4. Hartmann (1973) proposed that NREM sleep restores the body when it is physically injured or fatigued. The evidence is not overwhelming, but it does appear that NREM sleep could be involved in the normal physical restoration of the body. Perhaps, as Webb (1974) suggested, we sleep because it conserves energy and it is safer not to do much in the dark anyway!

Dreams

People have always been fascinated by dreams. Poets and philosophers have interpreted them either as romantic fantasies or as manifestations of the darker side of human nature. Many researchers have taken a more practical attitude toward dreams and have studied them in and out of the laboratory in order to more scientifically understand their place in human lives.

Freud's Theory of Dreams. One popular early theory of dreams was proposed by Sigmund Freud (1900), who believed that dreams were the road to the unconscious mind. He thought that conflicts that disturb us or events that we can't deal with during the day make their way into our dreams. Freud distinguished between the manifest dream content (what we remember about the dream) and the latent dream content (the actual thoughts and emotions in the unconscious dream).

In order to analyze a dream, we need to focus on each of the individual elements or symbols and ignore any connections between the parts of the manifest dream. The manifest dream is really a disguised representation of our unconscious wishes (which, according to Freud, are often unacceptable in society).

Freud believed a number of processes were involved in determining a dream's content. In displacement, the emotional feelings are displaced from one object to another one. For example, your hatred for one person might be expressed as hatred for someone else in a dream. In symbolization, the latent content of a dream is converted into manifest symbols. Freud believed that dreams disguised the images they presented and so it was necessary to interpret them. A great deal of Freud's interpretation focused on sexual symbolism. For example, he suggested that the male genitals are represented in dreams by symbols such as sticks, posts, trees, daggers, spears, revolvers, pencils, or hammers; the female genitals by pits, cavities, vessels, bottles, boxes, and pockets. The basic problem with this approach is that a symbol might not have the same meaning for every dreamer. For instance, other researchers find significantly fewer sexual dreams than Freud did.

Dream Content. Another approach to studying dream content is represented by Palumbo (1978) who suggested that dreams are a way to process the events of the day. Calvin Hall (1966) also believed that dreams are simply visual representations of daily experiences. Hall studied the dream content of thousands of subjects and found that, while individual differences occur, there are some general trends. Women tend to dream of familiar people, places, and events, while men tend to dream more of unfamiliar situations. One gender difference that occurs in a variety of cultures is that females tend to dream about males and females equally often but males dream more often (65%) about males (Hall, 1984). Hall contends that any analysis of a person's dreams must be highly individualized and cannot be generalized.

College students were surveyed for their most common dreams by Griffith and his colleagues (1958). Their study found 83% of the students reported dreams about falling and 77% reported dreams in which they were being attacked. A large percentage of dreams involved

Figure 5.6. Common Dreams

DREAM	Percentage of Students		
	Total	Male	Female
Falling	83	80	85
Being attacked or pursued	77	77	78
Trying repeatedly to do something	71	68	75
School, teachers, studying	71	60	84
Falling, with fear	68	62	73
Sexual experiences	66	93	36
Arriving too late	64	60	67
Eating delicious food	62	57	67
Being frozen with fright	58	53	64
A loved person is dead	57	49	67
Being locked up	56	55	58
Finding money	56	61	50
Swimming	52	47	58
Snakes	49	43	55
Being on verge of falling	47	52	41
Being inappropriately dressed	46	39	54
Dead people as though alive	46	40	53
Being smothered	44	42	47
Being nude	43	48	37
Fire	41	33	50
Failing an examination	39	34	44
Flying through air	34	32	35
Seeing self as dead	33	33	34
Being tied up	30	28	34
Killing someone	26	38	11

Here are the most common dreams of U.S. college students as reported in 1958 by Griffith, Miyago, and Tago.

school, sexual behavior, eating, being frightened, or having a loved one die. Fire was included in 41% of the reports, while failing an exam was in 39%. Other significant topics included finding money, swimming, snakes, being nude, and death. Many of these topics are probably items of concern to the student, while some of them seem unusual.

In a 1988 study, I asked over 300 college students what they dreamed about. Although many of the topics were similar to Griffith's 1958 findings (see Figure 5.6), there were some interesting differences. Falling (males 65%, females 86%) and being attacked (males 68%, females 89%), were frequently mentioned, but so were romantic situations (males 65%, females 86%), and being with family and friends (males 53%, females 81%). Sexual experiences were popular, but the older study's gender difference disappeared (in 1958—males 93%, females 36%; in 1988—males 76%, females 72%). I also found that students in 1988 appear to dream less about school, teachers, and studying (males 41%, females 70%) than in 1958.

Activation Synthesis Theory. Recently, the activation synthesis theory of dreaming was proposed by McCarley (McCarley & Hoffman, 1981). Essentially, this view states that during REM sleep, the brain activates itself and then synthesizes the information generated into dreams. Hobson and McCarley (1977) suggested that many dreams are the interpretation of brain activity. For example, they suggest that falling is the interpretation of vestibular activity; fear or being unable to escape is the interpretation of the muscular paralysis, and sexual activity is the interpretation of sex organ stimulation that occurs during REM sleep. Although the activation synthesis theory of dreaming is interesting, it has not yet been proved. Chase and Morales (1983) supported this idea and suggested that the rapid eye movements that occur during dreaming are just the result of central nervous system activity.

Estimates of time that lapses during a dream indicate that dream time is about the same as real time. In one experiment, Dement used an external stimulus, a spray of water, as a marker during REM sleep. When the dreamers were awakened, they usually incorporated the external stimulus into the appropriate time sequence in the dream. They interpreted the water as rain or a shower, depending on the content of the rest of the dream. While dreams remain a very private affair, psychologists are beginning to understand some of the complexities involved in the process.

Sleep Disorders

Sleep disorders include the dyssomnias and the parasomnias (DSM-III-R, 1987). In the dyssomnias, such as insomnia and hypersomnia, the chief symptom is a disturbance in the amount and quality of sleep one obtains. In the parasomnias, such as sleep terrors, bedwetting, and sleepwalking, the chief symptom is an unusual event that disturbs sleep.

Insomnia. The high demand for sleeping pills is a symptom of the widespread occurrence of insomnia, the inability to sleep. In a recent survey, 6% of men and 14% of women reported that they suffered from this type of sleep disorder. There are many causes for, and types of, insomnia (Kripke & Gillin, 1985). Some insomniacs fall asleep easily, but dream that they are awake. Hence, when they wake up, these people feel as if they were still trying to get to sleep. Others have trouble falling to sleep because of anxiety, fear, stress, depression, or other problems. Drugs, too, can disrupt the normal sleep cycle.

Some insomniacs suffer from a condition known as sleep apnea. They fall asleep easily, but then stop breathing and wake up gasping for air. People with sleep apnea might wake up several hundred times a night (Hall, 1986). Raymond (1986) reported that about 10% of men over the age of 40 have some form of sleep

**Figure 5.7. "The Nightmare"
by Henry Fuseli**
Freud's theory of dreams proposed that conflicts we can't deal with during the day find their way into our dreams. He distinguishes between the manifest and latent content of dreams and proposed several processes for interpreting them.

apnea. Obstruction of the air passage by the relaxation of the throat muscles or a malfunction in the brain might result in apnea but its cause is not completely known. It is possible that sudden infant death syndrome (SIDS), or crib death, may be caused by sleep apnea. Hales (1986) suggested that the newborn infant may not yet have the neural structure required to wake it up when breathing stops, and hence it suffocates.

Narcolepsy. A form of hypersomnia, narcolepsy is a sleep disorder characterized by inappropriate daytime attacks of sleep. The narcoleptic person unpredictably falls asleep during the day. EEG records show that the narcoleptic goes directly into REM sleep, and since this stage is associated with muscle paralysis, it can be very dangerous for the individual. Sometimes the attack is brought about by an intense emotion, such as laughing, surprise, or sexual arousal. One symptom of narcolepsy is the occurrence of hypnagogic hallucinations (Dement, 1976). These are very vivid dreams that occur as the narcoleptic enters a sleep attack. Often the dream is a continuation of prior waking events, creating the illusion of reality and resulting in a frightening experience.

The episode lasts for less than 15 minutes, and the person then gradually wakes up and continues with daily activities. We don't know what causes narcolepsy, but researchers suspect that it has to do with inadequate amounts of the neurotransmitter dopamine or abnormal REM functioning in the daytime (Erlich & Itabashi, 1986). Sometimes the disorder can be treated with stimulant drugs, such as amphetamines.

NREM Sleep Disorders. There are several parasomnias (sleep disorders) that occur in Stages 3 and 4 of NREM sleep, including sleep talking, sleepwalking (somnambulism), bed-wetting (enuresis), and sleep terrors (pavor nocturnus). They are, for the most part, not dangerous, and are often found in children. In many cases, the child eventually grows out of the behavior.

Sleepwalking (somnambulism) reaches a peak in children about 12 years old. It tends to run in families, suggesting a genetic base. An accepted treatment for sleepwalking is to make sure that the sleepwalker does not hurt himself. Bed-wetting (enuresis) can have a physiological cause, but often appears to have a psychological basis. There are several behavior therapies used to treat it, such as training the child to recognize the feeling of a full bladder by having him or her wait as long as possible before urinating. Waiting until the child outgrows the problem is also a common treatment. Sleep terror disorder (pavor nocturnus) occurs when children wake up screaming and terrified, but cannot recall why. It usually begins at around 4 years of age. Webb suggests that it is possible that the terror results from a rapid shift from Stage 4 sleep into waking. Again, the best treatment seems to let it run its course.

The NREM sleep disorders have the common characteristic that the sleeper often does not remember them the next morning. This fits with the concept that NREM sleep is not a mentally active state of consciousness. Other altered states of consciousness are experienced less frequently than sleep.

Biological Rhythms

People function on a variety of time cycles. We have seasons of the year, days of the week, and hours of the day. Scientists are interested in the degree to which we are influenced by our external environment versus internal biological rhythms.

An interesting biological rhythm is the circadian cycle (from the Latin words, "about a day"). Our body appears to be genetically programmed to function on roughly a 24-hour cycle. An early test of this concept was carried out by sleep researchers Nathaniel Kleitman and B. Richardson, who in 1938, stayed in the Mammoth Cave for 32 days. With no light/dark alterations, these scientists maintained an average "day" of 28 hours. They found that their functioning was best when the active parts of the day corresponded to the natural rhythm.

Most people have peak performance at a particular time of the day, with several smaller peaks distributed at other times. Some people function best in the morning, while others have their peak in the afternoon or evening. While there are large variations among individuals, a given person's cycle stays about the same from day to day.

If our normal rhythm is disrupted, we tend to become anxious. For example, many people have difficulty adjusting to swing-shift work schedules. And pilots and air travelers who cross time zones often report a time lag, during which they suffer physical complaints until they get readjusted (jet lag).

Other cycles also influence our behavior. Women's menstrual cycles can affect mood. And all of us probably have other cycles that are not understood completely. Understanding the biological rhythms of an individual may help psychologists understand human behavior more completely.

THOUGHT QUESTIONS

1. How could you identify your biological rhythms?
2. How could knowledge of your biological rhythms help you in everyday behaviors?
3. Should we try to behave according to our rhythms or change our rhythms in accordance to our behaviors?

PSYCHOACTIVE DRUGS

A drug is any foreign chemical substance that alters the functioning of a biological system. Many substances can serve as drugs, including pain relievers, alcohol, nicotine, caffeine, antibiotics, clinical drugs, and illegal psychoactive drugs. A psychoactive drug causes changes in behavior and cognition by modifying conscious awareness. Psychopharmacology is the science of the effects of psychoactive drugs on behavior and cognition. Some psychoactive drugs, such as alcohol, nicotine, and opium, have been consumed for centuries. Others, like tranquilizers, are the products of recent medical research. Still others, like LSD and PCP, have appeared in the illegal marketplace within the past several decades. As indicated earlier, people have always been interested in producing altered states of consciousness through drugs.

With repeated use, a person can become psychologically and physiologically dependent upon a drug. A person has developed psychological dependence when he or she craves the drug even though it is not biologically needed by the body; it often involves learning that the effect of the drug is pleasurable or effective in

Figure 5.8. Drug Addiction
Drug addiction is characterized by psychological and/or physiological dependence. It is a major problem today. It affects all areas of a person's life.

helping to cope with problems. Some drugs cause physical dependence, or addiction, a condition in which the habitual user's body becomes biochemically dependent upon the drugs.

Physical dependence is characterized by tolerance and withdrawal. The habitual use of some drugs leads to tolerance, in which larger and larger doses of the drug are required to produce the same effect. If the dependent person stops taking the drug, he or she will experience withdrawal symptoms, which are very unpleasant physical reactions. For example, with heroin the withdrawal symptoms include vomiting, diarrhea, loss of appetite, anxiety, and sweating; with alcohol they can include nausea, insomnia, and sometimes hallucinations and seizures. In this section we will review the major types of psychoactive drugs. These are usually divided into five categories based on how they influence behavior (Julien, 1985) and include depressants, opiates, stimulants, psychedelics, and the antipsychotic drugs. Psychologists are interested in the kinds of experiences produced by various drugs, the kinds of behavior associated with drug taking, and the nature of dependence on drugs. They are also interested in types of therapy for abusers of drugs, as well as the use of drugs in the treatment of mental disorders. We discuss the therapeutic use of drugs in chapter 14, "Therapy."

Figure 5.9. Alcohol Abuse
Alcohol is a widely used intoxicant that is quickly absorbed into the bloodstream. It affects physical coordination and perception, and can cause fatal automobile accidents when people drink, then drive.

Depressants

Depressants (or sedative-hypnotics) are central nervous system-acting drugs that have a sedative, or sleep-inducing effect. The general group includes alcohol, anesthetics (such as ether), barbiturates, antianxiety drugs, and tranquilizers (such as Librium and Valium). In small amounts, depressants produce tranquilizing effects. In high doses, they can induce sleep and, in even higher doses, coma and death.

It is important to note that the effects of depressants are additive. Thus, if you are taking barbiturates, and also take alcohol, you will become extremely sleepy. All of the depressants produce feelings of excitement when given in very small doses, because they affect inhibitory, before excitatory, synapses in the brain. Depressants operate on the arousal-sleep circuits in the brain (Julien, 1985).

Alcohol. Alcohol is the most frequently used depressant drug available today. In cultures throughout the world, ethyl alcohol is widely accepted as a legal intoxicant. While it varies widely in concentration, from less than 6% in beer to about 50% in hard liquor, what is important is the absolute amount in the bloodstream. Alcohol is quickly absorbed into the bloodstream from the stomach and intestines. It is then metabolized in the liver, where it is converted to carbon dioxide and water (Julien, 1985).

Alcohol appears to affect individuals in different ways, depending upon personality and expectation. In a 1979 experiment using dogs, I found that alcohol increased or decreased aggression, depending on the dominance status of the subject. Although people often assume otherwise, Briddell and Wilson (1976) showed that alcohol depresses human sexual responsiveness. Alcohol in large doses disrupts REM sleep, motor coordination, thinking, and perception, and therefore has a disastrous effect on automobile driving. There are over 10 million alcoholics in the United States, with psychological and social problems ranging from depression and loss of family life to physiological problems such as liver disease and memory loss.

One current concern is fetal alcohol syndrome (FAS), in which infants born to women alcoholics have congenital malformations. FAS babies often have brain defects, problems in speaking, retardation, and are underweight and premature at birth (Coles & colleagues, 1987). Much research is needed in the area of fetal alcohol syndrome.

Barbiturates. The barbiturates are drugs that can be used for mild sedation (Amobarbital), anesthesia (Methohexital), and as a treatment for insomnia (Nembutal or Seconal), or anxiety (Phenobarbital). They relax the muscles, produce a state of euphoria, and with increasing doses, sleep. Research indicates that barbiturates interfere with the arousal neurotransmitter norepinephrine (Kolb & Whishaw, 1985). They are highly addictive, with both physical dependence and tolerance developing in the user. Overdoses of barbiturates can end in coma or death.

Antianxiety Tranquilizers. The first benzodiazepine, chloridiazepoxide (Librium) was marketed in 1960. Librium and Valium (diazepan) are among the most widely prescribed drugs in this country as antianxiety minor tranquilizers, useful for treating anxiety, psychological pressure, and sometimes insomnia. Excessive use of these depressant drugs can produce symptoms such as disorientation and aggression. The additive effects of benzodiazepines and alcohol are severe disruptions of visual and motor coordination needed for driving (Julien, 1985).

Opiates

Opiates or narcotic analgesics refer to drugs whose effect on the body is similar to morphine, the *analgesic* (pain-relieving) ingredient derived from the opium poppy plant. Opiates include naturally occurring drugs such as codeine, morphine, and heroin, and synthetic drugs such as methadone, Darvon, and Demerol. Methadone has been used to treat dependence on morphine. The medical uses of narcotics include relief of pain, treatment of diarrhea, and suppression of coughing.

Opiates affect the central nervous system, eye, and gastrointestinal tract. Julien (1985) reviewed evidence that suggests that narcotics are able to relieve pain by depressing the pain receptors in the brain and spinal cord. It appears that opiates act similarly to the natural pain-relief substances, the endorphins (see chapter 3, "Sensation and Perception").

Heroin and other illegally used opiates can produce a sense of pleasant euphoria and well-being and can significantly decrease sexual interest (Abel, 1984). The user quickly develops a tolerance and addiction, however, and must take increasingly larger amounts to achieve the same feeling. Heroin addiction is often associated with criminal behavior because the addict needs large amounts of money to continue to buy enough of the drug to support the habit.

Stimulants

Stimulants are drugs that increase central nervous system activity and behavior speed, and produce feelings of alertness or even euphoria. They can help us stay awake when necessary, but often a cycle of arousal-depression develops, producing overall negative effects. Stimulants include common drugs such as caffeine and nicotine, and stronger drugs such as amphetamine and cocaine. The clinical antidepressants we discuss in chapter 14, "Therapy," are also classified as stimulants.

Caffeine.   Caffeine is probably the most widely used stimulant in our society. Whether you drink a cup of coffee in the morning to get going, drink tea or Coke at lunchtime, or eat a chocolate bar in the afternoon, you are getting a dose of caffeine. Julien reports that, in general, caffeine increases glucose production in the cells, which provides more energy and speeds up bodily

Figure 5.10.   Common Stimulant Drugs
Coffee and cigarettes contain stimulants that affect behavior. Caffeine and nicotine are both central nervous system stimulants.

activities. It affects the cerebral cortex of the brain, producing mental alertness. With frequent doses, the user may experience insomnia, agitation, anxiety, and rapid breathing.

It appears that caffeine is physically addictive, and many people develop psychological dependence on it (thus needing their "morning coffee" to wake up). Withdrawal symptoms (headaches, irritability, and nausea) are produced if the user stops taking caffeine. There is currently concern about the effect of caffeine on a pregnancy, although definitive answers have not yet been procured. All the major cola companies are now marketing no-caffeine colas to attract people who are concerned with their intake of caffeine.

Nicotine.   Nicotine is a stimulant contained in the tobacco of cigarettes. It is absorbed by the lungs and distributed by the bloodstream. In general, nicotine has many of the same effects as caffeine. Nicotine appears to stimulate neurons which are sensitive to acetylcholine.

One side effect of nicotine is that it reduces muscle tension, which might be why people claim it relaxes them. Nicotine induces psychological and physical dependence. Withdrawal symptoms include headaches, nausea, irritability, and insomnia. It is now known that nicotine affects the fetus during pregnancy resulting in increased probability of miscarriages and premature babies. Despite health hazards and the Surgeon General's warning on all cigarette packages that smoking is dangerous to people's health, many people still continue to smoke. However, due in part to the program established by Surgeon General Koop, there is an increasing awareness of the dangers of smoking, as evidenced in "no smoking" areas in public areas.

Amphetamine. Amphetamine is a much stronger stimulant than caffeine or nicotine, producing arousal of the central nervous system and increasing internal bodily processes such as heart rate and breathing. Large doses can lead to restlessness, insomnia, shaking, and sometimes *amphetamine psychosis,* which is characterized by marked changes in personality. Structurally, amphetamine is similar to the neurotransmitter norepinephrine, and some psychologists believe research with amphetamine abuse may lead to insights into causes of abnormal behaviors. Amphetamine's trade name is *Benzedrine*, and its close derivatives are *Dexedrine* and *Methedrine*.

During the past several decades, amphetamines and other stimulants, such as Ritalin and Cylert, have been used to treat *attention deficit disorder* (hyperactivity) in children. These children are hyperactive in the classroom and cannot focus their attention on the curriculum. When given stimulants, their attention and concentration improve. This effect was once thought paradoxical, but research on hyperactivity and attention has demonstrated that stimulants make sense. The actual reason is not known, but some researchers believe that it is possible that hyperactive children have brains that are developing at a slower-than-average rate, and the stimulant speeds up the brain functioning so the children can concentrate. Amphetamines are sometimes used to treat the sleep disorder narcolepsy. Amphetamines also suppress appetite, but because people quickly develop a tolerance, they are not effective as diet pills. Although there are some valid medical uses of amphetamines, they are also widely used illegally.

Cocaine. Cocaine is a powerful stimulant derived from the leaves of the South American coca plant. Cocaine was identified as the active ingredient in coca leaves in 1844. In the late nineteenth century, it was often used in medicine, and many claimed it had great beneficial effects, including Sigmund Freud who used it to relieve depression. Although recent Coca-Cola commercials advertise their product as "the real thing," Coca-Cola has not contained cocaine since 1906, when the medical world decided that it wasn't as beneficial as first believed.

The most popular way of taking cocaine, or "coke," is to snort it by inhaling it through a straw into the nose. It can also be ingested, injected, or smoked. A recently introduced potent form, called crack, comes in pellets and is smoked in a pipe. Crack is made by mixing baking soda and water with the crystalline form of cocaine and heating it. Crack cocaine has become extremely popular in recent years because it is relatively inexpensive and produces its effects quickly.

Cocaine produces stimulant effects similar to amphetamines. It increases heart rate and breathing, causes dilation of the pupils of the eyes and constricts blood vessels. Cocaine is an effective local anesthetic, numbing nerve endings with which it comes into contact. Psychologically, cocaine causes an increased state of alertness, a feeling of energy, and a general sense of euphoria. Side effects include sweating, anxiety, irritability, and occasional hallucinations. Unlike amphetamines cocaine effects last a short time, often only minutes; then withdrawal symptoms occur, including a desire for more of the drug, and depression. Like amphetamines, cocaine produces its effects by increasing the utilization of the neurotransmitter norepinephrine in the central nervous system.

Antidepressant Drugs. As we discuss in chapter 14, "Therapy," the antidepressant drugs are used to treat depression. Like other stimulants, they increase the levels of neurotransmitters, including norepinephrine and dopamine. Two major classes of antidepressants include MAO inhibitors (which include Parnate, Nardil, and Marplan) and the tricyclic antidepressants (which include Tofranil, Norpramin, Elavil, and Adapin). Because these drugs do not produce euphoria in healthy individuals, there is little recreational abuse of them (Julien, 1985).

Psychedelic Drugs and Marijuana

The psychedelic drugs are sometimes referred to as hallucinogens because at high doses they result in hallucinations, but they also have other effects on behavior and perception. They may excite the nervous system, producing not only a change in emotional feelings, but also in the user's perceptions of the external world. Psychedelic drugs vary widely in their effects, which seem to depend on the taker's expectations and the settings in which the drug is experienced. The most common hallucinogens are LSD (lysergic acid diethylamide), mescaline (which is derived from the peyote cactus), and cannabis (source of both marijuana and hashish). Although marijuana is not truly a hallucinogen, at high doses it can cause psychedelic experiences, and is included in this section.

Hallucinogens. The effects of drugs such as *LSD* and *mescaline* include: brightly colored visual illusions and vivid dreamlike thoughts; a sense of existing outside the body; or a sense of unity between the body and objects in the environment; and intense emotions ranging from feelings of well-being to terror. The social and

Figure 5.11. Major Psychoactive Drugs

Drug Classification	Slang terms often used	Chemical or trade name	Medical uses	How taken usually	Immediate effects of use	Physical dependence	Psychological dependence
DEPRESSANTS							
Alcohol	booze, juice	ethyl alcohol	antiseptic	swallow	reduce anxiety	yes	yes
Barbiturates	blue devils, barbs, candy	Seconal, Nembutal	sedation, anxiety relief	swallow, inject	euphoria, reduce anxiety	yes	yes
Antianxiety Tranquilizers		Librium, Valium	anxiety relief	swallow	none	yes	yes
OPIATES							
Codeine	schoolboy	Methyl-morphine	cough, pain	swallow	euphoria	yes	yes
Morphine	white stuff	Morphine sulfate	pain relief	swallow, inject	euphoria	yes	yes
Heroin	horse, smack	Diacetylmor-phine	pain relief	swallow, inject	euphoria	yes	yes
Methodone	dolly	Dolophine amidone	pain relief	swallow, inject	aid in withdrawal	yes	yes
STIMULANTS							
Caffeine	caffeine	caffeine	migraine headache	swallow	alertness	yes	yes
Nicotine	smoke	nicotine	emetic	smoke, chew	alertness, relaxation	yes	yes
Amphetamine	speed, bennies	Benzedrine	narcolepsy, hyperactivity	swallow, inject	alertness, active	yes	yes
Cocaine	coke, crack, snow, dust	cocaine	anesthesia	inhale, inject, smoke	excitation	yes	yes
Anti-depressants		Tofranil, Nardil	relieve depression	swallow	none	?	?
PSYCHEDELICS							
LSD	acid, trips	lysergic acid diethylamide	none	swallow	sensory distortion	no	no?
Mescaline	mesc	3, 4, 5 trimeth-oxyphenethy-lamine	none	swallow	sensory distortion	no	no?
PCP	angel dust	phencyclidine hydrochloride	veterinary anesthesia	swallow	disorientation	no	no?
Marijuana	pot, grass	Cannabis	glaucoma	smoke, swallow	euphoria, relaxation	no	yes?
ANTIPSYCHOTIC DRUGS							
Thorazine		chlorplo-mazine	treat psychosis	swallow, inject	relaxation	?	?

Source: Compiled by author from various sources.

physical setting seems to have an important role in determining whether the "trip"—an altered state of consciousness generally from 6 to 14 hours—is a pleasant or a bad experience. Partially due to unfavorable publicity, including studies suggesting that taking LSD might produce genetic defects in one's offspring, usage has declined sharply from the late 1960s peak.

Research has linked the action of LSD to a decrease in the effectiveness of serotonin neurons in the brain. In chapter 2, "Biology of Behavior," we learned that the neurotransmitter serotonin is involved in sleep and perception. Apparently, sensory information is incorrectly interpreted when LSD is present. The perceptual changes are usually visual and tactile. Tolerance to LSD rapidly develops, but there does not appear to be evidence of physical dependence.

A drug that became popular in the 1970s is phencyclidine hydrochloride (PCP), often called "angel dust." PCP was developed as an anesthetic in 1956, but, because of its side effects of producing disorientation and delirium, it was declared unfit for humans. It was approved, however, as a veterinary anesthetic. PCP acts like a hallucinogen, and can have dangerous and unpredictable effects on people.

Marijuana. An ancient and still very popular drug, reports of the effects of marijuana date back to about 2700 B.C. The cannabis sativa plant grows throughout the world, especially in tropical regions. Marijuana is a mixture of the leaves and flowers of the cannabis plant; its active ingredient is *THC* (delta-9-tetrahydrocannabinol). Marijuana contains a fairly low dose of THC whereas hashish is much more potent. People who use marijuana do so for a variety of reasons. Some believe that it increases their awareness and creativity, while others take it with friends to increase sociability and a feeling of warmth. Some people take it because they are curious, or because they hope it will help them escape from problems. The most common psychological effects of marijuana include a sense of well-being, feelings of relaxation and happiness, an altered perception of time and space, and a vivid awareness of sensations. Some research has shown that with moderate doses of marijuana, subjects tested in laboratory settings showed impairment of short-term memory and of the capacity for complex thinking. Higher doses result in confusion, hallucinations, and feelings of panic (Miller & Branconnier, 1983).

The effects of marijuana appear to be highly subjective, individual, and dependent upon the expectations of the user. When it is used in social settings, its effects might be described as mildly mood altering. Marijuana use does not appear to develop physical dependence, but tolerance for the drug has been noted. Many claims have been made pro and con about marijuana; confirmation of these claims must await further research.

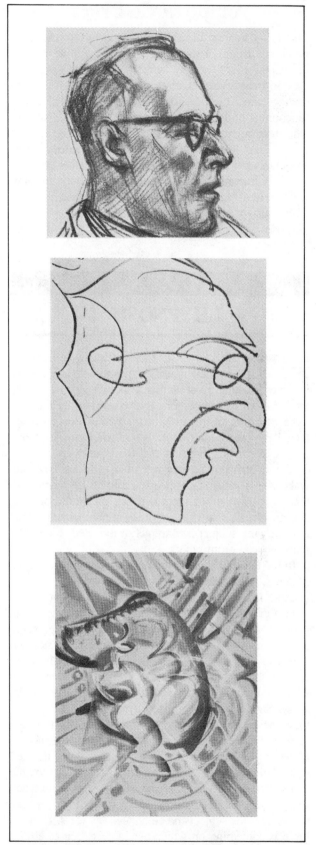

Figure 5.12. Effects of LSD on Artistic Drawing
LSD causes changes in perception. These drawings illustrate its effects. The first was done before the drug was taken.

Antipsychotic Drugs

The last category of psychoactive drugs is the antipsychotic drugs, or major tranquilizers. As we discuss in chapter 14, "Therapy," the antipsychotic drugs are used to treat several disruptions of psychological functioning called the psychoses by appearing to alter the functioning of dopamine in the brain. Psychotic patients who have been treated with antipsychotic drugs appear calmer and less anxious than they had been. Chlorpromazine (trade name Thorazine), which helped to create a dramatic change in the way psychotic patients were treated, was marketed in the United States in 1955. These drugs are not usually used for recreational purposes.

HYPNOSIS

Hypnosis is an altered state of consciousness that is characterized by heightened suggestibility. Hypnotism involves producing a dreamlike trance in people through the use of verbal suggestion. Hypnosis was once thought to be a form of sleeping (the word hypnosis comes from the Greek word for sleep), but recent evidence from EEG experiments indicates that the brain-wave pattern of the hypnotized person resembles various types of wakefulness rather than sleep. It should be mentioned that not everyone considers hypnosis an altered state of consciousness; some suggest it is simply a normal state in which the subject is extremely motivated to comply with requests from others.

In the late 1700s, a Viennese physician, Franz Anton Mesmer, demonstrated a technique called animal magnetism, in which magnetized rods in a tub of water generated an electrical current that produced seizures in patients. Mesmerism later became known as hypnotism as the emphasis shifted to producing an altered state of consciousness through verbal suggestion. In the latter part of the nineteenth century, French physician Jean Charcot thought hypnosis was a way to help people relax. Sigmund Freud utilized hypnosis as one way to view the unconscious mind (the other way was through dreams). However, he decided that hypnosis was not as effective as other methods, and thus abandoned its use.

Techniques and Susceptibility. There are many techniques used to induce hypnosis; most of them have several features in common. The setting should be one that relaxes the subject and eliminates any fears. Usually there is something on which the subject focuses attention. It can be an object (such as a watch on the end of a chain) or a repetitive sound. The hypnotist repeatedly gives the subject the suggestion that he or she feels comfortable and is relaxed; he or she tests to make sure the subject is relaxing when entering the hypnotic state.

Several hypnotic susceptibility tests are available, such as the Stanford Hypnotic Susceptibility Scale and the Barber Suggestibility Scale. These tests have various tasks that identify an individual's susceptibility, such as having subjects close their eyes, lower their hand, and react to a posthypnotic suggestion. There is a wide variation in individuals' susceptibility to hypnotism, and psychologists have not yet identified a distinct "hypnotizable" personality. When people are hypnotized, their altered state of consciousness is characterized by an extraordinary increase in their normal openness to the influence of suggestion. Ernest Hilgard (1975) reported that the best subjects for hypnosis are those who have good imaginations and the ability to fantasize.

Theories of Hypnosis. There are several theories of hypnosis, including the trance theory, the sociological role theory, and the task-motivation theory (Wallace & Fisher, 1987). According to the trance theory, hypnosis involves an altered state of consciousness in which the subject is in a heightened state of suggestibility (Hilgard, 1979). Hilgard suggested in his neodissociation theory that consciousness can be split into several streams of thought that are partially independent of each other. The hypnotized subject is not aware of all of the events happening in each of the levels of consciousness.

Sarbin and Coe's (1979) sociological role theory states that hypnotized subjects are in a normal state of consciousness and are trying to meet the role expectations set up by the hypnotist and society. Barber (1969) also argued in the task-motivation theory that hypnotism is not an altered state of consciousness but rather is a normal state of consciousness in which the subject is motivated to attend to the suggestions of the hypnotist. Currently, there is not agreement on one theory of hypnosis.

Uses of Hypnosis. Hypnosis has been used for a variety of purposes, such as to control pain, change behavior, improve memory, and modify perception. In the 1800s, hypnosis was used as anesthesia for surgical patients but with the advent of anesthetic drugs, hypnosis was no longer used for this purpose. It has been successfully used to reduce pain during childbirth. Hilgard and Hilgard (1983) suggested that hypnosis allows the individual to dissociate consciousness into two levels, and that under hypnosis the pain is not experienced at a conscious level of awareness.

One of the most common uses of hypnosis has been in controlling everyday behavior problems such as smoking and obesity. By providing suggestions that smoking or overeating is bad for health and encouraging a positive self-image, hypnotists are able to help people change bad habits. Anderson (1985) found that using

Figure 5.13. Meditation
In meditation the subject concentrates on blocking out distracting stimuli, and focuses on one specific thought or image. This can reduce physical and emotional tension.

hypnosis to control obesity was most successful when subjects were more susceptible as measured on the Stanford Hypnotic Susceptibility Scale and when hypnosis was used along with other behavior modification techniques because of the tendency of some individuals to revert to their undesirable habits.

Hypnosis has also been used to help individuals remember past events. Psychologists have hypnotized witnesses to help them remember details of a crime. While sometimes the witness makes up information (or is influenced by the hypnotist's suggestions), at other times this procedure has produced valuable information (Sheehan & Tilden, 1983). A recent study by McConkey and Kinoshita (1988) found that subjects who were hypnotized were able to recall significantly more pictures, which they had been shown a week earlier, than subjects who were not hypnotized.

In a controversial technique called hypnotic age regression, an individual under hypnosis is asked to recall information about events that occurred at a much earlier date (for example, during childhood). Although this use of hypnosis does not always produce positive effects, this altered state of consciousness continues to intrigue psychologists.

MEDITATION

For perhaps thousands of years, people in the Eastern world have been altering their awareness by means of meditation. And in recent years, hundreds of thousands of individuals in Western industrialized nations have become regular meditators. Meditation is the practice of some form of relaxed concentration that can block distracting sensory stimuli. Goleman (1977) reported that by focusing their attention on a single sound, sight, movement, or thought, accomplished meditators can refresh themselves emotionally and even physically.

Effects of Meditation. Studies of meditators have reported that meditation can produce a wide variety of psychological and physiological effects. A number of studies have found that meditation can enhance self-esteem and confidence in subjects (Hjelle, 1974). It appears capable of reducing stress, anxiety, high blood pressure, and can help individuals control asthma, insomnia, or excessive fears.

Some of the physiological changes that can occur during meditation were described in a comprehensive study by Wallace and Benson (1972). They found that transcendental meditation was able to help individuals reduce oxygen consumption, increase electrical resistance of the skin, decrease the heart rate, increase the EEG alpha-wave activity and decrease the overall amount of air breathed. Wallace and Benson pointed out that these changes do not occur in hypnosis.

Types of Meditation. There are several forms of meditation, including Zen, yoga, and TM (transcendental meditation). Zen is the oldest form of meditation. The meditator must begin by counting his or her breaths. Then the individual focuses on breathing, trying to eliminate all other stimuli. With practice, the Zen meditator is able to produce an altered state of consciousness.

In yoga meditation, the individual alters his or her state of consciousness by modifying autonomic processes such as heart rate, blood pressure, and digestion. The yoga meditator assumes a particular position (lotus), focuses on a visual object, and repeats a word or phrase called a mantra. Again these procedures allow the yoga meditator to produce an altered state of consciousness by blocking out environmental stimuli.

TM is a form of yoga in which the subject repeats a specific mantra (sound) over a period of time, while trying to block out all other stimuli. The person practicing TM can take any comfortable position (unlike yoga in which the lotus position must be assumed). The goal of all meditation is to block out normal awareness to provide an altered state of consciousness.

Evaluation of Meditation. Herbert Benson (1975) studied individuals who practiced TM and concluded that most of the effects of meditation can be achieved by producing a "relaxation response." A number of other studies have also concluded that meditation does not produce an altered state of consciousness, but rather a relaxed state in which physiological arousal is significantly lowered (Shapiro, 1985). Relaxation techniques are widely used in therapy to treat a variety of fear and anxiety problems as we discuss in chapter 14, "Therapy."

David Holmes and his colleagues (1983) did not find

any significant differences between people who practiced TM and individuals who rested quietly. Changes in heart rate, blood pressure, and respiration were similar in both groups. The question of whether meditation produces an altered state of consciousness or a state of extreme relaxation has not yet been conclusively answered, but psychologists do recognize its benefits in dealing with stress and anxiety.

BIOFEEDBACK

The biofeedback approach to altering consciousness usually involves the use of a device that permits the individual to monitor and influence one or more bodily processes that are not normally subject to voluntary control. Essentially, the person is responding to his or her own internal biological cues. The subject has electrodes or a transducer attached to the surface of the body to pick up the physiological activity. The bodily processes include brain waves, skin resistance, muscle tone, blood pressure, or skin temperature.

One commonly practiced form of biofeedback uses an EEG monitoring device that permits a person to generate alpha brain waves of 8 to 12 cycles per second. By generating such brain waves to the exclusion of all others, one can enter a type of consciousness known as the alpha state, which is characterized by a relaxed, tranquil, composed, yet fully aware state of mind.

Accomplished meditators—without a biofeedback machine, but usually only after long training and practice—typically can achieve the alpha state.

Neal Miller was one of the pioneers in this field. He reported the results of an experiment (Miller & Banuazizi, 1968) in which rats learned to increase or decrease their heart rates when rewarded for doing so. Miller (1973) also conducted research on the ability of humans to control various "involuntary" internal biological functions.

People have been taught to gain conscious control over a wide variety of processes, including their own heart rates, blood pressure, temperature, and other bodily functions. The biofeedback method is gaining acceptance as a therapeutic technique for treating emotional, behavioral, psychosomatic, and even organic problems. Tension headaches, vomiting, anxiety, and even ulcers, can be helped through biofeedback techniques (Roberts, 1985). These techniques for altering consciousness are constantly being improved and tested for new applications. ■

It is important to remember that the study of consciousness—whether it is the waking state or an altered state—is extremely subjective, since we must rely on the subject for much of our data. People sometimes have trouble understanding altered states of consciousness such as sleep because they are such a normal part of our everyday existence. However, research is helping people sleep better and relax more fully, and is helping psychologists treat a variety of problems.

Drawing by Henry Martin; © 1983 The New Yorker Magazine, Inc.

"This concludes the conscious part of your day. Good night."

CHAPTER REVIEW
What You've Learned About Sleep and Consciousness

1. Consciousness is the processing of our sensations, thoughts, and feelings at various levels of awareness. Waking consciousness is the awareness of sensations and thoughts while we are awake and alert. In an altered state of consciousness there is a redirection of attention.

2. There are two types of sleep: REM, or rapid-eye-movement sleep, and NREM, or non-rapid-eye-movement sleep. In REM sleep, the heart rate accelerates, the eyes move rapidly about, breathing becomes variable, and the EEG is similar to the waking state. In NREM sleep, the heart rate and breathing slow down and muscular tension is absent. When we sleep, we pass through the four stages of NREM sleep and then come back to REM.

3. NREM appears to be influenced by serotonin produced in the raphe nucleus. REM is influenced by the locus coeruleus, and is affected by norepinephrine and acetylcholine. One theory suggests that REM sleep is involved in memory, whereas NREM sleep helps with physical growth and tissue repair. A recent theory proposes that REM sleep clears the brain of memories that interfere with thought and memory.

4. Everyone dreams each night, mostly during REM sleep. Early theories of dreaming suggested that dreams are where our unconscious conflicts reside. Current theories suggest that dreams are extensions of our everyday experiences. In one survey people reported dreaming about falling, being attacked, school, sexual behavior, eating, being frightened, or having a loved one die. The activation synthesis theory of dreaming suggests that dreams are the interpretation of brain physiological activity.

5. Insomnia is the inability to sleep. In sleep apnea, the person immediately awakens because he or she can't breathe. Narcolepsy is an inappropriate daytime attack of sleep. Other sleep disorders occur in NREM sleep and include sleep talking, sleepwalking, bed-wetting, and night terrors.

6. A psychoactive drug causes changes in behavior and cognition by modifying conscious awareness. Psychological dependence occurs when a person craves the drug. In physical dependence, or addiction, the habitual user's body becomes biochemically dependent upon the drug. Psychoactive drugs include depressants, opiates, stimulants, psychedelics, and the antipsychotic drugs.

7. Depressants (or sedative-hypnotics) are drugs that have a sedative effect. In large doses, alcohol disrupts motor coordination, thinking, and perception. Infants born to women alcoholics might have congenital malformations. Barbiturates are used for mild sedation, anesthesia, and as a treatment for insomnia or anxiety. Antianxiety minor tranquilizers are useful for treating anxiety.

8. Opiates (or narcotic analgesics) are drugs whose effect on the body is similar to morphine. Opiates include naturally-occurring drugs such as codeine, morphine, and heroin, and synthetic drugs such as methadone, Darvon, and Demerol. Medical uses include relief of pain, treatment of diarrhea, and suppression of coughs.

9. Stimulants are drugs that increase central nervous system activity and produce alertness or euphoria. Caffeine is probably the most widely used stimulant in our society. Nicotine produces effects similar to caffeine. Amphetamines have been used to treat sleep disorders. Cocaine is derived from the coca plant. Antidepressant drugs treat depression.

10. The psychedelic drugs excite the nervous system, producing not only a change in emotional feelings, but also in the user's perceptions of the external world. They are called hallucinogens because at high doses they can result in hallucinations; they include LSD, mescaline, and PCP. Marijuana, derived from the cannabis plant, produces changes in time perception, attention, and mental organization.

11. Hypnosis is an altered state of consciousness characterized by heightened suggestibility. Techniques require a subject to relax and focus attention on something such as a repetitive sound. The best subjects are those who have good imaginations and the ability to fantasize. Hypnosis has been used to control pain, improve memory, and modify perception.

12. Meditation is the practice of relaxed concentration which blocks distracting stimuli. It appears to be capable of reducing anxiety, increasing resistance to anger and depression, and improving a person's self-esteem.

13. Biofeedback involves the monitoring and influencing of a person's own bodily processes such as heart rate, blood pressure, and muscle tension.

LEARNING AND COGNITIVE PROCESSES

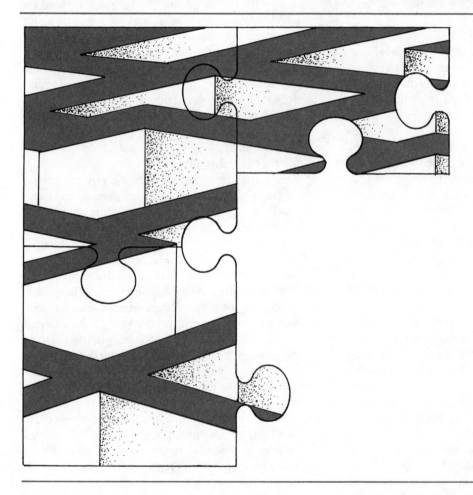

Part III surveys learning and the cognitive areas of psychology. In this section, learning, memory, language and thought processes, and the concept of intelligence are covered.

After reading Part III you should be able to:

Define classical and operant conditioning

Describe the effects of reinforcement on learning

Define short-term and long-term memory

Identify techniques for memory improvement

Explain how language and thought are related

Describe some basic theories of intelligence

Identify the influence of genetics and environment on intelligence

Chapter 6	Learning

One of the most significant contributions of experimental psychologists to learning theory is the result of their research on the basic processes of learning. Major attention has focused on the association of stimuli and responses and the effects of reinforcement and punishment on behavior. Psychologists have also studied cognition and the biological constraints of learning.

Chapter 7	Human Memory

Practical suggestions for improving our ability to learn and remember is one outcome of the study of memory. Psychologists are interested in how information is entered, stored, and retrieved from our memory systems. Recent attention has focused on how information proceeds from sensory memory to short-term and long-term memory stores.

Chapter 8	Language and Intelligence

Part of what makes us unique is our ability to use language to communicate and to use thought to solve problems. The cognitive processes of language and thought are involved in intelligence. A number of important theories of intelligence have been proposed, and a variety of IQ tests have been developed to measure it accurately.

LEARNING

One of the most significant contributions of experimental psychologists to learning theory is the result of their research on the basic processes of learning. Major attention has focused on the association of stimuli and responses and the effects of reinforcement and punishment on behavior. Psychologists have also studied cognition and the biological constraints of learning.

Can you imagine two pigeons playing Ping-Pong together? Harvard psychologist B. F. Skinner reported on a demonstration of this unlikely behavior. Skinner found in 1962 that, under the proper circumstances, pigeons are capable of learning fairly complex, sophisticated patterns of behavior, including how to play Ping-Pong.

The Ping-Pong table was about 8 inches wide, 16 inches long, and 8 inches high. (See Figure 6.1.) It was constructed so that a pigeon could approach the edge of the table and peck at the ball. The surface was sloped slightly toward the edges so the ball would roll to a player. A trough at each end of the table allowed the ball to trip a switch at the other end of the table to provide food for the other pigeon. Wires prevented the pigeons from jumping onto the table itself.

In a pigeon Ping-Pong game, the human experimenter starts the ball in the middle of the table. The ball rolls toward the edge of one side. Each bird is expected to peck at the ball as it approaches to send it to the opposite side of the table. If it succeeds in causing it to roll off the other end of the table, that bird is rewarded with food. However, if an opponent pecks the ball and successfully returns it, the first pigeon must peck at it again. This procedure continues until one player misses the ball and the other bird gets the food reward. How could Skinner get these pigeons to learn the skills necessary to play the game of Ping-Pong?

He began by working with one pigeon at a time. First, he motivated a pigeon by making sure it was hungry. Then he glued a Ping-Pong ball to the edge of the table, and gave the pigeon a little food whenever it pecked at

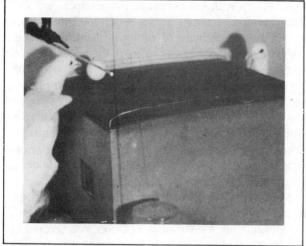

Figure 6.1. Operant Conditioning
Harvard psychologist B. F. Skinner was able to shape the behavior of pigeons so that they pecked at a Ping-Pong ball in order to get food. Eventually, the pigeons were able to play a modified version of Ping-Pong. Shaping animal behavior is a technique of operant conditioning.

the ball. In the beginning the pigeon did not show very much pecking behavior, but after receiving food for pecking, this behavior gradually increased.

When the bird had learned to peck consistently, Skinner unglued the ball so it could move about. The food reward was given only when the pigeon was able to

drive the ball a certain distance. Gradually, the distance the ball had to travel before the pigeon received food was increased. Then Skinner began to delay giving food until the ball went to the opposite side of the table. Although the pigeon's behavior occasionally deteriorated, eventually Skinner was able to train the bird to continue to peck even if it did not immediately receive the food reward.

Finally, Skinner had trained pigeons to the point that they were ready to play an actual "game" of Ping-Pong. In a typical game, the pigeons were able to return the ball five or six times before scoring a point. The pigeons worked hard to peck at the ball until they received food. They watched the ball as it came toward them, and usually got in the correct position to send it back.

Through the gradual shaping of behavior by using a food reward, Skinner was able to teach the pigeons the fairly complex (for a pigeon) game of Ping-Pong. Using similar procedures, Skinner was able to get a variety of animals and people to learn numerous complex behaviors. The procedures he developed are currently being used in schools, mental hospitals, and homes to help people learn more efficiently. Since the learning procedures were developed with animals, they can be successfully used with young children, the retarded, and others who cannot talk. The shaping technique is a very powerful tool used by psychologists today.

CHAPTER OBJECTIVES
What You'll Learn About Learning

After studying this chapter, you should be able to:

1. Define learning.
2. Identify the types of stimuli and responses involved in classical conditioning.
3. Outline the basic principles of classical conditioning (acquisition, extinction, spontaneous recovery, generalization, and discrimination).
4. Explain how taste aversions might be acquired through classical conditioning.
5. Identify three applications of classical conditioning in everyday life.
6. State Thorndike's law of effect.
7. Define shaping and describe an example.
8. Outline the basic principles of operant conditioning (acquisition, extinction, spontaneous recovery, generalization, and discrimination).
9. Define reinforcement and describe the major schedules of reinforcement (continuous, fixed interval, variable interval, fixed ratio, and variable ratio).
10. Contrast and give examples of the different types of reinforcement (primary and secondary reinforcement, and positive and negative reinforcement).
11. Describe the procedures of aversive conditioning (escape conditioning and avoidance conditioning).
12. Define punishment and list the variables that contribute to its effectiveness.
13. Identify three applications of operant conditioning in everyday life.
14. Compare classical conditioning and operant conditioning.
15. Describe the major forms of cognitive learning (insight, latent learning, and observational learning).
16. Outline the biological constraints on learning (instinctive drift, imprinting, and the continuum of preparedness in learning).

WHAT IS LEARNING?

From the moment we wake up until we fall asleep, most of what we do involves learning. We get up, shower, dress, eat, walk, study, talk, listen to music—all because we have learned how to perform these behaviors. In fact, learning is so important in our lives that we would find it difficult to think of situations that do not involve learning in some way.

Psychologists usually define learning as the relatively permanent change in behavior or behavioral ability of an individual that occurs as a result of experience. There is some variation in the emphasis of different perspectives; the behavioral viewpoint focuses on the actual change in behavior and the cognitive perspective emphasizes the change in the ability to exhibit the behavior.

There are several features of this definition we need to discuss. First, learning involves a relatively permanent change. This refers to the fact that the individual's behavior is modified and continues to remain different in the future. The term relatively permanent distinguishes learning from temporary changes in behavior caused by motivation, fatigue, or drugs. For example, when we are tired, we behave differently than usual (perhaps we go to sleep or become sloppy in our work), but this is a temporary change and thus does not reflect learning. Likewise, motivations such as hunger or thirst might temporarily alter our behavior, but after we have eaten or have had a drink, we revert back to our former behavior. Learning only includes relatively long-lasting changes.

Second, learning involves a change in the individual's behavior or ability to exhibit a behavior. Often a distinction is made between learning and performance. The actual behavior that is observed is called performance, whereas learning is inferred from the behavior. Performance can be thought of as the combined result of learning and motivation. Let's assume that you read this chapter and know the definition of learning when you go to class. But even though you have learned the definition, you do not show it until motivated to do so (perhaps when taking a test). How does your instructor know you have learned the information? He or she observes your performance on the test and infers from your behavior that learning has taken place. While we often talk as if performance and learning were equivalent, there is a difference. Typically, you learn much more than you exhibit (unless motivated to do your best).

Third, learning results from behavioral experience in the environment. In order to learn, we need to perceive events in our environment, and to associate or connect those events with our behavior. For instance, we learn that certain restaurants serve better food than others through our experience of eating in them, and change our behavior by continuing to eat in the better ones. We learn how to play tennis by practicing until we become good players. We learn that certain television programs are more entertaining than others by watching them and change our behavior by continuing to watch the more entertaining ones. Experience in the environment is necessary for learning to occur, and thus behavioral changes caused only by physical growth, maturation, or injury are not examples of learning.

Most psychologists study an individual's behavior in terms of specific actions, which are called responses. If we looked at an individual in isolation, and ignored his or her surroundings, we would not make much headway in understanding behavior. Clearly, we must also consider the individual's environment, the events taking place outside the body. Only in relation to the environment do an individual's movements—taking a pill, kissing a baby, walking a tightrope, dancing a waltz, or writing a letter—become meaningful responses. Like behavior, environment must also be broken up into useful units, which psychologists call stimuli. Environmental stimuli cause us to give particular responses. The red traffic light that signals us to stop our car at an intersection is an example of a stimulus.

The pigeons in our opening story had to learn how to play Ping-Pong. Their modified ability to play can be seen in the change from random pecking to pecking the ball in a way that would score a point. This change came about because they experienced a food reward when they showed the expected behavior. They continued to show the learned behavior at future Ping-Pong matches, thus demonstrating that the learning was relatively permanent.

Learning involves associations between the events in the environment (stimuli) and our behavior (responses). Many theorists argue that reinforcement, or reward, is necessary for learning to take place, whereas others suggest that reward provides the motivation to exhibit what has been learned. We will discover many variables that influence learning as we go through this chapter.

CLASSICAL CONDITIONING

Picture in your mind a research laboratory in Russia. The year is about 1904 and the researcher is the Russian physiologist Ivan Pavlov, who has recently won the Nobel Prize for his work on the digestive process in dogs. He has been measuring saliva and other internal

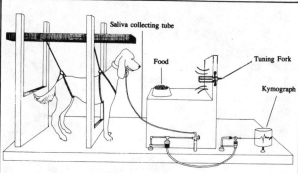

Figure 6.2. Classical Conditioning
The apparatus pictured is similar to that used in Pavlov's famous early experiments on conditioning. Pavlov trained dogs to salivate at the sound of a bell. In classical conditioning, the conditioned stimulus (CS, a bell) is presented just before the unconditioned stimulus (US, food). After several pairings, the conditioned stimulus evokes the conditioned response (CR, salivation).

secretions produced by dogs when they eat and digest their food.

Pavlov has discovered that his dogs began salivating before he fed them. In fact, upon careful observation, the dogs were salivating when they saw the experimenter, the food dish, or even when they heard footsteps coming into the lab. Pavlov decided to study this anticipatory response in its own right, and by doing so, greatly influenced the future of psychology.

He conducted one famous experiment in which he rang a bell just prior to administering food to a dog. At first, the dog showed no particular reaction to the bell. But, after several trials in which the dog heard the bell just before being administered food, it began to salivate in response to the bell alone. What had originally been a neutral stimulus now caused the dog to salivate. The dog had learned to interpret the sound of the bell as a signal that it was about to be fed.

Pavlov did not stop here. He gave the dog a number of trials in which he only rang the bell (and no food was given). When the bell alone was used as a stimulus, after several trials the dog's salivation response declined drastically. Pavlov found, however, that when he gave the dog a rest for a day or two, again it quickly responded only to the bell for several more trials before stopping (Pavlov, 1927).

Pavlov conducted a large number of experiments to study the associations of responses and stimuli. For neutral stimuli, he presented lights, and sounds of buzzers, bells, and metronomes. He usually followed one of these stimuli with food (meat powder) but also

BIOGRAPHICAL ☆ HIGHLIGHT ☆

Ivan Petrovich Pavlov, shown here in the center with a white beard, was born in 1849 in Ryazan, Russia, at the beginning of one of the most fertile intellectual eras in Russian history.

In accordance with his father's wishes, he attended the local theological seminary until a growing interest in the natural sciences led him to rebel against his inherited destiny. He went on to obtain a medical degree from the Imperial Medicosurgical Academy in 1879. He then studied physiology in Germany briefly before being appointed professor of pharmacology at the St. Petersburg Institute of Experimental Medicine in 1890.

He won the Nobel Prize in 1904 for his research on the physiology of digestion. At this time, he began research on conditioned reflexes in dogs, thus becoming the pioneer in classical conditioning. Pavlov spent the rest of his life studying conditioning, which he believed was a useful research method for studying physiology. He engaged in research actively until his death at the age of 87 in 1936.

used a weak acid solution, or even a mild electric shock. The responses measured were often salivary, but also included flexing the leg (after a shock). Pavlov referred to these responses as "reflexes," and was interested in how the physiological pathways in the brain that produced the newly acquired reflexes were formed.

Pavlov gave the name conditioning to the formation of this new bond or association between a neutral stimulus and the response. Today, this type of learning is called classical conditioning, or sometimes Pavlovian or respondent conditioning. The term "conditioning" is usually used to signify a relatively simple form of learning that is often studied scientifically. Learning is a much broader term which incorporates conditioning as well as other forms of acquiring new behaviors (Houston, 1986).

Classical Conditioning Terminology

We begin by discussing four important terms in classical conditioning: unconditioned stimulus, unconditioned response, conditioned stimulus, and conditioned response. The unconditioned stimulus, or US, is any stimulus that provokes an automatic or reflexive reaction in an individual. Examples of common unconditioned stimuli include: loud noises, a pin-prick, and an object rapidly approaching you. The particular response elicited by the US is called the unconditioned response, or UR. Examples of unconditioned responses include: tensing the body in response to hearing a loud noise, jumping in response to being pricked by a pin, and ducking in response to an object being thrown at you. In Pavlov's original experiment, the US was food, and the UR was the dog's salivation. The term "unconditioned" response refers to a behavior that does not have to be learned as a response to a stimulus in the present situation. It may be a genetically programmed reflex, or it may have been previously learned. The important point is that the subject automatically shows the unconditioned response when presented with the unconditioned stimulus.

If the US is repeatedly presented immediately after some neutral stimulus, such as Pavlov's bell, the neutral stimulus alone will become sufficient to elicit the response. The originally neutral stimulus is then called conditioned stimulus, or CS. The newly learned response to the CS is the conditioned response or CR.

I like to think of classical conditioning as "stimulus substitution," in which the US is replaced by the CS, and the response stays about the same. Although this particular interpretation is somewhat simplistic, it will help you grasp the general idea of classical conditioning. The CR,

Figure 6.3. Example of Classical Conditioning
In everyday life, a loud noise is often an unconditioned stimulus (US) that elicits a startle, an unconditioned response (UR). If the sight of an overinflated balloon precedes the loud noise of it bursting, the balloon becomes a conditioned stimulus (CS). The next time a balloon is seen, it might elicit a startle, a conditioned response (CR).

for our purposes, is essentially the same as the UR, although it is important to remember that they are elicited by two different stimuli (Houston, 1986). Thus, to understand classical conditioning we must identify the response shown by the subject when the stimulus is presented. If the stimulus previously caused the response, it is the US and if the stimulus was just learned, it is the CS.

A famous experiment was conducted in 1920 by John Watson and his assistant, Rosalie Rayner. Although not strictly pure classical conditioning, it exemplifies the principles we are discussing. Watson was interested in how human emotions were learned. He tested an 11-month-old baby named Albert for reactions to a variety of stimuli, including a white rat, a rabbit, masks and a ball of cotton. "Little Albert's" response was positive to all of these things and he readily touched them when given the chance. In order to produce a fear response, when Albert reached out to touch the rat (CS), Watson produced a loud, unpleasant noise (US) behind the child by striking a hammer on a steel bar. Albert, of course, responded with a fit of crying (UR). After five or six trials, the mere sight of the rat alone (CS) caused Little Albert to burst out in tears (CR). Watson had conditioned Little Albert to associate a loud noise with one of the stimuli, the white rat. Watson suggested that many emotions, both positive and negative, are learned in this manner.

Classical conditioning is involved in every aspect of our lives. For instance, you probably still associate the smell of certain foods with your enjoyment of a particular occasion in your life. You feel warm and tingly when you see that special someone. And hearing your special song on the radio brings back happy memories. Classical conditioning is indeed involved in a wide variety of situations.

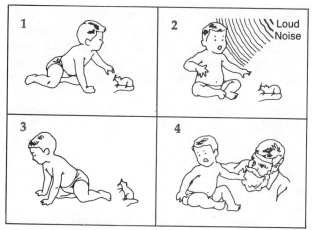

Figure 6.4. Little Albert Experiment
John B. Watson in his experiment with Little Albert, an 11-month-old baby (*above*) studied how emotions are learned. He presented (**1**) a white rat (CS) and (**2**) a loud noise (US) to Little Albert. After several pairings, (**3**) Albert showed fear (CR) of the white rat. Later, (**4**) Albert generalized the fear to stimuli that were similar to CS, such as a beard. *Below:* the youngster reacts to the scarecrow's beard in a manner that is similar to Little Albert's generalized fear.

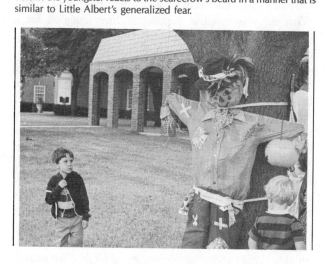

Basic Principles of Classical Conditioning

To understand how classical conditioning works, it is necessary to identify and examine its basic principles. These include acquisition, extinction, spontaneous recovery, stimulus generalization, stimulus discrimination, and higher order conditioning.

Acquisition. A great deal of research has examined the variables that have an impact on the acquisition of classical conditioning (Klein, 1987). The interstimulus interval between the CS and US is an extremely important variable. For classical conditioning to take place effectively, the CS usually comes first, followed by the US usually within half a second. Pavlov discovered in 1927 that the timing of the CS was a crucial factor in conditioning. If the CS was presented at the same time as the US, too long after it, or too long before it, it had little or no effect on the dog's behavior.

There are several procedures in classical conditioning that vary the temporal relationship of the stimuli, including forward delayed conditioning, forward trace conditioning, simultaneous conditioning, and backward conditioning. Overall, the forward delayed conditioning procedure is the most effective, followed by forward trace conditioning and then simultaneous conditioning (Sherman, 1978). Backward conditioning is not very effective, and indeed can sometimes lead to opposite effects.

In delayed conditioning, the presentation of the CS precedes the onset of the US, and the termination of the CS is delayed until the US is presented (either at the US onset or during the presentation of the US). In Watson's study, the rat (CS) was presented before the loud noise (US) and remained in view of Little Albert until the loud noise was presented.

In many situations, the CS is a discrete event that is presented and terminated before the US is presented. Examples of discrete events include the noise of a gun being fired, the flash of a strobe light, one ring of a telephone, and the sound of a single firecracker exploding. This is the procedure of trace conditioning, which can be very effective if the interstimulus interval is very brief. Pavlov used trace conditioning when he rang the bell once and then one second later presented the food. Even though trace conditioning is often used, it is not as effective as delayed conditioning.

Although Pavlov restricted his own research to dogs, other investigators have studied classical conditioning in many animals as well as people. In many situations, the optimum time interval between the CS and US is about one-half to 2 seconds (Klein, 1987). However, there is variability among species and the particular response being conditioned. For example, in conditioned taste aversion, discussed later in this chapter, the successful interstimulus interval can be hours rather than seconds.

In simultaneous conditioning the CS and the US are presented at exactly the same time. Pavlov found that conditioning was very weak when the bell and food were presented together. One explanation is that there is no time for the subject to anticipate the US and thus the CS does not take on the properties of the US.

In the procedure sometimes called backward conditioning, the US is presented and terminated before the presentation of the CS. If Pavlov had presented the food and then after the dog ate, presented the bell, the bell alone would not elicit much salivation, since it no longer signals that food is imminent. Backward conditioning is controversial because many psychologists argue that it does not work.

In the above examples, it is assumed that the CS is originally a truly neutral stimulus. Often, however, both

Figure 6.5. Temporal Relationships

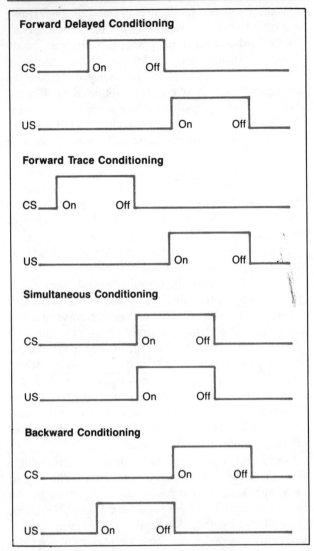

Forward Delayed Conditioning

CS _____ On _____ Off

US _____ On _____ Off

Forward Trace Conditioning

CS _____ On _____ Off

US _____ On _____ Off

Simultaneous Conditioning

CS _____ On _____ Off

US _____ On _____ Off

Backward Conditioning

CS _____ On _____ Off

US _____ On _____ Off

In classical conditioning, the conditioned stimulus (CS) presented immediately before the unconditioned stimulus (US), is known as forward delayed conditioning. If the CS is presented and terminated before the US is presented, the procedure is known as forward trace conditioning. Sometimes the CS and US are presented at exactly the same time and the process is known as simultaneous conditioning. When the CS is presented after the US, it is referred to as backward conditioning.

stimuli have meaning to the subject, and the labeling of them is arbitrary. What usually happens is that the first stimulus (called the CS) takes on the properties of the second stimulus (called the US). This can be demonstrated with a simple illustration. Suppose you have a child who loves honey and hates medicine. Your child is sick and must take medicine, so you decide to use classical conditioning to accomplish your task. Which would you give first, the medicine or the honey? Think about it very carefully, because if you do the wrong thing, your child will come to hate honey as well as the medicine.

If you give honey (CS) first, and then medicine (US), your child will come to hate (CR) honey. However, if you give the medicine (CS) first, and then the honey (US), the medicine will become associated with the honey, and after a couple of pairings, the medicine alone will be liked (CR), or at least tolerated.

The CS becomes stronger as the number of conditioning trials containing the US increases (Adams, 1980). That is, if you only pair the CS and US once or twice, the CS alone will not be as effective as it would be if you paired the stimuli a half-dozen times. Pavlov needed to have a number of pairings before the bell alone would elicit salivation.

Extinction. I once had a guinea pig who loved lettuce. Within a few weeks, she would squeal every time the refrigerator door was opened, because she often received lettuce shortly thereafter. The guinea pig had become classically conditioned to squeal (CR) at the sound of the refrigerator door being opened (CS). Then the price of lettuce went up and I no longer fed her any. What do you suppose happened? She squealed for a while, but then the squealing became weaker and died out altogether. The squealing had been extinguished.

Extinction is the elimination of a CR by presenting only the CS without the US. Pavlov found that when the bell was presented by itself without any meat powder following it, the dog salivated less and eventually stopped altogether. The US is sometimes referred to as the reinforcement, and thus we say that extinction occurs when reinforcement is withdrawn.

Spontaneous Recovery. Extinction does not necessarily stop the CR permanently. If the subject is given a rest in which the CS is withheld, a later presentation of the CS alone may bring on at least some of the old CR, although it is likely to be weaker and disappear fairly quickly. This sudden reappearance of a CR after extinction is called spontaneous recovery. This occurs even though the US has not been presented after extinction began.

I went on a vacation and took my guinea pig with me. When we arrived home, I happened to open the refrigerator and the guinea pig squealed loudly and clearly, even though she had not had any lettuce for a long time. Likewise, Pavlov found spontaneous recovery in his dogs. After he had extinguished their response to the bell, they were returned to their home cages. The next morning, they spontaneously recovered, and salivated at the sound of the bell, even though it had not been repaired with meat powder.

Stimulus Generalization. After Little Albert had been conditioned to fear a white rat, Watson and Rayner discovered that he began to cry when shown other furry objects—a rabbit, a dog, a fur coat, and even a mask of Santa Claus. He was exhibiting the principle of stimulus generalization. That is, once the CR (crying) was condi-

Figure 6.6. Classical Conditioning Paradigm

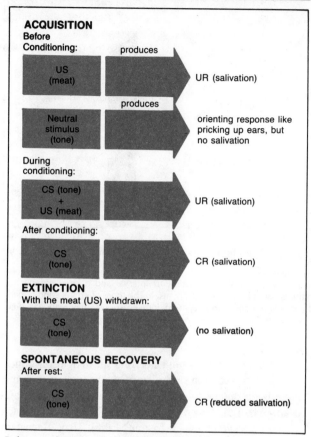

ACQUISITION
Before Conditioning:

US (meat) — produces → UR (salivation)

Neutral stimulus (tone) — produces → orienting response like pricking up ears, but no salivation

During conditioning:

CS (tone) + US (meat) → UR (salivation)

After conditioning:

CS (tone) → CR (salivation)

EXTINCTION
With the meat (US) withdrawn:

CS (tone) → (no salivation)

SPONTANEOUS RECOVERY
After rest:

CS (tone) → CR (reduced salivation)

Before conditioning, the unconditioned stimulus (US) of meat elicits the unconditioned response (UR), or salivation from the dog. During conditioning, the conditioned stimulus (CS), the bell, is presented immediately before the US. After several pairings, the bell (CS) alone elicits the conditioned response (CR). During extinction, when the US (meat) has been removed, the CS (bell) becomes less and less effective in eliciting the CR. In spontaneous recovery, after a rest period, the CS is again briefly able to elicit the CR.

tioned to the CS (rat), stimuli similar to the CS became sufficient to elicit the CR. The greater the similarity between the new stimulus and the original CS, the stronger the CR.

Once Pavlov had the dog responding to the sound of a bell, he tried other signals and found that sounds similar to the bell would also elicit the CR. For example, Pavlov found that the sound of a buzzer or of a metronome would also cause the dog to salivate.

The phenomenon of stimulus generalization has been observed and well documented in both animal and human studies. It seems that many of our fears are learned through classical conditioning and stimulus generalization. For example, an individual who is bitten by a large dog may later find that he or she is not only fearful of all large dogs but of small dogs and other similar animals as well.

Stimulus Discrimination. If organisms were to generalize their learned responses to one particular type of stimulus to all remotely similar stimuli, the result would be a vast array of unadaptive behaviors. We usually learn to limit our responses to relevant stimuli. Indeed, the capacity for adaptive living depends upon how well we learn to recognize and respond to the critical features of the environment. This process is called stimulus discrimination, and is important in successful adjustment.

Pavlov also identified this phenomenon in his dogs. Once the dogs had been conditioned to the sound of a bell, through stimulus generalization, they would also salivate in response to the sound of a buzzer. But then if the buzzer was never followed by the US, whereas the bell always was, the CR to the buzzer would soon cease to occur. The dogs would learn to discriminate between the two stimuli, never salivating to the one but always to the other.

Discrimination learning is important in our everyday lives. Reading would be extremely difficult if we could not discriminate between similar letters, like *b* and *d*. We learn to respond to people on the basis of individual behavior and personal characteristics, not stereotypes.

Higher Order Conditioning. The potential complexity of the role of classical conditioning in our lives has one final principle. Pavlov and his colleagues discovered that a CS could sometimes work as a US. If still another neutral stimulus was constantly presented before a particular CS, it too would bring on a CR. For example, they injected a dog with morphine, which produced vomiting. After that, the dog would vomit at the mere sight of a needle, thus exhibiting a CR. They then found that various stimuli occurring before the sight of the needle—the smell of alcohol, the box containing the needle, or even the sight of the laboratory—might be sufficient to elicit the CR.

In higher order conditioning, the CS is paired with a new neutral stimulus, which takes on the properties of the CS. Higher order conditioning is not the same as stimulus generalization. It is no longer a question of responding to stimuli similar to the original CS. Rather, the individual is now responding to stimuli that are totally unlike the original CS but associated with it in time. Thus, the victim of a dog bite may subsequently develop fears and apprehensions that will cause him to avoid the street in which the event took place.

Higher order classical conditioning is a common phenomenon. It is often successfully used in advertising. For example, you probably have seen model/actress Brooke Shields in an advertisement for blue jeans or Michael Jackson in a commercial for a popular soda. Consumers presumably have learned to respond positively to these stars and thus will also respond favorably to the advertised product. Another example is the development of test anxiety. Let's assume that as a child when you went to school (CS) you were threatened by a bully

Figure 6.7. Acquisition, Extinction and Spontaneous Recovery of Classical Conditioning

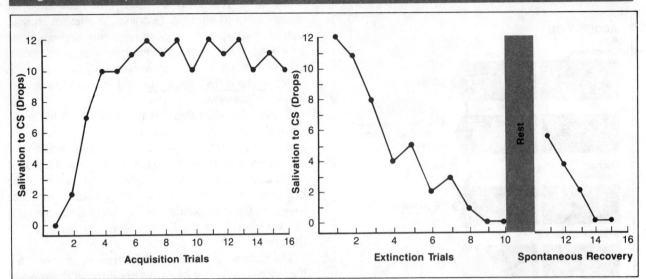

During acquisition, the conditioned stimulus and unconditioned stimulus are paired. A short interstimulus interval and a large number of conditioning trials result in effective acquisition. During extinction, the conditioned stimulus is presented by itself. The more often the conditioned stimulus is presented by itself, the less effective it becomes in producing the conditioned response. A conditioned response may reappear after extinction if the CS is withheld for awhile and then presented later (after Pavlov, 1927).

(US) and became very upset (UR). School then caused anxiety (CR). If you were then given a test in school, the test would become associated with school, and through higher order conditioning also elicit anxiety. Of course there are many ways that test anxiety can develop, such as having people tell you that you will probably fail a test or actually failing a test yourself.

Conditioned Taste Aversion

Do you have a particular type of food that you do not like? Do you know why? For many people, conditioned taste aversion, or CTA, might be due to situations where they become ill (often with the stomach flu) after eating a meal which often contained something new. One example is my "Big Mac attack" which I experienced as a graduate student. I loved Big Macs from McDonald's and often treated myself to them in the evening. One night, I woke up in terrible pain, and eventually found myself in the hospital awaiting surgery for kidney stones. After I recuperated from the operation, I headed for McDonalds, only to find that every time I started to eat a Big Mac, I felt nauseated. I had developed a conditioned taste aversion. The kidney stone was the US, the severe stomach pain was the UR, the hamburger was the CS, and the stomach pain was the CR. Luckily I learned about extinction, and the taste aversion eventually disappeared. But for awhile, the "Big Mac attack" slogan had special meaning for me.

It is currently difficult to look in a journal dealing with animal learning and not find an article on conditioned taste aversion. Many animals, as well as humans, have been quick to learn to avoid particular tastes and odors when the tested substance is followed by stomach distress (Braveman & Bernstein, 1985). Ilene Bernstein reported finding conditioned taste aversion in children with cancer who were undergoing chemotherapy. She believes that studying CTA might help prevent the dangerous loss of appetite experienced by many chemotherapy patients (Bernstein, 1985).

People who use poison to get rid of rats often discover an interesting set of events. Upon introduction, the new poison is extremely effective and kills many rats. However, shortly afterward, the poison seems ineffective because the rats will not eat it. This phenomenon, sometimes called bait shyness, is an example of conditioned taste aversion (Garcia, 1981). Rats are nibblers—they nibble a little of a variety of foods. When a rat nibbles on the poison, it is likely to become very sick. If it survives, it has learned to avoid substances tasting like the poison.

John Garcia and his colleagues tested taste aversion in the laboratory in 1966. They allowed rats to drink sweetened water, and then produced gastrointestinal distress, or a stomachache, by giving them either X-irradiation or a chemical called apomorphine. They found that when given the opportunity a few days later to drink the sweetened water, the rats refused. The X ray or chemical (US) that caused the stomachache (UR) had been associated with the sweetened water (CS), so that it also came to be associated with illness (CR).

Figure 6.8. Conditioned Taste Aversion (CTA)
We encounter CTA when we become ill after eating a particular food. If you enjoyed eating escargots, but later became sick, you would probably dislike the appearance of snails the next time, and would avoid eating them. CTA has likely helped in our survival as well as the survival of other species.

A study that I completed in 1981 shows that conditioned aversion can also be formed in social situations. I paired two gerbils together for five minutes and then had one of them, by injection of lithium chloride, experience a stomachache. When placed together again two days later, the stomachache gerbil appeared to be afraid of the other gerbil. He had learned to avoid another animal because he associated it with the stomachache. This research suggests the possibility of liking or disliking others due to classical conditioning.

Conditioned taste aversion differs from regular classical conditioning in several respects. CTA often occurs in one trial requiring only one pairing of the CS with the US instead of several. The interstimulus interval for CTA can be hours rather than seconds. There is currently a scientific debate going on to determine whether CTA is a unique form of learning or a special case of classical conditioning. At any rate, you should be aware of the possible effects of conditioned taste aversion in your everyday life.

Applications of Classical Conditioning

By this time, you will recognize that classical conditioning plays an important role in our lives. The principles of classical conditioning have been used to help improve the human condition. The applications of classical conditioning in treating behavior problems are discussed in detail in chapter 14, "Therapy," and several examples of therapies involving classical conditioning are provided here.

Mowrer and Mowrer (1938) developed a treatment for enuresis, or bed-wetting. A child with this problem sleeps on a pad into which a wire mesh that is connected to a bell has been sewn. Should the child wet the bed, an electrical circuit is completed causing the bell to ring (US). This in turn awakens the child (UR). After several repetitions of this cycle, in which bed-wetting has caused him to be awakened by the bell, the child begins to associate the sensation of pressure in his bladder (a previously neutral stimulus) with waking up. In a short time, the need to urinate (now a CS) becomes sufficient in itself to awaken the child (now a CR) so he can get up and go to the bathroom.

Classical conditioning has also been used in predation control. Because they like to eat sheep, this natural predatory instinct of coyotes are a problem to sheep farmers. We could kill the coyotes, but since all wild animals need to be protected this approach would probably not be appropriate. Instead, Gustavson and Gustavson (1985) described a study in which they conditioned the coyotes not to eat the sheep. They took sheep meat (CS) and sprinkled it with a chemical (US) that would produce a stomachache (UR) in the coyotes. After the coyotes ate the treated meat, they avoided the live sheep (CR). This humane application of conditioned taste aversion might be used to control other predators as well.

Finally, classical conditioning can be used to help people reduce fears. Counterconditioning involves pairing the stimulus (CS) that elicits fear with a stimulus (US) that elicits positive emotion (UR). For example, a person who is afraid of snakes, but loves chocolate ice cream is shown a snake and then given the ice cream. While the person is busy eating the ice cream, classical conditioning helps associate the snake with good feelings.

Classical conditioning appears to be involved both in the formation and elimination of our emotional reactions. You should try to become more aware of the stimuli in your environment that elicit responses from you. Then put to work the principles of classical conditioning to help you understand how you learn the many emotions you experience.

OPERANT CONDITIONING

About the time Pavlov was experimenting with conditioned reflexes in dogs, an American experimental psychologist, Edward L. Thorndike, was observing trial and error learning in cats. In a typical study, he placed a cat in a small cage and left some food outside, in full view of the hungry cat. At first, the cat moved restlessly about. Then it began clawing at the bars of the cage and at the objects in it. Eventually, when the cat pulled the right string or pushed the right knob, the door of the cage opened, and the cat rushed out and pounced on the food. Thorndike then put the cat back in the cage and let it try again. In each successive trial, the cat took less time to find the right way to get out of the cage (Thorndike, 1911).

The cat had definitely learned something, but classical conditioning did not fit this situation. Pulling and pushing were not reflexes but rather voluntary responses; there was no unconditioned stimulus that automatically elicited them. Thorndike called this form of learning instrumental conditioning, stating that the individual is instrumental in producing a response.

To explain this form of learning, Thorndike proposed his law of effect: Any response that produces satisfaction

in a given situation becomes associated with that situation, and when that situation occurs again, the response is more likely to be repeated. Conversely, a response that brings discomfort in a certain situation will be less likely to occur when the situation arises again (Thorndike, 1932). The law of effect applies to learning responses that affect (or change) the environment, which in turn affects the individual. And it is because these responses make a satisfying difference that they are repeated.

The person who has probably done the most to shape the direction of the form of conditioning called operant conditioning is the well-known behaviorist, B. F. Skinner. He named the behavior that comes to be controlled by its consequences, or effects, *operant behavior* because its function is to operate on the environment. He called the behavior Pavlov studied "respondent behav-

Figure 6.9. Edward L. Thorndike
An early American psychologist who conducted research in the area of instrumental learning, Thorndike proposed the law of effect, which states that a response that produces satisfaction will be repeated.

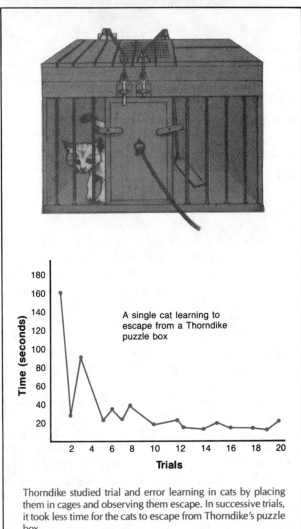

Figure 6.10. Instrumental Conditioning

A single cat learning to escape from a Thorndike puzzle box

Thorndike studied trial and error learning in cats by placing them in cages and observing them escape. In successive trials, it took less time for the cats to escape from Thorndike's puzzle box.

ior," because the reflexes are elicited responses to preceding stimuli. In contrast to the respondent behavior, the operant behavior is first emitted more or less as a random act. This behavior becomes learned, or operantly conditioned, only when it is regularly followed by reinforcement. *Reinforcement* is an event that increases the probability that the behavior which precedes it will be repeated. Reinforcement can generally be thought of as a reward.

Shaping (Successive Approximation)

Assume that you are a psychologist and your task is to get Little Tommy to wear his glasses. Tommy is four years old and does not like his glasses because his sisters laugh at him and call him names when he wears them. How would you help Tommy wear his glasses willingly?

After you are finished with this chapter, here is what you might do. First, ask Tommy's mother not to feed him before bringing him to the session. And make sure that he loves Reese's Pieces. (What little boy doesn't love E.T.'s favorite candy?) Prepare the treatment room by taking everything out except one table in the center. Place the glasses on the table. When Tommy's mother drops him off, tell her to wait in your office, on another floor.

Bring Tommy in and lock the door. He might cry and try to escape. You do nothing. Eventually he looks at you. You run over and give him a Reese's Piece. He cries some more. Nothing. Then he stands up and takes a step toward the table on which his glasses have been placed. One Reese's Piece. He stops and looks around. Nothing. When he takes two steps toward the table, one Reese's Piece. He moves back to the door. Nothing. He takes two steps forward, placing him where he was before. Nothing. Finally he walks over to the table. A Reese's Piece (or maybe two). He stands there. Nothing. Then he reaches out toward the glasses. A Reese's Piece. Then he stands there. Nothing. Eventually, he picks up the glasses and puts them on. Two Reese's Pieces. He may take them off but when he puts them back on he gets a Reese's Piece only if he keeps them on for 10 seconds. Then 30 seconds. Then 1 minute. Then 5 minutes.

When he reaches this point (which might take more than one session), you bring Tommy's mother back and give her the candy. She continues to reinforce him with the candy as long as he wears the glasses. You also arrange for his mother and sisters to say nice things to him and to include him in activities which he finds reinforcing. Eventually, other reinforcers take the place of the candy, and he will continue to wear the glasses because with them he can see better.

Figure 6.11. Shaping (Successive Approximation)
The trainers at Marineland in Rancho Palos Verdes, CA, have succeeded in training a killer whale called Orky to perform tricks by reinforcing the kind of behavior that gradually approximates the desired trick. This is an example of shaping.

You have been using shaping with Tommy. Shaping, or successive approximation, is a gradual process that begins with the reinforcement of some behavior that approximates, or gets closer, to the final behavior desired (Skinner, 1953). When that response has been conditioned, reinforcement is withheld until the subject emits a response just a little closer to the end goal desired. With careful giving and withholding of reinforcements, the subject can gradually be made to perform complex responses that he would never perform in an "uncontrolled" environment.

This technique really works. Many animal trainers regularly make effective use of shaping, as do some sports coaches. As illustrated in this chapter's opening story, Skinner has used shaping techniques in the laboratory, where he got two pigeons to play a form of Ping-Pong. In fact, this basic approach to conditioning is so successful that it has become popular with psychologists in helping people in mental institutions and educational settings.

Can you think of other situations in which shaping might occur? A second-grade teacher helping students write? A friend of yours getting you to go to a movie? An instructor helping students give correct answers on tests? Or a parent helping a child overcome shyness? Shaping is a very common phenomenon in our lives.

Basic Principles of Operant Conditioning

In operant conditioning, it's "what comes afterward that counts." Much of our everyday behavior is based on its effects, as Thorndike pointed out with his law of effect. If we do something and we get rewarded, we will do it again. If we do it often enough, we will form a habit.

Acquisition. Shaping is a very effective way to acquire or learn a behavior through operant conditioning. But we often do not need to shape a behavior. We often discover what gets reinforcement through trial and error learning, as in Thorndike's cats.

Much of the early basic work on operant conditioning was done with <u>mazes</u> and <u>Skinner Boxes</u> (or operant chambers). In maze learning, a subject has to travel through the maze before being reinforced. In Skinner Boxes, we train a subject, most commonly a rat or a pigeon, who finds itself in a box (or a cage) that features a depressible bar (or other manipulative device) and a cup that presents food pellets (or other reinforcers). The Skinner Box was designed by B. F. Skinner to study operant conditioning in animals.

First, the experimenter checks the operant level of the behavior being studied. The *operant level* is the rate at which the subject makes the desired response without getting direct reinforcement from the experimenter. In this instance, the operant level, or *baseline,* is the rate at which the subject depresses the bar without getting food. The experimenter then turns on a mechanism that dis-

penses food into the cup as soon as the subject presses the bar. Typically, the subject will be moving about the Skinner Box more or less randomly. Sooner or later, the subject will probably push down on the bar, immediately receiving a food pellet. Later, the same thing happens again. If the subject has not eaten for some time, it soon begins to press the bar faster and faster until it reaches the maximum rate at which the food pellets may be dispensed. The subject is undergoing operant conditioning. If the subject didn't by chance touch the bar, the experimenter could always use the technique of shaping.

In order for the acquisition of operant conditioning to occur, the subject must be motivated to want whatever is used as *reinforcement.* If reinforcement is food, then the subject should be hungry. It is important that reinforcement follows the response because the response then occurs more frequently. We discuss the concept of reinforcement more fully later in this chapter.

Extinction. In operant conditioning, extinction is the withholding of reinforcement. As we discussed earlier in classical conditioning, when there is no reinforcement (the US in classical conditioning), the frequency of the behavior decreases and often eventually disappears altogether. For example, when a rat operantly conditioned in a Skinner Box is in extinction, at first its behavior may become more variable and more frequent. Fairly soon, however, the rat depresses the

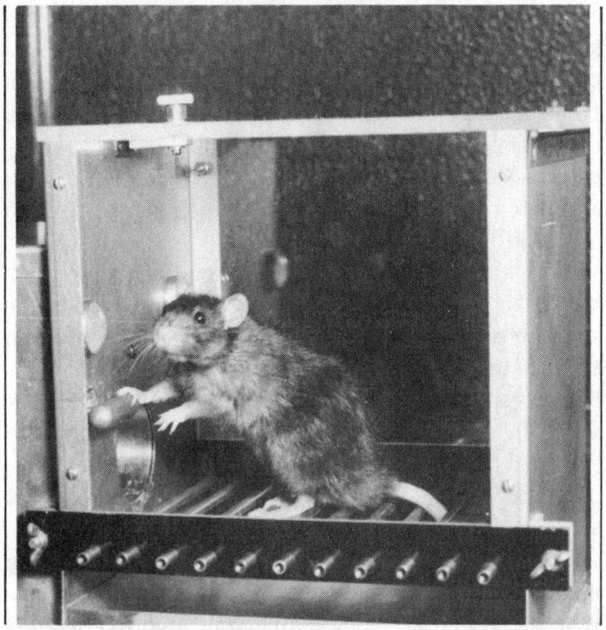

Figure 6.12. Reinforcement: The Skinner Box
Reinforcement is used to teach a rat to press a bar by rising on his hind legs and bending forward. This is accomplished by strengthening the animal's natural behavior each time he comes close to the bar.

Figure 6.13. Stimulus Discrimination
Behavioral psychologist B. F. Skinner has observed that a pigeon can learn to distinguish between stimuli (red disk and orange disk) in order to receive reinforcement (food).

lever less and less, and eventually no longer shows the bar-pressing behavior.

What do you do when you do not receive reinforcement for your behavior? What if you studied hard for your tests, but continually failed them? Or you worked all week and then found there was no paycheck? Chances are good that you would stop studying or stop working (at least at that job).

There are many factors involved in the extinction rate. The stronger the original learning, the longer you will continue to respond. As we discuss later in the chapter, the number of reinforcements, the delay of reinforcement, and the schedule of reinforcement are all important factors. You might even create some internal reinforcement when the observable reinforcement is absent. For example, you could tell yourself you really enjoy working, and do it just for fun. Sooner or later, however, you will decrease your response rate when your behavior is no longer followed by reinforcement.

Spontaneous Recovery. Spontaneous recovery, the occurrence of behavior that had been extinguished, can appear after a rest period. Rats that have been on extinction in Skinner Boxes will begin to press the lever again when placed back in the Skinner Box after a rest period. Likewise, after a break, you might be ready to try hard again in your studies the next semester.

Generalization and Discrimination. Many fathers have found, to their dismay, that when their young children learn to say "daddy," they begin to call all men by that name. Individuals tend to emit similar responses to stimuli that are similar to ones that have in the past led to reinforcement. This is stimulus generalization. If we find that we enjoy a particular kind of food, chances are very good that we will go to all of the restaurants that specialize in serving it.

The child who calls the man next door, as well as the mailman, "daddy" soon learns that the name applies only to one man. Through the process of stimulus discrimination, the parents selectively reinforce the child only when he calls the father "daddy." Likewise, if we find that one hamburger restaurant is consistently better than another, we will begin to eat there exclusively.

Generalization and discrimination also occur when a pigeon is in a Skinner Box. A pigeon who has learned to peck at an illuminated red disk (with food as a reinforcer) will continue to peck at the disk, although at a lower rate, when the color of the disk is changed from red to orange. If, however, the pigeon receives no food after pecking at the disk while it is orange, its pecking at it will soon extinguish. If, when the disk turns red, it begins pecking again, it shows stimulus discrimination.

BIOGRAPHICAL ☆ HIGHLIGHT ☆

B. F. SKINNER

Burrhus Frederic Skinner is probably the most famous, influential, and controversial figure in contemporary American psychology. He was born in the small railroad town of Susquehanna, Pennsylvania, in March 1904. After graduating from Hamilton College in 1926 with a degree in English, he tried writing, but eventually gave it up, because he felt he had nothing important to say. He became interested in psychology and earned his Ph.D. from Harvard University in 1931.

He taught for several years at the University of Minnesota and Indiana University. During this time he wrote two of his most important books, *The Behavior of Organisms* (1938) and a novel, *Walden Two* (1948), the latter of which is an account of a utopian society run in accordance with operant principles. Skinner returned to Harvard in 1948, where he has since remained.

B. F. Skinner has made numerous contributions to the science of behavior. He has strongly influenced the area of learning that he named operant conditioning. His Skinner Box is now a standard apparatus for the experimental study of animal behavior. Much of his work involved the study of how reinforcement schedules influence learning and behavior. His *Beyond Freedom and Dignity* (1971) is a nonfiction examination of his utopian society, in which he explains why we must understand how we control behavior in everyday life. In his 1987 book, *Upon Further Reflection*, Skinner presents his views on issues ranging from world peace and evolution to education and old age.

Reinforcement

Reinforcement is any event that increases the probability that the behavior that precedes it will be repeated. If a behavior is immediately reinforced, we will show the behavior again. Food is a reinforcer when we are hungry. Water is a reinforcer when we are thirsty. Money, praise, and attention can all serve as reinforcers in the right circumstances. Reinforcement is most effective if it is given immediately after a behavior. If it is delayed, its power is diminished.

Schedules of Reinforcement. Continuous reinforcement, in which every correct response is reinforced, quickly produces a high rate of responding. However, continuous reinforcement provides little resistance to extinction. When the rat, for example, no longer gets any food pellets, the rate and number of bar presses fall off rather quickly. Resistance to extinction is the most common measure of the "strength" of a conditioned operant response.

When resistance to extinction is the measure of response strength, one would think that the more times the response has been reinforced, the greater the number of responses after reinforcement is discontinued. But an operant response can be made even stronger if it is not always reinforced during conditioning. This partial reinforcement produces a response that takes longer to extinguish than continuous reinforcement does and is

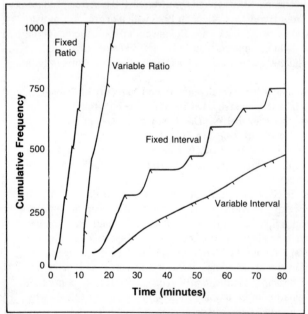

Figure 6.14. Schedules of Reinforcement

These are typical rates of pigeons responding under different partial reinforcement schedules. "Ratio" refers to number of responses before reinforcement occurs; "interval" refers to time periods before reinforcement occurs. Short diagonal lines indicate occurrence of reinforcement (after Skinner, 1961).

called the partial reinforcement extinction effect. Flaherty (1985) argued that the partial reinforcement extinction effect is important in nature since it motivates animals to continue to seek goals even when they have experienced several unsuccessful attempts. Recent research (Pittenger & Pavlik, 1988) has also found the partial reinforcement extinction effect in humans. Who will go on spending dimes longer, the person operating a slot machine which reinforces him or her only occasionally, or the person operating an out-of-order pay phone, which has previously always provided reinforcement?

You might think of schedules of reinforcement as being on a continuum. On one end is continuous reinforcement, where reinforcement is given after every response. At the other end is extinction, where no reinforcement is given. In between is intermittent, or partial reinforcement, where reinforcement is given after some of the responses. Partial reinforcement schedules are based on two properties: the time interval between reinforced responses, and the ratio of unreinforced responses to reinforced responses. Ferster and Skinner (1957) describe the four basic partial reinforcement schedules: fixed interval, variable interval, fixed ratio, and variable ratio.

In the fixed interval (FI) schedule the subject receives reinforcement for the first response shown after a given time interval (Ferster & Skinner, 1957). For example, in a FI two-minute schedule, the subject is reinforced once every two minutes. After a reinforcement is given, no further responses are reinforced until the two minutes have elapsed. Then the next response is reinforced. The fixed interval schedule is probably the most common everyday form of reinforcement. For instance, people work hard to receive a weekly paycheck. Students study to receive a test grade at the end of the semester. And children are "good" all week to receive their allowance.

In a fixed interval schedule, the subject tends to rest immediately after a reinforcement and then increases frequency of responding just before the next reinforcement occurs. Think about your study behavior. Chances are good that right after an exam you relax awhile, and then increase your study activity as the time for the next exam draws near. If you made a graph of the behavior, you would see that the fixed interval schedule results in a characteristic scalloping effect in a cumulative response curve.

In the variable interval (VI) schedule, the subject is reinforced for the first response given after a particular time interval, which is changed for each trial (Ferster & Skinner, 1957). One trial may have a two-minute interval, the next a four-minute interval, and the third a one-minute interval. There is an overall average time interval, but each trial is different.

An example of the variable interval schedule might be

an instructor who gives unannounced quizzes. At the beginning of the semester, the students are told that there will be six quizzes, on the average of one every three weeks, but that they can be given at any time. What would your study pattern be under these circumstances? You would probably study at a fairly steady pace throughout the semester. Another example of the VI schedule is calling someone on the telephone. Success in reaching your friend is dependent upon an interval of time that varies from one incident to the next. The variable interval schedule produces steady responding, but sometimes at a fairly low rate.

In the fixed ratio (FR) schedule, a certain number of responses must be made before reinforcement is given (Ferster & Skinner, 1957). For instance, reinforcement might be given after every three responses. A good example in industry is piecework, where the worker must produce a certain number of items for a certain amount of money. FR results in a fairly high rate of continuous responding. There is just a little scallop effect between reinforcements. If you know the instructor only calls on you after you have raised your hand 10

times, you will pause immediately after being called on, and begin to increase hand raising as you approach the next reinforcement.

The fourth partial reinforcement schedule is the variable ratio (VR) schedule. Here the number of responses required for reinforcement to occur varies. There is an overall average, but for each trial, the number changes. An example of variable reinforcement is the slot machine used in gambling establishments. The machine provides reinforcement, but you can never tell when it will occur. Thus, your response rate is steady and high, with no scalloping effect on a cumulative response curve. Other examples are the salesperson who continues to work hard because he or she never knows when the next reinforcing customer will come along, or the person who buys a lottery ticket each week in the hopes of hitting it big someday.

Primary and Secondary Reinforcement. Psychologists distinguish between primary and secondary reinforcement. Primary reinforcement is effective without having been associated with other reinforcers. Food is a primary reinforcer for a hungry person. Water is a primary reinforcer for a thirsty person. Food and water satisfy basic physiological needs and serve as reinforcers without being paired with other reinforcers.

Secondary reinforcement is effective only after it has been associated with a primary reinforcer. For instance, what can you do with money? It's dirty, often smells, and is sometimes difficult to carry around. Why is it

Figure 6.15. Example of Variable Ratio Schedule of Reinforcement
A slot machine provides reinforcement, but the gambler can never be sure whether the next bet will pay off. This results in a high rate of response.

Figure 6.16. Reinforcement in Everyday Life

Reinforcement		
	Primary	**Secondary**
Usually Positive	Food	Money
	Water	Tokens
	Sex	Esteem
	Sleep	Grades
	Sensory stimulation	Status
		Approval
Usually Negative	Shock	Low esteem
	Pain	Ridicule
	Extreme temperatures	Exclusion
	Loud noise	Violation of personal space
	Physical pressure	

There are many types of reinforcement in everyday life. Primary reinforcers are effective without having been associated with other reinforcers. Secondary reinforcers are effective only when associated with primary reinforcers. Positive reinforcers strengthen a response when they are presented. Negative reinforcers strengthen the behaviors that caused them to be removed.

reinforcing to find a twenty-dollar bill? Obviously, it is valuable to you because it is associated with other reinforcers, such as food. Money is a secondary reinforcer.

We learn about secondary reinforcers through the process of classical conditioning. Would you work hard for a poker chip? Studies have shown that chimpanzees, children, and adults will all work for poker chip tokens, if the tokens can later be cashed in for food or other objects of value. Higher order conditioning may take place when the token (a conditioned reinforcer) is traded for money, which is traded for a gift coupon, which is traded for a hamburger. Other examples of conditioned secondary reinforcers include praise and attention.

Positive and Negative Reinforcement. As we learned earlier, Thorndike's law of effect states that any response that produces satisfaction in a given situation becomes associated with that situation, and when that situation occurs again, the response is more likely to be repeated. Reinforcement can thus be thought of as something satisfying or pleasant to the individual that causes the individual to repeat the behavior that preceded the reinforcement. The discussion so far has concentrated primarily on positive reinforcement such as food, which, when presented, strengthens the response it follows. But much of our behavior is controlled by negative reinforcement, which, when removed, strengthens the behavior (Skinner, 1953). Have you ever had a stone in your shoe? When you removed it, the feeling of relief is negative reinforcement. Escaping from a hot, crowded room, removing a splinter from your finger, and running away from someone who is yelling at you are all examples of negative reinforcement.

Many students have difficulty distinguishing between these two terms. Remember that reinforcement always increases the likelihood that the behavior will occur again. Think of positive as presenting and negative as removing. Then, essentially, as far as the individual is concerned, positive reinforcement means he or she is presented something pleasant that increases a response, and negative reinforcement means something unpleasant is removed and that also increases a response. Although somewhat simplistic, this will help you differentiate the two terms in a given situation. Both types of reinforcement lead to an increase in behavior.

Figure 6.17. Reinforcement and Punishment

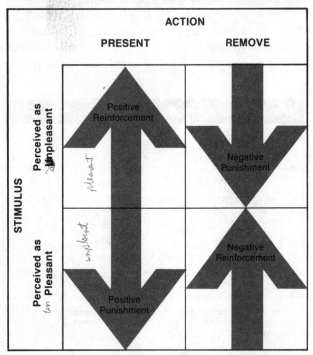

The impact of an event depends upon whether it is presented or removed after a response is made, and whether the subject perceives it as pleasant or unpleasant. Any event that increases responding is called reinforcement and any event that decreases responding is called punishment; any event that is presented is called positive and any event that is removed is called negative. Each square defines one possibility: Arrows pointing upward indicate that responding is increased; arrows pointing downward indicate that responding is decreased. For example, if a subject perceives an event that is presented as pleasant, the subject's rate of responding is likely to increase, and we say that positive reinforcement has occurred.

Aversive Conditioning

Negative reinforcement occurs when a response leads to escape or avoidance of stimuli that are aversive—annoying, unpleasant, uncomfortable, or painful to the individual. Psychologists studying aversive control of behavior have used mainly two types of procedures: escape conditioning and avoidance conditioning.

Escape Conditioning. In escape conditioning the subject is presented with an aversive stimulus from which he or she must learn to escape. If a particularly traumatic scene appears during a movie someone is watching, he or she might escape (at least visually) by closing his or her eyes. Likewise, if someone gets into a scalding shower, he or she is most likely to escape as quickly as possible so as not to get burned.

In the laboratory, psychologists sometimes use mild electric shocks to condition a subject. A rat learns very quickly to escape from an electrified floor by running up a pole to a safe platform. Leeming and Little (1977) studied escape conditioning in houseflies. The experimenters placed the houseflies in a tube that was divided into two sections. One section was lighted and hot, while the other was dark and cool. The houseflies quickly learned to escape from the hot section to the cool section.

Avoidance Conditioning. In avoidance conditioning the subject learns to avoid an unpleasant stimulus by

Figure 6.18. Aversive Conditioning
Behavior can be modified by aversive stimuli. To make smoking unenjoyable this therapist gives a slight electric shock to the smoker each time he takes a puff from his cigarette. The smoker can see in the mirror opposite how his hand shakes at each shock. He has also been surrounded by cigarette butts and the smell of tobacco that add to his unpleasant experience.

responding appropriately before it begins. Perhaps we have had very poor service in a particular restaurant and thus avoid that establishment thereafter. We learn to avoid getting traffic tickets by following established rules of the road and being harmed by locking our cars in high crime areas.

In a classic laboratory experiment, a dog was placed in a cage made up of two compartments separated by a small hurdle. A light came on and a few seconds later the dog was shocked. The dog needed very little training to learn that it could avoid the shock by jumping the hurdle into the other compartment just after the light came on and before the shock began (Solomon & Wynne, 1953). Once learned, avoidance behavior is very persistent; when the warning stimulus occurs, the avoidance behavior is likely to be repeated.

What happens if an animal cannot escape or avoid an aversive stimulus? Seligman and Meier (1967) conducted a study similar to Solomon's, except that the dogs were restrained and could not escape the shock. After a few shocks, the dogs gave up even trying to escape. Learned helplessness is a phenomenon observed in humans as well as animals. Its possible relationship to depression is discussed in chapter 12, "Stress and Adjustment."

Punishment

Punishment decreases the likelihood that the behavior preceding it will be repeated. It is, in many ways, the opposite of reinforcement. Although not always called positive and negative punishment, you can think of punishment in these two distinct forms. You can present something unpleasant (positive punishment) or you can remove something pleasant (negative punishment). Skinner (1953) described punishment as either presenting a negative reinforcer or withdrawing a positive reinforcer. In either case, if the preceding behavior decreases, this is defined as punishment (Skinner, 1988).

The presentation of something aversive or unpleasant after a behavior will lead to a decrease in the behavior. Scolding a child, assessing a fine, and shocking a rat are examples of positive punishment. The removal of something pleasant after a behavior will usually also lead to a decrease in the behavior. Taking away a teenager's car

Figure 6.19. Punishment
Prison as a form of punishment is meant to decrease undesired behavior, but the overcrowded and sometimes inhuman conditions of prison life can have negative effects. The resentment inmates may have for unusually bad prison conditions may increase, rather than decrease undesired behavior.

keys, withholding visiting privileges, and keeping a child inside school during recess are examples of what is meant by negative punishment. Often, when people speak of punishment, they are referring to positive punishment.

The effectiveness of punishment varies widely, and is often dependent upon the characteristics of its presentation (Schwartz, 1984). In particular, proximity, consistency, and intensity are important variables. Proximity is the closeness of the aversive stimulus to the punished behavior. The closer the punishment follows the behavior, the more effective it is. For example, let's assume you want to housebreak your new puppy. Unless you

catch it in the act, you will not be very effective. If, after leaving it alone all afternoon, you arrive home to discover an accident, scolding will most likely have the effect of teaching it to run away from you when you open the door.

Consistency means always following the behavior with punishment. Intensity refers to the strength of the punishment. Other things being equal, usually more consistent and intense punishment results in a more effective reduction in the undesired behavior.

Punishment might have undesirable side effects. Azarin (1959) has shown that aggression is often produced by intense punishment. There are ethical considerations

Computers and Programmed Learning

Operant conditioning has been used in developing programmed learning. According to B. F. Skinner (1958), the purpose of programmed learning is to manage human learning under controlled conditions. Typically, a textbook or machine presents the material to be learned in a series of very small steps, called frames. Each frame contains some information and a statement with a blank that the student fills in. The student then uncovers the correct answer (by moving a paper down the page) before going on to the next frame. Each frame introduces a new idea or reviews material covered earlier. The agreement between the uncovered answer and the student's own response reinforces correct responses, making it likely that they will occur again. Moreover, shaping is employed, in that the frames start from the student's initial knowledge and in small steps proceed to the final knowledge. The student is therefore usually correct and continues to be reinforced, which keeps him at the task until completion.

The principles of programmed learning have been incorporated into a method of instruction that is usually called Personalized System of Instruction (PSI). PSI is a self-paced instruction format where each student works his or her way through the course material, which is broken down into small steps. Each student must "master" the material in one unit through a quiz before moving on to the next unit. Because of active student participation, small steps, immediate feedback, and reinforcement, PSI can be very effective (Reiser, 1984; Gage & Berliner, 1988).

Currently the principles of programmed learning are being applied to a form of education called computer assisted instruction (CAI). The computer can be used to present learning material and help students learn through a variety of techniques such as multiple-choice quizzes, fill-in-the-blank, simulations, and personality tests (Pettijohn, 1985).

The advantages of the computer are that it can be continuously available, provide immediate feedback,

Figure 6.20. Computer Assisted Instruction
The principles of operant conditioning and programmed learning are currently being applied to the educational technique of computer assisted instruction. The computer is used to present learning material and then test the student's knowledge. Studies show this procedure to be effective in helping a student learn.

and allow students flexibility in studying and testing (Quintanar, Crowell, & Pryor, 1982). With the advent of microcomputers such as the Apple and IBM PC, programmed learning is becoming an attractive way to implement in the classroom some of the basic principles of operant conditioning (Kulik, Kulik, & Gangert-Drowns, 1985).

THOUGHT QUESTIONS

1. How can programmed instruction improve education? Can it be utilized at different levels of education?
2. How could programmed instruction be utilized outside the classroom to help people learn more efficiently?
3. Will the computer replace the teacher? Why or why not?

in the use of some punishers such as imprisonment or electrocution for certain crimes. Anthony Burgess suggested in his 1963 novel, *A Clockwork Orange*, that violence and crime might effectively be controlled if a society is willing to accept the side effects, including resentment, hate, and the tendency to aggress.

There is an ongoing debate on the use of punishment to control behavior (Landers, 1988). Some clinical psychologists support the use of aversive stimuli such as electric shock to treat severely mentally retarded or autistic individuals who do not effectively communicate with others. Recently an electric shock device called the Self-Injurious Behavior Inhibiting System was introduced to help parents and clinicians reduce head banging behavior in autistic children. On the other hand, some states have banned the use of aversive stimuli in therapy. B. F. Skinner released a statement in which he argued that brief and harmless stimuli that suppressed self-destructive behavior in autistic children might be justified. However, Skinner and others urge the exploration for nonpunitive alternatives such as reinforcement.

It is important to note that reinforcement and punishment are defined by their consequences. If it increases behavior, it is reinforcement; if it decreases behavior, it is punishment. As an illustration, imagine that there is a disruptive student in a classroom. The instructor constantly yells at the student. Is this reinforcement or punishment? If the student quiets down, it is punishment. But if the student increases the disruptive behavior, it is reinforcement. Perhaps the student feels ignored, and this is the only way to get noticed. Regardless of the motivation of the student, it is the consequence of events that defines the procedure either as reinforcement or punishment.

Applications of Operant Conditioning

Operant conditioning has become a very influential area of psychology, because it has successfully provided practical solutions to many problems in human behavior. Operant principles discovered in the laboratory are now being employed to improve teaching techniques so that even slow or unmotivated students can learn faster and better. Behavior modification is the application of operant conditioning techniques to modify behavior. It is being used to help people with a wide variety of everyday behavior problems, including obesity, smoking, alcoholism, delinquency, and aggression. For example, people with the eating disorder, anorexia nervosa, have been helped to gain weight and animals such as primates have been trained to assist handicapped individuals by feeding and caring for them. It has been successfully used in child rearing, in school systems and in mental institutions.

Some therapeutic uses of behavior modification are explained in detail in chapter 14, "Therapy," such as the token economy method of behavior modification, a

Figure 6.21. Behavior Modification
Operant conditioning techniques are often used to modify behavior in school learning, child rearing, or animal training. One of the most frequent techniques is to give the subject reinforcement after a desired response has been given.

study with psychiatric patients in a mental hospital who had difficulty performing expected behaviors (Ayllon & Azrin, 1968). The researchers chose a number of simple grooming behaviors, including face washing, hair combing, teeth brushing, bed making, and dressing properly. The researchers first recorded baseline, or normally occurring frequencies of the behaviors. Then they gave the patients a token every time the proper behavior was performed. The tokens could be exchanged for food and personal items at the hospital drugstore. The patients significantly increased their frequency of the desired behaviors when they were reinforced with tokens.

Another practical application of reinforcement was suggested by David Premack in 1965. The Premack Principle states that of any two responses, the one that is more likely to occur can be used to reinforce the response that is less likely to occur. People prefer doing certain things more than others. For example, a child might prefer to play outside rather than practice the piano. A parent could then use the playing response to reinforce (and increase) the occurrence of piano practice by promising more play time only after practice was finished. Likewise, a child is more likely to watch television than perform household chores. Thus television watching could be used to reinforce doing chores. If a student likes going to the movies more than studying, he or she could use going to the movies as a reinforcer to increase study behavior. Or if someone enjoyed talking on the telephone more than reading a book, he or she could use telephone conversation as a reinforcer for reading. The Premack Principle is used regularly by many people, even if they are not aware of it.

It has even been suggested that the principles of operant conditioning can be used efficiently to control a society. B. F. Skinner, in his 1948 novel, *Walden Two*, presented a utopian society guided by operant conditioning principles. His 1971 book, *Beyond Freedom and Dignity*, caused a controversy by presenting his ideas on how operant conditioning could be utilized in an actual society. Although most people are not willing to accept Skinner's utopian ideal, the principles of operant conditioning are being applied in our everyday lives.

Comparison of Classical and Operant Conditioning

Classical and operant conditioning share many of the same basic principles and procedures. For example, Kimble (1961) has pointed out that the basic principles of acquisition, extinction, spontaneous recovery, and stimulus generalization are common to both types of learning.

There are several differences, however, between classical and operant conditioning (Houston, 1986). While a basic feature of operant conditioning is reinforcement, classical conditioning relies more on association between stimuli and responses. A second distinction is that much of operant conditioning is based on voluntary behavior, while classical conditioning often involves involuntary reflexive behavior.

Klein (1987) pointed out that these distinctions are not as strong as they once were believed to be. For example, Neal Miller (1978) has demonstrated that involuntary responses, such as heart rate, can be modified through operant conditioning techniques. It now appears that classical conditioning does involve reinforcement. And many classical conditioning situations also involve operant behavior. For example, let's assume that Tina was conditioned to fear rats like Little Albert. She would first learn to associate the rat with the loud noise through classical conditioning. Then presentation of the rat would produce a fear reaction and Tina would learn to escape from the aversive stimulus through operant conditioning (negative reinforcement). This is sometimes called the two-factor theory of avoidance conditioning (Mowrer & Lamoreauz, 1942).

Perhaps the best distinctions are the particular procedures developed by the psychologists in each area. Current approaches to learning emphasize the general phenomenon of learning, rather than the uniqueness of each approach.

COGNITIVE LEARNING

Classical and operant conditioning are both examples of association learning. Another type of learning relies more on cognitive processes. Cognitive learning proposes that the learner utilizes mental structures and memory to make decisions about behaviors. The types of cognitive learning include insight, latent learning, and observational learning.

Insight

Learning by insight is one type of cognitive learning, as we discuss in chapter 8, "Language and Intelligence." In a classic 1927 experiment, Gestalt psychologist Wolfgang Köhler observed a chimpanzee trying to reach a bunch of bananas hung just out of reach. The animal jumped at the bananas several times, but soon stopped and looked around the cage. Then after a minute or so, the chimpanzee stacked a couple of boxes together, climbed up and easily reached the bananas.

Köhler called this an example of insight or sudden

Figure 6.22 Insight Learning
With no clues to a solution, the chimpanzee must decide how to reach the bananas. Through insight he solves the problem by stacking the boxes to reach the food.

perception of the relationship of the cognitive elements necessary to solve a problem. In this situation, there was no gradual shaping of the response with reinforcement. Köhler argued that cognitive processes allowed the animal to learn the solution to the problem without having to try alternatives through a trial-and-error approach.

Recently Epstein and colleagues (1984) replicated Köhler's banana problem with pigeons. Because moving boxes and eating bananas were not usual behaviors for pigeons, the researchers, by using a food reward, first trained the birds to push a box and then to jump on it and peck at a picture of a banana. What happened when the pigeons were placed in a new cage with a box and a banana hung too high to reach? Like Köhler's chim-

panzees, the pigeons found that they couldn't reach the banana from the box in its original location. They waited awhile, and then solved the problem by pushing the box to a new location under the banana. The researchers argued that the pigeons showed insight when solving the problem.

Latent Learning and Cognitive Maps

Cognitive factors are also central to latent learning. Latent learning occurs when an individual acquires knowledge of something but does not show it until motivated to do so. Edward Tolman, in his 1932 book, *Purposive Behavior in Animals and Men*, suggested that purpose was important for learning. He argued that understanding was the key to learning and reinforcement was only necessary to motivate an individual to perform the behavior that was learned.

In one experiment (Tolman & Honzik, 1930), three groups of rats were run through a complex maze on 17 consecutive days. One group never received food reinforcement upon reaching the end of the maze and performed poorly throughout the experiment. The second group always received reinforcement and continued to improve (chose fewer blind alleys) throughout the study. The third group did not receive reinforcement for the first 10 days, but were always reinforced the last 7 days of the experiment. This group did poorly the first 10 days, but as soon as they began to receive reinforcement, they did as well as the group that was always reinforced. Tolman argued that this third group had

Figure 6.23. Cognitive Maps

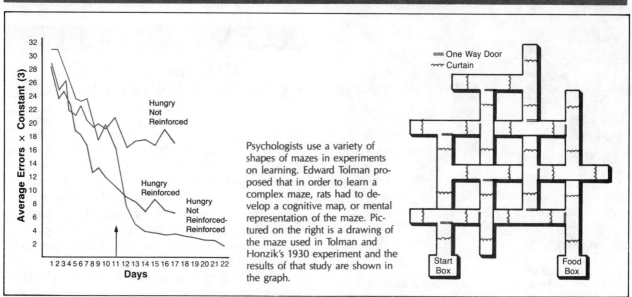

Psychologists use a variety of shapes of mazes in experiments on learning. Edward Tolman proposed that in order to learn a complex maze, rats had to develop a cognitive map, or mental representation of the maze. Pictured on the right is a drawing of the maze used in Tolman and Honzik's 1930 experiment and the results of that study are shown in the graph.

learned the maze, but had not shown it until motivated. They showed latent learning.

Tolman (1948) suggested that the rats had developed a cognitive map or mental representation of the maze. Cognitive maps help us learn in a goal-oriented way. For example, if you were driving somewhere and the road was closed, you could rely on your cognitive map of the streets to help you decide on an alternate route. A cognitive map is similar to the concept of scheme used by Piaget in his theory of cognitive development (see chapter 3, "Development").

Observational Learning

Another form of cognitive learning is observational learning. Social psychologist Albert Bandura (1977) argued that reinforcement is important in learning. But like Tolman, Bandura held that reinforcement is largely involved in motivation rather than the learning process itself. This approach is currently called *social learning theory*.

One of the best-known studies by Bandura is the 1961 experiment in which he and his colleagues looked at the influence of observational learning on aggression in children. As described in chapter 10, "Emotion," nursery school children observed adults interacting either passively or aggressively with an inflated life-size doll. The children were able to imitate the adult role model of aggressive behavior, especially when the behavior was

reinforced. While not absolutely conclusive, a number of research studies have shown that when children observe violence in television shows, they behave more aggressively. But when nonaggressive role models are available, children can easily learn to behave in socially cooperative ways (Gelfand & Hartmann, 1980).

Bandura (1986) suggested that many kinds of behavior are learned through observation. Children often acquire appropriate behaviors and gender roles such as dressing up like mommy, shaving like daddy, or cooking through observation and imitation of their parents. Often the behaviors are neither reinforced nor explained to the children but parents serve as models whom their children observe and from whom they learn.

In order for observational learning to be effective, four steps must occur (Bandura, 1977). First, we must pay attention to the role model. We tend to do this most often when we are motivated and believe the behavior has some relevance to us. This might help to explain why students sometimes have difficulty learning academic course concepts but can readily learn sports activities or memorize the latest popular songs. Second, we must store our observations in our memory system. Third, we must be able to remember what we have learned when we are motivated to behave in the appropriate fashion. And fourth, our behavior must be reinforced if we expect to repeat it with any regularity.

Cognitive learning is involved in many day-to-day situations. We use insight to solve problems and utilize what we have observed to make decisions about our behaviors. We discuss the role of cognitive learning in a variety of applications throughout the textbook, including the areas of problem solving and thinking (chapter 8), motivation (chapter 9), personality (chapter 11), and social behavior (chapter 15).

Figure 6.24. Imitation
Children learn behavior patterns through imitating adults. Here we see a young girl striking a pose similar to that of her instructor.

THE BIOLOGICAL CONSTRAINTS ON LEARNING

There is no doubt that conditioning plays a role in teaching both humans and animals various forms of behavior. The manipulation of stimuli, responses, and reinforcements influences learning in natural settings and experimental environments alike. This is why whales and porpoises can be made to perform so beautifully in oceanarium shows, why even people with severe mental handicaps can learn to function fairly normally, and why computer-assisted instruction has proven so effective in school classrooms. Do these successes of learning theory mean that conditioning can be used to train any animal (or person) to perform any behavior? Although some learning theorists have argued exactly this, recent evidence indicates that there are biological limits on what an individual can learn.

Instinctive Drift. Instinctive drift, the process in which conditioned behavior moves toward more instinctual behavior, is an example of the biological limits on learning. For instance, Keller and Marion Breland (1961) easily trained a raccoon to pick up coins and deposit them in a container in order to get a food reward. But the animal soon began holding on to the coins and eventually just rubbed and handled them instead of depositing them. Although the raccoon had been successfully conditioned, there appeared to be a limitation on the strength and lasting power of the learning process. Raccoons have a strong natural instinct to handle and wash their food before eating. This instinctual "washing" behavior proved to be stronger than the operantly conditioned action of placing the coin in the container. The concept of instinct is described in more detail in chapter 11, "Motivation," where we also discuss the related subjects of species-specific behavior and ethology.

Imprinting. Instinctive influences on learning have forced psychologists to take a close look at how biology prepares the individual for learning during development. Newborn ducklings, and some other animals, learn to follow their mothers—or any moving object—11 to 18 hours after hatching (Hess, 1959). This form of early learning in a *critical period* is called imprinting. A critical period is a brief time during which an individual is very sensitive to changes in the environment and will be greatly influenced by it. And if certain learning that normally takes place in that period does not occur, the individual can have a hard time learning it later. After being imprinted, the ducks will continue to follow the imprinted object in the future. Some of the most influential work on imprinting has been conducted by the Nobel Prize recipient, Konrad Lorenz. Among his most memorable studies was one in 1937 in which he allowed goslings to imprint on him instead of the mother goose— and they followed him around wherever he went.

Imprinting is highly adaptive for the species. The babies need to stay close to the mother for protection, and to learn species identification. Psychologists are not sure whether imprinting takes place as part of the attachment process in humans. At any rate, imprinting is a good example of how heredity influences learning and behavior.

Continuum of Preparedness. Martin Seligman (1970) has proposed a continuum of preparedness in learning which helps place the biological constraints on learning in perspective. According to Seligman, animals are biologically prepared to associate some stimuli and responses more readily than others. At one end of his

Figure 6.25. Imprinting
This is a form of learning in which very young animals learn to follow their mothers. Most imprinting occurs in birds, and takes place within 18 hours of hatching. Ethologist Konrad Lorenz demonstrated that young geese will imprint on any moving stimulus by acting as the stimulus himself. These geese preferred Lorenz to their natural mother even at a later time.

continuum is *prepared learning*, such as conditioned taste aversion, where the association is formed after one pairing. In the middle is *unprepared learning*, where the subject can learn but only after a number of trials. Examples might include rats pressing a lever in a Skinner Box, or people learning to spell words. At the other end of the continuum is *contraprepared learning*, where the subject cannot learn, or does so only after many trials. An example would be teaching a dog to yawn for food.

The concept of preparedness can help explain some of the research findings in the field of emotion. Seligman reported in 1972 that fears in people usually involve animals or danger, which could be due to our evolutionary past, when it was important for *Homo sapiens* to learn to escape or avoid dangerous predators. Earlier, we discussed the study of Little Albert quickly learning to fear a rat. Another study done a few years later (Bregman, 1934) found that, although it was easy to get children to fear animals through classical conditioning, it was impossible to get them to fear inanimate objects.

Earlier we discussed conditioned taste aversion, and showed how quickly the subjects were able to associate taste with stomachache. A 1966 study by Garcia and Koelling demonstrates the importance of the animal's preparedness in determining whether learning successfully occurs. The researchers compared the ease with which rats could associate internal (taste) and external (noise and light) stimuli with internal (poison-induced stomachache) and external (electric shock-induced pain) consequences. Rats first drank salty water in the presence of clicking noises and flashing lights (each lick produced a click and a flash of light). Half of the subjects drank water with lithium chloride (a salt that produced a stomachache) whereas the rest received an electric shock. Later, half of each group was given pure water in the presence of noise and lights, while the other half received water flavored with sodium chloride, a harmless salt in quiet surroundings. Rats that had been poisoned significantly preferred the pure water with clicks and lights. However rats that had been shocked drank significantly more of the salty water when in quiet conditions. Thus, some animals are more prepared to associate certain stimuli and responses than others.

Psychologists are discovering that before they plan an experiment the biological constraints on learning must be considered. Both the species being studied and the particular responses and reinforcers used must be carefully matched to increase the likelihood of success. By studying the biological constraints on learning, psychologists understand better the complex process of learning. ▪

By now, you should be aware of the importance of learning in your life. The techniques of operant and classical conditioning can be used in a variety of ways from training pigeons to playing ping-pong, to modifying human behaviors. Everything you do and think involves learning in some way. Because learning is basic to our individual behaviors, we refer to the principles and applications of learning throughout the rest of the text. We next turn to the topic of memory, the process of storing what we learn for later use.

"PERHAPS, DR. PAVLOV, HE COULD BE TAUGHT TO SEAL ENVELOPES."

CHAPTER REVIEW
What You've Learned About Learning

1. Learning is the relatively permanent change in behavior or behavioral potential of an individual that occurs as a result of experience. The actual behavior that is observed is called performance, whereas learning is inferred from the behavior.

2. In classical conditioning, described by Ivan Pavlov, the unconditioned stimulus (US) is a stimulus that provokes an automatic response, the unconditioned response (UR). If the US is repeatedly presented following a neutral stimulus, the neutral stimulus

becomes the conditioned stimulus (CS), and gains sufficient power alone to provoke the conditioned response (CR). The CS comes first, and takes on the properties of the US.

3. When the conditioned stimulus is presented by itself, after a while the conditioned response is extinguished. If the subject is given a rest during extinction, he will show spontaneous recovery and respond again briefly to the conditioned stimulus. Once a CS becomes effective, other similar stimuli also elicit the conditioned response, a process called stimulus generalization. In stimulus discrimination, the subject learns to respond only to a stimulus that is paired with the US.

4. Conditioned taste aversion occurs when an individual experiences stomach distress after eating something. This phenomenon, sometimes called bait shyness, is a unique form of classical conditioning because it can occur with one trial and the inter-stimulus interval can be hours rather than seconds.

5. Classical conditioning plays an important role in our lives. Applications of classical conditioning include treating bedwetting and behavioral problems, controlling predators, and reducing fears.

6. Thorndike's law of effect states that any response that produces satisfaction in a given situation becomes associated with that situation. When that situation occurs again, the response is more likely to be repeated.

7. Shaping is the gradual process of reinforcing successive behavior approximations to achieve some goal. Examples include training an animal, treating behavior problems, helping students learn, and treating shyness.

8. In operant conditioning, extinction is the withholding of reinforcement. After a rest period, spontaneous recovery may occur. Stimulus generalization is responding to stimuli that are similar to ones that have been reinforced. Stimulus discrimination is learning to respond only to stimuli that lead to reinforcement.

9. Reinforcement is defined as any event that increases the probability that the behavior which precedes it will be repeated. Continuous reinforcement, or reinforcing every correct response, leads to rapid acquisition and rapid extinction of a behavior. In partial reinforcement schedules, the subject is reinforced after some responses and not others. The four schedules of partial reinforcement are fixed interval, variable interval, fixed ratio, and variable ratio.

10. Primary reinforcement, like food, is effective without having been associated with other reinforcers. However, secondary reinforcement, such as money, works only after it has been paired with primary reinforcers. Positive reinforcement is anything that, when presented, strengthens the response that precedes it. Negative reinforcement is anything that, when removed, strengthens the response that precedes it.

11. Negative reinforcement occurs when a response leads to escape or avoidance of stimuli that are aversive. In escape conditioning, the subject is presented with an aversive stimulus from which he must learn to escape. In avoidance conditioning, the subject learns to avoid an unpleasant stimulus by responding appropriately before it begins.

12. Punishment decreases the probability of the behavior preceding it being repeated. Punishment can consist of presenting something unpleasant (such as a scolding) or removing something pleasurable (such as the car keys). Effective punishment depends upon a variety of variables, including proximity, consistency, and intensity. Punishment can have unpleasant side effects.

13. Operant conditioning has many applications in everyday life. Behavior modification, programmed learning, and token economies are useful in child rearing, school systems, mental institutions and animal training. The Premack Principle states that of any two responses, the one that is more likely to occur can be used to reinforce the response that is less likely to occur.

14. Classical and operant conditioning share many of the same basic principles, including acquisition, extinction, spontaneous recovery, and stimulus generalization. While a basic feature of operant conditioning is reinforcement, classical conditioning relies more on association between stimuli and responses. Much of operant conditioning is based on voluntary behavior, while classical conditioning often involves involuntary reflexive behavior.

15. Cognitive learning proposes that the learner utilizes mental structures and memory to make decisions about behaviors. Insight involves the sudden perception of the relationship of the cognitive elements necessary to solve a problem. Latent learning occurs when an individual acquires knowledge of something but does not show it until motivated to do so. In observational learning, the individiual observes another performing a task.

16. There are biological constraints on what can be efficiently learned. Instinctive drift is the process of learned behavior moving toward innate patterns. Imprinting is a form of learning in birds, occuring within hours after hatching, which involves following a moving object. The continuum of preparedness states that animals are prepared to associate certain stimuli and responses, but unprepared to learn other associations.

HUMAN MEMORY

Practical suggestions for improving our ability to learn and remember is one outcome of the study of memory. Psychologists are interested in how information is entered, stored, and retrieved from our memory systems. Recent attention has focused on how information proceeds from sensory memory to short-term and long-term memory stores.

The scientific study of remembering verbal materials began with the German psychologist Hermann Ebbinghaus. He became interested in the process of human memory, and developed procedures to measure it objectively, contributing significantly to the study of human memory. His major book, *On Memory*, published in 1885, is still read today.

Using himself as a subject, Ebbinghaus memorized lists of unrelated words and later tested himself to find out how many he could remember. At first, he worked with ordinary German words. But some words were more familiar and had more associations for him than others, and were thus easier to remember. So he decided to make up new words that would be equally unfamiliar to him and that would have no associations. These *nonsense syllables* (or trigrams, as they are also called) usually consist of a consonant, a vowel, and a consonant. For example, such "words" as DAJ, FUP, and CIN might be chosen as nonsense syllables for someone who speaks English. They can be pronounced, but have no literal meaning in the language of the person using them.

Ebbinghaus created over 2,000 nonsense syllables that he used to test his memory. His basic method of testing memory (called serial learning) required him to memorize a list of about 15 nonsense syllables until he could repeat it without making any mistakes. He read each word at a specified rate set by a metronome until he finished the list. Then he would try to recall the list perfectly. If he could not recite it without errors he read the list again and retested himself.

In order to determine how much he forgot within a

Figure 7.1 Ebbinghaus's Forgetting Curve

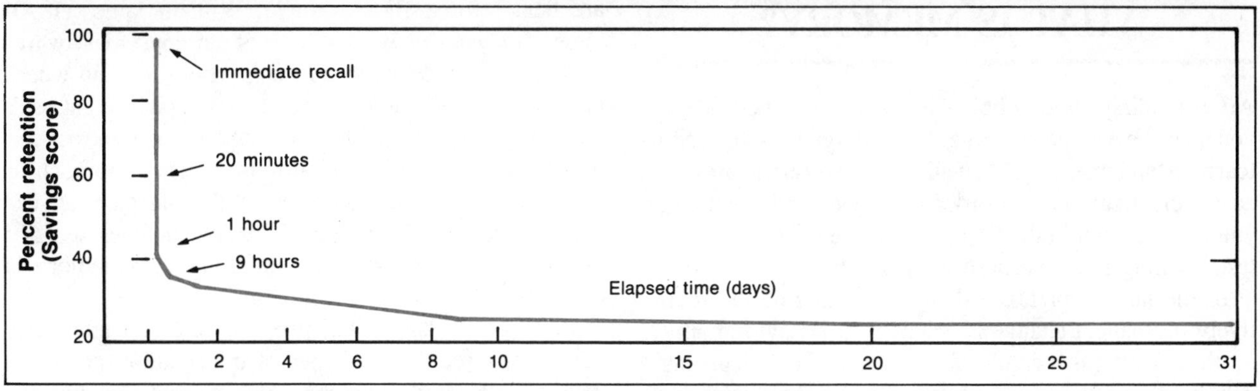

Ebbinghaus demonstrated that a greater memory loss occurs in the first 20 minutes after learning than in the remaining 31 days.

given period of time, he would wait and then retest himself. Inevitably he would forget some of the items on the list. So next he would relearn the list until he could again recall it perfectly.

In order to assess the amount of forgetting that occurred, Ebbinghaus developed the "memory savings" measure. He took the number of times he needed to repeat the list until he could recall it perfectly during the first session and subtracted from it the number of times he took to memorize the list during the second session. This difference was called the savings. If the savings score was converted to a percentage (by dividing the savings by the number of times needed during the first session), it served as a comparative measure of memory. For instance, if learning took 12 times during the first session and 6 times during the second, there was a savings of 50%, meaning that 50% of the material had been forgotten.

Ebbinghaus was especially interested in the amount of material that was forgotten at various time intervals after the original learning took place. In his classic study, he learned a list perfectly and then relearned it after a period of time elapsed (from 20 minutes to 31 days). The dependent variable was the savings score.

He found that the forgetting curve was steep immediately after learning, and slowed down over time. After 1 hour about 50% of the material had been forgotten, but by 6 days, the loss had leveled off. Eventually, forgetting stops altogether. Ebbinghaus thought perhaps the memory became permanent and did not weaken after a certain period of time. (See Figure 7.1.)

Ebbinghaus also found that when a person memorizes a list of unrelated words, he or she is most likely to remember those occurring near the beginning and end of the list, while the words in the middle are quickly forgotten. For example, you can immediately recall the first or last letter of the alphabet, but you probably have considerable difficulty remembering the 14th letter. The findings of Ebbinghaus have led to extensive research in the area of memory.

CHAPTER OBJECTIVES
What You'll Learn About Human Memory

After studying this chapter, you should be able to:

1. Define memory.
2. Describe the memory processes of encoding, storage, and retrieval.
3. Describe the iconic and echoic sensory memory stores.
4. Identify the processes of attention and pattern recognition.
5. Identify the variables that influence encoding in short-term memory.
6. Describe the characteristics of short-term memory.
7. Compare maintenance and elaborative rehearsal.
8. Compare the three types of long-term memory.
9. Define the concept of metamemory.
10. Identify three procedures used in verbal learning and memory.
11. Identify three measures of memory retention.
12. Compare the three theories of forgetting.
13. Identify five techniques for memory improvement.
14. Identify the steps of the SQ3R study technique.
15. Describe the biological basis of memory.

WHAT IS MEMORY?

After reading about Ebbinghaus and his experiments, you may be wondering what the difference is between learning and memory. Actually, the two terms are not easily distinguished. In order to remember something, you must learn it in the first place, while the only way to test learning is to measure what is remembered.

In the last chapter, we defined learning as the relatively permanent change in behavior or behavioral ability that occurs as a result of experience. Thus, learning can be thought of as acquiring new information or behavior skills. Memory involves storing the information that is learned so it can be retrieved and used at a later time. The process of memory overlaps the processes of perception (perceiving the stimuli that are being learned), learning (acquiring associations among stimuli), and consciousness (being aware of certain information at any point in time).

In order to have a memory of something, one needs to acquire (or learn) the behavior (or information), retain it until it is needed, and then be able to retrieve it. When psychologists study memory, they are interested in the retention level, which is simply the amount of information accurately stored after learning has taken place. Retention is measured by asking a person to retrieve previously learned information. *Forgetting*, or retention loss, is the part of the original learning that cannot be retrieved.

There has been a long history of attempting to describe the stages that our memories go through as they are being stored. For example, William James (1890) viewed *primary memory* as part of our conscious awareness, and *secondary memory* as part of the mind where knowledge is stored until it is needed to be brought back into consciousness again. This model was reintroduced in the 1960s as the information-processing approach to memory. As we discuss later in this chapter, an expanded version of this model, which includes sensory memory, short-term memory, and long-term memory, is currently dominant in psychology.

Brewer and Pani (1983) proposed that our memories consist of three distinct types of information: personal, generic, and skill. Personal information includes our specific experiences; generic information includes general knowledge we have gained not associated with a particular experience, such as our attitudes about school, our knowledge of VCRs, or our vocabulary; skill information includes behavioral and cognitive abilities, such as riding a bicycle or solving a crossword puzzle.

In chapter 6, "Learning," we made a distinction between learning and performance, indicating that learning was inferred from the actual performance of an individual. In the same way, we cannot know what an individual remembers until the person demonstrates it by retrieving the selected information. Psychologists use the techniques of recall, recognition, and savings as measures of memory retention. We begin this chapter with a look at the processes involved in our memory system.

BIOGRAPHICAL ☆ HIGHLIGHT ☆

HERMANN EBBINGHAUS

Hermann Ebbinghaus was born in 1850 to Lutheran merchants in Barmen, Germany. At the age of 17, he entered the University of Bonn, where he developed an avid interest in philosophy. However, his studies were temporarily interrupted when in 1870, at the outbreak of the Franco-Prussian War, he enlisted in the Prussian army. He resumed his studies a year later, and received his Ph.D. in 1873.

In 1885, the year of the publication of his most important book, *On Memory*, he was appointed professor of philosophy at the University of Berlin. Several years later, he accepted a position at Breslau where he remained until his death in 1909.

Ebbinghaus's contributions to psychology are numerous. In addition to founding two psychology laboratories in Germany, he also founded and edited a major journal that did much to advance psychology in its early days. His famous work on memory set a precedent for experimental psychology. Ebbinghaus helped to bring clear and precise experimental techniques to the science of psychology.

He was highly popular as a lecturer, and his sense of humor, informal style, and personal charm endeared him to students and colleagues alike. He died of pneumonia in Breslau at the age of 59.

MEMORY PROCESSES

What if someone asked you the name of the author of your psychology textbook? You might give one of three responses: "I never learned it," "I completely forgot," or "I can't quite remember." These three responses correspond roughly to the three basic components of our memory system: encoding, storage, and retrieval.

The first step is encoding, the process of putting information into our memory system (Murdock, 1974). If we don't learn or experience something first, we cannot remember it at a later time. The stimuli that we perceive or are aware of must be transformed in some way into data that can be deposited into our brain's memory banks. Essentially, encoding is the process in which the nervous system develops a representation of the stimuli that we perceive.

There are a number of variables that influence the effectiveness of the encoding process. We must perceive the event, and pay attention to its characteristics. We should be motivated to remember, and find the information meaningful or relevant to our lives. And if we practice or rehearse the information, the likelihood of successfully remembering it increases significantly.

Once we have encoded, or put the information into our memory, we need to store it. If we don't store it, then it's forgotten. The second step, storage, is the process that retains information in our memory system for some length of time. The processes of encoding and storage are not easily distinguishable, since each depends upon the other for successful memory to take place.

Although we might prefer our stored memories to be like a video recording that can be played back perfectly, research has demonstrated that our memory is a dynamic process that is continually changing to accommo-

date new information (Loftus, 1980). Currently, it is believed that three separate memory stores exist—sensory, short-term, and long-term—with memories being transferred among the three.

The third step in memory process is retrieval, pulling information out of the memory system. We don't know what is stored until we retrieve it. Sometimes the information is adequately stored, but not easily accessible at that moment. For example, have you ever taken a test and gone blank on some of the questions, only to remember them completely as soon as you leave the classroom? The test answers were in your memory but you had difficulty retrieving them. The success of retrieval obviously is closely tied to the effectiveness of encoding and storage. For this reason, the distinction among these processes is not always clear.

STAGES OF MEMORY STORAGE

One useful way of approaching memory is to distinguish between processes and structures (Atkinson & Shiffrin, 1971). As we just discussed, memory processes—including encoding, storage, and retrieval—help us place information into our memory systems, keep it there, and then pull it out when needed. Memory structures are concerned with the stages of memory storage. For example, the capacity of memory, the duration of storage, how information is stored and organized, and the form of the information are questions concerning memory structures. Psychologists consider the three memory stores (sensory, short-term, and long-term) to be cognitive structures of the mind.

Currently, memory theories are dominated by the

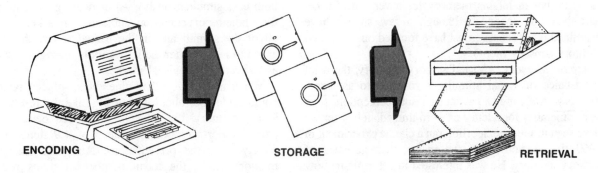

ENCODING   **STORAGE**   **RETRIEVAL**

Figure 7.2. Information Processing Theory of Human Memory
Currently the area of human memory is dominated by the information processing theory which compares the way our memory works to the way a computer works. In both instances, information is encoded into the system, is stored for some period of time, and ultimately is retrieved so that it can be used.

information-processing theory of memory. Information-processing theory relies on mathematical and computer models to describe the flow of information through the memory system. There are numerous models of memory currently available and we cannot hope to describe them all. One of the most popular is the separate-storage model. Atkinson and Shiffrin (1971) developed a model which contains three memory stores: sensory register, short-term store, and long-term store. Since many information-processing theories have these three memory storage structures, we will use this as the basis for our discussion of the storage process.

Sensory Memory

A stimulus from the environment persists for a brief time in our perceptual-nervous system even after it has been terminated. For example, when a photographer uses a flash, you tend to see "light flashes" for a while afterward (even though the actual flash is no longer used). The perceptual persistence of a stimulus after its termination in the environment is called a stimulus trace.

Sensory memory refers to the memory store that sensory information first enters in the memory system. The stimulus trace information in sensory memory is in a relatively raw form, waiting until it can be processed further. The sensory register, or sensory memory, is crucial to the correct functioning of our memory system. We are exposed to an enormous number of sensory stimuli (sights, sounds, smells, tastes, and touches) every moment we are awake. We need to be able to keep the relevant stimuli in our system until we decide which are important and therefore process them further into a more permanent form.

Sensory memory has several important characteristics that distinguish it from the other memory stores (Matlin, 1983). The information in sensory memory is a fairly accurate representation of the environmental stimuli but is unprocessed. Sensory memory has a very large capacity, but maintains memory for a very brief time, less than one second. Although a few studies have examined other senses, most have focused on visual and auditory sensory memory.

Iconic Memory. Visual sensory memory, the brief persistance of visual stimuli, is referred to as iconic memory. An icon is a particular visual perception, such as our memory for a letter or word immediately after we have seen it. George Sperling ran a classic experiment in 1960 that demonstrated the major characteristics of sensory memory. He was interested in determining how much people could see in a brief exposure to the stimuli.

Prior research indicated that when people are presented a number of letters for a very brief time, they often reported that they had seen more than they could remember. Following is an array of letters typical of what Sperling used in his research project. Glance at it for 50 milliseconds ($^1/_{20}$ of a second) and try to recall as many items as possible.

$$
\begin{array}{cccc}
X & B & R & G \\
F & S & L & C \\
Z & N & T & P
\end{array}
$$

When the stimuli are presented for a brief time and then the subject is immediately requested to remember as many items as possible, it is called the *whole report* procedure.

If you are like most of Sperling's subjects, in the whole report procedure you could remember a mean of 4.3 items out of the 12 presented. This is a measure of your immediate memory span. You would also have a tendency to forget the items while you were writing them down, indicating the brief time span of sensory memory.

Sperling next told subjects that he was going to ask them to give a *partial report* or recall a specific row. He indicated which row by means of a high (top row), medium (middle row), or low (bottom row) auditory tone. If, immediately after presentation of the items, he indicated a particular row, he found that subjects could recall 3 or 4 items from the row. Sperling concluded the subjects actually had a memory for a mean of 9.1 of the 12 items. He also found that if he delayed asking for a partial report by one second, the subjects' scores dropped down to about the level of the whole report (4.6 items). Thus, Sperling demonstrated that iconic memory has a large capacity but a very brief (less than 1 second) time span. (See Figure 7.3.)

Echoic Memory. The brief persistence of auditory stimuli after the sound itself has ended is called echoic memory. A classic study was reported by Darwin, Turvey, and Crowder (1972) that tested echoic memory. Subjects wore headphones which could present three different three-item auditory sequences (such as J 3 H or 4 T F) at the same time (to the left ear, right ear, and both ears simultaneously). After hearing the stimuli in the whole report condition, subjects were asked to recall all of the stimuli and in the partial report they were asked to recall either the left, middle, or right sequence as indicated by a visual marker.

When asked to recall all nine items, subjects typically could remember about half (4.2). Like the results with iconic memory, the subjects performed better in the partial report condition (a mean of 4.9 items immediately after the presentation). Also like the iconic memory study, the mean number of items recalled decreased with a delay of the partial report cue, to a rate of about 4.3 items with a delay of 4 seconds.

Wingfield and Byrnes (1981) suggested that typically echoic memory lasts about 2 seconds. Why is echoic

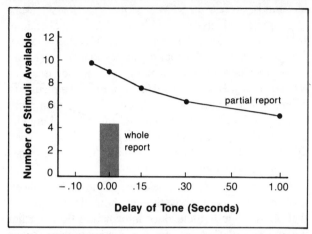

Figure 7.3. Sperling's Sensory Memory

Sperling (1960) found that when subjects were asked to immediately recall a portion of an array of numbers and letters, they were able to remember significantly more than when they tried to remember the entire array. This suggests that the capacity of sensory memory is large but quickly decays in less than one second.

memory longer than iconic memory? Speech requires more time than vision. For instance, we might be able to see a dozen letters in 50 milliseconds (msec), but it would take longer to listen to someone reading them to us. It therefore is necessary to keep sounds in sensory memory long enough to hear a complete phrase so that it makes sense to us.

Attention and Pattern Recognition. As we mentioned earlier, we store raw, unprocessed sensory information in sensory memory. Two processes that help us begin to analyze the information so it can be transferred to short-term memory include attention and pattern recognition. Attention is the process of focusing on certain stimuli. When we pay attention to certain sensory stimuli in sensory memory, they can be processed further (Baddeley, 1986). Attention functions as a gate that determines what we have available to remember. As we discuss in chapter 8, "Language and Intelligence," a condition in which the individual does not pay attention is called attention deficit disorder. A child with this condition has a difficult time remembering, creating academic and behavioral problems in the classroom.

Once we select information from sensory memory through attention, the next processing step is pattern recognition. In pattern recognition we compare the selected information with the information already permanently stored in our memory. When we see an "A," we compare the distinctive features of this stimulus with template patterns in our memory in an attempt to identify it. We are able to recognize a wide variety of sensory stimuli in this fashion. Research has shown that the context in which we experience a stimulus and our motivation and expectations can influence pattern rec-

ognition. After we pay attention to sensory information and analyze it through pattern recognition, we are able to transfer it into our short-term memory.

Short-Term Memory

Information is placed in the short-term memory (STM) when the individual attends to a stimulus. There are various terms used for this stage of memory, including working memory, immediate memory, active memory, and primary memory (Klatzky, 1980). Essentially, short-term memory is where we hold the information we are aware of at any one point in time. In a way, it is our consciousness and is important in a variety of tasks such as thinking, reading, speaking, and problem solving. We use our short-term memory when we remember a phone number we just looked up, during a conversation with another person, and when deciding what to purchase at the grocery store.

Unlike the extensive storage capacity of sensory memory, short-term memory capacity is severely limited to about seven pieces of information. The duration is less than 30 seconds before the information is lost. Also unlike sensory store, we can maintain information in our short-term memory longer if we continue to rehearse it.

Encoding in STM. Encoding involves placing information into the memory system. Do we encode into memory everything we see? Many stimuli bombard our senses and we must use pattern recognition and selective attention to screen out irrelevant information while focusing on significant stimuli. We tend to remember information that we have an interest in and are motivated to learn. For example, in a textbook we most easily remember practical material or information that is interesting to read. Two important variables in encoding information are meaningfulness and chunking.

Meaningfulness refers to the informational value of the material. High-meaningful material is encoded more easily than low-meaningful material. Read the following letters and then, without looking, try to recall them in order: T—HED—OGS—AW—TH—ECA—T. How well did you do? This string of letters had very little meaning for you. However, we can increase the meaningfulness of these letters dramatically by rearranging the grouping. Here are the same letters again. THE—DOG—SAW—THE—CAT. This time you should have no trouble remembering the letters because they are arranged in meaningful units (words). Whenever possible, we should try to remember information in a meaningful way.

Another reason you did better the second time is a phenomenon called chunking. This is the encoding process of combining stimuli (above we combined the

Figure 7.4. Chunking

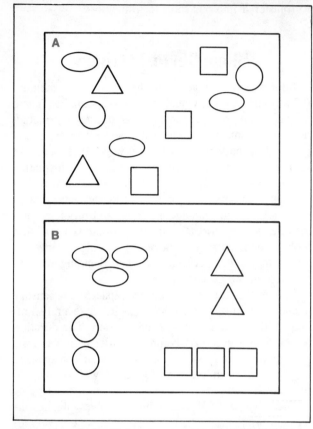

If you look at picture **(A)** for a few seconds, you will probably have trouble remembering how many figures you saw. But if you were to look at picture **(B)** for the same amount of time you should be able to recall them. Although there are as many figures in B as in A, they are grouped or chunked in B and are thus easier to count and remember.

letters into five words). It has been found that our ability to remember items presented a short time earlier is restricted to about seven pieces of information. Chunking may help us improve our memory because each chunk may contain more information. For example, XHNQC represents five chunks, the same number as the word groups presented in the earlier dog-and-cat example. A practical application of chunking is to reduce your study notes to fewer phrases, so you will do better on tests.

Information Code in STM. When discussing sensory memory, we stated that the sensory stimuli accurately reflected the environmental stimuli. That is, visual information was coded visually and auditory information was coded acoustically. What code is used in short-term memory? Research suggests that we are most likely to use an acoustic code storing information in terms of how it sounds. For example, assume we just looked up the zip code for a friend who lives in Pinckney, Michigan and learn that it is 48169. How would we store it in our short-term memory until we

could write it down? Chances are good that we will repeat the number over and over again and by rehearsing its sounds, store it in STM.

Some individuals are capable of using a visual code in short-term memory. A small number of children (about 5%) have such good visual memories that they are said to have photographic memory, or eidetic imagery (Haber, 1980). In one study, Haber presented a picture to children who studied it for 30 seconds and then were able to answer extremely detailed questions about the picture. The subjects reported that they could still "see" the image of the picture. This ability usually declines with age, and adults rarely possess it.

Capacity of STM. The storage capacity of short-term memory is severely limited. Sometimes it is said that STM is the bottleneck of information flow. Earlier we mentioned that we could remember about seven chunks of information. George Miller (1956) was so impressed by this finding (and the fact that Ebbinghaus had earlier reported the same results), that he called it the magic number 7. Most people can remember 7 ($\pm$ 2) items of information for a short time. This is why we can easily remember a telephone number of seven digits for the short time it takes to place the call after looking up the number.

The digit-span memory test is often used to test short-term memory. Following is a list of numbers. Read it once slowly, and then write down as many of the numbers as you can remember.

1 8 7 9 1 9 1 3 1 4 9 2

Most people remember about five to nine numbers. Do you remember how you can increase your memory of these numbers? Try the date of the first psychology laboratory, the founding of the school of behaviorism, and the discovery of America. These are three dates: *1879, 1913,* and *1492.* Now I bet you can easily remember all 12 items (since now they are in three chunks of information).

Recently some memory researchers have suggested that memory capacity is determined by the number of items that can be processed in a couple of seconds (2 or 3) rather than the number of chunks. Some research indicates that as the size of the chunk increases, fewer chunks can be held in memory. For example, Zhang and Simon (1985) found that when items are encoded on the basis of sound, we can hold seven items in STM. But when the items are encoded on the basis of meaning, we can only hold about three chunks of information. Although additional research is needed to clarify this area, we can conclude that the capacity of STM is definitely limited.

Retrieval in STM. We are able to quickly retrieve information from our short-term memory. Saul Sternberg (1966, 1969) conducted a series of experiments to

STM: maintenance rehearsal
        elaborate rehearse

Figure 7.5. Sternberg's Short-Term Memory

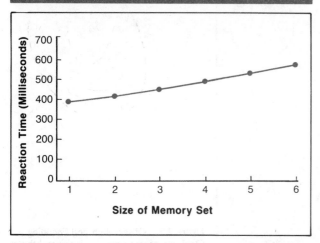

Sternberg (1969) found that the time to scan information in short-term memory increased as the number of items increased. This suggests that we use serial processing to scan short-term memory.

Figure 7.6. Peterson and Peterson's STM

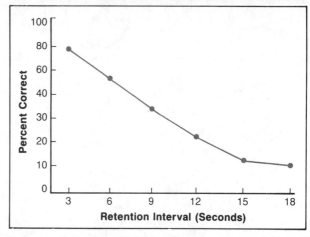

Peterson and Peterson (1959) found that a nonsense syllable was quickly forgotten if subjects could not rehearse it. This suggests our short-term memory retention time is less than 30 seconds.

determine whether people scan items in short-term memory one at a time (*serial processing*) or all at once (*parallel processing*). In one study, he presented a display of from one to six different digits to a subject for 1.2 seconds. Then he presented a test digit and the subject had to decide whether the test digit was included in the display just shown. If parallel processing occurred, the length of the display should not influence the reaction time, but if serial processing occurred, the reaction time should increase with an increase in the length of the display.

Sternberg found that it took a minimum of 397.2 msec (each second contains 1000 msec) to respond when one item was in the display and increased by 37.9 msec with each additional item. This indicated an average scanning rate of about 27 digits per second. An interesting finding was that the reaction time was the same whether the response was a "yes" or a "no." In other words, subjects did not stop responding when they found a match, but continued searching the entire display. This process is called an exhaustive search. Thus Sternberg concluded that people perform an *exhaustive serial search* when retrieving information from STM. (See Figure 7.5.)

Duration of STM. A classic experiment was conducted in 1959 by Lloyd and Margaret Peterson to determine the duration of short-term memory. They presented subjects with a nonsense syllable followed by a number. When the subjects heard the number, they were to immediately count backward by threes until told to stop. Then they were to give the nonsense syllable. Sounds easy, right? Try it on a friend. For instance, try BEQ and 409. Then in 18 seconds ask for the letters. Chances are good that your subject will not be able to remember the letters after this amount of time. In the

Peterson and Peterson study, fewer than 10% of the nonsense syllables could be remembered after 18 seconds. This finding is sometimes called the Brown-Peterson effect because Brown (1958) discovered the same phenomenon at about the same time (See Figure 7.6.)

Rehearsal. There is a way to keep information in the short-term memory store for a much longer time. The Atkinson-Shiffrin model of memory (1971) includes a rehearsal buffer in the short-term memory store. Rehearsal may take two forms—maintenance or elaborative rehearsal (Craig & Watkins, 1973). Maintenance rehearsal is simply repeating the material over and over again without thinking about it. We would use maintenance rehearsal if we wanted to remember a phone number long enough to make the call.

Theoretically, it is possible to keep information indefinitely in short-term memory through maintenance rehearsal. At one time it was believed that maintenance rehearsal contributed to the transfer of information from short-term memory to long-term memory, but more recent evidence suggests that maintenance rehearsal alone does not effectively facilitate transfer, no matter how often it occurs. For example, Nickerson and Adams (1979) found that less than half of the people they asked could identify a penny correctly from a group of very similar models. Just looking at pennies does not help us permanently store the information.

Apparently, some organization is necessary for transfer of information into long-term memory. For instance, you have undoubtedly made many telephone calls, rehearsing the numbers and perceiving the letters on the phone. Which two letters of the alphabet are missing? Like most people, you probably don't know. Exposure to stimuli alone is ineffective, and therefore as you study,

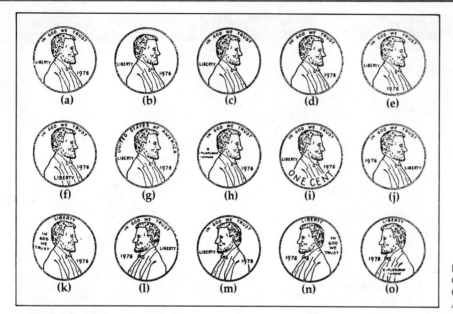

Figure 7.7. Observation and Encoding
Only one of these pennies is the real thing. Can you pick it out? (after Nickerson and Adams, 1979).

just going over your notes by rote will not significantly affect your test score. Greene (1987) pointed out that maintenance rehearsal strengthens the information about the item itself rather than associations with other items, and thus any positive results are seen more on recognition tests rather than recall tests. Elaborative rehearsal is thinking about the meaning of the material and trying to form associations with information already in memory. Elaborative rehearsal is much more effective because it involves a deeper level of processing (Craig & Lockhart, 1972). Rehearsing information correctly helps to encode it into long-term memory.

Long-Term Memory

Through elaborative rehearsal, you are able to encode information so that it enters long-term memory. The key to encoding in long-term memory is to organize the material and make it meaningful. In a sense, long-term memory incorporates the best of both sensory and short-term memory stores: its capacity is fairly unlimited as to amount of material and length of time, and it appears to be relatively permanent. We continue to add information to our long-term memory throughout life. Some of this information, such as our name, is always readily available. Other information, such as the name of our kindergarten teacher, is available only part of the time.

Depth of Processing. Closely related to elaborative rehearsal is the concept of depth of processing. As described by Craig and Lockhart (1972), the depth-of-processing approach does not incorporate separate memory stores, but rather views memory as having different levels of depth. Information that is irrelevant or incidental will not be remembered as well as information

that is meaningful and that the subject is motivated to learn. Meaningful material can be processed more deeply.

Hyde and Jenkins (1969) tested the idea of depth of processing in an experiment employing three groups of subjects. The first group was told to try hard to remember a list of words, and they did quite well. The second group was told to check to see whether the words in the list contained the letter e. This procedure is irrelevant to memory and should result in "shallow" processing. Indeed, they found the subjects in this group did rather poorly. The third group was also not told to try to remember the words, but to rate each word for its pleasantness or unpleasantness. This task involves searching the memory for other associations and thus encoding the meaning of the word. The researchers found that this deep processing procedure did result in memory as strong as that of the group that was instructed to try hard to remember. When we want to remember something, we should try to think about its meaning and its association with similar information. We could incorporate deep processing into our study routine for improved performance.

Procedural, Semantic, and Episodic Memory. Endel Tulving in 1972 distinguished between two types of long-term memory—semantic memory and episodic memory. Then in 1985, he expanded his theory to include three long-term memory systems. He proposed a classification scheme in which episodic memory is a subsystem of semantic memory and semantic memory is a subsystem of procedural memory.

Procedural memory is the most basic type of memory, and involves the formation of associations between stimuli and responses (Tulving, 1985) as when animals or humans learn to respond behaviorally in adapting to

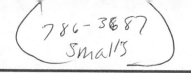

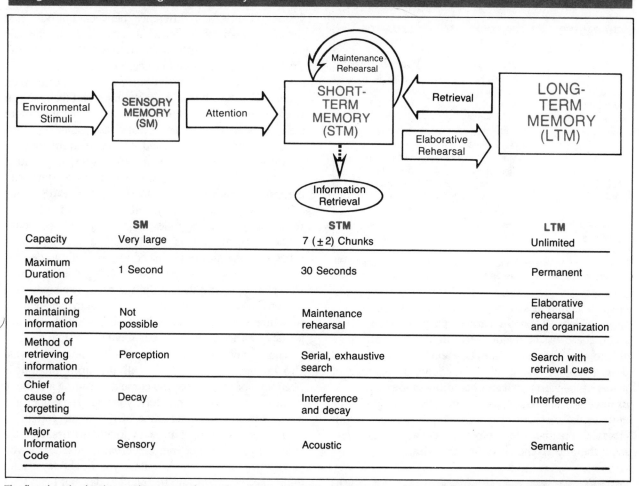

Figure 7.8. Three Stages of Memory

	SM	STM	LTM
Capacity	Very large	7 (±2) Chunks	Unlimited
Maximum Duration	1 Second	30 Seconds	Permanent
Method of maintaining information	Not possible	Maintenance rehearsal	Elaborative rehearsal and organization
Method of retrieving information	Perception	Serial, exhaustive search	Search with retrieval cues
Chief cause of forgetting	Decay	Interference and decay	Interference
Major Information Code	Sensory	Acoustic	Semantic

The flowchart for this theory of memory indicates that all incoming information first passes through Sensory Memory before it enters Short-Term Memory (STM). There it can be maintained by rehearsal and either successfully encoded for storage in Long-Term Memory (LTM) or forgotten. A summary of the characteristics of each stage of memory is included beneath.

their environment. Remembering how to ride a bicycle, how to eat a lobster, or that you were sick after eating tomato soup would involve procedural memory.

Semantic memory has the additional characteristic of allowing the individual to develop mental models of the environment. Whereas procedural memory results in overt behavior, semantic memory can involve cognitive activities. Knowledge that is used in everyday experience, such as 2 plus 2 equals 4, it's dark at night, or add an *s* to form the plural of a word, are examples of semantic memory. Access to information is automatic in semantic memory, and retrieval often involves answering the question "what."

Episodic memory, according to Tulving, is the highest memory system, and provides the additional characteristic of retaining knowledge about personal experiences (Tulving, 1985). Sometimes called autobiographical memory, it includes events that have personal meaning for us. Remembering that we had chicken for dinner last night or that we saw a movie with Ella Jean and Don last week are examples of episodic memory. Like semantic memory, this form involves cognitive activities. However, episodic memory is more personal, involves a time frame, and retrieval often involves answering the questions "when" and "where." In amnesia (a form of forgetting), the individual still possesses general facts and comprehension (semantic memory), but cannot remember personal information (episodic memory). You might think of semantic memory as a dictionary and episodic memory as a diary.

Occasionally an event is so major in importance that it leaves a vivid impression in episodic memory and significantly more details than usual about it can readily be retrieved. This type of memory is called a flashbulb memory (Brown & Kulik, 1977). For example, what were you doing on January 28, 1986, when you heard the tragic news about the Challenger space shuttle explosion? Chances are good that you can recall many details about your experiences that day.

In a study of flashbulb memory Reynolds and Tak-

Figure 7.9. Episodic and Semantic Memory

CHARACTER-ISTIC	EPISODIC MEMORY	SEMANTIC MEMORY
Source	Sensation	Comprehension
Units	Events	Facts, Ideas
Organization	Temporal	Conceptual
Reference	Self	Universe
Registration	Experiential	Symbolic
Temporal	Present	Absent
Affect	More affect	Less affect
Vulnerability	More chance of disruption	Less chance of disruption
Access	Deliberate	Automatic
Queries	Time? Place?	What?
Reports	Remember	Know
Development	Later in life	Early in life
Amnesia	Affected	Unaffected

Tulving proposed that episodic and semantic long-term memory differed in several important aspects. This chart shows that comparison.

ooshian (1988) asked people where they were on a specific date 19 months earlier. They found that even where there was no major event, all of the subjects were able to give a general description and 54% gave detailed descriptions of that specific day. Some of this kind of research suggests that flashbulb memories are only examples of episodic memory, and are not produced by any special mechanism (McCloskey & Cohen, 1988). Research continues to explore the variables that determine the effectiveness of our memories.

Figure 7.10. Flashbulb Memory
An extraordinary event usually imprints itself in our memory with such sudden clarity that we can vividly recall a great deal of detail about it many years later. Do you remember where you were and what you were doing when the space shuttle Challenger exploded on January 28, 1986?

Retrieval in LTM.   As defined earlier, retrieval is the process of pulling information out of our memory system. There is a difference between episodic and semantic memory in retrieval success rate: episodic material is more difficult to retrieve than semantic. There is usually no need to remember all of the details of our personal life. What did you eat for dinner a week ago last Tuesday? It was probably important then, so you wouldn't eat the same thing the next day, but now more than likely it is not of any great consequence.

How should you proceed to try to remember a personal event (episodic memory)? A study by Whitten and Leonard (1981) suggests that you should start with the most recent experience and work backwards. They asked college students to recall the name of a teacher from each of the 12 grades of primary and secondary school. One group was asked to come up with names randomly, one group was asked to start with grade one, and one group was asked to start with grade 12. Those who started with grade 12 did the best. The study also demonstrated that remembering one item can help in remembering a contiguous item, thus showing the importance of association in our memory system.

The importance of association is shown in what Brown and McNeil (1966) call the tip-of-the-tongue phenomenon: the closer you come to recalling a name or a word, the more accurately you can remember the number of syllables and some of the letters (often, as Ebbinghaus in our opening story found, the first or last). What was the name of your kindergarten teacher? If you cannot instantly recall the name, you might say something like, "I can picture her plain as day, but I can't get the name yet. . . . It rhymes with spoon. It's right on the tip of my tongue. I know it. Moon. No, it's Kuhn. Mary Kuhn. Yes, I remember her well."

Organization of information in long-term memory significantly increases the success of retrieval. Sometimes events and experiences are well organized, but often we must produce our own organization scheme. In subjective organization, the individual organizes information in some type of order. Tulving (1962) gave subjects lists of unrelated words and asked them to recall as many as possible. Those who created an organizational framework by creating associations among words were able to remember significantly more than those who tried to recall the words randomly. A useful suggestion is to organize your course material to facilitate retrieval on tests.

Sometimes when we attempt to retrieve information from long-term memory we cannot remember all of the details. Reconstructive memory involves combining the actual details of an event with other information that tends to fill in the gaps. For example, suppose you were asked to describe your 10th birthday party. You probably can remember some details, but not everything. In an

Eyewitness Testimony

We have all watched television shows in which the victim picks the criminal out of a lineup. And many of us have been asked to recall details of certain events to help someone solve a problem. Do we always remember our perceptions correctly? Or are our recollections of what we hear and see influenced by other variables? Recent research by Elizabeth Loftus of the University of Washington has focused on these questions as reported in her 1979 book, *Eyewitness Testimony*.

In a number of studies, Loftus found that memories of eyewitnesses were influenced by assumptions and social variables. For example, in one study subjects saw a short film of an automobile accident and then were asked questions about it. Part of the subjects were asked how fast the car was going when it passed a barn along the road, while others were asked how fast the car was going along the road (no mention of the barn). When questioned later, over five times as many subjects who had been asked the first question replied that they remembered seeing the barn than those who had been asked the second question (no mention of the barn). Just the fact that the barn had been mentioned caused the subjects to incorporate it into their memory. Loftus points out that many times we supplement our recollection of events with sensible but possibly false information.

In another study, Loftus and her colleagues showed subjects slides of the events leading up to an automobile accident. Slides for two groups were identical except for one slide in which half of the subjects saw a stop sign and the other half saw a yield sign. Next, subjects were asked a series of questions which included the assumption of either a stop or yield sign. When shown pairs of slides later and asked to identify the one they had previously seen, if the assumption had been given of the correct sign, 75% correctly chose the one they had previously seen, while if the assumption had been given of the incorrect sign, only 41% correctly chose the one they had previously been exposed to. Thus, our memory of what we have seen can be altered by inaccurate information.

Figure 7.11. Eyewitness Testimony
Would you be able to remember all of the details of an emergency situation? Research shows that it is difficult for most people to accurately recall specific information in these situations.

In chapter 8, "Language and Intelligence," we discuss the concept of set. Apparently, we tend to become accustomed to seeing certain things and our memory is set to continue to interpret information accordingly. What we perceive and what we remember is often important because in jury trials people can be falsely identified as the criminal due to faulty perceptions, beliefs, or memories. Research such as Loftus's helps us understand the importance of careful investigation of eyewitness testimony.

THOUGHT QUESTIONS

1. What factors might explain the faulty account of an event by eyewitnesses?
2. What other situations depend on our memory of our perceptions?
3. Should eyewitness testimony be allowed in court? What safeguards do we need?

effort to reconstruct the event, you will, perhaps, remember your brother was sick that year and couldn't attend. Because he normally attended you might use that detail to reconstruct the rest of your party.

Eyewitness Testimony. An important application of reconstructive memory is the area of eyewitness testimony. Elizabeth Loftus (1983) pointed out that during an interview, inaccurate or false information could be given to a witness, thereby causing the witness to reconstruct an unreliable account of the incident. Loftus (1984) suggested that accuracy of the memory of witnesses is especially a problem when identifying people

of a different race, since many people have difficulty distinguishing features of members of another race and therefore are more likely to make inaccurate identifications.

Metamemory. Metamemory refers to the knowledge of one's own memory ability (Cavanaugh & Perlmutter, 1982). People appear to have a fairly good idea about how well they are able to remember things. If your psychology teacher asked you if you knew his or her birthday, you would not have to think too long before indicating you do not have that information stored in your memory. Likewise, you would probably be able to predict that it would be more difficult to memorize a list of Chinese words than a list of English words. Metamemory is concerned with how much people know about their memory systems and how accurately people can predict how difficult a memory task will be.

Children are often unable to predict how well they will remember things. Yussen and Berman (1981) tested seven-year-old children and found that they predicted they would be able to remember nine words from a list. However, they actually could only remember four words.

Eugene Lovelace (1984) recently examined metamemory in college students. He displayed a series of 90 words, and after each word the subjects predicted how well they would be able to recall the word. The results showed that subjects were able to predict accurately how well they would do on the recall task.

Leal (1987) asked her university students to predict their performance prior to taking examinations. She found that the students were able to adequately assess their exam readiness. Intons-Peterson and Fournier (1986) reported that college students used external memory aids (taking notes or asking someone else) more than internal memory aids (mental rehearsal or imagery) to prepare for an exam. The students appeared to be able to evaluate and select effective strategies for remembering. From the research we can conclude that metamemory is well established by college age.

FORGETTING

The opposite but equally important factor in the process of remembering is the process of forgetting. It would probably be annoying if not impossible to think abstractly, to rationalize, to organize material to function effectively, if we were not able to forget some of the insignificant material that enters our memory every day. Forgetting refers to the apparent loss of memory. Here we discuss the methods of studying and measuring forgetting and review its major theories.

Verbal Learning and Memory

As discussed in our opening story, a significant amount of learning and memory involves language, learning to respond to, or with, words or symbols. The study of verbal learning pioneered by Ebbinghaus focused on learning associations between verbal units and the time it takes to forget the associations. Three basic procedures used in studying verbal learning and memory include: serial learning, free recall, and paired-associate learning.

Serial Learning.   In serial learning the stimuli are

BIOGRAPHICAL ☆ HIGHLIGHT ☆

ELIZABETH F. LOFTUS

Elizabeth F. Loftus was born in 1944 in Los Angeles. Her mother was a librarian and her father a doctor. Her interests include both mathematics and psychology, which helps to explain her double major at the University of California at Los Angeles. Then she went on to obtain her Ph.D. in psychology from Stanford University in 1970.

Loftus's early research centered on learning and problem solving with computers. Eventually, she became interested in how human memory functions and coauthored several books on memory. She wanted to become involved in more socially relevant kinds of research and got her chance in 1974 with a grant to study the effects of leading questions on witnesses' memory of traffic accidents.

In her 1979 book, *Eyewitness Testimony* (which won a 1980 National Media Award, Distinguished Contribution), she described her theory of how perceptions can modify human memory. Leading questions can have a permanent effect on the memory of a witness. This research helped her to become one of the nation's leading legal consultants in the area of eyewitness testimony in trials.

Elizabeth Loftus is professor of psychology at the University of Washington. She has written several books with her husband, Geoffrey Loftus. Her interests continue to focus on understanding how the human memory is shaped by perception and experience.

always presented in the same order, and the subject has to learn them in the order in which they are presented. We used serial learning when we learned the letters of the alphabet or months of the year.

Ebbinghaus read a list of nonsense words at a steady pace (such as LOQ, BAJ, NUR, SEB, and CIV). When he thought he knew the entire list, he tried to reproduce the items in the correct order. If he could not remember the list perfectly, he repeated the procedure until he could.

As mentioned in our opening story, a common finding is that items at the beginning and end of the list are remembered better than those in the middle, called the serial position effect. Remembering items in the beginning of the list is due to the primary effect, whereas the recency effect is used to explain remembering items at the end of the list.

Free Recall. In free recall, the order of presentation of the stimulus items is varied on each trial, and the subject can learn and remember the items in any order. An example of such a list would be the names of people invited to a party. Free recall is often used to study how people organize their memory and what strategies are used to retrieve information. As we mentioned earlier, people tend to use subjective organization when learning unrelated stimuli.

Paired-associate Learning. In paired-associate learning, the subject is presented with a series of pairs of items (for example red-bike, girl-horse, tree-dog). In subsequent trials, he or she is given any of the first items

Figure 7.13. Paired-associate Learning Task

QEW	GUX
QEW-ZAJ	GUX-PIW
KEZ	WUJ
KEZ-FUH	WUJ-BOF
QOS	DAQ
QOS-MIF	DAQ-ZUY
XAJ	CEJ
XAJ-NUX	CEJ-KOJ

In this test of memory, a series of pairs of nonsense words is first presented to the subject until he or she can remember them all. On subsequent trials, the first syllable (stimulus) is presented alone, and the subject must remember the second syllable (response).

of the pair (the stimulus) and attempts to produce the second item (the response). You might use paired-associate learning in learning vocabulary words of a foreign language.

Measures of Retention

After Ebbinghaus learned a list of nonsense syllables, he would wait a given length of time and test for forgetting. In order to test the amount of forgetting that has taken place, psychologists commonly use three measures of retention: recall, recognition, and savings.

Recall. In recall (reconstruction), the subject is required to retrieve learned information from memory. In *free recall* the subject can remember the information in any order without any cues. In cued recall, the subject is helped by cues or aids to remembering. For example, in serial recall, each item acts as a cue for the next one. Research suggests that we tend to organize our memories, and provide our own cues if none are given. If we were asked to recall the 10th letter of the alphabet, very likely we would start at the beginning and count off letters until we reached the letter *j*. We would provide the cues we needed to retrieve the correct response from our memory. Some very common types of recall tests used in school include the essay test, short answer test, and fill-in-the-blank test.

Recognition. A second measure of memory retention is recognition. In recognition the subject is required to identify items which were previously learned and ignore new items that are used for distraction. A true-false or multiple-choice test is a good example of a test of recognition. Subjects often do better with recognition tests than recall tests. The recognition test requires that you do one task—identify the correct item. The recall test requires two tasks—first you must retrieve the item from memory and then you must identify it as being the correct one. You engage in recognition tasks every day. For example, you use recognition when you pick your

Figure 7.12. Serial Position Effect

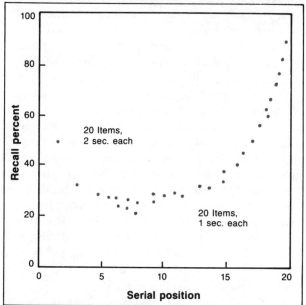

In an experiment in which subjects were shown a list of words for a brief time, they were better able to recall the words at the beginning and the end of the list.

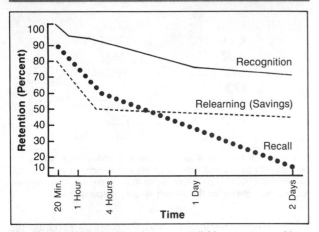

Figure 7.14. Nonsense Syllables

Three measures of retention of nonsense syllables are compared here. Although there is substantial forgetting for all three measures, recognition produces the best retention curve, followed by savings, and then recall. (After Luh, 1922.)

coat out of many from the coatrack, or when you identify a friend.

The difference between recall and recognition is nicely illustrated in a study conducted by Bahrick, Bahrick, and Wittlinger (1975) to test the memory of high school graduates for the names and faces of their former classmates at times ranging from 3 months to 48 years ago. The subjects who had graduated 48 years ago were able to recall only about 20% of their classmate's names, but could recognize almost 80% of their faces.

Savings. A third measure of retention is savings (relearning), in which the subject first learns a task and then is required to relearn it at a later time. Ebbinghaus used the savings technique in the research described in our opening story. The number of trials or amount of time to relearn the material subtracted from the number of trials or the time it originally took to learn it is divided by the original score to obtain a percent savings score. For example, someone might take 18 trials to learn a list of words the first time, but only 12 trials to relearn it two weeks later. This is a savings of $33^{1}/_{3}\%$ ($18 - 12 = 6$; $6 \div 18 = .333$ or $33^{1}/_{3}\%$). Much of what we learn seems to be forgotten, but we often find that it is relatively easy to relearn it, indicating that some of it had still been retained. An important implication of this is that while you will forget much of what you learn in school, once you learn it, it will be easier to relearn it in the future.

Theories of Forgetting

Sometimes we can remember things that happened to us as children, while at other times we seem to forget what happened to us yesterday. Are memories permanent, or do they tend to fade with time? And if memories are permanent, why can't we retrieve needed information whenever we want to? Forgetting refers to the apparent loss of memory. There are several major theories of forgetting, including decay, interference, and motivated forgetting (repression).

Decay. According to the traditional theory, sensory impressions and acquired knowledge of facts leave memory traces that fade away with time or decay through disuse. This is a commonsense theory, and is believed by many people. But there is very little experimental evidence that decay occurs to memories in our long-term memory store. We already know that we tend to forget things after a time, but not all memories fade away like photographs in old newspapers or unused paths in a forest. Sometimes we can recall a fact today that we could not remember yesterday. And, under hypnosis or through electrical brain stimulation, we can sometimes remember occurrences from our past that we are unable to recall while fully conscious and alert. Decay might operate in short-term memory, where information fades within 30 seconds if not rehearsed but that does not seem to be the case with long-term memory. We need another theory to help explain the unavailability of material in long-term memory.

Interference. Most psychologists currently believe that once information is properly encoded and stored in long-term memory, it is fairly permanent. The reason we cannot retrieve information at one time but can at another is because of interference from other information that was also learned. The interference might come from information learned before (proactive interference) or after (retroactive interference) the information being tested for. Whereas decay appears to be a problem of storage, interference is a problem of retrieval.

In proactive interference, information learned earlier interferes with retrieval of information learned later. If you already speak French when you begin studying Spanish, you probably will experience some difficulty in remembering newly learned Spanish words because your knowledge of French interferes with your memory of the corresponding Spanish word.

To test for the effects of proactive interference in the laboratory, psychologists have subjects in the experimental group learn List A, while subjects in the control group rest (and thus do not learn the list). Then both groups are required to learn List B, a new list of items. Finally, after a given period of time, both groups are tested for retention of List B. If proactive interference took place, the experimental group that had previously learned List A will not be able to remember List B as well as the control group, because List A items interfere with remembering List B items. (See Figure 7.15.)

In retroactive interference, newly learned information interferes with the memory of previously learned information. After you have studied Spanish until you

Figure 7.15. Procedure to Test for Interference

	STEP 1	STEP 2	STEP 3
PROACTIVE INTERFERENCE			
Experimental Group	Learn List A	Learn List B	Recall List B
Control Group	Rest	Learn List B	Recall List B
RETROACTIVE INTERFERENCE			
Experimental Group	Learn List A	Learn List B	Recall List A
Control Group	Learn List A	Rest	Recall List A

The chart above illustrates the procedure for testing the effects of proactive and retroactive interference on memory. If the experimental group's recall performance is not as good as the control group's performance, then interference has occurred.

are fairly fluent, and have meanwhile neglected your French, you might find that when reaching for a French expression you only remember the Spanish translation.

Psychologists test for the effects of retroactive interference by first having both the experimental and control group learn List A. Then the experimental group learns List B while the control group rests. Finally, after a given period of time, both groups are tested for the memory of List A. If retroactive interference took place, the experimental group that had recently learned List B will not be able to remember List A as well as the control group. The newly learned material interferes with the earlier learned material. (See Figure 7.15.)

Interference theory sounds reasonable, and helps account for the fact that some of our memories last an extremely long time. However, much of the work on interference has been on nonsense syllables or unrelated words, and its applicability to everyday situations is not yet fully known. Psychologists are still investigating why interference occurs at some times with some memories, but not at other times (for example, during a test, but not afterwards).

Motivated Forgetting. One last theory we cover suggests that sometimes we forget because we want to. Motivated forgetting (repression), is a term used by Freudian psychologists (see chapter 11, "Personality") for the process of forgetting something that is anxiety-arousing. Although repression is often a personality problem, it can result in a loss of memory. For example, let's assume that you have a dentist appointment this afternoon. While your dentist is always careful, there is

still some pain involved in having your teeth drilled and this causes you to be anxious. The Freudian psychologist might suggest that you could become so involved in other activities that you forget to go to the dentist. In this situation, you might be motivated to forget your appointment.

Psychologists do not agree on any one theory of forgetting. However, current research on memory processes promises to help shed more light on the processes of memory and forgetting.

IMPROVEMENT OF MEMORY

Most people complain at one time or another that their memory is not as efficient as they would like it to be. Part of the problem is likely to be the technique used to encode, store, and retrieve information rather than the memory system itself. In this section, we will look at several methods for improving memory.

Memory Enhancement Techniques

Psychologists have developed a number of procedures to enhance memory. For example, practice activities, organization, and special memory techniques are effective memory enhancement techniques.

Practice Activities. Suppose you have a week to learn a fairly important role in a play, but your schedule allows you only 14 hours to memorize all the lines. You want to know what pattern of learning would best enable you to have those lines down cold by the end of seven days. Should you work on them in two stretches of seven hours each? Or should you devise some other schedule? Psychological research suggests that massed practice, or "crash" learning of as much material as possible in long continuous stretches, would *not* be the ideal method. The most effective method would be distributed practice, in which the memorization process is spaced out over an extended period of time. Underwood (1983) explained that less interference is likely when you use distributed practice than when you try to learn all at once.

In most situations, we will remember material longest and most accurately when we have overlearned it. Despite the way it sounds, overlearning does not mean too much learning. Rather, overlearning means that the material has been rehearsed over and over again following its initial learning. Of course, it is always helpful if the material we are trying to learn interests us. But in every case, the more we rehearse beyond the first "perfect" performance, the longer we will be able to remember the material that we have learned.

A memory lasts longest when the material is familiar, and review following learning helps to keep the material familiar. Students who regularly review assigned reading and lecture notes generally do better than those who study the material only when assigned or just before an exam.

To remember written or verbal material, even material whose content need not be learned word for word, it helps a great deal to actually recite, or repeat from memory, the material just read. This active recitation or elaboration has a far greater effect on long-term memory than does mere passive reading, even when the material is clearly understood in the first reading.

In general, the better we encode and store informa-

Improving Your Memory

This chapter contains many suggestions for improving your memory. In addition, there are a number of excellent "help" books available which give practical advice to people who would like to be able to remember things better. One of the more popular books currently out is a paperback by Laird Cermak called *Improving Your Memory*. Cermak's book is a nontechnical review of practical suggestions to help you improve your memory, including attention, organization, mediation, imagery, and mnemonics.

The first suggestion is to increase *attention* in order to focus on the information we want to remember. You've heard it said again and again, but you must pay attention if you want to remember better. When reading, focus on the material and don't let your mind wander. When listening to a lecture, concentrate on the information and don't daydream. Attention brings information into our short-term memory.

Organization is important in memory improvement, and is usually considered essential for retrieval of information. Organization in putting information into the system saves time in trying to retrieve it later. In some ways, memory can be thought of as a filing cabinet, and an organized filing system saves the individual time and frustration in finding particular information. The key is to associate new information with information already in the system. The key organizational techniques include mediation, imagery, and mnemonics.

Mediation helps you organize and remember material by making words, sentences, or other connections out of the information. For example, you could insert a word between two words you are trying to remember. If you needed to remember milk and bread you might insert the word white. Then you can associate both white milk and white bread.

Imagery is the technique of making mental pictures of the material to be remembered. It is important to make the images as vivid or bizarre as possible. For example, with milk and bread, you might picture a huge water fountain made out of a loaf of bread, with milk flowing out of it.

The third technique for organizing material in memory is *mnemonics*. Mnemonics sometimes combines mediation and imagery, but uses an already existing organization scheme. A mnemonic is like a peg on a pegboard in that it allows you to hang information on the peg. For example, you might already know "one is a bun," "two is a shoe." Then you imagine milk flowing out of a big bun and bread stuffed into a shoe. The key to all of these memory techniques is to personalize them and make them work for you. Good luck!

THOUGHT QUESTIONS

1. What types of information could you memorize with these memory techniques?
2. How could these memory suggestions be applied to studying for a test?
3. Can a person's memory be too good? If you remembered everything you ever did, what would you do with this knowledge?

Figure 7.16. Pegword Mnemonic Technique

Rhyme with Pegwords	Words to Memorize	Pegwords	Visual Image
	1. steak	bun	
One is a bun			
Two is a shoe			
Three is a tree			
Four is a door	2. milk	shoe	
Five is a hive			
Six is sticks			
Seven is heaven	3. eggs	tree	
Eight is a gate			
Nine is a line			
Ten is a hen			
	4. bread	door	

Imagery and association are involved in many mnemonic devices. In the pegword mnemonic technique, you first memorize the short rhyme. Then, using these words as pegs, you create a visual image of each of the words you wish to remember.

tion, the easier it will be to retrieve. This chapter contains a number of useful encoding suggestions for improving memory, including chunking, selective attention, and depth of processing.

Mnemonic Techniques. Examples of chunking, organizing, and logically relating the components of material to be recalled may be encountered in various learning experiences. What they have in common is the need to reduce the information to be remembered to the most manageable and, therefore, the most memorizable form.

Mnemonic techniques are strategies for improving memory by organizing and encoding information to aid memory performance (Bellezza, 1981). One mnemonic technique is to combine items to be remembered into words or *phrases*. For example, to learn the colors of the spectrum, you might remember the name "Roy G. Biv," which should help you remember red, orange, yellow, green, blue, indigo, and violet.

Imagery is important in a number of mnemonic techniques (Bellezza, 1981). A mnemonic that utilizes imagery is the pegword technique, which typically starts with a rhyme or series in which the key words serve as

"pegs" to associate with other items to be remembered. (See Figure 7.16. and application box.) Another, used originally by Greek orators, is the method of loci (places). You first memorize a series of familiar locations, such as the rooms in a house, buildings on a street, or even parts of the body. For example, you might take a mental walk through your house and come up with *living room, dining room, kitchen,* and *bedroom.* Once you have these places learned, you are ready to memorize the new words. You pair a word with a location, and form a vivid image. For example, if you had a grocery list, you might have items such as milk, bread, eggs, and steak. Your images might include milky white living room furniture, a huge table made out of bread in the dining room, fried eggs as burners on your stove, and a huge cow sitting in your bed. In order to remember your grocery list, you then go through the sequence of rooms, recalling the vivid images you formed in each room. (See Figure 7.17.)

One way to improve encoding of material for easier retrieval is to employ a device that logically relates and organizes the components. In this way, a person can easily learn an apparently complex list that could go to

Figure 7.17. Method of Loci Mnemonic Technique

Location	Intend to Remember	Visual Image
Living room	Bread	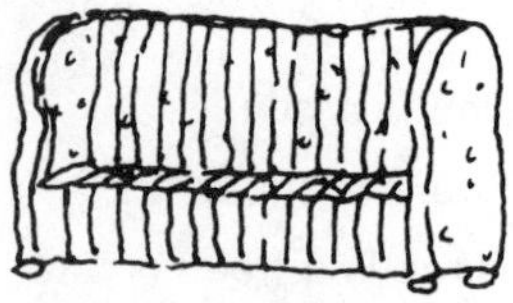
Kitchen	Eggs	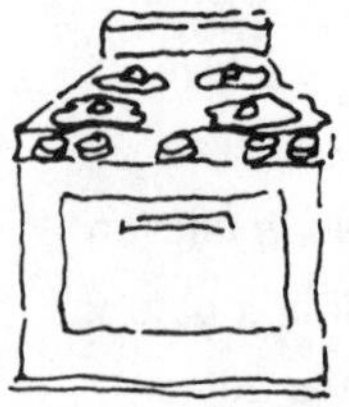
Bedroom	Meat	

Another technique to remember a list is the method of loci. You first memorize a series of familiar locations, such as rooms in your house, and combine them with the items you want to remember. Finally, you form a visual image of these combinations.

infinity: *0, 2, 5, 7, 10, 12, 15, 17, 20, 22, 25, 27, 30, . . .* Can you come up with a rule that organizes these numbers? Use this formula: Beginning at zero, add two, then add three, then add two, then add three again, and so forth. Instead of trying to memorize the entire list, you have greatly simplified your task by reducing it to merely two actions (adding two and then three alternately) which can be readily learned. You are no longer memorizing an imposing list of items, but organizing the items by finding the relationship between the items and remembering that relationship.

Henry Ellis (1987) described a memory strategy called ARESIDORI, which he said was a mnemonic code for the important variables in improving memory. ARESIDORI stands for attention, rehearsal, elaboration, semantic processing, imagery, distinctiveness, organization, retrieval, and interest. We have discussed these concepts and variables throughout this chapter.

Context and Memory. Psychologists have found that remembering is easier when we do it under conditions that are similar to those that we originally learned in. If possible, study under conditions similar to those that will exist in the test situation. For example, study at a desk, rather than lying on the floor. Study under quiet conditions, rather than with the radio playing. Ideally, you should study in an environment that is as similar as possible to the environment in which you will take the test. And while you are taking the test, think about the environment in which you studied to retrieve information through context associations.

State-dependent learning refers to the phenomenon that we remember best when we are in the same state of consciousness that we were in when we originally learned the material (see chapter 5, "Sleep and Consciousness"). A number of studies have demonstrated that if a person learns while in a drug-induced altered state of consciousness, he or she will remember it most efficiently when in the same state. Of course, this also means that information you learn when in waking consciousness will be recalled best when you are in waking consciousness. Sometimes other influences (such as environmental cues) will outweigh the effects of state-dependent memory. Try to study when you are alert and in the same state of waking consciousness that you will be in when taking a test.

A related phenomenon is the finding that emotional

mood states can influence memory. Bower (1981) reported that subjects who were either sad or happy when they learned material recalled the information significantly better when they were later in the same mood. Bower suggested that this is why we are able to remember more negative experiences when we are depressed. Thus, you need to think positively when you are studying for and taking your exams.

SQ3R Study Technique

Much of the material in this chapter can be applied immediately as you study in school. A particularly good technique for organizing some of these principles of learning and memory is the SQ3R study technique originally developed by Francis Robinson (1970). As you learn to use this technique, you should find you are able to identify the parts of this chapter that apply to the various sections of the SQ3R formula. SQ3R study technique stands for survey, question, read, recite, and review.

The first step in studying is to *survey*. If you are reading a chapter of a textbook, you should quickly glance through the entire chapter, noting the headings, style, length, and general format. This step focuses your attention on the material and helps prepare you for effective studying.

Question simply means to look at the chapter and ask yourself questions about it. What does a heading mean? What are the important points in the chapter? What does a word mean? You make up questions about the chapter by quickly looking through it. The questions are designed primarily to motivate you to study the material carefully. In this book, you could turn the chapter objectives into questions. Again, the question step prepares you for effectively studying the material.

A critical step is to *read*. It's important that you actively read the material. Read for a purpose, even if the purpose is just to find out what is in the chapter. Read to answer the questions you have developed. Carefully note important terms, including the italicized or underlined words and phrases. Your main job in reading is to obtain the main ideas and important details. Active reading is important for effectively remembering what you have studied.

The fourth step is to *recite*. Recitation means recalling what you have read. It is rehearsing the main ideas and important details in your memory. You can simply recall the information, but a better technique is to organize it and form associations to other ideas you have already remembered. Recitation is an excellent way to discover what you can remember about the chapter material.

The last step of the SQ3R study formula is to *review*.

Reviewing the material helps to keep it fresh in your mind. Essentially you quickly reread the chapter to make sure you have covered it all. Then you recite the information to yourself and read over any notes you have taken. If you review regularly, you should have no problems when the big test comes.

BIOLOGY OF MEMORY

We can reasonably assume that our memories have a biological basis in our brain. And yet the vast amount and complexity of information we must encode and store seems to defy any simple explanation. Psychologists have been trying to discover the biological basis of memory for some time.

Karl Lashley (1950) spent many years trying to identify the engram, or memory trace, in the brain that holds specific memories. He conducted many experiments in which he trained rats and then destroyed parts of their brain. He concluded that memory is not stored in any one specific part of the brain and that the degree to which memory is hurt depends on the amount of brain destroyed (called the law of equipotentiality). In other words, memory depends on the size of the total brain and not on any specific location.

At about the time that Lashley was concluding his research efforts, Donald Hebb (1949) presented his biological theory of memory consolidation. Consolidation is the neural process of making memories more permanent. As new material is learned, neurons in a particular circuit are stimulated and fire. With rehearsal or practice, the circuit is repeated over and over, and through this consolidation procedure, the chemical events at the synapses change into a permanent record of the information. While all the details have not yet been worked out, many psychologists accept that a process similar to the one Hebb proposed is probably responsible for the biology of memory.

Some research has been used to test Hebb's theory of consolidation and gain new information on the biology of memory. One line of research concentrated on disrupting the repeating electrical circuits. Chorover and Schiller (1965) gave rats electroconvulsive shock at various times after they had been trained. The researchers found that the shock produced retrograde amnesia, or forgetting of the information, when administered a brief time after learning took place. In other research studies, electrodes have been implanted in specific areas of the brain to test the effects of electrical stimulation at particular locations immediately after learning has taken place. Several brain areas have been suggested as potential memory processing sites, including the hippocampus, the midbrain reticular formation, and the frontal cortex.

It is likely that different brain sites are involved in different types of memories (procedural, semantic and episodic). Richard Thompson (1985) suggested that the cerebellum plays an important role in procedural memory. In classical conditioning experiments in which rabbits were taught to blink their eyes when a stimulus was presented, the neural circuits in the cerebellum were activated.

The hippocampus and thalamus are involved in the development of semantic and episodic memory (Herbert, 1983). Many researchers and clinicians have reported that patients with damage to the hippocampus are not able to form new memories (Squire, 1987). Research has also suggested that the thalamus plays a key role in creating a memory trace (Mishkin, 1982).

Another line of research has concentrated on the neurochemistry of memory. In an experiment with rats, James McGaugh (1983) found that the hormone epinephrine significantly increased the rat's memory of a maze. Other studies have found that the adrenal hormone ACTH and the pituitary hormone vasopressin aid the memory of rats in learning tasks (Messing & Sparber, 1985).

Scopolamine, a drug which decreases the level of the neurotransmitter acetylcholine, impairs memory in rats (Murray & Fibiger, 1986). Humans who were given a dose of scopolamine also showed temporary memory deficits (Beatty, Butters, & Janowsky, 1986). Likewise, drugs that temporarily increase levels of acetylcholine tend to help improve human memory (Bartus & colleagues, 1982). Unfortunately, there are side effects, and so this is not presently a feasible way to improve memory.

Information on how memory operates has been obtained from studies of brain-related memory deficits. A recent topic of great interest is Alzheimer's disease, a disorder in which the individual gradually loses all memory. Research on this brain degenerative disorder (Davies, 1985) suggests that it is caused by a deficiency of the brain neurotransmitter acetylcholine. This research gives insight into the role acetylcholine plays in memory and also may provide a lead in the treatment of Alzheimer's disease.

Although progress has been made, there is still much to discover about the biology of memory. However, it is likely that the specific chemical code will eventually be broken. ■

The study of memory, begun with Ebbinghaus, continues today providing a rich array of information about human memory. This chapter can be very useful to you if you apply the principles discussed to everyday life. You can only retrieve information that you have properly encoded and stored. While some people seem naturally to have better memories than others, research has clearly shown that memory can be improved through practice and utilization of the memory techniques. Can you now remember the name of your kindergarten teacher? How about the three measures of retention in memory? You will probably be able to find out shortly how much of the memory chapter you remember. Do you remember when your next test is scheduled?

"The matters about which I'm being questioned, Your Honor, are all things I should have included in my long-term memory but which I mistakenly inserted in my short-term memory."

Drawing by Fisher; © 1983 The New Yorker Magazine, Inc.

CHAPTER REVIEW
What You've Learned About Human Memory

1. Memory involves encoding and storing information that is learned so it can be retrieved and used at a later time. The amount of information accurately stored is called the memory retention level.

2. Encoding is the process of putting information into the memory system. Storage is the process that retains information in the memory system over time. Retrieval is the process of pulling information out of the memory system.

3. Information processing theory is a model of memory that includes three memory stores: sensory memory, short-term memory, and long-term memory. Sensory memory refers to the memory store that sensory information first enters in the memory system. It has a large capacity, but maintains unprocessed information for a brief time, about half a second. Visual sensory memory is called iconic memory, and auditory sensory memory is called echoic memory.

4. Attention is the process of focusing only on certain stimuli. In pattern recognition we compare the information selected through attention with the information already permanently stored in our memory.

5. Important variables in encoding in short-term memory include meaningfulness (informational value) and chunking (combining stimuli).

6. We tend to store information in short-term memory the way it sounds (acoustic code). The capacity of short-term memory is about seven (plus or minus two) chunks of information. If you attend to a stimulus, it can be transferred into short-term memory, where it can be held for up to 30 seconds before it decays. We use a serial, exhaustive search to retrieve information from short-term memory.

7. Maintenance rehearsal (repeating information without thinking about it) can keep information in short-term memory for a longer time. If you use elaborative rehearsal (thinking about the meaning of the information) you can transfer information into long-term memory, where it can remain indefinitely.

8. The key to encoding in long-term memory is to organize the material and make it meaningful. Procedural memory involves the formation of associations between stimuli and responses. Semantic memory can involve cognitive activities, such as knowledge used in everyday experience. Episodic memory involves knowledge of personal experiences, and is the highest form of long-term memory.

9. Metamemory refers to the knowledge of one's own memory ability.

10. Verbal learning is learning to respond to (or with) words or symbols. Three basic verbal learning procedures developed by Ebbinghaus include: serial learning, free recall, and paired associate learning.

11. Retrieval is the process of pulling information out of memory. Psychologists commonly use three measures of retention: recall, recognition, and savings.

12. Forgetting refers to the apparent loss of memory. Decay refers to the fading of the memory trace, especially in sensory or short-term memory. Interference theory suggests that memory is permanent, but we can't remember something because of other competing information learned before (proactive interference) or after (retroactive interference) the information being tested for. Motivated forgetting, or repression, is a term used by Freudian psychologists for the process of forgetting something that is anxiety-arousing.

13. There are many techniques that can be used to improve memory, including distributed practice, overlearning, review, active recitation, encoding techniques (chunking, selective attention, depth of processing, organization), mnemonic techniques (phrases, method of loci), and retrieval techniques. Mnemonic techniques are ways of improving memory by combining and relating chunks of information.

14. SQ3R stands for survey, question, read, recite, and review—the five steps in this study technique, which you can learn easily and utilize in your current studies.

15. The biological theory of memory consolidation suggests that memory becomes more permanent over time due to chemical changes at the neuron synapses. Memory resides in various brain sites including the hippocampus and thalamus.

LANGUAGE AND INTELLIGENCE

Part of what makes us unique is our ability to use language to communicate and to use thought to solve problems. The cognitive processes of language and thought are involved in intelligence. A number of important theories of intelligence have been proposed, and a variety of IQ tests have been developed to measure it accurately.

Ethical considerations sometimes prevent us from carrying out certain experimental studies that might help improve our understanding of human behavior. In the area of intelligence, we cannot, for instance, take children and place them in poor environments to see if intelligence will decline. Once in a while, however, the proper conditions are found in a natural setting which allow us to learn about effects that are otherwise unobtainable. Harold Skeels reported in 1966 on his now classic study of environmental influences on intelligence.

In the 1930s, Harold Skeels was a psychologist for the state of Iowa. One day, he tested the intelligence of two baby girls living in an orphanage. Both girls were extremely retarded mentally, and spent most of their time just sitting and staring into space. The orphanage's administration then decided that the babies were unadoptable and sent them to an institution for the mentally retarded. A year later, Skeels had an opportunity to retest the girls, and found them to be completely changed. Now they were active, alert, and had test scores which were near normal.

What could produce such a change? Skeels guessed that the environment was responsible. The orphanage was overcrowded and poorly staffed, and the children received little individualized attention. At the institution, the girls lived with women who "adopted" them and gave them lots of attention and affection.

Figure 8.1. Environmental Stimulation
Drama workshop at the Lorna Hodgkinson Sunshine Home for the mentally handicapped. Aldo Gennaro (center), therapist and theater director, is developing a program of creative abilities for disabled people.

Skeels next arranged for a controlled experiment to study the effects of the environment on intellectual functioning. The experimental group consisted of 13 mentally retarded children from the Iowa Soldiers' Orphans Home who were transferred to the Glenwood State School. The mean age of the children was 19.4 months, with a range of from 7.1 to 35.9 months. The children had a mean IQ of 64.3, with a range of from 35 to 89.

The control group consisted of 12 children in the orphanage who were given a medical examination the same time as the experimental group. The mean age of the control group was 16.6 months with a range of from 11.9 months to 21.8 months. The mean IQ for this group was 86.7, with a range of from 81 to 103.

The children in the experimental group were placed in wards with older girls who spent much time playing with them. The control group's environment was typical of an orphanage. Few contacts with adults were possible because of overcrowding.

The experimental group gained an average of 27.5 IQ points, and their mean IQ at the end of the experimental period was 91.8. The length of the experimental period varied, since as soon as a child showed normal intelligence, she was placed in an adoptive home or returned to the orphanage. Two years after the close of the study, 11 of the experimental children were in adoptive homes, and had a mean IQ of 101.4. The control group had a loss in IQ of 26.2 points, and ended the study with a mean IQ of 60.5.

Skeels concluded that an environment which is caring and stimulating can cause a dramatic increase in IQ in retarded children. An unstimulating environment, on the other hand, can cause IQs to decline. He did not test the possibility of genetic differences between the experimental and control groups. However, the study did provide convincing evidence of the importance of the environment in normal intellectual development.

CHAPTER OBJECTIVES
What You'll Learn About Language and Intelligence

After studying this chapter, you should be able to:

1. Define cognition and identify the topics in cognitive psychology.
2. Define language and describe the structure of language (grammar).
3. Outline how language develops in infants and children.
4. Compare the two major theories of language development.
5. Explain how language and thought are related.
6. Define concept formation and identify the types of concepts.
7. Identify three theories of problem solving.
8. Outline effective problem solving strategies and identify three variables that can interfere.
9. Outline the area of creativity.
10. Define the concept of intelligence.
11. Outline the major theories of intelligence.
12. Identify the characteristics of tests.
13. Describe the development of the Stanford-Binet Intelligence Scale.
14. Describe the Wechsler Intelligence Scales.
15. Outline the genetic influences on intelligence.
16. Outline the environmental influences on intelligence.
17. List the levels of mental retardation and identify the major causes of mental retardation.
18. Describe intellectually gifted people.

WHAT IS COGNITION?

Skeel's research project is among many which were designed to determine the influence of environment or heredity on intelligence. Intelligence, the capacity to learn and behave adaptively, is one of the topics studied in cognitive psychology. Other areas of cognitive psychology include perception, attention, memory, language, thinking, concept formation, problem solving, and artificial intelligence (Solso, 1988). In this chapter, we focus on language, thinking, problem solving, and intelligence.

What is cognition? Most psychologists would agree that cognition, or mental processes, involves the acquisition, storage, retrieval, and utilization of knowledge (Matlin, 1989). Examples of cognition include learning something and placing the information in our memory system; communicating through language by manipulating mental symbols; solving problems or acting intelligently utilizing information that we have previously learned and stored in memory.

The cognitive areas of language, thinking, problem solving, and intelligence are closely interrelated. *Language* is a form of communication utilizing manipulation of symbols to convey meaning to others or to oneself. Language can help us communicate with other people and can also help us think. *Thinking* can be defined as the cognitive or mental activity of manipulating symbols. For humans, thinking usually involves language. We use thinking to solve problems, make decisions, and act intelligently. *Intelligence* is defined as the capacity to learn and behave adaptively. Intelligence utilizes the ability to communicate through language, and can be improved through practice solving problems.

As we discussed in chapter 1, "The Study of Psychology," cognition currently plays a major role in psychology. In fact, we defined psychology as the science of behavior and cognition. Historically, psychology began with a strong cognitive orientation (Wundt's school of structuralism involved the study of conscious experience through introspection). However, during the early part of this century, behaviorists effectively eliminated cognition as an area of study in psychology. It was not until the 1960s that psychology began once again to incorporate cognitive processes into its theories and methods. The information-processing theory that was borrowed from computer science provided the ideal theoretical perspective for the study of cognitive processes (see chapter 7, "Human Memory"). Currently there are very few areas in psychology that do not include a cognitive approach.

Not all psychologists, however, support the pervasive influence of cognitive processes in psychology. Behaviorist B. F. Skinner (1987) accused cognitive scientists of loosely defining terms, speculating about internal unseen processes, and misusing terms such as storage (arguing the brain is not an encyclopedia or museum). He argued that the cognitive psychologists went too far and are not as productive as they could be. Thus, he proposed letting psychology become a behavioral science again.

An interesting area of cognitive science that has received considerable attention is artificial intelligence. The goal of artificial intelligence (AI) is to simulate human cognition. Researchers have written computer programs to learn more about how we process information. Alan Turing (1950) argued that the laws governing the thinking process could be simulated through a computer. As computer programs of AI are tested, we are learning about language, memory, thinking, problem solving, and intelligence. Although the actual activities of cognition cannot be observed directly, cognitive processes are an important force in our lives.

LANGUAGE

One of the ways we differ from lower animals is in our advanced ability to easily learn and utilize language. Other animals have developed communication systems, and recently some primates have been taught the rudiments of language. But only we humans, with our complex brain and higher mental functioning, have developed the complex system of communication called language.

The Structure of Language

Language is the principal means of communication in people utilizing the manipulation of symbols to convey meaning to others or to oneself. Language allows us to represent ideas and objects that are not restricted to the present time period. We can talk about the past and future, as well as the present.

Psycholinguistics is the psychological study of how we convert the sounds of language into meaningful symbols that can be used to communicate with others. Psycholinguists are concerned with the cognitive processes involved in the acquisition and use of a language.

Grammar. You can find most of the words in the English language in an unabridged dictionary. But no one would ever try to publish a list of all the sentences in English, since their number is probably infinite. Yet

Figure 8.2. Phonemes in American English

Vowels

ee as in h*ea*t	*ah* as in f*a*ther	*ʌ* as in t*o*n	*au* as in sh*ou*t
ı as in h*i*t	*aw* as in c*a*ll	*uh* as in th*e*	*ei* as in t*a*ke
ɛ as in h*ea*d	*U* as in p*u*t	*er* as in b*ir*d	*ou* as in t*o*ne
ae as in h*a*d	*oo* as in c*oo*l	*oi* as in t*oi*l	*ai* as in m*i*ght

Consonants

t as in *t*ee	*m* as in *m*e	*sh* as in *sh*ell	*zh* as in gara*g*e
p as in *p*ea	*n* as in *n*o	*h* as in *h*e	*l* as in *l*aw
k as in *k*ey	*ng* as in si*ng*	*v* as in *v*iew	*r* as in *r*ed
b as in *b*ee	*f* as in *f*ee	*th* as in *th*en	*y* as in *y*ou
d as in *d*awn	*θ* as in *th*in	*z* as in *z*oo	*w* as in *w*e
g as in *g*o	*s* as in *s*ee		

The basic speech sounds in a language are called phonemes. The numbers of phonemes vary in different languages and in different dialects within a language (after Denes & Pinson, 1963).

almost every time you hear a sentence, you understand it, even if you have never heard it before. Since you could not have learned the meaning of the sentences beforehand, how do you understand it?

The answer is that you understand the rules of the language. This set of rules, called grammar, can be used again and again to produce and understand innumerable sentences. Every fluent speaker of a language is familiar with its grammar, a general term that includes the rules for the sounds, (phonemes), structure (syntax), and meaning (semantics) of a language.

Basic Units of Language. Language consists of basic speech sounds that are called phonemes. The *m* sounds in mother, music, and memory are all similar and thus represent one phoneme. Some languages have as few as 15 phonemes, while other languages have as many as 85 (Bourne & colleagues, 1986). The English language contains about 40 different phonemes. As many students soon discover, it can be extremely difficult to learn a foreign language that contains phonemes not found in their native tongue.

Phonemes are combined into morphemes, the smallest meaningful units of a language. Many morphemes are words, like *swim, teach,* and *hit.* Other morphemes are prefixes or suffixes which must be combined with other morphemes to form meaningful words. For example, the suffix *er* can be added to the word *teach* to form the new word *teacher.* The 40 phonemes in the English language can be combined to produce over 100,000 morphemes, which can be combined to produce over 500,000 words in the English language.

Syntax. A subset of rules of grammar, that governs the order of words in sentences, is called syntax. The

rules of syntax help structure the language by regulating the way nouns and verbs form phrases, which in turn form sentences. Without syntax, language would not be meaningful. For example, can you decipher this first stanza in Lewis Carroll's famous nonsense poem, *Jabberwocky*?

> 'Twas brillig, and the slithy toves
> Did gyre and gimble in the wabe:
> All mimsy were the borogoves,
> And the mome raths outgrabe.

Given enough time, you might be able to make some sense out of these lines.

If *Jabberwocky* is too much for you, try to decipher this sentence: "Ran Tom house quickly the into." You should be able to reorder the words to form the sentence the proper way: "Tom quickly ran into the house." Actually, there are 720 potential word orders in this sentence, but only one is syntactically correct. We learn syntax early in childhood, and can usually tell when something is wrong, even though we might not be able to explain the formal rules (Chomsky, 1965).

Semantics. The study of the meaning of language is called semantics. Psychologists are trying to identify how we learn to put words together to make meaningful sentences. There are several theories of semantics. The learning theory views meaning as simply associations to words that we have learned.

More recently, the information-processing approach suggests that people process words using semantic memory. Apparently we learn the rules of semantics at a very young age.

Psycholinguists distinguish between surface structure and deep structure of sentences. The surface structure is simply the sequence of morphemes we hear or see in a sentence. The deep structure is the actual meaning of the sentence. "Mommy kissed Karen" and "Karen was kissed by mommy" have different surface structures, but both have the same deep structure, or meaning. Psycholinguist Noam Chomsky (1968) has proposed that we are able to relate the surface and deep structure of sentences through transformational grammar rules. These rules allow us to take ideas (deep structures) and convert them into meaningful sentences (surface structures).

When we wish to communicate something, we begin with a meaningful thought, select phrases to express the idea, and produce speech sounds that make up sentences. This process is called top-down processing by psycholinguists. When we want to understand language produced by someone else, we reverse the process and use bottom-up processing. Here we listen to the speech sounds and interpret the sounds as meaningful words that fit together in sentences that convey meaningful thoughts and ideas.

Figure 8.3. Transformational Grammar Rules

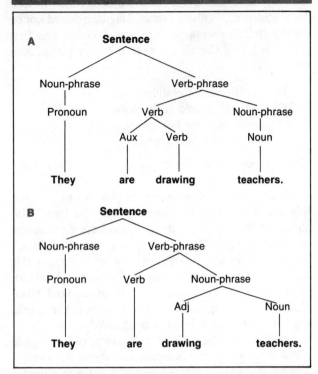

We use language rules to convert ideas into meaningful sentences. As shown here, the same sequence of words can have different meanings. In **A**, some people (they) are drawing pictures of the teachers. In **B**, the teachers (they) are identified as "drawing teachers" (after Chomsky, 1965).

Figure 8.4. Vocabulary Development

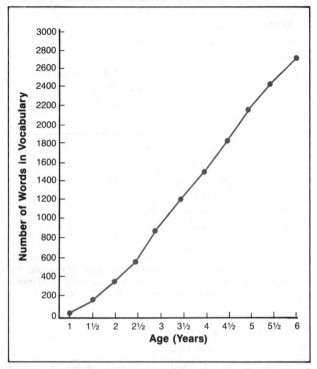

Children learn the basic structures of their language by age 3 and acquire a fairly extensive vocabulary by age 6 (after Smith, 1926).

Language Development in Children

Newborn babies often begin producing sounds within minutes of their birth. Historically it was thought that babies made random noises right up until they began to talk. However, Kaplan and Kaplan (1971) described four distinct stages of sound production occurring during the first year of life. The first stage occurs when babies begin to *cry* at birth. The second stage begins at about the end of the first month, when babies *coo* and vocalize. At around 6 months, babies begin to *babble*, the third stage. This babbling may contain sounds from many languages other than the one the baby will eventually acquire. In the fourth stage, starting at about one year of age, some sort of patterned *speech* can emerge.

Recent research has shown that babies are more aware of their early environment than was previously believed. Shortly after birth, infants react differently to the sound of their mother's voice than to that of an unfamiliar woman (DeCasper & Fifer, 1980). It has also been reported (Delack, 1976) that babies babble differently depending on the environment (crib versus with mother).

By about one year of age, babies say their first word, often "mama" or "dada." During the second year, babies develop their vocabulary by adding one word at a time. They use one word to communicate the meaning of a complete sentence (holophrastic speech) at this stage. Children say "juice" to mean "I would like some juice to drink, please." Most parents quickly learn what the child's words mean and respond appropriately (if not, the child usually communicates displeasure by crying or acting frustrated).

The next stage in language development, telegraphic speech, begins at about 2 years when children begin to use two-word sentences, like "my ball" and "Karen sleeping." They tend to include important words and leave out the rest. Even at this stage, children show an innate understanding of syntax allowing them to construct grammatically correct sentences. For example, they are likely to correctly say, "drink juice" rather than "juice drink" to indicate that they are thirsty.

Later, at 3 or 4 years of age, their sentences become longer and more complex. For instance, instead of "Cara Sue play," the child now says "Cara Sue plays with me." At this age, children begin using the past tense, and a variety of words. The size of their vocabulary grows rapidly, and by the time children enter school at the age of 5, they generally have a vocabulary of several thousand words.

Theories of Language Development

How do children acquire the language of their culture? Children everywhere learn to produce all the fundamental structures of their language within the first three years of life and have a vocabulary of several thousand words by about age 5. Children exposed early in their development to two different languages can easily learn to speak both fluently and with no foreign accent in either.

As a person grows older, however, it becomes more and more difficult to learn to speak a foreign language with fluency. In fact, it is extremely difficult for, say, an American in his or her thirties to learn to speak French as well as a Parisian does, even after years of living in Paris. Yet that American's 5-year-old son will catch up with his French playmates in a matter of months. This is currently happening in our country with Southeast Asians and other immigrants. Their children are able to pick up the English language very quickly at school and from friends, while their parents find it very difficult to learn English. Today some schools are making use of this early ability to learn a foreign language and offering a second language in elementary school, instead of waiting until later.

While force of habit and the interference of one's native language undoubtedly play some part in an adult's difficulty in learning another language, many psychologists think the difficulty may also be biologically influenced. Maturation may set the stage for a critical period of language development early in life.

Social interaction seems crucial for both the acquisition and the maintenance of spoken language. Younger people who have suffered long isolation usually come away mute and often never fully recover language. The most famous case is that of Victor, the Wild Boy of Aveyron, who after seven years in isolation, was discovered running wild in the forest of southern France. The boy was 12 years old at the time of his capture. The greatest scientists in France tried to rehabilitate him. In doing so, they created techniques of special education for the retarded and the deaf that are still in use today. But they never managed to teach Victor to speak normally. In the movie, *Greystoke, the Legend of Tarzan*, we again saw the great difficulty of trying to teach language to someone as an adult. The above examples illustrate the importance of other people in maintaining language performance.

Besides the *critical period hypothesis*, which states that if a person doesn't learn to speak during childhood, he or she will never learn to speak fluently, there are two major theories of language development—learning and biological.

Figure 8.5. The Wild Boy of Aveyron
One way scientists have been able to learn how a person comes to an understanding of concepts is to study children who, for various reasons, grew up without learning language. The Wild Boy of Aveyron was an animal-like child with no speech abilities when he was captured. This photo is from François Truffaut's film *The Wild Child*, a dramatization of the story of Victor, the Wild Boy of Aveyron.

Learning Theory. Because infants and children need to be around other people to develop language normally, many psychologists have emphasized the role of learning in language development. B. F. Skinner (1957) emphasized *reinforcement* in his theory of language acquisition. He argued that parents reinforce children for producing sounds that are recognizable as language. Through the process of shaping and reinforcement, children eventually learn which sounds and words will get them what they want.

Imitation also plays an important role in language development. Children try to imitate the words and phrases their parents use most frequently (Moerk, 1980). Many times, the children will repeat sentences they have heard others make, often in a simplified version. For example, "The bus will be coming soon" becomes "Bus coming." Children acquire the essence of language rules ("He goed to the store" and "My foots hurt") rather than pure imitation of complex sentences. Parents reinforce the structure of sentences and eventually the grammar is learned.

Biological Psycholinguistic Theory. As psycholinguists developed a better understanding of the complexity of adult language performance, it appeared unlikely that a small child could learn all the required rules of language in just a couple of years through reinforcement or imitation alone. Many psychologists currently accept Chomsky's psycholinguistic theory (1965) that children are biologically programmed to acquire language. Chomsky believes children are born with an internal language acquisition device (LAD) that

Figure 8.6.   Noam Chomsky
Chomsky proposed that children are biologically programmed to understand and acquire language. His revolutionary theories caused many learning and developmental psychologists to reexamine their methods and assumptions.

allows them to interpret the adult speech that they hear and to make their own sentences with the correct rules of grammar.

An interesting demonstration that children are acquiring rules as they master language comes from a study by Jean Berko (1958), who tested 4- to 7-year-old children to see whether they knew rules of sound change. The mere fact that a child correctly uses the plurals of nouns or the past tense of verbs does not prove that he or she knows the rules of grammar, since those particular forms may have been learned by imitation. On the other

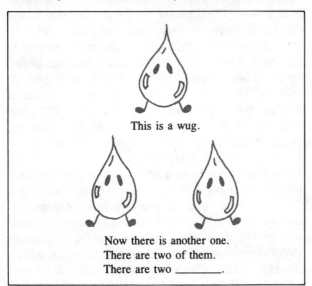

This is a wug.

Now there is another one.
There are two of them.
There are two _____.

Figure 8.7.   Test for Learning Syntax
Wugs, the imaginary figures Berko (1958) used in her experiments to test young children's ability to acquire the rules of grammar.

hand, suppose you show the child a picture with two objects and then ask that the following sentence be completed aloud: "This is a wug. Now there is another one. There are two of them. There are two _____." If the child correctly pluralizes the nonsense syllable ("wugs"), he or she knows the rule.

Berko also found that children successfully applied rules to nonsense syllables to form the past tense and the possessive: "This is a man who knows how to mot. He is motting. He did the same thing yesterday. What did he do yesterday? He _____." "This is a niz who owns a hat. Whose hat is it? It is the _____ hat."

Psychologists currently recognize the importance of environmental factors, while also realizing that biology plays an important role in language development. Future research will attempt to unravel the complex relationships that exist between biological and learning influences on language development.

THINKING

What comes to mind when you think about thinking? Do you envision a writer hard at work, or someone with a wrinkled forehead concentrating on a test? Thinking includes a wide variety of cognitive, or mental, activities: a student trying to remember an answer on a test; an employee contemplating asking the boss for a raise; a young child deciding whether to have chocolate or strawberry ice cream for dessert; or a man searching for lost car keys.

Psychologists cannot directly observe thinking, so it must be inferred from what a person does. As we discussed earlier, thinking is part of the area of cognitive psychology. Thinking can be defined as the cognitive or mental activity of manipulating symbols. For humans, thinking usually involves language, but can also involve mental images (Richardson, 1983).

Language and Thought

Does the language we speak influence the way we think and perceive the world around us? Benjamin Lee Whorf (1956) thought so. Most people believe that reality exists in much the same form for all people of sound mind. And all languages are similar in that they all have to deal with that reality by providing names for objects, qualities, actions, and relationships.

Whorf proposed in his linguistic relativity hypothesis that the perception of reality differs according to the language of the observer. More precisely, he contended that the world is experienced and conceived in different ways in different cultures and that language is the cause of these differences. There are two forms of the Whorfian hypothesis: the strong form states that language determines thought, while the weak form states that language influences thought.

Hopi Indian language has one name for everything that flies—except birds. Insects and airplanes are called by the same name in ordinary conversation without causing any special problems. That category would seem unnatural to us since it is far too general. But our word "snow" must seem extraordinarily general to Eskimos, who find it natural, and indeed necessary, to distinguish between slushy snow, hard-packed snow, falling snow, and melting snow. The Eskimos may have many more snow terms than we do, but they have half as many basic color terms. While we make a clear distinction between the colors green and blue, the Eskimos have one name to describe both.

What do these differences in language and culture demonstrate? A strong form of the Whorfian hypothesis would predict, for example, that Eskimos cannot distinguish as well as we can between blue and green. Most psychologists, however, make more moderate claims about the relation between cognition and language. For instance, Eleanor Heider (1972) compared the language and color-naming abilities of Americans and Dani, a primitive tribe from New Guinea. The Dani have only two basic color names, "mola" for bright colors and "mili" for dark colors. If the Whorfian hypothesis is correct, these two cultures would think about colors differently. When she showed her subjects colored chips, the Dani did indeed classify them into two categories, whereas the Americans used a larger number of categories to name colors. Then she showed subjects one color and 30 seconds later asked them to select that color from among 40 colored chips. None of the subjects had any difficulty matching the exact color. Even though the Dani did not have different words for different colors, they could still easily identify all of the individual colors. Thus, language was not necessary for thought in this case.

While Whorf's linguistic relativity has not received strong support recently, there is little doubt that language has an effect on our thinking and behavior. By knowing what a word means, you may increase your attention to the term and look for examples of it. For instance, now that you know the definition of shaping (from chapter 6, "Learning"), you may be more alert to find examples of shaping in your environment. It is also possible that language shapes our attitudes. Sexism and prejudice may be easier to learn with the language we use. For example, when a language uses masculine words (policeman, mailman) to refer to occupations available to both sexes, a sex-role stereotype is created which could affect our thinking and our behavior. The relationship between language and other cognitive processes, like thinking, is extremely complex, and will require much more research to obtain definitive answers.

Concept Formation

Psychologists use the term concept formation, or concept learning, to refer to the development of the ability to respond to common features of categories of objects or events. A concept refers to a set of features with one or more properties in common. Concepts allow us to classify objects and events. In learning a concept, you must focus on the relevant features and ignore those that are irrelevant (Bourne & colleagues, 1986). For instance, paperbacks and hardcover editions are all books. But you must also discriminate on the basis of relevant features: a stack of papers is not a book. What is the crucial feature of a book? Perhaps it is the presence of a binding. Most concepts, however, cannot be formed on the basis of a single critical feature.

Types of Concepts. Johnson-Laird and Wason (1977) identified two general types of concepts: natural, everyday types and formal systematic types. We use language to identify natural concepts intuitively in everyday life. For example, fruits, birds, or fish are natural concepts because each category includes objects that have similar characteristics. Sometimes natural concepts can cause confusion, as when we attempt to classify penguins, whales, or tomatoes.

Natural concepts are important to us in a number of ways. Without concepts, each object in our lives would be unique, making thinking difficult or impossible. Being able to utilize concepts helps improve our memory, as we can easily form associations and categorize things we want to remember; we do not have to constantly relearn what objects are each time we encounter an unfamiliar one. For example, we recognize an automobile as a transportation vehicle regardless of the particular model.

Formal concepts have clear and unambiguous rules that specify exactly which attributes or features define the category. Rules let us know how the features must be combined for a particular concept. For example, male dogs include the rule that the animal must be a dog and must be a male. Solso (1988) described five types of formal concepts defined by rules that psychologists have studied: affirmative, conjunctive, disjunctive, conditional, and biconditional. The affirmative rule is the easiest to learn, as it includes all instances of an attribute. For example, all males would include every single male animal or plant.

Many concepts are defined by the conjunctive rule in which objects or events must have two or more distinct

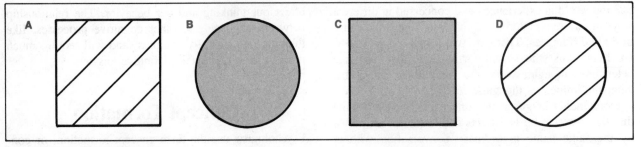

Figure 8.8. Types of Concepts
If the figures (above) are defined by two categories: square and striped, then **A** represents a conjunctive concept. If the figures (above) are defined by a category of either square or striped, then **A**, **C**, and **D** represent a disjunctive concept. Find the figure defined by the conjunctive concept of colored and square.

features to belong to the class in question. For example, a philosopher in ancient Greece defined "human being" with the conjunctive concept, "animals having two legs and no feathers."

Other concepts are defined by the disjunctive rule, in which any one of two or more different features define the concept. The concept of a strike in baseball is disjunctive. A swing missing the ball, the failure to swing when the ball passes directly over the plate, or a hit landing outside the baselines (foul ball) all qualify separately as strikes. As you might expect, disjunctive concepts are generally harder to learn than conjunctive ones.

The conditional rule states a specific situation to define a concept. For example, "if the stimulus is round, then it must be white." (Note that if white, it could be any shape, and thus this rule applies only in one direction.) The biconditional rule extends the condition in both directions. For instance, "if round, then white and if white, then round."

Learning Concepts. Most of the words we use refer to concepts and not to particular things. Proper nouns such as "William James" and "California" are exceptions. In learning some of their first concepts, children commonly focus not on names but on the functions of objects. For example, a spoon is something to eat with, and a pan is something to cook in. Other early concepts are based on groupings of objects that are similar in some respects: liquid things, moving things, or soft things.

Several theories have been proposed to explain how we learn concepts. The stimulus-response *association theory* was proposed by Clark Hull (1920). He argued that we learn to associate a particular response (the concept) with a variety of stimuli that define the concept. For instance, we associate the concept "dog" with all of the characteristics of dogs (four legs, fur, tail, bark) and are able to generalize the concept to unfamiliar dogs.

The *hypothesis testing theory* was proposed by Jerome Bruner and his colleagues (1956). Bruner believed that we develop a strategy of testing our hypotheses about a concept by making guesses about which attri-

butes are essential for defining the concept. While this tends to be the method used by subjects in an experiment, it might not be appropriate in everyday life (perhaps because we often use natural concepts rather than formal concepts in everyday life).

Eleanor Rosch (1978) suggested that the natural concepts in everyday life are learned through examples rather than abstract rules. Her *exemplar theory* proposes that we learn the concept of dog by seeing a wide variety of dogs and developing a *prototype* of what the typical dog is like. Busemeyer and Myung (1988) studied prototype learning in college students by presenting a series of exemplars and asking the subjects to reproduce the prototype. This type of study allows researchers to gain an understanding of the concept learning process.

Over the years, everyone is faced with an infinite number of complex stimuli. How we choose to group and sort them into concepts will depend upon our experiences with the environment, interests, beliefs, and values. Consider the concept "job." To one person it may mean an unpleasant task, while to another it is a means of achieving fulfillment. Concept formation is a form of thinking that helps us to better understand the world we live in, as well as ourselves.

PROBLEM SOLVING AND CREATIVITY

A chimpanzee sees a bunch of bananas suspended from the ceiling, well out of his reach. He stands up and makes a grab for them, but cannot get close. He then moves a box to a spot underneath the bananas, climbs on it, and reaches up. Still, he cannot quite make it. Finally, he takes another box, sets it on top of the first one, climbs on top of them, and takes the bananas. He has solved a problem.

Our 20-month-old son followed the same procedure in

problem solving. He wanted a cookie from the cookie jar on the kitchen counter. After looking around, he pushed a chair over to the counter, climbed onto it, and then proceeded to help himself to several cookies.

We have a *problem* whenever difficulties get in the way of achieving a goal. Throughout our lives, we are continuously faced with problems that we must successfully solve. Some problems are simple, such as deciding what clothes to wear for the day. Other problems are much more complex, such as deciding upon a career or a marriage partner.

Theories of Problem Solving

As you might imagine, there are many ways to approach problem solving. Generally, psychologists have studied problem solving from one of three viewpoints: *learning, insight,* and *information processing.*

Learning Theory. The earliest approach to problem solving was based heavily on learning theory and emphasized the role of *trial and error.* As we discussed in chapter 6, "Learning," Edward Thorndike studied trial-and-error learning in cats early in this century. As the cats attempted to escape from the puzzle boxes, they learned to show particular types of behaviors. Through trial and error and association of reward with behavior, the cats solved problems.

People also use trial-and-error learning in solving problems. My computer programming skills are minimal, and so when a program I am working on does not run properly, I change each statement randomly until I learn what works. Have you ever had a radio not work? Chances are that you used trial and error to remedy the

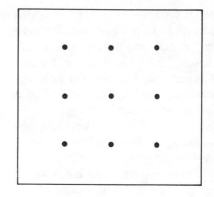

Figure 8.10. Nine Dot Problem
Scheerer (1963) said that people maintain assumptions that interfere with problem solving. Connect all nine dots with four straight lines without lifting your pencil from the paper or without going through any dot more than once. Solution on page 192.

situation. Perhaps you checked for loose wires or weak batteries, or made sure the switches were properly set. Trial-and-error learning is often used when we don't have other information to guide us.

Insight Theory. Trial-and-error learning is different from the method used by the chimpanzee to get the bananas mentioned above. The chimp demonstrated a far greater degree of *insight* in his situation, a sudden grasping of the means necessary to achieve a goal. Sometimes when we face a difficult problem, we become frustrated and feel we will never find the solution. Then, suddenly we see things in a different light, and the solution is so easy it amazes us.

The Gestalt psychologist, Wolfgang Köhler, described his experiments on the insight approach to problem solving in *The Mentality of Apes* (1925). Köhler presented problems to animals that could not be solved by simple trial-and-error learning. In one study, a chimpanzee named Sultan was trying to obtain a banana which was out of his reach. There was a short stick in the cage and a longer stick out of his reach outside the cage. Sultan first tried to get the banana with the short

Figure 8.9. Insight in Problem Solving
Gestalt psychologist Wolfgang Köhler studied learning by insight. Here the chimpanzee appears to think about the problem of getting fruit into his cage and then solves the problem by using the sticks together. By insight, the subject gains a sudden perception of the relationship of the cognitive elements necessary to solve a problem.

stick, but failed. He sat for a while looking around the cage. Then quite suddenly he rushed over, used the short stick to pull the longer stick into his reach, and then quickly used the longer stick to pull in the banana. Köhler cited this as an example of insight. Psychologists don't know how insight operates, but do realize that it can be a useful approach to problem solving.

Information Processing Theory. The third approach cognitive psychologists have used in recent years employs the terms and concepts of *information processing* in analyzing problem solving. The emphasis in information processing is on the active role of the problem solver in (1) formulating the problem; (2) transforming it in ways that facilitate its solution; (3) laying out a strategy for solving it; and (4) using the information or feedback that he or she receives while proceeding through the successive stages toward the solution.

The information processing approach to problem solving often makes use of flow charts and computer simulation. A flow chart is a diagram showing the possible choices at each step in solving the problem. This helps the problem solver visualize the choices and understand the potential outcomes. Computer simulation is the procedure in which the computer is programmed to approximate some event or activity. Computer programs of *artificial intelligence* are used in perception, memory, language, and problem solving (Solso, 1988). For example, computers have been programmed to play chess by determining strategies and outguessing opponents (in a fashion similar to what humans do).

All three approaches have validity because there are many kinds of problems and many ways of solving them. Human problem solving involves both trial and error and insight. Threading a needle requires few insights, but may take several unsuccessful attempts before finding the one that works. Solving a riddle, however, usually involves a sudden insight, the so-called "aha" reaction. However, insight itself requires past experience, which may have been largely trial and error. Sometimes solutions are a result neither of sudden insights nor of trial and error, but of understanding some general principles and applying them systematically to the problem. Writing a computer program or solving an algebra problem are two examples of this kind of problem solving that cognitive theorists find especially interesting. Still other problems are solved not by insight, trial and error, or understanding, but by the rote application of memorized rules. Some students who barely pass their courses may employ this process.

Problem-Solving Effectiveness

Our success in solving problems is influenced by several factors. One of these is perception. Unless we properly perceive the problem and what is relevant to its solution, we will be unable to solve it. Another factor is motivation. As you would expect, increased motivation improves problem solving—but only up to a point. Very intense levels of motivation actually interfere. You can be so anxious to achieve something that your anxiety

---

Figure 8.11. A Flow Chart in Information Processing

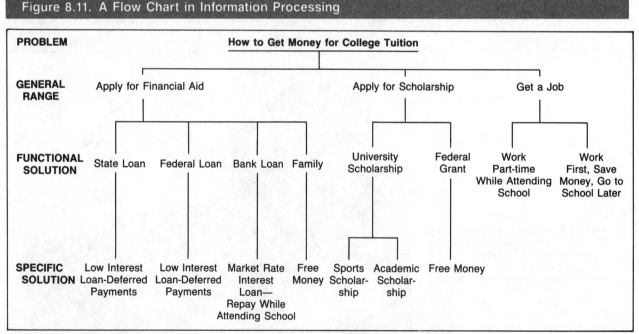

Much as a computer processes information in a logical step-by-step fashion, a flow chart can aid in the solution of a complex problem by visualizing the stages of decision making.

prevents you from succeeding. And for humans, language is perhaps the most valuable and important tool involved in solving problems. Its use mediates between the problem and the solution. For most problems, the use of language is indispensable in the organization of thoughts leading to a solution.

Stages in Solving Problems. Psychologists believe people generally go through three or four steps in solving problems. The insight approach to problem solving includes the steps of preparation, incubation, illumination, and verification.

In the first stage, *preparation*, we study the problem carefully and collect information that might be used to solve it. We consider as many possible solutions as we can.

When we have exhausted all the possibilities, we need to go into the second stage of problem solving called *incubation*. We need to rest from the problem and let our brain continue to sort out the possibilities. Some psychologists suggest that sleep is a good incubating activity.

Sometimes the *illumination* stage is called the "aha" phenomenon. Suddenly we get an insight into a very likely solution to the problem. It's as if a light bulb in our brain is suddenly illuminated.

In the last stage, *verification*, we test out the solution which seems most likely. If correct, then the problem is solved. If not, then we go back to the preparation stage and collect more facts that could lead to new hypotheses or ideas.

A more general theory of problem solving (Bourne & colleagues, 1986) includes the steps of preparation, production, and evaluation.

In the *preparation* step, we become aware of the problem and try to understand all sides of it. We often try to obtain additional information about the problem so we can feel comfortable working on it.

In the *production* step, we consider as many solutions as possible. This may require obtaining additional information or applying a solution strategy to the information we have.

Finally, in the *evaluation* step, we evaluate the appropriateness of our solutions. If successful, we have solved the problem. If not, we go back to preparation and production to try again.

The IDEAL program for solving problems was proposed by Bransford and Stein (1984). They suggested that the steps in problem solving include the following: *Identify* the problem that you are going to solve. *Define* the problem by collecting all of the available information. *Explore* all of the possible strategies for solving the problem. *Act* on the strategy most likely to solve the problem. And *look* at your solution and evaluate the effectiveness of your strategy.

Strategies. A good aid in solving a problem is prior

Figure 8.12. The Two-String Problem
This problem requires the subject to tie two hanging strings together although one cannot be reached while the other one is held. Insight comes when the subject realizes that an object can be attached to one string and then that string can be swung like a pendulum. This enables the subject to grasp both strings and tie them together.

practice in solving similar problems. Psychologists' best guess about what occurs during such practice is that the problem solver develops strategies and plans for attack. Consider how an absolute beginner might play Twenty Questions. When told that the object is animal, his first question might be "Is it a dog?" His second question might be "Is it a cat?" The experienced player has developed a more successful strategy of starting with the most general questions (for example, "Is it human?" or "real?" or "live?" or "a whole animal?") before narrowing down to more specific questions.

Two important strategies in problem solving are algorithms and heuristics. With an algorithm, or random search strategy, every possible solution is tried until the correct one is found. For example, the three letters in the anagram NFU would be rearranged until the correct solution, FUN, is found. Sometimes algorithms can efficiently be used in computer programs, but they are often confusing. People do not use algorithms too often in everyday problem-solving situations, partly because they don't work for some problems and partly because they usually take an extremely long time. Even computer programs used in artificial intelligence research do not often utilize algorithms (especially when heuristics are available).

A heuristic is a rule-of-thumb problem-solving strategy in which a person selectively tests solutions most likely to be correct (Matlin, 1989). For example, we would most likely try a vowel in the middle to produce FUN, without having to try all of the other solutions. Heuristics are quick solutions, but they sometimes do not work (as when they prevent us from trying new ideas).

This strategy might involve a means-end analysis, in which we evaluate the difference between the current situation and the desired outcome. For example, in a chess game, we test what the outcome of various moves might be before we actually make a move (Pfau & Murphy, 1988).

Learning to Learn. A well-known experiment with monkeys by Harry Harlow (1949) illustrates the advantages of prior problem-solving experience. Harlow first taught the monkeys to choose which of several objects concealed food. Each monkey had to select from among a triangle, a circle, and a square. Eventually, the monkeys learned that the food was always underneath the triangle, no matter what its position in relation to the other objects. When Harlow changed the location of the food to, say, the circle, the monkeys took much less time to learn to uncover the circle than they had taken to learn to uncover the triangle. The "skill" in this problem-solving situation transferred quickly because of prior experience with the original problem. Harlow calls this learning to learn.

Mental Sets. Previous practice and experience with solving problems sometimes hinders future problem solving. This frequently occurs when the new problem appears on the surface to be similar to the familiar one, but actually requires a different solution. Difficulty arises because we tend to develop mental sets, that is, our thinking becomes standardized and we approach new problems in fixed ways, and, as a result, other possible approaches do not occur to us.

What are the missing letters in the following series?

A E F H ? ?

If you studied these letters closely, you will notice that these letters of the alphabet are all made up of straight lines (the ones omitted have curved lines in them). Thus, the ones that would come next would be I, K, and L.

Now, with that experience, find the missing letters in this series:

O T T F ? ? ?

This series should be more difficult for you because you are probably attempting to solve it by examining physical characteristics of alphabet letters. If so, you have formed a mental set. In this case, that information was irrelevant to the solution of the new problem. These are the first letters in the numerical counting series (one, two, three). Therefore, the missing letters are F, S, and S, for five, six, and seven.

While mental set can interfere with problem-solving effectiveness, remember that sometimes learning to learn can overcome this difficulty. Let's try one more series of letters:

M T W T ? ? ?

If you were now thinking of words that began with these letters, you probably recognized the days of the week. The missing letters are F, S, and S for Friday, Saturday, and Sunday. The important point is to be aware of the potential for mental set to occur.

Functional Fixedness. When we habitually use an object in a certain way, we often do not think of new uses for it that could help solve other problems. Its function has become fixed. Such functional fixedness is a special case of a mental set that interferes with successful problem solving. Several studies indicate that

Figure 8.13. Water-Container Problems

Problem No.	Capacity of Containers			Obtain Exactly These Amounts of Water
	Container A	Container B	Container C	
1	21	127	3	100
2	14	163	25	99
3	18	43	10	5
4	9	42	6	21
5	20	59	4	31
6	23	49	3	20
7	10	36	7	3

Using the capacity of the containers A, B, and C, find a method of measuring out the exact amount of liquid called for, in the column to the right.

the longer we use an object in a certain way, the less likely we are to find new uses for it. A common table knife, for example, is normally used for eating. When we want to attach the leads from an antenna to a television set, its possible use as a screwdriver may not occur to us, especially if we have at hand a "real" screwdriver. The same sort of functionally fixed thinking led to the design of the first automobiles, which strongly resembled horse-drawn carriages. There are, of course, limits as to how fixed our uses are: a shovel is something we dig with, but most of us would not hesitate to use it to kill a poisonous snake that happened to slither our way while we were digging a hole.

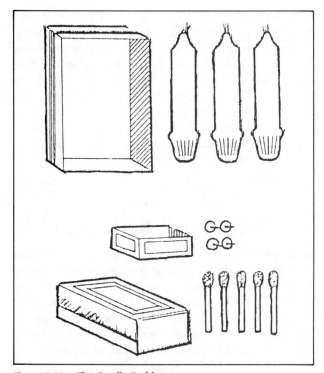

Figure 8.14. The Candle Problem
Using only a candle, thumbtack, and a box of matches, how would you mount the candle on a wall or bulletin board?

Confirmation Bias. A major obstacle to effective problem solving is confirmation bias, the tendency to selectively seek information that confirms our hypothesis. An effective problem-solving strategy is to try to find cases that disprove our hypothesis. But instead we only seek proof, limiting our knowledge. Peter Wason (1968) asked subjects to discover the rule that applied to a three-number series, such as 2, 4, 6. Most subjects tried other series that increased by 2, such as 1, 3, 5 or 8, 10, 12. These are examples of the rule. But most subjects were surprised to find that the rule was not "increase by 2," but rather "increase in magnitude." They should have tested the rule by trying to disprove it rather than trying to prove it. For example, 1, 2, 3 or 8,

10 would have also been positive examples, and would have forced the subjects to rethink their hypothesis.

Creativity

Since creativity involves coming up with new or unusual responses to familiar circumstances, it is closely related to the ability to solve problems. Psychological research on creativity has focused primarily on two areas: measuring creativity in people and identifying the personality traits of people who are recognized as highly creative.

Measurement of Creativity. Guilford (1967) distinguishes between *convergent thinking*, coming up with the single correct response, and *divergent thinking*, coming up with new and unusual responses. Intelligence tests typically measure convergent thinking, whereas divergent thinking is more involved in creativity.

There are a number of creativity tests, including the *Divergent Production Test* and the *Remote Associates Test*. In general, creativity tests ask the person to do such things as make up an ending for a story, name as many uses as possible for common objects, elaborate on drawings of simple geometric forms, or come up with words related to a series of other words. For example, you might be asked to list all the uses of a knife you can think of in one minute. Responses are scored for originality (how unique or different your answers are from others), usefulness (how relevant and practical your answers are), and quantity (how many different responses you came up with).

Research on the measurement of creativity has produced mixed results. Although results tend to be reliable, there is little evidence of validity outside of the test situation (Anastasi, 1988). And many psychologists question whether in fact the tests tap all that is involved in creativity (Weisberg, 1986). In general, the skills measured by intelligence and creativity tests tend to overlap (Sternberg & Davidson, 1982). People with higher intelligence generally tend to be more creative than people with lower intelligence.

Characteristics of Creative People. In addition to being related to intelligence, creativity is influenced by a variety of other factors. Although there is no one particular personality profile for all creative people, there are some tendencies which have been observed. Teresa Amabile (1983) reviewed much of the research on the influences on creativity in people. She concluded that creative people tend to enjoy doing things because of internal motivation. They tend to have the freedom to choose their own activities, and live in a stimulating and exciting environment. Creative people often tend to be independent and don't need external motivation, that is, social approval when solving problems.

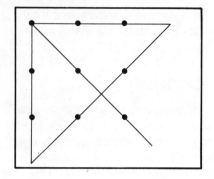

Solution to the nine dot problem for Figure 8.10. (after Scheerer, 1963).

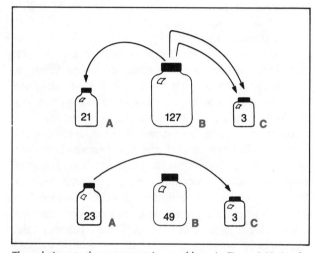

The solutions to the water-container problems in Figure 8.13. involve the formula B − A − 2C = desired liquid as shown in the top drawing. A mental set in solving problems 1–5 usually prevents the easier solutions to problem 6 (A − C) as shown in the bottom drawing and problem 7 (A + C) (after Luchins & Luchins, 1959).

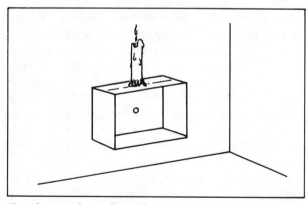

The solution to the candle problem in Figure 8.14. involves the ability to perceive that materials can be used in an unusual manner. The box, for example, need not be used as a container. This illustrates how functional fixedness can interfere with the solution to a problem.

Amabile (12983) suggested several things that could increase creativeness in children and adults. It is important to provide a stimulating environment for children, in which they are encouraged to be independent thinkers. Parents and educators should emphasize children's strengths and expose them to cultural diversity. Adults can increase creativity by learning to relax, having

freedom of choice in making decisions, reducing stress, and receiving encouragement from employers, family and friends. Research is continuing in an attempt to understand the environment in which people can best express creativity.

DEFINITION AND THEORIES OF INTELLIGENCE

Intelligence is a factor by which most people identify themselves or their behavior at any given point in time. "I wish I were as smart as you." "That was a stupid thing to do." But attempts at defining intelligence have been difficult if not confusing and controversial. Is it one specific ability, or several? Is it innate or learned? Is it static or changeable? Definitions of intelligence have often derived from theories of intelligence and these in turn may have been derived from measurements of observed behavior that indicate the components of intelligence.

Definition of Intelligence

Although everyone seems to have an idea about what intelligence entails, not all definitions are the same. In 1982 Robert Sternberg reported on his attempts to discover what psychologists and laypersons with no expertise in psychology think about intelligence. Through surveys, he found that when academic experts define intelligence, they usually speak of the abilities to verbalize, solve problems, and achieve goals. Laypersons, on the other hand, usually associate intelligence with verbal ability, practical problem-solving ability, and social competence. Although there was a great deal of overlap, Sternberg found that the psychologists stressed motivation ("works hard," "is persistent," "gets involved") whereas the layperson emphasized social-cultural aspects ("sensitivity to other people," "is honest with self and others").

Intelligence is a difficult concept to study, partially because we cannot observe it physically and partially because it is such a common term that in everyday language it is often misused (Green, 1981). Sometimes, a circular definition of intelligence is used: Intelligence is what is measured by intelligence tests, and intelligence tests measure intelligence. While this definition doesn't spell out the characteristics of intelligence, it is possible to discover them by examining intelligence tests themselves. Most stress verbal skills, quantitative skills, and problem-solving skills, the same characteristics that many think of when describing intelligence.

David Wechsler, the creator of a number of intelligence tests, considers intelligence to be the capacity to understand one's world and the resourcefulness to cope with the challenges of that world (Wechsler, 1975). Thus, you are intelligent if you know what is happening around you and if you are able to meet the challenges of your environment. For example, people in business are considered intelligent if they understand the financial world and are successful in making a profit. Students are considered intelligent if they understand the course material and are able to earn above-average grades.

A similar approach is to define intelligence as the skills necessary for success in a culture (Vernon, 1979). Intelligence is a culture-bound concept in that the particular skills necessary for success vary by culture. Verbal and mathematical skills are important in American culture, but speed and accuracy in throwing a spear might be more valuable in a hunting culture.

Sternberg (1986) suggested that while the particulars may be debated, there appears to be a consensus on what kind of behavior is considered intelligent. Sternberg stated that the ability to learn from experience and the ability to adapt to the environment are essential ingredients in a definition of intelligence and thus we define intelligence as the capacity to learn and behave adaptively.

Theories of Intelligence

Over the years, a large number of formal theories of intelligence have been proposed. Here we review some of the most influential ones: Charles Spearman's g factor; Louis Thurstone's seven primary factors; J. P. Guilford's model; and Robert Sternberg's triarchic theory.

Spearman's Factor Theory. Students who do well in one class usually have few problems with other classes or in participating in extracurricular activities. Charles Spearman (1904) proposed a theory of intelligence which included a general factor *g*, that gave a person the ability to achieve success in a wide variety of intellectual tasks. But Spearman also noted most people were best in one or two particular areas, and so he included specific factors *s* that allowed a person to excel on particular tasks. For example, students who have trouble in psychology may excel in mathematics. The combination of the *g* and *s* factors provides the specific intelligence level of an individual.

Thurstone's Primary Mental Abilities. Louis Thurstone (1938) believed that intelligence was determined by seven primary mental abilities rather than one general unknown factor. The seven abilities include:

verbal comprehension, numerical ability, memory, perceptual speed, spatial ability, verbal fluency, and reasoning and were incorporated in Thurstone's *Primary Mental Abilities Test*. The different abilities of an individual would explain why someone might excel in mathematics but do poorly in history. However, Thurstone later found that people who do well in one area also do well in others, suggesting that there may be some general factor underlying the various abilities. For example, verbal comprehension and reasoning were highly correlated, and could be considered what Spearman called the *g* factor.

Guilford's Model of Intelligence. One of the most sophisticated theories of intelligence was proposed by J. P. Guilford (1967, 1982). He suggested that there are three separate dimensions interacting in intelligence: contents, operations, and products. Contents include information a person is thinking about. Operations are the actions of a person. Products are the result of thinking about the information. Through a statistical technique, Guilford was able to determine five types of contents, five types of operations, and six types of products. If these three dimensions are thought of as sides on a cube, it can be demonstrated that 150 different mental abilities might determine intelligence.

Sternberg's Triarchic Theory of Intelligence. Yale University psychologist Robert Sternberg (1985, 1986) recently proposed the triarchic theory of intelligence. After studying theories and tests of intelligence, he concluded that intelligence was a much broader concept than what was previously assumed. The triarchic theory consists of three parts: componential, experiential, and contextual subtheories of intelligence.

The *componential subtheory* deals with the relation-

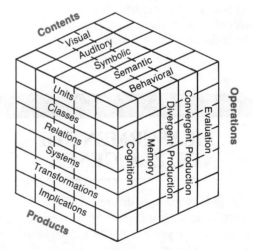

Figure 8.15. Guilford's Model of the Structure of Intelligence
This model proposes that intelligence consists of 150 independent abilities which result from the interaction of five types of contents, five operations, and six types of products (after Guilford, 1982).

ship of intelligence to the internal world of the individual. A component is a mental process. Metacomponents are processes that we use in planning and evaluating the behaviors that we exhibit. Performance components are the cognitive processes used when we actually solve problems. Knowledge-acquisition components are important whenever we learn something new. These form the core of the theory, and are used when gaining experience in new situations and solving problems.

There are two components to the *experiential subtheory*: the ability to deal with novel, unfamiliar tasks and situations and the ability to automatize information processing. We are able to perform complex verbal and mathematical mental tasks efficiently only because much of the procedure is automatic. For instance, reading requires operations that can be done without conscious thought. An inability to automatize cognitive processing results in less intelligent performance.

The *contextual subtheory* includes the components of adaptation, environmental selection, and environmental shaping. To be intelligent, one must adapt to the environment and at the same time, be able to decide when to select a different environmental situation. For instance, it is important to adapt to the work environment but if the values of the company we work for are incompatible with our own, the intelligent thing to do would be to change jobs if possible. When we can't adapt to our environment, and it is not possible to select a new one, intelligence helps us shape our present environment. In the work example, we might try to convince our boss to view things differently.

Sternberg (1986) argued that existing intelligence tests do not measure all of the intellectual skills included in the triarchic theory. The ideal test of intelligence would be one that takes components, experience, and context into consideration. We presented Sternberg's triarchic intelligence theory in detail because it is currently considered to be a major contribution to the field, and will be influential in the future.

MEASURMENT OF INTELLIGENCE

Do you remember the different tests you've taken throughout your school career? Some were designed to predict how well you would do in the future, while others measured how much you knew at the time. While both kinds of tests measure your abilities, they have different functions. Psychologists are interested in both aptitude and achievement tests.

Characteristics of Tests

Aptitude tests are designed to predict what a person can accomplish in the future with proper training. The General Aptitude Test Battery is commonly used to test the ability of people to achieve success in a wide number of occupations. These tests measure such concepts as musical potential, athletic ability, writing potential, or general intellectual capacity.

Many colleges require high school students to take the Scholastic Aptitude Test (SAT) or the American College Test (ACT) prior to admission. The SAT and ACT are multiple-choice tests that measure verbal and mathematical abilities of students. The basic idea is that knowledge gained in high school and expressed on the test should be a fairly good predictor of how well the student will do in college. As such, they are predictive tests, but also rely on measurement of the achievement of the test takers.

The SAT was first given in 1941, and although the questions are continually changed, they have been designed to remain equivalent. Thus, it is possible to compare the scores of students who take the test each year with previous years. In the 1960s and 1970s, the SAT scores dropped significantly. This has been attributed partially to the fact that in the 1960s more students took the test to get into college (Astin & Garber, 1982). Zajonc (1986) proposed that the decline was due to the large number of postwar babies born in the 1940s and 1950s, since as the number of children in a family increase, the family's resources must be spread out and each child would have a slightly lower IQ than in only-child families (we discuss Zajonc's theory later in this chapter). He also predicted that as families became smaller in the 1960s, the scores would increase in the late 1980s (which is what is apparently happening).

Achievement tests are designed to measure what a person can do at the time the test is given. A final examination that measures how much of the material you have mastered in a course such as this one is an example of an achievement test. Undoubtedly, you have taken many achievement tests in school.

Intelligence tests are usually aptitude tests designed to measure a broad range of mental capabilities. These tests are often used to predict future academic success. Alfred Binet devised the first real intelligence test for this purpose. Actually, aptitude tests depend to a certain degree on the achievement and knowledge of the test taker. Achievement and aptitude tests could be thought of as a continuum, with intelligence tests closer to the aptitude end.

What makes a good intelligence test? Originally, Binet developed the intelligence test to predict future academic success. The value of an intelligence test to predict achievement depends on several important factors: validity, reliability, standardization, objectivity, and practicality.

Validity, as discussed in chapter 1, "The Study of Psychology," refers to the degree to which a test actually measures what it is intended to measure. A valid intelligence test would measure intelligence, not memory, speed, guessing ability, or vocabulary. Reliability is the degree to which a person's score at one time is the same at a different time. A reliable intelligence test would yield consistent scores from one time to the next.

Standardization is the process of obtaining a sample of scores representative of the population, and necessary in interpreting a particular subject's score. For example, if a friend of yours tells you that he or she received a score of 179 on a test, how would you know whether this was a good score? It would help if you knew that the test contained a possible 200 points, the mean score was 125, and the range for the class was 75 to 190.

Psychologists standardize tests so that they can interpret individual test results. The first step is to define the population serving as the standardization group. For example, we might wish to know how an individual compared to other adult Americans, and so we would standardize the test on the American adult population. Or a population might include all high school seniors in the United States. After the population is identified, we need to obtain a representative sample, one that will allow us to describe what the entire population is like.

An intelligence test should be objective. Objectivity assures that a test's results are not affected by the personal feelings and biases of the examiner. Ideally, a test should be constructed so that any qualified person can administer and score it, and obtain the same results as any other scorer.

An intelligence test should also be practical. Practicality provides that a test can be administered easily and scored in a reasonable amount of time. Chances are good that psychologists would not be interested in a new test requiring five people to administer and 16 hours to complete.

Tests which are valid, reliable, standardized, objective, and practical meet the general requirements for use. Developing intelligence tests which meet all of these requirements is a difficult task.

Intelligence tests can be divided into individual or group tests, depending on the method of administration. Originally, only individual tests were used. However, during World War I the United States Armed Forces needed to test many individuals quickly. A group intelligence test, the Armed Forces General Classification Test, was developed for this purpose. We discuss two important individual intelligence tests next.

The Stanford-Binet Intelligence Scale

Alfred Binet was the director of the psychological laboratory at the Sorbonne, Paris, when he was asked by the French government to devise a test that would

ALFRED BINET

BIOGRAPHICAL ☆ HIGHLIGHT ☆

Alfred Binet was born in 1857 in Nice, France. He received a doctorate in 1894, based on his research on the nervous system of insects. In 1894 Binet was appointed director of the psychology laboratory at the Sorbonne. He spent the next several years studying topics such as handwriting, hypnosis, perception, and thinking. In 1895 he started an important journal, *L'Annee psychologique*.

Around 1900 he began publishing research on thinking that he had been conducting on his two daughters. In 1904 he was asked to help identify students in the Paris school system who needed special education because of their low level of intellectual functioning. Binet and his colleague, Theodore Simon, published the first intelligence scale in 1905.

Binet and Simon tested mentally retarded children and set guidelines for the degree of retardation. They decided that a child with a mental age of less than two years would be called an idiot. An imbecile had a mental age of between two and seven years, while a moron had a mental age above seven. While modified, this type of classification is still used today.

During the next several years, Binet spent much of his time testing children and revising the intelligence test, first in 1908 and again in 1911, the year of his death. Binet's early work on intelligence testing has stimulated an enormous amount of research in this area of psychology.

Figure 8.16. Examples from Stanford-Binet Intelligence Scale

AGE	TASK
2	**Naming parts of the body.** Child is shown a large paper doll and asked to point to various parts of the body.
3	**Visual-motor skills.** Child is shown a bridge built of three blocks and asked to build one like it. Can copy a drawing of a circle.
4	**Opposite analogies.** Fills in the missing word when asked: "Brother is a boy; sister is a _____. "In daytime it is light; at night it is _____." **Reasoning.** Answers correctly when asked: "Why do we have houses?" "Why do we have books?"
5	**Vocabulary.** Defines words such as *ball, hat,* and *stove.* **Visual-motor skills.** Can copy a drawing of a square.
6	**Number concepts.** Is able to give the examiner nine blocks when asked to do so.
8	**Memory for stories.** Listens to a story and answers questions about it.
9	**Rhymes.** Answers correctly when asked: "Tell me the name of a color that rhymes with Fred." "Tell me a number that rhymes with free."
12	**Verbal absurdities.** Tells what is foolish about statements such as, "Bill Jones's feet are so big that he has to put his trousers on over his head."
14	**Inference.** Examiner folds a piece of paper a number of times, notching a corner with scissors each time. Subject is asked the rule for determining how many holes there will be when the paper is unfolded.
Adult (15 years and older)	**Differences.** Can describe the difference between "misery and poverty," "character and reputation." **Memory for reversed digits.** Can repeat six digits backwards (that is, in reverse order) after they are read aloud by the examiner.

See Age 12 in the chart to the right.

It is possible to gauge a person's mental age by the answer given to each one of these questions. It is assumed that a person may be able to solve more complex problems as he or she gets older.

predict which children could most benefit from special education classes. Binet and his colleague, Theodore Simon, published the *Binet-Simon Intelligence Scale* in 1905. This test consisted of 30 tests of varying difficulty which were used to measure the functioning level of Paris schoolchildren.

Binet knew that reasoning and problem-solving ability increased with age. He tested children of different ages to determine the ability of each age level. This led him to establish the concept of mental age—what the typical child of a given chronological age (counted in years) can do. For example, a child who does what a typical 5-year-old can do has a mental age of 5, and a child who can do what a typical 10-year-old can do has a mental age of 10. If a 10-year-old child can do only what the typical 5-year-old can do, the 10-year-old has a mental age of 5 and could probably benefit from special educational training. School systems now had a test that would identify those children not working at their own chronological age level.

Lewis Terman of Stanford University revised Binet's test and in 1916 published what is known as the Stanford-Binet Intelligence Scale. In his revision, Terman contin-

ued the use of the concept of the intelligence quotient (IQ), as an index of intelligence. An IQ is simply the ratio of a person's mental age to chronological age. It describes the performance of an individual relative to that of others of the same age. The individual's mental age (in years and months), as determined by the test, is divided by the individual's chronological age and the result is multiplied by 100 to eliminate fractions. In mathematical terms,
$$IQ = \frac{MA}{CA} \times 100.$$

The Stanford-Binet Intelligence Scale has been revised several times since 1916 to reflect current knowledge and word usage. It takes about 45 minutes to administer to a child and up to $1\frac{1}{2}$ hours to test an adult. The scoring system has also been changed so that an IQ is no longer simply a ratio of MA to CA. Now the examiner begins with the test nearest the person's mental age. If the subject passes all the items on this level, he or she is tested at the next level. The highest level at which all items are passed is called the basal age. To this is added a score for items passed at still higher levels. The term IQ is still used to express the result of the intelligence scale. The average score is still 100, with

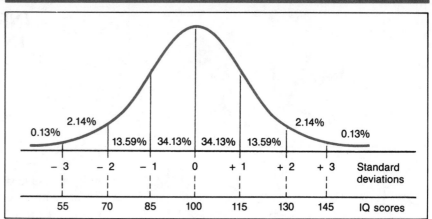

Figure 8.17. IQ Score Distribution

0.13% 2.14% 13.59% 34.13% 34.13% 13.59% 2.14% 0.13%

| Standard deviations | − 3 | − 2 | − 1 | 0 | + 1 | + 2 | + 3 |
| IQ scores | 55 | 70 | 85 | 100 | 115 | 130 | 145 |

Scores from the WAIS-R are described in various categories. Overall, the distribution of scores forms a normal curve; most individuals fall into the middle categories.

deviations in both directions. This distribution of IQ scores forms what is called a *normal curve*.

When Lewis Terman revised Binet's original IQ test, he standardized it based on a sample of middle-class white Americans. Obviously, this does not represent the entire American population. It was not until 1972 that the Stanford-Binet Intelligence Scale was standardized based on a representative sample of young Americans which included the diversified range of races, nationalities, economic, and social classes. It is also interesting to note that with revisions, the norms have had to be readjusted to account for the fact that over the years, people are doing better on the test (and hence raising the performance of the "average" test taker).

The 4th edition of the Stanford-Binet Intelligence Scale was published in 1986 and represents an extensive revision of the earlier test (Anastasi, 1988). The content has been significantly broadened, and now includes 15 separate tests in 4 areas: verbal reasoning (vocabulary, comprehension, absurdities, verbal relations); quantitative reasoning (quantitative, number series, equation building); abstract/visual reasoning (pattern analysis, copying, matrices, paper folding and cutting); and short-term memory (bead memory, memory for sentences, memory for digits, memory for objects). Some of the tests are designed for particular age groups, and so no one is given all 15 tests. The typical administration might include 8 to 13 tests (Anastasi, 1988). The 4th edition was standardized based on a sample of 5,000 people from 47 states ranging in age from 2 to 23 years.

The Wechsler Intelligence Scales

With the Stanford-Binet Intelligence Scale one score represents global intelligence. Another approach is represented by the tests of David Wechsler, who published the Wechsler-Bellevue Intelligence Scale in 1939 and the widely used Wechsler Adult Intelligence Scale (WAIS)

in 1955. Wechsler, who was a psychologist at Bellevue Hospital in New York, had several reasons for developing a new test of adult intelligence. The Stanford-Binet Intelligence Scale was originally designed for children and depended heavily on verbal skills. The recent 1981 revision of the Wechsler Adult Intelligence Scale (WAIS-R) was standardized for 1,880 Americans. This sample represented the general population in sex, race, age, and geographical distribution. The WAIS-R is currently the most widely used psychological test (Anastasi, 1988).

The WAIS-R is divided into subscales that measures verbal skills (information, comprehension, arithmetic, similarities, digit span, and vocabulary) and performance skills (digit symbol, picture completion, block design, picture arrangement, and object assembly). The subscales are standardized with a mean of 10 and standard deviation of 3 so that the subject's strengths and weaknesses can be compared easily. Wechsler's intelligence tests give a verbal IQ, a performance IQ, and a full-scale IQ (combined). Each scale has a mean of 100 and a standard deviation of 15.

Wechsler used the deviation IQ, which measures the extent to which a subject's score is different from the average score of 100 for a particular age group. Approximately 67% of the scores fall between 85 and 115, and about 95% fall between 70 and 130. Because of the deviation IQ it is possible to compare the IQ scores of people of different ages.

Wechsler has developed intelligence measures for children also. The 1974 revision of the Wechsler Intelligence Scale for Children (WISC-R) is used for ages 6 through 16, and the 1989 revision of the Wechsler Preschool and Primary Scale of Intelligence (WPPSI-R) is used for ages 3 through 7. Differences between the performance and verbal scores on the WISC-R can be used to help diagnose certain childhood disorders such as dyslexia and other learning disabilities (Sattler, 1982). Scores on the WISC-R correlate fairly well with the Stanford-Binet Intelligence Scale.

General Information
1. How many wings does a bird have?
2. How many nickels make a dime?
3. What is steam made of?
4. Who wrote *Paradise Lost*?
5. What is pepper?

General Comprehension
1. What should you do if you see someone forget his book when he leaves his seat in a restaurant?
2. What is the advantage of keeping money in a bank?
3. Why is copper often used in electrical wires?

Arithmetic
1. Sam had three pieces of candy and Joe gave him four more. How many pieces of candy did Sam have altogether?
2. Three men divided eighteen gold balls equally among themselves. How many golf balls did each man receive?
3. If two apples cost 15¢, what will be the cost of a dozen apples?

Similarities
1. In what way are a lion and a tiger alike?
2. In what way are a saw and a hammer alike?
3. In what way are an hour and a week alike?
4. In what way are a circle and a triangle alike?

Figure 8.18. Samples of Questions Based on the WISC-R
These drawings and questions are simulated examples taken from the Wechsler Intelligence Scale for Children (WISC-R). Because IQ tests cannot be reproduced, these questions are paraphrased but closely resemble those found in an actual test.

INFLUENCES ON INTELLIGENCE

If you take a minute to list all of the possible influences affecting a person's intelligence, you probably will come up with items such as diet, school, friends, training, community, relationships, and experiences. These might be grouped together under the general heading of environment. You might also include factors such as parents, instinct, personality, nature, ancestors, and family. These can be grouped together as biological and, especially, genetic influences. Intelligent behavior, like all behavior, is the result of the interaction of heredity and environment.

While it seems logical to assume that heredity and environment both contribute to intelligence, the degree to which each contributes is currently highly controversial and has wide-reaching implications for education and society. If intelligence is determined almost exclusively by heredity, as some claim, then nursery school, special education, and enriched environments will not have a significant impact on the intellectual growth of children, and we should not waste money on programs such as these. If, on the other hand, environment plays a significant role in determining intelligence, we may need to undertake massive revisions in the structure of the educational system to succeed in producing the maximum intelligence in each member of society. There may also be important cultural and political implications if we conclude that, due primarily to genetic factors, one race is significantly more intelligent than others. Because of the controversial nature of IQ, it is therefore important to review carefully what we do know about the genetic and environmental determinants of intelligence.

Genetic Influences on Intelligence

We pointed out in chapter 2, "Biology of Behavior," that we are limited when investigating heredity and human behavior. Much of the information we have on the contributions of heredity to intelligence comes from studies of the correlation between IQ and the degree of genetic relatedness.

Genetic Relationship and IQ Correlation. In general, the closer the genetic relationship, the higher the correlation (measurement of the relationship between two variables) between individual IQs. A large number of studies was reviewed in 1981 by Bouchard and McGue, who found the highest IQ correlations between

Figure 8.19.   Identical Twins Reared Together
Monozygotic, or identical twins, not only share 100% of their genes, but also often share extremely similar experiences. As a result, they tend to have very similar IQs.

Figure 8.20. Genetic Relationship and IQ

Relationship	Correlation
Monozygotic twins	
Reared together	.86
Reared apart	.72
Dizygotic twins	
Reared together	.60
Siblings	
Reared together	.47
Reared apart	.24
Parent/child	.40
Foster parent/child	.31

The closer the genetic relationship between two individuals, the higher the correlation between their IQs. Identical twins who were reared together have the highest IQ correlations (after Bouchard & McGue, 1981).

identical twins (sharing 100% of their genes) who were reared together in the same environment. Nonidentical twins (sharing 50% of their genes) were found similar to normal siblings (also sharing 50% of their genes). Unrelated people reared apart show virtually no correlation of IQ.

Much of the research on human heredity and intelligence has been done on twins. In 1976, when Loehlin and Nichols reviewed data from over 6,000 pairs of twins, they found a correlation of .62 in the IQs of nonidentical twins and .86 in the IQs of identical twins. In IQ studies, the more similar the IQs, the higher the correlation. So this data means that identical twins have IQs that are more similar than the IQs of nonidentical twins. This evidence strongly supports the notion that heredity influences intelligence in people significantly.

Unfortunately, some of the twin data had to be discarded. The British psychologist Cyril Burt conducted what was considered to be the most complete study of separated twins. His research showed extremely high correlations between the separated twins, no matter what conditions the individual twins had been reared in. After Burt's death, it was discovered that much of his data and indeed, even his colleagues, did not exist (Hearnshaw, 1979).

There have been other problems with twin data. Twins that had been separated early in life were difficult to find, and when they were found, it was discovered that they often had been reared in similar environments, by relatives, or by adoptive parents who were similar to the biological parents. However, a number of recent studies have continued to report a high correlation between IQs of pairs of twins (Bouchard, 1984). Wilson (1983) reported IQ correlations of .88 for MZ twins and .54 for

DZ twins at 15 years of age in 500 pairs of twins in the Louisville Twin Study.

Adoption Studies.   Adoption studies are another type of research in human behavior genetics. A number of studies have shown that the correlation between IQs of adopted children and their biological parents was much higher than the IQs of children and their adoptive parents. For example, a study called the Texas Adoption Project has reported IQ correlations between children and their biological mothers of .28 and between children and their adoptive mothers of only .15 (Horn, 1983). In the Minnesota Adoption Study, Scarr and Weinberg (1983) also found a stronger correlation between the IQ scores of adopted children and their biological parents than their adoptive parents. On the basis of studies like these, most psychologists agree that heredity does play a significant role in determining intelligence.

Race, Genetics, and Intelligence.   One of the most controversial issues in the relationship of heredity to intelligence concerns the issue of race. It is a fact that blacks score an average of 15 points lower on IQ tests than do whites (Hall & Kaye, 1980). While there have been many explanations for this finding, Arthur Jensen (1969) caused a controversy in the academic community by suggesting that intelligence was due nearly exclusively (80%) to hereditary factors. Let's take a look at the facts to try to understand why Jensen reached his conclusion, and what alternate conclusions might be reached.

Jensen used the data that was available to him in the late 1960s. What did the twin studies reveal at that time? Erlenmeyer-Kimling and Jarvik's 1963 data indicated correlations of .87 for identical twins reared together and .75 for identical twins reared apart. Since identical

Education and Learning Disabilities

You probably are aware of the term learning disability (LD) from elementary school. The term, which became popular in the 1960s, usually refers to any of a variety of learning problems experienced by a student. The problems do not include retardation, emotional disturbances, or physical handicaps, but rather include situations in which students do poorly in school even though adequate teaching is provided, and the intellectual capacity of the students is above normal. Kirk and Gallagher (1986) estimated that between 2% and 4% of students have severe learning disabilities, and many more have some degree of difficulty with learning in school.

Students with a learning disability have problems with at least one of the following: understanding written material, understanding mathematical concepts, listening, writing, and speaking (Warner, 1988). Essentially, these students have a weakness in their ability to learn. Academic skills problems include academic skills disorders, language and speech disorders, and attention-deficit hyperactivity disorder.

In the academic skills disorder of *developmental reading disorder*, or *dyslexia*, the student has difficulty learning to read written words adequately. The student has a normal intelligence level, but is not able to interpret visual information. He or she turns letters around, for instance, a *b* becomes a *d*. This is also called mirror reading. Oral reading is characterized by slowness and substitutions of words. Dyslexia is usually detected in early elementary school. In mild cases, reading therapy can completely eliminate the problem, whereas in more severe cases, the person exhibits symptoms throughout life.

Other *academic skills disorders* include developmental arithmetic disorder and developmental expressive writing disorder. The chief characteristic of *developmental arithmetic disorder* is significant impairment in the development of arithmetic skills that interferes with normal academic or daily activities. The student (who is typically identified by the third grade) often has problems understanding mathematical concepts and operations, remembering steps in solving equations or following sequences, and learning the basic mathematical formulas. A student who has *developmental expressive writing disorder* has great difficulty with spelling, grammar, punctuation, and organization. His or her writing skills are significantly worse than what is expected for the particular grade level and experience.

Language and speech disorders include a broad range of langauge-processing problems. In *developmental articulation disorder*, the student fails to correctly articulate speech sounds at the appropriate age. Often speech sounds are omitted, substituted, or misarticulated. Speech therapy almost always provides complete recovery. Impairment in development of speaking is called *developmental expressive language disorder*, and is characterized by difficulty in acquiring new vocabulary words, in using simple grammatical structure, and in using limited sentence structure. Impairment in the development of language comprehension is called *developmental receptive language disorder*. It varies in severity, and might include difficulty in understanding sentence structures or in processing auditory information. Many children with this problem can eventually acquire normal language skills.

Attention-deficit hyperactivity disorder (ADHD) is characterized by inattention, impulsiveness, and hyperactivity (DSM-III-R, 1987). The symptoms often become worse in situations which require sustained attention, such as listening in the classroom or working on school assignments. Inattention results in not completing tasks or appearing not to listen to others. Impulsiveness is shown when the individual interrupts others, fails to wait one's turn, and to completely understand an assignment before beginning. Hyperactive behavior results in the individual having difficulty remaining quiet, moving excessively, fidgeting, and constant manipulating of objects.

In school, ADHD is most characterized by excessive motor activity. Often the student (usually a male) has low self-esteem, experiences depression and underachieves. The problem often begins before age 4 but is usually not recognized until the child begins school. Sometimes the treatment includes administrating stimulating drugs, such as Ritalin, caffeine, or amphetamines. Barkley (1987) described ADHD as a neuromaturational delay and argued that a variety of assessment methods should be used when deciding the severity and treatment of the problem.

The general attitude toward students with learning disabilities is to help them maximize educational opportunities. In many school systems, learning disability specialists are able to suggest special techniques for students to use when studying. For example, students with reading problems might listen to taped textbooks, or have someone read the textbook to them. Word processors can help students with writing problems improve spelling and organization. Those who confuse oral and written information are encouraged to tape record lecture notes. If they have difficulty taking tests, study skill training can often help. Students often do better when they gain confidence and these kind of techniques may help them gain it.

THOUGHT QUESTIONS

1. What is meant by the term learning disabilities?
2. How would you diagnose a student with an LD problem?
3. Should we identify and label LD students, or does this make things more difficult for them in school?

twins share identical genes, the lower correlations are apparently determined by environmental influences. Thus, in 1969 Jensen reasoned that intelligence was determined by about 80% genetic and 20% environmental influence.

There are other possible interpretations of the data. For example, the .87 correlation for identical twins reared together is actually determined by both genetic and environmental factors. These twins not only share identical genes, but they also share nearly identical environments. It could be argued that environment is contributing much more than the .13 figure first suggested by the data. Remember also that Burt's false data was included in these studies.

Keep in mind also that these correlations are for group data, and tell us nothing about individual scores. Indeed, there is more variation within a particular race than between two races. Thus, we cannot make a prediction about an individual from this group data.

Until recently, most IQ tests were standardized for white, middle-class people. This being true, it is no wonder that other races do not score as well as whites. The IQ tests themselves could very well be biased. A number of attempts to construct a truly culture-fair intelligence test have shown little success, and we are left with less than ideal testing instruments.

Recent studies have suggested that environmental differences that exist between races are extremely important in IQ determination. For instance, data from the Minnesota Adoption Study reported by Scarr and Weinberg (1983) found that when black children were adopted by white families at an early age, their IQs were more similar to the white IQ averages. They concluded that it appears unlikely that genetic differences between the races can be used exclusively to explain IQ differences.

New IQ data from over 10,000 cases was reviewed by Plomin and DeFries (1980). The new data suggests a heritability of around .50 rather than the higher figure (.80) determined by Jensen from the older data. Differences in the sample size, data collection techniques, IQ test revisions, and representativeness of samples, help account for the lower heritability figure. Thus, while psychologists recognize the importance of heredity, it alone does not adequately explain differences in IQ. Heredity operates within an environment—the topic to which we now turn.

Environmental Influences on Intelligence

Psychologists also agree that environmental factors are important in determining intelligence. But determining what exactly in the environment is crucial for high intelligence is a difficult task.

Measurement of Environment and IQ. One line of research examines differences in IQs of identical twins reared in different environments. Since these twins share identical genes, any differences found could be attributed to the environment. Bouchard and McGue found in their 1981 review of twin studies a correlation in IQs between identical twins reared together of .86 and a correlation between identical twins reared apart of .72. Theoretically, both correlations ought to be 1.00 if heredity were the only factor, since the genes are identical. The lower correlations would seem to be due then to environmental influences. When reared in different homes, the different environmental experiences produce a correlation of only .72. Even when reared together, each twin has different personal experiences, resulting in a correlation of .86 and demonstrating the influence of the environment.

A great many studies show the importance of environment on intelligence. Remember the study by Cooper and Zubek (1958) from chapter 2, "Biology of Behavior," in which genetically identical rats showed differing maze-learning performance depending on whether they were reared in an enriched or restricted environment? Other studies have found diet to be important. Stock and Symthe's 1963 study of children in South Africa found that malnourished children had IQs that were an average of 20 points lower than children who were fed a well-balanced diet.

The family setting appears to be an extremely important environmental variable. In our opening story, we saw the importance of adult interaction when young orphan children of low IQs were placed with institutionalized mentally retarded adult women who gave the children much attention. The IQs of these children jumped almost 30 points within two years, while a control group of children who remained in the orphanage actually dropped. Studies have shown that middle-class families are more likely than lower-class families to provide extensive verbal interaction with children, thus increasing the probability of higher IQs (Bradley & Caldwell, 1984).

The Colorado Adoption Project is a study of 200 adoptive families and 200 control families. While the study is still going on, Plomin and DeFries (1983) reported that environmental family influences were extremely important in the early development of cognitive abilities.

Robert Zajonc, a social psychologist at the University of Michigan, looked at the data collected on almost 400,000 young men in the Netherlands, and concluded that intelligence declines with family size as well as birth order. The larger the family, the lower the IQ of the children, and later-born children tend to have lower IQs than early-born children.

Zajonc and Markus (1975) constructed a theoretical

Figure 8.21. Environmental Influences on Intelligence
Environment can have both a positive and a negative effect on intelligence. A stimulating and secure environment can significantly improve IQ.

model to explain the influences of family size on intelligence. Essentially, the model proposes that with every new child the family's potential intellectual environment is reduced. Zajonc explains that the family's average score decreases because the resources of the parents are spread out over the increased number of children. Not everyone agrees with Zajonc's results. Other researchers have pointed out that social class, cultural expectations, and economic factors may be much more influential on intelligence than family size.

Another important influence on intelligence involves what we expect of an individual. For example, if a student is expected to do well, he or she probably will, and if a student is expected to fail, he or she probably will fail. In chapter 1, "The Study of Psychology," we described the Rosenthal and Jacobson (1968) experiment in which school children were administered an IQ test, which was disguised as an "intellectual blooming test." Those randomly chosen students who the teacher believed would bloom, actually did increase their scores significantly on the second IQ test. Of course, expectancy also works the other way. If you come from a minority group, a lower social class, or, for whatever reason, the teacher did not expect you to do well, chances are that you will perform poorly.

We learn from these studies that environment has a significant effect on intelligence. But it is very difficult to measure environmental influence, and the effects seem to be complexly interwoven. As we have seen, psychologists have been interested in the influences on intelligence for a long time.

What can we conclude about the effects of heredity and environment on intelligence? At the present time, we cannot design and measure the relevant variables in a way that will answer the question specifically. We can conclude that both genetic and environmental influences are extremely important in the determination of intelligence. Since our genes are set at birth and immutable, it makes sense to concentrate on improving the environment to maximize individual success.

Environmental Enrichment Programs. A number of researchers have investigated methods of increasing intelligence through environmental enrichment programs. Recall the opening story of Skeels' study in which orphanage children improved IQ scores when transferred to a mental institution that provided stimulation and individual attention. Many studies have shown some degree of improvement in the IQ scores of those placed in stimulating environments.

Within the past couple of decades, preschools have become popular in the United States. Three- and four-year-old children are sent to preschool a couple of hours a day for a couple of days a week. The expectation is that the preschool will provide opportunities for the children to develop socialization skills, motivation, confidence, and knowledge that will translate into better performance in later years. Although the effects are generally not dramatic, there is some evidence that some programs can enhance the intelligence of school children (Zigler & Berman, 1983).

The Head Start program is a large-scale preschool for four-year-old children from disadvantaged backgrounds. Like most preschools, Head Start emphasizes socialization as well as academic skills. Although there are

Figure 8.22. Head Start Program
Children who experience the Head Start program generally become better students. A stimulating preschool environment improves their social and intellectual development.

varying degrees of success in Head Start programs around the United States, the increased attention to the importance of nutrition and early environmental enrichment has generally paid off by producing a greater number of better students (Lazar & Darlington, 1982).

An example of an enrichment program designed to help elementary and secondary school children improve cognitive skills is Feuerstein's (1980) instrumental enrichment program. The program is designed to help students through a series of exercises, such as comparisons of objects, that promote abstract reasoning. Sternberg (1986) argued that improving intellectual skills is an important objective for educators today.

THE EXTREMES OF INTELLIGENCE

As mentioned earlier in the chapter, the distribution of IQ scores falls into a bell-shaped or *normal curve*. Most individuals fall toward the middle, with fewer and fewer getting very high or very low scores. Wechsler designed the deviation IQ so that 95% of IQ scores fall between 70 and 130. The extreme upper $2^{1}/_{2}$% and lower $2^{1}/_{2}$% of cases are considered extremes of intelligence—mental retardation and intellectual giftedness.

Mental Retardation

Usually, an individual who scores below 70 on an IQ test, has problems in adaptive behavior (such as language skills and social competencies), and experiences these problems prior to age 18, is considered mentally retarded. Tests of adaptive behavior include the *Adaptive Behavior Scale* and the *Vineland Social Maturity Scale*. It is estimated that about 3% of Americans are mentally retarded.

Levels of Retardation. Not everyone classified as mentally retarded is affected to the same degree. The range goes from individuals who are extremely slow learners to individuals who are incapable of doing anything for themselves. As mentioned in the biographical highlight, Binet originally classified the mentally retarded as morons, imbeciles, and idiots. If you have ever heard jokes using these labels, you will understand why they were changed to reflect more descriptive terms.

The DSM-III-R (1987) divides the mentally retarded into four classifications: mild, moderate, severe, and profound. Individuals in the mild retardation classifica-

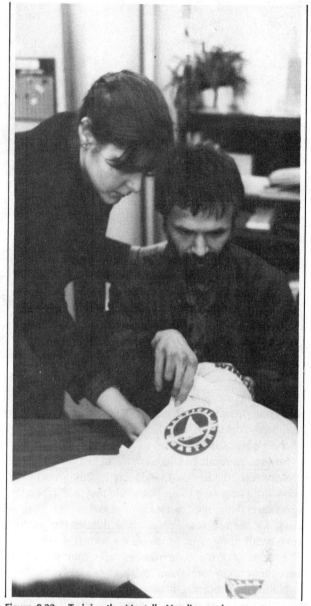

Figure 8.23. Training the Mentally Handicapped
Many mentally retarded individuals can lead happy, productive lives. In a class at the Young Adult Institute in Manhattan, this adult is being trained to perform simple skills.

tion have IQs of between 50 and 70. This classification comprises the largest group (85% of all mentally retarded individuals) and includes within it a great deal of variability. Adults who are mildly retarded may have a mental age of anywhere between 8 and 12. Some of the higher-functioning individuals can be fairly successful in family and occupation, and few of them need institutionalization. Most of these individuals, however, have difficulty dealing with abstract ideas.

Moderate retardation refers to a much smaller group (10%) of retarded individuals who have IQs of between 36 and 49 and a mental age of about four to seven. They can read and write on an elementary level, but they need

Figure 8.24. Special Education
The mentally retarded benefit from their participation in special education. Here two mentally handicapped children share a story.

constant supervision and are often placed in institutions and group homes. Some people in this category work in sheltered workshops, and many are productive members of their community.

Severe retardation includes those individuals with IQs of between 20 and 35. Individuals in this group (3%) show little language usage but while they are dependent upon caretakers, they can learn to perform some routine tasks for themselves. Profound retardation refers to a very small number of people (2%) with IQs below 20. They cannot learn even routine tasks and are totally dependent upon caretakers for their existence.

Until fairly recently, it was common to provide separate classes in school for all mentally retarded individuals. This practice did not help them as much as was expected. The Education for All Handicapped Children Act of 1975 changed this and required that children must

be taught in the least restrictive environment. For the higher functioning individuals, this means mainstreaming into regular classrooms as much as possible. Currently the developmentally handicapped (DH) are taught in regular classrooms unless they have special needs which can best be met elsewhere.

Causes of Retardation. Psychologists are interested in researching the causes of mental retardation, treating the mentally retarded, and preventing future cases of retardation. The factors that cause mental retardation are varied, and often we do not know the cause for certain (Hallahan & colleagues, 1985). However, two general categories are identified—genetic and environmental.

Genetic causes of mental retardation include biochemical disorders, such as PKU (phenylketonuria) and chromosomal disorders. An extra chromosome number 21 (resulting in three number 21 chromosomes, rather

Figure 8.25. Levels of Mental Retardation

Level	Percent	IQ	Functioning Ability
Mild	85%	50-70	Educable
Moderate	10%	36-49	Trainable
Severe	3%	20-35	Custodial
Profound	2%	0-19	Totally Dependent

The functioning ability of the mentally retarded is variable and depends on many factors (adapted from DSM-III-R, 1987).

Figure 8.26. The Intellectually Gifted
Several stereotypes of the gifted have been recently dispelled. Rather than being thin and weak, the gifted tend to be physically strong and well adjusted. Daniel Lowen of Cocoa Beach, Fla., challenged one answer to a question on the Preliminary Scholastic Aptitude Test in 1981. As a result, his score and some of the scores of 240,000 other students were raised. The question was, if two pyramids are placed together, how many exposed sides would the new figure have? The pyramids had a total of 9 sides and students were expected to subtract the 2 sides that are hidden when the pyramids are joined, arriving at the answer of 7. But Lowen answered 5, subtracting the 2 hidden sides from 9 and subtracting 2 more sides, reasoning that 4 exposed sides in the new figure merge to become only 2 sides. He made a model to demonstrate his point.

than the usual two), can cause a form of mental retardation known as Down's syndrome. Older mothers are more likely to have children with Down's syndrome. As their ova (eggs) get older they are exposed to a greater volume of potential environmental hazards (such as heat or X rays), which could cause the chromosomes to remain as a pair rather than splitting normally.

Overall, it appears that general genetic factors usually result in mild mental retardation, while specific factors result in more severe retardation. For instance, there are some genes which contribute to intelligence and some which contribute to mild retardation. If two individuals with IQs of 60 were to reproduce, the genes that resulted in their particular IQs would likely produce offspring with IQs also in the 60s. On the other hand, a specific gene, such as the one which produces phenylketonuria, can cause severe mental retardation.

There are many possible environmental causes of mental retardation. During pregnancy, the use of harmful drugs, smoking, a poor diet, or infectious diseases (such as German measles or chicken pox) can be factors. And birth complications may cause brain injury to the baby, or early in life the young child may ingest poison or contract certain infectious diseases (such as meningitis).

The general family environment—such as that found in homes where children are neglected or abused or in homes where little is done to motivate children—can contribute to mild retardation. But often a specific accident, such as ingesting poison or being dropped on the head, can result in severe retardation. Remember that genetic and environmental factors interact to produce any behavior, including mental retardation.

The Intellectually Gifted

At the upper extreme of the IQ scale are the intellectually gifted individuals. A person with an IQ above 130 is usually labeled as gifted, although some psychologists and educators prefer a cutoff of 140. Teachers often refer outstanding students for consideration for inclusion in a school's gifted program. Sternberg and Davidson (1985) suggested that gifted individuals are able to effectively utilize the cognitive components of intelligence (planning and evaluating performance, and learning new information).

Contrary to what many people believe, gifted individuals are not always the stereotyped "eggheads" who wear thick glasses (from reading 20 hours a day), are thin (malnourishment from skipping meals to study) and physically weak (from never lifting more than a book). Actually, people with high IQs tend to be superior in many areas including sports, occupation, interpersonal relations, and academic achievement. However, Gardner (1983) pointed out that sometimes gifted individuals perform no differently than normally intelligent people. A study in which gifted, general, and special learning needs students were compared found that gifted students tended to score highest both in academic and social self-concept, whereas the special learning needs students scored lowest on all measures (Colangelo, Kelly, & Schrepfer, 1987).

The most famous study of gifted children was started by psychologist Lewis Terman in the 1920s. He selected over 1,500 children with IQs above 140, and followed them as they developed into adulthood. Terman found that, as children, these individuals generally were physically healthier, better adjusted, and happier than a control group of other children (Terman, 1925).

Follow-up studies have shown that these gifted children grew up to be very successful adults (Goleman, 1980). Overall, the group was healthier, happier, more successful, and wealthier than the average person.

Recently, there has been a general trend in schools to develop programs for intellectually gifted students (Horowitz & O'Brien, 1986). Gifted children are now being challenged in and out of the classroom by enriched activities that allow them to develop their potential to the fullest. As more research is conducted in the area of giftedness, our schools will become better equipped to provide an education designed to maximize each student's intellectual capacity. ■

This chapter has pointed out that the cognitive processes of thinking, problem solving, language, and intelligence are so much a part of our everyday behavior that it is impossible to stop them. Intelligence is a difficult term to define properly, and yet, as we have shown, most people understand what is meant by intelligent behavior. All behavior, including intelligence, has genetic and environmental determinants, as shown in the opening story on how Skeels increased the IQ of retarded children. Intelligence influences other cognitive processes, such as learning, memory, language, and perception. We will see how these topics relate to intelligence in the chapters that follow.

"You mene I've bin spending this whol term with a defektiv reeding machin?"

CHAPTER REVIEW
What You've Learned About Language and Intelligence

1. Cognition, or mental processes, involves the acquisition, storage, retrieval, and utilization of knowledge. Cognitive psychology includes the study of the mental activities involved in perception, memory, language, thought, problem solving, and intelligence.

2. Language is a form of communication utilizing the manipulation of symbols to convey meaning. Grammar is the set of rules that determines the structure of the language required for understanding. The basic speech sounds of a language are called phonemes. Phonemes are combined into morphemes, the smallest meaningful units of a language. Syntax is the subset of rules of grammar that governs the order of words in phrases and sentences. The meaning of language is called semantics.

3. Language tends to develop in a regular pattern. Infants begin to cry at birth, vocalize at one month, babble at six months, and speak at one year. During the second year, infants use one-word sentences, called holophrastic speech. At about two years of age, children begin telegraphic speech in which they use two-word sentences. Eventually their sentences become longer and more complex, and their vocabularies become larger.

4. According to the learning theory of language, parents reinforce children for producing sounds that are recognizable as language, and children try to imitate words and phrases used by parents. According to the biological psycholinguistic theory of language, children are biologically programmed with an internal language acquisition device (LAD).

5. Thinking is the cognitive activity of manipulating symbols. For humans, thinking usually involves language. Whorf's linguistic relativity hypothesis states that the language of the observer influences thinking and perception.

6. Concept formation refers to the development of the ability to respond to common features of categories of objects or events. Natural concepts are used intuitively in everyday life, whereas formal concepts have clear and unambiguous rules which specify which attributes define the category. The rules include affirmative, conjunctive, disjunctive, conditional, and biconditional rules.

7. Theories of problem solving include trial and error learning, insight into the reorganization of the perceptual field, and information processing.

8. Most people go through the steps of preparation, production, and evaluation when solving problems. Strategies in problem solving include algorithms and heuristics. Experience is often useful in helping us learn to solve problems, but sometimes leads to mental sets, functional fixedness, or confirmation bias, which can interfere with successful problem solving by making it less likely that we will approach problems in new ways or devise novel uses for objects we have become accustomed to using in specific ways.

9. Since creativity involves coming up with new or unusual responses to familiar circumstances, it is closely related to the ability to solve problems. The skills measured by creativity and intelligence tests tend to overlap. Creative people tend to be internally motivated, to have freedom to choose their activities, and to live in a stimulating and exciting environment.

10. Intelligence can be defined as the capacity to learn and behave adaptively. Most intelligence tests stress verbal skills, quantitative skills, and problem-solving skills.

11. Spearman's theory of intelligence includes a general factor and specific factors. Thurstone's theory is based on seven primary mental abilities, including spatial ability, perceptual speed, numerical ability, verbal meaning, word fluency, memory, and reasoning. Guilford includes 150 abilities, arranged in 3 dimensions: contents, operations, and products. Steinberg's triarchic theory consists of 3 parts: cognitive components of intelligence, experience and intelligence, and context of intelligence.

12. Aptitude tests are designed to predict what can be accomplished in the future with proper training, whereas achievement tests are designed to measure what can be done at the present time. Intelligence tests are usually aptitude tests designed to predict a broad range of mental abilities. An intelligence test should be valid (actually measure intelligence) and reliable (consistent). It must be standardized and also objective and practical.

13. The first intelligence test was designed in 1905 by Alfred Binet to identify students in the Paris school system who needed special education. Binet defined mental age as what the typical child of a given chronological age could do. Terman revised Binet's test and in 1916 published the Stanford-Binet Intelligence Scale. Terman used the intelligence quotient, or IQ, to refer to the ratio of mental to chronological age (IQ = $\frac{MA}{CA} \times 100$).

14. Wechsler published several intelligence scales, including the Wechsler Adult Intelligence Scale (WAIS-R) and the Wechsler Intelligence Scale for Children (WISC-R). The WAIS-R measures verbal skills (information, comprehension, arithmetic, similarities, digit span, and vocabulary) and performance skills (digit symbol, picture completion, block design, picture arrangement, and object assembly).

15. Intelligence is determined in part by genetic factors. In general, the closer the genetic relationship between two individuals, the higher the correlation (relationship) between IQs. Thus, identical twins reared together have the highest IQ correlation, and IQs of adoptive children correlate more highly with the biological parents than with the adoptive parents.

16. Intelligence is also significantly influenced by environmental factors. Identical twins reared apart have lower IQ correlations than those reared together, suggesting that the environment influenced the difference. Studies show that diet, adult interaction, social class, and family size all have an influence on intelligence.

17. Individuals with IQs below 70 are classified as mentally retarded. There are four different levels of retardation: mild, moderate, severe, and profound. Genetic causes of mental retardation include biochemical disorders (such as PKU) and chromosomal disorders (such as Down's syndrome). Environmental causes of mental retardation include maternal diet, smoking, infectious diseases during pregnancy (German measles), or the child ingesting poison or contracting infectious diseases (meningitis) early in life. Overall, general factors usually result in mild retardation, while specific factors result in more severe retardation.

18. At the upper extreme are intellectually gifted individuals with IQs greater than 130. Studies suggest that gifted individuals are typically healthier, happier, wealthier, and better adjusted than average individuals.

MOTIVATION AND EMOTION

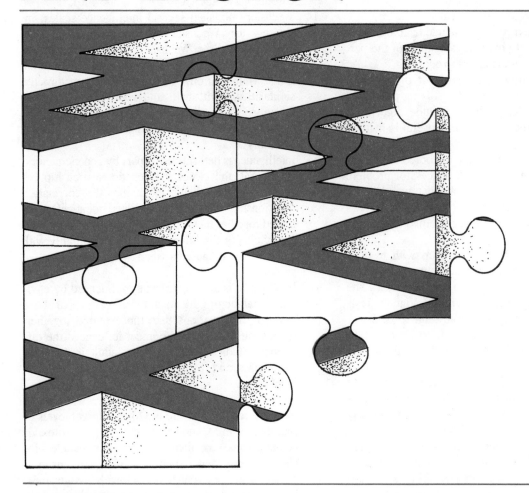

Part IV includes the theories and research into the explanation of human behavior. In this section the topics of motivation and emotion are explored.

After reading Part IV you should be able to:

Describe various theories of motivation

Identify the basic biological motives

Define stimulus motives

Outline learned social motives

Describe various theories of emotion

Explain the role of emotion in communication and human sexuality

Chapter 9   Motivation

The area of psychology that attempts to explain why we do the things we do is called motivation. Psychologists have studied motivation from a variety of approaches, including drives, incentives, arousal, and heredity. Much attention has focused on the motives of hunger, sex, curiosity, and achievement.

Chapter 10   Emotion

Although not easily understood, emotion is very important in our lives. Psychologists have developed a variety of theories to try to explain emotions. Love and nonverbal communication have been studied intensively in recent years. A current area of interest to psychologists is human sexuality.

Chapter 9

MOTIVATION

The area of psychology that attempts to explain why we do the things we do is called motivation. Psychologists have studied motivation from a variety of approaches, including drives, incentives, arousal, and heredity. Much attention has focused on the motives of hunger, sex, curiosity, and achievement.

In chapter 6, "Learning," we discussed how, with food as a reinforcer, a rat could be trained to press a lever in a Skinner Box. In 1954, in the psychology laboratory of McGill University, rats in Skinner Boxes were also trained to press levers; but in this experiment, instead of food, they received electrical stimulation to the brain.

James Olds and Peter Milner were interested in understanding whether the electrical stimulation of certain areas in the brain would produce behavior that would be motivated either by reinforcement or punishment.

Originally, Olds and Milner implanted an electrode (a thin piece of insulated wire) into the brain of a rat and placed the rat in a large box. Every time the rat went to a preselected corner, it was given a mild electric shock. The rat went to the designated corner several times before going to sleep.

The researchers thought, at first, the electrical stimulation was motivating curiosity in the rat; however, it quickly became apparent that pleasure was reinforcing the rat's behavior. Eventually the researchers were able to shape the subject through successive approximation so that it would go to any preselected corner; it was as if they were giving the rat food as reinforcement.

Next the subject was placed on a T-shaped platform and every time it turned right it received a shock. The animal quickly learned to turn right. Then when the shock was given only when the rat turned left, it quickly reversed and always went left. The electrical shock was indeed extremely reinforcing.

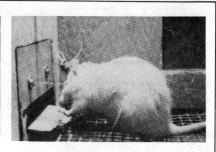

Figure 9.1. Electrical Brain Stimulation
Olds and Milner (1954) implanted electrodes in the brains of rats and observed that bar pressing behavior increased dramatically when the rats were reinforced with electrical stimulation of the brain.

In order to test which areas of the brain produced the most motivation in response to the electrical shock, a Skinner Box was used. Instead of food being presented each time a subject pressed the lever, an electric shock was delivered. In this way, motivation could be measured as the frequency of lever pressing.

The very first subject tested proved beyond doubt that electrical stimulation to the brain could produce reinforcing effects. After about 5 minutes of learning, the rat began pressing the lever once every 5 seconds. When the researchers turned the electric current off, the rat pressed the bar several times and then, without stimulation, went to sleep. When experimenters turned the current back on and gave the rat a shock, it immediately began pressing the lever again until the electricity was terminated, and then it would go to sleep once more.

Olds and Milner then began to search for the most reinforcing sites in the brain. When the electrode was placed in sensory or motor areas of the brain, the lever pressing remained at about 25 times per hour. However, certain areas of the brain produced a pleasurable response with lever-pressing rates of 200 to 5,000 times per hour and other areas produced pain or distress so that the subject pressed the lever once and never pressed it again.

After testing many areas of the brain, the researchers found the areas that appeared to produce the most pleasure from stimulation were the hypothalamus and mid-brain nuclei. When electrodes were implanted in these areas, the rats pressed the lever from 500 to 5,000 times per hour. Some of these brain sites were so reinforcing that hungry rats preferred the electrical stimulation over food. Some of the subjects continued to press the lever more than 2,000 times per hour for 24 continuous hours.

The behavior of the rats with implanted brain electrodes is often referred to as self-stimulation. The work of Olds and Milner has been replicated in monkeys and has formed an important basis for understanding the brain's role in motivation. Further research by Olds and Milner as well as other experimenters has shown the brain reward circuit to include a variety of areas such as the septal area and especially the medial forebrain bundle, a large nerve tract that runs from the brainstem to the cortex.

The discovery of pleasure centers in the brain was important in motivation research because it provided evidence that reinforcement of behavior has a physiological basis. This helped psychologists further understand the role the brain plays in motivation.

CHAPTER OBJECTIVES
What You'll Learn About Motivation

After studying this chapter, you should be able to:

1. Define the concept of motivation.
2. Describe the instinct theories of motivation.
3. Describe the drive theory of motivation.
4. Describe the incentive theory of motivation.
5. Describe the arousal theory of motivation.
6. Outline Maslow's humanistic theory of motivation.
7. Outline the cognitive theory of motivation.
8. Describe the biological motive of hunger.
9. Outline the biological motive of thirst.
10. Outline sexual motivation.
11. Identify the stimulus motive of curiosity.
12. Describe the stimulus motive of competence.
13. Describe the learned social motive of achievement.
14. Identify the learned social motive of power.
15. Identify the learned social motive of affiliation.

WHAT IS MOTIVATION?

In many ways, motivation is central to the study of psychology. People constantly engage in purposeful or goal-oriented behavior, and underlying all such behavior are motives. Motivational concepts allow us to account for the variability in behavior, both in an individual and between individuals (Mook, 1987).

Motives arouse and direct the individual's behavior toward some goal. There are three major categories of motives: biological, stimulus, and learned social. The *biological motives*, such as hunger, thirst, temperature regulation, and sex, have a definite physiological basis. The *stimulus motives*, such as sensory stimulation, exploration, curiosity, contact comfort, and competence, cause the individual to seek out sensory stimulation through interaction with the environment. They are internal and unlearned, but do not appear to have a specific physiological basis. The *learned social motives*, such as achievement, power, and affiliation, are determined largely by learning and focus on social experiences.

Motivated behavior is initiated and directed toward a goal, and varies in intensity and persistence (Houston, 1985). Motivation, then, can be thought of as the forces that initiate and direct behavior, and the variables that determine the intensity and persistence of that behavior. As examples of these variables, when we are hungry, we initiate food seeking, and when we are bored we initiate activity to relieve the boredom. This *initiation* can be prompted from within the individual or from the external environment. For example, we might be hungry because of low blood sugar level (internal) or because we just saw a delicious dessert (external). Motivation also provides *direction* for our behavior. For example, when we are hungry, we seek food, rather than read a newspaper.

Motivation determines the intensity and persistence of our behavior. *Intensity* has to do with how strong the behavior is. For instance, you might be a little hungry and if food is readily available, you would eat, but if there is no food in the immediate vicinity, you would probably engage in some other behavior. On the other hand, if you are extremely hungry, you would most likely engage intensively in food seeking behavior, doing whatever it took to obtain your goal. How motivated we are will influence our *persistence*. Sometimes we will persist in obtaining a goal for a long time, while at other times we will give up after a brief try.

Psychologists often measure motivation by observing what individuals do (initiation); how they make choices (direction); noting the strength of their behaviors (inten-

sity); and how long they engage in them (persistence). Motivation is not observed directly, but rather is inferred from the performance of subjects (Beck, 1983). For instance, if a person selects a horror movie over a romantic comedy, we infer that the person is meeting a need by doing so.

Sometimes we can manipulate the level of motivation, such as when researchers temporarily deprive animals of food to increase their motivation to work for food. Parents might also motivate their children by manipulating the level of reward (praise or money) given for certain behaviors.

THEORIES OF MOTIVATION

Because motivation is so vastly complex, many approaches have been developed to try to explain it. The basic question is *why* do we do what we do. Although many motives overlap, it is useful to study each approach separately. In this section we will survey major approaches to motivation: instinct, drive, incentive, arousal, humanistic, and cognitive.

Instinct Theories

Theories that attribute motivation to biologically determined factors, to instinctive patterns of behavior, were at one time highly influential in the United States. Instinct theories continue to be central to the work of ethologists, and sociobiologists argue that even social behavior is genetically programmed.

Instinct. Early zoologists and psychologists noticed that some behaviors of animals seemed universal and stereotyped. That is, every member of the species showed the same behavior pattern. These observers defined instinct as a behavior that is inherited by all members of the species.

The instinct theory dominated psychology in the early years of this century. Major psychologists such as William James (1890) developed elaborate instinct theories to explain human behavior. To James, instincts were impulses that produced behaviors. He believed that although people normally expressed instincts automatically, they could modify their instincts by learning and experience. Rather than absolute responses, reflexes, or learning, he viewed instincts as tendencies to act in a given way. In fact, he thought instincts formed the base from which we develop habits through our experiences.

According to James, people possess all of the instincts

Figure 9.2. Instinct
Because primates develop more slowly than most mammals, the young of the species have developed life-saving instincts peculiar to mammals. Young primates, such as the potto pictured here, are protected during their long, helpless infancies by an innate biological drive to cling tightly to their mothers. The clinging instinct assures the infant of never being separated from the mother, who must walk about looking for food or sometimes run, climb a tree, or swing from limb to limb to escape danger.

Figure 9.3. Ethological Study
Ethologists study animals in their natural environment. Many ethologists study fixed action patterns, or species-specific behaviors, which are stimulated by releasers in the environment. This female stickleback fish exhibits courtship behavior that is specific to her species when the male approaches her.

of lower animals, plus a variety of uniquely human ones. Some of the instincts proposed by James include: curiosity, shyness, modesty, fear, playfulness, sympathy, cleanliness, jealousy, sociability, and rivalry. With his list of instincts, James tried to argue that human behavior had a biological basis through instinct.

The early instinct theories did not last very long in psychology. Kuo (1921) argued that the behaviors attributed to instinct were actually learned. He also indicated that these instincts were caused by environmental stimuli rather than innate internal factors. Tolman (1923) also argued that the major problem with the motivational concept of instinct was that it didn't really explain behavior, but rather only described it. In the 1920s American psychology became dominated by behaviorism (see chapter 1, "The Study of Psychology"). Instinct theories disappeared in the American psychological literature, but continued to flourish in the work of the European zoologists called ethologists.

Ethology. Ethology is the science of the behavior of animals in their natural environment. Ethology focuses on inherited rather than learned behavior. The ultimate goal of ethologists is to discover how instinctive behavior evolved among related species and now improves survival. In the 1930s Konrad Lorenz and Niko Tinbergen became the leaders of this approach. Ethology

grew steadily, and in 1973 the Nobel Prize for physiology was awarded to Lorenz, Tinbergen, and Karl von Frisch for their work in identifying animal behavior patterns.

The first step for the ethologist is to form an ethogram, which is a detailed description of all the behaviors shown by the species. Theories are then proposed to explain the development and adaptive function of each behavior. Experiments are next conducted to test these theories. For example, Lorenz (1965) found that newly hatched greylag geese, who normally follow the mother goose, will follow any large moving stimulus that is presented to them shortly after hatching. This process, termed *imprinting*, has the function of bonding the new bird with its mother for survival (see chapter 6, "Learning").

Many of the behaviors described in an ethogram consist of fixed action patterns (FAP). FAPs are unlearned, inherited, stereotyped behaviors that are species-specific, or shown by all members of a species (Alcock, 1984). Fixed action patterns are stimulated by specific cues from the environment, called releasers (sign stimuli). Releasers are especially important in social behaviors such as aggression or courtship. For example, Tinbergen (1952) reported that stereotyped courtship behavior was released in the female stickleback fish when the male stickleback swam toward her in a particular zigzag fashion.

The ethological, or species-specific, approach to animal motivation has influenced many comparative psychologists once again to include biological concepts in their theories of the behavior of different species of animals (Hinde, 1970). In fact, genetic and evolutionary principles are currently having an impact on human psychology in a controversial theory called sociobiology.

Sociobiology. Why would parents sacrifice their lives to save their children? Why do all cultures have elaborate courtship rituals and devise complex kinship rules? Is there an evolutionary basis for human behaviors such as helping, aggression, mate selection, parenting, and territoriality? According to Edward O. Wilson (1975), the answer to these questions is explained by the theory of sociobiology.

Sociobiology is the study of the genetic basis of social behavior. A key concept in this theory is that an individual is genetically programmed to show behaviors that help pass the genes on to the next generation. The literature in animal behavior is full of observations of ritualized courtship patterns and territorial aggressive displays. There are innumerable examples in the animal kingdom of a parent sacrificing its life for its young. For instance, a mother meadowlark might flutter around as if she had a broken wing in order to distract a cat from her babies.

Sociobiology is controversial because it proposes that not only is human biology genetically based, but that human social behavior is also. Because it applies the theory of evolutionary biology to the study of social behavior, sociobiology makes some interesting predictions about human behavior (Barash, 1982). Since passing one's genes on to the next generation involves reproduction, the human endeavors of mate selection, courtship, and parenting are considered extremely important. Sociobiology predicts that people will engage in behaviors that will help them genetically.

Richard Dawkins (1976) argued that the behavior of people is motivated basically by selfishness. Even if they don't marry and have children, people still work hard to get their genes into the next generation. Each child has 50% of a person's genes, but each niece or nephew has 25%. Thus, if a person can get his or her brothers or sisters to have four children, this is considered to be genetically the same as if he or she had two children.

In courtship and mate selection, males and females have different reproductive strategies (Wilson, 1981). The worst thing for a male, according to this theory, would be for his mate to become pregnant by someone else. Why? Because the offspring wouldn't be his biologically. So males want a long engagement (at least nine months) so they can be sure she is not already pregnant by someone else. A female, on the other hand, looks for someone who pampers her (and will pamper her baby) and shows a great deal of devotion. She wants protection, so she looks for a male who has status, power and wealth.

When they do get married, who is older? Sociobiological theory would predict the male, since he matures a couple of years later than the female, takes time to acquire wealth, and is better able to protect his mate. A research study by Chris Paterson (1982) suggests men are likely to be two years older than their wives at marriage. When first married, with whose parents might a couple live? They often live with the husband's parents, so his parents can help keep an eye on his wife. When they move out and eventually have a baby, whose mother comes to help? Hers, because her mother is the only grandparent who knows absolutely it is her grandchild. Why do people have children in the first place? One important reason is parental pressure. A successful parent is one who becomes a grandparent, since this assures that the genes will be perpetuated into future generations. And finally, why do parents sacrifice for their children? Because the children carry the genes on into the next generation. Sociobiologists have not yet had enough time to test many of their predictions, and thus they will have to wait before they can draw any firm conclusions.

Freud's Motivation Theory. Freud (1915) believed that behavior is caused by internal instincts (the German word *treib* can be interpreted as instinct, impulse, or drive). According to Freud, psychic energy, or libido, builds up in the personality structure called the id whenever there is a need (see chapter 11, "Personality," for a discussion of Freud's personality theory). He also believed that there are two main instincts: the life instinct and death instinct. The life instinct, or eros, serves to help the individual and the species survive. Sex is the major expression of this life instinct. The death instinct, or thanatos, includes aggression and destruction. Thus to Freud, motivation is often associated with sex or aggression.

Freud proposed that instincts have four characteristics: source, impetus, aim, and object. The instinct's *source* is the bodily need that activates motivation. The *impetus* is the intensity or strength of the motivation. The *aim* of an instinct is satisfaction, which is achieved by reducing the bodily need. And the instinct's *object* is the means by which the need is satisfied. For example, we might be hungry (source) and motivated to eat (impetus). We can reduce our hunger with food (aim) and thus eat (object). Freud's theory has been criticized because it does not predict behavior, but rather only attempts to explain what has already happened. It served, however, as an early model of the drive concept, to which we turn next.

Drive Theory

The term drive was first used by Woodworth in 1918 to describe the internal forces that push us toward doing something. He argued that different drives motivate different behaviors. For instance, the hunger drive motivates eating and the thirst drive motivates drinking. Woodworth described the characteristics of drive as direction, intensity, and persistence (which we defined earlier in this chapter). The concept of drive is often associated with the process of homeostasis.

Homeostasis. If you plot your hunger, you would find that it appears periodically (three or four times a day, counting a late-night snack), and when it does, it leads to a particular behavior (eating) which satisfies it. After reaching the goal of eating, you aren't motivated by hunger again for a while.

The hunger motive follows a cycle that illustrates the concept of homeostasis. This concept was introduced by Walter Cannon in 1939 to illustrate how the internal bodily processes are maintained in a stable state of balance. The easiest example of a homeostatic mechanism is temperature. We may set the thermostat in our home on 70°. When the temperature goes below this setting, the heating system comes on. Similarly, when our body temperature rises, we perspire to cool the body, and when our body temperature drops, we shiver to warm it. Hunger and thirst are two other biological motives that operate within a homeostatic cycle.

Hull's Drive Theory. The drive concept of motivation is often associated with Clark Hull's (1943) theory,

since his theory was extremely influential in the development of learning and motivation theory in psychology. Hull was influenced by the concept of homeostasis, and proposed that an organism is motivated to maintain it.

When there is a deviation from homeostasis, a biological need is created. This need (which often results from deprivation) produces a psychological arousal, or drive. A drive provides the energy for goal-directed behavior that will restore homeostasis and thus reduce the drive. For example, you have a biological need for water. When you go without drinking for a while, this need creates a psychological drive called thirst. Thirst leads to drinking behavior. After you reach your goal of drinking, your thirst drive is reduced and rests until your body needs more water. This cycle of homeostasis is repeated again and again as the individual maintains internal balance. Hull's drive theory is sometimes referred to as a *push* motivation theory, since the individual is pushed by inner forces toward reducing the drive and restoring homeostasis.

Hull (1952) devised a very influential model that explained how the strength (intensity) of a behavior is related to the processes of learning and motivation. His basic formula was:

$$E = H \times D \times K$$

Originally, he theorized that the strength of a response (E) depended upon the strength of a learned habit (H) and the strength of the motivating drive (D). Eventually, he concluded that motivation as a totally internal force was inadequate, and added the concept of incentive (K) to the formula. Incentive involves external stimuli such as reinforcements. For instance, we are more motivated to perform when provided a large reinforcement rather than a small reinforcement. We turn next to a discussion of the concept of incentives.

Incentive Theory

In contrast to the push motivation theory of drive, psychologists have also proposed a *pull* theory, in which external stimuli, called incentives, pull the individual toward some goal. Sometimes there is no deprivation that causes a biological need leading to a psychological drive to restore homeostasis. Rather we are motivated by an external stimulus, called an incentive, that pulls us toward some goal. For example, you may be tempted to eat a delicious dessert even when you are full after a big dinner. Incentives are objects or events in the environment that motivate the individual in the absence of any apparent biological need. You had no need for the dessert even though you were motivated to eat it.

Incentives can be either positive or negative. We are motivated to obtain positive incentives, whereas we are

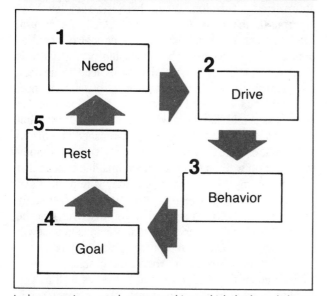

Figure 9.4. Homeostasis and Drive Reduction

1. Need
2. Drive
3. Behavior
4. Goal
5. Rest

In homeostasis, a need causes a drive, which leads to behavior designed to reach a goal and then allows the individual to rest. This cycle is repeated when a new need arises.

Figure 9.5. Incentive Motivation
External stimuli, called incentives, motivate us to avoid punishment or reinforce pleasure. A delicious dessert is an incentive to eat even if we do not have a biological deprivation which produces a need.

motivated to avoid negative incentives. For example, a positive incentive might be delicious food whereas a negative incentive might be pain. There are several distinctions between drives and incentives. Drives are produced internally, are unlearned, biological, and cyclic. Incentives, on the other hand, are produced externally, are learned, and do not depend on deprivation.

Incentive theory is similar to the motivational theory of hedonism. Hedonism is basically the seeking of pleasure and avoidance of pain. The theory of hedonism proposes that external stimuli motivate the individual because they are associated with the reinforcement of pleasure or the avoidance of punishment (Petri, 1986). Incentives play an important role in motivating human behavior.

Arousal Theory

The arousal theory of motivation focuses on the level of energy necessary to regulate our overall arousal. Sometimes we need to increase our arousal level by walking, looking, feeling, or other sensory active behaviors. At other times we already are highly aroused and need to lower the arousal level by sleeping, being quiet, or engaging in other forms of relaxation. The arousal theory emphasizes the whole individual and states that in order to understand behavior we need to study how the individual regulates his or her arousal level. The fundamental principle of arousal theory of motivation is that arousal occurs on a continuum from very low levels (such as in sleep) to extremely high levels (such as in

anxiety and strong emotions). Behavior is motivated as the arousal level changes, with some intermediate level of arousal producing the most efficient behavioral adaptation.

Optimum Level of Arousal. Donald Hebb (1955) proposed that we are motivated to maintain an optimum level of arousal. If our arousal level drops too low, we are motivated to do something to increase it. And if our arousal level becomes too high, we try to reduce it. The particular behavior is not as important as the goal of maintaining an optimum level of arousal.

He suggested that sensory information from the environment provided two functions: information and arousal. When our senses are stimulated, the neural impulses are carried to both the reticular formation (arousal) and cortex (information interpretation). The *cue function* of a sensory stimulus provides information about the environment, whereas the *arousal function* provides arousal stimulation. Hebb argued that motivation involves the arousal of the brain through the reticular formation so that the brain can interpret the sensory information and the individual can decide on direction.

The arousal theory differs from the drive theory in that in the drive theory the individual is motivated to decrease arousal by achieving some goal. In arousal theory, we sometimes increase and sometimes decrease the arousal. When we are bored, we find some excitement; we might go to an amusement park or talk to some friends to increase our arousal level. When we are overstimulated, we escape to find peace and quiet; we go off by ourselves, take a nap, or just relax to reduce our level of arousal.

Arousal and Performance. It has long been noted that the relationship between arousal and performance is an inverted-U function. When there is a very low level of arousal, the individual will be asleep. As arousal levels increase, the individual's alertness also increases until a point is reached when optimum performance is obtained. Additional arousal increases lead to anxiety, disorganization, and a decreased level of performance.

To understand arousal and performance, imagine that your class is told that there will be a test next Friday, but it will not be graded. In fact, when finished you are to toss it in the waste basket. You probably would not study much nor do well on this test. Now, imagine instead that the class learns that the test next Friday is important and that it will count as a regular test. Now, you will study and do well. Lastly, imagine that you discover that the test next Friday is so important that previous grades will be thrown out, and your course grade will be based exclusively on this one test. You would probably be very anxious about this test and might not do as well as you would if it were only a regular test. Test performance is likely to be best when arousal (motivation) is moderate. At either extreme, performance declines.

Figure 9.6. Optimum Level of Arousal
If our overall arousal level becomes too low, we are motivated to engage in a behavior to increase it as illustrated by these adventurous people.

The optimum level of arousal depends on the individual and the particular task, and predicts that the optimum motivation level for good performance decreases as the difficulty of the task increases (Berlyne, 1960). With a very easy task, you will need a high level of motivation to perform well. Think of that "easy" course you're taking and how difficult it is to do all of the assignments unless you force yourself. With a task of medium difficulty, performance is best when arousal (motivation) is moderate. But with a very difficult task, the optimum arousal level is fairly low. Think of your "tough" course, and how it doesn't take much to create such a panic that you study extremely hard. Over the years the relationship between arousal and performance has come to be known as the Yerkes-Dodson Law by many psychologists.

Sensation Seeking. The optimum arousal level is different for each individual (Weiss, 1987). Marvin Zuckerman (1979, 1984) has been investigating what he calls the dimension of sensation seeking. People with high optimum levels of arousal will seek thrills and adventure. These people may climb mountains, drive race cars, ride roller coasters, and enjoy action movies. High sensation seekers might also be more likely to use recreational drugs, become involved in illegal activities or be more easily aroused sexually (Zuckerman & Como, 1983). People with low optimum levels try to keep stimulation low. They may prefer reading a good book or watching a sunset. High-sensation seekers may have low levels of internal arousal, and thus depend on external stimulation to raise their internal level of arousal. On the other hand, low-sensation seekers may have internal levels of arousal that are already high and thus don't require any additional stimulation.

Sensation-seeking tendency may help explain criminal behavior. The EEGs of some criminals are lower than might be expected. It is possible that if the brain's overall arousal level is lower than usual, the person must do something to raise it. If socially approved activities do not raise arousal to its optimum level, then perhaps

Figure 9.7. Arousal and Performance

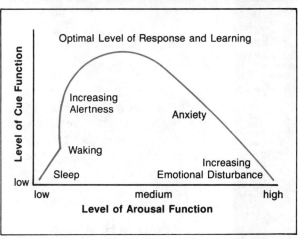

A certain amount of arousal is necessary for optimum performance, but additional stimulation leads to a decreased level of performance. This relationship is represented by an inverted U-shaped curve (after Hebb, 1955).

illegal behavior, such as committing a robbery, may provide the necessary stimulation. Although this theory is largely speculation, it does suggest the importance of recognizing individual differences in optimum arousal level.

A large number of research studies also have verified the wide variations in the sensation-seeking tendency of people (Mineka & Henderson, 1985). Zuckerman (1984) developed the sensation-seeking scale to measure four characteristics of sensation seeking as a personality trait. *Thrill and adventure seeking* is the characteristic of selecting activities that involve danger and adventure. *Disinhibition* involves engaging in uninhibited behaviors such as parachuting from a plane. *Experience seeking* involves gaining a wide variety of novel experiences, such as traveling. *Susceptibility to boredom* is the tendency to avoid routine activities.

Maslow's Humanistic Theory

Many psychologists view human behavior as being motivated by more than just strictly biological forces. One theory of human motivation, which is unusually broad in its design and appeal, is the humanistic theory proposed by Abraham Maslow, which has had an important influence on the psychology of motivation. In *Motivation and Personality*, Maslow stated that a theory of motivation must take into account the whole person, and should be based on a hierarchy of needs, which if successfully satisfied, leads to the full realization of one's potential (Maslow, 1970, 1987).

Physiological Needs. According to Maslow, physiological needs include motives such as hunger, thirst, sex, exercise, and rest. A person is dominated by the physiological needs until some of them have been satisfied at least partially. Note that higher needs in the hierarchy can become stronger when physiological needs start to be met. Maslow believed that the physiological needs were adequately met in most people in our society. After that, the individual is motivated by the safety needs.

Safety Needs. Motives such as security, stability, dependency, protection, freedom from fear and anxiety, and need for structure and order are safety needs. Security, protection, and safety become dominant forces in a person's life until they can be satisfied. Children prefer routines and familiar surroundings, and often experience problems when things are greatly disturbed. As we grow up, except for emergencies, the safety needs are largely met. When you feel safe and secure, you then begin to develop other social needs—the next highest level.

Belongingness and Love Needs. Motives such as love and affection are included in belongingness and love needs. As these needs dominate, we feel a desire for friends, family, and social contact. We need to belong to a group or family. Maslow suggests that when the family moves, children often have difficulties because they have many needs to be met quickly. As adults, we need

ABRAHAM H. MASLOW

Abraham H. Maslow was born in Brooklyn, New York, in 1908. He studied primate behavior at the University of Wisconsin, where he received his doctorate degree in psychology in 1934.

Early in his scholarly career, Maslow was drawn to the study of human motivation and personality. His work in this area upset strict behaviorists, whose explanations of motivation and personality failed to account for what Maslow called the whole person. His theory of the hierarchy of needs, which leads to the "self-actualized" individual, was a strong catalyst for the founding of humanistic psychology. Maslow successfully bridged motivation and personality in his theories of needs, self-actualizing persons, and peak experiences.

Maslow is considered an important figure in contemporary psychology. His career was a formidable one. For 14 years he taught at Brooklyn College, and then went to Brandeis University as chairman of the Psychology Department. In 1968 he was elected president of the American Psychological Association. In 1969 he went to the Laughlin Foundation in Menlo Park, California. He wrote two very important books: *Toward a Psychology of Being* (1968) and *Motivation and Personality* (1970). Abraham Maslow died of a heart attack in 1970.

Figure 9.8. Maslow's Need Hierarchy

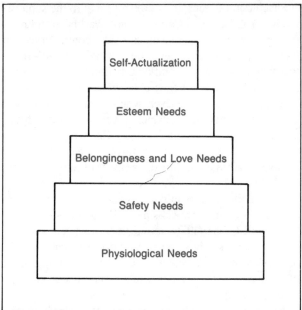

Self-Actualization

Esteem Needs

Belongingness and Love Needs

Safety Needs

Physiological Needs

This humanistic theory of motivation proposes a hierarchy of needs, which, if satisfied, leads to self-actualization, the full realization of one's potential.

to give and receive love. We can satisfy these needs through marriage, work, or social activities. If we do not satisfy the belongingness and love needs, Maslow believes that psychological problems may develop.

Esteem Needs. A high evaluation of oneself, self-respect, achievement, and recognition by others are considered esteem needs. We need to achieve competence if we want to gain other people's respect. When we earn recognition, attention, and status, we satisfy the esteem needs and feel self-confident and important. If we do not satisfy them, we tend to feel inferior and helpless.

Self-actualization. The final need in Maslow's hierarchy is self-actualization. When the physiological, safety, love, and esteem needs have been satisfied, the individual is motivated to reach the *growth* need of self-actualization. This refers to the attainment of the individual's special potential, to the person's becoming what he or she is capable of becoming. Self-actualization is highly individualized, since each of us has different sets of abilities. Maslow believed that self-actualization is rarely reached, and if it is, it is usually in older people who have had the time and experience necessary to achieve this level. We discuss Maslow's self-actualization theory in more detail in chapter 11, "Personality."

Although Maslow's theory of motivation has been influential in psychology, his ideas have been broadly criticized. Many of the people he considered to be self-actualized were either friends or people who were dead.

Therefore, a major problem with his hypothesis is reliability. Also, some research that tried to test the theory as a developmental model failed to support it (Goebel & Brown, 1981). Apparently, one does not necessarily move through the hierarchy as one grows older.

While Maslow's theory has been useful in helping us understand ourselves, it is important to remember that human behavior is so complex that the best way to study it is a thoroughly multidimensional approach.

Cognitive Theory

The cognitive approach to motivation emphasizes thinking and perceptual interpretation. While the theory of cognitive motivation is currently very popular in psychology, it has been discussed for many years. As we discussed in chapter 6, "Learning," Tolman (1932) proposed a cognitive theory of purposive behavior which states that as individuals learn that certain behaviors lead to certain goals, they develop cognitive expectancies that motivate them to exhibit those behaviors.

An expectancy-value theory of motivation was developed by Julian Rotter (1954). Basically, he argued that behavior is the result of our expectations of achieving goals and the value that those goals have for us. We are motivated to maximize the value of our behavior choices. For instance, suppose you need to choose between studying for an exam or going to a movie. If passing the course is a high priority (high value) and you believe you need a good exam grade to pass the course (expectation), you will probably spend the night studying rather than going to the theater. In chapter 11, "Personality," we discuss Rotter's theory that people vary in their expectancies about the source of reinforcement. Expectancy theory is also important in achievement motivation, which we will cover later.

Attribution involves the cognitive process of determining the motives of someone's behavior. Fritz Heider (1958) proposed the naive psychology approach in which a person decides the causes of behavior. According to Heider, we attribute behavior to forces within the individual (disposition forces) or forces in the environment (situation forces). *Dispositions* include ability and motivation, whereas *situations* include task difficulty and luck. As an example, you notice that the student next to you received an outstanding grade on a test. Do you attribute the performance to the person's intelligence and hard work (dispositions) or the fact that it was an easy test or the student was a lucky guesser (situation)? Heider suggested that you are probably biased toward a dispositional attribution. We discuss the current approach to attribution theory in chapter 15, "Social Psychology."

BIOLOGICAL MOTIVES

Biologically, organisms are prepared to engage in behaviors that facilitate survival. What are the biological (primary) motives? Biological motives have a definite physiological basis, and are biologically necessary for survival of the individual or the species; they include hunger, thirst, body temperature regulation, avoidance of pain, and the sexual drive. Some of these motives are satisfactorily explained by the drive theory, while others need additional theories for a complete understanding. In this section we discuss the biological motives of hunger, thirst and sex.

Hunger

It's noon, and as you look around the crowded cafeteria, you realize that many people seem to feel hungry at the same time. What motivates us to eat at certain times? Hunger is not always associated with a conscious internal sensation, and we sometimes find ourselves eating ravenously without having had any previous awareness of hunger pangs. Many times, external cues are used to signal initiation of eating behavior. When asked if they are hungry, many people consult their watches rather than their stomachs.

Peripheral Factors. When someone says he or she is hungry, the sensation most often reported is the feeling of a slight ache in the stomach. In a famous study

Figure 9.9. External Cues for Hunger
Although hunger has a biological basis, many times we are influenced by external cues that signal eating behavior.

by Cannon and Washburn (1912), a subject swallowed a balloon which allowed the experimenters to record stomach contractions and compare them to the subject's feelings of hunger. Cannon and Washburn found a strong association between stomach contractions and feelings of hunger. However, later studies demonstrated that when it contains an inflated balloon, the stomach is full, and that it is otherwise fairly quiet even when it does not contain food. Even when stomachs of humans and animals have been surgically removed, the subjects eat regularly. The stomach does influence the size of a meal that is eaten, probably through receptors in the stomach wall that monitor the amount of nutrients in the meal (Deutsch, 1983).

The duodenum, or initial segment of the small intestine, has been implicated as a mechanism to stop eating. Smith and Gibbs (1976) found that when fats and proteins enter the duodenum, a hormone called CCK (cholecystokinin) is released. CCK travels through the bloodstream to the brain where a signal to stop eating is released.

However, research by Deutsch and Hardy (1977) which found that rats find CCK aversive, indicates that the role of blood hormones in stopping eating is still unclear. Recent studies have reported conflicting claims on the role of CCK in stopping eating behavior through brain regulation. It now appears likely that CCK influences the termination of eating in humans by inhibiting stomach muscles, thus delaying the emptying of the stomach and shortening the length of a meal (McHugh & Moran, 1985).

Several other theories that attempt to explain eating behavior involve body temperature, mouth factors, body fat, and glucose levels. The glucostatic theory of hunger, first proposed by Jean Mayer (1953) argued that hunger occurs when glucose metabolism in individual cells is low. Later research has shown that the liver monitors glucose levels and when glucose levels in the liver are high, eating is suppressed (Russek & colleagues, 1980).

Brain Centers. We know that the hypothalamus is important in controlling eating behavior. In chapter 2, "Biology of Behavior," we learned that the hypothalamus played a key role in motivation of behavior, including eating, drinking, and sex. Two distinct areas of the hypothalamus are important in hunger. The lateral hypothalamus (LH) appears to be involved in initiating eating behavior, whereas the ventromedial hypothalamus (VMH) stops eating behavior.

While we are not certain how the lateral hypothalamus functions in hunger regulation, we do know that it facilitates the release of insulin and digestive secretions of the stomach (Morley, Bartness, Gosell, & Levine, 1985). It appears that the ventromedial hypothalamus (the satiety center) influences the cessation of eating behavior by monitoring glucose levels and other

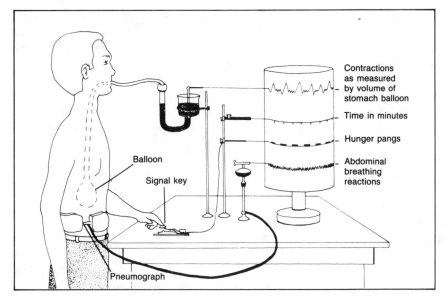

Figure 9.10. Cannon and Washburn Experiment
In an attempt to measure stomach contractions during hunger, Cannon and Washburn (1912) had a subject swallow a balloon and indicate when he felt hunger pangs.

chemicals in the blood. When the lateral hypothalamus is damaged, it produces a condition called aphagia, in which the individual does not eat at all. When the ventromedial hypothalamus is damaged, it produces hyperphagia, a condition in which the individual continues to eat until he or she becomes obese.

Obesity. How many times have you heard people complain that after they go on a diet and lose weight it always comes back? Can those of us who are overweight help ourselves, or are we doomed to remain fat? The causes of obesity are complex, but psychologists are beginning to understand that the overweight person is not just someone without willpower.

In 1971 Stanley Schachter reported some interesting parallels between the behavior of rats that have a dam-

Figure 9.11. Amount of Effort Required to Eat

	Normal Weight (number of subjects)		Obese (number of subjects)	
	Eat	Not Eat	Eat	Not Eat
Almonds Still With Shells	10	10	1	19
Almonds Without Shells	11	9	19	1

Schachter (1971) found that obese subjects were less willing than normal-weight subjects to shell almonds in order to eat them.

aged ventromedial hypothalamus and obese human beings. Both obese people and VMH damaged rats are less active, tend to eat faster, are more sensitive to taste (and eat more when the food tastes good), and are less willing to work for food. For example, in one experiment, Schachter gave people almonds to eat. When they were without shells, both obese and normal subjects ate them, but when they were in their shells, only the normal-weight subjects went to the trouble of shelling and eating them. The obese subjects would not work to shell the almonds!

Richard Nisbett (1972) proposed a set-point theory of obesity. He suggested that, unlike the rat with a damaged VMH, the obese human might have a normal functioning hypothalamus. Perhaps the level is just set higher than usual, and the person eats to maintain the higher set point. Nisbett feels that perhaps the set point is determined by the number of fat cells in the body.

Obese people tend to have many more fat cells than do normal-weight people. Scientists believe that the number of fat cells is determined in the first couple of years of life, and is the result of heredity and early eating habits (Grinker, 1982). When you diet, you cause your fat cells to shrink, but you do not eliminate them. Then when you begin to overeat, the fat cells are enlarged, and you gain weight again.

McMinn (1984) pointed out that when a person decreases food intake, the body compensates by decreasing the metabolism rate. Thus, when you diet you actually use less energy. This can, of course, be counteracted by additional exercise with the dieting. Judith Rodin (1981) pointed out that basal metabolism slows down as we age, thus making it more difficult to lose weight in middle adulthood.

Schachter developed a theory of obesity in which he suggested that while overweight people are no more

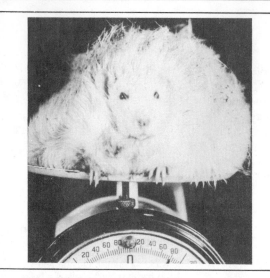

Figure 9.12. Hypothalamus and Overeating
This rat ate itself into these proportions after experimenters destroyed the ventromedial hypothalamus, the part of the hypothalamus that stops eating behavior.

sensitive than normal-weight people to internal cues (stomach contractions), they are much more sensitive to external cues (time and the sight, smell, and taste of food). These conclusions have practical implications for people trying to lose weight.

First, overweight people should shun situations in which external food cues are especially tempting. For example, they should avoid spending excessive time in the kitchen, and try not to have snack foods readily available.

Overweight people can learn to establish eating patterns similar to those of normal-weight people. Since overweight people cannot depend on cues to stop them from overeating, they can use smaller plates, take smaller bites, chew food longer, and leave the table earlier.

In order to become more aware of external cues, they can keep a food diary, including a list of what they eat, when they eat, how they feel when they eat, and under what circumstances they eat.

Eating Disorders

Although most people eat to maintain normal or above normal weight, some individuals have a problem with eating enough to stay healthy. Two major eating disorders are anorexia and bulimia.

Anorexia nervosa is an eating disorder in which the person becomes severely underweight because of self-imposed restrictions in eating. The problem is most often seen in young women and teenage girls as young as 14 years of age (Fosson & colleagues, 1987). Criteria in diagnosing anorexia from the American Psychiatric Association (DSM III-R, 1987) include intense fear of being overweight and loss of 15% of body weight without any physical problem that could account for it. Although cases of male anorexics have been reported, the vast majority of cases are female, with the disorder affecting as many as 1% of the female teenage population.

The causes of anorexia have not been fully identified, but appear to include social, psychological, and physiological influences. Societal pressures for being thin, as portrayed in the media, appear influential and apparently affect females more than males. The anorexic believes that she is overweight even when she is extremely thin, suggesting a perceptual self-image problem (Striegel-Moore, Silberstein, & Rodin, 1986). Other causes focus on physiological mechanisms such as a malfunctioning hypothalamus, endocrine disorder, and brain tumor (Muuss, 1985).

People suffering from bulimia nervosa eat large amounts of calorie-rich food in a short time and then purge the food by vomiting or using laxatives. Young women are most likely to experience bulimia, with incidence levels of 4 to 13% of primarily college females (Halmi, Falk, & Schwartz, 1981). While many bulimics are normal weight individuals, about 50% are anorexics.

Johnson and Larson (1982) suggested that women with bulimia tended to be sad, lonely, irritable, passive, and emotionally unstable. A number of studies have reported people with bulimia have poor body images, high levels of anxiety, and generally suffer depression (Hinze & Williamson, 1987). A recent study by Davis and his colleagues (1988) found that the mood of bulimic subjects was more positive than a control group just before a normal meal, but more negative than usual just before a binge eating episode, suggesting the importance of emotions on the behavior of people with bulimia.

Psychologists are trying to understand the causes of anorexia and bulimia. Unfortunately, often the affected individuals are noticed only after the disorder has been continuing for some time. Efforts that focus on positive self-image and emotional stability appear to help. Much more research needs to be conducted to discover the complex influences on these eating disorders.

THOUGHT QUESTIONS

1. What are the characteristics of anorexia and bulimia?
2. Why are women most likely to have these eating disorders?
3. How might these eating disorders be treated?

Thirst

Normally we feel thirsty when our mouths and throats are dry. But this is not the whole story. Recent research has demonstrated the importance of the kidneys and hypothalamus in maintaining thirst homeostasis.

Cells in the lateral preoptic area of the hypothalamus called osmoreceptors are sensitive not only to the relative amount of water in the blood, but more particularly to cellular dehydration due to the amount of salt, which becomes concentrated as the body dehydrates from loss of water (Peck & Novin, 1971). An increase in the amount of salt in the blood will thus cause the anterior hypothalamus to signal the pituitary gland to secrete antidiuretic hormone (ADH), which causes the kidneys to slow down their production of urine. This restores body fluid. At the same time, the hypothalamus signals the brain's cortex to create a thirst drive to force the increased water intake needed to restore the normal salt level (Epstein, 1982).

Prolonged water deprivation also results in the stimulation of receptors in the kidneys. The kidneys then secrete the hormone renin that produces angiotensin in the bloodstream. This causes the kidneys to retain more water, stimulates the subfornical and cortex areas of the brain to create a thirst drive (Simpson & Rottenberg, 1973). Drinking more water then restores homeostasis.

Sexual Motivation

Food, water, and a moderate temperature are all necessary to keep us alive. Our drives to obtain these needs are like our drives to get enough air, to eliminate bodily wastes, to sleep, and to avoid pain. Deprivation of the goal tends to increase the drive. The longer an organism is deprived of food, the more active it becomes in searching for it (up to the point where lack of nourishment begins to slow the organism down).

Uniqueness of the Sex Drive. Sex, on the other hand, is unique. Although sex is classified as a biological drive, it is neither necessary to sustain individual life nor is it activated by deprivation. Although sex is necessary for continuation of a species, the life of an individual member of that species is not threatened by the lack of a sexual outlet.

While the male cannot be aroused for a brief period after ejaculation, and both sexes may cease sexual activity through sheer exhaustion, the sexual impulse is fairly independent of the amount of sexual deprivation. And among human beings, higher psychological variables are also involved in stimulating or suppressing the motivation for sexual activity. Another way that sex is unlike the other biological drives is that individuals actively seek its arousal, since an increase in the drive is rewarding in itself. Both humans and animals will work

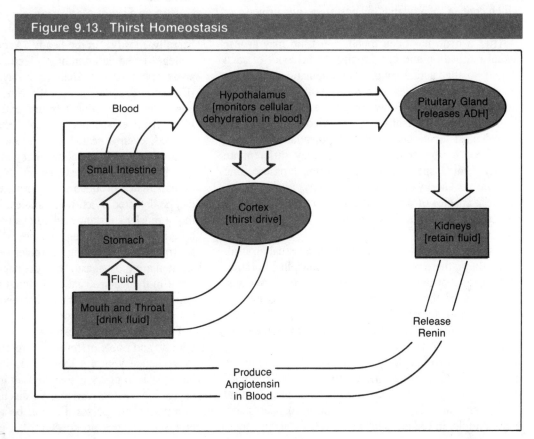

Figure 9.13. Thirst Homeostasis

Blood

Hypothalamus [monitors cellular dehydration in blood]

Pituitary Gland [releases ADH]

Small Intestine

Cortex [thirst drive]

Stomach

Kidneys [retain fluid]

Fluid

Mouth and Throat [drink fluid]

Release Renin

Produce Angiotensin in Blood

Thirst involves a variety of bodily organs and processes, including the brain, kidneys, and mouth.

for sexual arousal as a reward, even when there is no consummation and even though consummation produces only momentary satiation.

Animal Courtship and Mating. Although humans and other primates can be ready for sex at virtually all times, among most lower animals sexual activity is motivated largely by hormones (from ovaries or testes) plus instincts. Most commonly, when the female ovulates, her sex glands release the hormone estrogen into the bloodstream, making her sexually receptive during the period referred to as estrus.

Courtship in animals is the behavioral process whereby sexually mature individuals of a species become mating pairs. Often sensory cues in courtship attract a potential mate. Chemical cues often serve as sexual attractants in animals. Pheromones are chemicals secreted by the body which are used in communication with other members of the same species. We know that pheromones play an important role in the sexual behavior of lower animals. For example, the female cockroach produces a pheromone that attracts males from great distances. As the male cockroach approaches and his antennae touch the female, he begins to exhibit pre-copulatory behavior. It has been shown that the urine of male mice can cause the sexual cycles of female mice to become regulated. Among mammals, many males have scent glands that secrete pheromonal substances that attract females. For instance, deer rub their hind legs, which contain scent glands, against trees, and urine from female dogs can attract males from miles away.

After a mate has been found, courtship may arouse sexual motivation and synchronize the behavior of each animal so that actual mating, or copulation, can take place. Different species have evolved different behavior patterns in courtship. However, there are some common functions that courtship serves (Alcock, 1984). An animal must locate and identify a potential mate. Specific cues in the courtship pattern may differentiate closely related species, thus preventing crossbreeding and wasted energy on infertile matings. For example, different species of ducks have different head courtship movements, and other species do not respond to these movements.

Visual or auditory cues often enhance sexual arousal. In monkeys, there is a swelling and change in coloration in the genital area of the female during estrus. And just the sound of the male cooing may provide enough stimulation for female pigeons to ovulate. Tactile stimulation may also be important in sexual motivation, as evidenced by the fact that female cats are stimulated by the male to ovulate only during copulation. This is adaptive in that it allows the cat to retain her egg until male sperm are available. In many animals, postural adjustments are required for copulation to take place. For example, in rodents such as the rat, the female must

Figure 9.14. Animal Courtship
All male animals have certain courtship behaviors, designed to attract a female, that precede mating. One of the most spectacular displays in the animal kingdom is put on by the peacock. During mating season, the male will spread his beautiful plumes in hopes of attracting the female of his choice.

remain motionless and raise her hindquarters for the male to mount her successfully. The stereotyped courtship and mating activities among animals is another cue that sexual behavior is largely under biological control.

Human Sexual Motivation. For human beings, sex is a very important source of motivation, but it is, literally, mostly "in the head." According to one study, college freshmen attending a lecture reported that they spent about 20% of their time daydreaming about sex (Cameron & colleagues, 1968). Since human sexuality is controlled by the higher brain centers that enable us to learn from experience, sexual behavior in humans is learned, even if sexual arousal and orgasm are innate.

Some researchers believe that pheromones may play a role in human sexual attraction also. It is possible that human males produce a pheromone in their urine that can be detected by certain females. Research has shown that a musky substance called exaltolide can be detected by adult mature women, but not by premenstrual girls, postmenopausal women, or males of any age. And most women are most sensitive to the odor of exaltolide at the point in their menstrual cycle that they are most able to conceive. It appears, then, that people are sensitive to smell in sexual attraction.

Personal tastes in sexual partners and practice vary widely, and one's preferences are culturally shaped and may change within a lifetime (Kelly, 1988). Though it has a basis in biology, sex plays an important role in our psychological motivation. We discuss human sexuality, as a part of our personality, our behavior, our emotions, and our attitudes, in chapter 10, "Emotion."

Figure 9.15. Sexual Motivation
In people, a wide variety of factors influence sexual behavior including biological needs as well as environmental stimuli.

– STIMULUS MOTIVES –

There appear to be certain motivating factors for behavior that are internal and unlearned, but do not have a physiological basis. Stimulus motives cause the individual to seek out sensory stimulation through interaction with the environment. Stimulus motives that we cover include sensory stimulation, curiosity, and competence.

Sensory Stimulation

Have you ever noticed how difficult it is to do absolutely nothing? Even when we rest, we still think about things and often we daydream. If, at a certain time, we are not experiencing enough stimulation, daydreaming may provide that stimulation. People like to keep busy, even if what they are doing is not all that important.

As we discussed in chapter 4, "Sensation and Perception," there is evidence that a lack of *sensory stimulation* is aversive. Experiments have been carried out in which adult humans were subjected to sensory deprivation (Heron, 1957). The sensory-deprived subjects soon began to think illogically, occasionally to experience hallucinations, and to show impaired performance on a wide

variety of cognitive tasks (Goldberger, 1982). It appears that without an external, changing world to focus our senses on, our inner world begins to break down, and develops a need to create its own stimulation. Internal stimulation, however, never quite meets all the needs that external stimulation does. This is why solitary confinement for prisoners is such an effective punishment, and why people are motivated to increase arousal levels when in restricted conditions for any length of time.

Exploration and Curiosity

Misty and Silver always rush around sniffing the bushes and trees whenever they are let out in the backyard. These two dogs are exhibiting exploration, or sensory inspection of the environment. It's important to know our environment, with its pleasures and its dangers. The curiosity motive causes us to seek out a certain amount of novelty and complexity, and with no other apparent motivation, we seek out and explore new environments.

Curiosity and exploration are often seen in babies. Berlyne (1966) showed that even young babies prefer to look at complex patterns rather than simple ones. And babies are constantly exploring their environment, touching, tasting, looking, and listening.

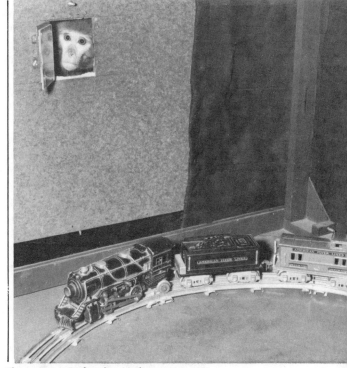

Figure 9.16. Exploration Motive
Butler and Harlow (1954) reported that monkeys were motivated to learn simple tasks if they were rewarded by the novel stimulation of viewing a toy train.

Figure 9.17. Curiosity Motive
Exploration and curiosity are important motivators for behavior in animals, as illustrated by these monkeys working to unlock the boxes.

As we mature, we require ever-increasing novelty and complexity in our surroundings. We gradually lose interest in the same situation and prefer that new elements be added, though not too many at once. Young children will play for hours with very simple toys, but their older brothers and sisters require more elaborate (and expensive) playthings.

Curiosity is not unique to humans. Many animals will explore a new environment with no external reward other than the newness of what is perceived. In one study by Butler and Harlow (1954), monkeys learned simple discrimination tasks if they were rewarded by being allowed to look out of a window and see a toy train. Other experiments have demonstrated that monkeys will work to learn how to unlock puzzles, or to open boxes, even when there is nothing interesting inside.

Berlyne (1960) suggested that the explanation for the curiosity motive might be simply the optimum level of arousal tendency (discussed earlier in this chapter). We explore to raise our arousal levels, and we rest when we're too stimulated. Hebb (1966) argued that play and exploration will occur primarily when other needs are not great or demanding. Other psychologists feel curiosity might help keep track of important resources, such as food, water, shelter, and the location of friends and enemies. Whatever the answer, it is clear that we do have a need to explore the environment.

Competence

Do we engage randomly in activities in which we explore, manipulate, contact, and generally show a need for curiosity and sensory stimulation, or do our actions seem to have some purpose? A theory proposed by White (1959) suggests that we have a need to master the environment. The motivational theory of competence states that people are motivated to interact successfully with the environment. Other stimulus motives, such as curiosity and exploration, might just be ways we try to master the environment.

Even children work hard at walking, talking, and doing the basic things that will allow them to deal effectively with an increasingly complex environment. How do you feel when you have done something perfectly? Doesn't it feel great when you complete a crossword puzzle or solve a complex math problem? These feelings of competency continue to motivate us to even greater challenges. This might be why people spend hours trying to master computer and video games.

Intrinsic and Extrinsic Motivation. We could say that we do things for basically two reasons: because they are fun or pleasurable (intrinsic motivation), or because they will lead to something in the environment that we want (extrinsic motivation). This could describe the difference between work and play. You might read your textbook because you enjoy it intrinsically, or you might read it to earn a good grade (extrinsic motivation) in class. Or, more likely, it is a combination of both.

A study by Lepper, Greene, and Nisbett (1973) with nursery children demonstrates the effects of intrinsic and extrinsic motivation. The experimenters chose children who loved to draw pictures, and told some of them to draw for fun and others to draw for a reward. They found that both groups drew good pictures, but the group that drew for the reward (extrinsic motivation) tended not to want to draw pictures later on their own. In other words, their play became work, and they only worked when rewarded. Examples of how this principle works are all around us. You may really enjoy swimming, and stay around the pool as much as possible. But when you're hired as a lifeguard, suddenly your fun becomes work, and it's not quite as enjoyable.

Edward Deci (1975) proposed a theory of intrinsic motivation which states that we need to feel competent in controlling our environment. Intrinsic motivation causes behaviors that lead to this competency and control. We tend to do things that we enjoy and that we are good at. Our hobbies, our pastimes, our recreational outings are done largely because we find them satisfying. The rewards come from within us rather than from others.

More recently, Deci has expanded his theory of intrinsic motivation to emphasize the importance of self-determination (Deci, 1980; Deci & Ryan, 1985). He argued that not all extrinsic reinforcement decreases intrinsic motivation. Rewards that help people believe they have competency or self-determination can increase intrinsic motivation. Being able to determine for oneself what one does is extremely motivating. For instance, if a student receives an excellent grade on an exam for which he or she has purposively studied hard, the grade will probably encourage feelings of competency, and will likely motivate the student to continue to strive for excellence. If the student perceives the grade as an attempt to control behavior, intrinsic motivation will decrease; if it is perceived as a source of information about his or her competency, intrinsic motivation will increase.

Deci believes that we need to concentrate more on intrinsic motivation and self-determination in schools and workplaces. Too often educational and business systems depend on extrinsic reinforcement (grades or money) for control rather than self-determination. One way to utilize intrinsic motivation is to help people do what they enjoy. Teachers might have students choose individual topics to study, for instance.

LEARNED SOCIAL MOTIVES

The learned social motives are determined largely by learning and center around social experiences. Henry Murray (1938) developed a list of human needs that are basically learned social motives. He included in his list motives such as achievement, affiliation, aggression, autonomy, dominance, nurturance, understanding, and play. Some of these motives are covered in later chapters. In this chapter the social motives of achievement, power, and affiliation are covered.

Achievement

The need for achievement, the desire to perform at some high standard of excellence, or the desire to be successful, has received considerable attention from psychologists who study learned motives. David McClelland and John Atkinson tested people's need to achieve by having them make up stories to describe what is happening in ambiguous pictures. The themes of the stories were then analyzed to identify themes involving goals and striving for success (McClelland, 1958). This test is called the Thematic Apperception Test (TAT) and is discussed in chapter 11, "Personality."

Characteristics of the Achievement Motive. Within normal limits, the need for achievement is not strongly related to ability. But people who score high on tests of need for achievement tend to do better on verbal and mathematical tests and get better grades in school. McClelland and his colleagues (1953) found that people who rank high in the need for achievement frequently have parents who demand or reward their independence as early as the second year of life. As children, for example, they are encouraged to go to bed by themselves, entertain themselves, and choose their own clothes.

Figure 9.18. Achievement Motivation
Considerable differences occur among people in the need for achievement or the desire to perform at some high standard of excellence. Lily K. Lai is the director of public relations and public affairs of AT&T International and the director of corporate development of AT&T New York. Lai holds degrees from MIT, University of Kentucky, and University of Wisconsin.

McClelland (1985a) also found that they tend to assume personal responsibility for their behavior and prefer situations in which they receive feedback about their performance. They also tend to be innovative in their approach to solving problems. Veroff (1982) reported that men who scored high in achievement motivation were well adjusted in both their personal lives and their work lives.

Atkinson (1957) developed a model for understanding achievement motivation. His formula was:

$$T = M \times P \times I$$

The tendency to achieve success (T) equals the motive to achieve success (M) times the probability of success (P) times the incentive value of success (I). Thus, people who succeed must be motivated to achieve, believe there is a good chance of success, and value the achievement goal. For example, students are most likely to be successful when they are motivated to earn high grades, have a good chance of maintaining a high grade point average, and believe that high grades are important.

Fear of Failure. Research indicates that people who score low on the need for achievement tests also tend to have a high fear of failure (Atkinson & Birch, 1978). When they have a free choice of goals, those with low need for achievement and high fear of failure scores may pick either very easy ones (thus avoiding failure) or unrealistically difficult ones (thus avoiding blame because they cannot be criticized for failing). People high in achievement motive and low in fear of failure, however, tend to choose realistically challenging goals where they run the risk of failure but also have a chance of achieving the goal.

For example, McClelland (1958) had a group of children play a ringtoss game. The children with high need for achievement tended to stand at moderate distances from the peg, while those with low need for achievement stood either very close or very far from the peg. According to McClelland, the high achiever is apparently better prepared to face failure than the low achiever, although he or she is also more realistic about evaluating the chances for success.

Fear of Success. Most of the early results in achievement motivation testing are found in research with male subjects. Female subjects don't necessarily fit the same pattern. One hypothesis developed by Matina Horner (1972) to explain the difference in achievement motivation between men and women, is that at least in our society, women have a motive to avoid success. The socialization process most women undergo in this country creates in them the fear of negative consequences if they successfully compete in traditionally "male" achievement situations that have been defined as inappropriate for their sex. According to Horner, women are therefore faced with a conflict between their motive to achieve and their motive to avoid success. In one study, Horner asked men and women college students to complete a story about a person who was at the top of the class after first term finals. The men wrote about "John" while the women wrote about "Anne." Only 9% of the men showed fear of success in their stories, whereas 65% of the women wrote stories with a fear of success orientation.

This conclusion has been seriously questioned by others (Zuckerman & Wheeler, 1975). Later studies showed that both men and women included more fear of success in Anne than in John. Karabenick (1977) found that a high fear of success hurt performance of women competing with men only when the task was believed to be masculine. Perhaps the attitude of women is more one of not wanting to reverse sex roles than of avoiding success.

One line of research on fear of success has focused on black men and women. A 1974 study by Fleming found that 29% of black college women demonstrated fear of success, compared to 67% of black college men. In later studies, Fleming found the sex difference tended to disappear, as the sex difference among white subjects did in Horner's studies. Recently, Fleming (1983) reported that black men who were high in fear of success tended to be very successful socially at a predominantly white college, probably because they were sensitive about being too assertive and thus had been careful to conform and "fit" in in order to be accepted by their white peers. This research program demonstrates the complexity of fear of success as it relates to sex and race for achievement motivation.

Power

The need for power involves the desire to control or exert influence (Veroff, 1957, 1982). Power is one way that we can influence others when we want something from them. Winter (1973) found that people with a high power motive had problems establishing close interpersonal relationships, as they typically attempt to control the relationship. They also tend to take risks, drink alcohol more often, and behave more recklessly (for example, gambling or unsafely driving a car) than those with a low need for power.

Other research indicates people with a high need for power can be very successful in life (McClelland, 1978). They become leaders and are able to exert influence to accomplish things. McClelland pointed out that leadership does not necessarily mean a dictatorship. Successful leaders are able to make others feel important and often enter careers in which they can make an impact on others.

The power motive tends to operate in a similar

fashion for both men and women (Winter, 1982). However, because of differences in sex-role expectations, the expression of the motive might differ. For instance, Winter argued that men with a high need for power are more likely to fight, gamble, and take risks, whereas women are more likely to show more socially responsible behavior (such as taking action and making appropriate decisions). Most research suggests that the power motive is a fairly stable personality characteristic, learned early in life, and expressed in a wide variety of situations.

Affiliation

A person expresses his or her <u>need for affiliation</u> by seeking out and forming attachments to other individuals, and by working toward belonging to, and being accepted by, groups of people. The need is both a personality trait and a motive (McClelland, 1985b). As a personality trait, it remains fairly constant for each individual throughout life, although it varies from person to person. As a motive within the individual, it is a state that is aroused on some occasions much more than on others.

Individuals with a high affiliation motive are likely to be found with other people. Constantian (1981) conducted a study in which a group of students wore beepers around for a week, and at random intervals were asked to report what they were doing. He found that those with a high need for affiliation were significantly more likely to be interacting with others than were those who had a low affiliation motive. They also

Figure 9.19. Schachter's Study of Affiliation

Experimental Condition	Social Waiting Selection	
	Together	Alone or Don't Care
High Anxiety	20	12
Low Anxiety	10	20

In his study on the relationship between anxiety and affiliation among college women, Schachter (1959) found that the need for affiliation increases under high anxiety conditions.

tended to avoid competition and conflict, and hence did not often succeed in management positions. Some research suggests that people with a very high need to affiliate are less popular, more anxious about social relationships, and fear disapproval of others than those with simply a high need. Crowne and Marlowe (1964) reported these individuals tend also to score high on the need for social approval.

The need for affiliation becomes particularly intense during periods of anxiety. This became evident in a classic series of experiments conducted by Stanley Schachter (1959). He aroused the anxiety of female subjects by getting them to believe that they were about to participate in an experiment in which they would receive severe electric shocks. The subjects were greeted by an ominous-looking "Dr. Zilstein," who told them the scientific importance of the experiment and assured them that they would receive no permanent

Figure 9.20. Affiliation
Most people have a need to be with others. The need for affiliation is both a personality trait and a motive for behavior.

damage from the shocks. Clearly visible to them was a sinister piece of apparatus, embedded in a maze of wires. When given a choice of waiting for their turns alone in a comfortable waiting room furnished with magazines, or with the other subjects in an empty classroom, the large majority chose to wait together, demonstrating what has been termed the need for affiliation (see Figure 9.19.).

Schachter gave the same choice to another group (the control group), whose anxiety had not been aroused. They were also told they would receive shocks, but they would feel only a tingling sensation. This "low-anxiety" group showed much less interest in waiting in the company of other subjects. The arousal of the affiliation motive indicates that in some circumstances, at least, misery loves miserable company. Further research indicates that we choose to be with others during a frightening situation in order to see how others react, and to gauge the appropriateness of our own reactions.

People vary considerably in their need to affiliate with others, and this need affects their performance. In our society, a man who shows a need for social support may be thought to be weak, while the same apparent need may be thought charmingly feminine in a woman. The evidence indicates that all people need some social support—at least praise and assurance that they are competent and doing a good job—but that often the most seemingly independent people are the ones who received the most social support in early childhood. ■

Human behavior is extremely complex, and thus it isn't too hard to understand why any one theory of motivation cannot explain everything that we do. As discussed in the opening story, psychologists are working to discover how the brain influences our motivation. Research is also uncovering motives for biological functions such as eating and drinking as well as social interactions and personal achievement. The next time you take a break from studying, spend a minute considering the theories of motivation we have discussed in this chapter and review the possible motives for your decision.

CHAPTER REVIEW
What You've Learned About Motivation

1. Motivation can be thought of as the forces which initiate and direct behavior, and the variables which determine the intensity and persistence of that behavior. Motives arouse and direct the individual's behavior toward some goal.

2. Instinct is a behavior that is inherited by all members of a species. Ethologists study how instinctive behavior evolved among related species and how it now improves survival. An ethogram is a description of all the behaviors shown by a species. Fixed

action patterns are unlearned, inherited, stereotyped behaviors that are species-specific and are stimulated by specific cues in the environment, called releases. Sociobiology is the study of the biological basis of social behavior. Sociobiology proposes that human behavior is genetically based. Freud proposed that behavior is caused by life instincts (sex) and death instincts (aggression).

3. Drive involves the internal forces that push us toward doing something. The drive theory of motivation suggests that a biological need (such as for food) causes a psychological drive (such as hunger). This drive motivates the individual to engage in goal-directed behavior (eating). This cycle is called homeostasis, keeping the body's internal environment in balance.

4. The incentive theory proposes that stimuli in the environment motivate the individual in the absence of any apparent biological need. These incentives, like ice cream or money, are learned, and do not depend on deprivation. We tend to approach positive incentives and avoid negative incentives.

5. Sensory information provides both an arousal and a cue function. The arousal theory suggests that we have a certain level of arousal that we try to maintain by either seeking additional stimulation or avoiding excitement. The optimum motivation level for good performance decreases as the difficulty of the task increases. People with high optimum levels of arousal will seek thrills and adventure, whereas those with low sensation seeking needs try to keep stimulation low.

6. Maslow's hierarchy of needs is a humanistic theory that incorporates several different types of needs. People first must satisfy physiological needs, which include hunger, thirst, and sex. Safety needs include security, stability, protection, and freedom from fear and anxiety. Belongingness and love needs include motives such as love and affection. Esteem needs include a high evaluation of oneself, self-respect, self-esteem, and the esteem of others. When these needs have been met, people are motivated by self-actualization, the full realization of one's potential.

7. The cognitive approach to motivation emphasizes thinking and perceptual interpretation. People develop cognitive expectancies when they learn that certain behaviors lead to certain goals. Attribution involves the cognitive process of determining the motives of someone's behavior.

8. Biological motives have a definite physiological basis and are related to survival of the individual or species. Hunger motivation includes factors such as stomach contractions, the release of the hormone CCK and the monitoring of glucose levels by the liver. The hypothalamus monitors blood chemistry and influences the starting (lateral hypothalamus) and stopping (ventromedial hypothalamus) of eating. Recent work on obesity suggests that overweight people are more sensitive to external environmental stimuli, and have more fat cells than normal weight individuals.

9. Thirst is regulated by a variety of variables, including the mouth and throat, kidneys, and the hypothalamus. Low levels of water in the body cause the anterior hypothalamus to signal the pituitary gland to secrete antidiuretic hormone, which causes the kidneys to slow down production of urine. The hypothalamus signals the cortex to create a thirst drive.

10. The sex motive is unique because it is not essential for individual survival, doesn't depend on deprivation, and allows the individual to seek its arousal. Courtship in animals is the behavioral process whereby sexually mature individuals of a species become mating pairs. In people, learning and experience are important variables in sexual motivation.

11. Stimulus motives cause the individual to seek out sensory stimulation through interaction with the environment. They are internal and unlearned, but do not appear to have a physiological basis. Exploration is the sensory inspection of the environment, whereas curiosity is the seeking out of novelty and complexity to maintain an optimum level of arousal.

12. The theory of competence proposes that people are motivated to interact successfully with the environment. Intrinsic motivation causes someone to do something for internal satisfaction, whereas extrinsic motivation causes someone to work for environmental rewards. Deci proposes that intrinsic motivation leads to competency in controlling the environment.

13. Learned social motives are complex human motives determined largely by learning and social experience. The need for achievement is the desire to perform at a high standard of excellence. People low in achievement need are motivated to avoid failure. People high in achievement motive tend to choose challenging goals.

14. The need for power involves the desire to control or exert influence. The power motive is learned early in life and expressed in a wide variety of situations.

15. The need for affiliation is the desire to seek out and form attachments to other individuals. As a motive, the need for affiliation increases during periods of anxiety.

EMOTION

Although not easily understood, emotion is very important in our lives. Psychologists have developed a variety of theories to try to explain emotions. Love and nonverbal communication have been studied intensively in recent years. A current area of interest to psychologists is human sexuality.

In 1962 Stanley Schachter and Jerome Singer conducted an interesting experiment to test the influence of social and cognitive (thinking) factors on the determination of a specific emotion. They hypothesized that the emotions we feel are due to our interpretation of the physiological arousal we experience. According to the circumstances of the situation that caused the arousal, we attribute the arousal to a particular emotion.

They designed an experiment in which they deliberately produced physiological arousal in subjects, manipulated the explanation provided to the subjects on the cause of their arousal, and created emotional situations that could be used to interpret the nature of the arousal. The research began with 185 students at the University of Minnesota.

The subjects were told that the study was designed to test how their vision was affected by the use of vitamin supplements. All of the subjects (except the one who refused) received an injection of what they thought was a vitamin solution called "suproxin." Three-fourths of the subjects received an injection of epinephrine (adrenaline), whereas the others received a placebo (a harmless saline solution).

Epinephrine is a stimulant drug that produces effects similar to sympathetic nervous system activity that occurs in many emotions, including increased blood pressure and heart rate, trembling hands, flushed face, and rapid breathing. The reaction to the epinephrine generally began within 5 minutes of the injection and lasted about 15 to 20 minutes. The saline which was given as a placebo did not produce any physiological reaction in the subjects.

Schachter and Singer divided the subjects into three experimental groups (all of whom received epinephrine) and a control group (who received the placebo). The "epinephrine informed" subjects were told about the effects of the drug, and thus they were informed about the physiological arousal they experienced. The "epinephrine ignorant" group was not told anything about the effects of the drug. The "epinephrine misinformed" subjects were told that side effects might make them have an itching sensation, numb feet and a headache. The subjects who received a "placebo" and thus were in a control group were not told anything about what to expect from the injection.

After the injection, each subject sat in a waiting room with one other person (who was actually working with the experimenters). In some cases, the other person (one pretending to be euphoric and happy) carried on in high spirits by throwing wadded-up paper into a waste basket, playing with a hula hoop, or flying paper airplanes. In other cases, the subject sat with someone who acted bitter and angry and who generally complained about filling out a questionnaire and were dissatisfied with the testing situation. The subjects in the angry situation were asked to fill out a long questionnaire that included questions about all the food eaten in a typical day, whether the subject bathed regularly, how often the subject had sex, and how many extramarital affairs the subjects' mother had. All four experimental groups were tested in both the euphoric and angry situations, except the one in the epinephrine misinformed group, which was not tested in the angry situation, since it was planned as a control.

Two measures of emotion were used in the experiment. An observer recorded each subject's behavior through a one-way mirror, and each subject was asked to fill out a questionnaire on which he or she reported on his or her mood and physical reaction.

Physiologically, the subjects who received the epinephrine were significantly aroused and those who received the placebo were not (their pulse rates actually decreased in the placebo condition). On the self-report mood scale, the subjects in the euphoric condition reported more happiness when they did not have an explanation of their arousal than when they did. The subjects in the angry condition on the other hand, were, according to the experimenters, reluctant to report anger on the scale. However, the epinephrine ignorant subjects showed significantly more angry behavior than the epinephrine informed or the placebo subjects thus identifying their emotion from the environment.

When the subjects were physiologically aroused by the durg, they labeled the emotion according to the environment. Those ignorant of the drug's true nature were guided by the situation, that is, by which type of person they were with, and labeled the emotion accordingly. Those who knew the truth about the drug identified epinephrine correctly as the source of the arousal, and hence did not display the same situational emotion as the other group. Schachter and Singer concluded that we do interpret our arousal according to our environmental situation and label our emotions appropriately. This theory has come to be known as the arousal-cognition theory. Its results have not been accepted by all psychologists. We discuss some of the criticism of this experimental method later in the chapter.

CHAPTER OBJECTIVES
What You'll Learn About Emotion

After studying this chapter, you should be able to:

1. Define the concept of emotion.
2. Describe the physiological characteristics of emotions.
3. Outline the development and classification of emotions.
4. State the James-Lange theory of emotion.
5. State the Cannon-Bard theory of emotion.
6. State the Schachter-Singer arousal-cognition theory of emotion.
7. State the Plutchik functional theory of emotion.
8. State the opponent-process theory of emotion.
9. Define interpersonal attraction and identify three variables that influence liking.
10. Outline five important theories of love.
11. Describe how animals communicate with one another.
12. Describe how people communicate nonverbally.
13. Outline sex determination and define gender identity.
14. Outline the human sexual response cycle.
15. Identify the major human sexual behaviors and problems.

WHAT IS EMOTION?

One conclusion about Schachter and Singer's research is that different emotions appear to have a similar physiological arousal base. The words "emotion" and "motivation" both come from the Latin term *emovere*, which means to disturb or move away. Probably because they have a common origin emotion and motivation are similar in many ways. Emotions often accompany many of our motivations.

For a hundred years psychologists have tried to define emotion scientifically. There is no complete agreement on any one definition, partially because emotions are complex private events which are difficult to understand—in ourselves and in others.

Robert Plutchik (1980) reviewed 28 definitions of emotion that have been proposed over the past century. William James (1884) argued that emotion is the feeling of the bodily changes as a reaction to something exciting occurring in the environment. Sigmund Freud (1915) stated that emotions are involved with physiological discharges that result in feelings. The behaviorist John Watson (1924) defined emotion as hereditary pattern-reaction that involves the visceral and glandular systems. Robert Plutchik (1962) described emotion as a patterned bodily reaction brought about by a stimulus. Carroll Izard (1972) included neurophysiological, motor, and phenomenological aspects in his conceptualization of emotion.

Recently Frijda (1988) proposed several laws of emotion that emphasize the universal nature of our emotional experiences. For example, the law of situational meaning states that different emotions occur in response to different situations. The law of concern states that emotions occur in response to events that are important to an individual's goals and motives. The law of apparent reality states that emotions are caused by events the individual perceives as real. The law of change states that emotions occur in response to the individual's expected changes in favorable or unfavorable conditions. And the fact that continued pleasure loses its positive feeling is explained in the law of habituation.

We define emotion as a response to a stimulus that involves physiological arousal, subjective feeling, cognitive interpretation, and overt behavior. Psychologists have studied emotions from the four different approaches included in this definition: physiological arousal, subjective feeling, cognition, and behavior. Physiological arousal is a part of all emotions. While there are minor differences in the physiological mechanisms involved in separate emotions, physiological processes in emotion can be viewed as a general arousal

Figure 10.1. Components of Emotion
An emotion involves physiological arousal, subjective feeling, and cognitive intrepretive behavior.

phenomenon. Usually the stronger the arousal the more intense the emotional experience.

All of our emotions include the subjective feeling that is identified as the emotional experience. If asked what emotion you are experiencing right now, you might respond "I feel happy," "I am angry," or "I feel afraid." Scientists have difficulty studying feelings because they are such subjective experiences. Russell (1980) found that people tend to perceive emotions along two dimensions: arousal (the physiological component) and pleasantness (the subjective feeling component). Our subjective feelings are ordered along a continuum from unpleasant to pleasant.

Many psychologists believe that cognitive processes are essential to emotions, while others argue that cognition is not necessary and emphasize only the emotional experience instead. Averill (1983) suggested that cognition intervenes between the environmental stimulus and the resulting behavioral response. In other words, cognitive interpretation of the stimulus serves as the trigger for the emotional experience.

Currently, a debate on the importance of cognition in emotion is being conducted between two prominent psychologists. Richard Lazarus from the University of California at Berkeley argues that cognitive interpretation is essential and must come before the subjective feeling. University of Michigan psychologist Robert Zajonc (1984) argues that feeling is universal and cognition is independent and not necessary for the emotional experience. Zajonc states that we don't know whether animals think, but we do know that they show emotions and that much of emotional expression is nonverbal, suggesting an independence from cognitive activities. While we will discuss the role of cognition in emotional theories, keep in mind that the issue of cognition is not yet settled.

Overt behavior can be used to infer the emotional state of the individual. Sometimes we can interpret facial expressions or behaviors (Ekman, 1985). For example, laughing is almost always an indication of a pleasant emotion. Sometimes, however, the emotion is difficult to identify from the behavior alone. For example, why do we cry? Perhaps it's because we're sad at a funeral; or it may be because we're happy at a wedding. Or it may be because we're peeling onions. Interpreting emotion depends upon our understanding of a combination of physiological, feeling, cognitive, and behavioral elements.

Figure 10.2. Reaction to Fear
When we experience fear, our sympathetic nervous system becomes aroused and we are prepared to fight or flee.

CHARACTERISTICS OF EMOTION

As we learned in the opening story, different emotions often have a similar physiological basis. Because the physiology of emotions is the best understood component of emotion, we start our discussion here. Then we describe what is known about the development and classification of emotions.

Physiology of Emotion

You are walking home about midnight. You are all alone, and, although you know you shouldn't, you decide to take a shortcut through an empty parking lot. Halfway across, you begin to hear footsteps behind you. You turn around and see someone coming straight toward you. What physiological changes occur in your body?

The pupils of your eyes dilate so that you are able to see more of the emergency situation. The blood vessels leading to the stomach constrict and digestion falters, while those leading to the skeletal muscles dilate, assuring that enough blood will reach these muscles in case you have to fight or run. Your breathing and heart rate both increase to provide more oxygen and blood to all muscles. You sweat to reduce the heat you're generating. Your pancreas secretes the hormone *glucagon* into the bloodstream to trigger the release of sugar for extra energy. And the adrenal glands secrete the hormones *epinephrine* and *norepinephrine* so that these arousal reactions will continue as long as the emergency lasts.

These physiological changes are due mainly to the action of the *sympathetic nervous system*. In chapter 2, "Biology of Behavior," we learned that the sympathetic nervous system produces arousal in times of emergency, while the parasympathetic nervous system tends to relax the body during normal circumstances. Both of these systems are branches of the autonomic nervous system.

Although the general physiological arousal of the sympathetic nervous system is apparently similar for different emotions, a few studies found slight variations. Ax (1953) found that during the emotional state of fear, greater amounts of epinephrine and norepinephrine are both secreted than during other emotions. Ekman, Levenson, and Friesen (1983) found subjects who thought about emotional states showed physiological responses that differed slightly for each emotion. For instance, heart rate increased more when the subjects purposely posed for anger or fear than for happiness, and skin temperature increased more for anger than other emotions. Other studies have not found any differences among emotions. For example, Averill (1969) had one group of subjects watch a sad movie while another group watched a comedy. There were no differences between groups in physiological responses to the movies. Thus, any physiological differences that might exist with emotional states are minor.

The brain is also involved in emotions. The cortex is important for interpreting the emotion. The limbic system, especially the *hypothalamus* and *amygdala*, also plays a vital role in emotion. Paul MacLean (1968) proposed that the *limbic system* is involved in the emotions necessary for survival. Emotions such as fear, anger, and joy have evolved because they are related to survival behaviors such as hunting, protection, and mating.

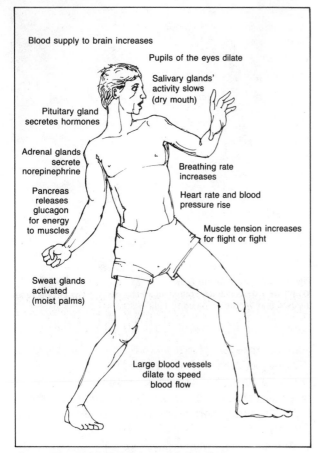

Figure 10.3. Physiological Arousal in Emotion
The entire body responds to an emergency situation through physiological arousal.

Labels in figure:
Blood supply to brain increases
Pupils of the eyes dilate
Salivary glands' activity slows (dry mouth)
Pituitary gland secretes hormones
Adrenal glands secrete norepinephrine
Breathing rate increases
Pancreas releases glucagon for energy to muscles
Heart rate and blood pressure rise
Muscle tension increases for flight or fight
Sweat glands activated (moist palms)
Large blood vessels dilate to speed blood flow

Some physiological arousal reactions can be measured with a polygraph (sometimes called a lie detector). Polygraphs are instruments that record a variety of physiological responses, including heart rate, respiration rate, blood pressure, and GSR (galvanic skin response). The GSR is a measure of a change in the electrical resistance of the skin. Our skin is capable of conducting a very slight electrical current. When we feel an emotion, we are likely to sweat, and there will be a change in the current flowing across the surface of the skin, because it conducts the electricity more readily when we sweat, thereby causing a change in the skin's electrical resistance (GSR). The polygraph measures this change.

The basic idea is that physiological arousal is an indicator of emotion which can be registered by a polygraph. In practice, however, polygraphs are far from perfect and are not accepted as evidence in court cases. Part of the problem is that the polygraph cannot always distinguish between the fearful, anxious, innocent person and the guilty one. While polygraphs do show that a person is physiologically aroused, they cannot interpret the particular cause of the arousal (Saxe, Doughterty, & Cross, 1985).

Development and Classification of Emotions

Are emotions innate or must we learn them? Charles Darwin (1872) suggested in *The Expression of Emotion in Man and Animals* that emotions are similar in animals and people and have evolved to aid in their survival. Dogs bare their teeth when they are aggressive. When people are outraged and scream at one another, they also bare their teeth. Darwin thought emotional expressions like baring the teeth are innate patterns of behavior.

Development of Emotions. Katherine Bridges (1932) was one of the first psychologists to study the development of emotions. In her naturalistic observation of 62 infants from the Montreal Foundling and Baby Hospital, she found a general excitement at birth with positive and negative emotions developing within a few months. As to the negative emotions, general distress appears first, with anger, disgust, and fear developing by 6 or 8 months. The positive emotions develop more slowly, with general delight becoming affection and joy during the second year of life. According to Bridges, a wide range of positive emotions are identifiable by the time an infant is 2 years old. Although this study has been influential in psychology, questions have arisen concerning the validity of generalizing the findings to home-reared infants and the reliability of the observations (Plutchik, 1980).

Carroll Izard and his colleagues (1980) have been studying the emotional expressions in very young infants. In one study, college students were able to identify

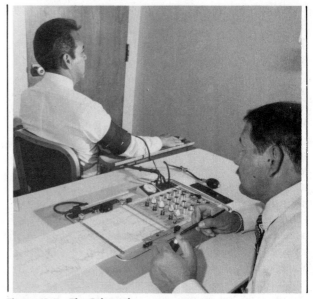

Figure 10.4. The Polygraph
Physiological responses such as heart rate, respiration, blood pressure, and GSR can be measured with the polygraph. Sometimes used as lie detectors, they actually measure only arousal and not the cause of that arousal.

Figure 10.5. Identifying Emotions
How do we identify emotions? Often facial expressions are used as clues, as suggested in this photo.

the facial expressions of 5- to 9-month-old infants as joy, fear, sadness, anger, and surprise. Although it is not possible to determine whether the infants actually experienced these emotions, they were able to show expressions at this early age that were interpreted as appropriate emotions.

Learning is also very important in emotion, and many emotions appear to be learned through conditioning. In chapter 6, "Learning," we learned that the fear response was classically conditioned in Little Albert. Although many emotional expressions appear universal, differences in learning are responsible for cultural variations. One early study by Klineberg (1938) demonstrated that some of the Chinese expressions of emotion are different from those in our culture. In the Chinese society, sticking out your tongue indicates surprise, while opening your eyes wide can suggest anger, and clapping can indicate disappointment. Despite cultural variations, it is recognized that emotions are a part of all human experiences.

Paul Ekman (1980) has been studying facial expressions of emotions. He found that people are capable of 7,000 possible facial muscle combinations which allow for a wide variety of emotional expressions. Since cultures throughout the world can correctly identify the emotions being expressed facially, he and his colleagues (1987) argue that emotions are biologically based.

According to Ekman (1985), lower brain stem areas produce spontaneous emotional expressions, whereas the cortex of the brain is involved in voluntary emotions. Thus, he predicted that differences between the left and right hemispheres should be apparent in voluntary but not spontaneous expressions of emotion. When he observed people who were smiling because of genuine enjoyment, their smiles were symmetrical, whereas when subjects were asked to pose, their smiles were asymmetrical, usually with an exaggeration on the left side of the face. Ekman argued that this might be one way to determine whether an emotion is real.

Classification of Emotions.   No one is sure how many emotions we can actually experience. Many psychologists have attempted to draw up lists of the basic emotions. William McDougall (1921) proposed a list of seven basic instincts, each with a corresponding emotion. Some of the instincts (with their corresponding emotions) included flight (fear), repulsion (disgust), curiosity (wonder), pugnacity (anger), and self-assertion (elation). While McDougall's theory is interesting, it was abandoned when psychology became dominated by behaviorism in the 1920s.

Today, psychologists have a number of classification schemes. Russell (1980) proposed the circumplex model of emotion, in which emotions are arranged in a circular pattern along two dimensions (arousal and pleasantness). The emotions tend to be paired as opposites, such as happy-sad, tense-relaxed, excited-bored, delighted-depressed.

Sylvan Tomkins (1964, 1981), in his facial feedback hypothesis, proposed that there are eight basic emotions: interest, surprise, enjoyment, distress, fear, shame, contempt, and anger. These emotions are innate and expressed through bodily reactions such as facial expressions. Tomkins argued that emotions are the intensified motives that in turn are a reflection of bodily needs.

Carroll Izard (1979) proposed that there are eight basic emotions: interest, joy, surprise, sadness, anger, disgust, contempt, and fear. Each basic emotion has its own neural network to the brain, its own characteristic behavioral reaction (usually involving facial expression), and its own subjective feeling. Izard suggested that the emotions we experience are innate and adaptive for the individual or species and therefore constitute the basic motivational system for human behavior.

One of the most complete classification attempts of emotions was described by Robert Plutchik (1980). Through extensive questionnaires, he arrived at eight basic emotions: joy, acceptance, fear, surprise, sadness, disgust, anger, and anticipation. These primary emotions can combine to form secondary emotions. For example, joy and acceptance form love, fear and acceptance form submission, and anger and anticipation form aggressiveness. If placed in a circle, the emotions across

Figure 10.6. Plutchik's Theory of Emotions

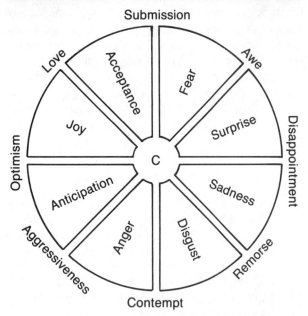

Figure 10.6. Plutchik's Theory of Emotions

The eight primary emotions can be arranged in a circle which helps demonstrate their relationships. Plutchik explains that these primary emotions combine to form secondary and tertiary emotions. The C at the center of the circle indicates that conflict results from the mixture of the emotions (after Plutchik, 1980).

from each other are opposites (for instance, joy and sadness).

In addition to combining, Plutchik stated that each basic emotion can vary in intensity, for example, grief, sadness, and pensiveness; rage, anger, and annoyance; terror, fear, and apprehension. Plutchik has developed the Emotions Profile Index (EPI) to identify personality dispositions based on emotional responses. He has developed an elaborate scheme relating emotions to adaptive functions and personality. For instance, the emotion of fear is expressed by escape behavior, serves the function of protection, and is associated with a timid personality. The emotion of anger is expressed by attack behavior, serves the function of destruction, and is associated with an aggressive personality. While psychologists have not completely agreed on definitions or classifications, research is continuing in this important area.

THEORIES OF EMOTION

Dozens of theories have been proposed to explain emotions. Perhaps because emotion is a private, subjective experience, or because it is such a conglomeration of potential feelings, we cannot agree on one definitive theory. Because of their historical value, several theories are notable, while a couple of contemporary concepts are gaining recognition.

The James-Lange Theory

It seems obvious to most of us that an emotion occurs before we act on it: we run away because we are afraid; we fight because we are angry; we cry because we feel sad. Working separately, William James (1884) and Carl Lange (1885) each came up with similar ideas that took the view of emotion that behavior precedes feeling. Usually called the James-Lange Theory of Emotion, it states, for instance, that we feel sad because we are crying. Our bodies automatically react to certain environmental stimuli and we recognize these reactions (both our behavior and the physiological arousal) as making up a certain emotion that we then feel. The physiological arousal and behavior come first and the subjective experience of the emotion comes second. Thus, we are angry because we are fighting, and we are afraid because we are trembling.

If recognizing a certain emotion is just recognizing a physical state of the body, then there must be different and quite distinct physiological states for each emotion. Some research suggests that there are some slight differences in the physiological arousal for different emotions. For example, McGeer and McGeer (1980) reviewed several studies that indicated that the hormone epinephrine is secreted during anger or aggression, while norepinephrine is more likely to be secreted during fear or anxiety. Other studies have not found this difference.

Figure 10.7. James-Lange Theory of Emotion
Have you ever been in an emergency situation and immediately afterward began to feel frightened? The James-Lange theory states that the feeling of fear comes after the physiological change and behavior.

Indeed, as shown in our opening story, many emotions appear to have the same physiological symptoms.

Sometimes it seems that in an emergency we react swiftly at the moment and then begin feeling the emotion a few minutes later. When we see a car approaching rapidly as we cross the street, first we jump quickly to safety and then we feel fear (or anger). Many scientists, however, have criticized the James-Lange theory for being untestable. And recent research indicates that emotions are much too complex to strongly support this theory.

The Cannon-Bard Theory

One criticism of the James-Lange theory was that most emotions have nearly identical arousal. Walter Cannon (1927) and Philip Bard (1928) both proposed that when a person perceived an environmental stimulus, the thalamus in the brain reacted. According to this theory, the thalamus simultaneously sends impulses to the cortex of the brain and controls the sympathetic nervous system in its general physiological arousal. Therefore, the emotional feeling and the physiological arousal occur at the same time.

The Cannon-Bard Theory of Emotion has been shown to be somewhat incorrect. The hypothalamus is central to the experience of emotion rather than the thalamus, as was first proposed. However, like the James-Lange theory, it is impossible to test accurately whether the feeling occurs with or after the physiological changes. As we learned in our opening story, a modern theory by Schachter and Singer emphasizes cognitive factors in influencing emotions.

The Schachter-Singer Arousal-Cognition Theory

Our opening story described the classic experiment conducted by Stanley Schachter and Jerome Singer in 1962. They argued that any differences that exist in the physiological arousal of emotions are relatively minor, and that cognition plays a major role in determining emotions. The Schachter-Singer Theory of Emotion states that in an emotion we are first physiologically aroused. Then we look for an environmental explanation for our arousal. We interpret our situation cognitively and label our arousal as an appropriate emotion.

Not all psychologists accept Schachter and Singer's results. For instance, Maslach (1979) found that subjects who were given an arousing drug always reacted negatively, regardless of the environment. The emphasis on cognition, however, has continued to play an important role in the study of emotion. Leventhal and Tomarken (1986) reviewed a number of studies that could not replicate Schachter and Singer's findings.

One criticism of the Schachter and Singer study

BIOGRAPHICAL ☆ ☆ HIGHLIGHT

WILLIAM JAMES

William James was born in New York City in 1842. He was the son of wealthy parents whose enthusiasm for their children's education sent young James traveling throughout Europe. His formative years were spent in the best schools of France, Germany, Switzerland, and the United States.

He vacillated from one interest to another, studying painting, chemistry, biology, and medicine. In 1869 he received a medical degree from Harvard University. Finally, at the age of 30, he accepted the teaching position at Harvard that launched his outstanding career in psychology.

In 1875 James established at Harvard one of the first psychology demonstration teaching laboratories in the world. Three years later, at the age of 36, he married a Boston schoolteacher and began writing his most famous work, *Principles of Psychology*, which, to his publisher's dismay, took him almost 12 years to complete.

James enjoyed great popularity as a lecturer at Harvard and was remembered by students as a vivacious personality whose extravagant sense of humor and picturesque language set him apart from the typical professor. His interests were tremendously varied: he wrote about such topics as habit, consciousness, personality, emotion, and religion.

James continued to write, lecture, and travel until his death in 1910 at his country home in New Hampshire.

focuses on the procedure they used to eliminate certain subjects (Plutchik, 1980). Out of 185 subjects, one did not permit the injection, 11 were eliminated because they acted suspiciously, and one was eliminated because of equipment failure. Apparently 20 of the placebo subjects had a decreased pulse rate and were thus eliminated. In the experimental condition 16 subjects were eliminated because they were self-informed. Therefore, of the original 185 subjects, only 136 were actually included in the final analysis. The experimenters could also be criticized for using heart rate as the measure of arousal, as heart rate by itself is not always an accurate measure. Even though it has been criticized, the Schachter and Singer theory of emotion has been very influential on research in this area and has helped focus attention on cognitive processes in emotion.

The Plutchik Functional Theory

Robert Plutchik (1980) described a functional theory of emotion. He perceived emotion as a chain reaction sequence: stimulus event, cognition, feeling, and behavior related to survival. For example, if you were approached by a stranger in a parking lot, the chain would include: the sight of the stranger (stimulus event), thinking of danger (cognition), experiencing fear (feeling), and running away (behavior). This sequence would be followed for an emotion whose function is protection.

Plutchik suggests that emotion has evolved to ensure

survival of the individual. He emphasizes cognition, and states that by thinking the individual is permitted to predict the future, thereby improving chances of adapting to the environment successfully. He does not stress physiological arousal, perhaps since this is the same in all situations. Plutchik's theory is an attempt to understand the function of emotions in our complex everyday world. Further research will be needed to determine the theory that best explains our emotional experiences.

The Opponent-Process Theory

Richard Solomon (1980) has developed a theory of motivation/emotion which views emotions as pairs of opposites (for example, fear-relief, pleasure-pain). The opponent-process theory states that when one emotion is experienced, the other is suppressed. For example, if

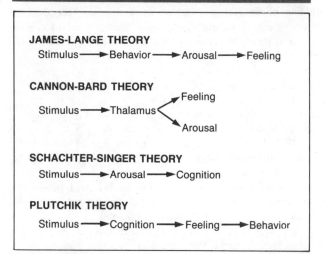

Figure 10.8. Theories of Emotion

The major theories of emotion are compared here. The James-Lange theory assumes that we are first physiologically aroused and then experience the feeling as emotion. The Cannon-Bard theory states that when a stimulus activates the thalamus, both physiological arousal and subjective feeling occur simultaneously. According to the Schachter-Singer theory, when physiological arousal occurs, we cognitively interpret it and lebel it as emotion. Plutchik's theory assumes a chain of cognition, feeling, and behavior that results in a function.

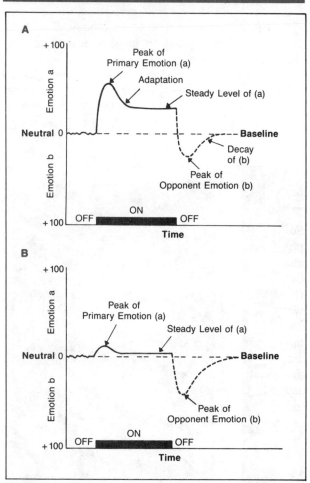

Figure 10.9. Opponent-Process Theory

R. Solomon views emotions as pairs of opposites. When one emotion is experienced (A) it triggers an opposing emotion after a period of time. With repeated stimulations (B) the opposing emotion becomes stronger, weakening the experience of the primary emotion and providing an aftereffect.

you are frightened by a mean dog, the emotion of fear is expressed and relief is suppressed. If the fear-causing stimulus continues to be present, after a while the fear decreases and the relief intensifies. For example, if the dog didn't move, your fear would decrease and relief that the dog didn't attack would increase. If the stimulus is no longer present, then the first emotion disappears and is replaced totally with the second emotion. If the dog turns and runs, you are no longer afraid, but rather feel very relieved.

Solomon and Corbit (1974) analyzed the emotions present when skydivers jump from planes. Beginners experience extreme fear as they jump, which is replaced by great relief when they land. With repeated jumps, the fear decreases and the post-jump pleasure increases. This theory attempts to explain a variety of thrill-seeking behaviors. It has also been proposed as a model of drug addiction. The drug originally produces pleasurable feelings but then a negative emotional experience occurs afterwards. Eventually, the drug user takes drugs not for their pleasurable effects, but to avoid the aversiveness of withdrawal symptoms. The opponent-process theory is an attempt to link emotional states with motivation, and is likely to become even more important in the future.

INTERPERSONAL ATTRACTION: LIKING AND LOVING

Songs and literature have immortalized one of the most potent emotions we experience—love. The area of psychology that includes liking, love, and friendship is called interpersonal attraction. Berscheid and Walster (1978) view interpersonal attraction as an attitude toward another person based on the tendency to evaluate another person positively. Interpersonal attraction has three aspects: cognitive, emotional, and behavioral. The cognitive aspect involves one's positive and negative thoughts and beliefs about another person; the emotional aspect one's positive and negative feelings; the behavioral aspect the way one acts.

Liking

People are social creatures who have a need to be with others (see affiliation in chapter 9, "Motivation"). Why are we attracted to certain people? How do we develop interpersonal relationships?

Influences on Interpersonal Attraction. Social psychologists have attempted to explain why we like certain people. In general, the research indicates three major influences: proximity, similarity, and physical attractiveness. We tend to like people who are in close geographical *proximity* to us. Our friends tend to be people in our neighborhood and people we see every day at school, work, or church. A classic study was conducted by Leon Festinger and his colleagues (1950), who measured friendship patterns among married students living in an apartment complex. They found that friendships developed between people who lived close to one another, with the person next door most likely to be a friend. One explanation of the role of proximity on liking is that we become more familiar with those people we see on a regular basis (Moreland & Zajonc, 1982).

Similarity research indicates that people like others who share similar values, intellectual ability, interests, and activity preferences (Wetzel & Insko, 1982). It is enjoyable to be with others who desire to do the things we like to do, and we are able to communicate more effectively with similar others. Hays (1985) reported that people who enjoy doing similar things and sharing experiences are most likely to become friends. In a way, we like others who are reflections of ourselves, as this makes us feel comfortable.

Physical attractiveness plays a major role in whom we decide to get to know better. In general, research indicates that physically attractive people are more likely to be perceived in a favorable way and are more likely to be sought after as friends (Dion & Dion, 1987). Why is physical attractiveness important? We tend to enjoy beauty and assume that beauty is associated with goodness and positive characteristics. We also increase our status when we are associated with attractive others.

Theories of Interpersonal Relationships. There are several theories that focus on the development of interpersonal relationships. The social exchange theory states that we evaluate the costs and rewards of our relationships (Homans, 1961). If the rewards outweigh the costs, then we continue the relationship, and if the costs are too high, we look for alternatives. Rewards might include status, information, money, emotional stability and enjoyment. Costs might include money, excessive effort, or any other unpleasant aspect of the relationship.

When we are in a relationship, we value fairness. The equity theory states that people are motivated to maintain a fair balance in relationships (Walster, Walster, & Bercheid, 1978). If one person is always giving and the other always taking, it obviously is an unfair relationship, and there is some pressure to balance it. If we feel as though we do not have equity in a relationship, we are more likely to search for alternatives than to continue in an unequal, unsatisfying one.

Theories of Love

In some cases the intimacy of knowing and liking someone can develop into a more intense and passionate relationship usually defined as the emotion of love. During the past couple of decades, social psychologists have helped us understand more about love. These findings and theories can help us understand our feelings and behaviors when we think we have fallen in love.

Fromm's Social Theory of Love.   Eric Fromm (1956) believed that people are products of their social environment. He suggested that we are lonely until we can relate to other people socially. Further, of all the possible ways of relating to others, the most complete relationship is the interpersonal union that we call love.

Fromm defined love as the active concern for the life and growth of another person. He described four characteristics of love: knowledge, care, responsibility, and respect. Love grows when we understand and have concern for another person, and accept the responsibility to help him or her every way we can. We must respect other people and acknowledge their unique qualities. According to Fromm, only through unselfish giving can we experience love.

Rubin's Liking and Loving Scales.   Zick Rubin presented his findings in this field in his 1973 book, *Liking and Loving.* He devised two questionnaires to measure liking and loving in people. The liking scale has 13 items which measure the degree of liking one person has for another. The research found that *respect* ("In my opinion, _____ is an exceptionally mature person"), and *similarity* ("I think that _____ and I are quite similar to one another") and a *favorable evaluation* ("I think that _____ is unusually well adjusted") were important factors in liking other people. Interestingly, when dating college couples were tested on the liking scale, Rubin found that women liked their boyfriends more than their boyfriends liked them.

Rubin then looked at love in dating college couples. He found in his loving scale that there were three major components involved in the emotion of love. According to Rubin, love involves *caring* ("I would do almost anything for _____"), an *attachment* ("If I could never be with _____, I would feel miserable"), and *intimacy* ("When I am with _____, I spend a good deal of time just looking at him/her"). This time, the scores for the men and the women were equal, indicating that in dating couples, love is reciprocal. Rubin also concluded that eye contact was one of the most valuable predictors of love. In one study, Rubin found that couples who looked into each other's eyes were more likely to remain together than those who did not look at one another. If you watch people who claim to be in love, you will probably find that they spend a great deal of time looking at one another.

Figure 10.10. Rubin's Liking and Loving Scale

Liking Scale

Respect
I would recommend _____ for a responsible job.
_____ is the sort of person whom I myself would like to be.

Perceived Similarity
When I am with _____, we are almost always in the same mood.
I think that _____ and I are quite similar to each other.

Favorable Evaluation
I feel that _____ is an extremely intelligent person.
It seems to me that it is easy for _____ to gain admiration.

Loving Scale

Caring
One of my primary concerns is _____'s welfare.
I would do almost anything for _____.

Attachment
If I were lonely, my first thought would be to seek _____ out.
It would be hard for me to get along without _____.

Intimacy
I feel very possessive about _____.
I feel that I can confide in _____ about virtually everything.

Pam's Psychometric Approach.   Alvin Pam, Robert Plutchik, and Hope Conte (1975) developed the "Love Scale" to measure the attitudes people have toward love. On the 40-item scale, they tested college students who were in love (but not married), who were dating, or who were friends with someone of the opposite sex. They found five factors which were very important in interpersonal attraction: *respect* ("He/she has better judgment than the average person"); *congeniality* ("You and she get along well as a couple"); *altruism* ("You like giving gifts to her/him"); *physical attraction* ("He/she is sexually attractive to you"); *attachment* ("You feel secure with him/her").

While all five factors are important, the researchers found certain trends: they reported that physical attraction and attachment are very important in love, whereas dating emphasizes congeniality and physical attraction, and friendship requires congeniality and respect. Through tests like this one, researchers believe that we can gain an understanding of a relationship.

Knox's Attitudes Toward Love Measurement. Another research approach is the measurement of attitudes toward love as people grow older. Knox (1970)

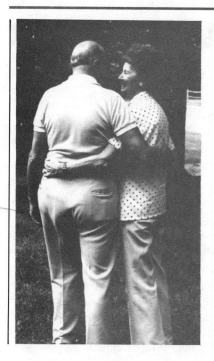

Figure 10.11. Love at Different Ages
People's attitudes toward love tend to change as they grow older. Knox reported that young unmarried people often have a romantic orientation toward love, which tends to become more practical after marriage. People married for many years tend to become more romantic again.

distinguished between romantic and realistic love; romantic love is mysterious and eternal and only occurs once in a lifetime. Romantic love is characterized by excitement, arousal, and urgency. Realistic love is practical, calm, and solid. A person with a practical outlook toward love carefully weighs the options before making a commitment. Romantic and realistic love may be thought of as opposite ends of a continuum, with people falling somewhere between two extremes.

Knox administered his attitudinal scale to high school seniors, people married less than 5 years, and people married more than 20 years. The high school students showed a romantic orientation, while the young married adults showed a more realistic orientation to love. He reasoned that the first years of marriage forced couples to cope with everyday problems such as paying bills and obtaining work. A very interesting finding was that people married over 20 years also showed a romantic orientation. These people presumably have overcome obstacles successfully and can now be romantic once again. Knox suggested that our attitudes toward love change as we go through life. We should mention that Knox's research did not actually survey the same people throughout their lives and thus cannot claim a developmental trend.

Passionate Love and Companionate Love. Walster and Walster (1978) distinguish between passionate and companionate love. Passionate love, or romantic love, is an intense emotional experience that includes sexual desire, elation, anxiety, ecstacy, and tenderness. Physiological arousal is high and the various emotional feelings often produce confusion. Walster and Walster stated that passionate love rarely lasts more than 6 to 30

months in a relationship, but can lead to a more stable companionate love.

Companionate love, or conjugal love, is characterized by deep attachment, trust, respect, affection, loyalty, and familiarity. It is much less intense than passionate love, but much more enduring. Companionate love includes a long-term commitment to a relationship. Rubenstein (1983) reported that its three important components were friendship, devotion, and intellectual compatibility. Passionate love is what Knox (1970) called romantic love, whereas companionate love is what Knox called realistic love.

Falling in Love. How do we fall in love? Let's put together some of the findings we have examined and describe the process. As already mentioned, proximity and similarity are important in liking someone. But the arousal of romantic love relies more on physical attractiveness. Karen Dion (1980) reported that when given a choice, people prefer others who are physically attractive. However, according to Ellen Berscheid (1983), the *matching hypothesis* best explains the process of love relationships (people tend ultimately to select someone of about the same attractiveness as themselves).

Berscheid and Walster (1978) suggested that in order for someone to fall in love, three conditions must be met. First, we must learn, through our culture, what love is. We are constantly exposed to films, books, songs, and stories of people in love. We thus learn what to expect when we are ready to experience this great emotion. Second, we cannot fall in love until we have an appropriate stimulus. Our prospective love partner should meet all the requirements we set up (proximity, similarity, and physical attractiveness). And, finally, we must experience a physiological arousal that we can label the emotion of love. As Schachter and Singer suggest, emotion is labeled according to the environmental circumstances. So if you are with someone of the opposite sex who is attractive and available, and if your heart is suddenly beating fast, you might very well call it love.

A study by Dutton and Aron (1974) examined the effects of anxiety and arousal on sexual attraction. Young men were interviewed by a very attractive young woman while crossing a bridge. Some of the subjects were on a swaying suspension bridge 230 feet above a raging river. Other subjects were interviewed on a wide, solid bridge near the ground. When the interview was completed, the woman said she'd be glad to explain the results of her class project in more detail when she had more time. She gave the subject her telephone number so he could call her if he desired. Four times as many men in the high arousal (high bridge) condition actually called than those in the low arousal (low bridge) condition. The psychologists concluded that the high-bridge subjects interpreted the arousal caused by the swaying bridge as attraction to the beautiful woman.

Sternberg's Triangular Theory of Love.   Yale University psychologist Robert Sternberg has recently proposed a triangular theory of love (1986) in which love consists of three components: intimacy, passion, and decision/commitment. The emotional component, *intimacy*, refers to the feelings in a love relationship that encourage closeness. They include respect, happiness, understanding, support, and intimate communication. The intimacy component is the core of a love relationship, and is found in a wide variety of love relationships, such as love for a parent, sibling, friend, or spouse.

The motivational component, *passion*, includes physiological arousal and is expressed by sexual desire. Other needs, such as self-esteem, affiliation, and dominance can also contribute to passion. In a love relationship with the opposite sex, often passion first attracts the lovers, and intimacy develops to sustain the relationship over time. In some cases, only passion is desired (for example, relationships with prostitutes).

The cognitive component, *decision/commitment*, consists of the short-term decision to love a person and the long-term commitment to continue with the relationship through good and bad times and helps to solidify it.

Sternberg (1987) proposed that the combination of these three components can determine eight different kinds of love. *Nonlove* refers to the absence of all three components, and characterizes most casual social interactions. *Liking* occurs when only intimacy is present, and characterizes friendships. *Infatuated love* results from only the passion component, and involves only the physiological arousal. It is usually associated with a short-term relationship. *Empty love* results when only

Figure 10.12. Sternberg's Theory of Love

Kind	Intimacy	Passion	Decision/ Commitment
Nonlove	No	No	No
Liking	Yes	No	No
Infatuated Love	No	Yes	No
Empty Love	No	No	Yes
Romantic Love	Yes	Yes	No
Companionate Love	Yes	No	Yes
Fatuous Love	No	Yes	Yes
Consummate Love	Yes	Yes	Yes

the decision/commitment component is present, and can occur in a love relationship that has become stagnant without passion or closeness. In some cultures where marriages are prearranged, empty love can be the first stage as the partners begin life together. *Romantic love* results from the presence of the intimacy and passion components, and is characterized by physical attraction and an emotional bond. When intimacy and decision/commitment are present, *companionate love* results, such as in a marriage after passion has died down. *Fatuous love* results from the presence of the passion and decision/commitment components. A whirlwind romance in which a couple meets, falls in love, and gets married very quickly is an example of fatuous love. Ultimately, either intimacy develops or the relationship is terminated. In *consummate love*, all three components are present. This is for many, the ideal in romantic situations, but often is difficult to maintain for long periods of time.

COMMUNICATION

Because people are so accustomed to using verbal language to communicate, they often forget that there are other types of communication systems. People can communicate with one another nonverbally. And animals have a variety of communication systems, including visual, auditory, and olfactory. In this section we discuss animal communication and human nonverbal communication.

Animal Communication

Some form of communication is necessary in socially organized groups of animals so that the members can maintain contact. The particular communication system used by a species of animal must be suited to the biological and social characteristics of that animal. J. P. Scott (1972) surveyed some of the communication systems used by different kinds of animals.

Many birds communicate with one another through sounds. Through particular calls or songs, a bird can identify its species; a male can attract a mate and/or keep other males out of his territory. Some birds, like parrots, can imitate the sound of human speech. Overall, the vocal communication system of birds appears to be biologically determined and limited to a few instinctive signals.

Through years of patient research, the "language" of bees was interpreted by the German ethologist (a scientist who studies animal behavior) Karl von Frisch (1967). When a bee finds a good supply of food, it returns to the hive and performs a dance to tell the other bees where the food source is located. Different dance movements indicate distances to the food source. For short distances, the bee does a round dance, while for longer distances, a figure-eight dance is performed that includes a particular number of tail wags (indicating precise distance). The dance also indicates direction from the hive so the other bees can easily find the food.

Pheromones. Odor is a form of communication used by many animals, from insects to mammals. Pheromones are chemical substances produced by an animal to communicate with another individual of the same species. E. O. Wilson (1968) showed that ants produce odor trails to food sources that other ants can readily follow. Pheromones are especially important in sexual communication in mammals.

A number of fascinating studies have focused on pheromone effects in mice. For example, when female mice are segregated from males, they stop having regular sex cycles. But when the female mice are exposed to the odor of the urine of a male mouse, all the cycles return in synchrony. If a pregnant female comes into contact with the odor pheromone produced by an unfamiliar male, she will abort and then become sexually receptive to the new mouse.

Recently, the role of pheromones in human communication has been studied. Bloom (1984) reported that people who lose the sense of smell sometimes also lose interest in sex. Morris and Udry (1978) found that when women applied perfume containing human vaginal secretions known to produce sexual arousal in monkeys, it sometimes (but not always) increased sexual activity in their husbands. Cutler and his colleagues (1986) reported that when underarm secretions of a woman were applied to the upper lip of other women, these women tended to have menstrual cycles that were synchronized to those of the donor. They also found that when underarm secretions of men were presented to women with irregular menstrual cycles, the cycles became significantly more regular than a control group that were presented alcohol only.

Primate Language Studies. The animal communication research that has been most controversial is that dealing with the ability of primates to learn and use language. Several early studies that tried to teach chimpanzees to talk resulted in failure. Then, in 1966 Beatrice and Allen Gardner of the University of Nevada began their study of language in a chimpanzee named Washoe. The Gardners concluded that chimpanzees could not learn to talk because their vocal apparatus was not capable of making the proper sounds. So they decided to teach their chimpanzee, Washoe, how to communicate using a nonvocal language—the American Sign Language—that was developed for communication in the deaf. The American Sign Language uses complex hand gestures and has its own distinctive rules.

Washoe learned the correct sign gestures at about the same rate as young children do. The Gardners did not speak around Washoe, but used signs to "tell" her what they were doing. Many activities and objects that might interest the young chimpanzee were introduced, just so the Gardners could sign about them. They also tried to be as responsive as possible to Washoe's signing: to answer her questions, to sign something more on any topic she initiated, to fulfill her requests. Gradually, Washoe learned the signs. By 1969, they reported, she had a vocabulary of 160 signs.

The amazing part of Washoe's language ability is not that she learned to "sign" the names of objects, but that she was able to use these signs to communicate. Washoe began spontaneously to combine the signs to make grammatically correct sentences. For example, one day when she wanted to play with Allen Gardner, she signed

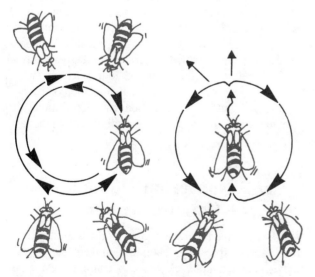

Figure 10.13. Communication Among Bees
Von Frisch realized that when a bee discovers nectar it indicates the direction and distance of the source to other bees in the hive through specific dance-like movements.

Figure 10.14. Primate Use of Sign Language
Susan Nichols has a conversation with the chimpanzee, Washoe, using American Sign Language. According to Gardner, Washoe has learned word signs and has acquired an elementary grammar.

Figure 10.15. Lana's Computer Communication
Duane Rumbaugh and his colleagues at Georgia State University taught Lana, a chimpanzee, non-verbal language skills by using symbols connected to a computer. Lana uses the computer console to ask for food, identify objects, and answer simple questions.

"Gimme tickle." She was also able to combine signs in meaningful ways. For example, when a window was open, she combined two signs to say "open window." Often when she had been scolded for disobeying, she said "come hug—love sorry."

The Gardners discovered that the development of language communication in Washoe was similar to the language development in human children. Washoe didn't just memorize names of objects—she actively learned and used the rules of the language. Since Washoe, there have been a number of other studies of language in nonhuman primates.

David Premack (1971) taught a chimpanzee named Sarah to communicate using plastic symbols with a variety of shapes to develop sentences. Among the other primates in similar studies are Lana, a chimpanzee who can communicate with the use of a symbol keyboard connected to a computer (Rumbaugh, 1977), and Koko, a gorilla who communicates with sign language (Patterson, 1978).

These studies demonstrate that primates can learn symbols for words. But do they use language in the same way as people? Herbert Terrace (1979) tried to teach sign language to his chimpanzee, Nim. After five years, Terrace concluded that while Nim could learn to imitate his trainer, he could not acquire the rules of grammar and develop complex sentences spontaneously.

However, other psychologists argue that Terrace's methods differ from other studies and that primates do generate unique sentences (deLuce & Wilber, 1983). For instance, Fouts and colleagues (1984) reported that

Washoe spontaneously uses sign language when communicating with other chimpanzees who have also been taught to sign. But when Lana's trainers re-examined the data, they concluded that Washoe could not develop beyond the language capacity of a 9-month-old human infant (Savage-Rumbaugh & colleagues, 1980). Terrace (1985) argued that apes do not understand the act of naming objects, but rather only acquire the words demonstrated by others.

More recently, research on Kanzi, a pygmy chimpanzee, has revealed the most advanced language abilities in a nonhuman primate (Savage-Rumbaugh & colleagues, 1985). Kanzi apparently uses symbols for concepts by pushing geometric shapes on a keyboard. His trainers reported that he produced creative solutions to problems, and even described future actions (which he then carried out). By no means has the controversy been settled, but we can conclude from these studies that primates can learn at least the rudiments of language.

Nonverbal Human Communication

We often learn a lot about people by the way they dress, their facial expressions, and the movements of their bodies. For example, clothes can communicate a person's feelings and personality. Think of the teacher who always wears a suit, and of another who dresses more casually. Who gives the more difficult exams? When asked this question, most people believe the formal one is more strict. However, many psychologists currently feel that the real key to understanding a person's emotions is the face.

Facial Expressions. Some scientists believe that many facial expressions, such as smiling, laughing, and crying, are almost universal among cultures, and have a genetic basis. Without speaking, how do you greet someone you recognize? Chances are that you raise your eyebrows. Eibl-Eibesfeldt (1972) found this eyebrow-raising greeting present in a wide variety of cultures. Children who are born blind develop the same facial gestures as sighted children do. The idea that emotional expressions are innate can be traced to Charles Darwin (1872) who proposed that animals and humans show a common pattern that has evolved over the years. Izard (1982) stated that Darwin's ideas still have a major influence on the psychology of emotion today.

In his facial feedback hypothesis, Sylvan Tomkins (1962) proposed that biological brain networks underlie each emotion and a specific facial expression is associated with it. Russell and Bullock (1985) found that young children show an ability to identify facial emotional expressions that are similar to that of adults, strengthening the argument that facial expressions are genetically controlled.

Joseph Hager and Paul Ekman (1979) conducted a study on the recognition of facial expressions at various distances. They chose six emotional expressions that had previously been shown to be reliable: happiness, sadness, surprise, fear, anger, and disgust. Subjects were able to identify the correct emotion at distances of up to 45 meters. They predicted that happiness and surprise could be recognized at even 100 meters. Hager and Ekman argue that facial expressions can communicate emotion over long distances and that people often use this information in social encounters.

More recent research, however, indicates that although facial expressions may be universal, the interpretation of emotion from facial expression is not always accurate. For example, Wagner and colleagues (1986) reported that subjects could reliably identify three emotions (happiness, anger, and disgust) that Ekman had found reliable but not another three (surprise, fear, and sadness). Russell and Fehr (1987) argued that the interpretation of a particular facial expression depends upon other expressions to which it is being compared. For instance, they found that a neutral face appears sad when compared with a happy face and happy when compared with a sad face.

Research on *social referencing* suggests that even infants are able to interpret facial expressions correctly and modify their behavior accordingly. Sorce and colleagues (1985) reported that when mothers stood at the deep end of a visual cliff (see chapter 4, "Sensation and

Figure 10.16. Facial Expressions

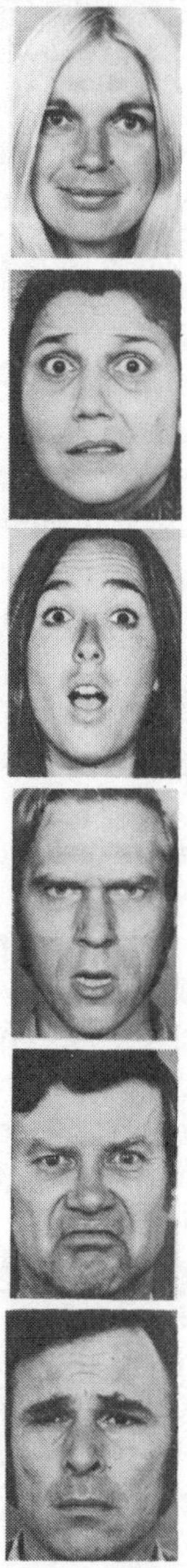

| | Ekman & Friesen (1969) | | | | |
	U.S. %	Japanese %	Brazilian %	Chilean %	Argentinian %
Happiness	97	87	97	90	94
Fear	88	71	77	78	68
Surprise	91	87	82	88	93
Anger	69	63	82	76	72
Disgust	82	82	86	85	79
Sadness	73	74	82	90	85

Ekman and Friesen (Ekman, 1973) believe that facial expressions of emotion are genetically based and universally recognized. As this chart from one of the experiments shows, people from different cultures had similar interpretations of these facial expressions. For example, 97% of Americans and Brazilians, and 87% of Japanese interpreted the emotion in the top photo as happiness.

Perception," and coaxed their infants to cross, the facial expression shown by the mother was important. Three-fourths of the infants crossed the deep end when she showed interest or joy, but very few (11%) crossed when the mother expressed anger and none crossed when the mother showed fear. When infants are confused about what to do, they utilize information provided by the facial expressions of others.

Some current researchers argue that when we smile or frown, sensory information is provided to our brain. Thus, it is possible that we are aware of being happy because we smile rather than we smile because we are aware of being happy (Cacioppo & colleagues, 1986).

An interesting proposal is that people might learn to control emotional feelings by controlling facial muscles. For instance, perhaps one therapy for depression might be to teach patients to smile more, thus helping them feel happier (McCanne & Anderson, 1987).

Eyes: Gazing and Staring. We often tend to judge people by the amount of eye contact we have with them. Research by Kleinke and his colleagues (1974) has shown that we tend to look more at people we like, and consequently when the level of eye contact is high, we interpret this positively. Kleinke also found that when a male and female interact, each considers low gazing as inattentiveness and high gazing as sincerity. However, males rated low-gazing females as less attractive, whereas females rated low-gazing males as more attractive. Kleinke (1986) reported research that indicated gazing behavior served a number of functions, including providing information on attraction and attentiveness, regulating social interaction, expressing intimacy, and exerting social control.

But if we look too long (stare) at someone, it is usually interpreted negatively. An interesting study by Greenbaum and Rosenfeld (1978) found that when a person stared at drivers stopped at red lights, the drivers drove off more quickly when the light changed. Thus, while we enjoy eye contact, we try to escape from people staring at us, who make us feel uncomfortable. Eye contact is also an important measure of love, as shown by Zick Rubin (1973), and discussed earlier in this chapter.

Body Language. We can convey information through the position and movement of the body. Body language can reveal emotionality, as when a person exhibits a nervous habit (biting the fingernails or wringing the hands). We often use *gestures,* or body movements, to accentuate what we are saying. Some people use them more than others. The clenched fist, the victory sign, the OK sign, the good-bye wave, blowing a kiss, and wiping the brow in relief are all popular gestures in our culture. There are some sex differences in nonverbal behavior. In our culture, men tend to sit or stand with legs apart and hands outward, whereas women tend to keep legs together and hands at their sides. Women also are better at interpreting nonverbal gestures, perhaps because of their nondominant status in many relationships (Matlin, 1987).

We can also use touching as a means of communicating. Often touching conveys affection, like a pat on the back, a handshake, a kiss, or a hug; although also it can suggest power, domination, and even dislike. Crusco and Wetzel (1984) found that when a waitress briefly touched a customer on the hand when she returned change from the bill, both male and female customers left larger tips. Sometimes touching affects the sexes differently. For example, Fisher, Tytting and Heslin

Figure 10.17. Gestures
People often use gestures to emphasize what they say or feel. Hand movements, such as those shown here, are usually recognized by people in the same culture.

(1976) stated that if they were touched by a library clerk when checking out books, female students responded positively (with positive evaluations of the clerk and library), whereas male students responded negatively. Women generally tend to respond more positively than men to touch in a variety of situations (Stier & Hall, 1984).

A little-studied nonverbal behavior is to have the tongue just slightly protruding from the mouth. Jones and colleagues (1987) found that people were less willing to interrupt others who had their tongues showing. In one situation, a clerk without the tongue showing was approached significantly more than another clerk who did have it showing. Perhaps this is why people often tend to avoid individuals with Down's syndrome (a form of mental retardation which is characterized by a protruding tongue and other attributes). When we make decisions about other people, we learn to recognize nonverbal cues and interpret them along with verbal information.

HUMAN SEXUALITY

Try to imagine life without sex. Our sexuality is a part of our personality, our behavior, our emotions, and our attitudes. Sexual identity becomes important as soon as we're born, as boy babies most often are wrapped in blue blankets while girl babies are wrapped in pink ones and have a bow in their hair. As children grow older, boys tend to identify with their fathers, while girls imitate their mothers. Then, at maturity, sex takes on new meanings. We experience new feelings about people of the opposite sex, and eventually may engage in various types of sexual behavior.

Sexuality has many meanings. It may be defined as our gender identity, or sense of being male or female; our sex role, or set of behaviors appropriate for our particular sex; and the act of copulation (sexual intercourse).

Sexual Determination

Most people would agree that it's easy to determine whether a person is male or female. Just look at the way they dress, walk, talk, and behave. Sometimes, however, it is not that simple. Dr. Richard Raskind was a Newport Beach, California ophthalmologist. He underwent a sex-change operation, and as Renee Richards became a female professional tennis player. The difficulty here is to decide whether the change in the physical appearance can determine sexual identity, or whether there must also be an internal hormonal change. The definition of sexuality is extremely complex.

Biological Determination of Sex. Sex, or gender, refers to the biological distinction of being male or female. Money and Ehrhardt (1972) described a number of biological determiners of sex. *Chromosomal sex* is the pattern of chromosomes that determine gender; males have an XY pattern and female an XX. Chromosomal sex is determined at conception when the chromosomes from the egg and sperm unite. *Hormonal sex* is the predominance of either male (testosterone) or female (estrogen) hormones in the body. After about six weeks, testes begin to develop and produce the male hormone testosterone if a Y chromosome is present. Without testosterone prenatally, genetic males would develop female sex structures. Or conversely, if male hormones are present prenatally (perhaps because of a drug given to the mother), genetic females might become masculinized and develop male genitals. When there is a contradiction between the predominant genital appearance and other biological sex determiners, the condition is called hermaphroditism. Depending on their appearance, these people may be raised as males or females. *Gonadal sex* is the presence of either testes (in the male) or ovaries (in the female) that produce the sex cells (egg and sperm) necessary for reproduction. *Genital sex* is the physical presence of either a penis (in the male) or a vulva (in the female). *Reproductive sex* includes all of the internal organs necessary for reproduction. And *assigned sex* is the sex decided upon by doctors and parents at the birth of a baby ("it's a girl" or "it's a boy"), largely based on the genital appearance.

Gender Identity and Sex Roles. While biological sexual determination takes place at conception, the learned, social sex role and gender identity of an individual develops at a slower rate. Gender identity is the psychological identification with a particular sex, the learned personal sense of maleness or femaleness in an individual. Gender identity is usually formed at about 3 years of age, when the child begins to master language skills.

Sex roles includes the set of behaviors and attitudes that determined to be appropriate for one sex or the other in a society. Even at very young ages, boys and girls are treated differently in our society (Tavris & Wade, 1984). They are taught appropriate behaviors for their particular sex, and are encouraged to incorporate these behaviors into their lifestyles. By the time they are mature young adults, they have learned the cultural norms regarding sex roles and sexual behaviors.

There are several theories of the development of sex roles and gender identity, although there is not complete agreement on the issues involved. The *psychoanalytic theory*, developed by Freud, proposes that children are

Figure 10.18. Gender-Identity Role
The personal sense of maleness or femaleness is a function both of biological sexual determination and learned cultural and social roles. Although attitudes toward appropriate male or female behavior are beginning to change, most people in our society still encourage stereotypical behaviors for boys and girls.

confused by the genital differences between males and females and tend to identify with the same-sexed parent. The *social-learning theory* argues that society reinforces certain behaviors in boys and other behaviors in girls. The child identifies with the same-sexed parent and imitates his or her behaviors (Block, 1983). The *cognitive-developmental theory* states that children naturally categorize themselves as male or female and then develop those behaviors that fit in with cognitive gender identity (Kohlberg, 1966). The *gender-schema theory* is recent and emphasizes the development of cognitions that classify behaviors as masculine or feminine. The child interprets the world from his or her gender's perspective (Bem, 1987).

John Money (1987) argued that gender identity and sex role were intertwined and could not be separated. Gender identity is the private perception of one's sex, whereas sex role, or gender role, is the public expression of one's gender identity. Money suggested that since gender identity and gender role were so closely combined, we should use the term gender-identity/role to describe this aspect of sexuality.

Human Sexual Response Cycle

Much of what we know about the physiology of the human sexual response comes from the work of William Masters and Virginia Johnson, who published *Human Sexual Response* in 1966. Masters and Johnson studied nearly 700 men and women as they engaged in over 10,000 sex acts. The researchers described four phases

of the human sexual response cycle: excitement, plateau, orgasm, and resolution.

Excitement Phase. The excitement phase is the beginning of sexual arousal. For both sexes, heart rate, blood pressure, and breathing increase. In the male, the increased blood supply to the genital region produces penile erection. In the female, the clitoris enlarges and vaginal lubrication occurs. In both sexes, the sexual flush or reddening of the chest may begin, along with erection of the nipples.

Plateau Phase. During the plateau phase, the physiological arousal becomes even more intense. Breathing, heart rate and blood pressure continue to increase. The penis and testes enlarge even further in males. In females, the vagina and breasts swell more as the blood supply increases. In both sexes body temperatures rise.

Orgasm. The climax of intense excitement is orgasm, during which the release of sexual tension occurs. In both sexes, there are rhythmic muscular contractions of the genitals every 0.8 seconds. In males, orgasm is accompanied by ejaculation, the sudden release of semen through the penis. Males can sometimes achieve orgasm within 5 minutes of the start of sexual activity, while females might require around 20 minutes.

Resolution Phase. The resolution phase is the time after orgasm that the body gradually returns to the unaroused state. In females, the size of the breasts, clitoris and vagina are reduced. In males, the penis loses its erection and the testes return to their normal size. In both sexes, the heart rate, blood pressure and breathing slowly return to normal levels. Some people also experience perspiration at this time.

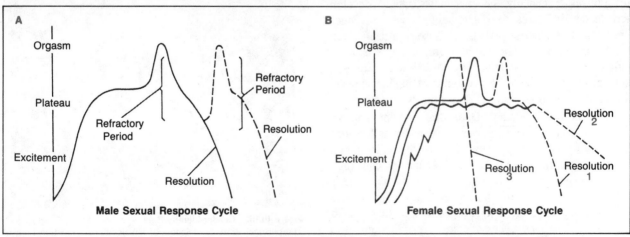

Figure 10.19. Human Sexual Response Cycle

Masters and Johnson (1966) reported that the human sexual response cycle can be described in four phases: excitement, plateau, orgasm, and resolution. In the male sexual response cycle **(A)** the dotted line shows the possibility of a second orgasm after the initial refractory period is over. The female sexual response cycle **(B)** shows several variations of sexual response. Pattern 1 shows multiple orgasm; pattern 2 shows arousal that fails to reach orgasm; pattern 3 shows several brief drops in the excitement phase followed by a rapid resolution phase.

During the resolution phase, males enter a *refractory period*, during which they are unable to have an erection or experience orgasm. There is considerable variability in the length of the refractory period, lasting from a few minutes to several hours, and it has a tendency to increase with age. Females do not enter a refractory period and can therefore experience multiple orgasms.

Sexual arousal in people is a complex phenomenon. While the physiological response is often caused by physical stimulation of the body's erogenous or pleasurable zones (areas such as genitals, breasts, mouth, earlobes), it can also be influenced by social and cognitive factors. In fact, just thinking about sex can cause arousal in many people.

Janet Hyde (1986) pointed out that knowledge of how the human sexual response works can be valuable to people. It can help them develop good lovemaking techniques; it can be useful in treating sexual problems; and it helps us better understand human behavior.

Human Sexual Behavior

How do we know what types of sexual behavior people engage in? Since sex is usually a very private and personal affair, the only way to obtain information is through surveys and interviews. In chapter 1, "The Study of Psychology," we discussed some of the difficulties of survey research. For instance, the reliability of the data depends upon the sample, the types of questions asked, and the honesty of the people responding.

Several major research programs examined sexual behavior in America. Alfred Kinsey and his associates surveyed over 11,000 men and women in the late 1940s and early 1950s. The Kinsey Reports were one of the first major scientific efforts to study sexual behavior. About 20 years later, in 1974, Morton Hunt interviewed over 2,000 men and women to determine contemporary sexual views and practices. While neither research project was perfect (because of the limitations of survey research), they do give some insights into American sexual practices. The following information is from their research findings.

Masturbation.   Masturbation is erotic self-stimulation to produce orgasm. There have been many myths about the evils of masturbation, but as yet no one has demonstrated any physical or mental harm. Even though masturbation was considered a deviant form of behavior in the 1940s, Kinsey reported that 92% of the men and 62% of the women had masturbated. Hunt found that the percentages were not much higher in the 1970s, but that both sexes began masturbating at an earlier age. Kinsey reported that there has recently been an increase in the rate of masturbation in married couples; he found about 40% of married men and 33% of married women

masturbated, while Hunt found the percentages to be 62 and 68 for men and women respectively. Masturbation decreases with increasing age, more so with men than women. Currently, according to Hunt, the majority of Americans do not see anything wrong either ethically or physically with masturbation.

Petting.   Petting is sexual contact with another person excluding intercourse. When petting precedes intercourse, it is referred to as foreplay. Kinsey reported that 89% of young men and 88% of young women had experienced petting. Hunt reported only slight increases: 95% for men and 90% for women. In the past, petting served as a compromise for people who wanted to be intimate but did not wish to have sexual intercourse. According to Hunt, petting is not as important today as it once was, since the frequency of sexual intercourse has increased greatly for young people.

Sexual Intercourse.   The number of people engaging in premarital intercourse has significantly increased over the past couple of decades. Kinsey reported that 71% of young men and 33% of young women had engaged in premarital intercourse. Hunt reported that 97% of men and 67% of women had experienced premarital intercourse. Thus, the change appears to be mainly due to the doubling of the number of women engaging in premarital intercourse. Data also indicate that people are engaging in intercourse at earlier ages than in the past.

Sexual intercourse with their spouse is the main sexual outlet for married men and women. However, while the incidence of extramarital sexual intercourse has not increased greatly over the years it continues to be engaged in by many people. Kinsey reported 39% of men and 20% of women had ever had extramarital sex, while Hunt reported 47% of men and 24% of women had engaged in this practice. What is interesting is that Hunt reported that men are tending toward extramarital sex as they grow older, while women tend to have affairs at a younger age than previously.

The frequency of intercourse diminishes with age, with young married couples engaging in it about three times a week, and couples over 45 years old engaging in it about once a week. Hunt reported that married couples used more variety in their lovemaking than Kinsey reported earlier.

Homosexuality.   A homosexual is a person whose sexual preference and activities are directed toward other people of the same sex. This person is sexually aroused by people of the same sex or engages in sexual activities with them. The term lesbian refers to a female homosexual, whereas gay often refers more to male homosexuals. A bisexual individual is sexually attracted to others of both sexes.

Kinsey reported that 37% of men and 13% of women had had at least one homosexual experience, while about

Figure 10.20. Homosexual Preference
Various theories have been proposed to explain homosexual preference but so far none have been successful. Perhaps because same sex behavior is not predominant in this society, many people misunderstand the physical and psychological needs of homosexuals who prefer to be accepted as complete human beings rather than as people with particular sexual preferences.

3% of males and 1% of females were exclusively homosexual. Hunt's data showed 2% of men and 1% of women had an exclusively homosexual orientation. Because of sampling problems, it appears that Kinsey overestimated the number of people having at least one homosexual experience, and that the number is more likely 25% for men and 10% for women (Pomeroy, 1972).

Although the majority of people feel that homosexuality is not normal (Levitt & Klassen, 1974), research shows that homosexuals are often well adjusted and happy (Bell & Weinberg, 1978). There is little agreement on the causes of homosexuality. One line of research suggests that the brains of homosexual men are more responsive to estrogen than the brains of heterosexuals (Blake, 1985). Psychoanalytic theory proposes that homosexuals have a problem in forming a gender identity with a parent. Social-learning theory suggests that early homosexual experiences were reinforcing and motivated individuals to continue. An important study by Bell, Weinberg, and Hammersmith (1981) found that sexual preference is largely determined before adolescents have had sexual experiences. Currently, psychologists do not really understand the causes of homosexuality.

An important point to remember about surveys on sexual behavior is that the results are suggestive of norms, but are not absolute facts. There is a great deal of variability in sexual behavior and since sex is usually a private matter, results of surveys cannot be totally trusted. Still, the results are presented here because they indicate the general trends in American sexual behavior.

Sexuality Concerns

Human sexuality is an important topic that researchers are currently studying intensively. Here we cover three concerns of current interest in sexuality: gender-identity disorders, sexual dysfunctions, and AIDS.

Gender-Identity Disorders. Gender identity is our learned personal sense of maleness or femaleness. This is ingrained in us from our earliest childhood, and most people have no difficulty with their self-perception of gender. For some individuals, however, there is an incongruence between the assigned sex and gender identity, a condition called gender-identity disorder. Most cases of gender-identity disorder can be linked back to childhood, although in rare cases, the problem can develop entirely in adulthood (DSM-III-R, 1987).

In gender-identity disorder of childhood a child experiences long-lasting and intense distress about his or her assigned sex and the desire to become the opposite sex. He or she often wants to wear clothes of the opposite sex and consistently asserts that he or she has or will have the anatomical structures associated with the opposite sex.

Sometimes a person feels trapped in the body of the

Figure 10.21. Transsexualism
An individual who feels trapped in the body of the wrong sex is a transsexual. Some, including professional tennis player Renee Richards, undergo sex-change operations to deal with the problem.

wrong sex. Such a person has a gender-identity disorder of transsexualism, in which the person who has reached puberty wishes to be the opposite sex (and had this desire for at least two years). The transsexual often suffers from anxiety and depression. Sometimes the transsexual will undergo sex reassignment surgery to treat the problem. We do not really know much about the causes of this disorder.

Sexual Dysfunctions.   The sexual dysfunctions refer to problems in normal sexual behavior, usually characterized by inhibitions in sexual arousal or problems in the sexual response cycle. The DSM-III-R (1987) identifies four problem areas: sexual desire, sexual arousal, orgasm, and sexual pain. A hypoactive sexual desire simply means that a person has very little interest in sexual activities (a "low sex drive"). Sexual arousal disorders are characterized by the inability of the male to attain or maintain erection or the female to attain or maintain lubrication. (Previously, this was referred to as impotence in the male and frigidity in the female.) A persistent inability to achieve orgasm is called inhibited female orgasm in the woman and inhibited male orgasm in the man. Premature ejaculation refers to the problem of the male not being able to delay ejaculation until he wishes to have it. Dyspareunia is painful intercourse, often caused by physical problems. Remember that these

problems can occur in normal healthy people and often can be successfully corrected.

Sexual Behavior and AIDS.   Sexually transmitted diseases have always played a role in sexual motivation and behavior (Masters, Johnson, & Kolodny, 1988). During the 1980s a deadly disease of this kind has emerged. Acquired immune deficiency syndrome (AIDS) is a fatal viral infection that can be sexually transmitted by men or women (or spread through the sharing of infected needles).

In 1987 the World Health Organization indicated that four main routes of infection had been documented:
Anal or vaginal intercourse.
Oral-genital intercourse.
Contact with semen; transplanted organs; or blood, such as on contaminated needles and syringes shared by drug users.
Transfer from mother to child, although it is not fully understood whether the transmission occurs before birth, during the birth process, or through breast milk during nursing.
The persons at highest risk of infection include homosexual males and intravenous (IV) drug users who transmit the virus through shared needles. Women can, however, contract the disease from infected needles, or by having sex with IV drug users or bisexual men who are infected. Unborn children can contract the disease from their mothers. Since mid-1985 blood used for

Figure 10.22. Sex and AIDS
The fatal disease of AIDS is a major influence in causing psychological and physical changes in human sexual behavior in the late 1980s.

transfusions is routinely checked for the virus, but prior to that time, the virus could have been transmitted to hemophiliacs and those needing donated blood, in the blood itself.

Because sexual activity with an infected person is the major means of transmitting or contracting AIDS, and since AIDS is a deadly disease expanding rapidly throughout the world, many organizations have attempted to educate the public about the nature of the disease and the means of preventing its spread. Chief among these in the United States have been the office of Surgeon General C. Everett Koop which sent a comprehensive, informational booklet on AIDS to every household in the summer of 1988. Among others was a group of students at Dartmouth College who put together a Safer Sex kit containing a condom, a lubricant, a rubber dam, and a brochure, *Safe Sex* published by the American College Health Association. This kit is designed to give college students the means and the information necessary to use condoms during sexual intercourse, one of the best ways to prevent the transmission of the AIDS

virus except for the choice to abstain from having sex.

Psychologists have begun to study the psychological aspects of this disease. They are involved in information programs aimed at preventing the spread of the disease and at allaying people's excessive fears about AIDS and how it can be acquired. Psychologists are also involved in helping the patient, his friends, and family deal with the social and psychological impact of the disease. It is believed that the fear of AIDS will alter the sexual motivation and behavior of people for many years to come (Meridith, 1984). ▪

Emotion is an important part of all our lives: it's what makes us human, as well as being a potent source of motivation in our society. As shown in our opening story, emotion is complex and involves both biological and cognitive processes. In addition to other areas of concern, psychology is trying to help people gain a better understanding of themselves through an understanding of their emotions. We turn next to personality, the study of the complete person.

"ALTHOUGH HUMANS MAKE SOUNDS WITH THEIR MOUTHS AND OCCASIONALLY LOOK AT EACH OTHER, THERE IS NO SOLID EVIDENCE THAT THEY ACTUALLY COMMUNICATE WITH EACH OTHER."

CHAPTER REVIEW
What You Learned About Emotion

1. Emotion is a response to a stimulus that involves physiological arousal, subjective feeling, cognitive interpretation, and overt behavior.
2. When emotion occurs, the pupils dilate, digestion stops, breathing and heart rate increase, sweating begins, and hormones are secreted. These physiological changes are due mainly to the action of the

sympathetic nervous system. The cortex is important in interpreting emotions and the hypothalamus is important in coordinating motivation and emotion. Polygraphs are instruments that record a variety of physiological responses, including heart rate, respiration, blood pressure, and GSR.
3. At birth, the newborn shows only a general re-

sponse, but specific emotions develop rapidly. Many emotions are shown by the time an infant is two years old. Emotions can be classified among a number of dimensions, such as Russell's model involving arousal and pleasantness. A recent classification scheme by Plutchik identifies eight basic emotions: joy, acceptance, fear, surprise, sadness, disgust, anger, and anticipation.

4. The James-Lange theory of emotion proposes that emotional behavior precedes the feeling (we feel sad because we are crying).

5. The Cannon-Bard theory of emotion states that when we perceive a stimulus the thalamus reacts and then simultaneously causes emotional feeling and arousal.

6. The Schachter-Singer arousal-cognition theory of emotion proposes that the emotion we feel depends upon the interpretation of our physiological arousal.

7. The Plutchik functional theory of emotion proposes that emotion occurs as a chain reaction: stimulus event, cognition, feeling, and then behavior related to survival.

8. Solomon's opponent-process theory of emotion states that emotions occur as pairs, and as one emotion is experienced the other is suppressed. With repeated trials, the first emotion weakens and the second one intensifies.

9. Interpersonal attraction is an attitude (involving cognitive, emotional, and behavioral components) toward other people based on the tendency to evaluate others positively. Interpersonal attraction includes affiliation, friendship, liking, and loving. Proximity, similarity, and physical attractiveness are important factors in determining whom we like.

10. Fromm described four characteristics of love: knowledge, care, responsibility, and respect. Rubin found three major components involved in love: caring, attachment, and intimacy. Pam, Plutchik, and Conte identified five factors important in interpersonal attraction: respect, congeniality, altruism, physical attraction, and attachment. Knox found developmental differences in the attitudes people have toward romantic and realistic love. Walster and Walster distinguished between passionate and companionate love. Berscheid and Walster suggested that in order to fall in love, a person must learn what love is, have an appropriate stimulus, and experience a physiological arousal that can be labeled as love. Sternberg's triangular theory of love proposes that love consists of three components: intimacy, passion, and decision/commitment.

11. Communication is necessary in socially organized groups of animals so that the members can maintain contact. The senses involved in animal communica-

tion may include hearing, seeing, taste, smell, or touch. A number of research studies have reported that primates can learn to use language. The Gardners taught Washoe, a chimpanzee, to communicate with sign language. Premack taught a chimpanzee named Sarah to use plastic symbols to communicate. Some psychologists question whether these studies actually demonstrate language learning in primates, or just the ability to imitate.

12. We learn a great deal about people through nonverbal communication. Facial expressions can communicate many emotions, including happiness, sadness, surprise, fear, anger, and disgust. Eye contact is important and we tend to judge people by the amount of eye contact we have with them. We tend to look more at people we like, but staring can be negatively interpreted. People convey information through body language, the position and movement of the body. We might use gestures or touching to accentuate communication.

13. Human sexuality is a part of our personality, our behavior, our emotions, and our attitudes. There are a number of determiners of sex: chromosomal sex (XX or XY chromosomes), hormonal sex (testosterone or estrogen), gonadal sex (testes and ovaries), genital sex (penis or vulva), reproductive sex (internal reproductive organs), and assigned sex (sex decided upon by doctors at birth). Gender identity is the learned personal sense of maleness or femaleness in an individual. Sex roles include the set of cultural behaviors appropriate for a sex.

14. Masters and Johnson have described the physiological basis of the human sexual response cycle. The excitement phase is the beginning of sexual arousal. During the plateau phase, the arousal becomes more intense. Orgasm is the climax of intense excitement during which the release from building sexual tension occurs. The resolution phase is the time after orgasm during which the body gradually returns to the unaroused state.

15. Kinsey's surveys around 1950 and Hunt's interviews in the 1970s provide us with an indication of the incidence of types of sexual behavior Americans engage in. The incidence of masturbation has not changed, although both sexes now begin to masturbate at an earlier age. The number of people engaging in premarital sexual intercourse has significantly increased over the past two decades and sexual intercourse remains the main sexual outlet for married couples. The incidence of homosexuality has remained extremely low over the years. Psychologists are studying problems in sexuality, including gender-identity disorders, sexual dysfunctions, and AIDS.

PERSONALITY AND ADJUSTMENT

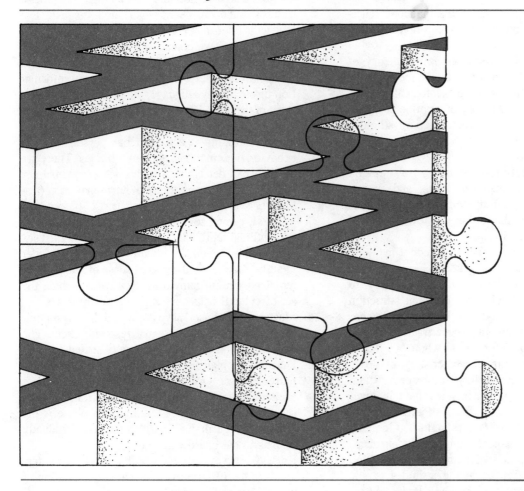

Part V focuses on individual differences in personality structure and adjustment to the demands placed on individuals. Personality, stress, and adjustment are covered here.

After reading Part V you should be able to:

Outline the personality theories of various psychologists

Describe and identify various methods of assessing personality

Identify the causes of stress in daily life

Describe the interaction of psychological and physical stress

Outline various techniques of adjusting to stress

Chapter 11   Personality

Many psychologists have proposed theories of personality in an attempt to explain human behavior. Personality assessment is important in many areas of psychology and a variety of methods have been developed to accurately measure personal characteristics.

Chapter 12   Stress and Adjustment

Stress, an unavoidable consequence of life, is anything that produces demands on people to adjust their behavior. Stress often has negative consequences, such as anxiety or burnout. Psychologists have studied a variety of adjustment techniques, some of which are more effective than others. Recently time management skills have been refined to help people better adjust to the demands placed upon them.

PERSONALITY

Many psychologists have proposed theories of personality in an attempt to explain human behavior. Personality assessment is important in many areas of psychology and a variety of methods have been developed to accurately measure personal characteristics.

Imagine yourself studying for a test. Would you be more likely to think "If I study hard I will earn a good grade" or "If the questions are easy I will do well"? If you answered that studying will help you earn a good grade, you probably have an internal locus of control whereas if you answered that the chance of having easy questions will help, you probably have an external locus of control.

Julian Rotter of the University of Connecticut has spent many years investigating this dimension of personality called locus of control. Rotter believes that there tend to be two types of people: internal people who believe that reinforcement is contingent upon their own behavior and that if they work hard they will be rewarded; and external people who perceive that reinforcement is independent of their behavior and who expect to be rewarded by luck or by the control of other people.

Rotter hypothesized that the perception of reinforcement is an important variable in understanding learning as well as personality. According to the social learning theory, reinforcement strengthens the individual's expectancy that a behavior will be followed by reinforcement in the future. As expectancies are developed, the individual acts in certain ways that ultimately lead to the development of his or her personality.

Rotter developed a test to measure this personality difference. Rotter's Internal-External Scale took many years of revisions to reach the final 29-item objective test published in 1966. For each item, he gives the subject a choice of two statements (one is indicative of an internal orientation, while the other reflects an external orientation). For example, an internal item might be, "In my case, the grades I make are the results of my own efforts." A similar external item might be, "Sometimes I feel that I have little to do with the grades I get." A subject is required to choose one of these statements. When the selections are totaled, the tester has a measure of the subject's internal or external locus of control of reinforcement. The actual score is the number of external choices selected by the subject (of 23 possible questions—6 questions are "fillers," designed to limit guessing by subjects).

Figure 11.1. Internal-External Locus of Control

For each pair of items, select A or B according to which more closely represents your beliefs.

___1. A. Promotions are earned through hard work and persistence.
   B. Making a lot of money is largely a matter of getting the right breaks.

___2. A. The number of divorces indicates that more and more people are not trying to make their marriages work.
   B. Marriage is largely a gamble.

___3. A. When I am right I can convince others.
   B. It is silly to think that one can really change another person's basic attitudes.

___4. A. In my experience, I have noticed that there is usually a direct connection between how hard I study and the grades I get.

   B. Many times the reactions of teachers seem haphazard to me.

___5. A. I am the master of my fate.
   B. A great deal that happens to me is probably a matter of chance.

___6. A. The grades I make are the results of my own efforts; luck has little or nothing to do with it.
   B. Sometimes I feel that I have little to do with the grades I get.

___7. A. In our society a person's future earning is dependent upon his or her ability.
   B. Getting promoted is really a matter of being a little luckier than the next guy.

Internal people perceive reinforcement to be within their control whereas external people perceive reinforcement to be controlled by outside forces. Shown here are sample test items similar to those in Rotter's locus of control scale. (The A items represent an internal locus of control whereas the B items represent an external locus of control.)

Rotter tested the internal-external locus of control scale on a wide variety of subjects, including college students, prisoners, and the general population. He found that the reliability of the test scores was high, and that they correlated with other measurements of personality. Thus, the test did measure the dimension of personality expected. His early testing found that both sexes tended to score about the same and that blacks tended to score more externally than whites.

More than 600 studies investigating internal-external locus of control have been reported. Some of Rotter and his colleagues' early studies exemplify the trend in results. For instance, Rotter has shown that lower-class children tend to be external, while children from richer families are more internal. He found that black college students who participated in civil-rights campaigns were more internal than those who didn't. Another study reported that internal students were more successful in changing peer attitudes about fraternities, while several other studies have shown that nonsmokers tend to be more internal than smokers. People who gamble were found to be more external. One recent study (Doherty & Baldwin, 1985) found that during the 1970s women began to score more externally than men. The internal-external dimension demonstrates a useful method of testing personality.

CHAPTER OBJECTIVES
What You'll Learn About Personality

After studying this chapter, you should be able to:

1. Define the concept of personality.
2. State the goals and requirements of personality theories.
3. Describe Freud's psychoanalytic theory of personality.
4. Outline Jung's analytical theory of personality.
5. Outline Adler's individual theory of personality.
6. Outline Horney's cultural theory of personality.
7. Outline Allport's trait theory of personality.
8. Outline Cattell's factor theory of personality.
9. Outline Eysenck's trait model of personality.
10. Outline the five factor personality model.
11. Outline Rogers's self theory of personality.
12. Outline Maslow's self-actualization theory of personality.
13. Outline Skinner's behavior approach to personality.
14. Outline Bandura's modeling theory of personality.
15. Outline Rotter's locus of control theory of personality.
16. Describe the personality assessment methods of interview and observation.
17. Identify four major objective personality tests and two major projective personality tests.

WHAT IS PERSONALITY?

We often use the term personality without really defining it. For instance, have you heard statements such as "Carole has a terrific personality" or "Henry's personality leaves much to be desired"? Hall and Lindzey (1985) point out that we use the concept of personality to evaluate other people. We also use personality to describe people. For example, we might use statements such as "Sharon has an outgoing personality" or "Louise has an aggressive personality."

Partially because the term is used in our everyday language and partially because it is so central to our study of psychology, psychologists have a difficult time defining personality. Gordon Allport reviewed nearly 50 definitions of personality in 1961 and many more have been suggested since then. In a very real sense, personality forms the core of psychology. It is the sum total of what a person is—including his or her actions, thoughts, and feelings. Because of the inclusive nature of personality, psychologists have a difficult time developing an acceptable definition. In this textbook, we define personality as the distinctive and enduring patterns of behavior and cognition that characterize a person's adaptation to life. Some of the more important definitions follow. Singer (1984) stated that personality is made up of one's public behaviors, including verbal and nonverbal expressions, and one's private motives, thoughts, and emotions. Psychologist Walter Mischel (1986) defines personality as an individual's overall, stable, and distinctive patterns of behavior in responding to people and environmental events—that is, each person's characteristic patterns of behavior that are consistent across a variety of situations. Of particular concern to personality theorists are those patterns that are characteristic of the person's interactions with other people. Feshbach and Weiner (1986) also stress social interactions when they define personality as the relatively enduring behavior patterns that distinguish people, groups, and cultures.

Psychologists who study personality are more interested in understanding the fairly stable aspects of a person's behavior than the occasionally uncharacteristic acts. For example, if someone who is normally quiet and polite once swore in public, that is not really an important aspect of his or her personality. Likewise, psychologists often focus on individual differences in behavior patterns. In order to understand individual behavior, we want to know what is distinctive about the person and makes that individual different from others. Thus, Byrne and Kelley (1981) view personality as the sum total of the relatively enduring dimensions of individual differences.

Psychologists called personality theorists try to discover complete and systematic explanations for people's styles of behavior. Their explanations go beyond merely categorizing people into types (although they do that too). They are also interested in the specific events that make people act the way they do. Some of the major personality theories that explain human behavior are explored in this chapter. The other major area of personality, assessment of individual differences, will be covered after we discuss the major theories.

GOALS OF PERSONALITY THEORIES

There are several important goals of personality theories. One is to organize the characteristics of personality. Theories provide a structure for integrating characteristics such as aggressiveness, emotionality, intelligence, sociableness, anxiousness, and passivity. Theories identify which characteristics are most important and how they are organized in individuals. This helps us understand the relationships among our different behaviors.

Another goal of personality theories is to explain personality variability (the differences and similarities among individuals). For instance, people have different reactions to jokes, different styles of dress, and different ways of reacting under stress. We can explain some of these differences fairly easily; others not so. The personality theorist provides concepts that trace the factors that influence the development of personality and everyday behaviors in individuals, and helps us understand why everyone is unique.

A third goal of personality theories is to describe the normal, healthy personality. Personality theorists have studied normal people as well as people with problems in the hope of determining what contributes to a healthy personality. Some of this information can be used to understand what is considered normal behavior within a culture. Theories also attempt to determine the relationship between personality characteristics and motivation. For instance, our behaviors often reflect our motives and over time contribute to our stable personalities.

Personality theories vary in a number of ways. They may focus on the past or present; the holistic or analytical point of view; the individual versus the situation; conscious or unconscious awareness; learning versus innate knowledge; childhood experiences versus adult experiences; and degree of optimism for the human race. Personality theories have a particular orientation and focus on specific aspects of personality. Try to identify the dimensions of each theory we cover in this chapter.

All of us have an implicit theory of personality that we use when we interact with others. The value of personality theories is that it helps reduce our confusion and indecision about ourselves and other people. Understanding our own theory, and being able to recognize it more easily helps us understand ourselves and others better.

There are several requirements that a good theory of personality should meet. It should be explicit, or expressed in precise words and symbols. It should be testable, so that it can be verified scientifically. And it should be alive, or exciting enough to get people to investigate and utilize it. Think about the functions and requirements of good theories of personality as we review some of the major theories that have been developed over the years.

PSYCHOANALYTIC THEORIES

The first systematic and comprehensive theory of personality to incorporate unconscious influences, dreams, sexuality, and instinctual urges was proposed by Sigmund Freud. He worked to discover how the unconscious mind and the motives of sex and aggression influences human behavior.

Psychoanalytic theories: unconscious ideas, thoughts, feelings, wishes, etc. shape our lives more than do the conscious. Life includes sex; death

Freud's Psychoanalytic Theory

The idea that our emotional lives are unconsciously represented in our dreams was revolutionary. The credit for it goes to Sigmund Freud, the "father" of psychoanalytic theory. Unlike most other complex theories about human behavior, Freud's ideas have filtered down through academic and professional circles to become part of the everyday thought and vocabulary of the average person.

Beginning his work as a medical doctor, Freud noted that his patients' reports of their dreams and thoughts, as well as their other conversational topics, seemed to form patterns that related to their emotional problems. Gradually, he developed his theory that our experiences in early childhood, especially those with sexual significance, have a lasting influence on our personalities, and are often the basis for our adult emotional problems. Freud was convinced of the importance of these early experiences, but, since many of them are usually forgotten or repressed, he concluded that we do not know the real reasons for much of our adult behavior because these reasons are unconscious.

Freud thought of personality as an iceberg, with only the tip showing above water. The part of personality that we are aware of in everyday life is our *conscious mind*. This is the tip of the iceberg. Below this is the *preconscious mind*, which contains information that we have learned but are not thinking about right now. Our preconscious mind contains things such as our birth date and our address. We can easily pull information in the preconscious mind into consciousness by concentrating. Beneath the preconscious level lies the *unconscious*

Personality, according to Freud, is the result of the interaction of the ego, superego, and id. The ego operates on the reality principle, which is a conscious awareness of the conflict between the id and the superego. The id contains instinctual, unconscious animal urges and the superego the ethical and moral values of a person's family and culture.

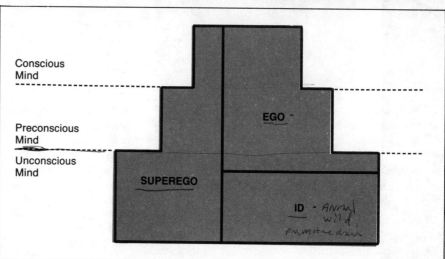

Figure 11.2 Freud's Psychoanalytic Theory

Conscious Mind

Preconscious Mind

Unconscious Mind

EGO

SUPEREGO

ID - *Animal, wild, primitive drives*

mind. Material in the unconscious mind is not readily available to us. Freud suggests that our fears and unpleasant memories are repressed into the unconscious mind.

Freud's theory of personality consists of three major concepts: id, superego, and ego. The id, which is present at birth, represents a person's most basic instinctual or biological drives. Freud claimed that the id operates on the pleasure principle, in which the instinctual drives unconsciously and impulsively seek immediate pleasure and consider nothing else (we discussed the motivational aspects of Freud's theory in chapter 9, "Motivation").

According to Freud, psychic energy, or libido, drives the id. The id contains two major instincts: the life instinct and death instinct. The life instinct, or eros, serves to help the individual and the species survive. Sex is the major expression of the life instinct, and provides motivation for a wide variety of human thoughts and behaviors. Freud suggested that the libido was largely sexual energy motivating eros. Eros was not limited to direct sexual motivation, but was believed to be involved in any pleasurable activity. The death instinct, or thanatos, includes aggression and destruction (Freud, 1939). Freud did not develop the concept of the death instinct as fully as he did the life instinct.

The superego consists of societal and parental values that have been instilled in the person. It is largely unconscious and restrains the impulses of the id. It represents the person's moral aspect and is idealistic

rather than realistic. The superego therefore includes the conscience (knowledge of the behaviors that are wrong) and the ego-ideal (knowledge of the behaviors that are correct).

The ego consists of a conscious faculty for perceiving and dealing intelligently with reality. It acts as mediator between the id (postponing its urges for immediate gratification) and the superego (recognizing that some of its inhibiting forces are irrational). The ego operates on the reality principle, and tries to find socially acceptable ways (according to the superego) to gratify the id. In the personality of a well-adjusted person, the ego is the dominant force.

According to Freud, an individual's personality is the result of the interaction of these three forces. In some ways the id represents "want," the superego "should," and the ego "can." The id, which is largely unconscious and rational, is expressed cognitively. Conflict can arise when the three personality structures interact. For instance, the id demands instant gratification, whereas the ego is able to wait. Which part of your personality would be active if you were thinking of cheating on your next examination? Sometimes when the conflict is great, we utilize defense mechanisms to reduce anxiety (we discuss defense mechanisms in chapter 12, "Stress and Adjustment").

In chapter 3, "Development," we reviewed the psychosexual stages proposed by Freud. Freud theorized that from birth through adolescence, the individual

SIGMUND FREUD

Sigmund Freud was born in 1856 to a lower-middle-class family, the son of wool merchants, in the Austrian town of Freiburg. When he was four his family moved to Vienna. His parents soon recognized and encouraged young Freud's intellectual capacities. After receiving his medical degree in 1881, he began to practice medicine; shortly afterward he met a young woman whom he eventually married.

Departing from the traditional academic setting of the psychological laboratory, he began to study mental disorders by clinical observation. Initially, Freud's theories shocked his highly conservative colleagues, most of whom either dismissed him entirely or countered him vehemently with caustic criticism. Freud refused to be discouraged by his adversaries, and continued his investigations with an almost obsessive fervor, gaining the support of only a handful of men who, like Jung and Adler, were themselves destined to make major contributions to psychoanalysis.

Freud spent nearly all his life in Vienna, and, when Nazi storm troopers invaded the city in 1938, he was soon arrested in his home and held in captivity until his stock of unsold books could be retrieved and burned publicly. Upon his release a few weeks later, he moved to London, where he lived out the last months of his life. In 1939 Freud died of cancer at the age of 83.

develops through five distinct stages. Each of these stages focuses on an area of the body that is of prominent concern to the individual at that particular time. Freud's psychosexual stages include the *oral* stage, *anal* stage, *phallic* stage, *latency* stage, and the *genital* stage. Freud considered these psychosexual stages crucial in the development of a healthy personality.

During the phallic stage, children must resolve the Oedipus (for boys) or Electra (for girls) complex. The name Oedipus complex is taken from the Greek play *Oedipus Rex*, in which a young man kills his father and marries his mother without knowing who they are. According to Freud, the young boy has sexual feelings for his mother and is jealous of his father. He experiences castration anxiety because he is afraid his father will castrate him. To resolve this conflict, the boy identifies with his father and suppresses his sexual feelings toward his mother.

The young girl in the phallic stage goes through the Electra complex, in which she feels inferior to boys because she lacks a penis. She blames her mother for her condition and loves her father because he has a penis. This penis envy eventually is resolved by suppressing her feelings toward her father and identifying with her mother. Freud believed that if the Oedipus/Electra complex was not resolved, the person would have difficulty relating to members of the opposite sex as an adult.

One of the major criticisms of Freud's personality theory centers on his perception of women as inferior. Freud argued that because women do not experience castration anxiety they do not develop as strong a superego as men do. However, research has demonstrated that gender has little or no effect on the development of a conscience or a superego.

Freud had attracted a close circle of followers, who joined with him to form the first psychoanalytic society. Given the distinctions between psychoanalysis as personality theory and as therapy, and considering the controversial nature of Freud's ideas, it is understandable that several members of Freud's circle, disagreeing with him on various aspects of his basic concept (especially his pessimistic view of humankind and his strong emphasis on sexuality), left the group and developed their own analytic approaches to personality and therapy. Three of the most important of these psychoanalytic theorists were Carl Jung, Alfred Adler, and Karen Horney.

Jung's Analytical Psychology

The personality theory of the Swiss psychologist Carl Jung is called analytical psychology. He thought that in addition to an individual personal unconscious, consisting of repressed thoughts and memories, there was also a collective unconscious shared by all humankind. Stored in the collective unconscious are universal human experiences repeated over centuries. The collective unconscious shapes our experiences, as a dried-up river bed gives shape to running water after a rainstorm. Jung called these unconscious universal ideas archetypes.

The aim of a healthy personality, Jung thought, was to achieve a kind of wholeness, in which all parts of the personality are fully developed and harmoniously integrated, rather than being fragmented as they are in most people. He called the process leading to this goal individuation. With awareness of both the bright side of our personality and its darker side, we can mediate between our animal instinct and the requirements of society, and achieve a feeling of balance, calm, and security.

The psyche includes all of the thoughts and feelings (conscious and unconscious) of an individual. According to Jung, the ego is the conscious mind, the part of the psyche that is concerned with thinking, emotion, memory, and perception. The ego is important because it provides stability in how we react to the world around us.

Jung argued that libido energy can be directed externally, called extraversion, or it can be directed inward, called introversion. The introverted person tends to be shy and withdrawn, whereas the extravert is sociable and outgoing. For each person, one of these attitudes becomes dominant and controls the ego and the other nondominant attitude becomes included in the personal unconscious.

In addition to the attitudes of introversion and extraversion, Jung proposed four psychological functions to describe how people deal with the world: thinking, feeling, sensing, and intuiting. *Thinking* and *feeling* are rational functions that people use to evaluate their experiences. Thinking involves making judgments and decisions, whereas feeling is determining whether an experience is pleasant or unpleasant. *Sensing* and *intuiting* are irrational functions because they are not used to evaluate. Sensation is simply the experience produced by stimulation of the sense organs. Intuition does not arise from external stimulation but rather from an internal source (for example, a hunch).

Jung combined the two attitudes and four functions to produce eight psychological types. The *thinking extraverted* type of objective and dogmatic. The *feeling extraverted type* is highly emotional and conforming. The *sensing extraverted type* enjoys new experiences and meeting new people. The *intuiting extraverted type* is creative and can motivate others. The *thinking introverted type* is aloof and focuses on ideas. The *feeling introverted type* tends to be quiet and shy. The *sensing introverted type* is sensitive and detached. And the *intuiting introverted type* is often eccentric and shy.

Figure 11.3   Freud and Colleagues
Standing, left to right, are A. A. Brill, Sandor Ferenczi, and Ernest Jones; seated are Sigmund Freud, G. Stanley Hall, and Carl G. Jung.

Jung's psychological types form the core of a personality test, called the Myers-Briggs Type Indicator (MBTI), which we discuss later in the chapter.

Adler's Individual Psychology

Alfred Adler's theory of individual psychology differed from Freud's in several fundamental ways. The theory focused on the uniqueness of each individual person. Adler minimized the importance of the unconscious and did not subscribe to the theory that sexuality was the basis for personality or disorders. Instead, he saw human beings as motivated primarily by a *drive for superiority*. Children develop an inferiority complex because they are so little and so dependent on adults. As children develop, they encounter things they cannot do and situations in which they do not meet the standards they set for themselves. People are thus constantly striving to *compensate* for their weaknesses. Sometimes, unfortunately, they overcompensate and develop a superiority complex, in which they exaggerate their abilities and characteristics.

Although Adler rejected Freud's notion that childhood experiences are all-important in determining the nature of the adult personality, he believed that they contribute, along with hereditary and environmental factors, to the development of the individual's style of life—patterns of thinking and behaving that persist into adulthood. The individual's lifestyle directs how the person will strive for superiority.

According to Adler (1939), each person must solve life problems in the areas of interacting with other people, having an occupation, and being in love. As the person deals with these problems, he or she adopts a particular type of lifestyle. The *dominant type* typically shows no interest in other people. The *avoiding type*

avoids the problems of life. The *getting type* is dependent on other people to provide for him or her. And the *useful type* interacts successfully with others. Adler's emphasis on cognitive and social processes has influenced a number of later personality theorists.

Also central to Adler's conception of personality is a human being's social nature. He believed that people are motivated by *social interest*, a capacity to love others, and a need to cooperate and work for social goals. Ideally, the individual's striving for superiority should be channeled into striving for social rather than selfish goals.

Horney's Cultural Psychology

Karen Horney was a physician trained in psychoanalysis. Like Jung and Adler, she broke with Freud, largely because of his emphasis on biological factors in personality. She believed social and cultural influences were very important influences and focused her theory on them. Horney was also distressed by Freud's views of women, and she rejected Freud's concept of penis envy. According to Horney, women envy the privileges that men enjoy in our culture, such as independence, success, sexual freedom, and strength (Horney, 1939).

Like Freud, Horney believed that early childhood was important. However, she stressed the social influences during childhood. Two basic needs in childhood include safety and satisfaction and if these are not met may result in basic anxiety. Children are basically helpless and need adults to care for them but may at the same time resent the need and develop a hostility toward the parent. But because this hostility is not allowed in our society, and because the child is dependent on the adult, the hostility is repressed, and may ultimately lead to basic anxiety, a feeling of loneliness and helplessness.

Figure 11.4. Karen Horney
Karen Horney (1885–1952), a personality theorist who practiced therapy in Germany and America, disagreed with Freud's stress on the sexual influence in the development of personality. She believed that environmental and social factors were more important than sexuality and that anxiety was a stronger motivating force in human behavior than the sexual drive.

In order to protect oneself from basic anxiety, the person attempts to gain love from others, complies with the wishes of others, or gains power over others. These strategies may be so successful that they eventually become part of the individual's personality. Horney identified several neurotic needs, which are irrational solutions to basic anxiety, as: affection, power, exploitation, prestige, achievement, perfection, and self-sufficiency.

Horney eventually proposed that rather than ten separate neurotic needs, there were three neurotic trends, or ways of adapting. The compliant personality (moving toward people) is characterized by a strong need to be loved and needed by others. The aggressive personality (moving against people) is characterized by a need to act aggressively in a world seen as hostile. The detached personality (moving away from people) is characterized by a need to maintain distance from others. Horney's personality theory is more optimistic than Freud's, probably because she does not emphasize the biological factors, but instead focuses on the social, and thus modifiable variables of personality.

The basic problem with much of the psychoanalytic approach to personality is that it emphasizes the unconscious, and therefore is not testable. Many psychologists were not convinced that psychoanalysis could explain completely the complexity of human personality.

A different approach is represented in the theories that try to describe personality rather than explain it. The trait theories of personality emphasize tangible qualities, rather than abstract unconsciousness.

TRAIT THEORIES

Some psychologists attempt to characterize personality through the use of traits—distinctive and stable attributes that can be found in people. Traits help to differentiate us from one another. Trait psychologists are interested in which attributes tend to occur together, indicating common underlying traits that can be identified. Typically these psychologists have based their personality theories on their observations of normal, healthy individuals.

Allport's Trait Theory

Gordon W. Allport (1961) defined personality as the dynamic organization of the psychophysical systems that determine characteristic behavior and thought of an individual. Personality is constantly changing (dynamic) and involves an interaction of biology and cognition (psychophysical). According to Allport, it is important to focus on the individual, an approach called idiographic, as each person is unique and has a distinctive personality.

In his early research, Allport referred to common traits (those shared by many people in a culture) and individual traits (those unique to a person). Later, he referred to common traits as *traits* and individual traits as personal dispositions.

Allport believes that individual personality can be understood through three types of hierarchical personal disposition traits: cardinal, central, and secondary. Cardinal traits are so dominant that they are expressed in everything the person does in life. For instance, the fanatical lover or the zealous religious person might represent expressions of cardinal traits. Allport believes few people have cardinal traits.

Rather than a single cardinal trait, most people have a small number of central traits. These form the core of our personality, and are developed by our experiences in life. Central traits can be measured in personality tests that include lists of adjectives. Allport (1961) asked college students to write a description of a friend, and found that the descriptions included about seven central traits.

Secondary traits are less important, situation-specific traits that help round out our personality. Things like attitudes, specific behavior patterns, skills, and preferences would be included in secondary traits. They are less dominant and are more likely to change in different situations.

Allport tried to measure an individual's traits in sufficient detail needed to classify the person and distinguish him or her from other people. He was the first personality theorist not to come from a psychoanalytic background. One criticism has been that since he took the ideographic approach, it is not possible to generalize from one person to another. However, his theory has been very influential in serving as a nonpsychoanalytic model of personality for other theories to follow.

Cattell's Factor Theory

Raymond B. Cattell wanted to go beyond the listing of personality traits; he wanted to understand how the traits are organized into particular clusters or patterns, and how these influence behavior. He studied under Spearman (who developed a factor theory of intelligence) and wanted to produce a mathematical model of the factors of personality. Cattell proposed the following equation to represent personality:

$$R = f(P,S)$$

The behavioral response (R) of a person is a function (f) of the individual's personality (P) and the situation (S). The most difficult aspect of this equation is to understand personality.

Cattell used a statistical procedure called factor analysis to determine the relationship among various personality traits. He defined a *trait* as the potential of a person to react in a certain way. Cattell used three measures to collect personality data: life records, which are observations of the person's behavior; personal questionnaires,

---

Figure 11.5. Sixteen Personality Factor Questionnaire (16PF)

The Primary Source Traits Covered by the 16PF Test

Factor	Low Sten Score Description (1–3)	High Sten Score Description (8–10)
A	*Cool,* **reserved, impersonal, detached, formal, aloof** Sizothymia	*Warm,* **outgoing, kindly, easygoing, participating, likes people** Affectothymia
B	*Concrete-thinking,* **less intelligent** Lower scholastic mental capacity	*Abstract-thinking,* **more intelligent, bright** Higher scholastic mental capacity
C	*Affected by feelings,* **emotionally less stable, easily annoyed** Lower ego strength	*Emotionally stable,* **mature, faces reality, calm** Higher ego strength
E	*Submissive,* **humble, mild, easily led, accommodating** Submissiveness	*Dominant,* **assertive, aggressive, stubborn, competitive, bossy** Dominance
F	*Sober,* **restrained, prudent, taciturn, serious** Desurgency	*Enthusiastic,* **spontaneous, heedless, expressive, cheerful** Surgency
G	*Expedient,* **disregards rules, self-indulgent** Weaker superego strength	*Conscientious,* **conforming, moralistic, staid, rule-bound** Stronger superego strength
H	*Shy,* **threat-sensitive, timid, hesitant, intimidated** Threctia	*Bold,* **venturesome, uninhibited, can take stress** Parmia
I	*Tough-minded,* **self-reliant, no-nonsense, rough, realistic** Harria	*Tender-minded,* **sensitive, overprotected, intuitive, refined** Premsia
L	*Trusting,* **accepting conditions, easy to get on with** Alaxia	*Suspicious,* **hard to fool, distrustful, skeptical** Protension
M	*Practical,* **concerned with "down-to-earth" issues, steady** Praxernia	*Imaginative,* **absent-minded, absorbed in thought, impractical** Autia
N	*Forthright,* **unpretentious, open, genuine, artless** Artlessness	*Shrewd,* **polished, socially aware, diplomatic, calculating** Shrewdness
O	*Self-assured,* **secure, feels free of guilt, untroubled, self-satisfied** Untroubled adequacy	*Apprehensive,* **self-blaming, guilt-prone, insecure, worrying** Guilt proneness
Q_1	*Conservative,* **respecting traditional ideas** Conservatism of temperament	*Experimenting,* **liberal, critical, open to change** Radicalism
Q_2	*Group-oriented,* **a "joiner" and sound follower, listens to others** Group adherence	*Self-sufficient,* **resourceful, prefers own decisions** Self-sufficiency
Q_3	*Undisciplined self-conflict,* **lax, careless of social rules** Low integration	*Folloiwng self-image,* **socially precise, compulsive** High self-concept control
Q_4	*Relaxed,* **tranquil, composed, has low drive, unfrustrated** Low ergic tension	*Tense,* **frustrated, overwrought, has high drive** High ergic tension

which provide self-descriptions of personality; and objective tests, which help identify clusters of personality traits.

He started by identifying surface traits, the observable characteristics of a person's behavior and personality. Cattell noticed that surface traits tend to fall into groupings or clusters that can often be described with a single word. The identity of these trait clusters is what Cattell calls source traits, or characteristics more basic to the core of an individual's personality.

Cattell developed a personality test called the Sixteen Personality Factor Questionnaire (16PF) to measure source traits. With this he could develop a trait profile, or graphic representation of the source traits. We discuss the 16PF Questionnaire later in the chapter.

Eysenck's Trait Model of Personality

Hans J. Eysenck believes that biology plays a major role in personality. He used questionnaires, observations, and physiological measures of personality when developing his theory (Eysenck, 1952). His conception of personality suggests that it develops through an interaction of four sectors: cognitive (intelligence), conative (character), affective (temperament), and somatic (constitution).

Eysenck (1967) believes that personality consists of behaviors and dispositions arranged in a hierarchy. At the lowest level is the *specific response*, an isolated behavior that occurs in a single situation. For example, you might observe Ben opening the door at school for a stranger. At a more general level is the *habitual response*, a pattern of behaviors that usually occur together. For example, Ben is often observed talking with others, leading groups, organizing meetings, and smiling when others are around. Next is the *trait*, a collection of related habitual responses. Because of the habitual response shown by Ben, we could say that he has the trait of sociability. Finally, the highest and most general level is the *type*, a collection of commonly displayed traits. Eysenck would argue that Ben displays the extraverted personality type.

Eysenck (1975) proposed three major personality type dimensions: introversion-extraversion, neuroticism (stability), and psychoticism. *Introversion* includes characteristics such as pessimism, thoughtfulness, carefulness, and quietness. *Extraversion* includes characteristics such as impulsiveness, activity, excitability, liveliness, and sociability. The *neuroticism* (or emotionality/stability) dimension goes from stable to unstable, and measures stress tolerance. The unstable end of this dimension includes characteristics such as moodiness, restlessness, and anxiousness, and the stable end is characterized by calmness, leadership, and the ability to be even-tem-

pered. The psychotic end of the *psychoticism* dimension includes characteristics such as aggressiveness, disregard for danger, solitariness and not fitting in with others. The traits of each dimension can be arranged along a continuum, such as when introversion-extraversion and stability-unstability are combined. For example, the stable-extraverted person might show traits such as leadership, responsiveness, and sociability, whereas the unstable-introverted person might be characterized as moody, rigid, anxious, and pessimistic.

An interesting aspect of Eysenck's theory is his suggestion that an individual's nervous system reacts to environmental stimulation in a way that influences personality. In particular, extraverts have low cortical excitation levels and therefore tend to seek outside stimulation. Introverts have high cortical excitation levels and thus tend to avoid external stimulation. Not all research supports the arousal aspect of his theory, but Eysenck's theory has been important in attempting to relate biology and personality and in utilizing the experimental approach in studying personality.

Five Factor Personality Model

Psychologists have continued to be involved in identifying the core traits which effectively describe personality, and currently there is considerable interest in the five factor model of personality traits. Tupes and Christal (1961) first proposed the model, which consists of the factors of extraversion, agreeableness, conscientiousness, neuroticism (emotional stability), and culture (openness to experience). Norman (1963) argued that these five factors could adequately describe personality. Little was done with the theory until the 1980s, when a number of psychologists confirmed that these factors are central in personality.

Costa and McCrae (1980) developed a classification scheme consisting of neuroticism, extraversion, and openness (in their NEO scale). Later they discovered substantial agreement between the NEO scale and the corresponding factors of the five factor model (McCrae & Costa, 1985). Additional support for several of the five factor variables (extraversion, agreeableness, and conscientiousness) was reported by Peabody (1984), who also found several other possible factors. Digman and Takemoto-Chock (1981) reported support for the five factor model when they reanalyzed six classic studies in personality. Amelang and Borkenau (1982) reported the same five factors when they tested German subjects, and McCrae and Costa (1987) again validated the five factor model with different questionnaires and observers. They argued that support for the five factor model is present and encouraged researchers and clinicians to utilize the model in future research and assessment of personality.

What are the traits represented in the five factor model? McCrae and Costa (1987) called the traits neuroticism, extraversion, openness, agreeableness, and conscientiousness. *Neuroticism* is characterized by worrying, nervousness, emotionality, insecurity, and self-consciousness. *Extraversion* includes traits of sociableness, affection, friendliness, warmth, person-orientation, and boldness. *Openness* is characterized by creativity, curiosity, independence, preference for variety, and liberalness. *Agreeableness* includes goodnaturedness, helpfulness, trust, agreeableness, and straightforwardness. *Conscientiousness* is characterized by carefulness, reliableness, organization, neatness, ambition, intelligence, and culturedness.

Some psychologists do not believe that personality can be classified so easily according to different traits. A more comprehensive approach to human behavior is seen in the personality theories of the humanistic psychologists.

HUMANISTIC THEORIES

Humanistic psychologists concentrate on the uniqueness of the human personality. Sometimes they are called *self* theorists because they emphasize the self (what is part of oneself and what is not). Humanistic theorists view the individual as essentially active in determining the potential course of his or her own life. Humanistic theorists tend to be optimistic, concentrating on human strengths rather than weaknesses; they stress the uniqueness of each individual, and maintain that the proper way to study a person is as a total entity that cannot be dissected into parts. We discuss the work of two representative humanistic theorists—Carl Rogers and Abraham Maslow.

Rogers's Theory of Self

Carl Rogers, who began his career as a psychotherapist, emphasizes the capacities that are distinctly human in contrast to the basic drives shared by all animals. He is thus very interested in free will, responsibility, and choice. Rogers sees our basic motives as good, healthy, and positive, as discussed in his 1980 book, *A Way of Being*.

Rogers suggested that there is an inherent tendency in each of us toward self-actualization, that is, toward developing all the capacities made available to us by our heredity. He believed that under ideal conditions, our

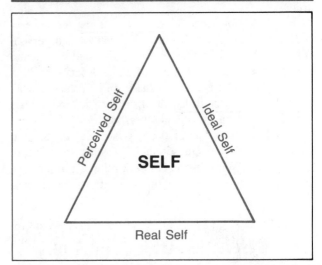

Figure 11.6. Rogers's Theory of Self

Personality, or the self, can be viewed as a triangle, with the real self (what the person is really like), perceived self (what the person perceives himself or herself to be), and ideal self (what the person would like to be) as the sides. Rogers argues that congruence among the aspects of the self will lead to self-actualization.

actions and feelings are determined by an innate wisdom and goodness, which, if unhampered, will result in a fully functioning person. This tendency toward self-actualization is our primary motivation and goal in life. According to Rogers, however, a healthy psychological environment is necessary for self-actualization to occur, one of total warmth and of our acceptance by others, which inspires corresponding self-acceptance.

Rogers contended that the individual organism interacts in the world to develop a phenomenal field, the sum total of both conscious and unconscious experiences. A part of the phenomenal field develops as the self, the individual's perception of "I" or "me" obtained through interactions with other people.

Rogers (1971) described personality (or self) as a triangle, with real self (what you are really like), perceived self (what you perceive yourself to be), and ideal self (what you would like to be), as the sides. Central to Rogers's person-centered approach to life is the idea that every person has an innate need for a positive self-regard, as well as positive regard from others. To the extent that a person distorts or denies experiences (because they conflict with the need for the positive regard of others), the self-actualizing tendency is hampered, and personal growth is impaired. Congruence results when there is a fit among the aspects of self. Thus, congruence helps us become psychologically healthy and reach self-actualization. Distorted or denied experiences produce incongruence and conflict between the self-image and the individual's true nature. The person must spend time and effort protecting a false image of self rather than in gaining actualization. The resulting tensions can cause psychological maladjustment.

When we show <u>unconditional positive regard</u> toward someone, we love and accept them without conditions (that is, regardless of what they do). <u>Conditional positive regard</u> occurs when we accept another only if she or he meets our conditions (for example, a child behaves for us or a friend doesn't embarrass us). Eventually, through conditional positive regard experiences, the individual develops *conditions of worth* (a conscience), defining what is acceptable or unacceptable about the self. A psychologically healthy person can integrate new experiences into the self-image. Even unwanted feelings such as hostility can be accepted as a part of the self without making the person feel unworthy.

According to Rogers (1961), the individual strives to be a fully functioning person in the *good life*. There are three characteristics of the process of developing the good life. An increasing openness to experience occurs when the individual is open to feelings and events without becoming defensive. An increasing tendency to live fully moment to moment is a second characteristic. And developing trust in one's organism refers to feeling comfortable with who one is and what one is becoming. When a person is developing the good life, he or she will experience a sense of freedom.

Maslow's Self-Actualization Theory

Another humanistic psychologist, Abraham Maslow, focused his theory of personality on the psychologically healthy person. Abraham Maslow is also a leading figure in the humanistic tradition, and did much to define humanistic psychology before his death in 1970. Like Rogers, he believed that people's basic nature is good, and that the individual has an innate motive to strive toward <u>self-actualization.</u>

Maslow conceived of human beings as born with a hierarchy of needs, as we discussed in chapter 9, "Motivation." When needs on the primary level are satisfied, then needs farther up on the scale make themselves felt. Maslow's need hierarchy included physiological needs, safety needs, belongingness and love needs, esteem needs, and self-actualization. The first four are called basic needs.

Self-actualization includes another group of needs called *metaneeds*, or growth needs. Among these are the needs for knowledge, justice, truth, and beauty. The metaneeds are not arranged in a hierarchical order as are the basic needs; one can be substituted for another. Maslow (1968) proposed that the individual's personality progresses naturally with the fulfillment of the needs,

Figure 11.7. Maslow's Self-actualization

- Efficient Perception of Reality
- Acceptance of Self and Others
- Spontaneity
- Problem Centering
- Need for Privacy
- Autonomy
- Continued Freshness of Appreciation
- Peak Experiences
- Identification with Humanity
- Deep Interpersonal Relationships
- Democratic Character Structure
- Strong Ethics
- Unhostile Sense of Humor
- Creativeness
- Resistance to Enculturation

Humanistic psychologist Abraham Maslow concluded that self-actualized people shared a number of common personality characteristics.

steadily moving toward self-actualization. Like Rogers, he maintained that a warm and supportive environment is vital for self-actualization. Without such an environment, the individual cannot satisfy the basic needs, and because of consequent anxiety, the person will not develop the self-actualized personality.

Maslow (1970, 1987) described a number of psychological attributes that characterize self-actualized individuals. Self-actualized people are realistic, with a good grasp of what is possible. They do not frustrate themselves by working for impossible goals. They accept themselves and others for what they are. Since they have resolved inner conflicts, they tend to focus their attention on problems outside themselves. But they need privacy, for they have their own needs apart from those of others. They are autonomous and independent, able to act without orders from others or from a desire to imitate others.

<u>Self-actualized people</u> appreciate other people in a fresh, unstereotyped way. They form a few meaningful and intimate relationships, rather than many shallow ones. They tend to be creative, original, and have a good sense of humor. They see each new person as a unique individual, and identify with humankind, seeing themselves as part of the human experience. Their values and attitudes are democratic; they have a passion to secure equal opportunity for everyone to develop into a self-actualized person (see Figure 11.12).

Although Maslow did not conduct empirical research on his theory, other psychologists have, particularly with the *Personal Orientation Inventory* personality test (Shostrom, 1964). Generally, the characteristics that Maslow identified as self-actualization correlated highly with other tests of positive mental health and adjustment. One study (Miner, 1984) did not find Maslow's theory to

Figure 11.8. Self-actualization
Abraham Maslow studied the biographies of people to help him obtain case studies of those who he thought had realized their full potential, or self-actualization. Eleanor Roosevelt, Martin Luther King, Jr., and Albert Einstein might be considered examples of people who achieved self-actualization.

be applicable to work situations; however, other research has suggested that upper-level executives were more concerned with actualization needs than were their subordinates. A study by Graham and Balloun (1973) found support for the theory in the general population. While most of us will never reach total self-actualization, this theory provides a view of the human personality which we can begin to understand and appreciate.

BEHAVIOR AND SOCIAL LEARNING THEORIES

The last approach to personality that we review comes from the learning tradition. We discussed the basic theories of learning in chapter 6, "Learning." Learning theory in this chapter emphasizes observation, imitation, reinforcement, and punishment in the development of personality. We cover the traditional learning approach to behavior and personality, and then we discuss the cognitive social-reinforcement approach.

Skinner's Behaviorism and Personality

Behaviorists rarely speak of such "abstract" traits as aggressiveness or the need for affection. Instead they observe people and conduct research to determine what produces particular behaviors. Since moral considerations prohibit most experimentation with people's personalities, behaviorists are limited in their ability to produce theories about the human personality. Moreover, behaviorists think it is virtually impossible to conduct research that either proves or disproves any one specific theory of personality.

Behaviorists such as B. F. Skinner generally believe that personality is defined as learned ways of behaving, which, like any behavior, follow the principles of reinforcement, extinction, generalization, discrimination, and punishment. Skinner concerns himself with the external forces operating on the individual, and does not treat the individual as an agent free to make decisions. If someone strikes another person, Skinner does not talk about aggressive drives, inner conflict, or an identity crisis. To explain this action, he attempts to get a history of the person's past experiences in similar situations. The individual may have learned that he or she can have his or her own way with particular types of people by striking them. With other people, striking out may have met with negative consequences, and thus this particular behavior pattern would be ineffective.

B. F. Skinner explained his behavioristic point of view in *Beyond Freedom and Dignity* (1971): "We can no longer afford freedom, and so it must be replaced with control, control over man, his conduct, and his culture." According to Skinner, the concept of freedom is an illusion. Skinner argued that, rather than making our own decisions freely, we are controlled by our environment. We are what our past experiences and environment cause us to be. For instance, a criminal's behavior is caused by the environment. Thus the treatment of criminals must focus on changing their environment,

Figure 11.9. Behaviorist Approach to Personality
Behaviorists, such as B. F. Skinner, believe that personality is a learned pattern of behavior. Reinforcement is a very powerful force in shaping behavior and hence personality, according to this view. Computer assisted instruction is one good example of how reinforcement can shape behavior. Receiving grades for schoolwork and money for work performed are other types of reinforcement.

which will in turn change their behavior (personality). Behaviorists such as Skinner argue that behavior is determined almost completely by external stimuli in the environment. Other psychologists suggest that cognition (thinking) is also very important, as we see in the next section.

Bandura's Modeling Theory

While Skinner's approach to personality (and indeed all of psychology) is based on reinforcement of behavior, Albert Bandura's (1977) social learning theory emphasizes the role of observation and modeling. It is possible to learn and modify one's behavior by observing someone and then imitating the action, with or without reinforcement.

Bandura (1978) viewed the *self* as a set of cognitive structures that direct a person's perception, thinking, and behavior. Actual reinforcement is not as important as the perception of reinforcement. Thus, if a person is happy and believes his or her actions are beneficial, the person will continue exhibiting the behavior.

People are able to provide their own reinforcement when it doesn't come from other sources. Bandura argued that *self-reinforcement* produces exactly the same effects on behavior as external reinforcement. People set goals for themselves and when their goals are reached, feel satisfaction, thus reinforcing the behaviors that led to the accomplishment of the goal. Eventually, patterns of behavior emerge that can be labeled personality.

Bandura (1982) also emphasized the concept of self-efficacy, or an individual's sense of self-worth and

success in adjusting to the world. According to Bandura, people are able to judge their levels of self-efficacy through several sources of information. The most important information is *performance attainment,* as prior achievements provide evidence of the capability of the individual. When people observe others perform successfully, they receive vicarious reinforcement, especially if they judge themselves to be similar to the performers. *Verbal persuasion*, or being told they can achieve their goals, increases their self-efficacy. And *physiological arousal* caused by excitement or fear can be used as a source of positive feedback. If, however, the observed model has extremely high standards, most people would likely not be able to meet those same standards, and hence would have low self-efficacy, low feelings of self-worth and importance.

The social learning approach of Bandura has been influential in a number of areas of psychology, including learning, adjustment, personality, therapy, and social. Many psychologists currently identify with this approach (Pervin, 1984). One criticism of social learning theory is that it emphasizes overt behavior and thus misses the internal emotional and motivating forces.

Rotter's Locus of Control Theory

In his social learning theory, Julian Rotter (1954) proposed that reinforcement is influential in shaping behavior and personality, but because humans are so complex, expectancies and cognitions are also involved significantly. Rotter views behavior potential as the probability that a particular behavior will be shown in a specific

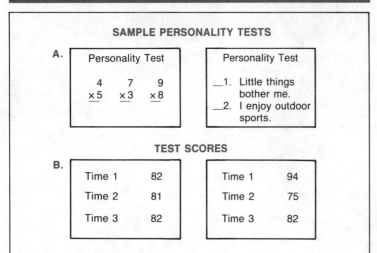

Figure 11.10. Requirements of Personality Tests

SAMPLE PERSONALITY TESTS

A.

| Personality Test |
| 4 7 9 |
| ×5 ×3 ×8 |

| Personality Test |
| __1. Little things bother me. |
| __2. I enjoy outdoor sports. |

TEST SCORES

B.

Time 1	82
Time 2	81
Time 3	82

Time 1	94
Time 2	75
Time 3	82

Personality tests should be valid and reliable. **A.** Which test is more likely to be a valid personality test? **B.** Which test scores are more likely to be considered reliable?

(Answers: In **A.** the second personality test is more valid. In **B.** the first set of scores is more reliable than the second.)

situation. Behavior potential depends upon two factors—expectancy and reinforcement value. Expectancy is the individual's belief that if he or she exhibits a certain behavior in a specific situation, it will result in reinforcement. Expectancy develops because of previous reinforcement in that and similar situations. Reinforcement value is the importance or value the person attaches to a particular reinforcement. For example, you will study (behavior potential) if you believe studying will lead to a reinforcement (expectancy) that you consider valuable (good grades). The preference for particular reinforcements comes from past experiences with them. The psychological situation results from the individual interacting in both internal and external environments. Rotter contends that behavior can only be predicted if the psychological situation is understood.

As we discussed in the opening story, Rotter has stimulated a great deal of recent research with his 1966 theory of internal-external locus of control. He extended his idea of expectancy to include generalized expectancies about the control of reinforcement for a person. People tend to have either an internal or external locus of control.

Internal people perceive that reinforcement is contingent upon their own behavior or attributes. They believe that if they work hard, they will be rewarded. They prefer situations that they have control over. Thus, internal people do not like gambling. They are less conforming and often have considerable power over their environment. They see the world as predictable and expect that consequences follow actions. If you believe that studying hard will lead to a better grade, you are likely to be labeled as internal.

External people tend to perceive that reinforcement is independent of their behavior, that it is controlled by external forces, by fate, or by luck. According to the external person, getting a good grade on a test depends on luck more than studying. External people cannot predict the consequences of their behavior; they tend to learn that there's nothing they can do to change things, so they give up easily.

Rotter stated that the orientation of people makes an important difference. According to him, one application of locus of control is that people cannot be helped in therapy until they begin to become internal. They must believe that their behavior does make a difference. It is possible that external expectancy actually leads to helplessness and depression, a topic we discuss in the next chapter.

PERSONALITY ASSESSMENT

Psychologists have developed a number of methods to measure and assess personality. In schools and businesses, in clinics and hospitals, and as part of their counseling and therapeutic work with patients, psychologists regularly administer personality tests. Their purpose is to discover a person's characteristic patterns of behavior. They can determine from the results of personality tests what tasks a person might be assigned in a job, what kinds of courses a student might be encouraged to take, as well as which therapy might best serve a disturbed individual.

Any measurement of personality should meet several requirements (see chapter 1, "The Study of Psychology" for discussion of research methods). Personality measures should be valid and reliable. Validity means that you actually measure what you intend to measure. In personality assessment, it means that you measure the subject's personality, rather than any temporary characteristics shown in the testing situation. Reliability means consistency or repeatability; each time you measure the individual's personality, you should obtain about the same results, if the test is reliable.

In addition, personality tests, like intelligence tests, should be standardized and practical. Standardization is the process of determining the norms, or standards, of the population you are working with. A test is standardized by giving it to a large group which is representative of the population. Practicality is important in personality assessment. Most people are less interested in taking a fantastic personality test that takes 16 hours to administer than a fairly good test that can be given in 2 hours.

Personality assessment by experienced psychologists often includes the interview. But this is usually supplemented by tests and observation.

Interview

Very likely, you were interviewed when you applied for a job, talked to your school counselor, or when someone else wanted to know how you accomplished something so well. During the interview, information about you was obtained by listening to what you said and observing how you behaved.

Interviews are sometimes classified as either unstructured or structured. In an unstructured interview no specific questions must be asked, but rather the conversation develops in whatever direction seems appropriate. In a structured interview a set of standard questions is designed to provide the information necessary to assess personality. Both types of interview can be useful in assessing personality.

While interviews can help assess personality, they obviously depend on the skill of the interviewer and the cooperation and honesty of the person being interviewed. The interviewer should be warm and friendly to encourage the subject to talk freely, but at the same time he or she must be objective in developing the personality assessment. Many times the person being interviewed may not want to cooperate, as in the case of criminals or the mentally ill. Especially when there is a problem with the effectiveness of the interview, the interviewer's observations are usually incorporated into the assessment.

Observation

Observation involves watching a person's behavior in everyday situations over a period of time. The ideal is naturalistic observation, where the person is observed in a normal environment (see chapter 1, "The Study of Psychology"). However, many times observations must be made in a clinical setting, as when psychologists are trying to diagnose behavior problems, or in artificial environments, such as an office (during a job interview). The observer records the subject's behavior, and then attempts to determine motivation and develop a personality description of the individual being observed.

Figure 11.11 Interview
Interviews are often used to assess personality. In a structured interview, a specific set of questions is asked, whereas in an unstructured inverview, the quesitons are determined by the interaction of the interviewer and subject.

Figure 11.12. Observation
In the observation technique of personality assessment, the psychologist records the behavior of a subject and then makes an assessment of the subject's motivation and personality.

Again, success in observation depends upon the skill of the observer and the cooperation of the subject. The observer must interpret correctly the behavior shown by the subject. And it is very likely that, when being observed, the subject's behavior will be somewhat different from normal. This problem is often overcome by making observations over an extended period of time, so that the subject can relax and behave in a normal manner.

In an attempt to standardize observations and make them more objective, psychologists have developed rating scales. A rating scale is a paper and pencil form that observers fill out in their assessment of a subject. To obtain the most accurate evaluation of a subject, several raters should be used. Ratings are used extensively in educational and industrial settings, but are also used to assess an individual's personality (Anastasi, 1988). Typically, the rating scale has a number of categories in which the characteristics shown by the subject are checked off. Self-rating scales might also be used, in which case the subject is asked to evaluate himself or herself by indicating which traits or characteristics apply. An elaborate form of a self-rating scale is the standardized objective test of personality, which we cover next.

Objective Personality Tests

Objective personality tests are administered and scored according to standardized instructions. Thus, no matter where or when you take the test, it will be given and scored in the same way, assuring objectivity in administration and interpretation. There are a number of popular objective tests in use today.

Strong-Campbell Interest Inventory. Edward Strong began developing a test in the 1920s to help people decide which occupations they were best suited for. The original test was called the *Strong Vocational Interest Blank* and matched a person's interests and activities with those of people in various occupations. If you go to the counseling center, you may be given the current version, the Strong-Campbell Interest Inventory (SCII), revised by Donald Campbell and J. C. Hansen in 1985.

This 325-item personality test asks the subject to evaluate a wide variety of specific activities, amusements, objects, and personalities. The SCII profile includes scores on six general occupational scales (realistic, investigative, artistic, social, conventional, and enterprising) as well as special scales (academic comfort and introversion-extraversion). The SCII shows that people engaged in different occupations tend to have different personalities. The differences include the kinds of hobbies engaged in, social activities enjoyed, school topics preferred, and the kind of material read. Thus, the personality of the test taker can be matched with people already in certain occupations, and the counselor's predictions for success can be guided thereby.

Minnesota Multiphasic Personality Inventory. One of the best known personality tests is the Minnesota Multiphasic Personality Inventory (MMPI). Originally developed in 1940 by Hathaway and McKinley to identify personality disorders, it is still the most widely used test for general personality assessment (Costa & colleagues, 1985). The MMPI consists of 550 items which are answered either true or false. The scores are used to develop a personality profile on 10 different scales. The MMPI items include statements such as "I believe I am being plotted against," "I do not tire easily," and "I am worried about sex matters." The subject's responses are compared to scores produced by *normal* adults, and can be used to identify a variety of personality disorders.

A recent analysis of the usefulness of the MMPI to analyze over 1,500 normal adults was reported by Paul Costa and his colleagues (1985). They identified only nine normality factors represented in the test. Because of its fairly narrow emphasis on factors of normal populations, they recommended supplementing the MMPI with other tests when working with normal personalities. While there are concerns about its effective use in normal populations, the MMPI is still a very useful measure of personality. (Lanyon, 1984). The MMPI was recently revised to correct some of these concerns.

California Psychological Inventory. The California Psychological Inventory (CPI) is a test currently used to measure personality in normal populations. The 1987 revision of CPI consists of 462 items which are to be answered true or false. Some of the scales of the CPI include dominance, capacity for status, sociability, self-acceptance, responsibility, self-control, and tolerance. Corporate personnel offices might use the CPI as part of their screening program for job applicants. Anastasi (1988) stated that the CPI is one of the better personality inventories in use today.

16PF. Raymond Cattell developed the Sixteen Personality Factor Questionnaire (16PF) to measure personality traits. Originally published in 1949, it has been revised several times, the latest for the questions in 1967 and the norms for interpretation in 1986. The factor analysis statistical technique was used to identify clusters of traits that have the same underlying cause and are consistently shown by subjects.

The 16PF (Form A) consists of 187 multiple-choice questions. Examples of questions that are similar to those on the 16PF include: "People say I'm friendly. A)

true B) uncertain C) false" or "When with other people I am: A) outgoing B) shy C) neither."

The test is scored by hand or a computer, and the result is a test profile in which the score for each of the 16 dimensions is graphed on a scale of 1 to 10.

The 16PF scale has been used to assess personality in a variety of situations, such as career counseling, personnel evaluation, marriage counseling, and adjustment screening (Anastasi, 1988). Although there has been some criticism of the reliability of the test (Lanyon, 1984), it is one of the most popular personality tests available (Fehr, 1983). (see Figure 11.5).

Myers-Briggs Type Indicator. In 1962, Isabel Briggs Myers and her mother, Katherine Briggs, published the Myers-Briggs Type Indicator (MBTI) to measure scientifically Jung's 1923 Type Theory. In recent years, the MBTI has become a very popular personality test, especially in academic settings. Jung's theory included the dimension of extraversion-introversion, perception (either sensing or intuition) and judgment (either thinking or feeling). The MBTI includes four dimensions that are used to generate 16 types. The four types include: extraversion-introversion, sensing-intuition, thinking-feeling, and judging-perception (Provost, 1984). Hanewitz (1978) reported that different types of people tend to go into different professions. For instance, teachers and social work students had high levels of intuiting and feeling whereas police officers and dental students scored high in extraversion, sensing and thinking.

Even with built-in factors to reduce lying, objective tests still depend upon the truthfulness of the answers provided by the subjects. One possible way to get around this problem is through the use of projective tests that provide ambiguous stimuli for which there are not clear-cut answers.

Projective Personality Tests

Projective personality tests present simple, ambiguous stimuli that will allow subjects to respond with projections of their own personality. Since there are no clear-cut correct answers, presumably this cuts down on any possible cheating. If the psychologist is experienced, projective tests can provide valuable insights into personality. However, it is sometimes easy to misinterpret a response, and an inexperienced tester can misuse the information obtained.

Rorschach Inkblot Test. One of the best-known projective tests is the Rorschach Inkblot Test. This test, developed by Hermann Rorschach in 1921, consists of 10 cards containing blots of ink (five black and five colored). The subject is asked to go through the cards and discuss freely what is seen. The examiner then asks

The MMPI

The MMPI (Minnesota Multiphasic Personality Inventory) is the most popular objective clinical personality test in use today (Lubin & colleagues, 1985). Since its conception in the early 1940s, over 5,000 studies have been published about it. What is the MMPI and what does it do?

The MMPI was developed to diagnose specific psychological disorders, such as depression and schizophrenia (a disorder of thinking and emotion which is discussed in chapter 13, "Abnormal Psychology"). Hathaway and Mckinley, the test's developers, gave hundreds of short statements to mentally disturbed patients. They then noted which statements the patients agreed with. The basic purpose of the test was to differentiate various types of mental patients as well as to discriminate between mental patients and normal people. The MMPI did indeed do that; certain types of people tend to give certain responses on the test. Thus, the test can be used to diagnose problems by first determining who actually has them.

The MMPI consists of 550 statements which the subject responds to with true, false, or cannot say. It was designed primarily for adults and has not been used for children. The items cover a wide range of topics, including attitudes on religion and sexual practices, perceptions of health, political ideas, information on family, education and occupation, and displays of symptoms known to be exhibited by certain groups of mentally disturbed people.

The test provides scores on a number of clinical scales. The scales include hypochondriasis (exaggerated concern about physical health), depression, hysteria, masculinity-femininity, paranoia, hypomania (excitability), psychopathic deviancy, psychasthenia (irrational fears and compulsive actions), schizophrenia (form of abnormal behavior), and social introversion (withdrawal). The original research compared the responses on the clinical scales of people known to have a particular psychological problem with those of a normal population. For the masculinity-femininity scale, scores of normal men and women were compared. The social introversion scale was tested on groups of college students who varied on the introversion-extraversion dimension. Several other validity scales were added to check on carelessness, lying, and misunderstanding of subjects.

The MMPI does a reasonable job of identifying personality traits that can be associated with certain types of psychological disorders. It has also been used, however, to describe variations in normal personalities. However, there are some difficulties in doing this. The original population of subjects might not be representative of all normal people, and test scores can be influenced by norms, experiences, and expectations of the

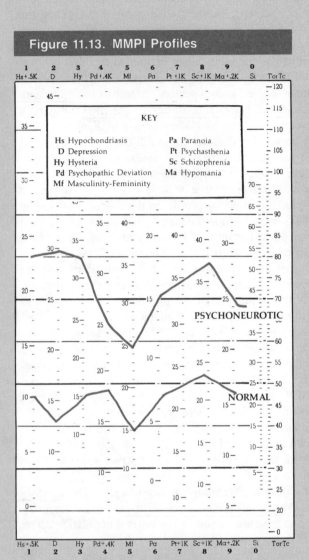

Figure 11.13. MMPI Profiles

KEY

Hs Hypochondriasis   Pa Paranoia
D Depression   Pt Psychasthenia
Hy Hysteria   Sc Schizophrenia
Pd Psychopathic Deviation   Ma Hypomania
Mf Masculinity-Femininity

PSYCHONEUROTIC

NORMAL

The MMPI is one of the most widely used objective tests of personality. Scores from the 550 true-false questions are used to develop a personality profile as shown here.

subculture. Still, if used properly, the MMPI can aid the trained psychologist in diagnosis of personality disturbances.

THOUGHT QUESTIONS

1. What is the MMPI used for?
2. If you were to take the MMPI, would your responses always be identified (or would they vary due to mood or immediate experience)?
3. Do you think it is ethical to give a personality test such as the MMPI to people who do not want to take it (such as institutionalized patients)?

Figure 11.14. Inkblot Test
In projective personality tests, such as the Rorschach Inkblot Test, subjects are asked to respond to relatively vague and meaningless stimuli. The assumption is that the individual's personality characteristics will be revealed through responses.

Figure 11.15. Thematic Apperception Test
In the TAT, subjects are asked to make up a story about the people in the picture. The test works on the assumption that subjects will project their own personalities into the photo. Who do you think the people in this photo are and what are they thinking?

questions which will help determine the assessment of personality. Rorschach's original cards are still used today. Because of the subjective nature of this kind of test interpretation, validity and reliability of this test are low. There are several systems that have attempted to improve objectivity in scoring. For example, one system scores responses based on location of inkblot, popularity of answer, and response content. A more recent inkblot test is the 1961 Holtzman Inkblot Technique (HIT), which uses 45 cards to assess personality. Holtzman developed the HIT to overcome the deficiencies of the Rorschach. Administration of the HIT is standardized, and scoring includes examination of 22 response variables. The scorer reliability is high, and a group form (using slides) produces a reliable measure. The HIT focuses on personality variables such as cognitive functioning, affective functioning, and self-concept. In general, it appears that the HIT is a useful projective test of personality.

Thematic Apperception Test. Another well-known projective test is the Thematic Apperception Test (TAT), which uses pictures of people in everyday settings, rather than abstract inkblots. The TAT was developed originally by Henry Murray in 1943. Subjects are shown the pictures one at a time and are required to make up stories about the people portrayed in the pictures. It is assumed that subjects will project their own thoughts and feelings into the stories. The test contains 19 cards

which require 2 hours of testing. Many examiners use only part of the cards.

The TAT has been used in a variety of settings. One of the most popular uses has been to measure the need for achievement, as discussed in chapter 9, "Motivation." Like other projective tests, there are problems in the TAT with the underlying assumptions such as the subjects always project themselves into the role of the hero in the story. Also John Atkinson (1981) has shown that temporary conditions such as hunger, lack of sleep, and frustration can affect a subject's responses on the TAT significantly. Despite the problems with the TAT, it is a popular projective test of personality and has been widely used.

There are many other projective tests of personality, including word-association tests, sentence-completion tests, and picture-drawing tests. Picture-drawing tests, such as the *Draw-A-Person* or the *House-Tree-Person* test have been especially useful in work with children, who often can't verbalize their feelings or problems adequately. The major objection to projective tests is one of misinterpretation. Still, they provide a glimpse of personality. ■

In some ways personality is the core of psychology. It is easy to see how all of the other topics covered thus far contribute to the development of personality—the distinctive enduring patterns of behavior and cognition that characterize a person's adaptation to life. As we saw in the opening story, personality theories allow us to predict how people will react in certain situations. This chapter is also a turning point. So far, we've been discussing the variables responsible for the healthy, normal individual's behavior. In the rest of the textbook, we use what we have learned to understand the topics of adjustment, abnormal behavior, therapy, social psychology, and applications of psychology.

"Who needs a super ego with 'Him' around?"

CHAPTER REVIEW
What You've Learned About Personality

1. Personality is the distinctive and enduring patterns of behavior and cognition that characterize a person's adaptation to life.
2. Personality theories organize the main themes of behavior, explain the differences and similarities among individuals, and define the healthy personality. Personality theories help us reduce our confusion and indecision about other people. A good theory should be explicit, testable, and alive.
3. Sigmund Freud's psychoanalytic theory of personality includes the conscious, preconscious, and un-conscious mind. Personality is the interaction of the id, ego, and superego. The id represents a person's basic instinctual drives which unconsciously and impulsively seek immediate pleasure. The id contains Eros (sexual) and Thanatos (aggressive) instincts and obtains energy from the libido. The superego consists of the societal values that have been instilled into a person (conscience). The ego consists of a conscious faculty for perceiving and dealing with reality.
4. Carl Jung's analytical personality theory includes

not only a personal conscious, but also a collective unconscious (consisting of archetypes) shared by all humankind. The goal of a healthy personality is to achieve individuation, in which all parts of the personality are fully developed and harmoniously integrated. Jung believed that the libido energy can be directed externally (extraversion) or internally (introversion). Jung identified 8 psychological types of personality.

5. Alfred Adler's individual personality theory states that people are motivated primarily by a drive for superiority, trying to overcome a sense of weakness. Also important in this theory is people's social interest, a capacity to love others and cooperate for social goals.

6. Karen Horney believed that in order to protect oneself from basic anxiety, a person attempts to gain love from others or gain power over others. She focused on neurotic trends of adaptation.

7. Some psychologists characterize personality through the use of traits, distinctive and stable attributes of people. Gordon Allport distinguished among cardinal traits, central traits, and secondary traits. Cardinal traits are so dominant that they are expressed in everything the person does. Most people have a small number of central traits which are developed by experience. Secondary traits are less important, situation-specific traits.

8. Raymond Cattell identified surface traits and source traits in his Sixteen Personality Factor Questionnaire (16PF). He started by identifying surface traits, the observable characteristics of a person's behavior and personality. Surface traits tend to fall into clusters, or source traits, the characteristics more basic to the core of an individual's personality.

9. Eysenck's conception of personality suggests that personality develops through interaction of cognitive, conative, affective, and somatic sectors. The personality hierachy includes specific responses, habitual responses, traits, and types. Eyesenck's types include introversion, extraversion, and neuroticism.

10. The five factor model of personality traits includes extraversion, aggreeableness, conscientiousness, neuroticism, and culture.

11. Humanistic psychologists concentrate on the uniqueness of the human personality. Carl Rogers believed that it is important to have congruence between our real self-image and our perceived self-image. Congruence helps us reach self-actualization, the development of all our capacities made available to us through heredity.

12. Abraham Maslow's humanistic theory also stresses people's innate motivation toward self-actualization. Maslow proposed that after meeting the lower, basic needs, people work toward self-actualization. Maslow studied the characteristics of the self-actualized person.

13. Learning theories view personality as behavior patterns that are learned due to experiences with reinforcements and punishments. B. F. Skinner proposed that external stimuli almost totally determine our behavior.

14. Albert Bandura's social learning theory emphasizes the role of observation and modeling. Self-efficacy is an individual's sense of self-worth and success in adjusting to the world.

15. Julian Rotter proposed that reinforcement and cognition are influential in shaping personality. Behavior potential, the probability that a particular behavior will be shown, depends on expectancy and reinforcement value. Rotter developed the locus of control theory, which classifies people as having internal or external beliefs about control of reinforcement. Internal people believe that their own actions control reinforcements, whereas external people believe that their actions have no influence on reinforcement.

16. Any measure of personality should be valid, reliable, standardized, and practical. In an interview, the interviewer obtains information about a person by listening to what is said and observing behavior patterns. Interviews can be structured or unstructured. Observation of a person's behavior in everyday situations over a period of time can aid in understanding personality.

17. Objective personality tests are administered and scored according to standardized procedures. The Strong-Campbell Interest Inventory (SCII) matches the personality of the subject with people in various occupations. The Minnesota Multiphasic Personality Inventory (MMPI) consists of 550 true-false items which can be used to identify a variety of personality disorders. The California Personality Inventory (CPI) consists of true-false items which are used to measure personality in normal populations. Other popular objective tests include the 16PF and the Myers-Briggs Type Indicator.

Projective tests assess personality by presenting ambiguous test stimuli that allow subjects to project their own personality. The Rorschach Inkblot Test consists of 10 cards containing blots of ink. The subject goes through the cards and freely discusses what is seen. In the Thematic Apperception Test (TAT), the subject is shown everyday-type pictures and is asked to make up a story about the people portrayed in the pictures.

empathy
positive regard
congruence

Chapter **12**

STRESS AND ADJUSTMENT

Stress, an unavoidable consequence of life, is anything that produces demands on people to adjust their behavior. Stress often has negative consequences, such as anxiety or burnout. Psychologists have studied a variety of adjustment techniques, some of which are more effective than others. Recently time management skills have been refined to help people better adjust to the demands placed upon them.

In his 1975 book, *Helplessness*, Martin Seligman described a theory to explain why some people seem to give up and become helpless: in a situation they have no control over, they eventually learn that the responses they make will not affect any particular outcome. Thus, people realize that trying to respond is useless, and so they give up and ultimately become depressed.

Seligman's research on learned helplessness began in the 1960s when he and his colleagues were looking at classical conditioning in dogs. In one study the experimenters trained four dogs to associate the sound of a tone with an electric shock by placing the dogs in a Pavlovian harness, a rubberized cloth hammock. The dogs received a series of 64 shocks on the hind feet. The shocks were inescapable, and they quickly learned to associate the sound of the tone with the pain of the shock.

The following day, the dogs were given an opportunity to avoid the shock. They were placed in a two-way shuttlebox that was divided by a small barrier set at the height of the dogs' shoulders. One-way mirrors allowed the experimenters to observe the subjects' performance. The experimenters sounded a tone, which was followed 10 seconds later by a shock to the side of the box that the dogs were in. Normal control-group dogs, who had not been conditioned to associate the shock with the tone, yelped and ran frantically about the box until they accidentally got over the barrier and escaped the shock. On the next trial, these "normal" dogs jumped more quickly over the barrier, and within a few trials they avoided the shock altogether by jumping as soon as the tone was sounded.

The behavior of the experimental dogs, who had previously been given the inescapable shock paired with the tone, was very different. At first they ran around, but very quickly they lay down and suffered the shock. On subsequent trials, these dogs didn't even attempt to escape; they gave up the effort. Ten trials were given in the shuttlebox. None of the subjects learned to escape or avoid the electric shock.

Seligman described the dogs' behavior as learned helplessness. Because they learned in the first part of the study that they could not escape the shock, they gave up in later experiences and didn't try to escape. They became helpless.

Seven days later, Seligman tested the dogs again in the shuttlebox for escape behavior. One dog escaped, but the others continued to show strong learned helplessness. Then the treatment to help the dogs overcome learned helplessness began. In Phase 1, the dogs were again placed in the shuttlebox, but this time the barrier was removed. In order to escape, the dogs only had to step across a 5-inch divider. In addition, the observation window on the "safe" side was opened and the experimenter called the dog to come over. Only one dog responded to this phase of the treatment.

In Phase 2, the subjects were placed in the shuttlebox with a long leash around their necks. Now the dogs were forced across the divider to the safe side by having the experimenter pull on the leash. A maximum of 25 trials were given per day until the subjects began to cross over without experimenter intervention.

One dog responded after Phase 1 (no barrier/calling).

Figure 12.1. Learned Helplessness
When people have no control over a situation, they eventually learn that their responses do not affect the outcome. This leads to what Martin Seligman calls learned helplessness.

One of the dogs who required Phase 2 (forced escape/avoidance exposure) began responding after 20 trials, whereas the other two required 35 and 50 trials of Phase 2 treatment. In a follow-up test, all of the dogs continued to respond positively, thus indicating that they were normal. Seligman had shown alleviation of learned helplessness in the dog.

He suggested that learned helplessness in people is acquired in a similar manner. He proposed further that this was a model of depression and that therapy for alleviating human depression should consist of techniques similar to that used on the dogs which would force the person to gain control over his or her life.

CHAPTER OBJECTIVES
What You'll Learn About Stress and Adjustment

After studying this chapter, you should be able to:

1. Define the concepts of stress and adjustment.
2. Identify the life changes and daily hassles that cause stress.
3. Describe the major psychological causes of stress (pressure, conflict, and frustration).
4. Describe anxiety.
5. Outline the stages of the general adaptation syndrome.
6. Describe the symptoms of burnout and identify four remedies for it.
7. Describe individual differences in reactions to stress.

8. Outline the problems of learned helplessness and shyness and describe how they are treated.
9. Identify three psychological factors that affect physical conditions.
10. Compare the Type A and the Type B behavior patterns.
11. Define well-being and identify three things that contribute to a sense of well-being.
12. Describe five major defense mechanisms.
13. Describe the process of task-oriented coping.
14. Describe the techniques of time management.

WHAT IS ADJUSTMENT?

Learned helplessness is one of the many reactions to stress. Although everyone has an idea of what stress is like, they find it difficult to define the concept. Some researchers define stress as a stimulus (stressor) that threatens us. Others view stress as the body's response to threats from the environment: in that context it isn't all bad. Sometimes stress and anxiety are equated as psychological reactions to stressors.

We define stress as anything that produces demands on us to adjust our behavior. These demands might tax our capacities. Stress includes threats to our well-being, pressures, and other changes which require us to adjust to new situations.

Stress can be caused by psychological or physical demands. For instance, conflict and frustration are examples of psychological demands. Physical demands might include infection, disease, or injury. We focus chiefly on the psychological causes of stress in this chapter.

How we react to the demands of stress in our lives is called adjustment. When we are threatened in some way or when excessive demands are placed upon us, we make changes in our behavior in order to protect ourselves. There are a variety of adjustment techniques, some successful and some not. To keep alert and productive we need some stress (Selye, 1980). But when excessive stress is present, we must do something to reduce it.

Brodsky (1988) described five views of adjustment. The *normality approach* views adjustment statistically to describe the average or typical person. Adjustment can also be viewed as *internal harmony*, or the absence of conflict. The *social competence* model defines adjustment as the ability to effectively interact with other people. The individual who is able to meet the *changing demands* of his or her environment is considered to be well-adjusted. The *self-fulfillment* approach to adjustment assumes internal harmony, social competence, and mastery of changing demands, but goes beyond to the personal goal of the realization of potential (or self-actualization).

Adjustment can be viewed part of a continuum of adaptation. Grasha and Kirschenbaum (1986) identified adaptation as the process we undergo when events in our lives force us to change. They argued that we tend to exhibit three kinds of adaptive responses to stress and demands in our daily life: maladjustment, adjustment, and competence. Maladjustment occurs when we utilize inappropriate abilities to respond to demands placed upon us. Adjustment occurs when we adequately re-spond to stress in our lives. However, when we behave in ways that go beyond just meeting the challenges of life to improving our lives and achieving our goals, we are exhibiting competence. Grasha and Kirschenbaum argued that maladjustment results in poor personal effectiveness and adjustment results in satisfactory personal effectiveness, but excellent personal effectiveness is only achieved through competence.

Critelli (1987) contrasted adjustment and growth as different but related processes. Adjustment involves reacting to the demands placed upon us whereas psychological growth involves acting spontaneously toward the goal of developing a mature personality. Sometimes adjustment is dominant in our lives whereas at other times we are motivated to grow and become a better person.

Adjustment is closely related to personality, as each individual adjusts to stressful demands in stable, unique ways. As in the study of personality, there are several viewpoints that contribute to our understanding of adjustment. The psychoanalytic model of adjustment emphasizes the importance of early experiences and unconscious motives and suggests that adjustment results from the absence of internal conflict. The biological view emphasizes overall physical and psychological health, and the physiological effects of stress on our health. The learning view emphasizes the importance of environmental demands and our learned responses to meet those demands. The humanistic approach emphasizes the role of the self and the tendency toward self-actualization. And the cognitive view emphasizes the role of the mental processes of perception, memory, and thinking in interpreting stress and our adjustment to it. We begin this chapter with a look at the causes of stress, and then examine how we adjust to the stressful demands in our lives.

CAUSES OF STRESS

Stress is unavoidable at some time in most of our lives. Most of us are aware of the negative sources of stress, but often forget about the positive sources. Hans Selye (1976) defined distress as damaging or unpleasant stress, such as the experience of anxiety or fear. We experience distress when we lose a loved one, do poorly on a test, or have a serious illness. Pleasant and satisfying experiences are due to what Selye called eustress. Examples of eustress include getting married, earning a high grade, or achieving success. Selye (1980) argued that stress is important in our lives, and that eustress, particularly, is

Figure 12.2. Social Readjustment Rating Scale

Life Event	Adult Group		Adolescent Group	
	Rank of Life Change Unit	Mean Value of Life Change Unit	Rank of Life Change Unit	Mean Value of Life Change Unit
Death of spouse	1	100	1	69
Divorce	2	73	2	60
Marital separation	3	65	3	55
Jail term	4	63	8	50
Death of a close family member	5	63	4	54
Major personal injury or illness	6	53	6	50
Marriage	7	50	9	50
Fired from work	8	47	7	50
Marital reconciliation	9	45	10	47
Retirement	10	45	11	46
Major change in health of family member	11	44	16	44
Pregnancy	12	40	13	45
Sex difficulties	13	39	5	51
Gain of a new family member	14	39	17	43
Business readjustment	15	39	15	44
Change in financial state	16	38	14	44
Death of a close friend	17	37	12	46
Change to a different line of work	18	36	21	38
Change in number of arguments with spouse	19	35	19	41
Mortgage over $10,000	20	31	18	41
Foreclosure of mortgage or loan	21	30	23	36
Change in responsibilities at work	22	29	20	38
Son or daughter leaving home	23	29	25	34
Trouble with in-laws	24	29	22	36
Outstanding personal achievement	25	28	28	31
Wife begins or stops work	26	26	27	32
Begin or end school	27	26	26	34
Change in living conditions	28	25	24	35
Revision of personal habits	29	24	35	26
Trouble with boss	30	23	33	26
Change in work hours or conditions	31	20	29	30
Change in residence	32	20	30	28
Change in schools	33	20	34	26
Change in recreation	34	19	36	26
Change in church activities	35	19	38	21
Change in social activities	36	18	32	28
Mortgage or loan less than $10,000	37	17	31	28
Change in sleeping habits	38	16	41	18
Change in number of family get-togethers	39	15	37	22
Change in eating habits	40	15	40	18
Vacation	41	13	39	19
Christmas	42	12	42	16
Minor violations of the law	43	11	43	12

Life change units measure stress. Research has shown that a large shift in life change units, positive or negative, can endanger a person's health. Holmes and Rahe (1967) used the scale to measure stress in adults, whereas Ruch and Holmes (1971) used it to examine the level of stress in an adolescent group. The rank of a life change unit is different for each group. Add the value of life change units for each change you have experienced during the past year to determine your level of stress.

necessary to motivate us to lead a full life. We focus on adjusting to the more negative aspects of stress in this chapter.

Life Changes and Daily Hassles

Our daily routine generates many sources of stress. But we also experience stress when we make more major changes in our lives. Here we compare these two types of stress.

Stress and Life Changes. Getting married, receiving a big pay raise, going on vacation, graduating from school, or getting a new job can be major sources of stress for many people. In fact, much of our stress comes from change in our lives which taxes our capacities to adjust our behavior to new situations.

Psychiatrists Thomas Holmes and Richard Rahe (1967) designed the *Social Readjustment Rating Scale (SRRS)* to study the amount and consequences of changes in our life because of stress (see Figure 12.2). They asked subjects to rate various changes in relationships in comparison to the changes caused by marriage (which served as an arbitrary guidepost). Each of the changes was assigned a *life change unit (LCU)* value which indicated the amount of stress it was likely to cause. Holmes and Rahe found that individuals who score over 300 life change units of both positive and negative events within a year have a higher probability of becoming ill.

A number of studies suggest that a large increase in life change units may indicate stress severe enough to endanger health. For example, in a 1974 study, Rahe and his colleagues found that victims who died of heart attacks experienced an average of a 150% increase in LCUs during the six months prior to the attack. Perkins (1982) reported that high LCUs were associated with a range of psychological and physical problems, from heart disease to psychological disorders.

Serious criticisms have been voiced concerning the

life change approach. Monroe (1982) pointed out that this type of research is correlational, and hence there can be other explanations for the data. Perhaps the problems existed prior to the life changes and even contributed to the changes. For instance, an illness might cause poor work habits or marital problems. A number of research studies have reported that negative life changes are much more likely to be associated with stress and illness than are positive life changes (Thoits, 1983). Rice (1987) reported that some researchers do not find any relationship between life change units and illness. Holahan and Moos (1985) suggested that variables such as personality, prior experience, and social support determine whether life change events will contribute to illness. At present, an understanding of the life changes and amount of stress is valuable in predicting difficulties, but the exact association is not completely known.

Daily Hassles.   Richard Lazarus and his colleagues (1985) argued that rather than major life change events, much stress is produced from the daily hassles that routinely annoy us. Lazarus (1981) defined hassles as petty routine annoyances, aggravations, or frustrations such as driving in traffic, preparing meals, the pressure of time, financial problems, communications problems, and making decisions.

According to Lazarus, the major life events themselves do not directly cause stress as much as they create numerous minor hassles that contribute to the overall stress level. For instance, a divorce or death of a spouse, while traumatic, often modifies the life of the sole or surviving spouse in such a way as to make him or her responsible for many details of life the other person had taken care of (making meals, washing clothes, paying bills, shopping, or maintaining the automobile). Lazarus and his colleagues found that the most frequent hassles include: too many responsibilities, maintaining an attractive physical appearance, loneliness, not enough time, and job dissatisfactions. It should be pointed out that Lazarus also found people had daily "uplifts" or satisfactions such as relating well with others, visiting, having enough money for something desired, listening to music, and sex. Some research suggests that these uplifts might be able to counteract some of the effects of stress (Cohen & Hoberman, 1983).

Major Psychological Causes of Stress

Here we review the major causes of stress in our daily lives. Along with physical stresses, such as illness, noise, or temperature extremes, there are three major psychological causes of stress: *pressure, conflict,* and *frustration*.

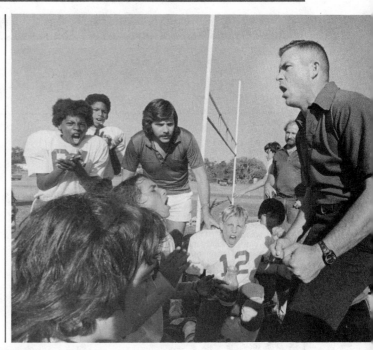

Figure 12.3. Pressure
Excessive demands made upon us by others or ourselves can result in stress.

Pressure.   Pressure occurs when we strive to meet the social and psychological demands we impose on ourselves and others impose on us. Internal pressure results when we attempt to maintain self-esteem by forcing ourselves to achieve higher standards: we study harder in school, try to be more popular with our friends, attempt to solve difficult challenges, and try to look attractive. We may feel pressured because there is not enough time to finish our work, or because we want to take on more than we are capable of effectively handling. Internal pressure is important for self-improvement. With internal pressure, we try harder to achieve more. Without internal pressure, we would not be motivated to improve and try harder. However, when we try too hard because of excessive pressure, the result is unhealthy stress.

External pressure results from the demands other people make on us. We try to please the people who are important in our lives. We may try to lose weight to please or attract a loved one, get high grades to make our parents proud, work hard to impress the boss, or compete to be successful so we will be admired by our friends. External pressure helps us adjust to a social environment. But when others make too many demands on us, or we find their demands too difficult to comply with, the result is stress. Sometimes different pressures act on us at the same time to produce a situation called conflict.

Conflict.   Conflict occurs when we experience incompatible demands or desires (Rice, 1987). In many cases, when the conflict is not resolved, the result is stress. Psychologists generally follow the lead of social psychologist Kurt Lewin (1935), who suggested that conflict can be described by two opposing tendencies: *approach* and *avoidance*.

In approach-approach conflict we are attracted to two equally desirable goals that are incompatible. Choosing one goal means giving up the other one. For instance, we can take psychology *or* biology, but not both. Or we can see only one movie at a time. When we experience approach-approach conflict, we often have difficulty in making a decision. Then after the decision is made, we have doubts about it. This leads to stress which would not have existed if we did not have to make the decision.

In avoidance-avoidance conflict we are faced with two equally undesirable demands that we must choose between. With either choice we are not going to be happy. For example, we might be terrified of water, but we don't want people to laugh at us for not swimming. Because the outcome will be negative, we are bound to experience stress. Our objective is to choose the alternative which is less likely to be stressful. There is a strong tendency for us to try to escape avoidance-avoidance

conflicts. For example, we might forget to bring a bathing suit to the swim party so that we can put off making a decision. Of course, this also creates its own type of stress.

In approach-avoidance conflicts we are faced with a single goal that has positive and negative aspects. We might really want a new car, but realize it will be too expensive. We really want to run for an office in student government, but we are afraid of the responsibility. In this type of conflict, we may try an alternative solution before we make the move, being aware that the consequences are not all positive. Or we may remain undecided and let the opportunity slip away.

Sometimes we experience conflict over two or more goals, both of which have positive and negative aspects. This situation is called a multiple approach-avoidance conflict (or double approach-avoidance conflict when only two goals are involved). For example, perhaps your family is considering a vacation, and the ideal destination (approach) is extremely expensive (avoidance) and a second choice would not be as much fun (avoidance) but would be more affordable (approach). Typically, we must make choices among several alternatives, all pos-

Figure 12.4. Conflict

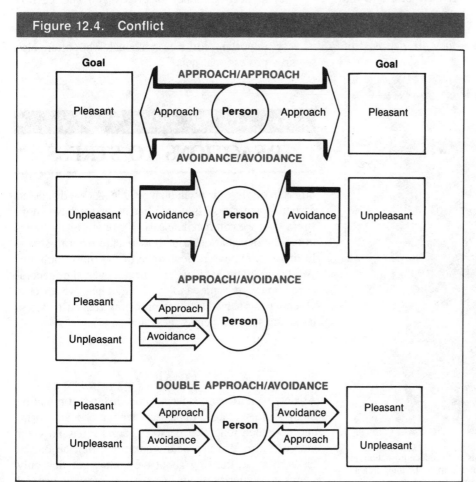

Conflict occurs, according to Lewin, when a person experiences demands or desires which are incompatible with each other. In approach-approach conflict, we are attracted to two equally desirable goals. In avoidance-avoidance conflict, we must choose between two equally undesirable demands. In approach-avoidance conflict, we have one goal that has positive and negative aspects. And in double approach-avoidance conflict we experience two or more goals both of which have positive and negative aspects.

sessing positive and negative features. As you can well imagine, almost anything we do will result in some stress. Conflict situations often produce frustration.

Frustration. Frustration occurs when a person is prevented from reaching a goal (Rice, 1987). When we experience frustration, we must either give up the goal or find another way to attain it. In either case, stress is produced. Coleman and his colleagues (1987) described some of the most common types of frustrations: delays, daily hassles, lack of resources, losses, and failure.

1. *Time Delays.* We live in a society where time is important, and we get upset when we are delayed. People are frustrated when they must wait in line at a store, when a phone number is busy, or when someone is late.

2. *Daily hassles.* As we discussed above, Lazarus and colleagues (1985) have identified numerous daily hassles, or routine irritations and aggravations that contribute to stress, often because they cause frustration. For instance, dropping an egg, misplacing a wallet, forgetting an appointment, or spraining an ankle all produce frustration, and ultimately increase stress level.

3. *Lack of resources.* Most people do not have enough money to purchase everything they desire. They also lack the ability always to perform their best and the capability always to succeed in everything they try.

4. *Losses.* When people lose something important, it frustrates them because it means they are deprived of

goals. If they lose money or possessions, they may not be able to purchase things that they desire. If they lose someone they love, they are deprived of the future of a relationship.

5. *Failure.* Failure frustrates people. Sometimes they fail to win, to get a high grade on a test, or to impress other people. Sometimes they feel as though they have failed, even when they do better than expected, because they have such high expectations for themselves. Then their failures may produce guilt.

Post-traumatic Stress Disorder. The pressures, conflicts, and frustrations we have discussed so far, while capable of contributing to severe stress, have mainly been common events that occur in our daily lives. Sometimes, however, people encounter extraordinary events, such as military combat, rape, earthquakes, assault, or an accident or disaster. People who experience severe distressing events such as these may develop post-traumatic stress disorder, which is characterized by repeatedly remembering the traumatic event, avoidance of anything associated with it, and arousal (DSM-III-R, 1987). They tend to have disruptions of sleep habits, and often become irritable and aggressive. The re-experiencing symptoms usually develop soon after the event, but may be delayed months or even years. The reaction may be mild, but is often severe, and disrupts the individual's entire life. Support from family and friends is very important for the individual who often also requires professional help.

Figure 12.5. Frustration
Many factors may block a person's goals and produce frustration and stress. They range from the loss of a relationship, to spraining an ankle in a championship game, to dropping an egg on the floor.

REACTIONS TO STRESS

Stress in our lives is often unavoidable. As we discussed earlier, some stress is good, but often we have more stress than we can handle easily. There are many topics in psychology that describe how people react to stress. In this section, we review some of the most common. We begin with anxiety, and next cover the general adaptation syndrome and burnout. Then we discuss several personal adjustment problems related to stress including learned helplessness and shyness.

Anxiety

Anxiety is a difficult concept to understand. It might be thought of as a vague unpleasant feeling of fear, worry, and apprehension. The person generally has no clear idea of the real cause of the anxiety. Often he or she tends to avoid thinking about the fears since that only seems to intensify them. Anxiety is often a general emotional response to stress. It is a fear of the demands placed upon the individual when the individual doesn't know what the demands actually are.

Anxiety is usually measured by examining self-reports, observing behavior, and recording physiological activity. Self-report responses include items such as feelings of uneasiness, impulses to escape, inability to concentrate, apprehension, vague fears, and tensions. Behavioral responses include avoidance, escape, and impairment in speech, coordination, and mental activities. Physiological measurement focuses on the sympathetic nervous system, and includes responses such as increased blood pressure, breathing and heart rate, sweating, and stomach distress (Grasha & Kirschenbaum, 1986).

Psychologists distinguish between trait and situation anxiety. Trait anxiety is anxiety which is long-lasting and a relatively stable personality characteristic. Some people are more anxious in general than others. A useful diagnostic tool in measuring trait anxiety is the 1953 Taylor Manifest Anxiety Scale. Situation anxiety is associated with a particular situation or event. For

Figure 12.6. Situation Anxiety
When under stress, people often experience anxiety. This condition might include feelings of uneasiness, inability to concentrate, avoidance responses, and increases in breathing and heart rate.

example, most people would be anxious when skydiving for the first time, regardless of their general overall anxiety level.

Anxiety can also be thought of as an emotion with important motivational consequences. A psychologically or physically painful experience is often associated with particular cues. A later presentation of these cues may lead to anxiety and an attempt to avoid any further encounter with them. A child who has been bitten by a dog may become anxious when he comes into contact with any dog. Since the anxiety makes him avoid all dogs, he may never give himself a chance to learn that dogs can be friendly.

Children experience anxiety mainly about such external events as punishment, physical harm, withdrawal of parental affection, and sudden intense changes in sensory conditions (such as sirens, the dark, and thunder). Anxiety in adults depends less on immediate physical threat than on their general security and self-concept, interpersonal relations, social expectations, and task completion (Grasha & Kirschenbaum, 1986).

It would not be in our best interest to be free of anxiety completely, since many things that arouse our anxiety are indeed dangerous (Brodsky, 1988). The uneasiness we feel while driving in heavy traffic in an unfamiliar city keeps us alert for the unexpected. But anxiety demands our undivided attention, and too much of it will impair performance that requires attention to other things. In the next sections, we focus on the physical consequences of stress and anxiety.

General Adaptation Syndrome

Obviously our emotions, anxiety, and stress affect our behavior and performance. But they also play a central role in the preservation of good health, and are critical factors in our survival of serious injuries and illnesses. Hans Selye (1976) theorized that our emotional reactions to stress produce important physiological changes. These changes can even result in a major illness that develops and progresses independently of the initial cause of the stress.

Selye referred to the pattern in which people respond to stress as the general adaptation syndrome (GAS). He believed that the response to stress is the same whether the stress is an illness, infection, physical danger, anxiety, psychological threat, or a change in life-style. The GAS consists of three distinct stages: the *alarm reaction*, the *stage of resistance*, and the *stage of exhaustion*.

The Alarm Reaction. The alarm reaction is the immediate response to stress. The body prepares for an emergency situation by increasing alertness and activating the sympathetic nervous system. The alarm reaction forces the individual to realize that stress is being

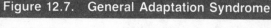

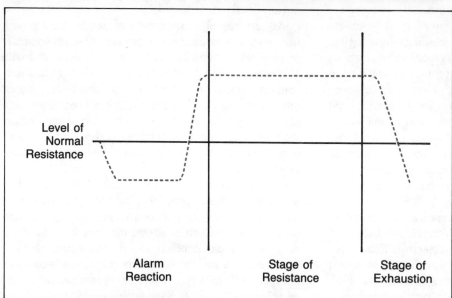

| Alarm | Stage of | Stage of |
| Reaction | Resistance | Exhaustion |

Selye noted that there is a pattern to the way in which people respond to stress. The general adaptation syndrome consists of the alarm reaction, stage of resistance, and stage of exhaustion.

experienced. Heart rate and blood pressure increase, adrenaline is released, digestion slows, and blood moves away from the skin. If there is a real physical danger, the alarm reaction is extremely useful. When the danger is past, the alarm subsides and the person can then relax.

However, sometimes the stresses of modern life do not pass, but remain with us day in and day out. We must always prepare for the next test or the next encounter with our employer. Our parents, friends, children, employers, classmates, and coworkers continue to place demands on us. And so the body responds by entering the second stage.

The Stage of Resistance.   When stress is prolonged, the body eventually builds a resistance to the effects of stress. According to Selye, people in the stage of resistance believe that they have overcome the negative consequences of stress and can handle the situation adequately. But the stress is still there and is still having negative consequences on the body. The body is in high gear and reacting as if an emergency is present. In other words, even though the person appears normal on the outside, there is an inner turmoil. If the stress continues, the individual enters the third stage, exhaustion.

The Stage of Exhaustion.   As the body continues to resist the stress, it begins to deplete its energy resources and eventually becomes exhausted. When the stage of exhaustion occurs, stress can even lead to ultimate death.

The exhaustion of the body's resources due to stress might account for *voodoo death*. Walter Cannon (1957) studied voodoo death, where people die as a result of having a curse placed on them. He concluded that rather than magic, death comes from exhaustion of the body's

resources. Because people believe they will die of the curse, their stress causes the sympathetic nervous system to operate so fast and furiously that they become exhausted.

Selye has made a fairly convincing case for the idea that the causes of stress are not as important as the body's response to it. He has shown how stress can play an important role in diseases such as asthma, diabetes, arthritis, colitis, allergies, and ulcers. However, research by others has indicated that different stressors can have different effects on the body. Mikhail (1981) argued that different people respond differently to stress and thus Selye's model is too narrow to be applied to everyone. Cognitive interpretation of a stressful situation can vary considerably from one person to the next. Other researchers are also beginning to study the consequences of long-term stress.

Burnout

We live in a society that constantly places demands on us. While most of us feel that we are able to deal with stress adequately, many people are not aware that they are burning energy too fast. Burnout is the depletion of our physical and mental resources. It occurs when we have more energy going out than we do coming in. Burnout is a major concern of mental health professionals.

Unfortunately, it's the "good guys" who often experience burnout. The achiever who takes on extra assignments, the executive who works extra hours, the student who takes extra courses, the teacher who gives extra help to students, and the police officer who logs extra time are all prime candidates for burnout. Because that type of person is hardworking, others take advantage of him or her and the work load increases; so he or she continues to work hard and take on even more responsibility. Then, as we noted in the general adaptation syndrome, stress persists until exhaustion or burnout occurs.

Symptoms of Burnout. In his 1980 book, *Burnout*, Herbert Freudenberger described some of the major symptoms: *Exhaustion*. The person feels tired and fatigued; he or she has exhausted his source of energy. *Detachment*. The person will often use detachment as a protective device. This is true especially in the helping professions where personal interaction on a continuous basis can be exhausting. *Boredom*. The person begins to question the value of activities and friendships; he or she becomes bored with life. *Impatience*. The person grows increasingly impatient with others who can't keep up; he or she becomes irritable with other people. *Sense of omnipotence*. The feeling that no one else can do it is common in burnout victims. They believe they must attend to all the details themselves. *Feeling unappreciated*. Burnout victims feel that other people don't appreciate all their hard work and effort. *Psychophysiological problems*. The stress eventually begins to show up in symptoms such as headaches, ulcers, asthma, or heart problems. Not everyone will show all of these symptoms, but they are indicative that burnout could be developing.

Occupation and Burnout. While burnout can occur to anyone in any situation, certain occupations are more likely to produce it. Christina Maslach has investigated burnout in caring professionals: nurses, teachers, counselors, doctors, therapists, police, and social workers. She described several occupational and demographic sources of burnout in her 1982 book, *Burnout: The Cost of Caring*. People in the helping professions often have too much contact with people. The doctor, social worker, or counselor might be seeing too many patients to provide the individualized care that they need.

Many times, people in these occupations feel they do not have control over their job. Supervisors tell them exactly what to do. They must follow the rules, with the result that frustration develops (Veninga & Spadley, 1981). A recent survey of mental health workers (Shinn & colleagues, 1984) found that the most common source of stress (47%) was job design (such as a high caseload). Many (44%) complained that administrators were incompetent or didn't give them the recognition they deserved. One third of the workers felt unable to meet their own high expectations and 23% cited their clients as sources of stress.

Overall, men and women experience burnout about equally (Maslach, 1982). Age is an important factor,

---

BIOGRAPHICAL ☆ HIGHLIGHT ☆

HANS SELYE

Hans Selye was born in Vienna in 1907. As early as his second year of medical school (1926), he began developing his now famous theory of the influence of stress on people's ability to cope with and adapt to the pressures of injury and disease. He discovered that patients with a variety of ailments manifested many similar symptoms, which he ultimately attributed to their body's efforts to respond to the stresses of being ill. He called this collection of symptoms—this separate stress disease—stress syndrome, or the general adaptation syndrome (GAS).

He spent a lifetime in continuing research on GAS and wrote some 30 books and more than 1,500 articles on stress and related problems, including *Stress Without Distress* (1974) and *The Stress of Life* (1976). So impressive have his findings and theories been that some authorities refer to him as "the Einstein of medicine."

A physician and endocrinologist with many honorary degrees for his pioneering contributions to science, Selye also served as a professor and director of the Institute of Experimental Medicine and Surgery at the University of Montreal. More than anyone else, Selye has demonstrated the role of emotional responses in causing or combating much of the wear and tear experienced by human beings throughout their lives. He died in 1982 in Montreal, where he had spent 50 years studying the causes and consequences of stress.

Figure 12.8. Stress and Performance
Air-traffic controllers are under constant stress because they cannot predict when a problem will develop. When too many demands are placed on people, they may not deliver peak performance.

Stress and Performance

We usually assume that it's important to reduce stress to prevent burnout. It is important to note that while burnout is the more commonly discussed extreme of stress, the opposite might also occur. Rustout is defined as the situation when the demands placed on the individual are much less than the capacity of the individual. Rustout can be just as bad as burnout.

In chapter 9, "Motivation," we discussed the theory of optimal arousal, which states that performance is best when the arousal level is medium. This concept has been applied by Walter Gmelch in his 1982 book, *Beyond Stress to Effective Management*. Stress is a fact of life, and it is important to learn how to use stress constructively to improve performance. We now look at Gmelch's ideas for optimizing performance through stress.

The relationship between stress and performance can be divided into several sections. First is the perceived ability of an individual to accomplish a task. Next is the actual work to be accomplished. How difficult is the work, and how much is required? Then we need to look at the individual's actual capacity to perform the assigned work. For example, if your capacity is too low for the work you're trying to accomplish, then you will experience burnout. If your capacity equals your work, you will experience peak performance. And if your capacity is greater than your work, you will experience rustout.

How can you utilize the concept of stress to maintain high performance? Gmelch gives several suggestions. If you are experiencing rustout (work is less than capacity), then you need to take risks, try new techniques, meet new people, and stay alert. In other words, you need to do whatever is necessary to increase stress or arousal to its optimum level.

If you are at peak performance (work is equal to capacity), you need to continue to remain in control. You should practice time-management skills, establish goals, and become aware of your stress points. In other words, you still have to work actively to keep performance at its peak level. If you don't, rustout or burnout will most likely result.

If you are experiencing burnout (work is greater than capacity), you need to reduce stress in order to optimize performance. You should learn the causes of your stress, and take steps to reduce it. You need to learn to say no to additional requests and delegate responsibility to others. You should learn time management skills, and practice dividing up large projects into smaller ones. The more you become aware of the relationship between stress and performance, the more you can make stress work for you.

THOUGHT QUESTIONS

1. What is the relationship between stress and performance?
2. Evaluate your work load compared to your capacity. Are you experiencing rustout, peak performance, or burnout?
3. Do people experience only one of these conditions, or could they experience different conditions in different endeavors, or at different times?

Figure 12.9. Burnout
When people experience too much stress for too long, they may experience burnout. This condition is especially prevalent in the helping professions. To help prevent burnout, set realistic goals and learn to relax.

Personal Adjustment Problems

Stress causes us to adjust. Most of us are able to cope with stress most of the time but sometimes we have more difficulty than usual in adjusting.

While most of us do not experience severe enough long-term stress to produce burnout, we usually experience some level of continuous stress. How much stress we experience at any one particular time depends upon a number of variables which include the stressors in our lives and our personality characteristics and coping abilities (Kessler & colleagues, 1985).

The number and severity of the stressors in our lives influence the degree of stress that we experience. In general, the more events that produce stress and the severity of each one, the more stress we have. O'Brien (1981) pointed out that stress is less when we are able to predict it. For example, if you were aware that an examination was scheduled for tomorrow, you should feel less anxiety than if you were surprised when you arrived at class. People who believe they have control over the situation experience less stress than those who don't have this perceived control (Phares, 1988).

Individual Differences in Reactions to Stress. Our personality affects how well we are able to handle stress. Kobasa (1982) has identified the hardy personality style of handling stress well. Characteristics of hardiness include commitment, challenge, and control. *Commitment* is characterized by a sense of purpose in life and a belief in what we are doing. *Challenge* involves being flexible and having a positive attitude toward the demands that are made on us. *Control* is the belief that we are responsible for ourselves, and can handle stressful situations. Depue and Monroe (1986) argued that racial differences exist in perceiving the degree of stress. For instance, in one study they found that minorities indicated starting work or reducing work time are stressful, whereas whites felt the birth of a child or going to jail was stressful.

Social support is also an important variable in how we react to stress. Cohen and Wills (1985) reported that people who have a social support system of family and friends are able to deal with stressful events better than those who don't. Our family and friends can provide assistance (financial or personal), can help us make properly informed decisions, and can support us emotionally when we are in need of a buffer from our stress. People with an internal locus of control tend to more effectively use social support to buffer stress (Fusilier & colleagues, 1987). Holahan and Moos (1985) reported that men tended to be more independent and self-confident when dealing with stress, whereas women tended to utilize family members as a support system. Marriage apparently does not alleviate stress for students in academic settings. For example, Staats (1983)

with young people burning out more than older people. The longer you work at something, the more likely it is that you adapt to it, or else go on to something else. Single people experience burnout more frequently than married people, perhaps because they don't have the same opportunity as married people to talk things out. People with a college degree but no postgraduate education seem to experience the highest levels of burnout, perhaps because they enter their professions in the middle, where they must deal constantly with problems above and below them in the hierarchy.

Solutions to Burnout. A number of remedies have been suggested to combat burnout. For instance, it's important to set realistic goals that are manageable and yet still challenging. Know your limits and don't continue to accept additional responsibilities beyond them. It's important to escape once in a while. Take a break, relax, and enjoy yourself before you tackle the job again. It's important not to become too involved emotionally with other people. Try to help others as much as possible, but try to remain professional. Experts now realize that social support groups are important aids in relieving tension in the helping professions. Whether in informal coffee hours or professional conferences, talking to others with similar responsibilities helps us feel better. And finally, many people in the helping professions are learning techniques of relaxation to help them deal with potential burnout.

Figure 12.10. Shyness
Zimbardo (1977) reported that more than 80% of people experience shyness at some time in their lives. It can involve a great deal of personal stress. Realizing that others are also shy is one step toward dealing with this problem.

reported that marriage did not affect the source of stress that college students tend to experience (which included not enough money, doing poorly on tests, and poor grades). Learning how to effectively use the resources that are available to us is important in handling the stress in our lives.

Learned Helplessness. As we discussed in our opening story, Martin Seligman (1975) proposed a theory to explain why some people seem to give up and become helpless. He believed that when people are in a situation in which there is no control, they eventually learn that any response they make will not affect any particular outcome. Behaviorally, they will stop responding. Cognitively, they will believe that responding is useless. Emotionally, they will experience anxiety and depression. Seligman suggested that learned helplessness is a serious problem in our society because, when ignored, it could develop into depression.

Seligman's original theory was based largely on animal studies, and did not predict human depression as well as it might. So he reformulated it to take the complexity of people into account (Peterson & Seligman, 1985). The reformulated theory of learned helplessness suggests that people have a need to believe that they have control over their lives. In particular, how do they answer the question "why?" when they encounter stressful events. For example, assume that you failed a test. You could attribute the failure to yourself (internal explanation) or to the situation (external explanation). You could assume the cause is permanent (stable) or temporary (unstable). For example, a stable cause might be low intelligence and an unstable cause might be the flu. And you could believe this situation is unique (specific) or part of a general pattern (global). Research suggests that people who are most likely to eventually

become depressed tend to use internal, stable, and global explanations for a failure. It is their fault, it is always their fault, and everything they attempt they fail. Obviously, if the event is truly uncontrollable, their behavior is not going to make a difference. But this one event may then be generalized to situations where the individual does have control and can contribute to a general feeling of helplessness.

Seligman suggests that parents sometimes encourage learned helplessness in children by not giving them more responsibility in making personal decisions. Teachers might encourage learned helplessness in students by not giving them more freedom in choosing assignments or learning from mistakes. As long as we tell others what to do, they learn that they have no control over the situation.

How can learned helplessness be prevented or treated? Seligman suggested that the basic problem in learned helplessness is that people expect that responding will not work. Therefore, they must be convinced that they do have some control over the situation. Parents can help children by giving them more responsibility. For example, let them choose to wear the red or the green jacket. Children will then feel they are important in making their own decisions. Teachers can let students experience mistakes. The most important factor is to convince people that they do make a difference. This concept is similar to Rotter's internal locus of control. When we feel we can control our life, we are much more capable of dealing with stress and anxiety.

Shyness. Shyness is a problem for many people and can involve a great deal of stress. Philip Zimbardo spent a number of years studying shyness and reported some interesting findings in his 1977 book, *Shyness.* He stated that shyness is the awareness of our inability to act even when we want to and know how. Sometimes shyness is a fear of negative evaluation from ourselves as well as others. When we are shy, we feel uncomfortable with other people. Shyness can create problems in meeting new people, making friends, standing up for our rights, and enjoying ourselves.

Zimbardo surveyed nearly 5,000 people and found shyness to be much more prevalent than one might expect. More than 80% of those surveyed reported being shy at some point in their life, and over 40% indicated that they were presently shy. The majority of people surveyed agreed that shyness produced negative consequences. Jones and Carpenter (1986) reported that shy people tend to experience loneliness and dissatisfaction with social relationships.

Shy people view shyness differently than people who are not shy. They tend to see their shyness as a personality trait that is always with them. People who are not shy tend to view shyness as a reaction that might occur in specific situations, but not as something inherent in personality. Some researchers believe shyness might be inherited, whereas others prefer to emphasize the role of learning. For instance, people who become shy might have overreacted at one time to events in which they were embarrassed or where others made fun of them. In order to prevent it from happening again, they withdrew from social situations (Phillips, 1981). What we do know is that shyness often occurs at an early age and is sometimes encouraged by society.

Zimbardo (1986) has developed a clinic to help shy students, but his ideas are appropriate for anyone with shyness. First, we should choose an atmosphere of nonevaluation where others will not be judging us and we feel confident. Second, we should realize that many other people are shy and that it is a perfectly normal experience. And third, we must try to develop assertiveness in interactions with others.

HEALTH PSYCHOLOGY

The field of health psychology is concerned with understanding the psychological influences on people's state of health, including how they stay healthy, why they become ill, and how their behavior relates to their state of health (Taylor, 1986). Health psychologists focus on a number of specific topics, including the promotion of health, the role of psychological factors in illness, the management of stress, and the improvement of health care and health care policy. In this section, we discuss the role of psychological factors on physical disorders,

Type A behavior pattern and health, and the promotion of health.

It has been estimated that up to 75% of all physician visits are motivated by stress-related problems (Charlesworth & Nathan, 1982). Health psychologists are studying the role of stress in various physical conditions such as hypertension and coronary heart disease; disorders of the immune system (such as AIDS), perhaps through endocrine reactions (Martin, 1987); and the possible relationship between stress and the course of cancer. Ultimately this information will allow us to modify stress-related behaviors in an approach called behavioral medicine.

Psychological Effects on Physical Conditions

The 1987 revision of the *Diagnostic and Statistical Manual of Mental Disorders (DSM-III-R)* states that psychological factors affecting physical condition include those that contribute to the initiation or aggravation of a specific physical condition (we discuss DSM-III-R in chapter 13, "Abnormal Psychology"). In the past, terms such as psychosomatic illness and psychophysiological disorder have been used. Although psychological and environmental stressors can affect physical conditions, they may also be due to strictly physiological causes.

DSM-III-R (1987) provides a listing of these conditions. They include obesity, tension and migraine headache, painful menstruation, acne, asthma, ulcers, cardiospasm, nausea, and colitis. Taylor (1986) described a number of the most extensively researched conditions, including ulcers, headaches, asthma, hypertension, and coronary heart disease.

Ulcers are holes in the lining of the stomach or duodenum. They are produced by excessive gastric-acid secretions from digestion processes which might be caused by stress, hostility, anxiety, and uncontrollable events (Bachrach, 1982). The autonomic nervous system then causes a reduction of blood to the protective mucus layer of the stomach and an increase in the secretion of acid. Some research suggests that people susceptible to ulcers may not show the appropriate physiological responsiveness to stress (Taylor & colleagues, 1982). Ulcers are generally treated through diet, medication, and relaxation techniques.

Migraine headache is the most common psychophysiological disorder with up to 10% of the population afflicted. The migraine headache is caused by arteries under the scalp of the head which become dilated and press on the pain-sensitive nerves in the area. It has been theorized that migraine headache sufferers have scalp arteries that are extremely sensitive to autonomic nervous system activity. Migraine headaches are often treated with stress reduction techniques, such as biofeedback and relaxation (Friedman, 1982).

Asthma is a problem characterized by increased responsiveness of the respiratory tract which results in the narrowing of the airways, thus causing breathing difficulties. Currently, it is believed that bronchial asthma is thought to be caused strictly by physiological factors, and that psychological and social stress are not direct causes (Alexander, 1981). However, psychological stress or emotional reactions such as fear, anger, or frustration can aggravate an asthmatic condition and increase its severity. Research indicates that the person with asthma can be helped by learning stress management techniques (Alexander, 1981).

Cardiovascular disorders include hypertension (high blood pressure) and coronary heart disease (CHD). Hypertension is an increase in blood pressure above acceptable levels (usually above systolic pressure of 160 and diastolic pressure of 120). The majority of cases of hypertension cannot be attributed to a specific organic cause, however, stress and anxiety appear to be important aggravating factors. Hypertensives seem to show excessive blood pressure reaction to stressful events. Sympathetic nervous system activity leads to sharp increases in blood pressure during stress, and then the blood pressure declines to normal. However, continued sympathetic arousal and constriction of the arteries may lead to hypertension.

Coronary heart disease (CHD) is the cause of nearly half of all deaths in the United States. It refers to any condition that causes a narrowing of the coronary arteries. A variety of risk factors are linked to CHD, including hypertension, obesity, diabetes, heredity, high-fat diet, high levels of cholesterol, smoking, inactivity, Type A behavior, and stress. In fact, stress is strongly implicated in half of the cases of CHD (American Heart Association, 1984). We discuss the relationship of stress and the Type A behavior pattern to coronary heart disease in the next section.

Type A Behavior

Do you like to do everything quickly? Have you even found yourself completing someone's sentence in order to speed the conversation along? Do you hate to wait in lines? Are you always trying to do several things at the same time? Are you competitive? Are you impatient with others who cannot keep up with you? Are you hard-driving? If you answer these questions with a yes, you may be a Type A behavior person.

Physicians Meyer Friedman and Ray Rosenman have investigated the long-term effects of stress-producing behavior patterns on heart disease. For 20 years they have been studying a personality pattern of behavior that causes stress. In 1974 they published a popular book entitled *Type A Behavior and Your Heart*, in which they summarized many of their research findings.

Type A behavior describes a particular type of personality. According to Friedman and Rosenman, Type A people tend to be competitive, aggressive, hard-driving individuals who are constantly under excessive stress. Type A people are impatient with others who cannot keep up with them. They compete unendingly; when there's no one to compete with, they race against time. Type A people hate delays and often they do several things at once (like read the mail while eating lunch). Type A individuals work extra hard to increase the level of their achievement. They are under stress *constantly*.

Type B behavior describes a different personality type. Sometimes Type B people are aggressive, competitive, impatient, and hardworking. But they also relax more. Type B people react to environmental demands and work hard when it is required. But they are not always in such a state of urgency that they experience constant stress.

Research on Type A and Type B people has shown that often Type A people are significantly more likely to develop coronary heart disease as they grow older. Type A and B individuals can be identified through a structured interview procedure developed by Rosenman and his colleagues which focuses on competitiveness, deadlines, ambitiousness, impatience, aggressiveness, and hostility. There are also several questionnaires available, including the *Jenkins Activity Survey* and the *Framingham Type A Scale* (Chesney & colleagues, 1981).

Research has shown that Type A people are especially affected by negative sources of stress over which they have no control (Carver & Humphries, 1982). They continue to respond to stress as if they had control, even if it is not possible for them to secure it. Matthews (1982) suggested that differences between Type A and Type B individuals become pronounced in situations that are competitive, require careful, slow performance, and are largely uncontrollable. Type A people can sometimes be more effective than Type B people when there are distracting conditions such as background noise because they are better able to attend to both the work at hand and the distraction and still accomplish the task.

Mark Pittner and his colleagues reported (1983) that Type A individuals showed higher blood pressure rates when exposed to an aversive stimulus, even when the subjects had no control over such stimulus. Kahn and colleagues (1980) suggested that Type A behavior might be the result of greater physiological reactions to stress rather than a cause of the reactions. They found, for instance, that Type A people undergoing bypass surgery showed a greater increase in blood pressure than did

Figure 12.11.   Type A Behavior
Friedman and Rosenman (1974) describe the Type A person as being a competitive, hard-driving individual who is constantly under stress. Type A behavior is associated with an increased risk of heart attacks.

Type B people, even though they were all unconscious.

Type A people show more sympathetic nervous system activity and more norepinephrine secretion than Type B people. Norepinephrine is a hormone that works with the sympathetic nervous system to prepare the body for emergency situations; high levels apparently contribute to CHD.

Recently it has been discovered that not all characteristics of Type A behavior contribute to an increased risk of heart disease (Wright, 1988). One line of research argues that hostility (stemming from a belief that people are generally selfish and mean and therefore cannot be trusted) is the core characteristic of Type A behavior that leads to CHD (Williams & colleagues, 1984). Dembroski and colleagues (1985) argued that an aggressive personality contributes to heart disease, but not other Type A characteristics, such as doing things quickly, being ambitious, or working hard. Spielberger and London (1982) found that people who react with anger to minor irritations are most likely to develop heart disease, while Spielberger and colleagues (1985) found that people who suppress anger are more likely to have hypertension. They developed the Anger-In Scale to measure the tendency to suppress anger. This scale

contains items such as "I keep things in" and "I am angrier than I am willing to admit."

Logan Wright (1988) recently reviewed the research on identifying the specific components of the Type A behavior pattern that significantly contribute to CHD. Originally he proposed a cluster of characteristics that included time urgency (concern with moment-to-moment time), chronic activation (always remaining active), and multiphasic activity (doing two or more things at the same time). After analyzing research data, Wright suggested that there are several independent factors that can contribute to heart disease including heredity, self-imposed non-Type A risk (smoking, diet), anger-in (tendency to suppress anger), anger-out with time urgency and chronic activations, and the traditional Type A pattern first identified by Rosenman and Friedman. Wright (1988) concluded that anger-in was the best predictor of CHD, followed by a combination of anger-out (expressing anger and irritability readily) and time urgency/chronic activation. Future research will continue to identify the specific characteristics and mechanisms that show a relationship between Type A behavior and coronary heart disease.

Friedman and Rosenman estimate that about 50% of

the adult white males in this country are Type A. Significantly fewer women exhibit Type A behavior, but as more women enter the competitive job market, it is likely that more of them will also become Type A. Research suggests that people can learn to modify their life-style and perhaps change from Type A to Type B, but more research is needed on ways to help people modify their behavior to avoid unnecessary coronary heart disease.

Adjustment and Well-being

Everyone would prefer to be well-adjusted and happy, but too often people experience so much stress that they are not as happy as they would like to be. Well-being may be defined as a subjective, positive, emotional state with general life satisfaction (Diener, 1984). It involves the way the individual feels about himself, and is due to achievement of goals in life. The successfully adjusted person is pleased with his or her life (Schwartz & Clore, 1983). In other words, the person is happy.

Staats (1983) reported that college students were generally happy if they were getting good grades, making friends, achieving goals, having enough money, and studying with good professors. Stassen and Staats (1988) found the American students were slightly happier and more satisfied than Canadian students. Both groups reported greatest satisfaction with health and lowest satisfaction with financial security. These students generally reflected the level of satisfaction found in the general population (Diener, 1984).

The most common contributors to a sense of well-being include family life, standard of living, work, marriage, and financial security. Diener (1984) reported that happy people tend to have high esteem, a satisfying love relationship, a meaningful religious faith, and are socially active. Maslow (1970) identified the characteristics of the self-actualized person in his humanistic approach (see chapter 11, "Personality"). Many of those characteristics are motives for the happy, well-adjusted individual.

Brodsky (1988) identified several characteristics of the person who is striving toward well-being. They include a strong positive affect, substantial satisfaction with life, and a reconciliation of values with realities of society. This person makes deliberate choices, perceives self-control, and takes some risks to obtain goals. In addition, the well-adjusted person is a unique person and has a good self-image. Future work in health psychology and adjustment will continue to explore adjustment and well-being, with the goal of helping more individuals reach this state of existence.

ADJUSTMENT TECHNIQUES

Everyone experiences stress in coping with the demands of daily living. People can give in to stress and become helpless, or they can adjust and learn techniques for confronting their problems head-on. Lazarus (1980) defined coping as the adjustment people make to stress. Coping involves solving the problems that cause stress and managing the emotions that accompany stress. In this section, we review various techniques that we use to adjust to stress. Some of them are clearly more effective than others. One of the most common coping techniques is the use of defense mechanisms.

Defense Mechanisms

Defense mechanisms are psychological techniques (first described by Freud in 1894)) with which we try to protect ourselves from anxiety and stress, to resolve conflicts within ourselves, and to preserve our self-esteem. Defense mechanisms have some useful functions, as described by Brodsky (1988). They help to protect us from very painful conflicts, which might otherwise cause so much stress that we would be overwhelmed. They allow us to maintain a positive self-evaluation, which can give us confidence. They allow us to deal effectively with short-term stress.

Defense mechanisms also have some negative aspects. They involve self-deception and ultimately prevent us from dealing with stress in an effective manner. They help us avoid the stress temporarily, but the stress is still there, and often manifests itself more intensely at a later time. We all use defense mechanisms, and as long as we don't use too many of them too often, they are not seriously harmful.

Repression. In repression painful memories and unacceptable thoughts and motives are conveniently forgotten or *repressed* so that they will not have to be dealt with. The individual unconsciously expends a great deal of emotional energy to keep them in the unconscious. We mentioned repression when we discussed theories of memory. An example of repression is the way we conveniently forget we have a dental appointment because we are fearful of the visit. A related defense mechanism is suppression, in which the individual consciously avoids thinking about something as a way of dealing with stressful situations.

Projection. In projection a person attributes her unacceptable characteristics or motives to others instead of herself. For example, the messy person might complain about the slob she has for a roommate. Or someone

Figure 12.12. Defense Mechanism of Fantasy
Freud suggested that defense mechanisms are used to avoid anxiety and conflict. In fantasy, a person daydreams that all problems are solved and everything is ideal.

who hates himself is convinced that others treat him badly because they hate him.

Fantasy. In fantasy a person escapes from stress and anxiety by daydreaming that everything is perfect and all the problems are gone. Everyone daydreams once in a while, and it is a good relaxation technique. We only have to worry when we have trouble separating fantasy from reality.

Regression. In regression a person retreats to an earlier, more immature, form of behavior. If we were hammering a nail and hit our thumb instead, we might yell and hop around the floor the way a young child would. Or when we are having a tense argument, we might break down and cry. The result is the stress is gone temporarily.

Compensation. The technique of compensation can help us deal with feelings of inadequacy by developing or focusing on a desirable characteristic. For example, if we are poor in mathematics, we might study extremely hard in English and do an outstanding job. Often compensatory behaviors are not entirely effective since they do not eliminate the basic weakness.

Rationalization. In rationalization the person makes up logical excuses to justify behavior rather than exposing the true motives. For example, if we do poorly on a test, we might tell others that our notes were stolen, or we were sick, rather than admit the truth that we didn't study. Of course if we really were sick, we would not be rationalizing.

Displacement. In displacement, we direct our aggression and hostility toward a person or object other than the one it should be directed toward. For example, if we have a difficult day at school, we might come home and yell at family members (who had nothing to do with our difficulties).

Sublimation. In sublimation the person redirects socially undesirable urges into socially acceptable behavior. A person who enjoys violence might become a police officer. A person who would like to beat up others might become a boxer. Or a person with strong sexual urges might become an artist who paints nude portraits.

Reaction Formation. In reaction formation a person masks an unconsciously distressing or unacceptable trait by assuming an opposite attitude behavior. For example, people who are basically shy or cowardly may act in forceful or even heroic ways to hide their fears— even from themselves. A person who hates kids might become an elementary school teacher. Or someone who hates animals might become the best-loved zookeeper of all time. How do you know if a person's behavior reflects true motives or is a reaction formation? It may be impossible to know for certain.

Some of the defense mechanisms appear to be useful, while others are so vague that they are useless. Still, the basic idea of the defense mechanism is that we can deal with stress by ignoring it or believing that it's not serious. Obviously, although they may postpone dealing with the stress temporarily, defense mechanisms are not very effective adjustment techniques in the long run. Task-oriented coping is often more effective in dealing with stress.

Coping Techniques

Coping techniques are ways of dealing with stress and anxiety. They are often done without thinking, and as such can be valuable ways of releasing tension. Coleman and his colleagues (1987) described several important stress-reduction coping techniques as well as more direct task-oriented coping strategies. These stress-reduction techniques do not solve the problems that lead to stress, but rather serve to temporarily reduce the stress so that the individual can attempt more direct adjustment.

Crying is extremely useful in releasing tension from a stressful situation. Although adults (especially men) are taught not to cry in our society, we all sometimes cry when the pressure gets too high. This helps us to release tension, relax, and become reoriented.

An important way of dealing with stress is *talking* your problem over with someone else. A number of therapies (to be discussed in chapter 14, "Therapy") are based on the premise that if you share your problem with someone else, you will feel better. Crisis hotlines are springing up everywhere and help people with problems talk them out anonymously. Often we overlook this simple technique for dealing with excessive stress.

Humor is an excellent way of reducing stress. We've all heard the old saying, laughter is the best medicine. It's important to keep things in perspective. If we can laugh about our mishaps, the stress is reduced and we can then deal with the situation more effectively. Through laughter we are able to more effectively accept hurt and disappointment and we can begin to solve our problems.

It is often useful to use *reflection* when thinking about our problems. I try to write them down and read them back to myself. Often we are so busy just trying to get by, that we forget to seriously think about things that are important in our lives. If we take time to think about a stressful situation, we will be able to evaluate our responses to stress and develop more effective methods of dealing with it.

An additional coping technique is to *obtain help* from others. Often we are not able to most effectively deal with problems by ourselves. It's often hard to admit to ourselves that we need outside help, but if we are to be successful in dealing with our problems, we must get help from other sources. Find information from the library. Visit a counselor. Talk to an instructor. See a friend. Do whatever will make us clearly put the problem into perspective. Then, once we have the proper perspective, we can begin task-oriented adjustment.

Adjustment aimed at realistically solving the problems that cause the stress is often the most successful. Task-oriented coping responses require that the person evaluate the stressful situation objectively and then formulate a plan with which to solve the problem. Three basic approaches to task-oriented coping include attack, withdrawal, and compromise.

In *attack*, the person faces the problem head-on. The first task is to survey the problem and determine a course of action. It is important to remain flexible and seek additional information and aid if the problem warrants it. For example, suppose you are doing poorly in your biology class. You first survey the situation and decide that you don't understand the material. Then you visit the instructor and arrange for a tutor to help you master the material. Because you attack the problem, you will very likely be successful and your grade will improve.

In chapter 8, "Language and Intelligence," we discussed the problem-solving theory of Bourne and colleagues (1986), which is effective in dealing with stress-related problems. The steps include preparation (understanding the problem and obtaining information), production (considering solutions to the problem), and evaluation (considering the appropriateness of the solution).

Sometimes it is wise to reassess the situation and decide to *withdraw*. When you have chosen an inappropriate goal that is unattainable, it's time to admit

Figure 12.13. Coping With Stress
There are many ways of dealing with stress when it begins to interfere with the ability to function in daily life. Meditation, biofeedback, and exercise are some effective stress reducers. President Bush jogs 2 miles, three or four times a week as one way of handling the pressures of his office.

defeat, leave the situation, and establish a new direction. For example, let's suppose that your grades in biology do not improve. You have your heart set on becoming a biologist, but you cannot pass the introductory course. If you have given it everything you have with no success, then it's time to withdraw. You can't persist until learned helplessness occurs.

When you are not likely to reach a particular goal, it's time to sit back and think about your options. Perhaps you could reach the goal through some other pathway. Maybe you could accept a substitute goal. For example, if you should find biology impossible, perhaps a degree in animal psychology would work out just as well. *Compromise* techniques allow us to readjust our goals and the means of obtaining these goals. Without them we would have trouble solving many of the problems that cause us stress and anxiety. Adjustment is often a matter of compromise.

There are many other techniques designed to reduce stress. In chapter 14, "Therapy," we discuss progressive relaxation, a technique for relieving stress by relaxing in the presence of stressful stimuli. A particularly effective approach to dealing with stress is stress inoculation. Donald Meichenbaum (1985) described three phases of stress inoculation: education, rehearsal, and implementation. In the *education phase*, specific information about what to expect is given to the individual. For instance, someone going into the hospital for an operation is able to cope better if he or she knows exactly what to expect. In the *rehearsal phase*, the person practices the threatening event in safe surroundings. For example, if I need to give a talk to a group of people, I rehearse at home until I am confident of myself. In the *implementation phase* the person actually carries out the plan. Stress reduction techniques also include a change in diet (for example, ingesting less caffeine), building a social support system, practicing meditation, using biofeedback, exercising, and implementing time-management techniques (see chapter 5, "Sleep and Consciousness," for a discussion of drugs, meditation, and biofeedback).

Time Management

For most people, in school as well as out, time management is the most difficult aspect of adjustment. Most of us have problems managing our time. We tend to put things off (procrastination) and wait until the last minute to do them. We often miss deadlines and then have to hurry to get back on schedule. We spend much of our time on unimportant things. We don't have a schedule and we don't know what goals are most important. In this last section, we discuss how to improve adjustment by learning how to manage time effectively.

An important point to remember is that we all have exactly the same amount of time. It does not matter whether we are rich or poor, we all own exactly the same number of minutes each day. So it is not a matter of getting more time. What counts is what you do with your time. If you use your time wisely, your adjustment will be easy and your stress level low. Williams and Long (1983) discuss some techniques for effective time management.

Before we even begin to implement time-management techniques, we must be motivated to manage our time. Commitment to solving our time problems and making time management a way of life is essential. Then we

---

Figure 12.14. Effective Time Management

- Develop Commitment to Time Management
- Assess Values and Beliefs
- Analyze Current Use of Time
- Set Goals and Decide Priorities
- Be Flexible in Setting Goals
- Work on Highest Priorities First
- Take Time to Plan Each Day
- Subdivide Large Goals into Small Tasks
- Develop List of "To Do" Activities
- Accumulate Similar Tasks to Do Together
- Avoid Procrastination and Perfectionism
- Learn to Say No to Requests
- Learn to Delegate Tasks to Others
- Become Effective Rather Than Efficient
- Evaluate Progress Toward Goals
- Build in Time for Relaxation

Time Management techniques help us successfully adjust to stress in our environment.

---

need to become fully aware of our current time usage strengths and weaknesses. One of the easiest methods of analyzing our current use of time is to keep a time log for a week. Every half hour throughout the day, record what we are doing. Then analyze how much time we are spending on various activities. For instance, we might find we are spending more time than we thought on traveling to and from our destinations each day, but less time on studying or socializing. We should be especially alert for potential time robbers, activities that take up a great deal of time but are not as important as some of our other activities.

In order to use the time we have effectively, we need to establish goals. Alan Lakein, in his 1973 book, *How to Get Control of Your Time and Your Life*, states that successful people are more likely to write a list of daily goals. We should write a list that we can monitor to check our daily progress. As we accomplish each of our goals, cross it off our list. By having an ongoing list, we will be able to channel our time into productive projects.

Once we have established our goals, we need to examine the behaviors that will lead to these goals. For example, we should group similar tasks. If we go to the grocery store, we should stop at the bank on our way there, so we won't need to make a separate trip. Likewise, while we're in the library studying, we should look up the assignment for English class; thus we won't need to return later for that purpose. Make sure that our daily activities are organized to expend our time effectively. If we have spare time between projects, we should use it to study or read or relax, rather than to worry.

There are numerous reasons why people have difficulty with managing time. Often we are overcommitted and end up doing more than we should. One easy technique is to learn how to say "no" to requests that we cannot adequately comply with because of a lack of time. We also can learn to delegate responsibilities to others when appropriate.

Procrastination is one of the most common time management problems. We have many reasons for procrastination, including fear of a large task, lack of motivation, interruptions, and general stress. Lakein proposed the "Swiss cheese technique" to help overcome procrastination. The basic idea is to poke holes in an overwhelming task to reduce it to bite-sized pieces. Divide a large task into small steps and begin with the easiest one. Then continue to complete small tasks until the large one is manageable. For example, perhaps your instructor assigned a term paper, but you have been procrastinating because it is such a huge assignment. Sit down and write an outline. Plan some time to go to the library to look up possible resources. Take a half hour to take a few notes from a resource or two. Now you have a good start on the term paper and should be able to continue to spend the required time to complete it.

The last step of a successful time-management pro-gram is to evaluate our program and make the necessary changes. For example, perhaps we are spending too much time on low priority tasks and need to modify the tasks we work on. We should be flexible in our time management goals and ready to modify our goals as we progress. Remember that our main goal is effective time management. Efficiency is doing things right and effectiveness is doing the right things. In other words, don't spend a lot of time doing things that are not very important. We should give ourselves lots of reinforcement when we progress toward our goals. And leave time for relaxation. Time-management skills help us adjust to stress by finding efficient solutions to our time problems. ■

Adjustment is an ongoing process. We can learn to be more successful in our adjustment, but there will always be new problems to solve. Stress is a fact of life. It's more important to learn to live with it than to try to eliminate it totally. As shown in the opening story on learned helplessness in dogs, learning may not always produce a positive outcome. But as we strive for successful adjustment and a state of well-being, we often learn how to cope with stressful demands made upon us.

"What do you mean '10 minutes'? I want my stress medicine *now*!"

CHAPTER REVIEW
What You've Learned About Stress and Adjustment

1. Stress is anything that produces demands on us to adjust our behavior. It can result from physical dangers or psychological threats. How we react to the stress in our lives is called adjustment. Adjustment might be viewed as a continuum from maladjustment to adjustment to competence.

2. The *Social Readjustment Rating Scale* measures the amount of stress caused by specific changes in life. A second approach is to study the daily hassles (annoyances, aggravations, frustrations).

3. Pressure occurs when we strive to meet the demands imposed on us by others (external pressure) and ourselves (internal pressure). Conflict occurs when we experience incompatible demands and desires. Types of conflict include approach-approach conflict, avoidance-avoidance conflict, approach-avoidance conflict, and multiple approach-avoidance conflict. Frustration occurs when we are prevented from reaching our goals. There are many types of frustration, including time delays, daily hassles, lack of resources, losses, and failure.

4. Anxiety is a vague unpleasant feeling of fear, worry, and apprehension and is often an emotional response to stress. It can be measured by examining self-reports, observing behavior and recording physiological activity. Trait anxiety is viewed as a stable personality characteristic. Situation anxiety is associated with a particular event.

5. The general adaptation syndrome consists of three stages. The alarm reaction is the immediate response to stress, in which the body prepares for an emergency by activating the sympathetic nervous system. When stress is prolonged, we enter the stage of resistance. As the body continues to resist, it eventually depletes its energy, and we enter the stage of exhaustion.

6. Burnout is the depletion of our physical and mental resources. The helping professions are most likely to experience burnout. Symptoms include exhaustion, detachment, boredom, impatience, and a feeling of being unappreciated. Some of the remedies include setting realistic goals, taking breaks, learning to relax, and using support groups.

7. How much stress we experience depends upon the stressors in our lives and our personality characteristics and coping abilities. Personality hardiness includes commitment, challenge, and control.

8. People who learn that their behavior is ineffective in reaching goals give up and experience learned helplessness. Seligman believes learned helplessness is related to depression. We can treat learned helplessness by helping people gain control over their environment. Shyness is an awareness of our inability to act when we want to and know how. Treatments include providing a nonevaluative environment, learning that shyness is common, and developing assertiveness techniques.

9. The field of health psychology is concerned with understanding the psychological influences on people's state of health. Psychological stress can create or aggravate certain physical conditions; the most extensively studied include ulcers, migraine headaches, asthma, and coronary heart disease.

10. The Type A behavior pattern produces stress and leads to heart disease. Type A people are competitive, aggressive, hard-driving, and impatient. Type B people react more to environmental demands, and are thus less subject to stress and heart disease. Specific aspects of the Type A behavior pattern, such as the tendency to suppress anger, may contribute to coronary heart disease.

11. Well-being is a subjective positive emotional state with general life satisfaction. Contributors to a sense of well-being include family life, standard of living, work, marriage, and financial security.

12. Defense mechanisms are psychological techniques developed from the ideas of Freud to help protect the individual from anxiety. In repression, painful memories are forgotten. In projection, unacceptable urges are attributed to other people. In fantasy, a person escapes from stress by daydreaming. In regression, a person reverts to earlier, more immature behavior. In rationalization, a person makes up logical excuses to justify behavior rather than exposing the true motives. In sublimation, a person redirects socially undesirable urges into socially acceptable behavior. And in reaction formation, a person behaves in a way that is opposite to the true unconscious motives.

13. Task-oriented coping involves realistically solving the problem that leads to stress. We can attack the problem head-on, withdraw if it looks impossible, or compromise when necessary.

14. For most people, time management is the most difficult aspect of adjustment. It is important to know how we spend our time. Successful time management requires that we establish goals, analyze tasks, organize activities, and evaluate progress.

ABNORMAL DISORDERS AND THERAPY

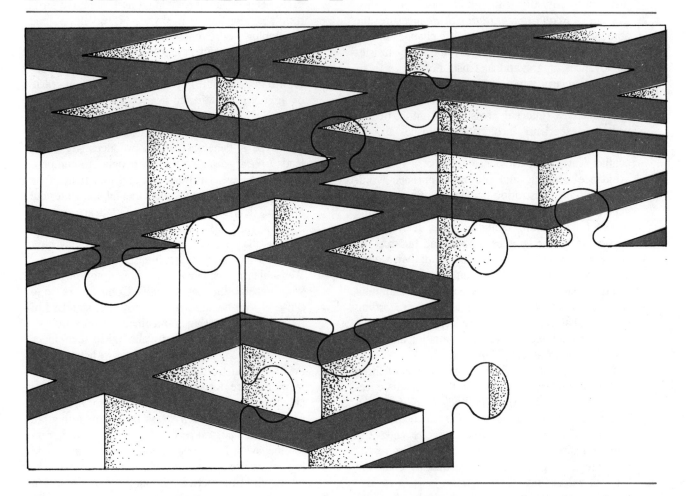

When there is a severe problem in personality, the area of psychology involved in its study is abnormal psychology. In this part of the textbook we cover abnormal disorders and the different types of therapies used to treat those disorders.

After reading Part VI you should be able to:

Outline the major models of abnormal behavior

Describe the clinical symptoms of schizophrenia based on the DSM-III-R

Outline the historical approaches to the treatment of abnormal behavior

Identify insight therapy

Describe behavior therapy

Describe biological therapy

Chapter 13   Abnormal Behavior

When an individual is not able to adequately adjust to daily life, he or she has an abnormal disorder. The milder types of abnormal behavior are called the anxiety disorders. The more severe abnormalities include depression and schizophrenia. Psychologists are trying to discover the causes of abnormal behaviors so they can more effectively treat them.

Chapter 14   Therapy

Treating individuals who have psychological problems has long been a major goal of psychologists. Psychoanalysis was the first major scientific attempt to treat psychopathology. Today, psychologists utilize a variety of therapeutic approaches, including insight, behavior, and group therapies. Sometimes drug therapy is incorporated into the treatment program.

ABNORMAL BEHAVIOR

When an individual is not able to adequately adjust to daily life, he or she has an abnormal disorder. The milder types of abnormal behavior are called the anxiety disorders. The more severe abnormalities include depression and schizophrenia. Psychologists are trying to discover the causes of abnormal behaviors so they can more effectively treat them.

David Rosenhan's 1973 article, "On Being Sane in Insane Places," is a classic study in how we diagnose abnormal behavior. He noted it is often assumed that mental patients exhibit specific symptoms that can be categorized in order to distinguish them from normal people. In order to verify this assumption, Rosenhan had eight normal people admit themselves to mental hospitals for diagnosis and treatment.

Rosenhan's eight "pseudopatients" included a graduate student, three psychologists, a psychiatrist, a physician, a painter, and a housewife. In the group were three women and five men. They were admitted to a total of twelve mental hospitals located in both the eastern and western parts of the country. The hospitals varied in size, age, research orientation, and staff-patient ratio.

When they arrived at the admitting offices of the hospitals, the pseudopatients complained of hearing voices. They said the voices were unclear, but seemed to say "empty," "hollow," and "thud." Other than complaining of these symptoms and giving false names and occupations, the pseudopatients were completely honest in their responses to all questions. They correctly described their relationships with other people, their frustrations as well as enjoyments. None of these conditions could be considered pathological. But as soon as they were admitted to the hospital, they stopped complaining of any symptoms, and behaved "normally" while trying to get released.

While in the mental hospital, the pseudopatients talked freely to the real patients and the staff. When asked how they felt, they responded that they no longer experienced any symptoms and they now felt fine. They cooperated fully with the staff (except they did not swallow any medication). The pseudopatients kept a record of observations in the hospital. At first these records were kept secretly, but it soon became apparent that no one cared what they did on the ward, so the pseudopatients openly wrote their observations.

Rosenhan's pseudopatients were told that they had to work to get out of the mental hospital as quickly as possible. This motivated them to cooperate fully and behave as normally as possible. The staff reports later confirmed that these pseudopatients were friendly, cooperative, and behaved normally at all times.

Not only were the pseudopatients not detected as fakes, but seven of them were diagnosed as having *schizophrenia* (a severe mental disorder) when admitted, and they were all discharged with a diagnosis of "schizophrenia in remission." In remission means that while the patient no longer shows the symptoms of a disorder, he or she might begin to show them in the future. Rosenhan pointed out that this diagnosis meant that the hospitals viewed the pseudopatients as continuing to have a psychiatric disorder, even though no abnormal symptoms were shown.

They had been kept in the mental hospitals for an average of 19 days (the range was 7 to 52 days), during which time staff personnel did not question their motives. Strangely enough, other patients did suspect that they were faking. During the first three admissions 35 out of a total of 118 real patients voiced suspicions that the pseudopatients were normal. Some patients even accused the pseudopatients of being journalists or professors checking up on the hospital.

Because normal people were so readily diagnosed as abnormal, Rosenhan ran a second study to see if the reverse was also true. The staff of a mental hospital not used in the first study was informed that one or more pseudopatients would attempt to be admitted within the following three months. Each staff member was asked to rate the likelihood that a new patient was actually a

Figure 13.1. A State Mental Hospital
Rosenhan's pseudopatients admitted themselves to mental hospitals in order to see how long it would take to be released once they no longer showed abnormal symptoms.

pseudopatient. Of 193 patients admitted, 41 were suspected (with high confidence) of being pseudopatients by at least one staff member. Nineteen were suspected by a psychiatrist and another staff member. Actually no pseudopatients were admitted during that time, again indicating the potential danger of labeling people in this situation.

Rosenhan's study demonstrates how easy it is in a mental hospital for normal people to be diagnosed as abnormal. He suggests further that the labels we use in diagnosing people are so general that they have little usefulness. And, as shown by the release diagnosis of "in remission," once one has been labeled as abnormal, it is extremely difficult to overcome that label. While some professionals question Rosenhan's research on methodological and ethical grounds, it does raise many questions about the diagnosis and treatment of the mentally disturbed.

CHAPTER OBJECTIVES
What You'll Learn About Abnormal Behavior

After studying this chapter, you should be able to:

1. Define abnormal behavior.
2. Identify the major models of abnormal behavior.
3. State the purpose of the DSM-III-R.
4. Describe the panic disorder and agoraphobia.
5. Describe the social and simple phobias.
6. Describe the obsessive compulsive disorder.
7. Describe the generalized anxiety disorder.
8. Describe the symptoms and theories of the mood disorder of depression.
9. Describe the bipolar disorder.
10. Identify the clinical symptoms of schizophrenia.
11. Describe the classification types of schizophrenia.
12. Identify the causes of schizophrenia.
13. Describe the delusional disorder.
14. Describe the organic mental disorders.
15. Describe the somatoform and dissociative disorders.
16. Describe the personality disorders and sexual disorders.

WHAT IS ABNORMAL BEHAVIOR?

The distinction between the psychologically normal and the abnormal can be tricky. But it is a very important distinction, for how individuals are labeled in this respect determines how society treats them: whether they are allowed the same freedoms as everyone else, are hospitalized for treatment, or, in times past, even put to death so their evil spirits could not infect others.

Defining abnormal behavior is a difficult task. The criteria that have been proposed tend to emphasize a particular orientation while ignoring other perspectives (Sue & colleagues, 1986). Abnormality is viewed differently from the medical, psychological, biological, legal, statistical, and anthropological perspectives. Strupp and Hadley (1977) argued that mental health can be approached from the point of view of society, the mental profession, and the individual. How abnormal behavior is defined has implications for research as well as therapy. For instance, if we define abnormal behavior as a disease (mental illness) or a biochemical imbalance, therapy would be very different than if it were defined as an inappropriate learned response.

While psychologists have not yet agreed on a single definition, there are some commonalities in abnormal behavior that can be incorporated into a working definition. Price and Lynn (1986) suggested subjective distress of the individual, behavior that is psychologically or socially disabling, and behavior that violates social norms as criteria of abnormal behavior. Sue and colleagues (1986) proposed personal discomfort, inefficiency in coping with daily demands, and bizarre behavior in a specific culture as criteria. Carson and colleagues (1988) viewed abnormal behavior as being deviant from social norms and maladaptive for the individual. In this book, we define abnormal behavior as behavior that (a) contributes to *maladaptiveness* in an individual; (b) is considered *deviant* by the culture; and (c) leads to personal psychological *distress*.

Maladaptiveness may be defined as gross inadequacy in the handling of the events of daily life. Should a person's state of mind become so confused that he or she is unable to efficiently accomplish even the ordinary tasks of day-to-day living, it is more than likely that he or she is in psychological trouble. Thus, the ability to adapt and function is a major criterion of sound psychological health.

A person may be judged abnormal if he or she behaves in a bizarre or highly deviant fashion. Such behavior can include *delusions* (the holding of obviously false beliefs), *hallucinations* (sensory experiences unrelated to the actual surroundings), and fears or odd rituals that serve no apparent purpose. Such behavior must, however, be seen against the background of the culture.

Perhaps the best indicator of psychological abnormality is the one that most closely resembles the criterion for determining physical illness—whether the person suffers acute distress. Depression, anxiety, and bodily complaints without corresponding physical ailments can all cause such subjective discomfort. The fact that an individual cannot easily eliminate such symptoms, and would welcome relief from them, is itself an indicator of psychological malfunctioning.

APPROACHES TO THE STUDY OF ABNORMAL BEHAVIOR

Sometimes abnormal psychology is a controversial field, as we saw in our opening story. Some professionals have great confidence in the classification schemes used, while others question the value of labeling people. Most psychologists recognize the need for a systematic approach to the study of abnormal behavior, and approve of some sort of classification scheme. This section reviews some of the major approaches used to study abnormal behavior, and describes how abnormal behaviors are classified.

Models of Abnormal Behavior

There are many different approaches to the study of abnormal behavior. We examine some of the representative models of abnormality in this first section.

Psychoanalytic Model. An approach to abnormal psychology stemming from Sigmund Freud's theories of personality is the psychoanalytic model. This approach suggests that abnormal behavior is the result of a person's inner conflicts. In chapter 12, "Stress and Adjustment," we discussed how we use defense mechanisms to deal with anxiety. When anxiety and conflict become too great for even the defense mechanisms to handle, abnormal behavior results. Thus, outward abnormal behavior is simply the symptom of some internal problem. The cure is to find the source of anxiety and solve the conflicts.

Biological Model. The idea that abnormal behavior is caused by biological factors is called the biological model. According to this approach, when the body's biochemical balance is upset, the person behaves abnormally. Historically, this approach was favored by psychiatrists, who are trained to treat disease. The cure is to alter the body biologically to restore balance. Thus, medical means, such as drugs or surgery, are used to treat abnormal behavior.

Learning Model. Many psychologists find it more constructive to view mental abnormalities not as diseases, but as learned social maladjustments. According to the learning model of abnormality, the standards of normality are simply the social standards of society.

Abnormal behavior is just the result of the individual's learning inappropriate role expectations. The cure is merely relearning the correct, socially acceptable behavior.

Cognitive Model. The cognitive model emphasizes inefficient thinking and problem solving as causes of abnormal behavior. The individual is not able to adequately meet daily demands because he or she cannot reason and logically understand the demands. The cognitive model is closely related to the psychoanalytic and

Insanity and the Law

In this chapter's opening story, we pointed out how difficult it is to define abnormal behavior. The issue becomes even more complicated when questions are raised in a court of law about a defendant's mental condition at the time he or she is alleged to have committed a crime. When the defendant pleads "not guilty by reason of insanity," the court must decide on his or her mental condition based on legal precedent. The issue of insanity is decided by a judge or jury after listening to testimony of experts, who are usually psychologists or psychiatrists.

It is important to remember that in a court the concept of insanity is legal rather than psychological. The insanity plea is used in situations where the defendant is judged to be incapable of knowing right from wrong because of a mental disorder. Although psychologists may examine the individual and testify in court, the final decision is a legal one made by the courts.

As you are probably aware, even the experts are not in agreement over insanity as a legitimate defense. In some cases, insanity is used as a means to avoid prosecution. Normally, if one is judged insane, he or she is committed to a mental hospital until cured. If later judged sane, he or she is set free, sometimes after only a light sentence. One proposal to help solve the problem is to replace the verdict of "not guilty by reason of insanity" with the verdict of "guilty but mentally ill." Individuals found "guilty but mentally ill" would be given the proper psychotherapy to treat their mental disorders, and when they were judged sane, they would be returned to prison to complete their sentences.

A related issue is the ability of the defendant to stand trial. In order to be brought to trial, an individual must understand the charge against him or her and be able to prepare a proper defense with a lawyer. Many times, instead of standing trial, the defendant is judged "incompetent to stand trial" and is committed to a mental institution for treatment. After being confined for a period of time, he or she is released if judged competent. Unfortunately, it is difficult to predict the future behavior of such a person. More research needs to be conducted on the legality of the insanity plea.

Figure 13.2. Insanity and Law
Insanity is a legal term for an individual who is judged not capable of knowing right from wrong. John Hinkley was sent to a mental institution rather than a prison because he was declared insane.

THOUGHT QUESTIONS

1. What is the insanity plea and how is it determined?
2. Why is insanity a legal rather than a psychological concept?
3. Do you believe we should continue to have an insanity plea? Why?

learning models. The therapeutic cognitive approach would be to help the patient understand his or her problems and learn to adequately solve them through thinking about the causes and consequences.

Legal Model. In the legal model, every society sets up its own laws and standards of behavior. If we break the law, our behavior might be considered insane, especially if we have no motive or cannot distinguish right from wrong. For example, walking naked down the street or harming oneself or others are examples of behavior that might be labeled legally insane. Recently, the legal definition of insanity has been a topic of debate. Because he was declared insane, John Hinckley was sent to a mental institution instead of prison for shooting President Reagan.

Statistical Model. Most abnormal behavior represents a magnification of some aspect of normal behavior. We have all experienced fear, daydreaming, fantasies, suspicions, or desires to escape from people and their demands. These experiences are not only normal, they are sometimes necessary for adjustment. Abnormal behavior occurs when some of these processes are magnified out of proportion to reality and become predominant. The statistical model defines behavior as abnormal when its frequency or extent is vastly different from the normal population's.

It should be clear, then, that defining abnormal behavior is a difficult task. There are many approaches, and psychologists have not agreed totally on one particular theory to explain abnormality. Before we review the various disorders themselves, we look at the classification of abnormal behaviors.

Classification and DSM-III-R

One of the most important tasks of clinical psychologists and other mental-health experts is to diagnose and classify abnormal behaviors correctly. The American Psychiatric Association attempted to develop a standard set of diagnoses of abnormal behaviors by publishing the *Diagnostic and Statistical Manual of Mental Disorders (DSM)* in 1952. The DSM was revised in 1968, and again in 1980. The latest edition, DSM-III-R was revised in 1987 and is currently used by psychologists and psychiatrists to classify abnormal behavior patterns; we refer to this revision throughout the textbook.

The purpose of the DSM-III-R is to provide conformity and continuity among mental health professionals in the diagnosis of mental disorders. The current revised edition emphasizes the patient's behavioral symptoms more than the assumptions of the underlying causes of the problem. Thus, it includes detailed criteria for classifying the various disorders. It is also more complex than earlier editions.

DSM-III-R classifies the individual on five axes, or dimensions. First, there is the primary diagnosis, which concerns the major problem and symptoms (Axis I). The individual's long-term personality characteristics or developmental problems are described (Axis II). Any physical problems that might be relevant to the disorder are also described (Axis III). The environment and sources of stress to which the individual is exposed are described (Axis IV). And finally, an evaluation is made on how well the individual has functioned in the past (Axis V). The extensive classification scheme is designed to help make more accurate diagnoses.

Not everyone is totally pleased with DSM-III-R. For instance, some psychologists argue that it is too specific in its classifications. For example, dependence on nicotine is included as a classification. Most people would probably not consider cigarette smoking a mental disorder. And the five axes make DSM-III-R complex to understand and use.

DSM-III-R was designed not to perpetuate a particular viewpoint, although it has been criticized for emphasizing the medical model. Some psychologists feel that it includes too many disorder classifications (more than 230). Others worry about the tendency to think that the syndromes have been explained when they have only been described (Robins & Helzer, 1986). And there is concern over the reliability of the diagnoses made with DSM-III-R. Some of the controversy is over the reclassification of disorders. For instance, homosexuality is no longer included as a psychiatric diagnosis, but several other controversial disorders are included in an appendix for "proposed diagnostic categories needing further study." The late luteal phase dysphoric disorder occurs in females who experience severe changes in physical and emotional functioning during menstrual cycles that cause marked impairment in social interactions. The sadistic personality disorder occurs when someone shows continual cruel, demeaning, and aggressive behavior toward other people. The self-defeating personality disorder occurs when a person shows a pattern of self-defeating behavior. Part of the concern about these proposed categories is that they focus on the potential prejudice against women.

We review some of the major classifications of abnormal behavior in DSM-III-R. We cannot possibly cover every one (of the 230), so we concentrate on the most relevant and representative examples of different types. Since anxiety and stress are often involved in behavior problems, we start with the anxiety disorders.

As we go through this chapter, you may recognize in your roommate, parents, friends, teachers, or even yourself some of the symptoms described. Chances are good that none of these people are abnormal. We all show little individual peculiarities or idiosyncrasies that make us unique. To be classified as abnormal, the

Figure 13.3. DSM-III-R Major Classifications

AXIS I CLINICAL SYNDROMES

DISORDERS USUALLY FIRST EVIDENT IN INFANCY, CHILDHOOD, OR ADOLESCENCE
- Disruptive Behavior Disorders
  - Attention-deficit hyperactivity disorder
  - Conduct disorder
  - Oppositional defiant disorder
- Anxiety Disorders of Childhood or Adolescence
- Eating Disorders
  - Anorexia nervosa
  - Bulimia nervosa
- Gender Identity Disorders
- Tic Disorders
- Elimination Disorders
- Other Disorders of Infancy, Childhood, or Adolescence

ORGANIC MENTAL DISORDERS
- Dementias Arising in the Senium and Presenium
  - Primary degenerative demantia of the Alzheimer type
- Psychoactive Substance-Induced Organic Mental Disorders
- Organic Mental Disorders associated with Axis III physical disorders

PSYCHOACTIVE SUBSTANCE USE DISORDERS

SCHIZOPHRENIA
- Catatonic Schizophrenia
- Disorganized Schizophrenia
- Paranoid Schizophrenia
- Undifferentiated Schizophrenia
- Residual Schizophrenia

DELUSIONAL DISORDER

PSYCHOTIC DISORDERS NOT ELSEWHERE CLASSIFIED

MOOD DISORDERS
- Bipolar Disorders
  - Bipolar disorder
  - Cyclothymia
- Depressive Disorders
  - Major depression
  - Dysthymia

ANXIETY DISORDERS
- Panic Disorder With Agoraphobia
- Panic Disorder Without Agoraphobia
- Agoraphobia Without History of Panic Disorder
- Social Phobia
- Simple Phobia
- Obsessive Compulsive Disorder
- Post-traumatic Stress Disorder
- Generalized Anxiety Disorder

SOMATOFORM DISORDERS
- Body Dysmorphic Disorder
- Conversion Disorder
- Hypochondriasis
- Somatization Disorder
- Somatoform Pain Disorder
- Undifferentiated Somatoform Disorder

DISSOCIATIVE DISORDERS
- Multiple Personality Disorder
- Psychogenic Fugue
- Psychogenic Amnesia
- Depersonalization Disorder

SEXUAL DISORDERS
- Paraphilias
- Sexual Dysfunctions
- Other Sexual Disorders

SLEEP DISORDERS
- Dyssomnias
- Parasomnias

FACTITIOUS DISORDERS

IMPULSE CONTROL DISORDERS NOT ELSEWHERE CLASSIFIED

ADJUSTMENT DISORDER

PSYCHOLOGICAL FACTORS AFFECTING PHYSICAL CONDITION

AXIS II DEVELOPMENTAL DISORDERS

DISORDERS USUALLY FIRST EVIDENT IN INFANCY, CHILDHOOD, OR ADOLESCENCE
- Mental retardation
- Pervasive Developmental Disorders
- Autistic disorder
- Specific Developmental Disorders
  - Academic skills disorders
  - Language and speech disorders
  - Motor skills disorder
- Other Developmental Disorders

AXIS II PERSONALITY DISORDERS

PERSONALITY DISORDERS

conditions would have to be fairly serious. While we all experience anxiety, severe abnormal behaviors are relatively rare.

ANXIETY DISORDERS

Anxiety disorders are fairly long-lasting disruptions of the normal pattern of living, characterized by anxiety. Anxiety is usually defined as a vague feeling of fear and apprehension. As we discussed in chapter 12, "Stress and Adjustment," anxiety might be thought of as a fear of the demands placed on the individual when the individual doesn't know exactly what the demands are. The person generally has no clear idea of the real cause of the anxiety; in fact, there is a tendency to avoid thinking about the fears, since that only seems to intensify them. The anxious person often develops specific ritualistic behaviors that serve to reduce anxiety temporarily, but that actually increase the problems because they don't solve them. Originally Freud used the term neurosis to describe abnormal behavior caused by anxiety. However, the term crept into popular usage and wasn't as specific as it might have been, and so in DSM-III and the DSM-III-R it was replaced with individual anxiety disorders.

We review four types of anxiety disorder: panic disorder and agoraphobia, social and simple phobias, obsessive compulsive disorder, and generalized anxiety disorder.

Panic Disorder and Agoraphobia

Panic disorder is identified by the occurrence of panic attacks, specific periods of intense anxiety characterized by shortness of breath, dizziness, faintness, trembling, sweating, nausea, numbness, chills or hot flashes, or a fear of dying. The person may feel apprehension and a sense of doom (DSM-III-R, 1987). Panic attacks may last from a few minutes up to an hour or more. They are unexpected and are not caused by anxiety-producing situations.

Usually panic disorders occur in young adults of both sexes. Panic attacks can occur several times a week, or in some cases, daily. The disruption of an important social relationship can predispose the panic disorder (Foa & colleagues, 1984). When panic disorder alone is experienced, there might be only a minimal impairment of social functioning; however, it is often accompanied by agoraphobia.

Agoraphobia occurs when the individual is afraid of

places or situations that would be difficult or embarrassing to escape from, especially if incapacitating symptoms occur. He or she may be afraid to be outside the home, in a crowd, or traveling; afraid of falling, becoming dizzy, or developing some embarrassing problem. Because of this intense fear, the person usually restricts travel. Sometimes he or she can travel with a companion, and is willing to endure the anxiety situation in order to accomplish something. Typically, agoraphobia develops in young adults, with females being more likely to develop the disorder than males. The individual may or may not also experience full-blown panic attacks but may have any of the symptoms individually. Recent research suggests that agoraphobia and panic disorder are often experienced together, and may have a common genetic basis (Noyes & colleagues, 1986).

Social and Simple Phobias

Phobias are acute excessive fears of specific situations or objects, fears which have no convincing basis in reality. Persons with phobias usually recognize their irrationality, but cannot overcome them without outside help. People can develop phobias about an endless variety of things. Some of the more common phobias are fear of being closed in (claustrophobia), fear of heights (acrophobia), fear of crowds (ocholophobia), fear of animals (zoophobia), and fear of the dark (nyctophobia).

Often fears toward specific objects are developed by simple classical conditioning. Fears become phobic when, without foundation, they interfere with daily living. For instance, they can prevent an individual from using public transportation, flying on an airplane, or going past the first floor of a building. When phobic persons encounter the objects of their phobias, typically they experience panic, nausea, and acute anxiety. On the other hand, phobias have the advantage of giving anxious persons reasons for anxiety and specific objects to avoid. Therefore, they can keep anxiety in check.

As we noted in chapter 6, "Learning," phobias do not develop at random, but rather appear to be learned from specific stimuli. A theory proposed by Martin Seligman (1972) states that we can learn phobias from stimuli that at some time in evolution were dangerous to people. Thus, phobias are often developed toward dogs, insects, snakes, heights, darkness, and storms. There is a trend away from a long list of Greek words indicating specific phobias. DSM-III-R classifies phobias into three general categories, *agoraphobia* (which we just discussed), *social phobia*, and *simple phobia*.

Social phobias are excessive irrational fears and embarrassment when interacting with other people. Social phobias include fear of assertive behavior, fear of criticism, fear of mistakes, and fear of public speaking. Social phobias often begin in adolescence and can be quite disruptive. The disorder is more common in males than in females. The individual with social phobia usually attempts to avoid the situations that cause the intense anxiety.

The individual with a simple phobia shows an excessive, irrational fear toward a specific stimulus. The most common simple, or specific phobias are directed toward dogs, snakes, insects, blood, closed-in spaces, and heights. Thus, one might have a simple phobia of snakes or a simple phobia of heights.

Figure 13.4. Social Phobia
An individual who fears situations and objects inordinately when there is no reason to be afraid, has a social phobia. An extreme fear of crowds, for example, can disrupt an individual's life and prevent him or her from enjoying many events such as football games.

The simple phobias exclude fear of social situations (social phobias), fear of having a panic attack (panic disorder), or agoraphobia. Females more often experience simple phobias, and the problem can begin at any age from childhood on. The simple phobias are fairly common, and since they usually are not too disruptive, often people do not seek treatment for them.

Obsessive Compulsive Disorder

One relatively common type of anxiety disorder is the obsessive compulsive disorder, which can take several forms. Anxious persons may have repetitive thoughts (obsessions) or constant urges to indulge in meaningless rituals (compulsions), which they find uncontrollable, irrational, and inconvenient. For example, they may imagine that someone is following them constantly or may check repeatedly to make sure a window is not open. The obsessions or compulsions cause significant distress, interfere with the individual's normal functioning, and are time-consuming (DSM-III-R, 1987).

Obsessions and compulsions are often combined in some way, such as constantly worrying about dirt together with washing one's hands every half hour. Or perhaps a person is afraid of being frozen, so he or she hoards blankets and sweaters. If the person has 1,000 sweaters, we can be pretty sure she is a compulsive. We all have thoughts and mannerisms that we perform almost automatically. In the obsessive compulsive, however, these thoughts and acts become so dominant that they disrupt life.

Obsessive thoughts often involve fears of being unable to control impulses. The individual may continually fantasize about killing a relative, walking naked in public, or screaming obscenities. The chances of carrying out these actions are practically nonexistent, but the fantasies continually and involuntarily recur to the point that the person having them is afraid of losing control. Any attempt to stop these thoughts, however, results in acute anxiety.

Compulsive acts are equally disruptive to the individual. They range from minor routines, such as checking doors three times to assure that they are locked or stirring coffee exactly five times, to complex rituals, such as dressing and undressing seven times before going out or adding the numbers on all visible license plates before crossing a street. Again, any attempt to stop the behaviors results in acute anxiety.

To judge accurately whether a particular behavior is obsessive compulsive, the social context must be taken into consideration. For example, we would not consider an airline pilot disturbed for compulsively checking out the airplane's instruments before each takeoff. Likewise, a few years ago my wife had a beer-can collection. She

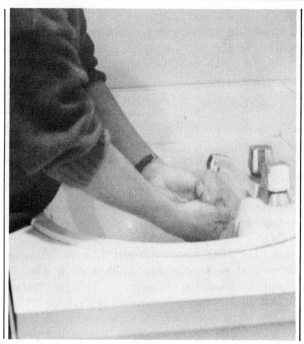

Figure 13.5. Obsessive Compulsive Disorders
An individual with an obsessive compulsive disorder may continually think about being contaminated or disorderly. These obsessive thoughts may lead to compulsive acts such as constantly washing or cleaning the house or constantly straightening the contents of drawers or closets even when they do not need it.

thought constantly about acquiring new cans and at times went out of her way to look at collections. If she had continued this hobby to the point of ignoring her family and becoming ill from not eating, then there would have been a serious problem (but, of course, she didn't). Obsessive compulsive individuals are relatively easy to treat, as this is usually considered a fairly mild form of maladjustment.

There are several theories of how obsessive compulsive disorders develop. The psychoanalytic model suggests that anxiety and guilt about some problem can overwhelm a person. The individual might find doing something else takes one's mind off the problem. Thus the cycle begins, and every time the anxiety is experienced, the ritualistic behavior is performed. The learning theory suggests that obsessive compulsive disorders develop in response to an anxiety-producing experience. When we are upset about something, we try various methods of reducing the anxiety. When we find something that works, we continue to do it. Dollard and Miller (1950) suggested that our compulsions may be behaviors which were rewarded in childhood. For example, washing our hands, getting dressed, or straightening our room often earned us praise. As adults, we exaggerate these childhood behaviors. Since they are associated with reinforcement, they temporarily reduce our anxiety. Recent research suggests that there is a biological basis for some forms of obsessive compulsive behavior and result in a person who is generally unable to adequately cope with daily demands (Turner & colleagues, 1985).

Generalized Anxiety Disorder

Individuals with generalized anxiety disorder live in a state of constant tension. Anxious people usually do not know why they feel as if something dreadful is about to happen; their anxiety is generally free-floating, or unattached to any particular object or situation.

Individuals with generalized anxiety disorder feel inadequate and helpless in the face of life and its challenges. Of course, we all have had anxious experiences when faced with trying situations (for example, incompleted work assignments or difficult decisions to be made). But somehow we get through the situation without severe trauma. People with generalized anxiety disorder, however, cannot function when faced with problems that most of us handle without much difficulty. They are constantly apprehensive and find endless problems to worry about. Even when things are going well for them, they cannot relax because there are always tomorrow's problems to worry about.

DSM-III-R lists 18 symptoms, 6 of which are required for a diagnosis of generalized anxiety disorder. Muscle tension symptoms include trembling, muscle tension, restlessness, and fatigue. Autonomic hyperactivity symptoms include shortness of breath, rapid heart rate, sweating, dizziness, dry mouth, nausea, chills, and frequent urination. Vigilance and scanning symptoms include feeling keyed up, an exaggerated startle re-

sponse, insomnia, and general irritability. The person must show these symptoms for at least six months to be diagnosed as having generalized anxiety disorder. Some evidence suggests that panic attacks can occur in individuals with generalized anxiety disorder (Barlow & colleagues, 1985).

Anxiety disorders represent the mild end of the continuum of maladjustment. While they are serious, as we see in chapter 14, "Therapy," they can often be treated successfully and the individual can then resume a productive life. Phobias are also often treated effectively with behavior therapy.

We turn next to the more severe categories of abnormal behaviors that are called psychotic disorders. The two major psychoses—the *mood disorders* and *schizophrenia*—are discussed here.

MOOD DISORDERS

When a person experiences a severe disruption in mood or emotional balance, we call the problem a mood disorder (formerly called an affective disorder). When emotions show an all-time low and we lose interest in life, we experience depression. At the other extreme of mood is mania, which is a highly excitable, highly active, unrealistic, optimistic state. DSM-III-R includes two major mood disorders. *Major depression* is characterized by a sad mood, filled with feelings of guilt and worthlessness. The *bipolar disorder* (which is some-

Figure 13.6. Depression
An individual who is depressed cannot adjust to the problems in life. He is usually sad and often has thoughts of guilt and worthlessness. Scientists have several theories that try to explain the basis for this affective disorder.

times referred to as manic-depression) is characterized by extreme mood swings from sad depression to joyful mania. Mania seldom occurs by itself.

Major Depression

Depression can vary widely in severity. In a mild form, it is normal for people to feel depressed when they have failed to achieve something or when they lose someone important to them. One review by Winokur (1985) found that people become depressed when they have problems at work, marital problems, or find they are incompetent in something they want to do. Some research suggests that men become more depressed than women when

their spouse dies (Stroebe & Stroebe, 1983). We may become mildly depressed when we have a fight with someone or receive a low grade on a test. As mentioned in chapter 12, "Stress and Adjustment," Seligman suggests depression is often an extension of learned helplessness. Mild depression usually lasts briefly and is followed by recovery.

A more serious problem is dysthymia, in which the person has a depressed mood much of the time for at least two years. Symptoms of dysthmymia include a major change in eating and sleeping habits (loss of appetite or overeating, insomnia or hypersomnia), fatigue, low self-esteem, poor concentration, and feelings of hopelessness (DSM-III-R, 1987). Dysthymia may be due to other nonmood disorders, such as anorexia or

Suicide

Suicide is often a real possibility in cases of depression. Roughly one out of ten thousand Americans commit suicide each year. While more women attempt suicide, three times more men actually die from suicide. Although the peak age for suicide attempts in our country is about age 30, recent studies indicate that the incidence of suicide is very serious among teenagers and the elderly (Peck & colleagues, 1985). Recently, the greatest increase in suicide rates is in the 15- to 24-year-old range (Hendin, 1985).

Why do people commit suicide? While there are many different individual reasons, most have to do with the fact that those who attempt suicide feel that life is not worth living. As we indicated in this chapter, feelings of hopelessness and guilt are prevalent in depression. If the situation looks hopeless, it might induce the depressed individual to commit suicide.

Some people believe that the act of suicide is a desperate plea for help. Leonard (1977) reported that nearly 80% of suicide victims provided some type of warning prior to the act itself. It appears that people who commit suicide are individuals who are unable to deal adequately with their stress and know of no other alternative.

There are some things which can be done to help prevent suicide, as discussed by Davison and Neale in their 1986 book, *Abnormal Psychology*. Getting potential suicide victims to promise not to commit suicide before seeing a counselor appears to be successful. Talking with them about how they feel might help reassure them until they can get professional help. If you are with a potential suicide victim, go with him or her to get help. A counseling center, hospital emergency room, or even a police station are places where professionals will know how to handle the situation. If indeed the person feels there is no reason to live, then the best treatment would seem to be that which provides hope.

Figure 13.7. Suicide
People who are severely depressed and feel hopeless may commit suicide. Scientists are trying to find ways to prevent this growing problem.

Psychologists do not understand exactly why people commit suicide. They hope through continuing research to improve their understanding and learn how to prevent this tragic waste of human life.

THOUGHT QUESTIONS

1. Why do people commit suicide?
2. Why is the suicide rate going up?
3. What is the best way to prevent a person from committing suicide? How can we ensure that he or she won't try again in the future?

drug use. The individual with dysthymia usually experiences minor impairment in social interactions, and is rarely hospitalized unless a suicide attempt occurs. The depression in dysthymia is moderate, compared to major depression which is more severe and incapacitating.

Symptoms of Major Depression. Major depression occurs when an individual experiences one or more major depressive episodes, the chief symptom of which includes a depressed mood and loss of interest in normal activities. Other symptoms can include sleep disruption, weight loss, fatigue, feelings of worthlessness or inappropriate guilt, inability to concentrate, and thoughts of death or suicide. These symptoms occur most of the time for at least a two-week period. People who are severely depressed describe themselves as sad and hopeless. They may have no motivation to continue living and may attempt suicide.

Major depression usually begins in early adulthood, but a major depressive episode may occur at any age, including infancy. A major episode usually lasts at least six months, and some of the symptoms can persist for a year or more. Impairment of the depressed individual varies from moderate disruption of normal relationships and activities to complete inability to function as a person. The largest problem in depression is the possibility of suicide.

Theories of Depression. Depression is a common maladjustment problem, and there are a variety of theories that attempt to explain how it occurs. Psychoanalytic theory focuses on unconscious conflict, and suggests that feelings of anger and hostility are displaced, or turned inward, and the result is that the person becomes so miserable that life is no longer tolerable. Thus, he or she gives up and becomes depressed. Beck's (1976) cognitive theory of depression emphasizes the negative and self-defeating thoughts of the person who is depressed. It suggests that when a person dwells on the negative for too long, low self-esteem and depression can result.

The learning theory (see chapter 12, "Stress and Adjustment," for a discussion of helplessness) suggests that depression is the result of learning to be helpless. This currently popular theory proposed by Seligman (1975) assumes that when people discover that they do not have control over their lives, socially, economically, or psychologically, they tend to give up. They tend to attribute their problems to their own personalities and believe they cannot improve (Abramson, Seligman & Teasdale, 1978). This might help to explain why depression is so common among the poor and helpless.

Other learning theorists speculate that depression results from the reduction of social reinforcement and activity (Heiby, 1983). For example, after the loss of a wife, a husband no longer has much intimate reinforcement or enjoyment, and other people do not expect

much from him. Soon he learns his new role, and continues to remain depressed. Treatment would consist of changing activity levels, reinforcements, or control over his life.

Some research focuses on the role of psychosocial factors in depression, especially on the possibility that the environment might affect changes in the brain (Thase & colleagues, 1985). Paykel (1982) reported that loss of a relationship (through death) often precedes depression. Roy (1985) found that children who lose a parent are more likely to become depressed as adults. In general, any major life event that significantly decreases an individual's self-esteem or increases his or her stress level might contribute to maladjustment.

A number of biological theories have been proposed for depression. Seligman (1975) found that dogs that had learned to become helpless had very low levels of the neurotransmitter norepinephrine. In their classic theory of mood disorders, Schildkraut and Kety (1967) proposed that low levels of dopamine and especially norepinephrine were involved in depression. Drugs that increase levels of norepinephrine have been successful in treating depression in humans (Cooper & colleagues, 1986). Some evidence exists that the loss of pleasurable reinforcement and enjoyment in Parkinson's disease patients is due to lowered levels of dopamine (Fibiger, 1984). A current theory of Janowsky and Risch (1984) suggests that depression and mania are caused by disturbances in the balance between the neurotransmitters norepinephrine and acetylcholine. Norepinephrine plays a role in the experience of pleasure in the brain when reinforcement occurs, thus linking the reinforcement-learning and biological theories. Recent research has focused on synaptic malfunctions and mood disorders (McNeal & Cimbolic, 1986). While the evidence is strong that a disturbance in the levels of neurotransmitters such as norepinephrine are involved in depression, at the present time the exact mechanism is not known. Some evidence also suggests that depression has a genetic component (Mendlewicz, 1985).

Bipolar Disorder

The bipolar disorder, or *manic-depression*, is characterized by unpredictable extreme mood swings. Sometimes the manic-depressive's mood swings wildly from great excitement to extreme melancholy. During the manic phase, the patient may become hyperexcited, talkative, boastful, uninhibited, and perhaps destructive. In this energy and excitement phase, he or she may talk about highly unrealistic projects. Then, suddenly without warning, the patient with bipolar disorder becomes so gloomy and experiences such profound feelings of worthlessness that he or she will refuse to eat and have difficulty sleeping and moving. In the depressed state, the individual with bipolar disorder behaves in exactly the same way as an individual with major depression (Perris, 1982). There are not nearly as many people with bipolar disorder (about 1% of the population) as with unipolar depression (from 10% to 20% of the population). The bipolar disorder occurs with equal frequency in men and women.

Some individuals experience a bipolar disorder called cyclothymia, which is a moderately severe problem with mood swings from hypomanic episodes to depression (but not as extreme as manic or major depressive episodes). A hypomanic episode is characterized by an elevated or irritable mood but is not severe enough to cause major disruption of normal functioning. It is also possible for an individual to have a seasonal pattern in a bipolar disorder, in which there is a relationship between an episode of bipolar disorder or depressive episode and the time of the year. Research is currently being conducted to better understand the effects of season and mood disorders.

SCHIZOPHRENIA

I met Jerry at a local mental institution. A group of students and I were walking up to one of the wards when a young man approached and said he would help guide our tour. He proceeded to tell us about some of the patients and the therapies used at the institution. Then he warned us about the gunman and told us that he had to go ring the church bell. But he stopped and began to laugh, saying that he didn't know why we had strawbe-

Figure 13.8. Artwork of an Individual with Schizophrenia
Schizophrenia includes a disruption of the normal processes of thinking, feeling, and perception. Here, the series of paintings by a schizophrenic patient becomes more bizarre as the disorder worsens.

313

rry jam in our pockets. Our tour guide, who had been with us the entire time, led Jerry back to his room. Later he explained that the best way to tell the patients from the workers was to ask for keys—only workers had keys.

Jerry had schizophrenia. Schizophrenia is the most common type of psychosis, and people with this disease tend to live in a world of their own imagining. Most hospitalized schizophrenics dress themselves, walk about, and indulge in such everyday activities as eating and smoking in much the same manner as everyone else. However, individuals with schizophrenia withdraw their interest in and concern for the events and people in the world around them. They are often preoccupied by fantasies, delusions, and hallucinations, which affect their speech and thoughts. Although there are several types of schizophrenia, most schizophrenics show some common symptoms.

Clinical Symptoms of Schizophrenia

As indicated in our opening story, there is quite a bit of controversy over labeling a person schizophrenic. Because it is the most common psychotic disorder, schizophrenia is sometimes used as a catchall for individuals who cannot be classified elsewhere. Some psychologists, like David Rosenhan, argue that mental health professionals are too ready to diagnose someone as having schizophrenia. It was to illustrate this point that he designed the study that had normal people admit themselves into various psychiatric hospitals, complaining of hearing voices. As we discussed in our opening story, while it would be extremely difficult to diagnose a disorder accurately from this symptom alone, seven out of eight of Rosenhan's pseudopatients were diagnosed as schizophrenic. This study demonstrated the danger in labeling people with clinical diagnostic terms. The DSM-III-R helps to classify people when sufficient symptoms can be seen clearly. Following is a brief description of the major symptoms of schizophrenia. The DSM-III-R identifies several areas in which individuals with schizophrenia typically experience disturbances. They include thinking, perception, affect (emotion), sense of self, volition, relationship to the world, and behavior.

Disruption of Content and Form of Thought. Many individuals with schizophrenia have delusions, or beliefs not founded on reality. Some schizophrenics have delusions of persecution, and believe that someone is trying to kill or hurt them. They also have thoughts of agents controlling their thinking and behavior, as well as difficulty separating reality from fantasy. A common delusion in schizophrenia is thought broadcasting, in which people believe that their thoughts are broadcast so others can hear them. Thought insertion, in which people with schizophrenia believe thoughts from others are inserted into their heads, is another common delusion.

Individuals with schizophrenia often have problems with the form of their thoughts, called formal thought disorder. Often their thinking is unorganized and incoherent. They appear to have trouble associating current information with previous knowledge. In addition, they show confusion and lack of insight. Ideas shift from one topic to another, even though there is no relationship between topics of thought.

Disruption of Perception. Individuals with schizophrenia often report having hallucinations, or sensory experiences with no sensory stimuli present. Often they are auditory hallucinations, such as hearing voices that talk to the patient or just make sounds. Tactile hallucinations may also be experienced, and usually involve a tingling or burning feeling. Sometimes visual or olfactory hallucinations occur, such as seeing snakes crawling around the room.

Disruption of Affect. Many individuals with schizophrenia show abnormalities of emotional response. Sometimes they are emotionally flat, and do not show any emotional arousal. They tend to stare straight ahead and appear apathetic. When they speak, their voice is monotone without any affective expression. Other individuals with schizophrenia show inappropriate emotional responses: for example, they laugh at sad news, or cry for no apparent reason; or they shift emotional moods quickly, and are not dependable in their reaction to a stimulus.

Disruption of Sense of Self and Volition. The sense of self is an important characteristic of the normal, healthy person. An individual with schizophrenia has difficulties in developing a personal identity, and may believe outside forces are directing his or her behavior.

A characteristic often observed in a person with schizophrenia is a disturbance in volition, or lack of goal-directed activation. The person does not show adequate motivation to follow through on an action. This, of course, causes the person to be unable to function properly in society.

Disruption of Relationships and Behavior. The individual with schizophrenia has great difficulty relating to other people. Often he or she will withdraw from social relationships. Because the person experiences delusions and hallucinations, he or she is unable to properly relate to the external world.

Especially in severe forms of schizophrenia, disturbances in behavior are observed. For instance, the person with schizophrenia may maintain a rigid posture, or exhibit stereotypical spastic movements, or other bizarre mannerisms.

Types of Schizophrenia

Schizophrenia usually begins during childhood or early adolescence. Diagnosis of schizophrenia requires that the symptoms be present for at least 6 months. Usually a *prodromal phase* occurs first, in which there is a definite deterioration in functioning. In this phase, the individual usually shows social withdrawal, neglect of personal hygiene, lack of motivation, and unusual perceptual experiences. During the *active phase* psychotic symptoms (such as hallucinations and delusions) are exhibited. Finally, after the active phase is a *residual phase* in which many of the prodromal phase characteristics are again evident.

DSM-III-R lists five major types of schizophrenia: *catatonic, disorganized, paranoid, undifferentiated,* and *residual.* They are often thought of as patterns of symptoms of the illness, rather than as distinct types of psychosis. They tend to overlap, and their diagnostic usefulness seems to be somewhat a matter of convenience.

Catatonic Schizophrenia. One fairly rare type of schizophrenia is catatonic schizophrenia, most often characterized by complete immobility and the apparent absence of the will to move and speak. The individual with catatonic schizophrenia is able, without shifting, to maintain the same—often quite uncomfortable—position for hours (called a catatonic stupor). Catatonics are sometimes suggestible, obeying the orders of others in a robot-like way. More often, they are negativistic, resisting outside efforts to change their position or even to feed them. They may also show selective amnesia (forgetting) for some events along with an extraordinary memory for others.

Disorganized Schizophrenia. The most severe personality disintegration occurs in disorganized schizophrenia. Previously, disorganized schizophrenia was called *hebephrenia* (from the Greek word "hebe" meaning childish or silly). Its onset most often occurs at an early age. It is characterized by flat or inappropriate emotions, including silliness and giggling, infantile reactions, bizarre behavior, incoherent speech and thought, hallucinations, and delusions.

Paranoid Schizophrenia. People with paranoid schizophrenia often have persecutory or grandiose delusions. With their often elaborately and logically constructed persecutory delusions, paranoids will often show great alertness, suspicion, and vigilance toward the "agents" who are "out to get them." They may also believe they are Christ or the object of a pursuit by the CIA; and may project feelings they think are "bad" onto others. This ability to transfer the bad part of themselves to others may result in feelings of omnipotence or all-powerfulness. Such grandiose delusions also provide paranoid schizophrenics with a rationale for why others

Figure 13.9. Catatonic Schizophrenia
An individual with catatonic schizophrenia sometimes maintains the same uncomfortable position for extended periods of time. This may be one way to avoid the anxiety of interacting with other people.

are persecuting them. One of the common symptoms of schizophrenia is sensory hallucination; paranoids may "hear voices" that confirm their supernatural powers. The individual with paranoid schizophrenia can be angry and at times violent. There is a chance the individual with paranoid schizophrenia can recover and function normally. The number of paranoid schizophrenics appears to be decreasing, whereas the number of individuals with undifferentiated schizophrenia is increasing.

Undifferentiated Schizophrenia. The above three types of schizophrenia show specific psychotic symptoms. Sometimes the individual with schizophrenia does not fit into any particular category, or shows symptoms of more than one type. This patient is labeled as having undifferentiated schizophrenia. This type, sometimes called simple schizophrenia, is characterized by a gradual loss of interest in the world, in social relationships, and in personal hygiene, as well as increased withdrawal, apathy, and emotional indifference. This person displays delusions, hallucinations, incoherence, or disorganized behavior, but because they do not meet all of the diagnostic criteria they cannot be categorized as a catatonic, disorganized, or paranoid type.

Residual Schizophrenia. Individuals with residual schizophrenia are without major psychotic symptoms but have had a schizophrenic episode in the past. They tend to exhibit symptoms such as social withdrawal, illogical thinking, and inappropriate emotions, although they can function fairly well. The individual who is classified as having residual schizophrenia is not quite "in remission" since the residual type still shows some signs of the disorder.

Causes of Schizophrenia

In the past 20 years or so, there has been considerable research into the possible biochemical and genetic causes of schizophrenia—specifically, research into the possibility that some genetically inherited substance in the brain might be responsible for schizophrenia. The disorder seems to run in families and the incidence of schizophrenia among identical twins, even those reared in different homes, is high. But environmental forces seem to intensify the influence of suspected genetic factors. Let's first look at environmental influences on schizophrenia.

Environmental Influences. Thorough investigation into the family background of individuals with schizophrenia usually indicates a history of very great stress on the child, so great that he escapes from an intolerable reality into a fantasy world (Zubin & Ludwig, 1983). There are two family situations most commonly linked to schizophrenia (Roff & Knight, 1981). The first involves a mother who is indifferent to the family, resulting in disorganization and stress. The second involves one parent (usually the mother) who completely dominates the spouse and children, but is not nurturant. In both cases, conflict and stress result in increased vulnerability in the children. In another study (Doane & colleagues, 1981), it was found that communication patterns in the family were related to schizophrenic tendencies in children. Specifically, unclear and conflicting messages, criticism, and hostility are more often found in homes in which children develop schizophrenia.

A number of early studies showed that schizophrenia is more prevalent in the lower socioeconomic groups (Hollingshead & Redlich, 1958). Lower-class people with schizophrenia show more physical and social symptoms of unhappiness, as well as more open friction with others. There are many possible but unproven reasons for these apparent class differences. They may be the result of less than adequate diagnostic procedures made available to poorer people; the poorer disturbed person is less able to hold a well-paying job; the poor and the rich may raise their children in ways that predispose the children to react to stress differently; being poor may also give rise to feelings of hopelessness. Research for an explanation for apparent class differences in the incidence of schizophrenia is scanty and more is needed.

Social learning theorists argue that schizophrenia is a learned behavior, produced through others' reinforcement of abnormal responses. If someone is ignored, then one way to gain attention is to show bizarre behavior. Laing (1964) suggested that schizophrenia occurs when an individual decides no longer to accept the pressures and demands of society, and thus turns inward to a self-made fantasy world. Psychoanalytic theorists like Freud believed schizophrenia was the result of regression to primary narcissism, the oral phase before the ego has developed. The narcissistic individual is totally controlled by the id, and seeks total self-gratification. None of the environmental theories have fully explained schizophrenia, and thus there is great excitement in the current research on possible biological causes.

Biological Influences. About 1% of the population has schizophrenia. But genetic research has shown that if one close genetic relative has schizophrenia, the chances are significantly higher that another will also have it. Twin studies have shown high *concordance* rates for schizophrenia (if one has it, the other does also), according to Zerbin-Rubin (1972). As discussed in chapter 2, "Biology of Behavior," schizophrenia concordance is much higher for monozygotic (identical) twins than for dizygotic (nonidentical) twins. Gottesman and Shields (1972) reported a concordance rate of 42% for MZ twins but only 9% for DZ twins. Adoption studies also demonstrate that genetic influences are very important in schizophrenia (Kety, 1983). Typically, even if separated, twins who are adopted are likely to have high concordance rates. However, a number of recent critiques have pointed out that with the current methodology, it is extremely difficult to separate the environmental and genetic influences (Abrams & Taylor, 1983). The exact genetic mechanism responsible for schizophrenia has not been identified. However, recent evidence suggests that genes affect biochemical reactions that may lead to schizophrenic behavior.

Over the years a number of biochemical theories of schizophrenia have been proposed. Researchers have suggested vitamin deficiencies, blood-protein abnormalities, and urine chemical irregularities as causal factors. Often in the past researchers overlooked the fact that people institutionalized for schizophrenia are usually on drug therapy, which may account for these chemical differences. The most promising current biochemical theory is the dopamine theory.

Wise and Stein (1973) reported that schizophrenics have significantly higher than normal levels of the neurotransmitter dopamine. Drugs called *phenothiazines*, which help treat schizophrenia by lowering dopamine levels, can, if not carefully monitored, produce symptoms of Parkinson's disease (which is normally caused by low levels of dopamine). Amphetamines tend to increase levels of dopamine and can lead to amphetamine psychosis, with schizophrenic symptoms (Angrist, 1983). Unfortunately, the data is not as clear-cut as we would like. Antipsychotic drugs do not help all schizophrenics. And, while these drugs lower levels of dopamine, they also interfere with the functioning of norepinephrine, serotonin, and acetylcholine and thus are not the complete solution to a complex situation. Research continues to try to find how neurochemicals are related to schizophrenia. There are some scientists who believe schizophrenia could be caused by a viral infection (Bower, 1985). Some viruses can affect the neurotransmitters, including dopamine. This line of research is still going on, and at the present time looks promising.

Neuchterlein and Dawson (1984) proposed a vulnerability-stress model of schizophrenia which states that some people have a biological tendency (predisposition), by inheriting particular genes, to develop schizophrenia if they are stressed enough by their environment. In particular, this theory suggests that certain people have difficulty processing information and maintaining attention. They overreact to social stressors and lack appropriate social competency and adjustment skills. Thus when a supportive family is not present, the stress is severe enough to push the individual toward schizophrenia. Thus, both biological and environmental factors are involved in the vulnerability-stress model.

We do not yet know exactly what causes schizophrenia. It seems to be produced and sustained by genetic, organic, biochemical, and environmental factors (Mirsky & Duncan, 1986). Like cancer, it probably isn't really one disorder, but rather a loose combination of physical and behavioral problems, only some of which we have identified. And like cancer, it is a disorder to which many people seem susceptible.

OTHER DSM-III-R CLASSIFICATIONS

As mentioned earlier in this chapter, there are over 230 clinical syndromes covered in DSM-III-R. In a textbook such as this, it is impossible to present each of these in detail. There are, however, some important disorders that students in general psychology courses should be familiar with. A brief review of other selected abnormal behavior disorders follows.

Delusional Disorder

The chief characteristic of the delusional disorder (formerly called paranoid disorder) is a persistent delusion not due to any other mental disorder (schizophrenia or a mood disorder), or to an organic factor. Other than the effects of the delusion on the individual's behavior, such as having great difficulties in interpersonal relationships, he or she is able to function fairly well. Recent research indicates that the delusional disorder is fairly rare and distinctly different from schizophrenia (Brennan & Henesley, 1984).

DSM-III-R identifies a number of delusions that are common to individuals with this disorder. They include erotomanic, grandiose, jealous, persecutory, and somatic. The *erotomanic delusion* involves believing that one is loved by another. In a *grandiose delusion* the person believes that he or she is extremely important. The *jealous delusion* involves believing that one's spouse or lover is unfaithful. In the *persecutory delusion*, the person believes that others are out to get him, and will try to poison, harass, hurt, frustrate, or kill him. The *somatic delusion* involves the belief that insects are inside the person, or certain parts of the body are not functioning properly.

Organic Mental Disorders

The organic mental disorders involve a disruption of psychological functioning due to a dysfunction of the brain. Primary degenerative dementia of the Alzheimer type refers to the progressive and deteriorating disorder in which cognitive abilities such as memory, thinking, and personality functioning are severely disrupted. In the early stages, the individual experiences memory impairment and social withdrawal. Eventually, personality changes occur and the individual's cognitive functions deteriorate to the point that he or she is incapable of caring for himself or herself. This disorder is much more common in people older than 65 years (senile onset), but does occur in younger individuals (presenile onset). Approximately 3% of the population over 65 have primary degenerative dementia of the Alzheimer type.

Organic mental disorders can also be caused by disease or by an accident. For example, brain tumors, exposure to lead, mercury, or other toxic chemicals, certain nervous diseases, or advanced syphilis all can produce psychotic symptoms. The severity of the psychosis, however, is a function not just of the physical damage, but also of the person's individual personality traits and previous psychological disposition.

People also develop psychotic symptoms because they have taken certain drugs. Such psychoactive substance-induced organic mental disorders are a growing problem among the users of drugs such as LSD and "crack" cocaine, which interfere with the normal functioning of the nervous system (see chapter 5, "Sleep and Consciousness," for a review of psychoactive drugs). DSM-

III-R identifies 11 classes of substances that can lead to organic mental disorders. They include: alcohol, amphetamines, caffeine, cannabis, cocaine, hallucinogens, inhalants, nicotine, opioids, phencyclidine, and sedatives.

Somatoform and Dissociative Disorders

The somatoform and dissociative disorders are ways that individuals deal with extreme stress and anxiety. The somatoform disorders focus on pain whereas the dissociative disorders focus on memory.

Somatoform Disorders. Somatoform disorders are generally characterized by physical symptoms for which there are no obvious physical causes. DSM-III-R identifies five major types of somatoform disorders: body dysmorphic disorder, conversion disorder, hypochondriasis, somatization disorder, and somatoform pain disorder.

The chief symptom of body dysmorphic disorder is a preoccupation with an imaginary defect in the physical appearance of a physically healthy person. Common complaints include excessive facial hair, skin spots, shape of various facial features, or rarely, of other body parts (hands, feet, breasts). The disorder often begins during adolescence or early adulthood, and often lasts for several years. Although social interactions are impaired, the individual is not usually incapacitated by this disorder.

In conversion disorder the person displays obvious disturbances in physical functioning that suggests a physical disorder, though medical examination reveals no physical basis for the problem. The symptoms can be those of paralysis, loss of sensation, blindness, or insensitivity to pain. People with these symptoms are often surprisingly undisturbed by them and show resistance to having them cured. They are not pretending and the symptoms are not imaginary; but these people are under the control of psychological processes of which they may be unaware. The relatively rare conversion disorder usually occurs during adolescence or early adulthood, and typically does not last long.

In hypochondriasis the person is preoccupied with the fear of having a serious or deadly disease. Medical examinations do not reveal any physical problem that could account for the complaints. The person may be preoccupied with normal bodily processes such as heart rate or breathing, or may focus on insignificant sores or an occasional cough. Often the person believes he or she has a fatal disease such as cancer or AIDS. Hypochondriasis occurs most often during young adulthood, and is equally common in men and women.

Somatization disorder occurs when a person (most often a woman) has numerous medical complaints for which no physical cause is evident. She might have headaches, backaches, allergies, painful or irregular menstrual periods, gastrointestinal cramps, vomiting, diarrhea, or dizziness. Year after year, the patient develops new symptoms that must be treated. Somatization disorder is closely related to hypochondriasis, the distinction being mainly that in hyponchondriasis the person is more concerned with fear of disease than in the symptoms of the disease itself, and the age of onset for somatization disorder is often adolescence rather than young adulthood.

The chief symptom of somatoform pain disorder (formerly called psychogenic pain disorder) is the preoccupation with severe pain for which there is no known organic cause. In some cases, there is a relationship between a stressful event and the occurrence of the pain, but in other cases, there is no evidence of any environmental stress. Although the somatoform pain disorder can occur at any time, it most often occurs in early adulthood, and occurs twice as often in women. In many cases, the person becomes incapacitated and can no longer work or function normally.

The somatoform disorders appear to help a person avoid anxiety because the pain and other symptoms excuse him or her for failing to carry out responsibilities. Note that these are different from the psychological factors affecting a physical condition discussed in chapter 12, "Stress and Adjustment." Those problems are real medical problems (such as ulcers, migraine headaches, high blood pressure) caused or aggravated by psychological stress.

Dissociative Disorders. The dissociative disorders involve a disturbance in memory, consciousness, or identity of an individual. Typically they are ways of escaping excessive anxiety through memory or identity loss. The DSM-III-R identifies four types of dissociative disorders. If the problem is primarily an identity loss, the individual must develop a new identity (multiple personality disorder) or reality is altered (depersonalization disorder). If it is primarily a memory loss, the individual cannot remember important personal events (psychogenic amnesia or psychogenic fugue).

Multiple personality is an extremely rare disorder in which several personalities are present in the same individual. One way to escape from overwhelming anxiety is to segment the personality into two or more alternatives that can more successfully deal with the situation. For example, one personality might be aggressive, while another might be shy, and the two are unaware of the existence of each other. Treatment of a woman called Sybil showed that she had 16 personalities. The most recent celebrated case is that of William Milligan, an accused rapist of coeds at the Ohio State University campus in the late 1970s who exhibited at least 24 different personalities.

Figure 13.10. Multiple Personality
In the extremely rare multiple personality disorder, one individual exhibits several different personalities. These personalities develop as a response to stress. Billy Milligan is a recent example of someone who may have 24 personalities.

Depersonalization disorder occurs when a person escapes from his or her own personality by believing he or she does not exist or that the environment is not real. The perception of the self is modified so that the individual can become detached from it. The person with depersonalization disorder often feels as if he or she is in a dream. The disorder often begins in adolescence or early adulthood, and may last for some time throughout the person's life.

Individuals with psychogenic amnesia lose their sense of identity, literally forgetting who they are, where they live, or what they do. It is a kind of selective amnesia, for they never forget their language or how to perform the tasks of daily life.

Disassociating oneself from personal commitments is probably a means of escape from overwhelming anxiety. Often a traumatic event has occurred prior to the development of the disorder. The person loses his or her memory and hence he or she is no longer responsible for obligations. It occurs most often in adolescents and young adults. Its onset is abrupt, and the disorder is usually temporary, with termination also abrupt and recovery complete.

Occasionally, the dissociated individual develops psychogenic fugue, and in addition to losing his or her memory, leaves the scene of his or her present life, going to a new geographic location and beginning life over as someone else by forgetting all of the unpleasant emotions connected with the old life. Often the fugue is less

severe than this, and consists of a brief travel period, after which the individual recovers and returns home. This rare disorder occurs most often during a natural disaster or a war. The dissociative disorders appear to be ways to deal with excessive anxiety or stress.

Personality Disorders

Personality disorders are problems in the basic personality structure of the individual. Personality disorders are often seen in other disorders, and are long-term impairments in social and personal functioning. When the characteristics are maladaptive and cause distress or impairment in adjustment they are called personality disorders. Personality disorders begin often in adolescence and continue throughout a lifetime.

DSM-III-R groups the personality disorders into three clusters. Cluster A includes paranoid, schizoid, and schizotypal personality disorders. The chief observation of individuals with these disorders is that they appear odd or strange in their daily functioning. Cluster B includes antisocial, borderline, histrionic, and narcissistic personality disorders. People with these disorders are emotional and dramatic, and can be antisocial. Cluster C includes avoidant, dependent, obsessive compulsive, and passive aggressive personality disorders. These individuals are seen as anxious and fearful.

One of the more serious personality disorders is the antisocial personality disorder, also known as *sociopathic personality* or *psychopathic personality*. DSM-III-R identifies the chief feature of this disorder as a pattern of irresponsible and antisocial behavior which begins in childhood or adolescence and continues into adulthood. It is much more common in males (4.5%) than in females (less than 1%) according to a recent study by Robins and colleagues (1984). As a child the individual has problems lying, stealing, fighting, and running away from home. In adulthood, the irresponsibility and antisocial pattern continues, as the individual does not honor obligations, fails to conform to social norms, and exhibits antisocial behavior such as destroying property and harassing other people. He typically does not experience guilt over his activities and feels no shame. Often he repeats the same mistakes and appears to be unable to learn from them. Some individuals with this disorder become criminals, but many just have very serious problems adjusting in society.

Sexual Disorders

The last major group of disorders concerns sexual adjustment. Some are quite serious disorders, while others are more common problems of adjustment. DSM-III-R divides the sexual disorders into two groups: the paraphilias and the sexual dysfunctions. As we discussed in chapter 10, "Emotion," the more common sexual dysfunctions involve an inhibition of sexual desire or problems in the sexual response cycle. Here we discuss the paraphilias, which are sexual deviations characterized by the need for unusual behaviors for sexual arousal which interfere with normal sexual activities. Paraphilia means deviant (para) attraction (philia).

The paraphilias are experienced almost exclusively by men. People who have a paraphilia tend to have repetitive sexual urges and fantasies that involve objects, humiliation, children, or nonconsenting people. DSM-III-R identifies eight specific paraphilias.

Exhibitionism is exposing the genitals to strangers in order to achieve sexual gratification. Fetishism occurs when a person prefers to become sexually excited by objects (fetishes). Frotteurism involves the obtaining of sexual arousal from touching and rubbing against a nonconsenting person, often in a crowd in a public place. Pedophilia is sexual activities with young children. Sexual sadism is inflicting suffering or humiliation on one's partner to achieve sexual arousal, and sexual masochism is achieving sexual arousal by receiving pain from one's partner. Transvestic fetishism involves ob-

taining sexual gratification from cross-dressing (usually a heterosexual man wears women's clothing when alone). In voyeurism a person derives sexual satisfaction from looking at people who are naked or engaging in sexual activities without their knowledge or consent.

There are many explanations for the paraphilias, but some psychologists believe that learning is extremely important in these disorders. The behavioral model suggests that somehow the person learns to be reinforced by the inappropriate stimulus. As we discuss in the next chapter, treatment often includes relearning the appropriate behavior. ■

Defining abnormal behavior is a very difficult task. The diagnostic categories in DSM have evolved as the psychology of abnormality has become more sophisticated. One of the potential dangers in the field of abnormal psychology is labeling a person as abnormal, as shown in the introductory story. There are many individual differences in personality, and what is thought to be abnormal in our society might be adaptive in another society. Psychologists try to understand abnormal behavior so they can treat it, as shown in the next chapter.

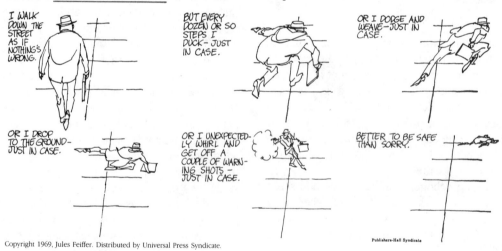

I WALK DOWN THE STREET AS IF NOTHING'S WRONG.

BUT EVERY DOZEN OR SO STEPS I DUCK— JUST IN CASE.

OR I DODGE AND WEAVE—JUST IN CASE.

OR I DROP TO THE GROUND— JUST IN CASE.

OR I UNEXPECTED-LY WHIRL AND GET OFF A COUPLE OF WARN-ING SHOTS — JUST IN CASE.

BETTER TO BE SAFE THAN SORRY.

Publishers-Hall Syndicate

CHAPTER REVIEW
What You've Learned About Abnormal Behavior

1. Behavior is abnormal when it contributes to maladaptiveness in an individual, is considered deviant by the culture, or leads to personal psychological distress.
2. There are a number of viewpoints on abnormal behavior, including the psychoanalytic model, the biosocial model, the learning model, the cognitive model, the legal model, and the statistical model.
3. The Diagnostic and Statistical Manual of Mental Disorders (DSM-III-R) was revised by the American Psychiatric Association in 1987. This is used today as a basis for diagnosing and classifying abnormal behavior.
4. The panic disorder is identified by the occurrence of panic attacks, specific periods of intense anxiety. Agoraphobia occurs when the individual is afraid of

places or situations from which it would be difficult or embarrassing to escape. The individual with agoraphobia is especially afraid to be outside the home, in a crowd, or traveling.

5. Phobias are acute excessive fears of specific situations or objects when such fears have no convincing basis in reality. Social phobias are excessive fears and embarrassment when interacting with other people. Simple phobias are excessive, irrational fears of specific objects, such as dogs, snakes, or closed-in places.

6. In the obsessive compulsive disorder, the anxious person may have repetitive thoughts (obsessions) or have constant urges to indulge in meaningless rituals (compulsions). Any attempt to stop the behaviors results in increased anxiety.

7. An individual with a generalized anxiety disorder lives in a state of constant tension and feels inadequate and helpless most of the time. Symptoms include trembling, restlessness, fatigue, rapid heart rate, sweating, nausea, and dizziness.

8. Mood disorders involve disruption of the normal emotional responses of the individual. In dysthymia, the person has a moderately depressed mood for at least 2 years. Major depression occurs when a person becomes unable to cope with daily activities. Depressed people are sad, have little interest in anything, have feelings of guilt, worthlessness, and inadequacy, and might have thoughts of suicide. Psychoanalytic theory suggests that feelings of anger and hostility are turned inward. Learning theory proposes that depression is the result of either learning to be helpless or a reduction in reinforcement from others. One physiological theory states that depression is the result of low levels of the neurotransmitter norepinephrine.

9. The bipolar disorder, or manic-depression, is characterized by unpredictable and extreme mood swings. In the manic state, the individual is hyperexcited, talkative, uninhibited, and perhaps destructive. Then, without warning, the patient becomes extremely depressed.

10. Schizophrenia is a severe form of psychosis. Schizophrenics show severe disturbances in the areas of thinking, perception, emotion, sense of self, volition, relationship to the world, and behavior. Often thinking is unorganized and incoherent. Many schizophrenics show delusions, or beliefs not founded on reality. They also have hallucinations, or sensory experiences with no sensory stimuli present. Many schizophrenics do not show any emotional arousal or show inappropriate emotional responses.

11. The individual with catatonic schizophrenia is sometimes immobile and does not speak, but at other times is aggressive. Disorganized schizophrenia is characterized by inappropriate silliness and bizarre behavior. In paranoid schizophrenia, the person often has persecutory or grandiose delusions. Undifferentiated schizophrenia is characterized by a gradual loss of interest in the world. Residual schizophrenia is the label given to a person who is currently without major psychotic symptoms, but who has had at least one prior episode.

12. Research suggests that the family life of a schizophrenic is extremely stressful. Learning theorists suggest that abnormal behavior increases because it is reinforced by others. Psychoanalytic theorists believe schizophrenics become narcissistic and totally controlled by the id. A genetic component is likely to be involved in schizophrenia. A biochemical theory proposes that schizophrenia results from excessively high levels of the neurotransmitter dopamine. The vulnerability-stress model proposes that some people have a biological tendency to develop schizophrenia when stressed by the environment.

13. The chief characteristic of the delusional disorder is a persistent delusion not due to any other mental disorder or to an organic factor. Common delusions include the erotomanic, grandiose, jealous, persecutory, and somatic.

14. Organic mental disorders involve problems in which there is a disruption of psychological functioning due to a dysfunction of the brain, whether caused by disease or accident. Psychoactive substance-induced organic mental disorders are psychotic symptoms caused by drugs and chemical substances.

15. Somatoform disorders are characterized by physical symptoms for which there are no obvious physical causes. They include body dysmorphic disorder, conversion disorder, hypochondriasis, somatization disorder, and somatoform pain disorder. Dissociative disorders involve a disturbance in memory, consciousness, or identity of an individual. They include multiple personality disorder, depersonalization disorder, psychogenic amnesia, and psychogenic fugue.

16. Personality disorders are problems in the basic personality structure of the individual. One of the most serious is the antisocial personality disorder. Sexual disorders include problems that people experience in their sexual adjustment. The paraphilias are sexual deviations such as fetishism, frotteurism, transvestism, pedophilia, voyeurism, exhibitionism, sadism, and masochism.

THERAPY

Treating individuals who have psychological problems has long been a major goal of psychologists. Psychoanalysis was the first major scientific attempt to treat psychopathology. Today, psychologists utilize a variety of therapeutic approaches, including insight, behavior, and group therapies. Sometimes drug therapy is incorporated into the treatment program.

Behavior therapy, the application of reinforcement and punishment to modify behavior, became popular in the 1960s. One of the best-known early studies in the type of behavior therapy known as token economy was conducted at Anna State Hospital in Anna, Illinois, by Teodoro Ayllon and Nathon Azrin. Ayllon and Azrin described their study in their 1968 book, *The Token Economy*.

The two psychologists worked in a ward in a mental hospital in which 44 female patients resided. The women, most of whom were diagnosed as psychotic (mainly schizophrenic), had been in the ward for an average of 16 years (the range was from 1 to 37 years). At the beginning of the study, many of the women did not cooperate and were difficult to manage. The women did not dress themselves, wash themselves, talk, eat properly, or keep their rooms neat. The hospital staff was frustrated and did not know how to control the patients except through the use of drugs.

Ayllon and Azrin set up a token economy program in which tokens (often small plastic pieces but could be check marks on paper or any small objects) were awarded when subjects (children, students, mentally

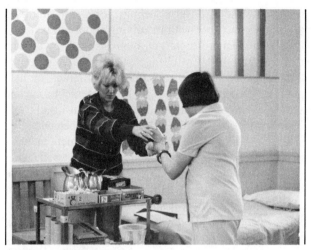

Figure 14.1. Token Economy
In a token economy, the subject works to earn tokens (or points) which may then be cashed in for something desired. The token is a secondary reinforcer and the desired event is the primary reinforcer. Here a resident of New Castle State Development Center in Indiana is purchasing items with tokens earned by successfully completing a bed-making program.

tokens they could go for a walk on the hospital grounds, for one token they could listen to a radio or watch a movie, and for 100 tokens they could go for a trip into town. For specified numbers of tokens the patients could also select commissary items such as candy, cigarettes, toothpaste, lipstick, gloves, or newspapers.

In one part of this study they recorded the total number of hours of on-work performance for the group. When reinforcement was contingent upon desired behaviors, the total for all of the patients was about 47 hours, which was maintained for 15 days. The next 15 days, no reinforcement was given, and performance fell quickly and drastically to about 10 hours per day, total time. The last 15 days of the study, reinforcement was again given and the performance swiftly returned to 45 hours, where it remained.

The results of this study were clear-cut. When the patients were being reinforced in the token economy system, desirable behaviors rose significantly, while undesirable behaviors greatly decreased. On the other hand, when the reinforcements were not awarded for desired, and withheld for undesired performance, the undesirable behaviors increased dramatically.

Ayllon and Azrin had demonstrated the effectiveness of behavior therapy in successfully modifying the behavior of even severely disturbed mental patients. An important aspect of the token economy study is not that schizophrenics could change the behaviors they exhibited (although this in itself is also important), but rather that the behavior of subjects could be quickly brought under the control of a reinforcement schedule. This valuable behavior modification technique has since been used with a wide variety of people, from the retarded and disturbed, to very healthy, normal individuals in schools, homes, and at work.

retarded, psychologically disturbed, employees, and many others) performed desired behaviors such as making beds, combing hair, brushing teeth, and eating properly and withheld when the desired behaviors were not performed. Another goal was to decrease undesired behaviors, such as being withdrawn, uncooperative and acting bizarrely. Tokens are effective because they permit immediate reinforcement of an appropriate behavior, are not prone to satiation effects, are portable (subjects and experimenter can easily carry them around), and are durable (Ayllon & Azrin, 1968).

The patients collected these tokens and were allowed to "cash them in" for privileges. For example, for ten

CHAPTER OBJECTIVES
What You'll Learn About Therapy

After studying this chapter, you should be able to:

1. Define therapy and identify its two major forms for psychological disorders.
2. Outline the history of the treatment of abnormal behavior.
3. Describe psychoanalysis.
4. Describe person-centered therapy.
5. Describe Gestalt therapy.
6. Describe reinforcement therapy.
7. Describe counterconditioning therapy.

8. Describe cognitive behavior therapy.
9. Describe encounter group therapy.
10. Describe family therapy.
11. Outline the evaluation of the effectiveness of psychotherapy.
12. Describe drug therapy.
13. Describe psychosurgery.
14. Describe electroconvulsive therapy.

WHAT IS THERAPY?

This opening story focuses on the application of behavior therapy in a mental ward. While many forms of therapy are practiced with the severely disturbed, many of the same techniques are being used to treat the more common problems that affect many healthy people. A primary goal of research into the causes and nature of emotional distress is the development of effective methods for aiding people with a variety of problems. Better treatments are emerging from the research of medical experimenters, the clinical experience of psychotherapists, and refinement of psychological theories.

This chapter describes many of the measures being taken to treat psychotics, to enhance their ability to cope more successfully with stressful life situations. They make it possible for people with a wide variety of mild and severe psychological problems to gain greater control over their feelings, thoughts, and actions, and thus to decrease the incidence and severity of abnormal behavior. People seek therapy for a variety of reasons, from improved self-understanding to the elimination of incapacitating distress. Others are forced into treatment by relatives or the court.

There are many types of professionals who are involved with people who need help with psychological problems. For instance, clergy are often involved in counseling sessions to help people with marital problems or who are having emotional difficulties. Family physicians may spot a potential problem and refer a patient to a trained professional. There are three major classes of professionals who provide therapy for psychological disorders. Psychiatrists are medical doctors who specialize in mental disorders. As an M.D., a psychiatrist can prescribe drugs or other medical treatment for patients. Clinical psychologists and counseling psychologists have graduate Ph.D. degrees in psychology, have typically worked in a mental hospital, and have had experience in counseling or psychotherapy. Psychiatric social workers have graduate training in social work and in counseling people and families.

There are two broad forms of therapy for mental disorders—psychotherapy and biological (or biomedical) therapy—which we cover in this chapter. Psychotherapy is the treatment of behavioral and emotional problems using psychological techniques. Psychotherapy includes a variety of approaches, including insight, behavior, and group therapies. *Insight therapies* are largely based on the assumption that behavior is abnormal because people do not adequately understand the motivation causing their behavior. Thus, insight therapies attempt to help people gain insight into their behaviors, thoughts, and feelings. *Behavior therapies* are more concerned with modifying abnormal behavior than with gaining insight into motivation. They assume that when the behavior changes, the underlying motivation also changes. *Group therapies* attempt to help people with problems by letting them interact in a group setting; through interaction they may gain insight into their motivations as well as change their behavior.

Psychotherapy is a broad category which includes many different approaches. Carson and his colleagues (1988) described some of the objectives of psychotherapy. According to them, it is used to reduce or eliminate maladaptive or abnormal behaviors. It is useful in increasing self-understanding, and in improving interpersonal competency. Psychotherapy can help a person solve an immediate crisis, as well as relieve personal distress over a longer period of time. Psychotherapy can help modify the environmental conditions contributing to the person's distress. And it can help the person modify misperceptions and inappropriate cognitions about the world. While a particular psychotherapy focuses on specific objectives, many of these objectives overlap. It is important to point out that this chapter covers only a few of the many forms of psychotherapy available. In one sense, each psychotherapist uses an individual, eclectic approach combining several types of therapy as may be appropriate for the patient.

Biological therapy is the treatment of behavior problems through biological techniques (Carson & colleagues, 1988). Biological therapy (or biomedical therapy) includes drug therapy, psychosurgery, and electroconvulsive therapy. The basic assumption of biological therapy is that a physiological disturbance causes the psychological disorder, and by treating the person biologically, the behavior will change. Biological therapy is usually used by a psychiatrist, since he or she has the appropriate medical training. The use of a particular therapy often depends upon the therapist, patient, and nature of the problem being treated.

HISTORICAL OVERVIEW OF TREATMENT OF ABNORMAL BEHAVIOR

For centuries, supposedly civilized societies looked upon psychologically abnormal humans as subhumans, to be tortured or locked away and forgotten. As a result, the history of the treatment of mental disorders and insanity makes a grim story. For hundreds of years, because of its bizarreness, insanity was associated with

Figure 14.2. Early Treatment of Mental Disorders
This drawing illustrates one of the torturous devices used in the treatment of mental disorders in the past.

Figure 14.3. Bicêtre Institution, 1793
This painting depicts Philippe Pinel ordering the release of the inmates who had been kept in chains at the Bicêtre mental hospital. Pinel, a French psychiatrist, campaigned for humane treatment of the insane at the end of the eighteenth century.

the supernatural, and the disturbed were thought to be possessed by demons or the devil. One "cure" that dates back to the Stone Age involves cutting a hole in the patient's skull to let out the evil spirits. In Europe, during the 17th and 18th centuries, hundreds of thousands of persons were tortured to "bring them to their senses." If that did not work, they were burned or hanged. Not only were the disturbed and insane miserable to begin with, but because they frightened other people, often they received treatment that made them worse.

In 1793, during the French Revolution, at the Bicêtre Asylum in Paris, Philippe Pinel brought about a startling new reform. He released the patients from their iron

chains and called for "wiser and more moderate restraints." He reported that a number of previously violent cases, once freed of chains, became relaxed and talked quite agreeably with those in charge. Although he was not the first to do so, Pinel attempted to classify the different types of mental disturbances and to suggest that different forms of insanity required different types of treatment. He showed the importance of keeping case histories and approaching each patient as worthy of individual treatment.

A major breakthrough for the mentally ill in America came in 1909 when Clifford W. Beers founded the National Committee for Mental Hygiene. Its purpose was to improve conditions in mental hospitals, create psychiatric research, enlarge the facilities for the care of the mentally ill, and make the public more aware of mental health.

Until quite recently, some modern treatments for psychological disorders included practices as "brutal" as many of those seen in asylums before Pinel. Psychosurgery, involving permanent destruction of portions of the brain, left thousands of patients with altered personalities, forced them to lead lives of limited potential and deprived them of normal experiences. Great strides are currently being made to provide better treatment of the psychologically disturbed. There has been a trend during the last couple of decades to get patients out of institutions and back into society. Here we look at some of the therapies used to treat some psychological problems.

INSIGHT THERAPY

Insight therapy is designed to help people better understand who they are and why they have various behavior tendencies. The assumption is that when people understand themselves and the motivation behind their behavior, they will have greater control over their lives. We review several types of insight therapy including psychoanalysis, person-centered therapy, and Gestalt therapy. We will start with one of the first insight therapies, Sigmund Freud's psychoanalysis.

Psychoanalysis

Therapists who have had psychoanalytic training, and have personally undergone psychoanalysis, are qualified to become psychoanalysts. Psychoanalysis is an intensive and prolonged exploration of the patient's unconscious motivation. The patient is assumed to have repressed conflicts from childhood that are still unresolved and causing anxiety and psychological problems. The goal of psychoanalysis is to bring the repressed conflicts to consciousness, so that the patient can deal with them as an adult. Although few professionals use psychoanalysis in exactly the way Freud did, it is important as many of the techniques are currently being employed in adaptations of the classical psychoanalytic approach. Psychoanalytic techniques include free association, resistance, dream analysis, and transference (Freud, 1949).

Free Association. In the classic psychoanalytic situation, the patient relaxes on a couch facing away from the analyst, and is encouraged to use free association, to say everything that crosses his or her mind, without letting normal inhibitions stop him or her from saying anything obscene, hostile, foolish, or illogical. The psychoanalyst expresses no disapproval or emotional reaction to what the patient talks about. As the therapist discerns patterns in the patient's associations, anxieties about certain topics, slips of the tongue, and reports of dreams, the patient is encouraged to explore the areas of past life that seem to be significant. The assumption is that, with conscious control of thought reduced to a minimum, the patient may reveal unconscious motives and associations.

Resistance. In principle, the patient will show resistance, unconsciously avoiding certain painful areas. The patient might suddenly change the topic or totally forget what was just said. If the therapist continues to prod, the patient interrupts the session by remaining silent, making jokes, or even becoming ill. In classical Freudian therapy, such areas are usually thought to be connected with real or imagined sexual experiences in childhood. Hence psychoanalysis focuses on these past causes of current problems.

Dream Analysis. As we discussed in chapter 5, "Sleep and Consciousness," Freud (1900) believed that dream analysis can help the therapist break into the patient's unconscious where true feelings can be expressed. Freud distinguished between the manifest dream content (what is remembered) and the latent dream content (the actual dream thoughts that occurred in the unconscious mind). The manifest dream is a disguised representation of our unconscious wishes, and thus the therapist must focus on using free association to gain insight into the latent content of the dream. Freud believed that "dreams are the royal road to the unconscious," and provide a way for the therapist to better understand the true nature of the patient's problems.

Transference. Transference is an important means of bringing out the patient's emotional conflicts. The analyst, remaining literally in the background and saying very little, becomes a blank figure on which the patient *projects* the attributes of significant figures in his emotional life—the hated or loved mother or father or sister or brother. Bringing these emotional reactions to life makes them recognizable for what they are and easier to deal with. Thus the patient *transfers* feelings onto the therapist.

In the course of analysis, the analyst begins to get a picture of the unconscious problems that are the source of the patient's difficulties. The analyst can suggest this picture to the patient, who then gains some insight into the problem. According to psychoanalytic theory, the patient must become aware of unconscious motives and conflicts, as well as understand how they are operating, before the maladaptive behavior patterns can be changed.

The classic form of psychoanalysis requires three to five visits per week over a period of five years or more, and can cost thousands of dollars. Since it requires an ability to verbalize feelings in a sophisticated way, and also an ability to respond rationally, its use is restricted to the nonfeebleminded and the nonpsychotic.

The classic form of psychoanalysis is rarely used today, partly because of the time and cost factors. Neo-Freudians, or psychoanalysts who came after Freud, often stress current behavior rather than historical conflict, and the ego as well as the id. However, psychoanalysis forms the basis for a variety of other therapies, many without specific names. Rather than free association, many analysts use a more direct probing technique. Psychoanalysis is important because it provided a frame-

Figure 14.4. Psychoanalysis
A therapeutic technique developed by Freud, psychoanalysis involves an intensive exploration of a patient's unconscious motivation. Here a patient is using free association to say whatever comes to mind.

work within which other forms of psychotherapy could be developed. One major therapy which is very different from psychoanalysis is person-centered therapy.

Person-Centered Therapy

Person-centered therapy (formerly called client-centered therapy) was founded by the humanistic personality theorist Carl Rogers. Its main assumptions are that every individual has an innate capacity to be healthy psychologically and self-actualized. Psychological maladjustment, according to this view, occurs when individuals deny important aspects of themselves, such as certain feelings and experiences because they regard them as "unacceptable." To get back into contact with themselves, instead of clinging to the images imposed upon them by others, they need an environment of acceptance which encourages free and open exploration of their personality. This will lead ultimately to self-understanding and mental health.

The function of the therapist is to provide a totally nonthreatening atmosphere of warmth and acceptance for the individual. To emphasize the active nature he or she plays in the process, the person receiving therapy is called a client rather than a patient. In this *nondirective* approach the therapist does not take an active role in directing the client to change his or her life, nor give advice or offer interpretations of what the client says. Rather, the therapist directs all efforts toward under-standing the client totally and clarifying the feelings and reactions he or she is expressing. Rogers thinks that the therapist should be genuine, sharing feelings with the client, while remaining a warm and sympathetic listener.

In his 1980 book, *A Way of Being*, Rogers described three core qualities—genuineness, unconditional positive regard, and empathy—that the therapist in person-centered therapy should have. Genuineness means being authentic, open, and honest. The therapist can help the client by being genuine in the relationship and by disclosing real thoughts and feelings when necessary. The therapist must view the client with unconditional positive regard, or total acceptance. The client must be treated always as a unique, important, and good human being. It is important to create an environment in which change can occur. The therapist must always have a positive, accepting attitude toward the client. The therapist must also show empathy for the client, and try to understand the client's feelings and perceptions. In showing empathy, the therapist reflects the feelings and ideas of the client, so the client can see himself or herself more clearly. Active listening (devoting full attention to what is being said) on the part of the therapist is essential in gaining empathetic understanding of the other person. Thus, the therapist does not interpret or evaluate what the client says, but rather lets the client form his or her own conclusions as the therapy progresses.

In the person-centered therapy situation, the client begins to feel free to explore his or her personality and

BIOGRAPHICAL ☆ HIGHLIGHT ☆

CARL ROGERS

Carl R. Rogers, the son of prosperous Illinois business people, was born in Oak Park, Illinois, in 1902. He was reared in a strict religious environment that placed great emphasis on the value of hard work and the sharing of responsibility. Rogers enrolled in the University of Wisconsin with the intention of studying agriculture. However, he soon decided to prepare for the ministry.

Leaving Wisconsin in 1924, he entered the Union Theological Seminary in New York. He became deeply involved in clinical work with disturbed children and his interests shifted to clinical psychology. He received his doctorate from Columbia University in 1931 and went to work at a guidance clinic in Rochester, New York. He taught at Ohio State University, the University of Chicago, and the University of Wisconsin, before settling at the Center for Studies of the Person in La Jolla, California.

Throughout his career, Rogers continued to work extensively with delinquent and underprivileged children, gathering the experience that led to his theory of nondirective, or person-centered therapy. He has written many influential books, including *Client-Centered Therapy* (1951), *On Becoming a Person* (1961), and *A Way of Being* (1980). He was a leader of the humanistic psychology movement until his death in 1987.

Figure 14.5. Person-centered Therapy Carl Rogers believed everyone has the capacity for developing psychological health. The function of person-centered or nondirective therapy is to provide a warm and accepting environment which encourages an open exploration of personality. Carl Rogers is pictured at the right leading a therapy session.

problems and to uncover experiences and feelings he or she had formerly suppressed. In the end, the client is expected to gain greater self-understanding and self-acceptance, which the person-centered therapist believes to be one and the same thing. The therapist believes also that the client's increased self-knowledge will facilitate discovery of more effective and rewarding ways of living and interacting with others.

Rogers believed that the person-centered approach applied to a wide variety of relationships, including therapist-client, parent-child, leader-group, teacher-student, or administrator-staff. Whenever the goal is to help the person develop, then the person-centered approach is appropriate. However, some concerns have been raised about Rogerian therapy. Evaluation focuses on self-reports of clients rather than actual behavior changes, thus making it difficult to measure the effectiveness of the therapy. Also, since the client must actively participate in the therapeutic process, the person-centered therapy is appropriate only for mild problems.

Gestalt Therapy

Another humanistic therapy was described by Frederick ("Fritz") S. Perls in his 1969 book, *Gestalt Therapy Verbatim*. Perls had been trained as a psychoanalyst, but because he couldn't support many of Freud's ideas, he broke away and developed Gestalt therapy. Gestalt therapy is designed to help people become more aware of themselves and of their responsibility for their own behavior; it focuses on the whole individual and the person's perceptions of self and the surrounding world. Like Rogers, Perls had an optimistic view of human nature, and believed that people develop problems when their innate goodness is frustrated.

The therapist observes nonverbal cues, such as voice, hand gestures, and eye movements; and then helps people become aware of their own feelings expressed through the nonverbal cues. The clients are encouraged to talk in the present tense and first person. Much of the therapy session is devoted to acting out emotions. It may involve other people who are present, or, if alone, the person *imagines* interactions with others. A goal of Gestalt therapy is to make people feel whole by helping them discover their feelings and reclaim the parts of personality that have been denied.

Like the other insight therapies, Gestalt therapy tries to improve the person's understanding of his or her own feelings. The emphasis of Gestalt therapy is on the present. The therapist takes a very active role in directing the person toward self-understanding. The therapist may laugh at, block, question, goad, or use any other technique necessary to get the person to achieve self-awareness and take responsibility for his or her own life. Also, again like other insight therapies, Gestalt seems to suit people with minor problems who have good verbal skills and fairly high intelligence; behavior therapy, the next type of therapy discussed, is not thus restricted.

BEHAVIOR THERAPY

In behavior therapy, the "symptoms" are treated as constituting the disorder itself. This is much different than in psychoanalysis, which treats emotional disturbances as symptoms of a disease whose roots extend far back into childhood. In behavior therapy, a disturbance in personality is considered a learned form of thinking, feeling, and behaving that can be modified through relearning. The aim of the relearning in behavior therapy is readaptation to present circumstances. Behavior therapy emphasizes learning new behavior to replace the old unwanted habits. It treats overt behavior by giving or withholding reinforcements, or by administering punishments. The therapeutic procedure is therefore more like training, using the principles of both classical and operant conditioning, than the gradual development of insight.

There are a great many types of behavior therapy that can be used singly or in combination, but most share a core of common characteristics (O'Leary & Wilson, 1987). Behavior therapists assume abnormal behavior is learned and can be modified through learning principles. The focus of therapy is to modify the current behavior in a wide range of settings rather than to try to determine its historical antecedents.

Reinforcement Therapy

Behavior therapy assumes that maladjusted behavior is learned, and thus to correct it, the subject must relearn appropriate behavior. As you will recall from our discussion of operant conditioning, *reinforcement* is very important in learning and maintaining new behaviors. Reinforcement therapy simply applies the operant conditioning principles of reinforcement to increase the frequency of desired behavior (and decrease the frequency of undesired behaviors). Skinner's 1953 book *Science and Human Behavior* was influential in helping behavior therapy, or behavior modification, gain support among therapists. O'Leary (1984) reported that a survey of the

1983 issues of the *Archives of General Psychiatry* and *The Journal of Consulting and Clinical Psychology* show that of the nondrug treatment studies, the majority involved a form of behavior therapy.

Shaping. Shaping (see chapter 6, "Learning") is a form of behavior modification that has been used successfully in therapy with emotionally disturbed and retarded individuals. Psychologist O. Ivar Lovaas (1977) used this conditioning technique to teach autistic children to speak. He did so by teaching them a series of new responses, each of which more closely approximated the ultimate desired response.

Lovaas gave each child a spoonful of food for every sound made. He also rewarded the child for looking at the teacher's mouth. When the child vocalized every 5 seconds or more often and spent at least half the time looking at the teacher's mouth, the next step began. For example, Lovaas said the word, "baby," every 10 seconds. If the child made any vocal response within 6 seconds of the adult's word, reinforcement was given. When the teacher's voice began to evoke a vocal response from the student fairly frequently, a further requirement for reinforcement was added: the pupil's reply actually had to match the teacher's.

Lovaas carefully chose the behavior to be reinforced. It had to be a syllable that the teacher was able to produce visibly. For example, the teacher said "ba" and held the child's lips closed with his finger, releasing them abruptly when the child exhaled; then the child was reinforced. On successive trials, the teacher moved his fingers away from the child's mouth, then to the cheek, finally touching the jaw.

In the next step, the teacher introduced a second sound, quite different from the first, and interspersed the

Figure 14.6. Reinforcement Therapy
In this form of behavior therapy, a reward is used to increase the frequency of the desired behavior. Here, autistic children are immediately reinforced with food when they interact with each other.

two sounds randomly. Other sounds were added, and in this way, the child built up a large stock of imitative syllables and words. A noticeable increase in the words learned by the end of this period indicated that the child had learned not just certain vocal responses but the principle of imitation as well.

Other studies have shown that shaping is useful in solving a wide range of childhood problems, including thumb sucking, hyperactivity, poor school performance, and even shyness. Franks (1984) reported that the rate of improvement using behavior modificaiton techniques was better than that obtained with other types of therapy. Parents can also use shaping to help children develop positive social skills and manners.

Extinction. In *extinction* all reinforcements are withheld when the unwanted response occurs. When all delusional or psychotic remarks made by a mental patient are ignored, there will often be a marked drop in the frequency of these statements. At the same time, more realistically oriented statements can be reinforced. The parents of a baby who cries at bedtime might use extinction to eliminate the unwanted behavior.

Sometimes we inadvertently reinforce undesirable behavior rather than using extinction. For example, a teacher may ignore a student's classwork, but as soon as the student misbehaves, the teacher yells at him or her. If the student has been deprived of attention, he or she may interpret this yelling as attention (reinforcement) and

Self-Directed Behavior Modification

It is possible to employ some of the principles of classical and operant conditioning in a program of self-directed behavior modification. You begin by choosing one problem to modify. Then you spend a week or so keeping a diary or journal of your normal behavior. The contents of this diary constitute the baseline data you will use to determine what aspects of your behavior need modifying and what actions and feelings that contribute to the problem may be susceptible to behavior modification.

Let's assume that you want to alter your habit of overeating or cut down on your smoking. In collecting your baseline data, you must include every instance of engaging in the target behavior, with entries indicating all the factors at work while you ate or smoked. You'll want to know how much you ate or smoked, whether you did so alone or with others, where you were, how you felt before, during, and after, and any other factors that might be related to your behavior.

Checking your completed baseline data you may discover that certain people, situations, or feelings seem to be cues or stimuli for your target behavior. By using the behavior modification technique of stimulus control, you can begin to master the forces compelling you to engage in some habit more than you feel is appropriate. If, for instance, you find that you eat too much when you are out with others, control that stimulus by removing it—eat alone. Similarly, if you seem to smoke most while watching TV or reading, confine your smoking to other occasions.

You can support your stimulus control efforts with a program of rewards or reinforcements for meeting certain behavioral goals. If you are in fact able to, say, restrict your eating only to mealtimes and only to the dining room, give yourself some predetermined reward, like the purchase of a book or an article of clothing. You can even set up your own token economy by awarding yourself points that add up to rewards you can collect

later. You can keep track of the points by carrying toothpicks or similarly portable counters in one pocket or part of a purse and transferring them to another spot as you meet some behavioral goal you've established as worth a certain number of points.

You can also alter your actions behaviorally by changing the sequence of events, doing things in a novel order and thus disrupting the stimulus-response pattern that may be sustaining your target behavior. And you can employ incompatible behavior, whereby you do something else, rather than your target behavior. For example, if you always seem to bite your fingernails unconsciously, in certain places at certain times, by becoming aware of the situations that reinforce that habit, and arranging to have something in your hands on those occasions, you will be acting incompatibly with the habit and weaken it.

The success you achieve with self-directed behavior modification depends largely on your willingness to go slowly and stay with the program. You have to keep complete baseline records, consistently use the chosen technique—failure to do so every time, and as soon as your target behavior is manifested, can make your problem worse than before—and try to concentrate on one problem at a time. Make sure that you understand the basic principles of behavior modification before you begin your program, and always keep your goals obtainable, and you should have success in modifying your behavior.

THOUGHT QUESTIONS

1. What is self-directed behavior modification?
2. What are some basic procedures in a behavior modification program?
3. What determines the success of a program? How can you measure success?

actually increase the misbehavior because it was able to elicit the attention denied previously. What would you do to correct the situation? An effective therapy is to ignore the undesired behavior (unless it is too disruptive) and reinforce the desirable behavior to increase its frequency.

The Token Economy. As discussed in our opening story, a token economy is a form of behavior modification in which desirable behaviors are immediately reinforced with tokens that can be exchanged at a later time for desired rewards such as food, television, or recreational activities (Kazdin, 1980). Reciprocally, sometimes tokens are taken away for undesirable behaviors.

As we saw in the Ayllon and Azrin study of a mental hospital ward, people's behavior quickly came under the control of the token reinforcements. When they briefly removed the tokens, the patients' undesirable behaviors again increased. As with other forms of behavior therapy, the token economy can be utilized with more severely disturbed individuals who do not have normal verbal capacities. Ayllon and Azrin found that a token economy could be administered easily by regular staff personnel. In recent years, token economies have not been used as frequently in mental institutions, partially because of the reduction in hospital staff as well as the trend toward hospitalization only for more severe psychological disorders (Carson & colleagues, 1988).

Token economies have also been used with the mentally retarded, and with normal people who need to change their behavior patterns in order to lose weight, manage their time, stop fingernail biting, and solve a host of other problems. In fact, your instructor may be using a form of token economy in your psychology class. How many tokens (points) do you need for an *A*?

Counterconditioning

The techniques of classical conditioning may be involved in behavior therapies. In counterconditioning, an unwanted response is replaced by conditioning a new response that is incompatible with the original one. An early study by Mary Cover Jones (1924) demonstrated counterconditioning. Jones was able to treat Peter, a young boy who was afraid of rabbits, by feeding him in the presence of a rabbit. Over a series of trials, the rabbit was brought closer and closer until Peter could pet the animal without fear. Essentially, the rabbit was presented prior to the food, and through classical conditioning, took on the properties of the food. A number of counterconditioning therapies have been developed.

Systematic Desensitization. An important application of counterconditioning is systematic desensitization, a technique that in supervised therapy programs is very valuable in treating fears, phobias, shyness, and related

Figure 14.7. Progressive Relaxation

BODY AREA	RELAXATION TECHNIQUE
Feet	Point your feet straight out and curl your toes tightly. Then release and relax.
Lower Legs	Point your feet toward your face as high as they will go. Relax.
Upper Legs	Keeping your legs straight, lift your feet off the floor 10 inches. Relax.
Stomach	Take a deep breath and tighten the stomach muscles as you hold your breath. Relax.
Chest	Push your shoulders back and hold as you slowly exhale. Relax.
Upper Arms	Tighten the muscles in both of the upper arms. Relax.
Lower Arms	Tighten muscles as you move your hand toward your arm. Relax.
Hands	Make a tight fist and hold. Relax.
Neck	Smile and tighten throat muscles. Relax.
Forehead	Push your eyebrows up and tighten muscles. Relax.

In this program of self-relaxation, you tense and relax each area of the body in turn.

problems. In systematic desensitization, individuals overcome anxieties by learning to relax in the presence of stimuli that had once made them unbearably nervous and afraid. First, patients are taught how to relax their muscles completely. Then, very gradually, anxiety-producing stimuli are introduced. As the patients learn to relax in the presence of these stimuli, stronger anxiety-arousing stimuli are added, until the patients are no longer made anxious by the original objects that caused them to seek help.

Systematic desensitization, a procedure developed by behaviorist Joseph Wolpe (1958) is based on the principle of reciprocal inhibition. This concept states that it is possible to break the bond between anxiety-provoking stimuli and responses manifesting anxiety by facing those stimuli in a calm, relaxed state. All this means is that there are actions or emotions that counter anxiety, and with them we can combat our tendency to feel anxious when encountering anxiety-provoking objects or situations. For example, eating seems to inhibit anxiety, which may be the reason so many people seem to choose eating—and overeating—as a way of dealing with anxiety. They usually do so unconsciously and unsystematically, and so often they just gain weight and still continue to experience anxiety. Desensitization is a more carefully planned approach.

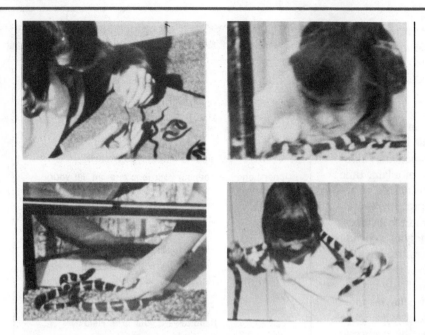

Figure 14.8. Treatment of Snake Phobia
Using both desensitization therapy and modeling, subjects were able to reduce significantly their fear of snakes. In desensitization, subjects are taught how to relax in the presence of stimuli which cause increasing degrees of anxiety. In modeling, subjects observe how models interact with snakes which helps lower their own fear levels.

A basic component of desensitization is the ability to relax. We can actually teach ourselves how to relax. So many of our problems involve stress, tension, and anxiety that acquiring the ability to relax quickly and easily and in a variety of situations is an important first step toward gaining significant control over our feelings.

Progressive relaxation is a simple form of self-relaxation. This technique was developed in 1929 by a physician named Edmund Jacobson. All you have to do is assume a horizontal position and in turn alternately tense, then relax, the various muscle groups in the body. This permits you to identify the lingering tenseness in different parts of your body by learning the difference between what a tense and a relaxed muscle feels like. It takes only a half-hour or so to begin learning the method, and after a few daily or twice-daily sessions, you should begin to notice that you are able to relax yourself totally with less and less practice or effort.

By using such self-relaxation before bedtime, people can overcome some of their insomnia. Practiced before encounters expected to be stressful, it can precondition a person to experience less tension and anxiety than he or she would usually manifest under the ordinary pressures of daily living. By reducing residual muscle tension, many people discover they are less troubled by nervous habits that in the past may have caused tensions.

In systematic desensitization, after subjects have learned how to relax successfully, the therapist helps them draw up an anxiety hierarchy. The hierarchy starts with a mild anxiety-arousing situation and proceeds to terrifying events that are unlikely ever to occur. For example, let's suppose you have a snake phobia. The least anxiety-provoking stimuli might include seeing a picture of a snake or a worm at a distance; the most

terrifying event might be actually handling or being bitten by a snake.

Now you are ready to proceed to relax in progressively more anxious situations. You might need a professional counselor for treatment, but in some cases, you can use systematic desensitization yourself. In a relaxed state, having freed yourself of muscle tensions, produce the least anxiety-arousing stimulus in your desensitization hierarchy. You experience it, in all its details and threatening aspects, until you begin to feel tense or anxious. You stop; using self-relaxation you relax yourself again, and repeat the procedure until that part of the hierarchy doesn't produce any anxiety. You continue the method, moving up the anxiety hierarchy a few steps each session, until even the most frightening aspect of your problem causes you no anxiety when you confront it head-on.

Another form of desensitization, covert desensitization, is an effective technique for helping an individual overcome fears by learning to relax in the presence of anxiety-arousing images. Many students experience anxiety when taking examinations. If you could learn to relax during a test, you would be able to focus on the test questions, and ultimately improve your grade in the course. Let's take test anxiety as an example of covert desensitization.

After you have learned to relax, you need to construct an anxiety hierarchy. You should have about 10 items which can be placed in a sequence from most anxiety-producing to least anxiety-arousing. The most threatening situation might be taking a test, not knowing any of the answers, and panicking. Next might be taking a test and knowing only half the answers. A little less threatening is sitting in the classroom waiting for your instructor to hand you the test. Then might come walking down the hallway toward the classroom where the test will be taken. A little less threatening still might be awakening the morning of the test and thinking about it. Then might come studying for the test the night before. Finally, might come scenes like reading the textbook or listening to a lecture a week before the test.

You need to find someplace quiet where you can relax. Once you've relaxed, imagine the least threatening item in your test anxiety hierarchy. As soon as you begin to feel anxious, stop imagining the item and practice relaxation again. Keep trying to imagine the stimulus until you can do so without feeling anxious. Then you're ready to try the next item on your hierarchy.

Continue until you have completed your anxiety hierarchy or until you have reached an item that you cannot relax with totally. The hierarchy should take several sessions to complete. If you experience much trouble, you need to divide the items up further. On the other hand, if you sail through the entire hierarchy, it is not threatening enough. Practice should help you decide on the procedure. When finished, you should be able to take tests without experiencing extreme anxiety.

Systematic desensitization is often successful (Spiegler, 1983). If the problem is fragmented into small enough parts, and if you proceed slowly and cautiously, even long-standing phobias and fears can usually be overcome.

Aversion Therapy.   In aversion therapy unwanted responses are paired with unpleasant consequences (see also chapter 6, "Learning"). Alcoholics, for example, can be given a slight electric shock every time they take a drink. Or they may take a drug that makes them nauseated when they consume alcohol. The new habits learned by such methods are fairly fragile and can soon be replaced, as discussed by Wilson and O'Leary (1980). If, however, the alcoholic, or person with any such specific problem, genuinely wants to rid himself of it, he may undergo aversion therapy to make it easier for him to break the unwanted habit.

Aversion therapy has been used to treat a variety of problems, including drinking, smoking, obesity, and sexual disorders. Usually the subject views, tastes, or imagines the problem stimulus while receiving an aversive stimulus. A person with a fetish for silk panties might view the panties while receiving an electric shock. Sometimes aversion can be accomplished by overindulgence. For example, you might form an aversion to chocolate ice cream if you ate three gallons of it at once.

Aversion therapy is controversial because of the ethical issues it raises. Some people question whether psychologists should ever be permitted to inflict pain on other people. Often aversion therapy is used with other methods, or when other methods prove ineffective.

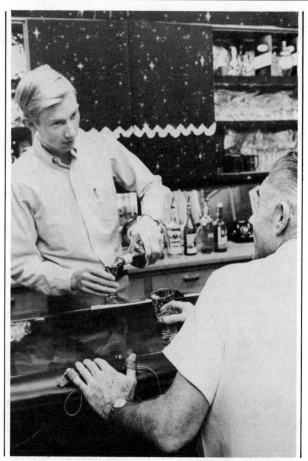

Figure 14.9. Aversion Therapy
When a subject undergoes aversion therapy, unwanted behaviors are associated with a negative stimulus. Here an alcoholic receives an electric shock to his hand each time he takes a drink.

Cognitive Behavior Therapy

Behavior therapy implies that behavior alone is modified, and that identical techniques should work on animals and humans. Recently, some forms of behavior therapy have included thinking or *cognition* in the treatment program (see chapter 8, "Language and Intelligence"). Cognitive behavior therapy involves modifying a client's cognitions through behavioral techniques. A basic assumption of cognitive behavior therapy is that a person's thoughts and feelings affect his or her behavior. The goal is to change the person's thoughts which will in turn have a positive effect on the person's adjustment. A number of different types of cognitive behavior therapy have been developed, most focusing on *cognitive restructuring*, the modification of the client's thoughts and perceptions that are contributing to his or her maladjustment. We discuss some of the most influential forms of cognitive behavior therapy here.

Rational-Emotive Therapy.   Albert Ellis (1984), the founder of rational-emotive therapy, argued that what we think has a significant influence on the way we

Telephone Crisis Centers

One problem with traditional forms of psychotherapy is that usually they take a long time and involve an intensive interaction between therapist and patient. Unfortunately, we don't have enough professional therapists to always have one available when a crisis arises. During the past decade or so, many community mental health centers have established telephone crisis centers to help deal with this problem.

The telephone crisis hot line is usually staffed by paraprofessionals. These are people who volunteer their time and are intensively trained in the techniques of phone usage in emotional and mental emergencies. Because they can remain anonymous, people with serious personal problems will phone and talk with anyone. The problems range from suicide, rape, and incest to loneliness, anxiety, and indecision. The concept works because someone is willing to listen. If the caller wants professional help, he or she is referred to an appropriate agency; the call may even be switched to a professional who can be reached by phone.

Speer (1971) has conducted research in this area and provides some suggestions for crisis hot line volunteers. First, the volunteer should be a good listener and try to develop empathy with the caller. Second, the volunteer must know where help can be obtained, including agencies, physicians, psychologists, or special centers for specific problems. Next, the volunteer should try to get the caller to promise to take some specific steps to solve the problem. And finally, it's important to reassure the caller that the crisis will end and life will not always seem so hopeless.

The popularity of telephone crisis centers has risen in recent years. However, evaluating their effectiveness is a difficult task. Speer has shown that about 95% of the callers do not call again. And since callers are usually anonymous, it's often difficult to do follow-up studies on them. Still, it seems likely that just having someone to

Figure 14.10.   Telephone Crisis Hotline
The telephone crisis hotline allows people with problems to talk to someone who will patiently listen. The benefits of this system consist of immediate attention from a volunteer paraprofessional and anonymity of the caller.

talk to can make a critical difference to a person contemplating suicide. And this type of service fills a gap that exists because there are insufficient professionals available at any given time.

THOUGHT QUESTIONS

1. What services do telephone crisis centers provide?
2. What are the advantages or disadvantages of having the telephone hot lines manned by volunteers?
3. Would everyone with a crisis problem call a hot line? What else could be done to help these people?

feel and act. In particular, psychological maladjustment occurs when we hold certain self-defeating, irrational beliefs about our experiences in the world. The rational-emotive therapy (RET) model suggests that a significant activating event (A) is interpreted by a person's belief system (B) and leads to an emotional consequence (C). When the consequence is an undesirable one, such as anxiety or stress, it is due to the individual's irrational beliefs. RET attempts to dispute (D) the irrational belief system by challenging it rationally, with the result that the disturbed consequences eventually disappear (Ellis, 1984).

Ellis compiled a list of common irrational beliefs. For example, one should be loved by everyone; one must

always be perfect in everything; one's self-worth is based on one's performance; a person has little control over emotions; and one should avoid life's problems. The aim of RET is to challenge beliefs such as these so the person can enjoy a happy, healthy life. For example, one of the irrational beliefs cited by Ellis is the belief that we must be competent in everything we do. Tom did not receive an *A* on his last test and now feels defeated and depressed. By understanding that everyone can't always come out on top, Tom can learn to accept himself, and in time even work harder to earn an *A* in that particular subject (or be satisfied with doing the best job possible).

Cognitive Therapy.   Aaron Beck (1976) argued that

many disorders are caused by the negative thoughts and feelings people experience. He developed a cognitive therapy to restructure these negative, self-defeating thoughts and modify the way people view the world. Beck has largely applied his cognitive therapy to depression, although recently he extended it to the treatment of anxiety disorders (Beck, 1985).

Beck's cognitive therapy assumes that depression results because people hold illogical ideas which are maintained by self-defeating behaviors. For example, if Bill does poorly on a test, he may believe he is stupid and will never do well and thus should quit school. Thus, Bill might tend to perceive the world as harmful (teachers are out to get him), overgeneralize from his limited experiences (he will never do well in anything), and magnify the significance of an event (failing the test is the end of the world). In cognitive therapy, Bill would be encouraged to develop hypotheses from his beliefs and expectations and test these hypotheses to determine if they are true. Eventually, the client learns to restructure cognitive processes to obtain a more objective, unbiased view of the world. A number of studies have supported the effectiveness of cognitive therapy (Wilson & colleagues, 1983).

Modeling.   Albert Bandura (1986) argued that modeling and imitation is extremely important in learning everyday behaviors, and observing others can help an individual deal with problems. In addition to reinforcement, Bandura proposed that cognitive factors were important in therapy. For instance, a person with a simple phobia of snakes was helped by observing someone (a model) handle snakes without fear (Bandura & colleagues, 1969). Children can reduce their fear of surgery when exposed to a model of the surgical event before the event.

Bandura (1977) described several functions of modeling in therapeutic situations. It serves a *learning function* by providing observers examples of appropriate behaviors. It has an *eliciting function* by providing appropriate cues (for instance, causing the client to relax when the model relaxes in an anxiety-producing situation). Modeling serves a *disinhibiting function* when the observer is not afraid to engage in an activity after seeing someone else do it (for example, children might lose their inhibitions about petting a dog if they observe other children petting it). Modeling can also serve an *inhibiting function* (children can learn not to pet the dog when they observe it biting someone else). Modeling has been applied to a variety of mild psychological disorders with great success.

Bandura (1982) recently argued that the success of therapy is due to the improvement of a person's sense of mastery, or self-efficacy. This, according to Bandura, involves both cognitive and behavioral therapeutic techniques. Many psychologists now believe that cognitive

factors are important in learning behavior and play a major role in psychological disorders such as phobias and depression. Future research will explore how cognitive therapy can help people change attitudes and maladaptive behaviors.

GROUP THERAPY

Group therapy involves the treatment of several patients at the same time. In group therapy the therapist tries to remain in the background, while patients discuss and share their feelings and problems with one another. Feedback is encouraged from other members of the group, rather than only from the therapist.

This method originally emerged as an alternative to the high cost of individual therapy, but it is now believed by many psychotherapists to be of value in its own right and with definite advantages for some patients. Patients may be helped by getting to know that other people have difficulties similar to their own. In addition, an individual in group therapy can see how a variety of people actually respond to him or her, and can try out new ways of reacting and responding with a group of people whom he or she knows and trusts.

In many cases, the individual therapies already discussed can be adapted easily to group situations. A group of people with test anxiety or fear of snakes can go through systematic desensitization together rather than alone. Gestalt therapy is often conducted in groups rather than individually. As you might imagine, there is an unlimited variety of group therapies. Not all groups are successful, however, and for any type of therapy it is important to weigh carefully the advantages and disadvantages before joining a group (Lubin, 1983).

Encounter Groups

In the past couple of decades, there has been a great deal of interest in encounter and sensitivity training groups. A group of people, usually no less than seven, and rarely more than twenty, get together with the aim of shedding their ordinarily polite social masks and expressing their real feelings. The group usually emphasizes verbal interaction, games, and other activities that encourage open displays of approval, criticism, affection, dislike, and even anger and tears, rather than the tact and inhibition of emotional expression that ordinarily govern our social behavior. The assumption in these groups is similar to that of person-centered therapy: the individual

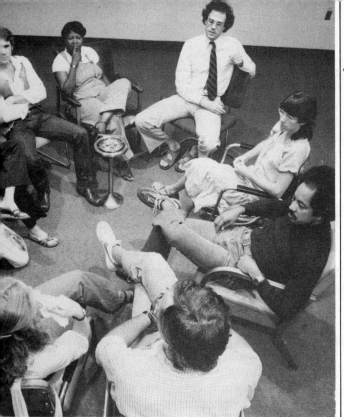

Figure 14.11. Group Therapy
When several people are treated simultaneously, there is opportunity for interaction with supportive others who often share similar problems. Group therapy includes such types as encounter groups and family therapy.

designed especially for <u>assertiveness training</u>. These groups help individuals stand up for their rights without violating the rights of others. Typically, a group of about a dozen people are told the problems of not being assertive and how the group can help build confidence. Then members of the group role-play in various situations that require an assertive response. Feedback and encouragement are provided by the therapist, until individuals feel comfortable being assertive (Carson & colleagues, 1988).

Most people in encounter groups do not consider themselves involved in psychotherapy. Rather it is thought that anyone can benefit from the experience in encounters where there is complete candor—something very rare in our everyday world. Some psychologists are concerned that these group experiences may trigger serious disturbances in some of the more troubled patients who participate in them. The success of these groups depends to a large degree on the skills of the leader and the personalities of the people involved. Caution is usually urged before joining a session that doesn't have the proper leadership.

Family Therapy

<u>Family therapy</u> assumes that ineffective communication and difficulty in interacting with members of the family unit are significantly involved in causing a problem (Gurman & colleagues, 1986). The task of the family therapist is to modify these social interactions and help improve communication patterns so family members can solve their own problems (Kutash & Wolf, 1986). In <u>conjoint family therapy</u>, the emphasis is on developing better relationships and self-esteem for all members of the family. <u>Structural family therapy</u> attempts to modify the organizational structure of the family so members can relate more positively and be supportive of one another. For instance, structural therapy might be used when the child has more power than a parent.

Often the therapist sees only one member of the family at a time, while at other times the entire family is in the therapy session together. The goal of family therapy is to work with a whole family to help them change unsuccessful patterns of behavior toward each other. A highly successful technique in family therapy involves making a videotape of the family members, in which they are interacting with one another in a normal situation. When people are able to view themselves "from the outside" in this way, they often find it easier to understand their unsuccessful behavior and to make progress toward improving it. While not everyone benefits from family therapy, for many it is a useful form of treatment.

When just husband and wife are treated together, it is

will grow in a positive way by resisting social restrictions and by interacting with others honestly and openly.

Sensitivity training groups originally tended to be less extreme than encounter groups, although the distinction between the two is thin, and the terms are often used interchangeably. The <u>sensitivity training group (T-group)</u> grew out of conferences on small-group dynamics held at the National Training Laboratory in Bethel, Maine, in 1947. Originally, T-groups were designed to help executives and managers become more sensitive or aware of their employees' needs. The emphasis has shifted toward individual growth in healthy people. Carl Rogers is credited with starting some of the first encounter groups when he trained counselors at the University of Chicago in the mid-1940s.

<u>Encounter groups</u> most often have a leader experienced at getting people to "open up." The group may meet for several hours a week over some period of months, or it may meet as a <u>marathon group</u> for 24 continuous hours or more, with individuals dropping out for naps. It is thought that the intensity and prolonged time of the marathon group will break down social resistance faster, and accomplish as much as groups whose meetings are interspersed over longer periods of time. The goals of encounter groups include: examining one's behavior and values, learning about people in general, becoming more successful in interpersonal relationships, and developing conflict resolution skills.

Related to encounter groups are groups that are

336

called <u>marital therapy</u>. Sometimes this form is called <u>couple counseling</u>, and includes nonmarried couples. What is essential is that both partners be treated together, so that they can better understand their relationship and improve their adjustment. One of the difficult tasks of couple counseling is helping each partner overcome their intense emotions to objectively view the relationship and the role each one plays in it. A study by Cookerly (1980) of the divorce rates of individuals undergoing marital therapy found that 56% of couples who underwent therapy together remained married for at least 5 years after the treatment. Of course, these couples would be likely to be the most motivated to maintain the marriage in the first place. Hahlweg and Markman (1988) argued that more efforts need to be placed on prevention of marital distress early in the relationship. A closely related form of therapy is called <u>divorce therapy</u>, and is aimed at helping people who are getting divorced make an easier transition into their new roles. Divorce therapy has not been used long enough to be fully evaluated properly.

EVALUATION OF THE EFFECTIVENESS OF PSYCHOTHERAPY

A true experimental test of the effectiveness of psychotherapeutic procedures would be complex, expensive, and probably impossible. It would require several groups of patients carefully matched for similarity of psychological disturbance, IQ, and family, educational, and economic background. One group would be treated with traditional psychoanalysis, one with person-centered therapy, one with behavior therapy, and another with group therapy. Also, we would need a control group whose members received no therapeutic help at all, since a study by Smith and Glass (1977) estimated that as many as one-fourth of all people with anxiety complaints get better without any professional help. Not only the extent of improvement would have to be measured, but also its duration.

Some investigations of therapists working with roughly the same methods suggest that there are common characteristics possessed by successful therapists. The more successful the therapist, the more likely he or she is to have strong feelings of warmth and liking for his or her patients; to be readily able to imagine himself or herself in the situation of the patient; to be free of anxiety or other disturbances; to be open and honest; and to have had considerable experience in treating patients.

Figure 14.12. Effectiveness of Psychotherapy

TYPE OF THERAPY	EFFECTIVENESS
Psychodynamic	72
Adlerian	76
Eclectic	68
Transactional Analysis	72
Rational-Emotive	78
Gestalt	60
Client-Centered	74
Systematic Desensitization	82
Implosive	74
Behavior Modification	78

(Effectiveness score = Client is better off than XX% of those untreated)

Smith and Glass (1977) reviewed the effectiveness of ten types of therapy and found that the patient who is treated, regardless of method, is generally better off than about three quarters of those not treated. Note many of the therapies are similar in their effectiveness.

We should point out, however, that some research has not found consistent results in the effectiveness of these characteristics (Parloff & colleagues, 1978). Not all therapists need all the qualities to successfully deal with all patients. The patient most likely to benefit from psychotherapy would have a moderate rather than a severe disorder and a high degree of motivation to overcome the problem. And, as one might expect, the patient's confidence in the therapist seems to aid the effectiveness of the therapy.

The task of evaluating specific types of psychotherapy is also extremely difficult because of the diversity of approaches used today. In a survey of 415 counseling and clinical psychologists, Smith (1982) reported that 41% were eclectic (integrated aspects of various types to create a unique type) in their approach to therapy. In this survey, 19% of psychologists use behavior or cognitive-behavior therapy, 21% used some form of insight therapy, and 19% indicated they used some other form of therapy. Thus, the majority (59%) of therapists do not readily fall into the categories of therapy we have discussed in this chapter.

Clearly, no certain measure of the effectiveness of the various forms of therapy has yet been devised. It is therefore largely up to the individual to decide which kind of therapy might best meet his or her needs. Otherwise normal people, who may be troubled by anxiety, mild depression, difficulty in getting along with others, and related common emotional and behavioral complaints, have a wide selection of therapeutic options.

Depending on their particular problem, on the character and skill of the therapist, and on their willingness to go along conscientiously with the therapeutic program they enter, they can confidently expect to see measurable results in a reasonable time. Howard and colleagues (1986) found that improvement was related to the number of therapy sessions participated in, with the greatest gains occurring within the first 6 months. Phillips (1988) argued that Howard's data base was limited, and that currently the most common length of psychotherapy (for all types and all problems combined) is six sessions. Psychoanalysis or some of the other insight therapies take a long time to see change and improvement; whereas behavior therapy can produce quite rapid results.

While Smith, Glass, and Miller's (1980) analysis of psychotherapy outcome studies found that the patient is better off than 80% of untreated controls, there is no evidence to prove that one form of therapy is always better than another.

Future research will continue to examine the characteristics that make psychotherapy effective, and practitioners will continue to refine their techniques to provide quality service for their clients. It seems likely that the characteristics of the therapist, the patient, the problem, and the therapy itself will be more closely matched in the future.

BIOLOGICAL THERAPY

Up to now we have discussed psychological therapies; this section deals with biological therapy, the treatment of behavior problems through biological techniques. The three major types of biological therapy, or biomedical therapy, are drug therapy, psychosurgery, and electroconvulsive therapy.

Drug Therapy

In the past three decades, remarkable discoveries of new psychoactive drugs have revolutionized treatment of psychological disorders. There are many types of drugs currently in use in drug therapy today. In chapter 5, "Sleep and Consciousness," we discussed the psychoactive drugs primarily that are not usually used to treat psychological disorders. In this chapter, we concentrate on three major classes of drugs used in the treatment of psychological disorders: antianxiety drugs, antipsychotic drugs, and antidepressant drugs. Remember that only therapists with M.D. degrees can prescribe these drugs, and that psychologists must work with medical person-

nel when drugs are used to treat psychological disorders.

Antianxiety Drugs. The antianxiety drugs, or antianxiety minor tranquilizers, are used to reduce anxiety. They are often given to patients under stress or experiencing pressure, tension, or insomnia. Sometimes antianxiety drugs are prescribed by general practitioners for people complaining of anxiety. Some people you know probably take Librium, Valium, Equanil or Miltown.

In small doses for short periods of time, when a person is in a stressful situation, these drugs do reduce anxiety and allow the person to function effectively. Unfortunately, sometimes people take large doses over a long period of time and misuse this potentially valuable aid to effective coping. Ideally, antianxiety drugs are used to relieve overwhelming anxiety, so that other forms of psychotherapy can treat the real problem.

Antipsychotic Drugs. Probably the greatest change in treating institutionalized schizophrenics occurred in 1955 when chlorpromazine was introduced in the United States. Antipsychotic drugs, also known as major tranquilizers, are effective in relieving the bizarre and antisocial symptoms of some schizophrenic patients. The antipsychotic drugs have made it possible for therapists to work with patients rather than just provide institutional custodial care. However, they have sometimes been abused. When given in large doses, they can sedate the patient to the point where he or she is incapable of responding to the environment.

As discussed in chapter 13, "Abnormal Behavior," a current theory of schizophrenia is that it results from high levels of the neurotransmitter dopamine. Among its actions, chlorpromazine reduces the level of dopamine usage in the brain. Future research will help us understand exactly how the antipsychotic drugs produce their dramatic effects.

Antipsychotic drugs are used extensively today, with the vast majority of institutionalized psychotic patients receiving regular medication. The trade name of chlorpromazine is Thorazine. Other often-used antipsychotic drugs include Mellaril, Stelazine, and Haldol. Sometimes antipsychotic drugs have been found to be more effective in modifying behavior than many forms of psychotherapy, but they produce maximum results when used with other forms of therapy.

Antidepressant Drugs. Antidepressant drugs, like imipramine, help to relieve depression. The most common trade names include Tofranil, Elavil, and Nardil. As described in chapter 13, "Abnormal Behavior," one current theory of depression suggests that it results from low levels of the neurotransmitter norepinephrine. Antidepressant drugs increase the levels of norepinephrine, and this probably contributes to their effectiveness.

Recently, there has been an increased interest in the drug lithium carbonate as an effective treatment for bipolar disorder. This simple inorganic salt was discov-

Figure 14.13. Drug Therapy

CLASS	GENERIC NAME	TRADE NAME
Antianxiety Drugs (minor tranquilizers)	chlordiazepoxide	Librium
	clorazepate	Tranxene
	diazepam	Valium
	meprobamate	Miltown
	oxazepam	Serax
Antipsychotic Drugs (major tranquilizers)		
phenothiazines	chlorpromazine	Thorazine
	fluphenazine	Prolixin
	perphenazine	Trilafon
	prochlorperazine	Compazine
	promazine	Sparine
	thioridazine	Mellaril
	trifluoperazine	Stelazine
butyrophenones	haloperidol	Haldol
thioxanthenes	chlorprothixene	Taractan
	thiothixine	Navane
Antidepressant Drugs		
tricyclics	amitriptyline	Elavil
	imipramine	Tofranil
	nortriptyline	Aventyl
	protriptyline	Vivactil
monoamine oxidase (MAO) inhibitors	isocarboxazid	Marplan
	phenelzine	Nardil
	tranylcpromine	Parnate
lithium	lithium carbonate	Lithane

There are a variety of drugs used in therapy. Antianxiety drugs are used to relieve feelings of tension. Antipsychotic drugs are used to treat symptoms such as those found in schizophrenia. Antidepressant drugs are used to relieve depression.

ered in Australia in 1949, but was not used in the United States for 20 years because it was considered dangerous and physicians had serious doubts about its effectiveness. It serves as a depressive for the manic state of the individual with bipolar disorders. Some research suggests that it might also help some forms of depression (Coppen & colleagues, 1982). There is concern over its side effects, however, and blood levels must be carefully monitored in patients. Research is continuing on the effectiveness and safety of lithium as a drug.

Drug therapy is currently the most widely-used biological therapy. It does, without a doubt, alter physiological reactions and consequently behavior. Another technique in biological therapy, popular before the introduction of drugs, is psychosurgery.

Psychosurgery

Psychosurgery was one of the earliest treatments for abnormal behavior. Some anthropologists suggest that the therapy practiced by cave dwellers consisted of cutting a hole in the skull to let the "evil spirits" out.

Patients who survived very likely behaved differently and probably were much calmer than before.

Modern psychosurgery is credited to Portuguese neuropsychiatrist Antonio Caetano de Abreu Freire Egas Moniz, who in 1935 began performing prefrontal lobotomies on people. In a *prefrontal lobotomy*, the frontal lobes of the brain are disconnected from the rest of the brain. When this surgery is performed on violent patients, they become calm. During the 1950s, thousands of patients received lobotomies, including those classified as having schizophrenia, depression, and even anxiety disorders.

Because of the frequent negative side effects, such as seizures, loss of emotionality, and problems in thinking, the number of lobotomies performed declined. Since the introduction of the antipsychotic drugs in the 1950s, extremely few psychosurgeries have been performed. Elliot Valenstein (1986) described the historical development of psychosurgery, and argued that the reason for its initial success was psychiatry's need to gain respectability by having a surgical treatment for psychological disorders. Overall, psychosurgery is usually reserved for cases where other treatments have failed to produce any effects. When necessary, newer techniques allow neurosurgeons to isolate an extremely small area of the brain that is malfunctioning or has a tumor, and precisely remove it.

Electroconvulsive Therapy

In the 1930s scientists began experimenting with convulsions as a therapy for schizophrenia and depression. One method was to inject insulin, which produced low blood-sugar level and coma. The other more popular method was electroconvulsive therapy (ECT), discovered by Italian physicians.

In electroconvulsive therapy (ECT), two electrodes are fastened to the patient's head and an electric current, about the same strength as household electricity, is passed between them for a very brief time. The patient goes through a brief period of extreme muscle contraction (a convulsion) and is temporarily unconscious. When the patient wakes up, he or she is drowsy and confused, but quickly recovers and shows less severe symptoms (sometimes ECT is incorrectly referred to as "shock" therapy). Side effects include temporary general disorientation and more serious memory impairments that can last for months (Palmer, 1981).

ECT is controversial and is not used as frequently as it was before the antidepressant drugs were introduced. It is generally reserved for the severely depressed. We do not know how it works, but it does produce some results in many severely depressed patients. It is, like psychosurgery, usually a last resort, as psychoactive drugs are generally much more effective in altering behavior. ▪

Many of the therapeutic techniques described in this chapter are extensions of everyday social interactions. Indeed, insight therapies such as psychoanalysis or

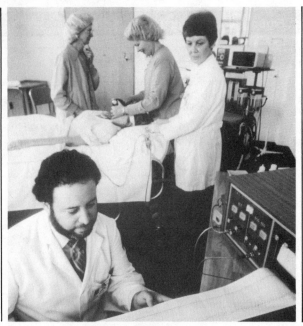

Figure 14.14. Electroconvulsive Therapy
When a patient receives electroconvulsive therapy (ECT) for severe depression, electricity is passed through the brain causing a convulsion. Scientists are not sure why it relieves symptoms of severe depression in some patients.

person-centered therapy have improved perception and self-understanding as their chief goals. As we saw in the opening story, reinforcement behavior therapy involves the application of learning and reinforcement principles, and is effective in a variety of situations from mental institutions to classrooms. Unfortunately, no one type of therapy is totally effective for all problems or all people. Success of a therapy depends on many factors, including the personalities of the therapist and patient, and the problem being treated. In the next chapter we explore some of the influences that create individual differences in social behavior.

"I BELIEVE I HAVE A NEW APPROACH TO PSYCHOTHERAPY, BUT, LIKE EVERYTHING ELSE, IT FIRST HAS TO BE TESTED ON MICE."

CHAPTER REVIEW
What You've Learned About Therapy

1. Professionals who provide therapy for psychological disorders include psychiatrists, clinical and counseling psychologists, and psychiatric social workers. Psychotherapy is the treatment of behavior problems using psychological techniques such as insight, behavior, and group therapies. Biological therapy treats behavior problems with biological techniques which include psychosurgery, and electroconvulsive and drug therapy.

2. Historically, people with behavior problems were treated inhumanely. There has been a trend during the past couple of decades to get patients out of institutions and back into society.

3. Insight therapy is largely based on the assumption that the behavior is abnormal because we do not adequately understand the motivation causing it. Psychoanalysis is an insight therapy developed by Freud that is an intensive and prolonged exploration of the patient's unconscious motivation. The patient is assumed to have repressed conflicts from childhood that are unresolved and hence causing problems. The goal of psychoanalysis is to bring the repressed conflicts into consciousness so that the patient can deal with them. Techniques employed by psychoanalysts include free association, resistance, dream analysis, and transference.

4. Person-centered therapy is an insight therapy developed by Rogers that is based on the assumption that every individual has an innate capacity to be psychologically healthy and self-actualized. The therapist provides a non-threatening atmosphere and lets the client choose the direction of the therapy. Therapists should show genuineness, unconditional positive regard, and empathy toward the client.

5. Gestalt therapy is an insight therapy designed to get people to become more aware of themselves and their responsibility for their own behavior. The therapist helps the person become aware of his or her own perceptions and act out his or her emotions.

6. Behavior therapy is concerned with modifying undesired behavior. Reinforcement therapy, one form of behavior therapy, is based on the assumption that abnormal behavior is learned, and therefore reinforcement can modify the behavior. The techniques of shaping and extinction are used in reinforcement therapy. In a token economy desirable behaviors are immediately reinforced with tokens that can be exchanged at a later time for desired rewards.

7. In counterconditioning, an unwanted response is replaced by conditioning a response incompatible with it. In systematic desensitization, individuals overcome fears and anxieties by learning to relax in the presence of stimuli that made them unbearably nervous. In aversion therapy, unwanted responses are paired with unpleasant consequences.

8. Cognitive behavior therapy involves modifying a client's cognitions through behavioral techniques. Cognitive restructuring involves the modification of the client's thoughts and perceptions that are contributing to his or her maladjustment. Rational-emotive therapy was developed by Ellis to get people to become aware of their irrational beliefs.

9. Group therapy attempts to treat problems by letting people interact in a group setting. Sensitivity training groups (or T-groups) grew out of efforts to help executives and managers become more aware of their employee's needs. There has been a shift toward self-awareness and self-growth in encounter groups. To be successful, an encounter group requires a leader experienced at getting people to open up and discuss their problems and feelings.

10. Family therapy and marital therapy are based on the assumption that communication and the social interactions of the family are causing the problem. The goal is to help family members change unsuccessful patterns of behavior.

11. No clear measure of the effectiveness of the various forms of therapy has been devised. Characteristics of the therapist, patient, problem, and therapy influence its effectiveness. Research indicates that psychotherapy often accelerates adjustment.

12. Biological therapy includes psychosurgery, and electroconvulsive and drug therapy. Drug therapy is the most widely used biological therapy and often alters behavior. Antianxiety drugs (minor tranquilizers) are used to reduce anxiety. Antipsychotic drugs (major tranquilizers) are used to relieve the symptoms of schizophrenia. Antidepressant drugs relieve depression, possibly by increasing the level of norepinephrine in the brain.

13. Psychosurgery, in the form of removing or destroying part of the brain, has never been very effective. Few such operations were performed after the 1950s, when antipsychotic drugs became available.

14. Electroconvulsive therapy (ECT) applies electricity to the brain to produce a convulsion. It sometimes relieves severely depressed patients, but is not as effective as antianxiety drugs.

SOCIAL PROCESSES

Part VII explores some of the influences others have on the individual. The areas of social psychology and psychology applied to industry, legal systems, and the environment are reviewed.

After reading Part VII you should be able to:

Define social psychology

Define how attitudes are formed and measured

Describe how groups affect behavior

Identify the areas in which industrial and organizational psychologists work

Explain how psychologists affect the social and physical environment

SOCIAL PSYCHOLOGY

Our behavior, thoughts, and feelings are often influenced by others. Person perception and attitude formation have long been major interests of social psychologists who are also involved in research on social influence and group processes. An important goal of social psychology is to understand social interaction and encourage people to become more helpful to one another.

Yale psychologist Stanley Milgram's 1963 experiment on obedience produced frightening results. Milgram's 1974 book, *Obedience to Authority*, describes the study. Milgram wanted a general cross section of people, so he placed an advertisement in the New Haven, Connecticut newspaper, offering $4 for anyone between the ages of 20 and 50 to participate in a 1-hour study of memory and learning. Subjects included teachers, post office workers, engineers, and laborers. Their education ranged from high school to professional degrees. Originally only men were tested, but women participated in some of the later studies.

The subjects were told that they were participating in a test to gauge the effects of punishment on learning. Each individual subject was asked to take the role of "teacher" and to deliver electric shocks to a "learner," who was actually a secret accomplice of Milgram. In a separate room, the "learner" was strapped into a chair, hooked up to the shocking device, and his responses were relayed to the "teacher."

Each "teacher" was provided with an impressive-looking (but actually harmless) electric shock generator, which, he was told, could deliver shocks ranging in intensity from 15 to 450 volts. The "teacher" decided on the strength of the shock to be administered and then actually pulled the switch. The "learner" had to memorize 40 word pairs, such as blue-box, and wild-duck. He was given an electric shock when he failed to remember one, the shocks becoming stronger if he continued to miss words. As part of the scenario, the "learner" deliberately made mistakes with 30 of the items.

Figure 15.1. Obedience Experiment
These photographs were taken at Yale University during the course of Milgram's experiments in obedience. **(A)** The "shock generator." **(B)** The "teacher/subject receives a sample shock from the generator. **(C)** The teacher sees the "learner"/confederate being strapped into the chair and connected to the shock apparatus. **(D)** The teacher refuses to administer any more shocks to the learner and gets up from his chair in protest.

The purpose of the study was to investigate obedience. As the shocks supposedly became stronger, (remember, no shocks were actually administered), the "learner" began to moan and cry out. At still higher levels, the "learner" demanded to be let out of the experiment, claiming to have a weak heart. At about 300 volts, he screamed in agony, then lapsed into silence.

Despite these apparent signs of the "learner's" distress, the experimenter urged the subject (teacher) to continue. If a "teacher" hesitated or resisted, the experimenter said, "You must go on."

Although many of the subjects showed signs of great conflict, 65% of them continued to administer what they thought were real shocks until the end of the study. Right up to the three highest possible voltages they pulled switches that delivered these shocks even to a screaming, protesting human being they were led to believe had a weak heart. Not one subject refused to participate in so seemingly cruel an exercise. They showed obedience to the authority represented by the "expert."

Milgram ran 18 different experiments in his study of obedience. The variables studied included proximity, personnel, institutional context, authority figure, and group decisions. Although there was considerable variability, generally, as physical proximity of the victim to the subject increased, the level of obedience fell significantly. Although some criticize Milgram's study of obedience on ethical grounds (Miller, 1986), it demonstrates how social psychology is often involved in understanding everyday behavior.

CHAPTER OBJECTIVES
What You'll Learn About Social Psychology

After studying this chapter, you should be able to:

1. Define social psychology.
2. Describe the process of person perception.
3. Describe the process of attribution.
4. Define attitude and outline how attitudes are formed and measured.
5. Describe how attitudes can be changed.
6. Outline the theory of cognitive dissonance.
7. Outline the concept of prejudice.
8. Outline the area of conformity.
9. Describe three techniques of compliance.
10. Outline the area of obedience.
11. Describe the processes that influence group effectiveness.
12. Define social facilitation.
13. Outline the area of competition and cooperation.
14. Outline the area of leadership.
15. Define aggression and outline four theories of aggression.
16. Outline the area of helping behavior.

WHAT IS SOCIAL PSYCHOLOGY?

It is hard to imagine a day in which our lives are not influenced by other people, directly or indirectly. We form impressions of other people every day. We make decisions about the motives of our friends and acquaintances, and decide whether we like new people that we meet. When we attribute motives to others (attribution) we rely on perceptual cues that we have learned through social interactions. Through our experiences and interactions with other people, we form and modify our attitudes. How we form these social perceptions is currently an important area of study in social psychology.

Another area of social psychology examines social influence on behavior. When we attend class, we sit politely and listen to the instructor. We also comply with requests, such as helping to hand out class papers. And, as shown in our opening story, we obey the orders of people in authority. These are social influences.

Social psychology also covers the influences that groups have on their members. In class discussions, a few people become leaders and guide the group's other members into the paths these discussions will take. Helping behavior and aggression are the final topics of social psychology that we will discuss in this chapter.

Although there are a number of variations, most psychologists accept Gordon Allport's (1985) definition of social psychology. Allport stated that social psychology is an attempt to understand how the thoughts, feelings and behavior of individuals are influenced by the actual, imagined, or implied presence of others. In this text we define social psychology as the study of how an individual's behavior, thoughts, and feelings are influenced by others. When someone asks us a question, we respond with an answer. Someone else's personality and physical characteristics can either attract or repel us. For instance, we are more inclined to notice an attractive person of the opposite sex than we are someone unattractive. We are also influenced indirectly by others: through books, movies, television, and newspapers people we have never met help shape our opinions and tastes.

Social psychology is a behavioral and social science and as such its emphasis is on the individual. However, it focuses primarily on interpersonal interactions, and the influences that other people have on the individual. Many basic topics that we have already discussed are relevant in this social approach to behavior. For instance, perception, learning, cognition, motivation, and personality all contribute to our understanding of social interactions. Other topics such as social influences, group processes, aggression and helping behavior, are uniquely social phenomena. As we go through this chapter, try to recall the previous topics and apply them in this new context.

Sears and colleagues (1988) discussed five major theories which currently dominate social psychology: learning, cognitive, motivational, sociological, and biological. The social learning theory proposes that social behavior is learned and maintained through the processes of observation, imitation, and reinforcement, and that learned behavior is particularly relevant in aggression. The cognitive theory focuses on thinking and language, and is important when discussing their effect on social perception and attitudes. The motivational theory emphasizes needs and desires, and is involved in determining social influence on behavior. The sociological theory views behavior as a group process. And the biological theory proposes that people have certain innate tendencies, which influence whether they will behave aggressively or helpfully. Social psychology is a complex area that covers a variety of topics from a number of different approaches. We begin this chapter with a look at how people develop impressions of others.

SOCIAL COGNITION

Social cognition is the process of understanding other people and ourselves (Fiske & Taylor, 1984). This area of social psychology explores how we make sense out of ourselves and other people by forming and utilizing information about the social world. Social cognition includes the study of attitudes, attribution, person perception, and prejudice. It stresses the cognitive functioning of the individual in everyday social situations. In this section, we discuss person perception, forming impressions of other people, and attribution, making inferences about the motives of ourselves and others.

Person Perception

Most people have an amazing ability to recognize and respond to the important aspects of another's personality. When we first meet people, we quickly determine whether or not we like them through the process of impression formation. Even hearing a bit of information about someone, or observing a person allows us to make judgments about them. Solomon Asch (1946) argued that we perceive people as wholes. Thus, when given only partial information, we tend to fill the gaps in our

Figure 15.2. Person Perception
The first impression we form of someone tends to be the overriding factor in interpreting later impressions of them. Physical attractiveness and manner of dress all contribute to first impressions.

impressions with traits of people similar to those we perceive. The process of person perception involves using the information we gather in forming impressions of people to evaluate them. Like perception, it is the process of interpreting sensations (see chapter 4, "Sensation and Perception"). However, in person perception, the sensations and information are produced by the behavior and characteristics of the people around us.

Osgood, Suci, and Tannenbaum (1957) developed the semantic differential procedure, in which they asked subjects to evaluate persons and objects by selecting which of a pair of traits was most descriptive. They found three dimensions were very important in rating people: evaluation (good-bad), potency (strong-weak), and activity (active-passive). They argued that evaluation was the most important dimension when forming an impression of other people.

First Impressions. Much research has centered around which is more important in forming lasting impressions of people: first impression (*primacy effect*) or last impression (*recency effect*). Asch (1946) reported that subjects who heard a personality profile of someone who was described as "intelligent, industrious, impulsive, critical, stubborn, and envious" rated the person as significantly more happy and sociable than other subjects who heard the exact same personality traits read in the reverse order. It appears the first words we hear, favorable or otherwise, are the ones which remain with us and influence our perceptions and behaviors.

In a classic experiment by Harold Kelly (1950), one group of students was told a new lecturer was "a very warm person, industrious, critical, practical, and determined." If this person came to give a talk to your class, how would you react? Would you be likely to interact

with the person or remain silent? Kelley found 56% of his students entered into class discussion with the lecturer, and the vast majority of students rated him as informed, considerate, sociable, popular, generous, and humorous. Another group of students were told that the guest was "a rather cold person, industrious, critical, practical, and determined." Now how would you react? Kelley found that only 32% of the subjects entered into class discussion with this person, and most rated him as self-centered, formal, unsociable, irritable and humorless. Of course, the only difference was the substitution of the word cold instead of warm in the description. Our first impressions do influence our behaviors.

Consistency and Positivity Bias. Research has shown that once we have formed a general impression of someone, we tend to interpret additional information about this person in a manner consistent with our general impression. The halo effect was demonstrated in a 1977 study by Nisbett and Wilson. These experimenters had college students view a videotape of a professor. In one version, the professor was warm and friendly, while in the other version, he acted cold and uncaring. Students who saw the warm version liked the professor better and rated all other characteristics in a much more positive fashion than did those subjects who saw the cold version.

We also tend to show person-perception bias when evaluating others through providing positive evaluations rather than negative ones (Sears, 1983). The tendency to evaluate others positively is called positivity bias. In one study, Sears reported that college students rated 97% of the college professors above average (in reality, only 50% could be above average, since 50% are below average). We empathize with people and thus evaluate them more highly if they are individuals rather than groups. Sears also reported that 74% of the time instructors were rated higher than the courses they taught, emphasizing the human element in the evaluation phenomenon (since the teacher and course provide roughly the same experience).

Physical Attractiveness. An important dimension in forming an impression of someone is what that person looks like. If he dresses sloppily, is clumsy, and is physically unattractive, we are inclined to dislike him, or in general think negatively about him, while to many people an attractive person can do no wrong.

Karen Dion (1972) reported that physical attractiveness does indeed influence other people's impressions. She had women read reports of severe classroom disruptions by elementary schoolchildren. In some cases the report was accompanied by a photograph of a very attractive child, while in other cases the photo was of an unattractive boy or girl. The subjects tended to blame the disruptive behavior on the ugly children, saying that it was easy to see that they were "brats." On the other hand, when the photo was of a beautiful child the women tended to excuse him or her.

Do adults notice attractiveness? Certainly, as shown in a study by Dion and her colleagues, Ellen Berscheid and Elaine Walster (1972). They showed college students photographs of attractive, average, and unattractive students, and asked them to rate the people in the

Figure 15.3. Physical Attractiveness
Research shows that physical attractiveness is an important influence on impression formation. Attractive people are generally seen as having more positive personalities and being more intelligent than unattractive ones.

photos on 27 personality traits. As expected, the attractive people received the most positive ratings.

Cunningham (1986) had male college students rate photographs of beauty contest finalists and ordinary college women, and then analyzed the differences in facial features between the two groups. One way that they differed was that the beautiful women had "widely spaced eyes, small noses, small chins, wide pupils, high eyebrows, and a big smile." These features were associated with positive personality characteristics, such as bright, sociable, and assertive. Thus, overall, research supports the claim that beautiful people are perceived as having excellent personalities.

Attribution

Are we able to observe a person's behavior and somehow decide what that person is really like? How do we attribute a person's personality to his or her behaviors? Attribution is the social cognitive process of determining the causes of behavior of other people and understanding their motives and personality. Essentially, we are interested in attributing the motivation for a behavior to either situational or dispositional factors. Situational factors involve the external environment, whereas dispositional factors involve the individual's internal personality. Common sense tells us that there are many times that we want to know whether a person's behavior is due to external or internal causes. For example, if someone does poorly on an exam, is it because the test is very difficult (external) or the individual does not know the material well (internal)? Through attribution, we are able to predict what a person is likely to do in a given situation, and we gain a better understanding of the person's motivation for engaging in certain behaviors.

Correspondent Inference Theory. Often we are interested in knowing more about an individual's personality. We usually observe the individual's behavior and then make inferences about his motivation and personality based on what we observe. Jones and Davis (1965), in their theory of correspondent inference, suggested that attribution is often successful because we focus on certain types of behaviors. People have many traits in common, but we tend to focus on the ways in which a person is different or unique from others. For example, try to describe the personality of someone who drives a car to work every day. It's a very difficult task, since most people drive cars to work. Now, try to describe the personality of someone who rides a lion to work every day.

Jones and Davis also suggested that we tend to focus on behaviors that could have only one motive. For example, John asks Mary for a date. Let's assume Mary is beautiful, sexy, rich and intelligent. Why did John ask

Figure 15.4. Causal Attribution

	Internal	External
Consensus	Low Others do not act this way in this situation	High Most others act this way in this situation
Consistency	High Person always acts same way in this situation	High Person always acts same way in this situation
Distinctiveness	Low Person acts same way in other situations	High Person does not act same way in other situations

Kelley stated that the factors of consensus, consistency, and distinctiveness must be considered in determining whether a behavior is internally or externally motivated.

her out? He might have any of several reasons. But let's assume that Mary is unattractive, poor, and intelligent. We now most likely assume John is interested in her mind.

Covariation Theory. Often the main task in attribution is to determine whether a person's behavior was caused by internal or external motives. Harold Kelley (1973) proposed a covariation theory to account for causal attribution. Kelley suggested we consider three factors (consensus, consistency, and distinctiveness) in determining whether a behavior was internally or externally motivated. Often these factors will covary (occur together), helping us predict causation. Consensus is the extent to which other people react in the same way the subject does in a particular situation. Consistency is the extent to which the subject always behaves the same way in a particular situation. And distinctiveness is the extent to which the subject reacts the same way in other situations.

If we conclude that we have conditions of low consensus, high consistency, and low distinctiveness, we attribute the subject's behavior to internal causes. If we have high consensus, high consistency, and high distinctiveness, then we attribute the person's behavior to external causes. For example, the mailman takes one look at your big dog and runs off down the street. If no one else avoids your dog (low consensus), the mailman always avoids your dog (high consistency), and he avoids all dogs (low distinctiveness), we conclude that he is afraid of dogs. If however, everyone avoids your dog, the mailman avoids your dog, and he doesn't avoid other dogs, we would conclude that he is afraid of your

dog because your dog is a vicious animal who bites people. Apparently, the process of attribution is so ingrained in us that we often don't realize that we use it.

Attribution Bias. In general, when trying to explain the behavior of others we often overestimate the role of disposition (personality, inner motivation) and underestimate the role of situation (external environment). This bias is called the fundamental attribution error (Ross, 1977). For instance, what if you asked a librarian a question and were met with a sharp, sarcastic reply? Chances are that you would explain this behavior as due to his unpleasant personality (disposition) rather than the possibility that he had a rough day or the job is very demanding (situation).

An interesting finding is that the fundamental attribution error holds true when we observe others, but not when we perceive our own behavior. If the person sitting next to you in class did poorly on an exam, you would probably conclude that he was not very bright. But what if you did poorly on an exam? Perhaps you might think the test was tricky, the instructor misled you, or there was not enough time to finish it. We tend to attribute the behavior of other people to internal causes, while we often attribute our own behavior to external causes. This tendency is sometimes called actor-observer bias (Jones & Nisbett, 1972). If we are aware of this attribution bias tendency, we can make more accurate attributions.

Attribution, Success, and Failure. Bernard Weiner (1974, 1986) described a model of attribution that focuses on the causes of success and failure. In addition to the internal-external dimension (disposition-situation), he added a stable-unstable dimension to the model, as well as a controllability component. Essentially we can attribute a behavior to effort (internal-unstable), luck

Figure 15.5. Weiner's Theory of Attribution

		Locus of Control	
		Internal	External
Stability	Stable	Ability	Task difficulty
	Unstable	Effort, Mood, Fatigue	Luck

According to Weiner, success or failure can be attributed to an internal or external locus of control as well as to a stable or unstable personality. He also added a controllability factor generally stating that success is due to internal controllable factors and failure to external uncontrollable factors.

(external-unstable), ability (internal-stable) or task difficulty (external-stable). In addition, each outcome could be due to controllable or uncontrollable factors. For instance, to what would we attribute the success of the school's football team's perfect record? We would probably agree it was due to effort and ability (both internal causes). What if the team had not won any games? Perhaps we would suggest it was due to bad luck and having to play teams out of our league (external causes). We tend to attribute success to internal causes and failure to external causes.

ATTITUDES

We may like carrots but dislike cabbage, and we may approve of a president's personality but disapprove of his politics. Our feelings, thoughts, and behavioral tendencies toward other people, objects, or ideas constitute our attitudes. Attitudes are learned dispositions that actively guide us toward specific behaviors. Petty and Cacioppo (1985) suggested that attitudes consist of long-lasting, general evaluations of people, objects, or issues.

The ABC model of attitudes divides the concept of attitude into three distinct components: affect, behavior, and cognition (Breckler, 1984). The affective component refers to our emotional reactions. The behavioral component refers to our actions that carry out our evaluations. The cognitive component refers to the thinking aspect of forming an attitude. Affect, behavior, and cognition are present in almost every attitude we have. Consider your attitude toward marijuana. All three components will be present: you will have cognitions about marijuana—that it is either harmful or harmless; you will have affective responses to marijuana, viewing it as positive and pleasant or negative and unpleasant; and you will either use it yourself or refrain from using it.

Attitudes are sometimes irrational. The cognitive component might be founded on factual arguments, or on unfounded ideas that we have accepted uncritically from other people. The emotional component might be based on direct personal experience (like going to the dentist) or lack of experience (like eating frog's legs); nonetheless, we can have definite feelings with or without personal experiences. The behavioral tendency component may appear to be the most irrational of all, particularly when we behave contrary to our stated attitudes (like refusing to give money to a beggar while professing to be generous).

Attitude Formation

Obviously, no one is born with a clear set of attitudes. Psychologists suspect that early childhood experiences are related to the development of attitudes, although later experiences can modify and sometimes change them radically. Both classical and operant conditioning are involved in attitude formation (Baron & Byrne, 1987).

Some attitudes are formed as a result of direct contact: a person severely frightened by a dog in childhood may continue to fear them throughout life. However, most attitudes are learned indirectly from other people. Parents teach certain attitudes deliberately—controlling TV viewing, selecting playmates, or sending children to special schools. McGuire (1985) pointed out the close similarity of the political attitudes of parents and children. But parents can also contribute to attitude development in quite inadvertent ways. The mother who encourages her daughter to play with dolls and wear frilly "feminine" clothes is laying the groundwork for a particular sex-role attitude, although she may be totally unconscious of doing so. The father, whose behavior encourages his son to avoid doing the dishes or housecleaning because they are "woman's chores," is also fostering sex-role attitudes.

Schools and peer groups play an important part in attitude development, for children learn a great deal about life by observing and interacting with their teachers and with other children. The social learning

Figure 15.6. ABC Model of an Attitude

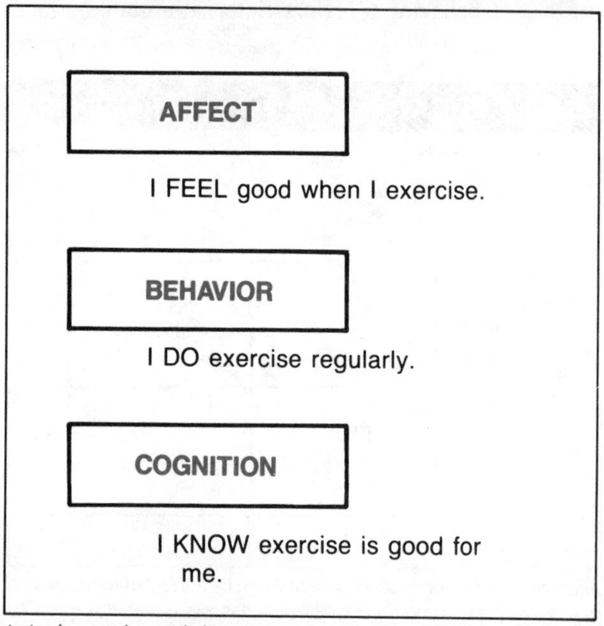

AFFECT

I FEEL good when I exercise.

BEHAVIOR

I DO exercise regularly.

COGNITION

I KNOW exercise is good for me.

Attitudes are learned dispositions that involve cognition, affect, and behavior. The three components (cognitive, emotional, and behavioral) can be found in all attitudes, and interrelate with each other.

Figure 15.7. Attitude Formation
Parents, families, schools, peer groups, and the mass media all contribute to the formation of attitudes in an individual.

theory proposes that the mass media have a powerful influence in shaping attitudes (Roberts & MacCory, 1985). In 98% of all American homes, the occupants view a television set an average of six hours a day. Some psychologists think we learn attitudes toward violence from TV. For example, between the ages of 5 and 14 the average child witnesses the annihilation of thousands of human beings on the television screen. This must have some effect on the child.

Another way we form attitudes is through inadvertent conditioning (see chapter 6, "Learning"). We adopt attitudes toward people or events because we associate them with pleasant or unpleasant experiences. For instance, we may adopt a negative attitude toward the Republican party because of the Watergate scandal, or we may form a favorable view of a city we have visited simply because the weather was great and we met people we liked.

Attitude Measurement

Since attitudes involve cognitions and emotions, they cannot be studied easily. Psychologists have devised several techniques for measuring attitudes. One approach is simply to ask people what their attitudes are, either by interview or by questionnaire. Interviews are particularly useful for in-depth studies of small numbers of people; questionnaires are quicker to complete and more useful for larger samples. If the questionnaire is given to a representative number of people, the findings can serve as a useful indicator of the attitudes of the general population. As we discussed in chapter 1, "The Study of Psychology," one problem with interviews and questionnaires is that we cannot always be sure that people are telling the truth.

To reduce the risk of inaccuracy in their findings, psychologists sometimes use *projective techniques* in studying attitudes. The idea here is to get people to project their attitudes in a way that they may not recognize, but that the trained psychologist will. For example, the subjects might be given a set of incomplete sentences to finish; their answers sometimes reveal truer attitudes than when they are questioned directly.

Social psychologists also use *behavioral measures*, which involve testing a person's actual behavior. For example, they might ask people to sign petitions or attend a rally for a particular cause. Or they might observe where a person ate and conclude that he or she had a positive attitude about the chosen restaurant. Recently, fast-food chains and soft-drink companies asked people to engage in taste tests, and used the results to indicate attitude preferences.

Social psychologists often use attitude scales, which consist of a series of statements expressing attitudes toward a particular issue. On a Likert Scale the subjects are asked to indicate their degree of agreement or disagreement with each of the statements, often using a five-point scale ranging from "strongly agree" to "strongly disagree." The responses are then computed, and the subjects can be ranked as having favorable or unfavorable attitudes toward the issue in question.

Attitude Change

People are bombarded from all directions by advertisements and persuasive communications designed to change their attitudes (and ultimately their behavior). As we watch TV or listen to the radio, we are exposed to countless ads that try to convince us to use specific products or vote for particular candidates. Psychologists

Figure 15.8. Attitude Change
Research on attitude change focuses on the communicator, the message, and the audience. Many variables interact to determine whether the audience will change its mind. Ronald Reagan, during his presidency, was known as the "great communicator."

are involved actively in these campaigns to change attitudes and behaviors. What is the most effective way to alter someone's attitude? The research into attitude change is divided usually into three areas: the source of the communication (the communicator), the communication itself (the message), and the receiver of the communication (the audience).

The Communicator. What are the characteristics of the successful communicator? Research suggests that successful communicators are credible, trustworthy, attractive, and similar to their audience (Petty & Cacioppo, 1981). The higher the communicator's social status and expertise, the more credible his message becomes. This is why advertisers use testimonials from professionals, as well as from popular athletes and entertainers.

We are more influenced also by someone we trust. Hence, as Eagly and Himmelfarb (1978) report, we look for what the communicator has to gain if we are persuaded; we are influenced more readily by someone who does not have a great deal to gain. For example, we would probably be more influenced to purchase a new Ford if the president of General Motors, rather than the president of Ford urged us to do so. Obviously, the president of General Motors has nothing to gain (and in fact much to lose) if we purchase a car from Ford.

We are persuaded more easily by attractive people, as demonstrated by Chaiken (1979), who asked college students to persuade other students to sign a petition. She found that those students who were most attractive were significantly more successful at persuading others to sign a petition than those who were unattractive. We like attractive people and perceive them as being friendly, trustworthy, and more like ourselves; thus we

can identify with him or her more easily, and therefore trust the message.

The Message. When trying to change attitudes, what is said is as important as who says it. Research on the message has focused on how different it is from the audience's previous views, whether opposition evidence should be included, and how emotional it should be. Eagly (1974) showed that attitudes are changed much more easily by mild persuasion (soft sell) than by a barrage of extreme propaganda (hard sell). Some religious and political groups overlook this fact and run the risk of being dismissed as fanatics.

Should we use two-sided arguments, or only present our own case? Often this choice depends on the audience. If our audience already favors our views, then a one-sided argument is more effective. If the audience is unfavorably disposed toward them, however, it is best to use the two-sided approach, as this gives us more credibility and helps build an immunity to the claims of the opposing side.

If we need to present both sides of an argument (or if someone else is presenting the other side), which side should be presented first for maximum impact? Petty and Cacioppo (1981) pointed out that if the attitude measurement is to take place several days after the talks, the primacy effect prevails and the side presented first is remembered best. However, if there is a length of time between the first and second talk, and the attitude measurement takes place immediately after the second talk, it has more impact due to the recency effect.

Under some conditions, the use of fear and other emotional appeals might change attitudes. Fear alone is likely to cause people to avoid the message completely. However, if the fear is coupled with instructions of what to do about it, it may be effective. For example, Leventhal, Singer, and Jones (1965) reported that college students were more likely to obtain a tetanus shot when presented with a fear message coupled with instructions about how to get the shot than when they were presented with the fear message only or the instructions only. But emotional appeals do not always work, and more research is needed before we can draw definite conclusions.

The Audience. It appears that some people are persuaded more easily than others. It is easier to convince people who have a need for a product. For example, if you are in the market for a new car, you will be more motivated to listen to car ads. Other research has shown that people with a high need for social approval will often be persuaded because they want others to like them. In general, more intelligent people will be more resistant to persuasion than less intelligent people. However, there are many individual differences, and at the present time the conclusions in this area are still somewhat tentative. For instance, recently Baumeister and Covington (1985) found that people with high self-esteem were as easily persuaded as people with low self-esteem, but they did not want to admit it. And Eagly and Carli (1981) reported that men and women were equally likely to change their attitudes.

Cognitive Dissonance

What is the underlying basis of attitude change? Leon Festinger theorized about attitude changes in his 1957 book, *A Theory of Cognitive Dissonance.* According to Festinger, the essence of persuasion consists of introducing material into a person's mind that, though inconsistent with existing attitudes, is difficult to dismiss. Some people are able to ignore inconsistencies, at least to some extent, but most people find that when they have two psychologically inconsistent ideas they will experience cognitive dissonance, an uncomfortable psychological state characterized by tension and conflict.

Cognitive Dissonance Theory. Naturally, individuals in such an unpleasant state will try to remove the source of their dissonance. They may do this either by changing one or the other of their dissonant (conflicting) attitudes or by adopting additional attitudes that will help reconcile the conflicting elements. As an example Festinger cites the case of a cigarette smoker who is presented with evidence that smoking causes cancer. This arouses cognitive dissonance, as the person does not wish to believe that the habit may be deadly. The smoker has several options. He or she can stop smoking, disbelieve the cancer report, or reason that the pleasures of smoking make the risk of cancer worthwhile.

Another example of how cognitive dissonance can be

Figure 15.9. Cognitive Dissonance
Festinger's theory of cognitive dissonance predicts that when people hold two inconsistent beliefs, they experience tension which drives them to reconcile their thoughts. Antismoking campaigns produce dissonance for smokers who enjoy smoking but know it is harmful.

aroused is when a person acts in ways that conflict with stated attitudes. In this case, the theory predicts that the person will change attitudes so that they will be consistent with existing behavior. The more willingly the person engages in behavior that is contrary to his or her attitudes, the more cognitive dissonance will be experienced, and the more he or she will be motivated to change attitudes.

Festinger and Carlsmith (1959) illustrated this principle in their classic study, in which they paid subjects who had engaged in an extremely boring, senseless experiment to tell other subjects that the experiment had been exciting and fun. The subjects were paid either $20 or $1. Cognitive-dissonance theory predicted that if a subject was paid $20, the money would justify that person's telling a lie and hence no dissonance would be experienced: the subject told a lie and was paid $20 for it. On the other hand, if the subject was paid $1, that would not justify the lie, and dissonance would be produced.

Later, the subjects were interviewed and asked their true feelings about the experiment. As predicted, the high-dissonance group reported that the experiment had been interesting and worthwhile, while the low-dissonance group, as well as a control group who were not asked to lie, felt the experiment was boring. The high-dissonance group had apparently adjusted their attitudes about the task, making them consistent with their actions.

Cooper and Fazio (1984) reported that the experience of dissonance is dependent upon two conditions. First, the behavior must lead to an aversive consequence (in Festinger's study, lying to someone would be aversive). Second, the person must assume personal responsibility in choosing the behavior (in Festinger's study, the subjects could say no). Croyle and Cooper (1983) found that dissonance is actually accompanied by physiological arousal which is interpreted negatively by the person.

Application of Cognitive Dissonance. Festinger's theory of cognitive dissonance spurred many other psychologists to research the applications of this theory. For instance, Axsom and Cooper (1985) had some patients in a weight loss program exert a great effort on a task at an initial meeting while others did not. Six months later, those who engaged in the difficult task were more committed to the weight loss program and had lost significantly more weight than those who did not have to do the task.

Elliott Aronson described some excellent examples of cognitive dissonance applied to an educational setting in his 1988 book, *The Social Animal*. Aronson described the typical classroom procedure: If teachers want students to learn, they often give them large amounts of external rewards. For example, when students perform well on a test, teachers give them *A*s, gold stars, or praise. But perhaps students learn their lessons only to obtain the high grades. Aronson suggests that if teachers provide inadequate rewards, the students will still learn, but for internal justification, not external rewards. In other words, if students can be convinced to learn without receiving high grades for the assignment, dissonance is produced which can be eliminated when the

students feel they actually enjoy the work. Inadequate rewards may influence many attitudes and behaviors in our society.

Self-perception Theory. Cognitive dissonance theory provided an explanation of attitude change, and has been widely accepted. Daryl Bem (1967) proposed an alternative explanation in his self-perception theory. He suggested that the formation and change in our attitudes are often based on our perceptions of our own behavior. For example, if we move into a new home and grow roses in our garden, we assume we must like roses and thus have a positive attitude toward them. In his reanalysis of Festinger's original study, Bem argued that subjects who received the large sum of money perceived themselves as doing it for the money, whereas those receiving the small amount of money perceived that they really believed the experiment was fun, and hence changed their attitudes. Self-perception theory works best when we don't already have strong attitudes toward something (Tybout & Scott, 1983).

Prejudice

Prejudice is an attitude of special interest to social psychologists. Prejudice is an unjustified attitude involving a fixed, usually negative, way of thinking about a person or object. Prejudices do not easily adjust to new information or experience; instead, new facts are either readjusted to fit into the existing pattern of prejudice, or simply ignored. For example, if racially prejudiced persons encounter a pleasant member of a disliked group, they will more than likely view him or her as "an exception to the rule" rather than change their attitude toward the group as a whole.

Like all attitudes, prejudice has cognitive, affective,

BIOGRAPHICAL HIGHLIGHT ☆

LEON FESTINGER

Leon Festinger was born in New York City in 1919. Being interested in psychology, he started college at the City College of New York, and after getting his bachelor's degree, went to the State University of Iowa, where he obtained his Ph.D. in 1942. He taught at a number of universities before going to Stanford University in 1955. In 1968, he went to the New School for Social Research in New York City, where he remains today.

Although Festinger has contributed a large number of concepts and theories to the field of social psychology, probably none has had greater impact that his ideas from his 1957 book, *Theory of Cognitive Dissonance*. Festinger views people as thinking animals who need to have balance in their thoughts as well as their actions. This idea of balance is key to his theory of cognitive dissonance. Much research is still being conducted today in social psychology to answer some of the questions cognitive dissonance has raised.

and behavioral components. The cognitive component of prejudice is the stereotype, an exaggerated and rigid mental image of a particular group of persons or objects. The stereotype is applied indiscriminantly to all members of the category and is often used to justify the negative feelings and behavior toward the group (Brewer & Kramer, 1985). Discrimination refers to the unfair behaviors toward members of the group. Common forms of prejudice include racism, sexism, and ageism.

Causes of Prejudice. Prejudice appears to have many causes; even individuals with the same prejudice can have different reasons for it. For example, usually people like people who resemble themselves or those they think resemble themselves. This generalization extends not only to similarities in skin color or other physical attributes, but also to tastes, interests, beliefs, attitudes, and values. Research has shown that we assume that individuals of our race share our attitudes and that those of a different race share different attitudes(Brewer, 1986). Another source of prejudice is the mutuality of attitudes in the community or subculture in which the individual is raised. Psychologists have discovered regional, cultural, and group differences in prejudiced attitudes. Individuals who move to different areas or become identified with different groups tend to alter their prejudiced attitudes to conform to the norms, or standards, of their new social environment.

Much of this culturally based prejudice is transmitted to the child at an early age by parents, neighbors, peers, schools, the media, and other influences. The transmission does not often involve direct teaching. Instead, children receive approval and disapproval for associating with particular playmates. They overhear conversations of adults, imitate their behavior, and take on their attitudes and thoughts.

Overcoming Prejudice. The government has enlisted the help of psychologists in dealing with racial prejudice, a real problem for a multiracial country devoted to the ideal of the individual's equal rights and opportunities. Psychologists have studied prejudiced people and tried to learn what causes prejudice and what functions it serves. They have discovered, for example, that prejudiced people lump other people into easily identifiable or stereotyped groups and treat them all alike, rather than as individuals. A racially prejudiced employer, for example, may simplify decisions about hiring by simply rejecting all applicants of a different race.

What can be done to decrease intergroup prejudice? Allport (1954) proposed the contact theory which included three conditions necessary for the reduction of intergroup hostility. First, there must be close contact on a regular basis (such as in school, work, and living situations). Second, there must be cooperative interdependence, in which both blacks and whites need each other to accomplish goals. And third, the contact must be of equal status. A number of recent research programs has confirmed this theory. For instance, Cook (1984) studied students in a school system, and found that the contact over a period of time decreased racial prejudice. Brewer and Miller (1984) pointed out that the requirement of equal status can be very difficult to achieve. For instance, in a school system, students might have certain dress codes for their particular group and might select different types of classes because of their interests and abilities.

Social psychologists have worked hard to reduce

Figure 15.10. Overcoming Prejudice
Psychologists have found that one of the most successful methods of overcoming prejudice is to have the prejudiced person interact with people he or she dislikes. Ideally, the interaction should be one that requires cooperation to reach some goal.

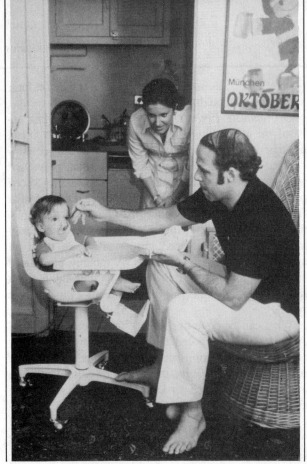

Figure 15.11. Gender Identity
Gender identity, or sex role, is an important part of our personality. The sex roles of men and women are not as divergent as was once believed. Researchers such as Sandra Bem show people can have traits of both sexes. Men in today's society no longer feel their identity threatened by performing tasks once believed to be strictly feminine.

qualities. Bem found that while many people score high on either the feminine or masculine scale, some people score high on both stereotype scales, a personality characteristic called androgyny. People who are androgynous are less likely to be influenced by sex stereotypes (Bem, 1975).

Research has shown that like racism, sexism continues to be a problem in our society. For instance, Zinkhan and Stoidain (1984) found that if a man and woman are waiting for service in a department store, the man is significantly more likely to be served first. Many studies have documented the bias that exists against hiring women for all types of employment. Kluegel and Smith 1986) argued that beliefs and stereotypes about women are often part of historical traditions, but are not readily acknowledged by most people. Continuing research and education will play a major role in helping to reduce prejudice of all kinds.

SOCIAL INFLUENCE

A great deal of human social encounters consists of influencing and being influenced by other people. We try to persuade our friends to go to the movies with us. We often ask favors of our friends. We tend to obey people in authority, such as police, teachers, and parents. Attempts at changing the attitudes or behavior of others can be thought of as social influence (Cialdini, 1988). The areas of social influence that have been most thoroughly studied include conformity, compliance, and obedience.

Conformity

Conformity has been studied extensively by social psychologists. Conformity is defined as the changing of one's behavior in order to fit social norms or expectations more closely. It is a major type of social influence. We know that we conform to social expectations a good deal of the time.

Social psychologist Solomon Asch conducted a classic experiment on conformity in 1955. He assembled several groups, each composed of seven college students. Each group was presented with a series of 18 cards on which four lines were drawn. One was the "standard" and the other three were comparison lines. One of the comparison lines was the same length as the standard line, and each student had to declare aloud which comparison line matched the standard line in each

racial prejudice. For instance, Kenneth Clark of the City University of New York has established a firm to help promote successful race relations. Clark has also written a number of books which explain the dangers of prejudice, in the hope of educating people and reducing the incidence of prejudice. Still, research shows that prejudice continues to be a problem in this society (Dovidio & Gaertner, 1986).

Sex Roles and Stereotypes. People sometimes hold beliefs about what men and women should be like. Often these sex stereotypes are learned as children but continue to influence the behavior of adults. For example, some people believe that women are interested only in babies, are overly emotional, and are always dependent on others. Men are sometimes viewed as interested only in money, as of high intelligence, and as leaders.

Sandra Bem (1974) developed the Bem Sex-Role Inventory (BSRI), a 60-adjective sex-role questionnaire to measure feminine and masculine traits in people. She found that specific traits were stereotypically associated with each sex. For example, feminine traits include being gentle, sensitive, warm, soft-spoken, and loving children. Masculine traits include being ambitious, dominant, competitive, aggressive, and having leadership

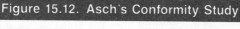

Figure 15.12. Asch's Conformity Study

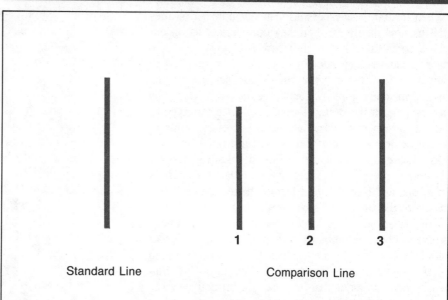

Solomon Asch (1955) found that subjects yielded to a majority over one-third of the time and gave wrong answers in a line comparison task. Which of the lines on the right is equal in length to the line on the left?

Standard Line   Comparison Line

case. But six of the seven subjects in each group were actually Asch's accomplices and had been coached beforehand to give incorrect answers on 12 of the 18 trials. For the first two cards, there was unanimous agreement. But then the majority started agreeing on occasional wrong answers.

The naive subjects yielded to the majority and gave a wrong answer on 36.8% or more of the trials. Students in a control group made mistakes less than 1% of the time. There were considerable personal differences: some subjects yielded all the time, some yielded only part of the time, and about 25% maintained their independence as a minority of one.

Why did some subjects seem to disbelieve the evidence of their senses? When Asch interviewed them, they gave three types of reasons for bowing to group pressure. Some believed the majority was wrong, but did not want to be "different" by giving the right answer. A second group, which included most of the subjects, did not trust their own judgment when the majority disagreed. They thought they knew the right answer but were not sufficiently sure of themselves. A third group suffered from an actual distortion of perception and claimed to perceive the lines the way the majority seemed to.

In some cases, conformity can be an end in itself. We learn that it is rewarding to be accepted and punishing to be rejected. If we deviate, we are subjected immediately to group pressure to conform. Conformity can also be a means to an end. Whenever we are unsure of ourselves in a new situation, we look to others to see how things are done. We internalize the appropriate norms and adopt the expected role.

Leon Festinger accounts for this latter type of conformity in his social comparison theory. We all have a need to evaluate the correctness of our opinions and the worth of our abilities. If some standard exists by which we can make these evaluations—a score on an examination, for example—we will use it. But how do we assess the correctness or adequacy of our views about politics, religion, athletic ability, or our social skills? We look to the other people around us. We ask their opinions, examine their performance, and compare our own behavior with theirs. Since everyone does this, our attitudes and behavior tend to converge, and we remain pretty much like one another. Festinger's theory also suggests why cultural norms retain their cohesion: we all validate them constantly to ensure that they will guide us through an ambiguous world.

There is no doubt that conformity to the majority plays an important role in our lives. But some psychologists, including French psychologist Serge Moscovici (1985), argue that minority influence is also important. He suggests that in order for a minority in a group to effect change, it must be consistent, coherent, and forceful. This attitude is interpreted as confidence by the majority, and eventually the majority may begin to question its own point of view. Mass and Clark (1984) pointed out that the minority is most likely to be successful when the suggestion or idea is similar to the majority except for a particular attitude. One of the advantages of minority influence is that it forces the majority to carefully evaluate its position on issues (Nemeth, 1986). It is currently not clear whether minority influence is a type of conformity or a separate social process.

Compliance

When insurance salespersons visit our home, first they tell us how nice it is; then they compliment us on our three beautiful children. Just before they get down to work, usually they ask for a small favor—a glass of water or to use the bathroom. These actions are designed for our compliance and to get us ready to comply by signing on the dotted line. Compliance is a type of social influence in which an individual changes his or her behavior because of a direct request from someone else. There are a number of techniques that can be used to obtain compliance, including ingratiation, multiple requests, and low-balling. Most of the techniques work much of the time with most people.

Ingratiation. The salesperson described above seeks to obtain compliance through ingratiation. He or she attempts to get us to like him or her through complimenting us on our home and children. Ingratiation is any technique that increases the attractiveness of a person trying to seek compliance from us. Ingratiation might include giving compliments, doing favors, agreeing with someone, or just being nice.

Multiple Requests. Often multiple requests are made in order to obtain compliance. The salesperson asked for a small favor (a drink of water) before he made the big request (buying insurance). This compliance technique of first making a small request and then making a large request is called the foot-in-the-door technique. A study by Freedman and Fraser (1966) demonstrates the effectiveness of this method. They called homemakers on the phone and asked them to answer several simple questions about the soap products that they used in their home. This was the small request. A few days later, they called back and asked if a 5-person crew could come into the person's home and take a complete inventory of all the products in the house. What would you say to such an enormous request? Almost 53% of the subjects agreed to this second request, compared to only 22% of a control group who had not been asked for a small request earlier.

In getting customers to buy more, salespersons frequently make a small request followed by a large request. For example, they might encourage you to purchase a less expensive model, and then when you agree, begin to talk about the advantages of the higher priced model, or about all the accessories that you certainly will need. This technique is very effective when the salesperson has the time to implement it. But can it also work when he or she doesn't have time to talk someone into it?

Psychologists Robert Cialdini and David Schroeder (1976) tested this idea in an experiment with solicitors for contributions to the American Cancer Society. They

Figure 15.13. Compliance
Research indicates that one way to obtain compliance is to first make a small request and follow it with a large request. This is called the foot-in-the-door technique.

reasoned that if they could get people to contribute anything, they might get them to contribute more. Thus, they had some of the solicitors add a phrase at the end of the standard request, "Even a penny would help."

Cialdini and Schroeder had two teams (each consisting of a male and female college student) use the standard approach ("I'm collecting money for the American Cancer Society. Would you be willing to help by giving a donation?"). Another two teams used the same approach, but added the "Even a penny will help" phrase at the end. Forty-two people were canvassed with each approach.

Which approach was more effective? With the standard approach, 12 out of 42 people donated, while with the penny approach, the teams received 21 contributions. Clearly, the small-favor penny pitch worked to increase contributions. But if the contributions were smaller (since even pennies were acceptable), then it still might not be as effective as the regular pitch. The standard approach earned a total of $18.55, while the penny approach earned a total of $30.34. Cialdini and Schroeder argued that the "Even a penny would help" was the equivalent of a small favor, and once a person made the decision to help, he or she would actually contribute a larger amount because he or she didn't want to appear cheap.

The foot-in-the-door technique is not always effective, however. Some research suggests that if the first request results in a bad experience for the person solicited, he or she is less likely to comply with the second request (Crano & Sivacek, 1982).

Surprisingly, the opposite technique is also successful. The compliance technique of first making a large request and then making a small request is called the door-in-the-face technique, or the rejection-then-retreat technique (Cialdini, 1988). Suppose someone comes to the door and asks you to subscribe to an expensive magazine for three years. After you refuse, he or she then asks if you will buy the current issue. Chances are good that you will comply with this second small request. Cialdini and his colleagues demonstrated the effectiveness of this technique in a 1975 study. When they approached college students and asked them if they would volunteer to serve as counselors for several hours a week for the next two years, none of them agreed. Then they asked the students if they would take a group of delinquents to the zoo. About 50% agreed to this smaller request, compared to only about 17% of a control group who had not received the larger request first.

Cialdini (1988) described a number of situations in which the door-in-the-face technique is often used. Labor negotiators might make extreme demands at first and then settle for more realistic requests later. Cialdini also described television script writers who deliberately put extreme statements in their scripts, knowing the censors would delete them, so they then could keep the statements they really wanted in the first place.

The Low-ball Procedure. A technique called the low-ball procedure is also used to obtain compliance. When shopping for insurance, I found that three salespersons quoted me a very low price. When I told them to write the policy, they suddenly "discovered" an error, and the premium was actually significantly higher. Often, people will continue to make the purchase even if it is more expensive. Cialdini (1988) described a couple of low-balling techniques used by some automobile salespersons. Sometimes the customer is offered a great deal, and is encouraged to like the car, then an error is "discovered" and the price is several hundred dollars higher than originally stated. Or an overgenerous trade-in allowance is offered and when the new car is picked up, a "reevaluation" reduces the allowance several hundred dollars. Since the customer really wants the car,

chances are good he or she will go ahead with the higher-priced deal anyway.

Cialdini and his colleagues (1978) tested the effectiveness of the low-balling technique on college students enrolled in a psychology course. They called the subjects on the phone and asked them to participate in an experiment for which they would get credit for the course. After the subjects agreed, they were told the study would start at 7 A.M. Over 55% of the subjects showed up for their appointments, compared to only about 24% of control subjects who were told about the 7 A.M. time *before* agreeing to participate.

By understanding the techniques used to obtain compliance, we can be more free to make our own decisions. Sometimes we are not asked for a favor, but are told what to do. The study of obedience has important implications for social psychology.

Obedience

When Adolf Eichmann was on trial for his role in the mass murder of Jews in Nazi Germany, he justified his action by stating that he was "just following orders." At the My Lai massacre in Vietnam, American troops led by Lieutenant William L. Calley opened fire on unarmed women and children, although there were no enemy forces in the vicinity. When Calley was charged with the crime, his defense was that he believed he was "acting under orders." During the Watergate investigation, some of the defendants claimed that they were following orders, or carrying out the demands of their superiors. Is this kind of behavior the result of a psychopathic personality? Or might a great many of us behave in a similar way in a similar situation?

In this chapter's opening story, we described Stanley Milgram's classic experiment on obedience. In this study, subjects were led to believe that they were participating in an experiment to test the effects of punishment on learning. The subjects served as "teachers," and had to deliver increasingly larger shocks when the "learners" made mistakes on a memory task. Actually, no shocks were given, and the real purpose of the study was to investigate obedience in the subjects who were the "teachers." As we indicated in our opening story, 65% of the subjects continued to deliver shocks at the 450-volt level, even when the "learner" complained of a weak heart and screamed to be released. The study demonstrated obedience to authority.

Milgram had conducted his study at Yale University, and it occurred to him that the subjects might be obeying him because of the prestige of the university and the belief that the experimenters must "know what they are doing." To test this idea, he set up his experiment elsewhere—in a run-down office in downtown Bridge-

Figure 15.14. Proximity Effect on Obedience

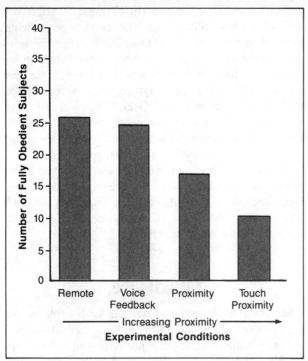

Milgram conducted four studies that examined the effect of proximity of the victim on the subject's level of obedience. The number of subjects out of 40 in each study who gave the maximum shock levels are presented here. In Experiment 1 (Remote Feedback), the victim-learner could not be seen or heard but pounded on the wall at 300 volts. In Experiment 2 (Voice Feedback), the learner's yells could be heard through the wall. In Experiment 3 (Proximity), the victim was in the same room as the subject. And in Experiment 4 (Touch-Proximity), the subject had to hold the learner's hand on a plate for the shock to be delivered.

port, Connecticut. And he claimed this time to represent a research firm rather than a university. Interestingly, the new subjects proved to be about as obedient as those in his Yale laboratory.

In the light of these findings, the attitude of the American public to the Calley trial should come as no surprise. Just before the trial, a national sample of Americans was asked about a hypothetical situation in which "soldiers in Vietnam are ordered to shoot all inhabitants of a village suspected of assisting the enemy, including old men, women, and children." The subjects were asked what they thought most people would do in that situation. Some 65% thought that most Americans would follow orders and shoot; and 51% thought they themselves would shoot women and children under those circumstances. To them, following orders was an obligation that outweighed all other considerations.

In a variation on his original experiment, Milgram (1965) introduced a second "teacher," also an accomplice, who flatly refused to continue to administer shocks when the "learner" protested. When Milgram instructed his real subjects to proceed with the shocks in

these new circumstances, 36 out of 40 sided with the other "teacher" and refused to obey orders. This experiment demonstrated that when the subjects administered the electric shocks they were doing so not out of any basic cruelty, but out of simple obedience to authority. They apparently would have preferred not to cause pain, yet they were unable to defy Milgram's orders until there was sufficient social support to justify their actions.

Why do people obey and how can we learn to resist when obedience is destructive? People with authority assume responsibility for decisions and actions, thus allowing others to more readily obey. Milgram argued that we learn to obey people in authority since this often results in positive reinforcement, which most people learned as children. As an experiment, Bushman (1984) had someone stop pedestrians and order them to give a dime to a person who appeared to need it for a parking meter. Significantly more people obeyed when the person giving orders was dressed in a firefighter uniform (nearly 80%) than when dressed in a business suit or old clothes (40%). The firefighter seemingly had authority and hence was obeyed. Milgram found several factors that might reduce the level of destructive obedience (Sears & colleagues, 1988). Obedience is reduced when the victim's suffering is immediate; if people are made to feel responsible for their own actions; and if people are taught to consider the motives of people in authority. If someone else resists an order for destructive obedience, others are likely to also resist. Although there are times when we should obey people in authority, we need to evaluate the situation to decide the most appropriate action.

GROUP PROCESSES

We are highly social animals, and we spend a great deal of our lives in groups—family, friends, classes, clubs, organizations, companies. Not every collection of people is a group, however; a number of people standing in line for a bus is simply an aggregate of individuals. The difference between a group and an aggregate of people lies in the fact that group members think of themselves as group members, have common goals, and interact with one another on that basis (McGrath, 1984).

Every group functions according to norms—the explicit or implicit rules and standards that regulate the behavior of members participating in the group situation. The norms may vary from group to group and depend on the values and objectives that members consider important and relevant. A weekend pleasure group may stress such norms as instant gratification and the enjoyment of leisure; a commercial group may stress such norms as deferred gratification for future profit and the value of a decent day's work; a baseball team may stress winning and teamwork.

According to Leon Festinger's 1953 research, two factors account for the emergence of norms in groups. One is the desire to strengthen common attitudes by reaching agreement on relevant issues and courses of action. Group members often spend a great deal of time routinely discussing and agreeing on the fundamental issues that brought them together in the first place. Unless there are expected norms that stabilize the group to ensure its smooth and mutually satisfying functioning, it is not likely to achieve its goals or to sustain the loyalty of its members.

The degree to which group norms influence an individual's behavior depends to some extent on whether or not the group is a reference group for that person. We all belong to a number of groups—some formal, some informal—but among these groups certain ones are more influential than others. These influential groups, which psychologists call reference groups, are those from which a person derives his or her values, attitudes, and identity. Reference groups may be large—such as a person's race, religion, native country, or political affiliation; or they may be small—such as a club or a team or a group of friends. But regardless of their size or formal status, the reference groups we belong to have a profound influence on our individual behavior.

Group Effectiveness

Most institutions in our society operate on the assumption that "two heads are better than one." Colleges, corporations, and governments are run by committees in the belief that group decisions are wiser and more efficient than decisions made by an individual working alone. But is this assumption always justified? The answer depends on several factors: the task, the size and composition of the group, the nature of the leadership, and the way the members relate to one another.

Group Tasks. Steiner (1972) described several types of tasks that groups might perform and the productivity of the group versus individuals. In additive tasks the contributions of each member are combined into the final group product. For example, pushing an automobile that is stuck in the mud involves the efforts of everyone, and the group is more effective than an individual. In disjunctive tasks, there is a single problem for the group to solve. The most competent person in the group usually finds the solution. A group of people working collectively will be more likely to hit on the right answer than one person working alone. For example, a group of people is more likely to solve a difficult crossword puzzle than a single individual; a group of scientists working on a cure for cancer is more likely to succeed than a scientist working alone. A conjunctive task requires all group members to work toward the goal, and productivity is limited to the least competent member. For example, if a group is tied together when

BIOGRAPHICAL ☆ HIGHLIGHT ☆

STANLEY MILGRAM

Stanley Milgram was born in New York City in 1933. His high school interests centered around science, as evidenced by his earning the school's gold medal in biology. Following graduation from high school he enrolled at Queens College of the City University of New York, where he majored in political science.

Eventually he decided to major in social psychology at Harvard University, where he studied with Solomon Asch and earned a doctorate in 1960. Milgram taught at Yale University and Harvard University before finally settling at the Graduate Center of the City University of New York in 1967.

Milgram conducted a large number of studies in social psychology. Perhaps the best known is his controversial obedience study described in his 1974 book, *Obedience to Authority*. Milgram's research was often creative and original. For example, he dropped letters from a helicopter to measure prejudice, asked people to hand a package to someone they knew to study communication channels, and took photographs of people to study social interactions.

Milgram received numerous awards for his creative contributions to psychology. He produced an award-winning film on his work on urban life and overload. Stanley Milgram died in December 1984 at the age of 51.

Figure 15.15. Groups
We spend a large amount of time interacting with members of groups. Each
group functions according to its own
rules called norms.

climbing a mountain, every member is essential, and if
even one does not keep up, the group is ineffective.
Here, often individual performance is better than a
group's. Hill (1982) noted that research has confirmed
Steiner's divisions, and that in most cases the performance of a group is better than the average individual
(but often worse than the best individual).

Brainstorming. Alex Osborn (1957) developed the
technique of brainstorming as a means to create innovative ideas in business advertising. Basically, a problem is
presented to the group and the members are to come up
with as many different solutions as possible in a brief
time. Osborn listed several rules, including not allowing
criticism during the session, and encouraging combinations of previous ideas. Brainstorming has been used in a
wide variety of situations and is currently used in
education, business, and social groups. Brainstorming
can also be done by individuals, and some research
shows that individuals can produce more solutions that
groups (Lamm & Trommsdorf, 1973).

Groupthink. Psychologist Irving Janis (1982) has
pointed out that some group decisions, which he terms
groupthink, can be dangerous. Groupthink occurs when
the members of a group are so committed to and
optimistic about the group that they feel it is invulnerable, and the members are so concerned with maintaining
consensus that criticism is muted. According to Janis, an
example of groupthink occurred in April 1980 when
President Carter and his advisers decided to use military
force to rescue the American hostages in Iran. The plan
was ill-conceived with major errors, and even though
there was some opposition to the plan, the majority

agreed and it was put into effect. It, of course, failed
completely. Nearly 20 years earlier, in 1961, one of the
worst military and diplomatic blunders in American
history was the result of groupthink. President John F.
Kennedy, on the advice of a group of brilliant statesmen
and advisors, launched the ill-fated invasion of Cuba at
the Bay of Pigs. Several members of the group had very
strong private objections to the plan, but the pressures
toward unanimity were so great that the dissenters kept
silent.

Janis (1982) suggested several precautions to prevent
groupthink in group decisions. The leader should encourage members to voice objections and doubts about
decision. The leader should be impartial in discussions,
rather than stating his or her preference at the outset. If
possible, several groups should independently work on
the same problem, so different proposals could be
evaluated. And after a decision has been made, a
"second chance" meeting should be held to air doubts or
alternatives. Janis suggested that groupthink is most
dangerous when it occurs in groups setting national
policies; therefore these precautions might not be war-
ranted for simple solving-problem sessions.

Group Polarization. Group discussion can often
stimulate ideas that would not have been thought of
otherwise, and groups can evaluate critically ideas that
an individual might accept too readily. But, on the other
hand, a solution may be evaluated according to the status
in the group of the person who offers it, rather than
according to its merits. It has also been found that
groups are more likely to take an extreme position than
an individual alone.

Theory of Social Impact

Bibb Latané has been involved actively in trying to understand the influence of others on social behavior. His early work with John Darley demonstrated that people are less likely to help someone in an emergency if there are other people around. The concept of *diffusion of responsibility* explains the bystander effect by saying that responsibility for helping is equally distributed among all of the people present. Hence, if you are alone, the responsibility of helping or not helping is totally yours, but if you are only one of four people, only 25% of it is yours.

Latané has also investigated the phenomenon of *social loafing*, which states that in a group of people each one contributes less than he or she would contribute alone. He found that when eight people clapped their hands, the sound was not eight times as loud as the sound of each one individually or that in a game of tug-of-war, the force was not multiplied by the number of people pulling on the rope.

Recently Latané combined much of his research into a new theory called the *theory of social impact.* There are several principles included in this theory. First, the more people present, the more influence they will have on each individual. Additionally, the more important the people are to the individual, the more influence they will have on him or her. This explains why someone is more nervous when delivering a presentation to a large group of important people than when he or she is delivering it to a small group of friends.

Second, the theory of social impact states that while the impact of others on the individual increases as the number of people increases, the rate of increase in impact grows less as each new individual is added. For example, if you are giving a presentation to three people and a fourth one joins the group, this is more significant than if you were giving a presentation to 31 people and one more joined. As shown in Latané's social-loafing study, eight people clapping do not produce a sound eight times as loud as the sound produced by each individual.

Third, each individual can influence others, but the more people present, the less influence any one individual will have. Thus, we are more likely to listen attentively to a speaker if we are in a small group than if we were in a large group.

Latané has tested his theory of social impact in a variety of situations. In his 1981 paper, he reports that people tip more if they have separate bills than if they share in a group bill. In parties of six, if each person is given an individual bill, the tipping is about 19%, while in groups of six with a group bill each individual contributes only about 13%.

Figure 15.16. Social Loafing
When we are part of a group, we tend to contribute less than what we would if we were alone, because we tend to feel less responsibility for the outcome of a situation.

In another study, Latané tested the hypothesis that Billy Graham would be more effective in front of small audiences. He researched the numbers of people who responded to Graham's appeal for converts in various-sized audiences. He found that when the audiences were small, people were more willing to sign cards allowing local ministers to contact them than when the audiences were large.

Social psychologists are just beginning to research the theory of social impact. Already it has made many predictions that could be useful in understanding human behavior. Further research will test the validity of these predictions.

THOUGHT QUESTIONS

1. What is the theory of social impact?
2. What are some of the predictions based on this theory?
3. Do you think it is likely that one theory can explain all of social behavior? Why? Why not?

The tendency for groups to make riskier decisions than an individual would make is called the risky-shift phenomenon (Stoner, 1961). Davis and his colleagues in 1976 discussed several possible reasons why risky-shift might occur. In a group situation, people feel less personal responsibility: if something goes wrong, no particular person will be blamed. People in a group generally tend to conform, and individuals do not want to be seen as deviating from the established norm. And it's possible that the group members who are the ones most likely to take risks are the same persons who can influence others to go along with them. Groups often do make risky decisions.

Originally, it was believed that groups always tended to move only in more risky directions. More recent research has shown that, although groups are likely to move to the extreme, it can be either the *risky* extreme or the *conservative* extreme (Isenberg, 1986). The tendency for a group to move toward an extreme position is called group polarization. The persuasive argument explanation for group polarization suggests that people gain information as the discussion develops, and thus the more persuasive an argument is that is proposed for a particular position, the more likely it will be adopted. The social comparison explanation emphasizes the tendency for members to compare their views with others in the group. As they discover some other members have even more extreme views than they, they align their opinions with the extreme view to appear as competent as those in the group.

Social Loafing. If a single person puts enough energy into a cheer to make a loud noise, theoretically a group of eight people should make a noise eight times as loud. This is not what happens, however. Bibb Latané reported in 1981 that in a group of people each person actually does less than he or she would do alone. This effect is called social loafing. Latané explains social loafing by his theory of social impact, which says that because each member of the group shares the responsibility equally, each individual performs at a somewhat lessened rate.

Cognitive factors also appear to contribute to social loafing. Jackson and Harkins (1985) argued that if people think others are not working as hard as they are, they are likely to also do less. It is likely that when people believe their contribution is not recognizable they do not feel a responsibility to try hard. Jackson and Williams (1985) reported that social loafing decreased when people believed they contributed something important to the group effort or when the task was very difficult. Social psychologists are just beginning to investigate social loafing, but it appears that leaders can lessen the effects of social loafing by helping each member of the group feel a sense of importance and responsibility.

Social Facilitation

Our behavior is sometimes different in front of a group than when we are alone. Social psychologists have known this basic fact for many years. The problem is that sometimes our performance improves when we have an audience, while at other times it deteriorates. For a long time no one could explain this audience effect.

In 1965 social psychologist Robert Zajonc proposed a motivational theory of social facilitation. His theory states that the presence of others enhances the emission of the individual's dominant response. Effectively, the presence of others causes an increase in arousal, which contributes to an increase in the dominant (most likely) response (see chapter 9, "Motivation").

If the dominant response is a well-learned behavior, such as eating, doing math problems, or running, then the presence of others (either as an audience or as coactors) will usually lead to improved performance. If, on the other hand, the response is a new behavior, not yet well-learned, then the dominant response will most likely be an impaired performance. In this case, if you add an audience, the arousal increases and leads to a decrement in behavior. Learning new nonsense syllables or learning a complicated maze are examples of behaviors in which the subject is likely to make many mistakes in the beginning.

The social facilitation prediction was tested in a study by Michaels and colleagues (1982) in a college student union. The researchers observed pairs of students while the students were playing pool. Then a group of four confederates approached the students and closely watched them continue to play. Zajonc's theory predicts that the good players should improve while the poor players should show decreased scores. This hypothesis was confirmed: the good players increased their accuracy from 71% to 80%, whereas the poor players decreased their accuracy from 36% to 25% when they were observed.

Recently, several other explanations for the social facilitation drive have been proposed, including Baron's (1986) distraction-conflict theory which states that others cause arousal because they distract the individual from the task. The past two decades have seen a great deal of research devoted to social facilitation (Guerin, 1986) and while all the particulars have not yet been settled, it is clear that social facilitation is an important phenomenon that can be used in everyday life. For example, when you are learning something new (such as the material in this chapter), you should study alone until you begin to master the material. Then, once you have learned it fairly well, study in a group so that social facilitation can improve your performance and prepare you for your test.

Figure 15.17. Social Facilitation
Zajonc (whose name rhymes with science) proposed a theory of social facilitation which states that the presence of others enhances the possibility of an individual's expected response. One application of this theory is that you should study alone when learning new material, but with others after you know the material fairly well.

Competition and Cooperation

In some groups, competition is dominant, whereas in others, cooperation is. Factors such as personality of the individuals, amount of communication, size of the group, and reciprocity determine whether individuals compete or cooperate in a social situation. These factors have been the focus of recent research conducted in laboratory game simulations of everyday situations. In this game theory approach there are two kinds of games of interest to social psychologists: zero-sum and non-zero-sum. In zero-sum games, the total gains and losses equal zero. For example, in chess or tennis there is a winner and a loser. In non-zero-sum games the sum of the payoffs is not zero. There is value in cooperation in non-zero-sum games, since if both players cooperate both can gain and no one has to lose. Two non-zero-sum games are described below.

The trucking game was developed by Deutsch and Krauss (1960) to explore the bargaining behavior of individuals in a social situation. Each player owns a trucking company and tries to make a shipment as quickly as possible. Each has a long route to the destination as well as a short route that converges into a one-lane road. In order to use the short-cut (and make

"money") the players have to cooperate and take turns using the road. However, each person also had control of a gate to prevent the other trucking company from using the road. The best strategy is to cooperate, and yet the researchers found that when the players had a weapon (the gate), the majority of the time was spent competing and threatening the other.

In the prisoner's dilemma, two prisoners are isolated and each is accused of a crime. If both prisoners do not confess, both receive light sentences (1 year) and if both confess, both receive heavy sentences (10 years). If one confesses but the other does not, the one who confesses is given a very light sentence (3 months) while the other receives a very heavy sentence (20 years). There is an advantage over a series of trials for both to cooperate and remain silent, but personal gain favors competition by confessing and hoping the other person does not. Typically, subjects show competition in this game also.

These games illustrate the factors that determine whether an individual competes or cooperates. Some research suggests that Americans are especially competitive, and that this characteristic is learned during childhood (Werner, 1979). There are personality differences, with some people always competing, some always cooperating, and some dependent upon the other person (they begin cooperating but compete if the other person does). Communication is also a very important factor. Wichman (1970) found that when there was no communication between individuals in the prisoner's dilemma, about 40% of the responses were cooperative, but if verbal communication were allowed, the cooperation level increased to around 70%. The size of the group also makes a difference. When the prisoner's dilemma was modified so groups could play, it was found that as the size of group increased, cooperation decreased (Komorita & Lapworth, 1982). Reciprocity also plays a role, since many people will go along with whatever strategy the other begins. Cooperation and competition are important forces in today's world and social psychologists are attempting to understand how groups and even nations can learn to increase cooperation.

Leadership

One element—leadership—is always present in groups, even in those informal groups that try to avoid it. A leader is someone who is able to exert influence over the other members of a group. He or she need not necessarily occupy a formal position of power. There can always be a "power behind the throne," some person who actually exercises more influence than the leader who has been designated officially or informally (Ridgeway, 1983). Usually group members agree who the

Figure 15.18. Leadership
There are many traits which leaders might possess. Of primary importance for a specific group is whether a leader has a task orientation or a group-maintenance orientation. In these photos, **A** is probably task orientation whereas **B** is likely to be group-maintenance orientation.

leader is. Leadership involves a number of qualities, such as the capacity to direct others effectively, to speak convincingly, to represent the group to the outside world, to initiate and organize programs of action, to mediate between disputing members, to raise morale, and to get consensus from the group members.

Social psychologists have been anxious to discern any consistent attributes shared by leaders in general. Initially, they focused on personality and attempted to establish recurrent character traits in leaders. But this research proved inconclusive. Leaders often are quite unlike one another, and the only commonly occurring characteristics seem to be that leaders are more intelligent and verbally fluent than nonleaders.

A subsequent situational approach focused on the position of leadership rather than on the person who held it. The assumption was that any person can be a leader as long as he or she can satisfy the current objectives of the group. Since the demands of the role will change over time, different persons will emerge to satisfy these elements (Fiedler, 1981). If a political group decides to initiate a fund-raising campaign, for example, leadership may pass from one who excels at politics to one who is good at raising money.

A more recent approach is based on "process," which attempts to take into account the broader relationships among leaders, members, and the group situation. The concept of a leader as a person who just gives orders is far too simplistic. The way he or she leads depends on the expectations and needs of the followers, as well as the varying demands of the situation.

Extensive research on leadership has demonstrated that one cannot label a leader "good" or "bad" without understanding the conditions under which he or she operates. There is a wide range of leadership styles, from democratic (consulting and persuading others) to

Figure 15.19. Frustration and Aggression
When we are frustrated, it can lead to aggression. Here two children both want the same puzzle. Since only one can have it, frustration will probably result in aggression.

authoritarian (making decisions alone and issuing orders). No one leader is effective in all situations, and a person who is quite inefficient in one environment might be a superb leader in different circumstances. For instance, authoritarian leaders are most effective in emergency situations where speed and efficiency outweigh any other considerations. Armies thus have a very authoritarian power structure. On the other hand, democratic leaders are far more effective in situations where group members are concerned about individual rights and where there is some disagreement about goals. Discussion groups usually adopt a democratic structure for this reason.

Halpin (1966) described two dimensions often present in leadership: task orientation and group-maintenance orientation. The task leader is the one who gets the job done. He can direct others to carry out task goals efficiently. The social leader is the one who tries to keep the people in the group happy with one another. He or she is the group-maintenance leader, and is more concerned with social interaction than task accomplishment. Often a group will have separate leaders for the task and social functions. Permanent groups usually need both types of leaders to carry out their long-term goals effectively.

Besides those described above, there are several additional ways in which other people have a great influence on individual behavior. These other people influence the individual in ways similar to groups. We end this chapter by reviewing the areas of social facilitation and helping behavior.

AGGRESSION AND HELPING BEHAVIOR

None of us live in this world alone. Our actions and reactions have either a positive or negative effect on those around us. Social psychologists are interested in discovering what influences people to help others or be aggressive and hurt others in social interactions. In this last section, we review what is known about aggression and helping behavior.

Aggression

Every time we pick up a newspaper or watch a television newscast, we are bombarded by stories of aggression and violence. The struggle in Central America, the war in the Middle East, the violence in Northern Ireland, and crime in the United States all remind us that people can be very aggressive creatures.

What is aggression? What causes it? How does it develop? How can it be controlled? Do people have to be aggressive, or is it learned? How can we reduce destructive aggression? The answers to these questions are being sought by social psychologists.

Definition of Aggression. Aggression is a difficult concept to define and is widely used and misused (Scott, 1975). To the layperson, it could be the behavior of a

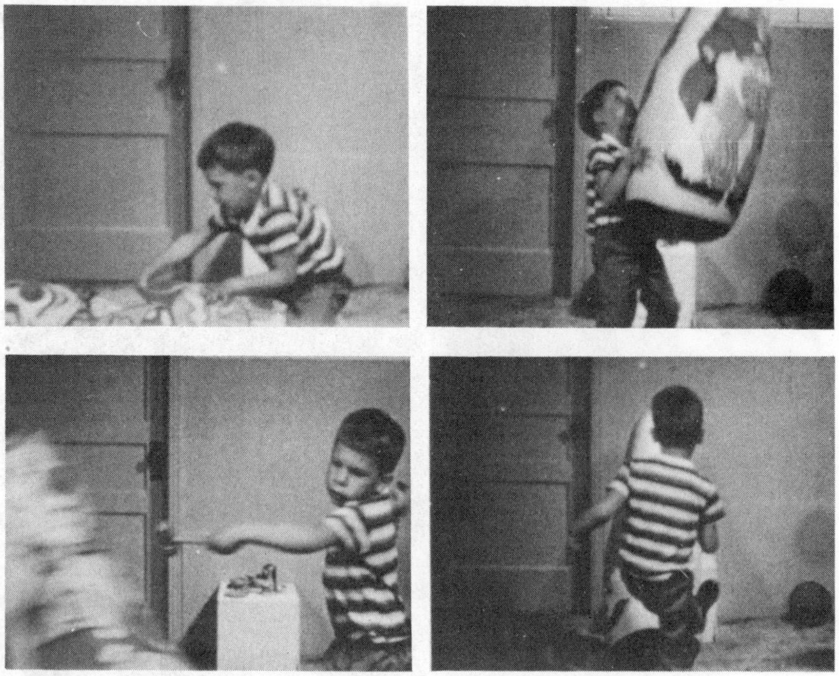

Figure 15.20. Imitation of Aggression
Bandura and his colleagues found that after children observed a film of adult aggression, they would imitate the aggressive behavior. This research supports the social-learning theory of aggression.

salesman closing a deal or of a bank robber in action; but it could also be an act of war by a nation. People continue to debate the scope of aggression. For example, a person may kill an insect, an animal, or another person. We may yell at someone or feel tense inside. Two animals may fight with claws and teeth or two people may fight with guns or knives. In order to understand aggression in the context of human behavior, psychologists often limit the scope of their research. We focus our discussion on destructive human aggression.

Social psychologist Robert Baron (1983) defined aggression as behavior intended to harm another member of the same species. This definition eliminates cross-species aggression (hunting), accidental aggression, and aggression toward objects in the environment. For social psychologists studying human aggression, it is behavior directed toward harming another person.

Aggressive behavior can take many forms. It may be physical behavior, such as attacking with fists or weapons, or it may be verbal behavior such as threats. Or it may be an indirect action, such as destroying the property of the enemy or harming his loved ones.

Aggression is a behavior, but it is accompanied by emotion (anger) and influenced by motivation. Roger Johnson (1972) pointed out that aggression is a multi-dimensional concept with many influences. Psychologists have studied the relationships between aggression and such factors as heredity, sex, territory, dominance, ecology, physiology, development, learning, and social organization.

Theories of Aggression. Aggression has been studied from four approaches: instinct theory, frustration-drive theory, social learning theory, and cognitive-neoassociationist theory.

The oldest theory of aggression holds that people are naturally aggressive. Probably the most famous proponent of the instinct theory was Sigmund Freud (1930) who argued in that aggression is the result of a death instinct (Thanatos) inherent in all human beings. Freud proposed that destructive energy builds up and has to be released through aggressive behavior.

A modern instinct theory of aggression has been proposed by the European ethologist Konrad Lorenz. Lorenz (1966) argued that people are aggressive because they evolved to survive. Other more powerful animals have inhibitions against harming one another. Because a human without weapons is fairly powerless against other people, Lorenz argues, he didn't develop the same inhibitions against fighting that most other species have. The instinct to be aggressive, combined with the development of weapons, has made the human the most dangerous animal in nature. The instinct theory takes a fairly pessimistic view of human aggression.

The frustration-drive theory provides a little more hope for people. The frustration-drive theory of aggression was proposed by social psychologists Dollard, Doob, Miller, Mowrer, and Sears (1939). The theory hypothesizes that frustration leads to the arousal of an aggressive drive to hurt the source of the frustration. For example, if you wanted to have a party but your best friend objected, your frustration might lead to aggression toward your friend. This theory suggests that all aggression is the result of frustration, and the way to control aggression is to eliminate potential frustrations

Figure 15.21. Television and Aggression
A great deal of research has been done on the relationship of watching television violence and behaving aggressively. No conclusive results have been reached but they suggest a positive correlation.

Television and Aggression

In 1982 the National Institute of Mental Health published a 10-year study of the effects of watching television. Its conclusion was that watching violence on television can contribute to aggressive behavior. The response from the television networks was that the research was incomplete. The question of television and aggression is complex and has not yet been fully answered.

We do know that the average household spends almost seven hours a day watching television. And we know that the level of violence on television is higher than it was 10 years ago. Does watching crime and violence on television influence children? The evidence suggests that it probably does.

Bandura's (1963) early research on young children's imitation of aggressive acts seen in a film suggests that we might learn aggression by watching television. Leonard Berkowitz (1974) has shown that in watching violence on television we learn to associate a variety of cues with aggression. He studied television-watching habits of a group of boys when they were 9 years old and then returned to examine them again 10 years later. He found that those boys who watched the most violence on

TV were the most aggressive when they were 19. Phillips (1983) reported that the number of homicides in the United States significantly increased after championship boxing matches were aired on television.

Opponents argue that perhaps the most aggressive children like to watch violence on television the most. Although it seems logical that we can learn to be aggressive through watching television, some research suggests that television violence reduces the tendency to become anxious when experiencing real aggression (Thomas, 1982). And some experts believe that we can take out our aggressive impulses through watching violence on TV. Thus, while it seems that television can teach us to be aggressive, the issue is not completely settled (Freedman, 1984).

THOUGHT QUESTIONS

1. How do we learn aggression?
2. Could we learn helping by watching television?
3. What should we do if we conclude that watching television increases aggression?

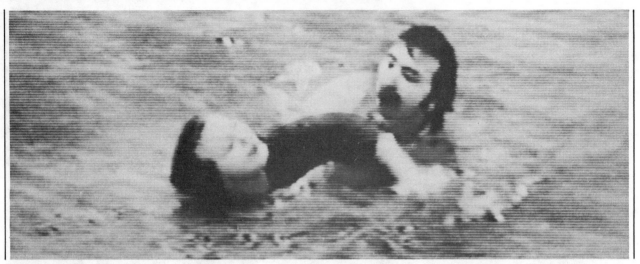

Figure 15.22. Altruistic Behavior
When we help others without expectation of a reward, we are engaging in altruistic behavior. This photograph shows Lennie Skutnik saving a victim of an airplane crash in the icy water of the Potomac River in January 1982.

in the environment. For example, if everyone had everything he or she needed or wanted, which unfortunately seems highly unlikely, there would be no frustration and hence no aggression.

Social learning theory proposes that aggression is a form of learned social behavior. Albert Bandura (1973) and Robert Baron (1977) represent the current view that aggression is learned through observation and imitation of other people and is maintained through positive reinforcement.

A classic experiment conducted by Bandura and his colleagues (1963) demonstrated the social learning concept of aggression. The researchers had children watch a film of an adult attacking a large inflatable "Bobo" doll that stands upright. The adult model used some unusual aggressive behaviors with the doll. Later, when the children were allowed to play with the doll, most of them imitated the aggressive behaviors shown by the adult in the film. They learned to be aggressive by observing someone else.

Children watch aggression on television and observe it in other children and adults. They then imitate the aggressive behaviors and are reinforced when they get what they want. The social learning theory suggests that the way to control aggression is to reduce the number of aggressive models available to children and to eliminate reinforcement when aggression occurs (Eron, 1982).

Berkowitz (1984) recently proposed the cognitive neoassociationist theory of aggression, which views aggression as a reaction to aversive events. Essentially, this theory states that when people experience aversive events they also experience negative affective states (unpleasant feelings of anger and irritation). This causes them to show aggression or escape behavior, depending upon the cognitive processes that interpret the situation.

For instance, if someone bothers us, we might lash out and behave aggressively, unless it is inappropriate and then we might just get away from the person. This theory is relatively new and has not been fully evaluated yet. However, it does make some predictions about behavior that are currently being tested.

An alarming recent statistic is the high rate of aggressive behavior in close relationships, such as families and dating couples (Laner, 1983). Straus and colleagues (1980) reported that nearly 75% of parents used some form of physical aggression on children (20% striking their children with an object). The causes of violence in families are varied, and include having grown up in a violent family with a great deal of stress and frustration. Overall, it appears that males are slightly more aggressive than females (Eagly & Steffen, 1986). Men tend to use more physical aggression than women and both men and women direct aggression more often toward men.

Aggression is a very serious problem for humankind. We need to increase research into the causes of aggression, and work to reduce aggression in our society. Baron (1983) suggested several techniques to control human aggression, including punishment, exposure to nonaggressive models, and training in basic social skills. J. P. Scott (1975) emphasizes the importance of scientific research in trying to make the world a safer place to live, and argues that the consequences of not reducing aggression are too painful to consider.

Helping Behavior

It is early evening. You are at home, relaxing. Suddenly you hear screams coming from your neighbor's home next door. It sounds like a fight, with crashes and bangs.

What should you do? Should you help? What if they consider the fight to be their personal business? What if it's only the TV? What if they begin to attack you instead? The decision to help is sometimes complex and difficult to make. Recently the question of helping received the attention of social psychologists.

We help others for a number of reasons. Sometimes we expect to be rewarded. Sometimes it's our job. Sometimes we do it just to be nice. Helping behavior is often called prosocial behavior, and when we help others without any expectation of reward for ourself, it is called altruistic behavior.

Steps in Helping Behavior. In their 1970 book *The Unresponsive Bystander: Why Doesn't He Help?* Bibb Latané and John Darley proposed a series of steps that we must go through before actually helping in an emergency situation. The first step is to notice that something is happening. If we don't pay attention to the problem, we will not be able to do anything. Next, we must correctly interpret the situation. We have to make sure that it is an emergency. We then must assume responsibility for taking action. If we believe someone else will take care of it, or that it is none of our business, then we will not help. After we decide that we must help, we must decide what to do. Should we call the police, rush in ourselves, get reinforcements, or announce politely that we are here to help? Finally, after we decide to help, we must engage in the helping behavior itself. Latané and Darley explain that unless all of the above steps are taken, helping behavior will not occur.

The Bystander Effect. Sometimes we see an emergency situation but we do not help. Social psychologists have discovered that we are actually less likely to help when other people are present. The fact that a single person by himself or herself is much more likely to help in an emergency than when he or she is in a group of people is called the bystander effect. Latané and Darley tested the bystander effect in numerous experiments. In a 1968 study, they had students fill out questionnaires, some in a room by themselves and others in a room with two other people. While they were working, smoke began to pour into the rooms. The lone subjects reported the smoke immediately, while the subjects in groups tended to ignore the smoke completely, even though it got so thick they couldn't breathe properly.

Latané and Darley explain the bystander effect by saying that when we are in a group a diffusion of responsibility occurs, so that each individual feels less responsibility to take action. Also, in a group you can preserve anonymity: no one recognizes you as an individual expected to help. Furthermore, we hesitate to become involved because of the possibility that there may not be an emergency after all and we would be

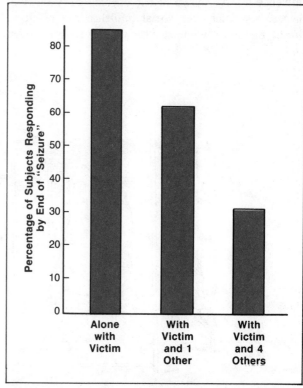

Figure 15.23. Diffusion of Responsibility

When other people are present, each person feels less responsible to take action. In one experiment on helping, Latané and Darley (1970) found that the percentage of subjects reporting a victim's seizure decreased dramatically as the number of people in the group increased.

embarrassed if we made the mistake of acting as if there is one when there really is not.

How can we increase the incidence of helping? Research has shown that people are more likely to help when they feel good (O'Malley & Andrews, 1983) and when they feel responsible. In this situation the presence of other people can actually increase the likelihood of helping (Yinon & colleagues, 1982). Some research has suggested that personality characteristics influence the probability of helping behavior (Amato, 1985). For example, people who have a strong need for approval or who have high moral standards are more likely to help. A person who has made a prior commitment to help is much more likely to carry through on that commitment. Eagly and Crowley (1986) reported that men are more likely to help than women, especially when helping is defined as a heroic act for a distressed stranger, but not necessarily when everyday friendship and family assistance are taken into account. Latané and Darley's research suggests that we need to help people recognize emergencies. Helping behavior is very important to a society, and social psychologists will continue to work to increase its incidence in emergency situations. ■

Social behavior is a major part of being human. We continually influence other people and they in turn influence us. As shown in our opening story on obedience, sometimes the social influence can result in drastic measures, while at other times we are not even aware of the influence. Many of the topics we discussed earlier are relevant when exploring social psychology. To become truly effective social citizens, we must understand the many ways that social interaction pervades our daily life.

© 1983 The Register and Tribune Syndicate, Inc.

CHAPTER REVIEW
What You've Learned About Social Psychology

1. Social psychology is the study of how an individual's behavior, thoughts, and feelings are influenced by others. Important areas in social psychology include social cognition, attitudes, social influence, group processes, and aggression and helping behavior.

2. Social cognition is the process of understanding other people and ourselves. Person perception is the process of developing an impression of another person from our perceptions. Once we form a general impression of someone, we tend to interpret additional information in a consistent manner, called the halo effect. Physical attractiveness and first impressions are important variables in impression formation.

3. Attribution is the process of determining the causes of behavior in a given individual. Situational factors involve the external environment, whereas dispositional factors involve the individual's internal personality. In covariation theory, conditions of low consensus, high consistency, and low distinctiveness lead to attributing a person's behavior to internal causes, whereas conditions of high consensus, high consistency, and high distinctiveness lead to attributing a person's behavior to external causes. Actor-observer attribution is the tendency to attribute the behavior of others to internal causes while attributing our own behavior to external causes.

4. Attitudes are learned dispositions that actively guide us toward specific behaviors. Attitudes include affective, behavioral, and cognitive components. Attitudes are formed through conditioning.

We develop attitudes from our experiences with our parents, schools, peers, and mass media. We can measure attitudes through interviews, questionnaires, projective techniques, and behavioral testing.

5. Research on attitude change has concentrated on the communicator, message, and audience. The effective communicator is credible, trusted, attractive, and similar to the audience. Two-sided arguments should be used when the audience is unfavorable, but single-sided arguments work best when the audience is favorable. Emotional appeals work only under certain conditions.

6. Festinger's cognitive dissonance theory states that when a person has two attitudes that are discrepant, tension is produced. The person tries to reduce this tension by changing attitudes. An extension of cognitive dissonance is the concept of inadequate rewards, in which a person develops an internal reward when the external rewards are inadequate.

7. Prejudice is an unjustified attitude involving a fixed, usually negative, way of thinking about a person or object. A stereotype is an exaggerated and rigid mental image of a particular class of persons or objects. Racial prejudice can be reduced when the prejudiced person interacts with members of the disliked group. Sex stereotypes are often learned when we are children. People who score high on both feminine and masculine scales are androgynous.

8. A good deal of human social encounters consist of influencing and being influenced by other people. Conformity is the changing of behavior in order to fit social norms or expectations more closely. We conform to avoid being different or to learn about our environment. The social comparison theory states that we use other people to judge our own perceptions and conform to others.

9. Compliance is a type of social influence in which an individual changes his or her behavior because of a direct request from someone else. Ingratiation increases the attractiveness of the person making the request. The foot-in-the-door technique is making a small request followed by a large one. The door-in-the-face technique is making a very large request and following it up with a smaller one. Low-balling is making an attractive offer and then changing it once it has been accepted.

10. Stanley Milgram extensively studied obedience, in which one person makes a demand of another. He has shown that when conditions were right, a large number of people tend to obey authority. In one classic study, Milgram found 65% of the subjects continued to deliver 450-volt shocks to a learner who complained of a weak heart.

11. We spend a great deal of time interacting in groups which function according to norms—rules and standards that regulate the behavior of its members. Groupthink occurs when the group makes decisions that individuals would not. Groups tend to make extreme decisions, a phenomenon called group polarization. People in groups tend to exert less energy than they would by themselves, a finding called social loafing. Latané's theory of social impact proposes that (a) the more people present, the more influence they have on each individual, (b) the rate of influence grows less as each new individual is added, and (c) the more people present, the less influence any one will have.

12. Zajonc's theory of social facilitation proposes that when in the presence of others, we tend to exhibit our dominant responses. Thus, when we are learning something new, we should practice it alone, but once it is well-learned, it's better to perform in front of an audience.

13. Social psychologists use the game theory approach to study competition and cooperation. Factors that influence competition or cooperation include personality, communication, reciprocity, and group size.

14. Groups have leaders, people who are able to exert influence over other group members. Research has not been able to totally define what makes a great leader. Two dimensions of leadership include task orientation and social orientation.

15. Aggression is behavior intended to harm another member of the same species. Aggressive behavior can be physical, verbal, or indirect. Aggression is a behavior accompanied by emotion and influenced by motivation. The instinct theory states that people are aggressive because of genetic tendencies. The frustration-drive theory proposes that frustration leads to the arousal of an aggressive drive to hurt the source of the frustration. The social learning theory views aggression as a behavior which is learned through observation and maintained through reinforcement. The cognitive neoassociationist theory of aggression views aggression as a reaction to aversive events.

16. When we help others without expectation of a reward it is called altruistic behavior. Latané and Darley suggest that in order to help in an emergency, we must notice something is happening, interpret it as an emergency, assume responsibility, decide what to do, and take action. The bystander effect is that a single person is more likely to help in an emergency than a group of people. Diffusion of responsibility means that each member of the group has only partial responsibility, with the result that none help.

Chapter 16

APPLIED PSYCHOLOGY

Psychologists are interested in applying their skills and research findings to practical problems. Some of the areas psychologists are involved with include industry, which is concerned with business and organizational behavior, police departments and prisons, sports, education, and environment, which is concerned with the effects of a person's surroundings on emotion and behavior.

Researchers, led by Philip Zimbardo, created a simulated prison in 1973 in a laboratory basement, using as subjects 21 healthy male undergraduate volunteers. Each person was to receive 15 dollars a day for 2 weeks. Nine of the students were randomly selected to be "prisoners" while the rest were divided into three shifts of "guards," who worked around the clock.

The experimenters tried to reproduce, as closely as possible, the same typically anonymous and dehumanizing conditions found in prisons. The "cells" were poorly ventilated because they had no windows. The prisoners wore identical uniforms with identifying numbers to simulate prison conditions. The guards took away all personal belongings and addressed the prisoners only by their identification numbers.

The guards were equally depersonalized. They wore identical khaki uniforms, one-way sunglasses that hid their eyes, and were given the usual articles of their trade: whistles, billy clubs, and handcuffs. Neither prisoners nor guards were given any specific instructions about how to behave, except that no physical violence was allowed.

Within a brief time, the "guards" and "prisoners" became totally absorbed in their respective roles. As the guards got more aggressive, the prisoners became passive and apathetic. No sense of solidarity developed among them. They spent only a tenth of their conversation talking about subjects unrelated to the prison situation. The rest of the time they talked about escape, the quality of the food, and the causes of their discontent.

At first, it was an exciting game, but quickly became frustrating. For instance, an hour after the prisoners went to sleep, the guards abruptly woke them and made them line up and repeat their ID numbers. The guards made the prisoners do push-ups until they were exhausted. When the prisoners revolted, they were placed in solitary confinement and even made to clean toilets with their bare hands. The guards then began using psychological tactics, isolating and recombining prisoners until the prisoners no longer trusted one another.

According to Zimbardo, within a few days, most of the subjects, as well as the experimenters, no longer knew where reality ended and the play roles began. A majority of the subjects began acting as though they really were prisoners or guards. Less than 36 hours after the experiment began, one of the prisoners had to be released because of extreme depression, although the guards suspected him of pretending. Another prisoner developed psychophysiological hives over his entire body and had to be hospitalized. A rumor spread among the guards that the ex-prisoners were going to break in and free the ones still remaining; even though there was no truth to the rumor, the guards stayed past their regular shifts to protect the prison.

Finally, after only 6 days, the experiment had to be halted. Zimbardo explained: "I didn't stop it because of the horror of what was going on, but because of the horror I felt at the idea that I myself could easily become the cruelest guard or the weakest of all the prisoners."

Even with his significant training in social psychology, Zimbardo was unprepared for the psychological influences that totally took control of the social environment. He quickly became convinced that behavior does not exist in a vacuum, but is due to a complex variety of variables which psychologists have only begun to understand.

This striking example of psychological research shows how the behavior of the individual can be shaped

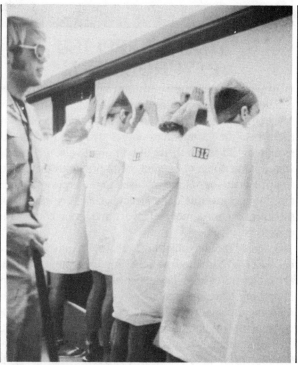

Figure 16.1. Simulated Prison Study
College students participated in a study which simulated a prison environment where they played the role of guards or prisoners. Zimbardo found both guards and prisoners soon took their roles too seriously. The study had to be ended early because of the possible negative consequences.

by the demands of the environment. The fact that the prisoners are convicted criminals or the guards may be rigid may have little to do with the brutalizing effect of prisons on both prisoners and guards. It also demonstrates how the study of psychology can shed light not only on questions about individual behavior, but also on questions of practical concern to society.

CHAPTER OBJECTIVES
What You'll Learn About Applied Psychology

After studying this chapter, you should be able to:

1. Define the area of applied psychology.
2. Describe the role of psychologists in assisting police departments.
3. Describe how psychologists are involved in the courtroom.
4. Describe how psychologists are involved in prisons.
5. Identify three tasks performed by psychologists in personnel psychology.
6. Identify the major theories of motivation in organizational psychology.
7. Describe the area of engineering psychology.
8. Identify the areas of research in consumer psychology.
9. Outline how personal space influences behavior.
10. Outline the effects of crowding on behavior.
11. Describe the effects of noise on behavior.
12. Describe how psychology is applied to sports.
13. Describe how psychology is applied to education.

WHAT IS APPLIED PSYCHOLOGY?

Although most people are aware of the contributions psychologists make to solving individual behavioral problems, they sometimes forget that the findings of psychological research are also of great value in dealing with a wide range of applied social problems that affect us all. Psychologists are involved in the areas of education, aging, juvenile delinquency, crime, crowding, job satisfaction, consumer behavior, and even courts and prisons.

Some of the information psychologists have gathered has already benefited society. For example, the basic principles of learning have been employed effectively in improving teaching techniques in the classroom and in reducing behavior problems in schools, homes, and institutions. Psychologists have investigated the effects of TV violence, created educational programs such as the popular Sesame Street, helped people find satisfying career occupations, and studied the causes of crime.

Applied psychology is concerned with helping to solve practical problems. Two large segments of applied psychology are clinical and counseling psychology, areas we have already discussed in chapters 12, "Stress and Adjustment," 13, "Abnormal Behavior," and 14, "Therapy." Historically, the other major applied area is indus-

trial psychology, which includes personnel selection, training, job satisfaction, and consumer behavior.

Currently, in addition to clinical and industrial applications, psychologists are involved in solving environmental problems; investigating crime, the legal system, and prisons; and improving mental health care in the community. Some other applied psychology specialties include sports psychology, medical psychology, traffic and transportation, pet psychology, and leisure psychology. Applied social psychology incudes such areas as the environment, health, and organization (Rodin, 1985). These areas are an extension of the principles of social psychology. You will notice the application of some of the research from the social psychology chapter in the topics discussed here.

Goldstein and Krasner (1987) stressed that basic and applied research are interrelated, and that applied psychology refers more to where the information is being used than to what is being used. They argued that areas of modern applied psychology include clinical, industrial, health, legal, educational, and sports applications.

The *Journal of Applied Psychology,* established in 1917, continues to have a heavy emphasis on industrial psychology applications. It also covers applications in settings such as police and corrections, urban affairs, government, health, and education. Until 1946 the scientific and applied (mainly clinical and industrial) areas had two separate organizations, the American Association for Applied Psychology for practitioners and the American Psychological Association for scientists.

BIOGRAPHICAL ☆ HIGHLIGHT ☆

PHILIP ZIMBARDO

Philip Zimbardo was born in 1933 in New York City. He entered Brooklyn College with the idea of majoring in the social psychology of race relations. Instead, for awhile he researched exploratory behavior in albino rats.

He received his bachelor's degree in 1954 from Brooklyn College. Eventually, Zimbardo returned to his first love and received his Ph.D. degree in social psychology from Yale University in 1959. He taught at Yale University and New York University before accepting a position at Stanford University in 1968.

Zimbardo has contributed to a wide variety of topics in social psychology. His early work included research on vandalism and cognitive social motivation. One of his best-known research projects was a functional simulation of a prison. More recently, he has become known for his research on the causes and treatment of shyness.

Zimbardo has received recognition for both his creative research and his outstanding teaching. He was given the APA Distinguished Teaching Award for Outstanding Contributions to Education in Psychology in 1975. In addition to his introductory psychology textbook, he has published several popular books, including *Shyness* (1977).

These two organizations merged into the APA in 1946, with the goal of advancing psychology as a science and a profession.

Although the applications of psychology to our social activities is wide and varied, the interests of psychologists discussed here will serve to illustrate how they are applying research findings to everyday behaviors. We begin this chapter with a look at the field of legal psychology.

LEGAL PSYCHOLOGY

After a rash of airplane skyjackings, the federal government called in psychologists to develop a profile of the typical skyjacker. Interviews with the skyjackers who had been caught and a study of their motives, life history, and methods of operation provided psychologists with data for a composite profile of the typical skyjacker, so that people concerned with the security of flights could recognize someone likely to try to take over an airplane. Developing profiles of potential criminals is but one of many roles psychologists play in law enforcement. Forensic psychologists work in police departments, courts, and prisons to detect and prevent crime and to assess and rehabilitate those convicted of criminal behavior.

Police Departments

To reduce the crime rate we need an effective police department. Police officers are under a great deal of everyday stress. They must deal with the public carefully, uphold the laws, ensure that people accused of a crime are treated fairly, and, when off duty, still be able to function socially. Psychologists are involved in selecting, training, and counseling police officers, and in helping to detect and prevent crime (Goldstein & Krasner, 1987).

Psychologists have skills in assessing personality, motivation, attitudes, perception, abilities, and adjustment. The methods of testing, observation, and interviewing, which have already been described in this textbook, can be helpful in selecting capable police officers (see chapter 11, "Personality"). Stotland and Berberich (1979) indicated that these methods should predict characteristics such as skills in human relations, communication, decision making, emotional maturity, and adjustment, which are necessary in police depart-

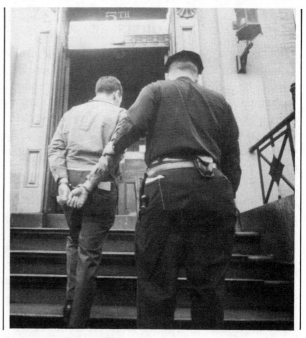

Figure 16.2. Police Officers
Psychologists are involved in the training and counseling of police officers. They help police deal with their high level of stress and may help develop and interpret methods of solving crimes.

ments because they need officers who can tolerate stress, behave objectively, act compassionately, and yet be firm and obedient.

Once the proper persons have been selected, they must receive instruction on how to carry out their duties. Psychologists can help teach police officers about motivation, personality, social interactions, prejudice, aggression, abnormal behavior, and various kinds of treatment. The psychologist is able to provide information about how to deal with problems such as drug abuse, aggression, youth delinquency, and race relations. This information is of immense value to the police officer who has to deal with these problems daily.

Police officers experience a high level of stress from exposure to danger, dealing with people, making crucial decisions, and scheduling their lives around the department's demands. Bartol (1983) reported the most significant sources of stress for police officers include lack of supervisory support, shiftwork, physical danger, and negative public image. Psychologists can help them deal with this stress. For example, Maslach (1982) reported that stress management workshops are routinely conducted by police departments.

Psychologists also assist police in the prevention and detection of crime. They compile criminal profiles. They advise on the techniques for interviewing suspects, on ways to deal with the public, and on methods of handling dangerous situations. Once a suspect has been arrested, psychologists often participate in the legal process as expert witnesses.

Courts

"But I saw it with my own eyes!" is a statement many of us have heard. But whether the person really saw it, or thought he did, may be debatable because perception is sometimes confused with sensation. However, as the Gestalt psychologists point out, perception and sensation are often quite different and in a courtroom where legal decisions are made, this distinction can be a critical difference.

Expert Testimony. To understand the crime and the people involved in it, most court systems need the assistance of psychologists and other specialists. Psychologists may be called as expert witnesses to give a clinical evaluation of a defendant or to evaluate scientifically the testimony and evidence. For example, psychologists might be asked to share their expertise in areas such as identification techniques, interpretation of memory, and identification of perception or motivation. They might also interpret a score on a personality or intelligence test.

Eyewitness Testimony. Imagine you are a juror watching a videotape of an automobile accident. If the prosecutor asks "How fast were the cars going when they hit each other?" what might you respond? What if the prosecutor asked "How fast were the cars going when they collided?" How about "bumped," "contacted," or "smashed"? A single word in a question can elicit quite different responses, even when the actual perception is the same. This study, described by Elizabeth Loftus in her 1979 book, *Eyewitness Testimony*, found that the highest speed was reported by a witness when the word used by the prosecutor was "smashed," and the lowest speed was reported when the word "contacted" was used. The analysis and application of courtroom eyewitness testimony is an important concern of applied psychology.

Psychologists are aware that perception and memory distortions can lead to inaccurate descriptions of events. For instance, Buckhout (1980) had subjects watch a film of a staged crime and then attempt to identify the "criminal" in a line-up. Only 14% of the subjects were able to identify the correct person. Other research suggests that there is no relationship between the confidence of the eyewitness and the accuracy of the testimony (Wells & Murray, 1983).

Does eyewitness testimony influence jurors? Yes, according to Leippe (1985) who had subjects participate in a mock robbery trial with all variables held constant except the testimony of the "eyewitnesses." In one situation, two witnesses (the victim and a bystander) both identified the defendant as the guilty person, whereas in another situation, one of the witnesses decided the defendant was not guilty. When the witnesses agreed, 70% of the jurors felt the defendant was guilty, compared to only 13% when the witnesses disagreed. Thus, eyewitness testimony does have a significant impact on jurors in a trial.

Jury Behavior. Research on the behavior of juries is probably the earliest interest of legal psychology. Early studies focused on how small groups make decisions. Research in social psychology on topics such as leadership, groupthink, and risk taking (which are discussed in chapter 15, "Social Psychology") is directly relevant to the functioning of juries.

More recent research on jury behavior has concentrated on interviewing jurors directly after a trial, or monitoring simulated trials with volunteer subjects (often college students) as mock jurors. Jury research has studied variables such as the personal background of jurors, the order of presentation of evidence in the courtroom, and the effects of the instructions given by the judge (Nemeth, 1981). Personality findings include the fact that younger jurors and those with more education are more likely to vote for acquittal than older ones or those with less education. Monahan and Loftus (1982) reported that the more similar in age and education the juror is to the defendant the more likely an easy sentence will be suggested.

Research has shown that the verdict reached by the jury depends to a large degree on the number and severity of the possible alternatives available to it. For instance, if the only possible verdicts allowable are first-degree murder and not guilty, more jurors will vote not guilty than when the possible verdicts are manslaughter and not guilty. Even fewer would vote for not guilty when more alternatives, such as negligent homicide or second-degree murder are added to first-degree murder and manslaughter as choices.

The order of presentation of evidence in a trial appears to have an influence on the decision of the jurors. Consistent with other research in social psychology, it has been found that a *recency effect* occurs. That is, information presented at the end of a trial is more persuasive than that presented at the beginning of the trial. A classic study was done by Weld and Roff (1938), who divided prosecution and defense evidence into distinct units. In one condition, subjects (mock jurors) were presented with all of the prosecution evidence first, followed by all of the defense evidence. In the other condition, part of the prosecution evidence was presented, followed by the defense evidence, with the rest of the prosecution evidence presented last. Subjects in the latter group were more likely to believe the defendant was guilty. While research such as this gives some insight into how jurors may function, it is important to remember that the research is not conducted under ideal conditions, and that it is impossible to predict human behavior infallibly in such settings.

Jury Selection

Sometimes psychologists help attorneys predict the behavior of individual jurors, and thereby enable the attorneys to select jurors they believe are sympathetic to their case. Christie in 1976 described the procedures used by psychologists to help select jurors.

The first step is to conduct a survey in the community in which the trial will be held. This survey is designed to help understand the prevalent attitudes on the issues which will be raised during the trial. It is also designed to match up some of these attitudes with specific demographic variables (age, sex, religion, occupation).

Next, information is obtained on each of the potential individual jurors, especially background information pertinent to the issues likely to be raised during the trial.

In the preliminary sessions, the behavior of the potential individual juror is observed in the courtroom. Then the psychologist collates all the information collected together and develops his predictions about the juror's behavior, as well as his possible interactions with the other jurors. Social psychological principles of small group behavior are helpful in making these predictions.

Finally, after the trial, the psychologist interviews the jury, as well as those prospective jurors eliminated in the jury selection sessions. Through these interviews, the psychologist can measure the effectiveness of his predictions.

Figure 16.3. Jury Selection
The process in which a jury is selected is complex and includes a wide variety of people. Psychologists are involved in conducting surveys and interviews, and making observations to help predict jury behavior.

While this area is still relatively young, there is some evidence that the predictions have been somewhat effective (Moran & Comfort, 1982). However, questions concerning the ethics of the involvement of psychologists in the process of jury selection have been raised. In the future, we will need to decide what limits should be placed on the applications of psychology in our judicial processes.

THOUGHT QUESTIONS

1. What is the procedure for predicting behavior of jurors?
2. Could these techniques be used in other situations? Name some.
3. Do you think it is ethical for psychologists to become involved in procedures such as jury selection? Why? Or why not?

Prisons

Once convicted, often a person is sentenced to a term in prison. In a prison setting, psychologists are frequently consulted in the evaluation of new prisoners, they counsel inmates, and train prison personnel.

Usually prison psychologists have clinical or counseling backgrounds. One of their important duties is to evaluate newly admitted prisoners. The new prisoner is given a battery of tests, including intelligence, interest, personality, and social tests (see chapter 11, "Personality") to determine how he is likely to respond to the pressures of confinement, whether he will become violent in prison, and how the prison system might best help rehabilitate him. Most prisons have educational opportunities (including college courses) and some type of vocational training program.

While the inmates are incarcerated, they may require some sort of counseling, either as part of an ongoing assessment of rehabilitation procedures, or to help them cope with the demands of prison life. In some cases, prisoners just need the opportunity to talk to someone who is interested in them as individuals. The outcome of counseling sessions can be an important factor in parole decisions, and so most inmates take them very seriously.

Like the police officer, the prison staff member is under a great deal of stress. Prison guards are especially vulnerable to the strains of the prison environment and need psychological counseling and training to teach them how to deal effectively with potential problems.

Among other psychologists concerned with the prison system are environmental psychologists, who assist in designing new facilities or help the staff understand the prisoner's need for personal space and privacy; correc-

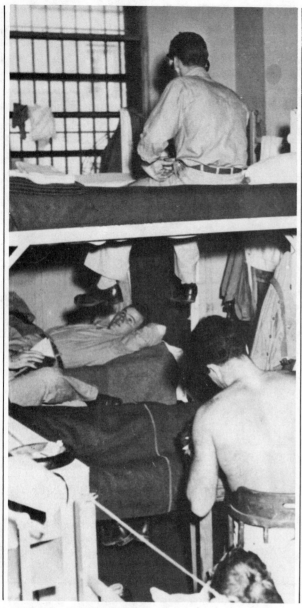

Figure 16.4. Prison Environment
Psychologists evaluate and counsel prisoners and train prison personnel. They may assist in the design of prison environment so that the need for personal space and privacy can be met. Ultimately, psychologists may positively influence the prison system itself.

tional psychologists, who make recommendations to parole boards; and educational psychologists, who set up and run educational programs for the inmates. (When I teach General Psychology at the local correctional institution, I am greatly impressed with the ability and motivation of my inmate students to learn the course material. In a small research study in 1978, I found my inmate students to be similar to my regular college students in both class performance and the need for social approval.)

Unquestionably, crime is one of the major social problems in America, more so than in most other countries. Some people feel that the only solution to the crime problem is to catch criminals and put them in prison to recognize the evil of their ways, acquire useful skills, and emerge rehabilitated and prepared to lead productive, law-abiding lives. But, as shown in our opening story, the simulated prison study by Philip Zimbardo indicates that our present-day penal system tends to bring out the worst in both prisoners and guards. According to Zimbardo's results, the flaw seems to lie more in the system than in the personalities of the individuals. Psychology can contribute much to prison reform (Monahan & Loftus, 1982).

INDUSTRIAL AND ORGANIZATIONAL PSYCHOLOGY

Industrial psychology, or industrial-organizational (I-O) psychology, is an area of applied psychology which will have a great impact on your life (Schultz & Schultz, 1986). Someday you will take a job. After you are hired, you will need additional training in the precise skills and procedures of that job. Your performance will be evaluated regularly for promotion and raises. You will be motivated to work hard and be happy when you achieve job satisfaction. While working, the environment will influence your performance. And when you get paid, you will become a consumer and purchase the goods you need or desire. Industrial or organizational psychology includes personnel psychology, organizational psychology, engineering psychology, and consumer psychology (Howell & Dipboye, 1982).

Personnel Psychology

Personnel psychology involves employee selection, training, and evaluation. In the process of selection, the employer decides what type of employee is needed, solicits and receives applications, and conducts interviews. Training prepares new employees for their jobs and helps older employees learn more effective techniques for doing their jobs. Finally, employees are periodically evaluated for promotions and pay raises. The personnel psychologist participates in all phases of an employee's career.

Selection. The basic idea of selection is to obtain the best applicant for the job. There are several steps involved in a successful selection process. First, a job analysis is undertaken to determine exactly what the new

Figure 16.5. Personnel Selection
The selection of new employees often involves personnel psychologists who may aid in the selection procedure. This usually includes evaluating an application blank, letters of recommendation, and conducting a personal interview with the applicant.

employee will be doing. It usually consists of a job description and personnel specifications. The job description is a detailed description of what the worker does and the conditions under which he or she works. It is obtained by examining published analyses of similar jobs, interviewing people already doing the job, or observing people as they work on the job. Personnel specifications describe the characteristics of the person required for the position and might include such things as personality, physical ability, mental ability, experience, and motivation (Howell & Dipboye, 1982).

There are numerous indicators involved in the process of employee selection, but the most common include application blanks, references, tests, and interviews. The *application blank* is virtually universal and is usually the initial step in the selection process. Customarily, the application requests routine biographical information, work experience, qualifications, and sometimes personal information (from finances to hobbies). Care is taken to meet guidelines of fair employment legislation (Landy, 1989).

A common selection technique is to require that the applicant submit the names of several *references* who can testify to the applicant's abilities, or provide several *letters of recommendation.* The major limitation of letters of recommendation is that they tend to be rather

positive regardless of the qualities of the applicant since the applicant often can choose who will write the letters.

Often the selection process includes tests of mental ability, aptitude, motor ability, and personality. These tests help the employer match the applicant with a particular job. The last method almost always included in the selection process is the personal *interview.* As we discussed in chapter 11, "Personality," an interview can be structured or unstructured, and depends for its success mostly on the ability of the interviewer (Hakel, 1982). In many cases, the structured interview is the more effective.

Training. Training is the process of learning something new. After someone has been hired, he or she is trained to perform the job efficiently. Along with developing job knowledge and skills, sometimes training programs serve to inform the employee about the organization and to modify employee attitudes and develop employee loyalty.

There are several steps in designing and conducting training programs. They are usually specific to the particular organization, so the first step is to decide the function of the training (to orient new employees, teach employees how to use machines, or help them improve their attitude). Then the actual training is conducted to meet the objectives that have been developed. Finally, the effectiveness of the training program is evaluated by observing the behavior and performance of the employees.

There are different types of training programs (Goldstein, 1980). Orientation training is designed to develop job skills and provide knowledge of the organization. Usually on-the-job training is handled by a supervisor who teaches an apprentice how to improve job performance. Off-the-job training is a professional type of instruction and may consist of lectures, programmed instruction, or simulations (practice in a simulated environment). Training programs for managers concentrate on social and psychological skills, and include techniques such as role-playing, sensitivity training, and business games (Decker, 1982).

Evaluation. Evaluation of performance is routine in most organizations. Functions of evaluation include: gaining feedback on effectiveness of selection procedures, recognizing areas that require additional training, providing feedback for employee improvement, and determining promotions and salaries.

In evaluating job performance, employers try to appraise for merit or to determine areas where the employee can be coached to improve performance. Anastasi (1988) stated that when appraising for merit, we often use rating scales, which are standardized forms for recording personal evaluation. There are several types of rating scales, including ranking employees from best to worst, forced-choice comparisons of statements about the worker, and behavior checklists. Anastasi (1988) pointed out that there are problems with many rating scales, including ambiguity, the halo effect, the error of central tendency (tendency to evaluate everyone in the middle range and avoid extreme ratings) and the error of leniency (tendency not to evaluate anyone negatively). Ambiguity can be decreased by having clear adjectives that everyone understands. One way to reduce the halo effect, for example, is to define the traits being measured in terms of specific behaviors (such as "is slower than average," "is late at least once a week," or "is always dressed neatly"). One way to reduce error of central tendency and error of leniency is to force *rankings* of individuals within the organization.

When appraising progress, the management by objectives (MBO) approach is often used. In this technique, originally developed by Peter Drucker to improve management-employee relations, the worker and supervisor jointly agree on objectives for the worker to accomplish, and then both evaluate progress toward these measurable goals. This can lead to increased performance and increased job satisfaction, both goals of organizational psychology. MBO is an extremely popular technique, and often is very successful for both the employee and management (Kondrasuk, 1981).

Organizational Psychology

Organization theory is often described as an interdisciplinary study that examines the structure and functioning of organizations and the behavior of the people within organizations (Mitchell & Larsen, 1987). Sometimes organizational psychology includes all of industrial psychology and all aspects of behavior of people in organizations. More often, however, the term organizational psychology refers to the area of industrial psychology derived from social and personality psychology. Robert Baron (1983) stated that organizational psychology is the field that focuses on understanding and predicting human behavior in organizational settings.

Howell and Dipboye (1982) defined organizational psychology as the area concerned with management functions and their implications for an organization. Employee motivation is one of the key areas of organizational psychology.

The Hawthorne Study. One of the most influential studies in organizational psychology began in 1924 at the Hawthorne plant of the Western Electric Company near Chicago (Roethlisberger & Dickson, 1939). The management was interested in how different types of working conditions, such as lighting and temperature,

ANNE ANASTASI

Anne Anastasi was born in New York City in 1908. As a child, she excelled in school, skipping several grades. She was admitted to Barnard College at the age of 15 and received her Ph.D. degree from Columbia University at age 21.

From childhood, Anastasi was fascinated with mathematics. In college, she began combining mathematics and psychology—an interest that led to her eventual contributions to psychological testing and differential psychology. She researched how trait development is influenced by genetic and environmental influences and how the measurement of traits is influenced by experiences and training. Her work has helped psychologists better understand testing and measurement.

Anastasi taught at Barnard College and Queens College of the City University of New York before she settled at Fordham University in 1947. She remained at Fordham University conducting research and teaching courses in psychological testing, applied psychology, and intelligence.

Among Anastasi's popular textbooks are *Fields of Applied Psychology* (1979) and *Psychological Testing* (1988). Both are currently used extensively in college courses. Anastasi has also been active in psychological societies, including the presidency of APA in 1971. In 1981 she received the APA Distinguished Scientific Award for the Applications of Psychology and in 1984 was awarded the American Psychological Foundation Gold Medal.

influenced productivity. Studies were conducted in which the illumination level was varied and productivity recorded. When brighter lights were installed, productivity increased. When poorer lighting was used, productivity still increased.

Eventually, the researchers realized that the workers were not responding just to the lighting level. Rather, they were motivated to work harder just because the management cared enough about them to try to find ideal working conditions. Although the original study had some flaws, the Hawthorne effect now refers to the fact that behavior can be influenced just by participation in a research study. Motivation can be extremely important in a work setting.

McGregor's Theory X and Theory Y. Douglas McGregor (1960) summarized two possible views of management in worker motivation. Theory X is the traditional view of direction and control. It states that the worker dislikes work and tries to avoid it. The function of management, therefore, is to force the employee to work through coercion and threats of punishment. The worker prefers in most cases to be directed and wants to avoid responsibility. The main motivator, therefore, for the worker is money.

Theory Y is the humanistic/self-actualization approach to human motivation. Sometimes called the human resources model, it states that work is natural and can be a source of satisfaction, and when it is, the worker can be highly committed and motivated. Workers often seek responsibility and need to be more fully involved with management to become motivated. Theory Y is most likely to be used when management utilizes worker participation in organizational decisions. In their book, *In Search of Excellence*, Peters and Waterman (1982) stated that one of the chief differences between American and Japanese management is that American managers tend to use Theory X and Japanese managers tend to use Theory Y (however, this appears to be changing).

In his book, *Theory Z*, William Ouchi (1981) described the characteristics of the Japanese companies that produce high employee commitment, motivation, and productivity. Many Japanese employees are guaranteed a position for life, increasing their loyalty to the company. Careful evaluation occurs over a period of time, and the responsibility for success or failure is shared among employees and management. Most employees do not specialize in one skill area, but work several different tasks, learning more about the company as they develop. And Japanese companies are often concerned about all aspects of their employees' lives, on and off the job. According to Ouchi, type Z organizations tend to have stable employment, high productivity, and high employee morale and satisfaction. Many of these outcomes are similar to Theory Y, and research

Figure 16.6. Employee Motivation
Research has demonstrated that people are motivated by a wide variety of needs. While basic maintenance needs such as salary and working conditions must be met, the greatest worker satisfaction is obtained only by meeting such needs as responsibility, achievement, and personal recognition.

will continue to evaluate the feasibility of implementing some of them in American companies.

Herzberg's Motivator-Hygiene Theory. Frederick Herzberg (1966) proposed the motivator-hygiene theory to account for motivation and job satisfaction. He calls the factors that lead to job satisfaction motivator needs. They include responsibility, the nature of the work, possibility for advancement, the chance for achievement, and recognition for a good job. Hygiene needs, or maintenance needs, include company policy, supervision, salary, interpersonal relations, and working conditions. If hygiene needs are met, they do not produce job satisfaction necessarily, but if they are not met, they do produce dissatisfaction.

Herzberg believes that there are two motivation systems for the worker: the need for personal growth (job satisfaction) and the need to avoid unpleasantness (job dissatisfaction). In many ways, the hygiene needs are similar to Maslow's basic needs, while the motivator needs are similar to Maslow's higher needs (see chapter 9, "Motivation"). In order for job satisfaction to occur, the worker must be able to experience personal growth and development on the job.

Unfortunately, research has not strongly supported Herzberg's theory, largely due to Herzberg's use of the *critical incident* approach, which confuses the job and the people involved (Thayer, 1983). The critical incident approach used by Herzberg involved asking employees to list specific events that they thought produced work satisfaction or dissatisfaction. Thus, it is difficult to identify a few universal variables that always lead to satisfaction or dissatisfaction with work for everyone. Psychologists now recognize that work motivation is influenced by many variables. Each individual has a unique personality, interests, abilities, and experiences. The work environment, including the physical and social structures, management, location, and task difficulty helps determine the compatibility between worker and job. Research continues to explore this important area.

Organizational psychologists have become interested in developing strategies to help workers develop quality of work life (QWL). Lawler (1982) suggested several strategies for improving QWL, including improving work conditions and security, including worker responsibility, and providing financial stability. Other strategies include increasing the worker's sense of self-worth and providing opportunities for social relationships to develop within the organization. QWL is an area of organizational psychology that will become more important in the future.

Engineering Psychology

Engineering psychology, or human factors psychology, is concerned with how work is performed, the design of equipment, and the work environment. The ideal objective of engineering psychology is to design a job so that anybody could perform it.

As early as the 1880s, Frederick Taylor went into plants with a stopwatch and timed how long it took to perform particular tasks. Then he set time standards by which workers were compared. In the early part of this century, Frank Gilbreth brought a camera into factories and took pictures of people working. Then he figured out ways to simplify the jobs. Essentially, time and motion studies helped people work more efficiently to increase productivity. Workers and labor unions have argued, however, that these studies only benefit the company and not the employees, who often feel they must continually work harder to be more productive.

Engineering psychology is concerned with designing the work space for efficient utilization by the worker. Research has discovered that materials and tools should be placed in the order that they are needed. Incidentally, this principle also holds for study areas. When you study, do you have all of your materials where you need them?

We often need to obtain information about the machines we use. Engineering psychology is concerned with producing information displays that are efficient and cost-effective. There are three categories of visual display: quantitative (information in numerical form, such as a thermometer); qualitative (information in three or more categories, such as cold, warm, hot); and dichotomist (information in two categories, such as on-off). Sleight (1948) examined the effectiveness of different types of quantitative displays. It was found that the semicircular display was more efficient than the horizontal, which was more efficient than the vertical. What type of speedometer does your automobile have?

Engineering psychologists are involved in technological projects such as nuclear power plants. After the recent Soviet Chernobyl nuclear power plant accident, psychologists will play an even more prominent role in designing equipment to prevent "human error." They are also working closely with NASA on the new space shuttle program to help design efficient control panels for the astronauts.

Engineering psychology also evaluates the physical and social conditions of the workplace (Prince, 1980). Research has examined factors such as noise, light, and color. Color can have an effect on our moods and perceptions. For example, a dark room seems smaller than a lighter-colored room. And in some situations, the colors of blue and green appear cool, while the colors of red and orange appear warm. It has been found that fish in an aquarium tend to relax and soothe the people around them. However, caution must be used in this area, since many studies have not been replicated, and often the effects are smaller than what would have been expected.

Finally, engineering psychology is concerned with the temporal conditions of work (Curry & Haerer, 1981). Research has been conducted on the hours of work, the 4-day workweek, flexible working hours, and rest periods during the workday. In general, shorter hours decrease boredom and fatigue and increase productivity. Companies that have converted to a 4-day week have generally experienced increases in productivity, a reduction in absenteeism, and increased employee satisfaction. Flexible working hours, or flextime, in which employees can help determine which time they will work (for example, 9am–5pm, 7am–3pm, or 8am–4pm, has also proven very satisfactory, both to employees and their companies. Productivity increases, absenteeism and tardiness is reduced, turnover rate is reduced, and employee morale is improved (Foegen & Curry, 1980).

Consumer Psychology

Consumer psychology deals with the behavior of the consumer when he or she goes out to purchase a product. It includes advertising, research on consumers, packaging, and psychological factors such as memory and perception (Bettman, 1986).

Advertising. Do you pay attention to advertisements? Probably, because as Schrank (1977) explained, advertising is a reflection of people's needs. Advertising makes promises to us, and we listen because we want to hear those messages. For instance, we must drink Coca-Cola because it's the "real thing," but we want Seven-Up because "no caffeine is good for you." And, of course, we might eat a hamburger at Wendy's because we know the answer to "Where's the beef?"

But advertising can be deceptive, according to Schrank. When an aspirin manufacturer tells us "no other aspirin is better," we assume that his product is the best, unless we know that all aspirin is alike. As another example, I bought a can of chocolate-flavored syrup only to find out that it contained no chocolate; it contained only chemicals to make it taste like chocolate.

Childers and Houston (1984) tested the importance of pictures versus words in advertising. When the experimenters asked the subjects to pay attention to the visual content of the advertisement, they remembered the name of the product better than when they were told to pay attention to the words. The use of color and repetition is also effective in getting people to remember a product. On the other hand, sometimes advertisers put too much information into an ad and consumers have difficulty remembering it, a phenomenon called information overload (Jacoby, 1984).

Advertisers sometimes use very attractive, seductive, and sexually appealing models. Sex appeal is used to sell everything from automobiles to after-shave lotion and soft drinks. Most consumers (as well as advertisers) assume automatically that the use of sexually attractive models will guarantee the success of a product. Actually, little research has been conducted in this area of advertising.

Sexually attractive models do get the attention of both men and women. People tend to look at ads using sexually attractive models more often than they look at other ads. But, research shows that often the wrong audience is reached with the ad. For instance, both men and women look at ads containing pictures of sexually attractive women, but the actual advertising message is read more often by women. Thus, using an attractive female to get men to read an ad often doesn't work. Likewise, ads using attractive males are actually read more often by men. While more research is needed in this area, it appears that sex in advertising is not always effective (Schultz & Schultz, 1986).

Consumer Purchase Process. There are many reasons why we buy something. In order to understand consumer behavior we must first examine individual, social, and cultural variables. For example, we may buy something because it makes us feel good, impresses other people, or is part of our ethnic heritage. Or we may buy something simply because it is on sale. To

Figure 16.7. Advertising
It is assumed that sexually attractive models will sell any product; however, research in this area is not conclusive. When you see an advertisement like this one, do you remember the product or the model?

understand the consumer purchase process, we need to take these cognitive, emotional, and motivational variables into account.

Lavidge and Steiner (1961) identified six stages the consumer goes through to reach the purchase stage:

1. *Awareness.* Learns that a product exists.
2. *Knowledge.* Learns what the product offers.
3. *Liking.* Develops favorable attitudes toward the product.
4. *Preference.* Begins to prefer the product.
5. *Conviction.* Believes that purchase of the product would be wise.
6. *Purchase.* Buys the product.

To illustrate this process, I bought a personal computer in order to help me write this textbook. I first became aware that the company made a computer. Then I began to study the characteristics of a number of different computers. I decided one was better than the others and developed a preference for it. I did this by reading current computer magazines and actually looking over various makes of computers. I developed a conviction that the computer would be useful to me, and eventually bought it (when it was on sale).

Consumer Behavior Research. What has research in consumer psychology found out about consumer

Figure 16.8. Consumer Psychology
The consumer is affected by such variables as advertising, cost, and availability. Because the consumer's perception of these variables as well as his or her own needs can be influenced rather easily, advertisers and marketing specialists seek to understand the psychology of consumer behavior.

behavior? Brettman (1986) described a number of findings. Consumer perception is important in pricing. For example, would you be more inclined to buy a product selling for $4.95 or $5.00? If you're like most people, $4.95 sounds much less expensive than $5.00.

Perception is also important in developing a brand image, or recognition of a particular brand of a product. A large number of studies demonstrate that people feel secure in buying a name brand (even if it is identical to an unknown brand). For example, Makens (1965) gave two identical samples of turkey meat to customers in a grocery store. One was labeled with a national brand, and the other one was an unknown brand (both samples were actually identical and were the national brand). Shoppers chose the sample marked with the national brand as being more tender and tasty. Other shoppers were given a choice between two unmarked samples of turkey, one tough and the other tender. Shoppers all thought the tender sample was the national brand.

When something happens to disrupt people's confidence in a product, a brand image can have serious problems, as shown when Tylenol capsules laced with cyanide resulted in the death of seven Chicago residents. However, because of its strong brand image and an aggressive advertising strategy to get customers back, McNeil Laboratory was able to win back the public's confidence.

How do people decide where to shop? A survey of over 500 people found that nearly 50% depended upon advertisements for information (Hirschman & Mills, 1980). Those people who relied on ads were more concerned with price and better informed about the product than those who didn't. Newspapers were the most widely used sources of information (35%), followed by mail brochures (7%), and television commercials (6%). What influenced the rest of the shoppers? Over 50% decided on where to shop at any particular time strictly by habit. Consumer behavior can be difficult to predict.

Psychology of Packaging. An important part of advertising is the package a product comes in. Several companies manufacture antihistamine tablets for allergies or colds. One brand's tablet is twice the size of another, even though they both contain exactly the same amount of drug. Which one sells more? More consumers believe the bigger tablet must be better (even though they are identical in strength). So size is important.

Dichter suggested (1975) that a package must satisfy the following six criteria to be effective: *convenience, adaptability* (for example, it must fit in a purse or medicine cabinet), *security* (for example, the new tamper-proof containers), *status, dependability,* and *aesthetic satisfaction.* The next time you buy a product, note whether you were influenced by the package.

Psychology sells many products. The shopper who understands how advertisers use psychology can become a wiser consumer.

ENVIRONMENTAL PSYCHOLOGY

Environmental psychologists are interested in discovering how the environment influences human behavior. Holahan (1986) described these variables as pollution, noise, crowding, and weather. Some psychologists consider environmental psychology a subarea of social psychology, whereas others view it as a unique and separate field of study. In this section we cover the variables of personal space, crowding, and noise.

Figure 16.9. Interpersonal Distance
Hall proposed that Americans have four distinct interpersonal distances that they use in social interactions: intimate, personal, social, and public. Social distance is appropriate for such activities as diplomatic meetings where the participants know of each other, but aren't necessarily friends. Here Secretary-General of the United Nations, Kurt Waldheim, (second from right) meets with President Anwar Sadat of Egypt (far right) in February, 1977.

Personal Space

People surround themselves with a "bubble" of personal space that they claim as their own, and they tend to become stressed when other people invade their "bubble." Our personal space protects us from too much arousal and helps us feel comfortable when we communicate with other people.

Interpersonal Distance. The study of the interpersonal distance between people was called proxemics by Edward T. Hall. From observing Americans, Hall (1966) concluded that four interpersonal distances were important in our social interaction: intimate, personal, social, and public.

Intimate distance is from 0 to 1.5 feet. What can be done at this close range? Vision is minimal, and we rely on our senses of smell and touch. Making love or comforting someone are intimate activities, usually restricted to private encounters, that can be performed comfortably at intimate distances. We tend not to get this close to people we are not intimate with and try to escape if we do.

Personal distance is from about 1.5 feet to around 4 feet. At this distance, touch is minimal (except perhaps when shaking hands), and vision and hearing become important. This is the distance we use to interact with friends. Within this range, normal conversations can take place easily. We might allow strangers into the outer limits, but reserve the inner limits strictly for friends.

Social distance extends from approximately 4 to 12 feet, and includes the space required for more formal social interactions. Hearing and vision are the primary senses involved. The social distance is often utilized in business, for example, in interviewing new applicants for employment or negotiating for a raise.

Public distance includes distances greater than 12 feet. Hall suggested that after 25 feet, interpersonal interaction is not possible. At this distance, there is little detail involved in communication. A public speaker (actor, politician) communicates only one way with an audience.

According to Hall, we feel uncomfortable when we are too close or too distant from another person. How do we learn appropriate social distances? Baxter (1970) suggested that we imitate others in our culture. He reported cultural differences in interpersonal spacing, with Mexicans being closest, white Americans next, and black Americans being farthest apart.

Sex differences have been reported in personal spacing, as well, with women usually being closer than men (Ashton & colleagues, 1980). Still other research suggests that interpersonal distance is influenced by social relationships. Women prefer more distance between themselves and an opposite-sex stranger than do men. Ashton and colleagues found that when they asked pairs of friends and strangers to stand at various distances from each other, both men and women felt more comfortable when an opposite-sex friend stood close (50 cm) than when a stranger stood at that distance. In general,

Figure 16.10. Invasion of Personal Space
Environmental psychologists Fisher and Byrne have found that there are sex differences in the reactions we have to invasion of our personal space. Males are most disturbed by an invasion from the front, whereas females are upset more with an invasion from the side.

women tend to stand closer when talking with friends than men do. Understanding these sex differences can help us appropriately behave in social situations with both men and women present.

Invasion of Personal Space. When sitting with a same-sex friend, do you tend to sit next to or across from the person? Research has shown that there are sex differences in seating preference which extend the interpersonal distance concept one step farther. Byrne, Baskett, and Hodges (1971) found that males prefer to sit across from someone they like, while females prefer to sit next to a friend.

Fisher and Byrne (1975) extended this finding by showing that males are most disturbed by an invasion from the front, while females dislike an intrusion on the side of their personal space. They had students invade other students who were working alone at tables in the library. The invasion came either from across or next to the subject. When interviewed later, males were most disturbed by invasions from across the table, while females were most disturbed by invasions from the same side of the table. Fisher and Byrne further found that males tend to "defend" the space on the library table in front of them by placing books on it, while females place their books to the side to block the area from which they fear incursions.

Understanding personal space can be applied to practical situations. For example, if we understand the "acceptable" or "appropriate" distance from someone in a given situation, we can communicate more effectively with that person. When we first meet someone we should be careful not to get too close (intimate distance), but should also not stay too far away (public distance), and we should not sit across from a man. It's also important to keep in mind the cultural variations that

exist. Sometimes we do not have a choice in regulating personal space. When too many people occupy too little space, we experience crowding.

Crowding

Environmental psychologists distinguish between the physical measurement of density and the psychological feeling of crowding. Density is defined as the physical area available to the given number of individuals present, while crowding is the psychological feeling of not having enough space available. Paulus (1980) concluded that while high density (a large number of individuals per area space) is usually necessary for crowding, it does not always produce the negative feeling of crowding. For example, at an enjoyable party or an exciting football game, we might have high density but not really think of it as being crowded. On the other hand, if we are on a deserted beach and someone else comes within view, we might feel crowded, even though the density is not high. Crowding is a psychological phenomenon.

There have been a number of animal studies on crowding; one of the most notable is John Calhoun's 1962 experiment using Norway rats. Calhoun placed a small population of rats in large enclosures with an abundance of food and water. The rats multiplied quickly and soon reached a high density. As the density reached maximum, the rats started behaving very strangely. The males became sexually motivated by females not ready to mate, young females, and even other males. Many became aggressive and violent. The females often ignored their young. Calhoun concluded that the crowded conditions caused normal social behavior to break down. This is not always the case, however.

Figure 16.11. Crowding
The psychological feeling of not having enough space is defined as crowding. People living in large cities are more likely to experience the psychological phenomenon of crowding.

In a 1980 study I was involved with, it was found that a litter of dogs could tolerate severe restrictions of space for short periods of time without any disruptions in the social hierarchy. Crowding research with humans also has produced conflicting results.

Most people think of crowding as definitely bad. It is usually assumed (but often unproven) that crowding automatically leads to aggression, violence, and crime. A number of studies have reported positive correlations between high density and negative social conditions, such as crime. For example, Schmitt (1966) found that as density of the population in Honolulu increased, the crime rate, death rate, and mental-disorder rate also increased. But Freedman (1975) argued that when social factors such as economic level, educational level, and ethnicity are taken into account, the relationship between crowding and crime disappears. Thus, it seems that the issue of crowding is more complex than we first believed it to be.

In research studies, usually it is found that performance decreases as density increases. But we feel less crowded with friends than with strangers. It is likely that someone with a large personal space need would feel crowded sooner than someone with a small personal space need. Sex differences have been reported by Freedman and his colleagues, with males usually experiencing more stress in high density situations.

The importance of cognitive factors in crowding was demonstrated in a 1984 experiment by Worchel and Brown. The experimenters showed either an arousing film (which was humorous, aggressive or sexual in content) or a nonarousing film to college students who were seated inappropriately close to one another. Subjects who were watching an arousing film attributed their arousal feelings to the film and thus did not experience crowding. However, subjects who were watching the nonarousing film could not attribute their arousal (actually caused by the inappropriately close seating arrangement) to the film and so felt crowded. Crowding, therefore, was dependent upon the perception of the source of the arousal.

In his 1975 book, *Crowding and Behavior*, Jonathan Freedman argued that crowding is neither good nor bad. Instead, in his density-intensity theory of crowding he suggests that as density increases, the intensity of our moods and behavior increases. Thus, if we expect to have a good time at a party and the party is crowded, we'll really enjoy ourselves. But if we expect to have a bad time, crowding makes us feel miserable. Baum and colleagues (1981) argued that when people are aware of the density level beforehand they will feel less crowded than those who do not know what to expect. In an urban setting, if crime is a dominant behavior, crowding will increase the crime level. But if positive social behaviors predominate, crowding will produce beneficial effects. Freedman argues that therefore it is important to make sure that positive social environments exist in high density areas.

Noise and Behavior

We measure noise with the decibel (dB) scale. The threshold for hearing is 0 dB. Normal conversation is about 40 dB, while the noise around a busy street is about 70 dB, and a rock band might be 120 dB. Long exposure to 90 dB can damage the eardrums. Sometimes noise is defined as any sound of a high enough intensity to inflict physical harm, but usually the definition in-

Figure 16.12. Noise and Behavior
The perception of noise as a stressful condition is a psychological phenomenon, but constant exposure to stressful noise, such as a busy street, or a nearby airport, can adversely affect behavior.

cludes the idea that noise is disturbing, either psychologically or physically. Thus, lower levels of sound can also be considered noise, especially when it is unpleasant and uncontrollable.

A study reported by Cohen and his colleagues (1986) found that children living on the lower floors of a high-rise apartment building had poorer hearing abilities and more problems with reading than children on the upper floors. The apartment building was built near a noisy freeway and the noise levels were blamed for the deficiencies of the children living on the lower floors. Smith and Stansfeld (1986) reported that noise also affects adults in daily life. For instance, people living in a noisy neighborhood tended to make more mistakes in simple tasks, forgot common things, and even dropped things more often.

Noise can be objectionable, but does it actually affect our social behavior? Yes, according to a number of research studies. For instance, Mathews and Canon (1975) found that people were less likely to help someone pick up dropped books when a noise of 85 dB was present. The same results were obtained whether the research took place in a laboratory situation or on a street where a lawn mower provided the noise. Other studies have shown that people living in noisy neighborhoods have fewer social interactions, are more aggressive, and tend to dislike their neighbors more.

Some research suggests that stressful noise can have an influence on our behavior even after we stop hearing it. In 1972 David Glass and Jerome Singer placed people in a noisy environment and either told them that they could control the noise (with a switch) or that they had no control over the noise. The group with control did not often use it, but when both groups were tested on a task afterward, the performance of the group who had control was significantly better. Glass and Singer proposed that noise is a source of stress and that uncontrollable stress leads to a feeling of helplessness. Thus, those in the group with control could relieve helplessness because of their belief that they could control its cause. This suggests that the psychological interpretation of environmental stressors such as noise, crowding, or heat plays an important role in determining our reactions to them.

OTHER APPLICATIONS OF PSYCHOLOGY

Psychology can be applied to a wide variety of areas, as we've seen thus far in this chapter. In this last section, we discuss two additional applications. Educational psychology is one of the oldest applied areas, and sports psychology is one of the newest.

Sports Psychology

Although the principles of psychology have been applied to sports for many years, it has only been in the past couple of decades that a formal discipline has developed. Sports psychology is the application of the principles of psychology to sport activities (Browne & Mahoney, 1984). Many of the topics discussed throughout the textbook are clearly relevant to the athlete and sports coach, such as motivation to play well, personality differences among athletes or coaches, social influences when playing, and attitudes toward sports and aggression.

Currently, sports psychology has three main areas of focus. It studies performance factors that concentrate on identifying and explaining the behaviors of athletes as compared to nonathletes. Second, sports psychologists are interested in social variables that influence performance, such as teamwork, cohesion, or goal setting by a team. And, third, sports psychologists have recently become interested in nonperformance factors related to sports, such as violence at games, the morality of athletes, their career development, and retirement. In this section we discuss personality and motivational influences on athletic performance.

Personality of Athletes. There have been many studies of the personality differences between athletes and nonathletes, in an attempt to identify the qualities that contribute to successful athletic performance. Overall, this has been an extremely difficult task, and has not resulted in many significant findings (Browne & Mahoney, 1984). In general, as might be suggested, successful athletes tend to be assertive, externally

motivated, dominant, self-confident, and have a high need for achievement.

Goldstein and Krasner (1987) argued that the lack of clear-cut personality profiles of successful athletes is likely due to the fact that there is such a wide variety of sports, and success depends on numerous variables other than just personality. In other words, the successful athlete is a successful person, who possesses the ability to do well in sports, and has had proper motivation and successful experiences. They suggest that future research should focus on the interaction of personality and situation rather than personality alone.

Motivation of Athletic Performance. The successful coach is one who can motivate athletes to exhibit their best performance. Alderman (1980) suggested several incentives that motivate athletes to perform well, including meeting the needs of independence, power, success, aggression, stress (excitement), affiliation, and excellence. Alderman found affiliation and excellence to be the most important motivators for athletes. Landers (1982) investigated the role that arousal plays in athletic performance and concluded that a medium arousal level is often more effective than being too "psyched up" for an activity. A relatively new technique for coaches is to help athletes learn how to monitor their arousal levels through biofeedback and control the excess arousal or anxiety (Paterson, 1984).

What is the optimum coaching strategy for motivating athletes? Duquin (1980) suggested that the successful athlete should be intrinsically motivated and not dependent upon the coach for reinforcement. For instance, my son's cross country running coach encourages the runners to compete against themselves, trying to beat their

Figure 16.13. Motivation of Athletic Performance
A successful coach is able to motivate athletes to perform their best. He or she understands the athlete's need for attaining success and excellence, as well as the need to control and utilize stress and arousal levels. Being too "psyched up" may result in a less than effective game or performance.

best time rather than competing against other people. The runners gain self-confidence and self-reward when they can set a new personal record. The coach needs to encourage team spirit and social cohesiveness. Emphasis should be on the success of the individual as a person and not only on the victory. These strategies are often successful in producing a winning team. It is important to remember that sports psychology involves the coach, the team members, the particular sport, the ability of the athletes, as well as personality and motivational factors.

Educational Psychology

We have all benefited greatly from the applications of psychology to education. Throughout our school years, our learning, thinking, and memory abilities have been guided and evaluated through procedures that educational psychologists designed. School psychologists give psychological tests to students, consult with students, teachers and parents, and try to help students adjust to academic requirements. You have probably had contact with school psychologists at various stages of your academic career. You are much less likely to have had contact with educational psychologists who often work behind the scenes conducting research or consulting with school officials to help maximize the effectiveness of the educational system. The field of educational psychology focuses on how students learn and how instructors teach (Thornburg, 1984).

Learning Applications. Much of what we discussed in chapter 6, "Learning," is relevant in educational psychology. The theories and techniques of learning, reinforcement, and punishment have been applied in the classroom for many years. For example, when students do well they are reinforced with praise, high grades, or leisure activities, and when they do poorly, they are punished with detentions, low grades, or threats. Edward Thorndike wrote *Educational Psychology* in 1903, where he emphasized the role of reinforcement in learning, and encouraged teachers to evaluate students' progress. John Dewey also contributed to the techniques used in education with his emphasis on "learning by doing." Since learning comprises the core of education, anything that enhances learning contributes to the success of education.

Instructional Process. In order to help students learn effectively, instructors have a number of tasks to perform. Gage and Berliner (1988) outlined several tasks involved in the instructional process. Teachers should develop a set of learning objectives that students are expected to achieve. They need to understand their students (personality, problems, interests, abilities) and how their students can best learn the information.

Teachers need to have an understanding of learning theories and psychological principles that influence the learning process. With this understanding, teachers must decide which teaching methods to use (for instance, lecture, discussion, demonstration, programmed instruction, computer-assisted instruction, or hands-on experience). Educational psychology provides results of research that investigates effective teaching methods. And finally, teachers need to evaluate the achievement of the students. Ultimately, education is a joint venture between teachers and students.

Learning Styles. Today's students are diverse and require a variety of teaching approaches to maximize learning. Understanding learning styles is one way to improve the educational process. Claxton and Murrell (1987) described four levels of learning style models. Differences in *personality* form the core, and affect the style of *information processing* used by the student. The *social interaction* model focuses on how the student behaves in the classroom, whereas the *instructional preference* the student has determines whether the teaching style is appropriate for effective learning.

There are a number of theories of learning style. The field dependent-field independent dimension is one example (Witkin, 1976). Those students who are *field dependent* prefer interpersonal interactions that might be found in areas such as social science and humanities. *Field independent* students prefer areas that involve analytic skills, such as mathematics and science. The Myers-Briggs Type Indicator has also been used to identify learning styles (Myers & Myers, 1980). As we discussed in chapter 11, "Personality," Jung's theory proposes that people perceive the world by sensing or intuition, and make decisions by thinking or feeling. These different types of students would learn best in an environment in which their style was matched with an appropriate instructional format.

Anthony Grasha and Sheryl Riechmann proposed six student learning styles. *Competitive students* are motivated to do better than other students and want to win at learning. *Collaborative students* prefer working with others as they learn and view the classroom as a social environment. *Avoidant students* are not interested in learning and would prefer to be elsewhere. *Participant students* enjoy class and take responsibility for learning what is required. *Dependent students* view the teacher as an authority and learn only what is required. *Independent students* prefer to think for themselves and are confident of their ability to learn. Hruska and Grasha (1982) reported that students become more independent and participate more as they get older. Women tend to be more collaborative than men in school, but otherwise sex differences in learning styles are not significant.

Perhaps Gregorc's (1986) model of learning style best illustrates how style of teaching and learning can be

Figure 16.14. Learning Styles
Educational psychologists have discovered that students have different learning styles. The challenge is to meet those diverse needs in one classroom. One effective way is to vary the presentation of material and the physical setting. Educational psychologists help both teachers and students improve the educational process.

matched, even in today's educational system. Gregorc proposed that students tend to vary on two dimensions, concrete-abstract and sequential-random. Students with a *concrete-sequential* style of learning tend to be organized, task-oriented, and focus on factual details. They need an instructional program that is structured and provides practical, hands-on experiences. Students with a *concrete-random* learning style tend to be independent risk-takers who focus on experiential components of learning. They need an instructional program that provides open-ended activities for them to explore and experiment with different options. Students who have an *abstract-sequential* learning style tend to be analytical and focus on theoretical aspects of learning. They prefer an instructional program that provides information and allows them to develop concepts and theories. Students with an *abstract-random* style of learning tend to be imaginative, flexible, and global. They need a program of instruction which involves interpretation of concepts and examples of applications.

Instructors can learn to help students with different styles of learning by presenting information in a variety of ways. For example, college instructors might provide an outline of the material for concrete-sequential students, use audio-visual materials for abstract-random students, give concrete-random students problems to solve, and give abstract-sequential students theoretical background information. Most can become better students if they understand their style of learning and attend to those activities that help them learn the course material.

Contributions of Psychology to Everyday Life

This chapter has touched on only a few of the many applications of psychology in our everyday lives. In the various fields of psychology, there are many more. By developing new methods of education and ways to increase the intellectual potential of individuals; by finding better ways to determine the effects of drugs; by treating the emotionally disturbed, the alcoholic, the drug addict, and the sexual deviate; by training the mentally retarded; by rehabilitating prisoners; by increasing cooperation and establishing effective communication between individuals; by learning how policy decisions can be made more effectively; by finding ways to reduce conflict between groups; and by increasing job satisfaction, psychologists help resolve our social problems.

In recent years the contributions of psychology have been enriched and broadened by research and clinical work in such areas as the biochemical foundations of behavior, which have revealed how and why people think and act as they do, and have suggested new means for treating emotional ailments long thought beyond the reach of therapy. Ethological studies examining basic animal behavior are demonstrating the limits and potentials of human learning. And advances in behavior therapy are opening new avenues to greater self-awareness and meaningful self-control.

Applied psychology is indeed intertwined throughout

our daily lives. New methods of training pets are being developed by animal behaviorists. The space program is going to need social psychologists to help establish societies on space stations. Medicine continues to depend more on public awareness for its effectiveness in treating disorders and encouraging health. As our society changes, career counseling psychologists will play a major role in helping people adjust to new careers and lifestyles. More time will be spent in leisure pursuits, and personality and motivation psychologists will help people relax and enjoy life as they engage in leisure activities. In our homes, schools, organizations, and recreational places, we will continue to enjoy the benefits of applied psychology.

In chapter 1, "The Study of Psychology," we learned that psychology is a relatively young science. Although already it has probed many of the mysteries of human behavior, there is still a great deal to be done. We need to encourage research at all levels, basic as well as applied, if we are to continue to make progress in our quest for knowledge. And on our journey of discovery we must chart a multidisciplinary course, as many different disciplines can guide us to our common goal—understanding ourselves and our environment. ■

I hope you have really enjoyed this textbook and will continue to apply what you have learned in psychology. Good luck!

CHAPTER REVIEW
What You've Learned About Applied Psychology

1. Applied psychology is the area that is concerned with helping people solve practical problems. Along with clinical and counseling psychology, applied psychology includes legal psychology, industrial psychology, environmental psychology, and educational psychology.

2. Forensic psychologists work in police departments and prisons to detect and prevent crime and to assess and rehabilitate those accused of criminal behavior. In police departments, psychologists are involved in selecting, training, and counseling police officers and assisting in crime fighting.

3. In court systems, psychologists serve as expert witnesses and conduct research on eyewitness testimony and on the behavior of juries. Psychologists may be called upon as expert witnesses to give a clinical evaluation of the defendant or to evaluate scientifically the testimony and evidence. Research on jury behavior has shown that the verdict depends in part upon the number of possible verdicts and severity of various possible penalties.

4. Some psychologists work in a prison setting. Their chief duties include evaluating new prisoners, counseling the inmates, and training the prison staff. Zimbardo's study of a simulated prison demonstrated the effects of a prison environment on the behavior of inmates and guards.

5. Industrial psychology is the area concerned with behavior in organizations and businesses. It includes personnel psychology, organizational psychology, engineering psychology, and consumer psychology. Personnel psychology includes selection, training, and evaluation of new applicants and current employees. Selection involves developing a job analysis, receiving applications and references, giving tests, and conducting interviews. Training programs help the employee develop job skills. Evaluation helps provide feedback on performance for promotions and improvement.

6. Organizational psychology involves the study of the social variables found in a work setting. The Hawthorne study demonstrated the influence of interest on performance levels. McGregor's Theory X and Theory Y illustrate the extremes of motivation expectations of managers. And Herzberg's motivator-hygiene theory attempts to explain the variables involved in job satisfaction.

7. Engineering psychology is concerned with how work is performed, the design of equipment, and the actual work environment. Areas in engineering psychology have focused on how to simplify work behaviors, how to design an efficient work space, how to display information efficiently, how to produce a pleasant work area, and how to maximize productivity by varying work time.

8. Consumer psychology is concerned with purchasing behavior. Consumer psychologists study the steps a consumer goes through before buying a product, how perception influences pricing and brand image, and how to effectively package and advertise a product.

9. Environmental psychologists are interested in discovering how the environment influences human behavior. When other people invade our personal space, we tend to become stressed. People usually maintain appropriate interpersonal distances. Four distances are: intimate (for lovers), personal (for friends), social (for acquaintances), and public (for audiences). Sex differences are found in seating preferences, with males tending to sit across from people they like and females tending to sit next to favored others. Since these seating preferences are favored for friends, they also produce the greatest disturbances when invaded by strangers.

10. Environmental psychologists distinguish between density (the physical area available to a given number of individuals) and crowding (the psychological feeling of not having enough space available). When in crowded conditions, we often show poor performance. Freedman's density-intensity theory of crowding proposes that crowding intensifies the already prevalent feelings and behaviors. Often performances decrease as density increases.

11. Noise is any sound loud enough to inflict psychological or physical harm or discomfort. Noise can result in hearing damage, reading deficits, and a decrease in helping behavior.

12. Sports psychology is the application of the principles of psychology to sport activities. Successful athletes are successful people who possess the ability to do well in sports and have had the proper motivation and experiences.

13. The field of educational psychology focuses on how students learn and how instructors teach. Educational psychologists study learning, the instructional process, and learning styles.

Glossary

Page references indicate where term is first defined.

A

ABC model Attitude model that divides the concept into three distinct components: affect, behavior, and cognition. 350

ablation Procedure in which a part of the brain is removed surgically. 38

abnormal behavior Behavior that contributes to maladaptiveness in an individual, is considered deviant by the culture, and leads to personal psychological distress. 304

abnormal psychology The subfield of psychology in which clinical and counseling psychologists diagnose and treat abnormal behavior. 304

absolute threshold The minimum amount of physical energy required to produce a sensation. 81

accommodation Process in cognitive development; involves altering or reorganizing the mental picture to make room for a new experience or idea. 60

acetylcholine A neurotransmitter involved in memory. 30

achievement test Test designed to measure what a person can currently accomplish. 192

acquisition In conditioning, forming associations in first learning a task. 133

action potential An electrical charge in a neuron (neural impulse) that travels down the length of the neuron. 30

activation synthesis theory Theory of dreaming that states that during REM sleep the brain activates itself and then synthesizes the information generated into dreams. 114

actor-observer bias Tendency to attribute the behavior of other people to internal causes and our own behavior to external causes. 349

acupuncture Oriental practice involving the insertion of needles into the body to control pain. 102

additive tasks Group tasks in which the contributions of each member are combined into the final group product. 361

adjustment How we react to stress; some change that we make in response to the demands placed upon us. 280

adolescence Period of human development between puberty and adulthood. 64

adoption studies Technique in human behavior genetics in which comparisons can be made between children and their adoptive parents as well as between children and their biological parents. 46

adrenal glands Endocrine glands involved in stress and energy regulation. 40

adrenaline A hormone produced by the adrenal glands that is involved in physiological arousal; adrenaline is also called epinephrine. 40

adulthood Period of human development after adolescence when one becomes an adult. 67

aerial perspective Monocular depth cue in which we use brightness, color, and detail to determine distance; closer objects tend to look brighter. 92

afferent neuron (also called sensory neuron) A neuron that carries messages from the sense organs toward the central nervous system. 29

affirmative rule Concept rule in which all of the instances of an attribute are listed. 183

afterimages Images that last in the nervous system for a brief time after being received; visual persistence. 94

aggression Behavior intended to harm another member of the same species. 368

aggressive personality In Horney's personality theory, the personality type that is characterized by a need to act aggressively in a world seen as hostile. 263

agoraphobia Disorder in which an individual is afraid of places or situations which would be difficult or embarrassing to escape from. 307

AIDS (acquired immune deficiency syndrome) A fatal sexually transmitted disease of the immune system that largely affects homosexual and bisexual men. 210, 251

alarm reaction The first stage in Selye's general adaptation syndrome. The alarm reaction is the immediate response to stress; adrenaline is released and digestion slows. The alarm reaction prepares the body for an emergency. 285

algorithm (random search strategy) A strategy in problem solving in which every possible solution is tried. 187

all-or-none law The principle that states that a neuron only fires when a stimulus is above a certain minimum strength (threshold), and when it fires, it does so at full strength. 30

alpha Brain-wave activity that indicates that a person is relaxed and resting quietly; 8–12 Hz. 109

altered state of consciousness (ASC) A state of consciousness in which there is a redirection of attention, a change in the aspects of the world which occupy a person's thoughts, and a change in the stimuli to which a person responds; a mental state qualitatively different from a person's normal, waking consciousness. 108

altruistic behavior Behavior which is directed toward helping others when there is no expectation of reward for oneself (and usually there are costs involved). 371

Alzheimer's disease An irreversible memory loss that often involves confusion and intellectual deterioration. 174

amacrine cells With the horizontal cells, they interconnect the neurons in the retina. 85

ambivalent attachment Type of infant-parent attachment in which the infant seeks contact but resists once the contact is made. 57

Ames room Experimental room constructed so that it looks normal even though the walls and windows are trapezoidal and one corner is much farther away from the observer than the other; a visual illusion. 88

amniocentesis Procedure of testing for genetic abnormalities during prenatal development. 52

amphetamine A strong stimulant; increases arousal of the central nervous system. 119

amplitude Intensity of sound waves; amplitude determines loudness of sound. 96

amygdala Brain structure in the limbic system that is involved in fear, aggression, and other social behaviors. 34

anal stage Psychosexual stage during which the child experiences the first restrictions on his impulses. 59

analytical psychology The personality theory of Carl Jung. 261

androgen Male sex hormone produced by the testes; androgen produces male characteristics such as facial hair and low-pitched voice. 41

androgyny Type of personality in which individual shows strong masculine and feminine characteristics. 356

angiotensin Substance in blood that helps regulate body fluid; involved in thirst motivation. 221

animism Process of attributing living characteristics to inanimate objects; for example, in young children, believing the sun is sleeping for the night. 61

anorexia nervosa Eating disorder in which an individual becomes severely underweight because of self-imposed restrictions in eating. 65, 220

antianxiety drug A minor tranquilizer that reduces anxiety; used in treatment of anxiety disorders. 338

antianxiety minor tranquilizers Drugs that are prescribed for treating anxiety, pressure, and insomnia. 117

antidepressant drug Any drug that relieves depression. 338

antidiuretic hormone (ADH) Hormone secreted by the pituitary gland to cause the kidneys to slow down their production of urine; this restores body fluids. 40

antipsychotic drug A major tranquilizer that relieves psychotic and schizophrenic symptoms. 122, 338

antisocial personality disorder Personality disorder in which the individual who engages in antisocial behavior experiences no guilt or anxiety about his actions; sometimes called sociopathy or psychopathy. 319

anxiety A vague feeling of fear and apprehension; a fear of the demands placed upon an individual which he or she is unable to clearly identify. 284, 307

anxiety disorder Fairly long-lasting disruption of the person's ability to deal with stress; often accompanied by feelings of fear and apprehension. 307

anxiety hierarchy A method of systematic desensitization that starts with a mild anxiety-producing situation and progresses to the most anxiety-producing. 332

aphagia Disorder in which the individual does not eat. 219

aphasia Disorder in which a person loses the ability to understand speech. 99

apparent motion Perceived movement of an object when in fact there is none; a visual illusion. 93

applied psychology The area of psychology that is most immediately concerned with helping to solve practical problems; includes clinical and counseling psychology, industrial, environmental, and legal psychology. 376

applied research Research conducted to help solve a practical or pressing question or problem. 15

approach-approach conflict When we are attracted to two equally desirable goals that are incompatible. 283

approach-avoidance conflict When we are faced with a single goal that has positive and negative aspects. 283

aptitude test Any test designed to predict what a person with the proper training can accomplish in the future. 192

archetypes In Jung's personality theory, unconscious universal ideas shared by all humans. 261

arousal theory Theory that focuses on the energy (arousal) aspect of motivation; it states that we are motivated to initiate behaviors that help to regulate overall arousal level. 214

artificial intelligence (AI) The area of cognitive science that simulates human thinking; the ability of computers to perform in ways that normally require intelligence. 178

asocial phase Phase in attachment development in which the neonate doesn't distinguish people from objects. 56

assertiveness training Training which helps individuals stand up for their rights while not denying rights of other people. 336

assimilation Process in cognitive development; occurs when something new is taken into the child's mental picture. 60

association areas Areas of the cortex of the brain that help integrate information. 34

association neurons (also called interneurons) Neurons connected with other neurons. 29

asthma Psychophysiological disorder characterized by increased responsiveness of the respiratory tract which results in the narrowing of the airways, thus causing breathing difficulties. 292

astigmatism Visual disorder in which the cornea of the eye has an irregular shape that distorts vision. 85

attachment Process in which the individual shows behaviors that promote proximity with a specific object or person. 56

attention Process of focusing on particular stimuli in the environment. 159

attitude scales A measurement technique for assessing attitudes; typically they consist of a series of statements with which subjects indicate agreement or disagreement. 351

attitudes Learned dispositions that actively guide us toward specific behaviors; they consist of feelings, beliefs, and behavioral tendencies. 350

attribution The cognitive process of determining the motives of someone's behavior, and especially determining whether the motives are internal or external. 217, 348

auditory canal Canal leading from the outer ear into the middle ear. 96

auditory nerve Nerve that carries auditory information from the ear to the brain. 97

autism A personality disorder in which the child does not respond socially to people. 58

autokinetic effect Perception of movement of a stationary spot of light in a darkened room. 94

autonomic nervous system The part of the peripheral nervous system that carries messages from the central nervous system to the endocrine glands, the smooth muscles controlling the heart, and the primarily involuntary muscles controlling internal processes; includes the sympathetic and parasympathetic nervous systems. 39

autosomes Chromosomes which carry genes that regulate various bodily processes and characteristics, such as eye color or intelligence. 42

aversion therapy A counterconditioning therapy in which unwanted responses are paired with unpleasant consequences. 297

avoidance conditioning Learning situation in which a subject avoids a stimulus by learning to respond appropriately before the stimulus begins. 144

avoidance-avoidance conflict Conflict that occurs when we must choose between two equally undesirable demands. 283

avoidant attachment Type of infant-parent attachment in which the infant avoids the parent. 57

axon The tail end of a neuron along which messages (neural impulses) are conducted; contains terminal buttons which release neurotransmitters into the synapse. 29

axon hillock The place at which the axon of a neuron meets the cell body. 29

B

Babinski reflex Reflex that occurs when you stroke the bottom of the baby's feet; the baby first spreads the toes out and then curls them in. 54

backward conditioning A procedure in classical conditioning in which the US is presented and terminated before the termination of the CS; very ineffective procedure. 133

bait shyness A form of conditioned taste aversion in which an animal learns to avoid eating a particular poison. 136

barbiturates Depressant drugs that can be used as tranquilizers to relieve anxiety or as sleep inducers. 117

basal age The age level at which a subject can answer test questions on an intelligence test correctly; basal age has replaced the ratio of the MA to CA. 194

basal metabolism The rate at which a body converts food to energy. 219

basic anxiety In Horney's personality theory, the feeling of loneliness and helplessness that people experience. 262

basic research Research conducted to obtain information for its own sake. 15

basilar membrane Partition in the cochlea of the ear; involved in sound sensation. 97

bed-wetting (enuresis) NREM sleep disorder in which the person wets the bed at night; occurs mainly in children. 115

behavior Anything you do or think, including various bodily reactions. Behavior includes physical and mental responses. 6

behavior genetics How genes influence behavior. 43

behavior modification Psychotherapy concerned with modifying the abnormal behavior symptoms, often through the application of conditioning principles; sometimes called behavior therapy. 147, 328

behavior potential In Rotter's personality theory, the probability that a particular behavior occurs in a specific situation. 269

behavioral measures In attitude measurement, techniques which involve observing or testing a person's actual behavior. 311

behaviorism The school of thought founded by John Watson; it studied only observable behavior. 10

belongingness and love needs Third level of motives in Maslow's hierarchy; includes love and affection, friends, and social contact. 216

BEM Sex-Role Inventory (BSRI) A 60-adjective sex-role questionnaire designed to measure feminine and masculine traits in people. 356

beta Brain wave activity which indicates that a person is alert, 13-30 Hz. 109

between-subject experiment An experimental design in which different subjects are included in the experimental and control groups. 18

biconditional rule Concept rule that extends the if-then rule in both directions. 184

binaural Condition in which sound is delivered to both ears simultaneously. 98

binocular depth cues Visual cues that depend on both eyes; used to detect distance. 92

biofeedback Practice wherein a person monitors his or her own bodily processes normally not under voluntary control in order to influence them. 124

biological model The approach to abnormality which states that abnormal behavior is caused by biological factors. 304

biological motives Motives that have a definite physiological basis and are biologically necessary for survival of the individual or species. 218

biological psychology (also called physiological psychology or psychobiology) The subfield of experimental psychology that is concerned with the influence of heredity and the biological response systems on behavior. 28

biological response systems Systems of the body that are particularly important in behavioral responding; include the senses, endocrines, muscles, and the nervous system. 28

biological therapy Treatment of behavior problems through biological techniques; major biological therapies include drug therapy, psychosurgery, and electroconvulsive therapy. 338

bipolar cells Cells in the retina of the eye; light causes the rods and cones to send electrical energy to the bipolar cells, then pass on neural impulses to ganglion cells. 85

bipolar disorder Affective disorder which is characterized by extreme mood swings from sad depression to joyful mania; sometimes called manic-depression. 312

blind spot Place in the retina where the optic nerve begins; a person cannot see at this location. 85

blinding technique In an experiment, a control for bias in which the assignment of a subject to the experimental or control group is unknown to the subject or experimenter or both (a double-blind experiment). 19

body dysmorphic disorder Type of somatoform disorder characterized by a preoccupation with an imaginary defect in the physical appearance of a physically healthy person. 318

body language communication through position and movement of the body. 246

bottom-up processing The psychoanalytic process of understanding communication by listening to words, then interpreting phrases, and finally understanding ideas. 179

brainstorming Technique in which a group attempts to come up with numerous creative solutions to a problem without evaluating or criticizing the ideas being presented. 362

brand image In consumer psychology, the consumer's recognition of a particular brand of product. 386

brightness Intensity of light; determined by wave amplitude. 83

brightness constancy Tendency to see objects as continuing to have the same brightness even though light or shadow may change their immediate sensory properties. 87

bulimia nervosa Eating disorder in which an individual eats large amounts of calorie-rich food in a short time and then purges the food by vomiting or using laxatives. 220

burnout The depletion of our physical and mental resources, due to stress; burnout occurs when we have more energy going out than coming in. 286

bystander effect Phenomenon in an emergency situation in which a person is more likely to help when alone than when in a group of people. 371

C

caffeine Stimulant drug that causes central nervous system arousal; often contained in coffee, tea, chocolate, and cola drinks. Causes alertness in people. 118

California Psychological Inventory (CPI) An objective personality test used to study normal populations. 273

cannabis sativa The plant from which marijuana is derived. 121

Cannon-Bard Theory of Emotion Theory of emotion which states that the emotional feeling and the physiological arousal occur at the same time. 237

cardinal traits In Allport's personality theory, the traits of an individual so dominant that they are expressed in everything the person does; few people possess cardinal traits. 263

cardiovascular disorders Psychophysiological disorders which involve the heart and circulatory system; include hypertension and coronary heart disease. 292

case study Research method in which the events of a person's life are reconstructed to gain insight into a current problem; a scientific biography. 17

castration anxiety The Freudian idea that the young boy is afraid his father will castrate him because the boy has sexual feelings for his mother. 261

catatonic schizophrenia A type of schizophrenia which is characterized by periods of complete immobility and the apparent absence of will to move or speak. 315

catatonic stupor Complete immobility and absence of will to move by someone with catatonic schizophrenia. 315

causal attribution Process of determining whether a person's behavior is due to internal or external motives. 349

CCK (cholecystokinin) Hormone involved in regulation of eating behavior. 218

central nervous system The part of the human nervous system which interprets and stores messages from the sense organs, decides what behavior to exhibit, and sends appropriate messages to the muscles and glands; includes the brain and spinal cord. 31

central tendency In statistics, measures of central tendency give a number that represents the entire group or sample. 22

central traits In Allport's personality theory, the traits of an individual that form the core of the personality; they are developed through experience. 263

cerebellum The part of the hindbrain that is involved in balance and muscle coordination. 33

cerebral cortex The outermost layer of the cerebrum of the brain where higher mental functions occur. The cerebral cortex is divided into sections, or lobes, that control activities. 34

cerebrum (cerebral hemisphere) Largest part of the forebrain involved in cognitive functions; the cerebrum consists of two hemispheres connected by the corpus callosum. 34

chemical senses The sense of smell and taste; sensory stimulation of the chemical sense receptors involves contact with chemical substances. 99

childhood The period of human development roughly between 2 and 11 years. 58

chorionic villus biopsy Prenatal test in which a sample of embryonic tissue is examined for genetic defects. 52

chromosomes Bodies in the cell nucleus which contain the genes. 42

chunking Process of combining stimuli in order to increase memory capacity. 159

classical conditioning The form of learning in which a stimulus is associated with another stimulus that causes a particular response. Sometimes called Pavlovian conditioning (after Pavlov) or respondent conditioning. 132

client-centered therapy An insight therapy in which the therapist remains nondirective, providing a warm atmosphere for the client to work out his or her problems; also called person-centered therapy. 327

clinical psychologist Psychologist who assesses psychological problems and treats people with behavior problems using psychological techniques. 324

clinical psychology Subfield in which psychologists assess psychological problems and treat people with behavior problems using psychological techniques (called psychotherapy). 12

closure Perceptual principle of organization consisting of filling in the gaps in a figure to perceive a complete form. 90

cocaine A stimulant derived from the leaves of the South American coca plant. 119

cochlea A spiraled organ in the inner ear which is involved in sound sensation. 96

cognition Mental processes, such as perception, attention, memory, language, thinking, and problem solving; cognition involves the acquisition, storage, retrieval, and utilization of knowledge. 178

cognition The activity that includes mental processes like dreaming, thinking, remembering, or solving problems. 6

cognitive behavior therapy A form of behavior therapy which identifies self-defeating attitudes and thoughts in a subject, and then helps the subject to replace these with positive, supportive thoughts. 333

cognitive development Changes over time in mental processes such as thinking, memory, language, and problem solving. 60

cognitive dissonance Theory of attitude change originally proposed by Festinger, which states that when people hold two psychologically inconsistent ideas they experience tension which forces them to reconcile the conflicting ideas. 353

cognitive expectancy The condition in which an individual learns that certain behaviors lead to particular goals; cognitive expectancy motivates the individual to exhibit goal-directed behaviors. 217

cognitive learning Type of learning that theorizes that the learner utilizes cognitive structures in memory to make decisions about behaviors. 148

cognitive map A mental representation of an area; concept used by Tolman in cognitive learning. 150

cognitive model The approach to abnormality which states that inefficient thinking and problem solving are causes of abnormal behavior. 305

cognitive motivation This approach to motivation emphasizes thinking and perceptual interpretation. 217

cognitive neoassociationist theory Theory that views aggression as a reaction to aversive events. 370

cognitive psychology The area of psychology that includes the study of the mental activities involved in perception, memory, language, thought, and problem solving. 12

cognitive psychology The area of psychology that includes the study of mental activities involved in perception, memory, language, thought, and problem solving. 178

cognitive therapy Therapy developed by Beck in which an individual's negative, self-defeating thoughts are restructured in a positive way. 335

collective unconscious Jung's representation of the thoughts shared by all humans. 261

color blindness Visual condition in which the person cannot discriminate all possible color variations. 86

color constancy Tendency to see familiar objects as the same color regardless of the illumination. 87

common fate Gestalt perceptual principle in which groups of stimuli, or objects moving together, are seen as a unit. 90

companionate love An emotion characterized by deep attachment, trust, respect, affection, loyalty, and familiarity; also called conjugal love. 241

comparative psychology Subfield in which experimental psychologists study and compare the behavior of different species of animals. 14

compensation Defense mechanism by which the individual deals with feelings of inadequacy by focusing on a desirable characteristic. 295

competence Condition that occurs when a person goes beyond just interacting successfully with the environment to improving his or her life and achieving his or her goals. 224, 280

compliance Type of social influence in which an individual changes his behavior because of a direct request from someone else. 358

compliant personality In Horney's personality theory, the personality type that is characterized by a strong need to be loved and needed by others. 263

compulsive acts Rituals performed by the compulsive-obsessive to reduce anxiety. 309

computer assisted instruction (CAI) The technique of using the computer to present learning material and help students learn; CAI has become popular with the advent of microcomputers. 146

computer simulation Process in which a computer is programmed to approximate some event or activity. 186

concept A set of features which share one or more common properties. 183

concept formation (concept learning) The development of the ability to respond to common features of categories of objects or events. 183

conception Reproductive process in which the egg cell is fertilized by a sperm, resulting in a zygote. 50

concrete operations period Stage in cognitive development; from 7 to 11 years, the time in which the child's ability to solve problems with reasoning greatly increases. 62

conditional positive regard Part of Rogers's personality theory; occurs when we accept someone only if he or she meets our conditions and expectations. 267

conditional rule Concept rule which uses if-then to define a concept. 184

conditioned reinforcer Reinforcement that is effective because it has been associated with other reinforcers; involved in higher-order conditioning. 144

conditioned response (CR) The response or behavior that occurs when the conditioned stimulus is presented (after the CS has been associated with the US). 132

conditioned stimulus (CS) An originally neutral stimulus that is associated with an unconditioned stimulus and takes on the latter's capability of eliciting a particular reaction. 132

conditioned taste aversion (CTA) An aversion to particular tastes associated with stomach distress; usually considered a unique form of classical conditioning because of the extremely long interstimulus intervals involved. 136

conditioning A term applied to two types of learning (classical and operant). Conditioning refers to the scientific aspect of the type of learning. 132

conduction The ability of a neuron to carry a message (a neural impulse) along its length. 29

conduction deafness Type of deafness resulting from structures in the outer or middle ear not functioning properly. 98

cones One type of vison receptor; cones respond to color variations in bright light. 84

confirmation bias When solving problems, the tendency to selectively seek information that confirms a hypothesis. 189

conflict Situation which occurs when we experience incompatible demands or desires. 282

conformity Type of social influence in which an individual changes his behavior to fit social norms or expectations. 356

confounding A situation in an experiment in which variables other than the independent variable also influence the dependent variable. 18

congruence In Rogers's personality theory, the state in which the different aspects of the personality—the real self, perceived self, and ideal self—are essentially the same. 266

conjoint family therapy Family therapy in which the emphasis is on developing better relationships and self-esteem for family members. 336

conjunctive rule Concept rule in which objects or events must have two or more distinct features to belong to the class in question. 183

conjunctive tasks Group tasks in which all members of the group are required to work toward the goal and productivity is limited to the least competent member. 361

conscious Being aware of experiencing sensations, thoughts, and feelings at any given point in time. 8

conscious mind In Freud's psychoanalytic theory, the part of personality that we are aware of in everyday life. 108

consciousness The processing of information at various levels of awareness; state in which a person is aware of sensations, thoughts, and feelings. 108

consensus In causal attribution, the extent to which other people react as the subject does in a particular situation. 349

conservation The theory that something stays the same even if it takes on a different form; Piaget tested conservation of mass, number, length, and volume. 62

consistency In causal attribution, the extent to which the subject always behaves in the same way in a situation. In punishment, it refers to the fact that punishment is most effective if it always follows the undesired behavior. 146, 349

consolidation The biological neural process of making memories permanent; possibly short-term memory is electrically coded and long-term memory is chemically coded. 173

consumer psychology Concerned with the behavior of the consumer when he goes out to purchase a product. 384

contact comfort In attachment, the comfort felt by infants in the touch of contact, especially when it is soft or warm. 58

contact theory Theory which states that contact and interaction can decrease intergroup prejudice. 355

continuity The Gestalt rule of perceiving a straight line as continuing to be straight. 90

continuous reinforcement Situation in which every correct response is followed by reinforcement. 142

continuum of preparedness Seligman's proposal that animals are biologically prepared to learn certain responses more readily than they are prepared to learn others. 151

control A goal of psychology; modifying behavior through manipulation of the environment. 7

control group Subjects in an experiment who do not receive the independent variable; the control group is used to determine the effectiveness of the independent variable. 18

conventional morality Level II in Kohlberg's theory; moral reasoning is based on conformity and social standards. 63

convergence Binocular depth cue in which we detect distance by interpreting the kinesthetic sensations produced by the muscles of the eyeballs. 92

conversion disorder Somatoform disorder in which a person displays obvious disturbance in the nervous system without a physical basis for the problem. 318

coping The adjustment people make to stress; coping involves solving the problems that cause stress and managing the emotions that accompany it. 294

copulation Reproductive mating in animals; process of joining an egg and a sperm. 222

cornea Outer membrane that covers the eyeball. 84

coronary heart disease (CHD) Any condition that causes a narrowing of the coronary arteries. 292

corpus callosum The nerve bundle which connects the two hemispheres of the cerebrum. 34

correlation Statistical technique used to determine the degree of relationship that exists between two variables. 19

correlation coefficient A statistical measure of the degree to which two factors are related; perfect positive correlation is +1.0, while no correlation is 0.0 and perfect negative correlation is −1.0. The stronger the relationship, the closer the correlation score is to 1.0. 19

correspondent inference theory Attribution theory which states that people observe an individual and then make inferences about his or her behavior. 348

counseling psychologist Psychologist who helps people with emotional or personal problems. 324

counseling psychology Subfield in which psychologists help people with emotional or personal problems. 13

counterbalancing An experimental design in which subjects receive all treatments, but in different orders. 18

counterconditioning A behavior therapy in which an unwanted response is replaced by conditioning a new response that is incompatible with it. 331

couple counseling Therapy for nonmarried couples. 337

courtship The behavioral process whereby sexually mature animals of a species become mating pairs. 222

covariation theory Attribution theory which states that certain factors (consensus, consistency, and distinctiveness) occur together, helping an individual predict causation. 349

covert desensitization A technique for helping an individual overcome fears by learning to relax in the presence of images of anxiety-arousing thoughts. 332

crack A potent form of cocaine made by mixing baking soda and water with the crystalline form of cocaine and heating it. 119

cranial nerves Set of 12 peripheral nerves that enter the central nervous system in the brain. The cranial nerves include sensory and motor nerves from the somatic nervous system. 33

creativity A process of coming up with new or unusual responses to familiar circumstances. 189

critical period Period of time during development in which particular learning or experiences normally occur; if learning doesn't occur, the individual has a difficult time learning it later. 54, 151

crowding The psychological feeling of not having enough space available. 388

crystalized intelligence Verbal reasoning and comprehension of cultural concepts. 70

cued recall Recall with cues to aid memory. 167

culture-bound The idea that a test's usefulness is limited to the culture in which it was written and utilized. 191

culture-fair Ideally, a test which is completely independent of cultural influences. 199

cumulative response curve Graphed curve that results when responses for a subject are added to one another over time; if subjects respond once every 5 minutes, they will have a cumulative response curve value of 12 after an hour. 142

curiosity motive Motive which causes the individual to seek out a certain amount of novelty. 223

cyclothymia A bipolar disorder which is a moderately severe problem with mood swings from hypomanic episodes to depression. 313

D

dark adaptation Process in which the retina's rods and cones adjust to changes in dim light. 84

death instinct (also called thanatos) Freud's term for an instinct that is destructive to the individual or species; aggression is a major expression of death instinct. 260

death instinct (also called thanatos) Freud's term for an instinct that is destructive to the individual or species; aggression is a major expression of death instinct. 212

decay Theory of forgetting in which sensory impressions leave memory traces that fade away with time. 168

decenter The ability to realize that your way of looking at the world is only one perspective. 62

decibel Unit for measuring loudness. 96

deep structure The actual meaning of a sentence. 179

defense mechanisms Psychological techniques to help protect ourselves from stress and anxiety, to resolve conflicts, and to preserve our self-esteem. 294

delayed conditioning A procedure in classical conditioning in which the presentation of the CS precedes the onset of the US and the termination of the CS is delayed until the US is presented; very effective procedure. 133

delusion The holding of obviously false beliefs; for example, imagining someone's trying to kill you. 314

delusional disorder Psychotic disorder in which the individual shows a persistent delusion not attributable to any other mental disorder; formerly called paranoid disorder. 317

demand characteristics In an experiment, the situation in which subjects feel they are required to act in a certain way; demand characteristics can bias the outcome of the study. 19

dendrites Projections that extend from the neuron and receive messages (neural impulses) from adjacent neurons. 29

density The physical area available to the given number of individuals present. 388

density-intensity theory Freedman's crowding theory; as density increases, the intensity of our moods and behavior also increases. 389

deoxyribonucleic acid (DNA) Organic molecules that genes are composed of; DNA has a double helix pattern that allows the gene to transcribe its message and direct the formation of biochemicals which can be utilized to ultimately produce the characteristics of the individual. 42

dependent variable The behavior or response that is measured; it is dependent on the independent variable. 18

depersonalization disorder Dissociative disorder in which the individual escapes from his own personality by believing that he doesn't exist or that his environment is not real. 319

depolarization Any change in which the internal electrical charge becomes more positive. 30

depressants Drugs that have a sedative effect. 117

depression In abnormal psychology, an affective disorder in which the individual shows very little emotion or arousal and loses interest in life. 310

depth of processing In memory encoding, how relevantly or meaningfully the material is encoded; meaningful material is processed more deeply. 162

depth perception Ability to judge distance to an object. 90

description A goal of psychology; recording accurate observations of behavior. 6

descriptive statistics Techniques that help summarize large amounts of data information. 22

detached personality In Horney's personality theory, the personality type that is characterized by a need to maintain distance from others. 263

development Changes in the physical, cognitive, and personality-social characteristics of the individual over time. 50

developmental norms The average time at which developmental changes occur in the normal individual. 54

developmental psychology Study of physical and mental growth and behavioral changes in individuals from conception to death. 14, 50

developmentally handicapped (DH) Individuals who are not able to learn as rapidly as classmates in school. Except for special needs, DH children are often mainstreamed in regular classrooms. 202

deviation IQ Intelligence test scoring method in which the extent to which a subject's score is different from average score for a particular age group is measured; first incorporated into intelligence tests by David Wechsler. 195

dichromat A person who is partially color blind; person lacks one of the three types of cones. 86

difference threshold The minimum amount of energy change required to produce a difference in sensation. 81

diffusion of responsibility Groups tend to inhibit helping behavior; responsibility is shared equally by members of the group so that no one individual feels a strong commitment. 371

digit-span memory test Test of short-term memory in which the subject is asked to recall a string of digits. 160

discrimination The behaviors toward members of a group which are unfair when compared to behavior toward others. 355

disjunctive rule Concept rule in which any one of two or more different features define the concept. 184

disjunctive tasks Group tasks in which there is a single problem for the group to solve and the most competent person usually finds the solution. 361

disorganized schizophrenia A type of schizophrenia which is characterized by a severe personality disintegration; the individual often displays bizarre behavior. 315

displacement Defense mechanism by which the individual directs his or her aggression or hostility toward a person or object other than the one it should be directed toward. 115, 295

dispositional factors The individual's internal personality factors in determining causes of behavior. 348

dissociative disorder Disorder which involves a disturbance in the memory, consciousness, or identity of an individual; types include multiple personality disorder, depersonalization disorder, psychogenic amnesia, and psychogenic fugue. 318

distinctiveness In causal attribution, the extent to which the subject reacts the same way in other situations. 349

distress Stress which is harmful or unpleasant; anxiety and fear are examples of distress. 280

distributed practice Learning material over an extended period of time, with breaks between sessions. 170

divorce therapy Aimed at helping people who are divorcing make an easier transition into their new roles. 337

dizygotic twins Nonidentical twins produced when two separate eggs are fertilized by two sperm at the same time. 45

dominant Form of a gene that is always reflected in the phenotype. 42

door-in-the-face technique The technique to obtain compliance from a person by first making a large request and then making a small request. 359

dopamine A neurotransmitter involved in moods. 31

dopamine theory The theory that schizophrenia is caused by high levels of dopamine. 316

Down's syndrome Form of mental retardation caused by having three number 21 chromosomes (trisomy 21). 203

dream analysis Psychoanalytic technique in which a patient's dreams are analyzed to discover true feelings. 326

drive Motivational concept used to describe the internal forces that push an organism toward a goal; sometimes identified as psychological arousal arising from a physiological need. 213

drug Any foreign chemical substance that alters the functioning of a biological system. 116

drug therapy A biological therapy in which drugs are given to modify abnormal behaviors. 338

DSM-III-R Diagnostic and Statistic Manual of Mental Disorders; latest edition was published in 1987 by the American Psychiatric Association. 306

duodenum The initial segment of the small intestine. 218

dyspareunia Painful intercourse, often the result of physical problems. 251

dyssomnia Sleep disorder in which the chief symptom is a disturbance in the amount and quality of sleep; they include insomnia and hypersomnia. 114

dysthymia Mood disorder in which the person suffers moderate depression much of the time for at least two years. 311

E

eardrum Thin membrane stretched across the inner end of the auditory canal. 96

echoic memory Auditory information that is encoded into the sensory memory store. 158

eclectic A unique, individual approach, often consisting of a combination of other approaches. 324

educational psychology Subfield in which psychologists help improve the effectiveness of textbooks, classroom organization, teaching methods, and test design. 13, 392

EEG imaging A brain research technique in which electrodes are placed on the scalp and the wires are connected to a computer to record brain activity. 38

efferent neuron (also called motor neuron) A neuron that carries messages from the central nervous system to the muscles and glands. 29

ego Psychoanalytic term for individual's sense of reality. 260

egocentrism Seeing the world only from your perspective. 61

eidetic memory Photographic memory; ability to accurately recall great detail after briefly viewing something. 160

elaborative rehearsal Thinking about the meaning of information and trying to form associations with information already in memory. 162

Electra complex The Freudian idea that the young girl feels inferior to boys because she lacks a penis. 261

electrical stimulation of the brain (ESB) Procedure in which a tiny electric current is sent into a precise location in the brain to alter behavior. 34

electroconvulsive therapy (ECT) Electricity is applied to the brain to relieve severe depression. 340

electroencephalography (EEG) Technique measuring brain-wave activity; the record is an electroencephalogram. 37, 109

electrophysiological Bodily measures which can be recorded electrically. 109

embryonic stage Stage in prenatal development; from about two to eight weeks, during which three layers of cells form. 50

emotion A response to a stimulus that involves physiological arousal, subjective feeling, cognitive interpretation, and overt behavior. 232

Emotions Profile Index (EPI) Test developed by Plutchik to identify personality dispositions in groups of people based on emotional responses to questions. 236

empathy In person-centered therapy, an attempt by the therapist to understand the client's feelings and perceptions. 327

encoding The process of putting information into the memory system. 157

encounter group Similar to sensitivity training group, this is a therapy where people become aware of themselves. 336

endocrine glands Ductless glands that secrete chemicals called hormones into the bloodstream. 40

endorphins Several neuropeptides that function as neurotransmitters. These opiate-like endorphins are involved in pain-killing, reinforcement, and memory. 31, 102

engineering psychology Area of psychology concerned with the design of equipment, the work environment, and how work is performed; also called human factors psychology. 14, 384

engram The physical memory trace or neural circuit that holds memory; also called memory trace. 173

environment The events to which individuals react that take place outside the body. Can also include internal events such as physiological functions. 130

environmental psychology Area concerned with how the physical environment influences human behavior. 13, 386

episodic memory Highest memory system; includes information about personal experiences and is a subsystem of semantic memory. 163

equilibration The interaction and balance of the processes of assimilation and accommodation responsible for moving the child through the periods of intellectual development. 60

equity theory Theory of interpersonal relationships which states that people are motivated to maintain a fair balance in relationships. 239

eros Freud's term for an instinct that helps the individual or species survive; also called life instinct. 212, 260

error of central tendency The tendency to evaluate everyone in the middle range and avoid extreme ratings when evaluating people with a rating scale. 382

error of leniency The tendency not to evaluate anyone negatively when evaluating people with a rating scale. 382

escape conditioning Learning situation in which a subject is presented with an aversive stimulus from which he must escape. 144

esteem needs Fourth level of motives in Maslow's hierarchy; includes high evaluation of oneself, self-respect, self-esteem, and respect of others. 217

estrogen Hormone secreted by female sex glands (ovaries) which makes the female animal sexually receptive; produces female characteristics in humans such as breasts and wide hips. 41, 222

estrus The period of sexual receptivity in a female animal. 222

ethics Code of conduct that ensures that research will be conducted properly and that subjects will not be harmed, mentally or physically. 20

ethogram A detailed description of all the behaviors shown by a species; this is the first step for the ethologist when studying animal behavior. 211

ethology The science of the behavior of animals in their natural environment. 211

eustress Stress which results from pleasant and satisfying experiences; earning a high grade or achieving success produce eustress. 280

excitement phase First phase in the human sexual response cycle; the beginning of sexual arousal. 248

exhibitionism A paraphilia in which an individual (usually a man) exposes the genitals to strangers in order to receive sexual gratification. 320

expectancy In Rotter's personality theory, the individual's belief that if he or she exhibits a certain behavior in a specific situation, it will result in reinforcement. In experimental research, a type of experimenter bias in which the experimenter subtly influences the outcome of an experiment; sometimes called the self-fulfilling prophecy. 19, 270

expectancy-value Theory of motivation which proposes that behavior is the result of expectations of achieving goals and the value placed on those goals. 217

experiment Research method in which environmental conditions can be controlled in order to discover the cause-effect relationship between two conditions. 17

experimental group Subjects in an experiment who receive the independent variable or treatment of interest. 18

experimental psychology Subfield in which psychologists research the fundamental causes of behavior. Many experimental psychologists conduct experiments in basic research. 14

experimenter bias Source of potential error in an experiment from the action or expectancy of the experimenter; the experimenter might influence the experimental results in ways that masks the true outcome. 19

expert witness In a courtroom, a person who is judged to be highly competent in the area under investigation and who can evaluate the evidence presented. 378

explanation A goal of psychology; understanding the influences on behavior. 7

exploration Sensory inspection of the environment. 223

external people In Rotter's theory, people who perceive that reinforcement is independent of their behavior. 270

external pressure Pressure which results from the demands made on us by other people. 282

extinction The elimination of behavior by, in classical conditioning, the withholding of the US, and in operant conditioning, the withholding of the reinforcement. 134

extraneous variables In an experiment, the conditions or influences that are not of interest to the researcher. 18

extraversion The personality concept in which the personal energy of the individual is directed externally; characterized by impulsiveness, outgoingness, and sociability. 261

extrinsic motivation Motivation outside of the individual; we do something for reinforcement from the environment. 224

eyewitness testimony In a courtroom, an account of an event by someone who saw it firsthand. 165, 378

F

facial expressions Communication of emotion through movement and position of facial muscles. 245

factor analysis A statistical procedure used to determine the relationship among variables. 264

family therapy Group therapy that treats the social interactions of the family unit. 336

fantasy Defense mechanism in which a person escapes from stress and anxiety by daydreaming that everything is perfect and that all the problems are gone. 295

fat cells The determining factor in the set-point theory of obesity; obese people tend to have more fat cells than normal weight people. 219

fear of failure Motivation in which an individual does not want to fail in a task; individuals who score low on need for achievement tend to have a high fear of failure. 226

fear of success Motivation in which an individual does not want to succeed on a task. 226

fetal alcohol syndrome (FAS) Condition in which defects in the newborn child are caused by mother's alcoholism. 52, 117

fetal stage Stage in prenatal devlopment, from eight weeks until birth. 52

fetishism Paraphilia in which a person prefers to become sexually aroused by objects (fetishes). 320

figure-ground relationship Perceptual organization rule that explains our tendency to separate a scene into a main figure and a background. 89

five factor model of personality tracts A trait theory of personality which includes the factors of extraversion, agreeableness, conscientiousness, neuroticism, and culture. 265

fixed action pattern (FAP) Unlearned, inherited, stereotyped behaviors that are shown by all members of a species; term used in ethology. 211

fixed interval (FI) schedule Schedule of reinforcement in which the subject receives reinforcement for the first correct response given after a specified time interval. 142

fixed ratio (FR) schedule Schedule in which the subject is reinforced after a certain number of responses. 143

flashbulb memory Memory of an event that is so important that significant details are vividly remembered for life. 163

flavor Property of food that is due to smell, appearance, texture, and temperature. 100

flextime Flexible working hours; type of working condition in which employees help determine the hours they work. 384

flow chart Diagram showing the possible choices at each step in solving problems. 186

fluid intelligence The ability to solve novel problems. 70

foot-in-the-door technique The technique to obtain compliance from a person by first making a small request and then making a large request. 358

forebrain The largest and most complex part of the brain; located in the front, it controls higher level functions. 33

forensic psychology Area of psychology that includes work in police departments, courts, and prisons to detect and prevent crime and assess and rehabilitate those accused of criminal behavior. 377

forgetting In memory, not being able to retrieve the original learning. The part of the original learning that cannot be retrieved is said to be forgotten. 166

formal concept Type of concept that has a clear and unambiguous rule that specifies exactly which attributes define the category. 183

formal operations period Period in cognitive development; at 11 years, the adolescent begins abstract thinking and reasoning. This period continues throughout the rest of life. 62

fovea The middle area of the retina in which the cones are clustered. 84

free association Psychoanalytic technique in which the patient says everything that comes to mind. 326

free recall A verbal learning procedure in which the order of presentation of the stimuli is varied and the subject can learn the items in any order. 167

frequency Number of peaks of sound pressure per second; determines the pitch of sound. 96

frequency distribution Tabulation of data which shows the number of times each score occurs. 22

frequency theory of hearing Theory of hearing that states that the frequency of vibrations at the basilar membrane determines the frequency of firing of neurons carrying impulses to the brain. 97

frontal lobes The part of the cerebral cortex that is involved in higher mental activities such as thinking. 34

frotteurism The paraphilia in which a person obtains sexual arousal from touching and rubbing against a non-consenting person, often in a crowd. 320

frustration Results from the blocking of a person's goal-oriented behavior. 284

frustration-drive theory Theory of aggression which states that aggression is caused by frustration. 368

functional fixedness A special case of a set that interferes with problem solving; the longer we use an object the less likely we are to find new uses for it. 188

functionalism School of thought which studied the functional value of consciousness and behavior. 9

fundamental attribution error Attribution bias in which people overestimate the role of internal disposition and underestimate the role of external situation. 349

G

ganglion cells Cells in the retina of the eye; the ganglion cells receive messages from the bipolar cells. Axons of the ganglions form the optic nerve. 85

gate-control theory of pain Theory of pain which proposes that there is a gate which allows pain impulses to travel from the spinal cord to the brain. 101

gender identity A person's sense of maleness or femaleness; the learned masculine or feminine identification with a particular sex. 56, 247

gender-identity disorder Incongruence between assigned sex and gender identity. 250

gender-identity/role Term that incorporates gender identity (the private perception of one's sex) and gender role (the public expression of one's gender identity). 248

gene The basic unit of heredity; the gene is composed of deoxyribonucleic acid (DNA). 42

general adaptation syndrome (GAS) Selye's theory of how the body responds to stress over time. GAS includes the stages of alarm reaction, resistance, and exhaustion. 285

generalized anxiety disorder Disorder in which the individual lives in a state of constant severe tension; continuous fear and apprehension experienced by an individual. 310

genetics The study of heredity; genetics is the science of discovering how traits are passed along generations. 42

genital stage Psychosexual stage during which the individual can relate in a positive sexual way toward other persons. 59

genotype The complete set of genes inherited by an individual from his or her parents. 42

genuineness In person-centered therapy, a characteristic of the therapist who is being authentic, open, and honest. 327

gerontology The study of late adulthood and aging. 68

Gestalt psychology A school of thought which studied whole or complete perceptions. 10

Gestalt therapy An insight therapy which is designed to help people become more aware of themselves in the here and now and to take responsibility for their own actions. 328

glucostatic theory Theory which states that hunger is due to low glucose metabolism in individual cells. 218

gonads The reproductive glands; ovaries in the female, testes in the male. 41

grammar The set of rules that structures a language. 179

grandiose delusion Distortion of reality; one's belief that he or she is extremely important or powerful. 315

group A collection of people who have a common goal and work toward that goal. 360

group polarization Tendency for a group to move toward an extreme position—either more risky or more conservative. 364

group therapy Treatment of several patients at the same time. 335

grouping Tendency to group stimuli to develop perceptions. 90

groupthink A situation that occurs when group members are so committed to, and optimistic about, the group that they feel it is invulnerable and so concerned with maintaining consensus that criticism is muted. 362

growth hormone Hormone secreted by the pituitary gland that helps regulate growth. 40

GSR (galvanic skin response) A measure of autonomic nervous system activity. In the GSR measurement technique a slight electric current is passed over the skin; the more nervous a subject is, the easier the current will flow. 234

gustation The taste sensation. 100

H

hallucination A sensory impression reported when no external stimulus exists to justify the report; often hallucinations are a symptom of mental illness. 314

hallucinogens Psychedelic drugs that result in hallucinations at high doses, and other effects on behavior and perception in mild doses. 119

halo effect The finding that once we form a general impression of someone, we tend to interpret additional information about the person in a consistent manner. 347

haptic sense Sense of touch. 101

hassles Petty routine annoyances, aggravations, and frustrations such as driving in traffic, preparing meals, the pressure of time, and communication problems. 282

Hawthorne effect The finding that behavior can be influenced just by participation in a research study. 383

health psychology Field of psychology that studies psychological influences on people's health, including how they stay healthy, why they become ill, and how their behavior relates to their state of health. 291

hedonism Theory which states that the individual is motivated to seek pleasure and avoid pain. 214

helping The act of providing aid or assistance to someone; sometimes called prosocial behavior. 371

heredity The natural capability of an individual to develop the characteristics possessed by his or her ancestors. 42

hermaphroditism Contradiction between predominant genital appearance and other biological sex determiners. 247

heuristic Problem-solving strategy; a person tests solutions most likely to be correct. 188

hierarchy of needs Maslow's list of motives in humans, arranged from the biological to the uniquely human. 216

higher order conditioning Learning to make associations with stimuli that have been learned previously (CSs). 135

hindbrain The back part of the brain which controls basic life-support of the body. 33

hippocampus Brain structure in the limbic system that is important in learning and memory. 34

holophrastic speech Speech of young children in which one word communicates the meaning of a complete sentence. 180

homeostasis The state of equilibrium which maintains a balance in the internal body environment. 40, 213

homosexual A person whose sexual preference and activities are directed toward other people of the same sex. 249

horizontal cells The cells that interconnect the neurons in the retina. 85

hormones Chemicals produced by the endocrine glands that regulate activity of certain bodily processes. 40

hospice Program of supportive services which provide physical, psychological, social, and spiritual aid for the dying. 71

hue The color we perceive; hue is determined by the wavelength of light. 83

humanistic Psychological school of thought which believes that people are unique beings. 216

humanistic psychologist Psychologist who concentrates on developing theories based on the uniqueness of the human personality. 266

humanistic psychology Psychological school of thought which believes that people are unique beings who cannot be broken down into parts. 12

hygiene needs In Herzberg's theory, the factors that can produce job dissatisfaction if not met. They include company policy, supervision, salary, interpersonal relations, and working conditions. 383

hyperopia (farsightedness) Visual disorder in which the eyeball is unusually short and so the image is focused beyond the retina. 85

hyperphagia Disorder in which the individual continues to eat until he or she is obese; can be caused by damage to ventromedial hypothalamus. 219

hypersomnia Sleep disorder in which an individual falls asleep at inappropriate times; narcolepsy is a form of hypersomnia. 115

hypertension An increase in blood pressure above acceptable levels. 292

hypnagogic hallucination Symptom of narcolepsy in which very vivid dreams occur as the narcoleptic begins a sleep attack. 115

hypnosis Altered state of consciousness characterized by heightened suggestibility. 122

hypnotic age regression Technique in which an individual under hypnosis is asked to recall information about events that occurred at a much earlier date (during childhood). 123

hypoactive sexual desire Condition in which person has very little interest in sexual activities. 251

hypochondriasis Somatoform disorder in which the individual is obsessed with fears of having a serious medical disease. 318

hypomanic episode Period in cyclothymia in which a person is in an elevated or irritable mood; not severe enough to cause major disruption of normal functioning. 313

hypothalamus Part of the brain's limbic system; involved in motivational behaviors, including eating, drinking, and sex. 34

hypothesis In the scientific method, an educated guess or prediction about future observable events. 15

hypothyroidism Condition resulting from underactive thyroid; symptoms are sluggishness, sleepiness, weight gain. 40

I

iconic memory Visual information that is encoded into the sensory memory store. 158

id Freud's representation of the basic instinctual drives; the id always seeks pleasure. 260

identification The process in which children adopt the attitudes, values, and behaviors of their parents. 58

illusion An incorrect perception that occurs when sensation is distorted. 94

imitation The act of repeating behavior observed in others; especially important in observational learning situations. 150

immediate memory span Sperling's measure of sensory memory capacity; subjects were asked to recall information immediately after it was presented to them. 158

impossible figure A figure that logically cannot exist; a visual illusion. 94

impression formation The process of developing an evaluation of another person from your perceptions; first, or initial, impressions are often important. 346

imprinting A form of early learning in which birds follow a moving stimulus (often the mother); may be similar to attachment in mammals. 151

inbred strain Genetically identical individuals produced by artificial selection. 44

incentive An external stimulus that pulls the individual toward some goal. 213

incongruence In Rogers's theory, a state in which the segments of an individual's personality do not fit together. 266

independent variable The condition in an experiment which is controlled and manipulated by the experimenter; it is a stimulus that will cause a response. 18

indiscriminate attachment phase Stage of attachment in which babies prefer humans to nonhumans, but do not discriminate among individual people. 57

individual psychology The personality theory of Alfred Adler; the individual psychology theory focuses on the uniqueness of each individual person. 262

individuation Jung's concept of the process leading to the unification of all parts of the personality. 261

induced motion Situation in which we attribute motion to an object that is not really moving; when we incorrectly attribute motion to figure rather than background. 93

industrial-organizational psychology Area of psychology that includes personnel psychology, organizational psychology, engineering psychology, and consumer psychology. 14, 380

infancy Period of the first two years of life during which the neonate becomes a small, achieving child. 52

inferential statistics Techniques that help researchers make generalizations about a finding based on a limited number of subjects. 24

inferiority complex Adler's personality concept which states that because children are dependent on adults and cannot meet the standards set for themselves they feel inferior. 262

information processing theory Memory theory that relies on computer models to describe the flow of information through the memory system. 158

ingratiation Any technique that increases the attractiveness of a person trying to seek compliance from us; examples include giving compliments, doing favors, or just being nice. 358

inhibited female orgasm A persistent inability of the female to achieve orgasm. 251

inhibited male orgasm A persistent inability of the male to achieve orgasm. 251

insight A sudden grasping of the means necessary to achieve a goal; important in the Gestalt approach to problem solving. 148

insight therapy Therapy based on the assumption that behavior is abnormal because people do not adequately understand the motivation causing their behavior. 325

insomnia The inability to sleep. 114

instinct Highly stereotyped inherited behavior common to all members of a species that often appears in complete form in the absence of any obvious opportunities to learn it. 151, 210

instinct theory Any theory which attempts to explain behavior as being determined by instincts; theory proposed by Freud that aggression is the result of a death instinct inherent in all human beings. 210, 368

instinctive drift The process of learned behavior moving over time toward more innate responses. 151

instrumental conditioning Operant conditioning. 138

intellectually gifted Upper extreme of intelligence, usually when an individual has an IQ score of 130 or higher; intellectually gifted individuals tend to be successful in life. 203

intelligence Capacity to learn and behave adaptively. 191

intelligence quotient (IQ) An index of a person's performance on an intelligence test relative to others in the culture; ratio of a person's mental age to chronological age. 194

intelligence test A test which is designed to measure a broad range of mental abilities; intelligence tests are often used to predict future academic success. 192

intensity Strength; in punishment, it refers to the fact that punishment is most effective if it is strong. 146

interference Theory of forgetting in which information that was learned before (proactive interference) or after (retroactive interference) causes the learner to be unable to remember the material of interest. 168

internal people In Rotter's personality theory, people who perceive reinforcement is contingent upon their behavior. 270

internal pressure Pressure which results when we attempt to maintain self-esteem by forcing ourselves to achieve higher standards. 282

interneurons (also called association neurons) Neurons connected with other neurons. 29

internship A period of time (usually one year) in which a person works under the supervision of others before being on his or her own, usually part of a clinical or counseling psychology program. 13

interpersonal attraction Our behavior and attitudes toward other people; can be positive or negative. 239

interposition Monocular depth cue in which one object partially blocks another; we assume the overlap is due to the first one being closer. 91

interstimulus interval Time interval between two stimuli; in classical conditioning, it is the elapsed time between the CS and the US. 133

interview Research method in which in-depth information is obtained through verbal interaction with a subject. 16

intimate distance Hall's closest interpersonal distance category, 0 to 1.5 feet. 387

intrinsic motivation Motivation inside the individual; we do something because we receive satisfaction from it. 224

introspection Method in which a subject gives a self-report of his or her immediate experience of an object. 8

introversion The personality concept in which the personal energy of the individual is directed inward; characterized by introspection, seriousness, inhibition, and restraint. 261

ions Electrically charged particles. 29

iris Colored part of the eye encircling the pupil. 84

irritability The characteristic of a neuron to change in response to stimulation. 29

J

James-Lange theory of emotion Theory of emotion which states that the physiological arousal and behavior come before the subjective experience of an emotion. 236

job analysis A review of the job that an employee will be doing; the first step in selection. 380

just noticeable difference (JND) Difference threshold: minimum amount of energy required to produce a difference in sensation. 81

K

kinesthesis The sense of bodily movement. 103

L

language Communication utilizing manipulation of symbols to convey meaning to others or one's self. 178

language acquisition device (LAD) Hypothesized biological structure that accounts for the relative ease of acquiring language, according to Chomsky. 181

late luteal phase dysphoric disorder Proposed DSM diagnostic category of females who experience severe changes in physical and emotional functioning during menstrual cycles that cause marked impairment in social interaction. 306

latency stage Psychosexual stage during which the child appears to have little need for erotic satisfaction. 59

latent dream content In Freud's dream theory, the true thoughts in the unconsciousness; the true meaning of the dream. 113

latent learning Learning which occurs when an individual acquires knowledge of something but does not show it until motivated to do so. 149

lateral hypothalamus (LH) Part of the hypothalamus involved in initiating eating behavior. 218

lateral preoptic area Area of the hypothalamus in which osmoreceptor cells are sensitive to the amount of water in blood and cellular dehydration due to the amount of salt. 221

law of effect Thorndike's proposal that when a response produces satisfaction it will be repeated; reinforcement. 138

leader Someone who is able to exert influence over the other members of a group. 365

learned helplessness Condition in which a person learns that his behavior has no effect on his environment; when an individual gives up and stops trying. 290

learned social motives Social motives in the human which are learned; include achievement and affiliation. 225

learning The relatively permanent change in behavior or behavioral ability of an individual that occurs as a result of experience. 130

learning model The approach to abnormal psychology which views abnormal behavior as due to faulty learning. 305

learning to learn Principle in which the skill learned in one situation is transferred to a new situation. 188

legal model The approach to abnormal psychology which views abnormal behavior as illegal. 306

lens Part of the eye which focuses on stimuli. 84

libido Freud's term for psychic energy that builds up in the id and powers motivation. 212, 260

life instinct (also called eros) Freud's term for an instinct that helps the individual or species survive; sex is the major expression of life instinct. 212, 260

life-span development Development of the individual throughout life, from conception to death. 50

lifestyle Adler's theory that people learn to deal with other people, occupations, and relationships in a particular style. 262

light waves A type of electromagnetic energy; light waves stimulate the eyes to produce vision. 83

Likert Scale A measurement technique which requests that subjects indicate their degree of agreement with a statement by marking a point along a scale. 351

limbic system The structures of the forebrain that control motivation and emotion. 33

linear perspective Monocular depth cue in which lines converging depict distance; example is railroad tracks receding in the distance. 92

linguistic relativity hypothesis Proposal that the perception of reality differs according to the language of the observer. 182

lobe One of the four parts of the cerebral cortex of the brain; the cerebral cortex is divided into the frontal lobe, temporal lobe, parietal lobe, and occipital lobe. Each lobe has certain distinct functions in interpreting information received by the brain. 34

locus coeruleus Area in the pons area of the brain stem that appears to be involved in REM sleep; this area inhibits muscle tone during REM sleep, paralyzing the person from acting out dreams. 112

locus of control Rotter's theory in which a person's beliefs about reinforcement are classified as internal or external. 270

long-term memory The permanent memory where rehearsed information is stored. 162

love An emotion characterized by knowing, liking, and becoming intimate with someone. 240

low-ball procedure The compliance technique of presenting an attractive proposal to someone and then switching it to a more unattractive proposal. 359

M

magic number 7 The finding that most people can remember about seven items of information for a short time (in short-term memory). 160

mainstreaming Educational practice of placing retarded individuals into regular classes whenever possible. 202

maintenance rehearsal Repeating information over and over without thinking about it. 161

major depression Severe mood disorder in which a person experiences one or more major depressive episodes. 312

major depressive episode Period in major depression in which a person is in a depressed mood and loses interest in normal activities; symptoms include sleep disruption, weight loss, fatigue, and feelings of worthlessness. 312

maladjustment Condition that occurs when a person utilizes inappropriate abilities to respond to demands placed upon him or her. 280

management by objectives (MBO) Procedure used in industry in which the worker and supervisor jointly agree on work objectives and evaluate the progress of the worker. 382

mania An affective disorder in which the individual is highly excitable, highly active, and extremely optimistic. 310

manifest dream content In Freud's dream theory, what is remembered about a dream upon waking; a disguised representation of the unconscious wishes. 113

marathon group Encounter group that meets for a continuous extended period of time (24 hours straight). 336

marijuana A psychoactive drug derived from the leaves and flowers of the cannabis plant. 121

marital therapy Family therapy where just the husband and wife are treated. 337

massed practice Learning as much material as possible in long continuous stretches. 170

masturbation Erotic self-stimulation to produce orgasm. 249

matched group design Experimental design in which the experimental and control groups are "matched" on as many variables as possible. 18

maturation The genetically controlled process of growth that results in orderly changes in behavior. 42, 50

maze A device for testing learning and exploration in animals; the subject must travel through a series of alleys until it reaches a goal box and is reinforced. 140

mean The arithmetic average, in which the sum of scores is divided by the number of scores. 22

meaningfulness The informational value of material to be learned; high meaningful material is better encoded. 159

medial forebrain bundle A tract of neurons that runs through the limbic system in the brain. 34

median The middle score in a group of scores that are arranged from lowest to highest. 22

meditation The practice of some form of relaxed concentration while ignoring other sensory stimuli. 123

medulla The part of the hindbrain which helps regulate blood pressure and breathing. 33

meiosis The process in which chromosomes in the sex cells divide to half of their number. Unlike the other body cells which have 46 chromosomes, each sex cell (sperm or egg) has only 23 chromosomes. 42

memory The process of storing information so that it can be retrieved and used later. 156

memory trace A hypothetical circuit that occurs because of learned information and fades over time due to disuse. 168

menarche Onset of menstruation in females. 64

menopause End of menstruation in women. 67

mental age The age level on which a person is capable of performing; used in determining intelligence. 194

mental retardation Lower extreme of intelligence range, when a person scores less than 70 on an IQ test and has problems adjusting. 201

mental set Condition in which a person's thinking becomes so standardized that he or she approaches new problems in fixed ways. 188

metabolism The biochemical process that produces energy for the body's maintenance. 40

metamemory The knowledge of one's own memory ability. 165

method of constant stimuli Method in psychophysics in which the experimenter determines the absolute threshold by presenting stimuli of varying intensities. 81

method of limits Method in psychophysics in which the experimenter determines the difference threshold by presenting stimuli of greater or less intensity than the original. 81

method of loci Mnemonic technique that associates places with words to be remembered. 171

midbrain Region connecting the hindbrain and forebrain. 33

migraine headache Headache caused by arteries under the scalp of the head which become dilated and press on pain-sensitive nerves in the area; psychophysiological disorder. 291

mild retardation Largest segment of the mentally retarded; includes individuals with IQs of 52 to 68. 201

Minnesota Multiphasic Personality Inventory (MMPI) An objective personality test which was originally devised to identify personality disorders. 273

minority influence Condition in which the minority members of a group are able to cause the majority to conform to their point of view. 357

miscarriage Spontaneous abortion during pregnancy, when the unborn life is terminated naturally. 52

mnemonic technique Method of improving memory by combining and relating chunks of information. 171

mode The most frequently occurring score. 23

modeling A process of learning by imitation in a therapeutic situation. 335

moderate retardation Level of mental retardation in which individuals have IQs of 36 to 51. 201

monaural Condition in which sound is delivered to one ear. 98

monochromat A person who can see only light and dark; a person who is totally color-blind. 86

monocular depth cues Visual cues that depend on only one eye; used to detect distance. 91

monozygotic twins Identical twins produced when one egg fertilized by one sperm divides into two individuals. 45

mood disorder Disorder in which a person experiences a severe disruption in mood or emotional balance. 310

moon illusion Illusion in which the moon looks larger on the horizon than when high in the sky. 95

moral development Development of individuals as they adopt their society's standards of right and wrong; development of awareness of ethical behavior. 63

Moro reflex Reflex that occurs when something in the environment changes quickly and the baby quickly extends both arms and brings his feet close to his body (startle reflex). 53

morpheme The smallest meaningful unit of a language. 179

motion parallax Monocular depth cue in which objects close to us seem to move faster than objects farther away. 92

motivated forgetting (repression) Theory which suggests that people want to forget unpleasant events. 169

motivation The forces which initiate and direct behavior, and the variables which determine the intensity and persistence of that behavior. 210

motivator needs In Herzberg's theory, the factors that lead to job satisfaction; they include responsibility, the nature of the work, advancement, and recognition. 383

motivator-hygiene theory Theory of Herzberg to account for motivation and job satisfaction. 383

motive Anything that arouses the individual and directs his or her behavior toward some goal. Three categories include biological, stimulus, and social motives. 210

motor division A part of the somatic nervous system that carries neural information to the skeletal muscles directing their voluntary movements. 38

motor neuron (also called efferent neuron) A neuron that carries messages from the central nervous system to the muscles and glands. 29

multiple approach-avoidance conflict Conflict that occurs when an individual has two or more goals, both of which have positive and negative aspects. 283

multiple attachment phase Later attachment stage in which the baby begins to form attachments to people other than the primary caretaker. 57

multiple personality A dissociative disorder in which several personalities are present in the same individual. 318

multiple requests Technique of making more than one request in order to obtain compliance. 358

myelin sheath A fatty substance that provides insulation for the axon; neural impulses travel faster in myelinated axons. 29

Myers-Briggs Type Indicator (MBTI) Objective personality test based on Jung's type theory. 273

myopia (nearsightedness) Visual disorder in which the eyeball is unusually long and the image is focused in front of the retina; nearsighted people cannot see long-range stimuli. 85

Müller-Lyer illusion A well-known illusion, in which two horizontal lines have end lines either going in or out; the line with the end lines going in appears longer. 95

N

naive psychology Heider's approach to motivation in which a person decides whether behavior is caused by forces within the individual or forces in the environment. 217

nanometer (nm) One billionth of a meter. 83

narcolepsy Sleep disorder characterized by inappropriate daytime attacks of sleep. 115

narcotic analgesics Drugs that have an effect on the body similar to morphine; relieve pain and suppress coughing. 118

natural childbirth Procedure in which little medication is used during labor and delivery so that through breathing and muscular control the mother can participate actively in the delivery. 52

natural concept Type of concept that is intuitively used in everyday life. 183

naturalistic observation Research method in which behavior of people or animals in their normal environment is accurately recorded. 15

Necker cube A visual illusion. The Necker cube is a drawing of a cube designed so that it is difficult to determine which side is toward you. 95

need A physiological deprivation that results in a drive to restore balance. 213

need for achievement The desire to perform at some high standard of excellence. 225

need for affiliation The desire to be with others. 227

need for power The desire to control or exert influence over other people. 226

negative afterimage Visual image which is the opposite colors of the original; occurs when you stare at an image and then look at a white surface. 86

negative reinforcement Taking from a subject something bad to increase the probability that the preceding behavior will be repeated. 144

neodissociation theory Hilgard's theory of hypnosis that states that consciousness can be split into several streams of thought that are partially independent of each other. 122

neonate Newborn infant immediately after birth. 52

nerve A group of neurons running together in the body. 29

nerve deafness Type of deafness resulting from damage to the auditory nerve. 98

neural impulse The electrical message that is conducted down the length of a neuron. 29

neuron A specialized cell that functions to conduct messages throughout the body. 28

neuropeptides Short chains of amino acids that can sometimes serve as neurotransmitters. 31

neurosis A Freudian term which was used to describe abnormal behavior caused by anxiety; it has been largely eliminated from DSM-III. 307

neurotic needs In Horney's personality theory, needs that are irrational in dealing with basic anxiety. 263

neurotic trends In Horney's personality theory, the ways that people adapt. 263

neurotransmitter Chemical which carries messages across the synapse. 30

neutral stimulus A stimulus which does not cause the response of interest; the individual may show some response to the stimulus but not the associated behavior. 131

nicotene A stimulant contained in the tobacco of cigarettes; it is absorbed by the lungs and distributed by the bloodstream. 118

NMR (Nuclear Magnetic Resonance) A method of studying brain activity using magnetic field imaging. 38

nodes of Ranvier Gaps along the myelin sheath of an axon. The nodes of Ranvier help the neural impulse travel quickly along the axon. 29

noise Any sound of a high enough intensity to disturb an individual. 389

norepinephrine A neurotransmitter involved in moods. 31

normal curve When scores of a large number of random cases are plotted on a graph, they often fall into a bell-shaped curve; as many cases on the curve are above the mean as below it. 22

norms The explicit or implicit rules and standards that regulate the behavior of members in the group situation. 360

NREM (non REM) Nonrapid eye-movement sleep; type of sleep in which the eyes are very slowly moving back and forth; a restful sleep time. 109

O

obedience Type of social influence in which an individual gives the behavior required. 359

obesity A condition of being significantly overweight. 219

object permanence The ability to realize that objects continue to exist even though we can no longer see them. 61

objective personality tests Measures of personality administered and scored according to standardized instructions. 272

objectivity A test's results are not affected by the personal feelings and biases of the examiner. 193

observation Research method which involves watching an individual's behavior in everyday situations over a period of time; also called naturalistic observation. 271

observational learning In social learning theory, learning by observing someone else behave; people observe and imitate in learning socialization. 150

obsessive compulsive disorder Anxiety disorder in which the individual has repetitive thoughts (obsessions) which lead to urges (compulsions) to engage in meaningless rituals. 309

obsessive thoughts Repetitive thoughts in the obsessive compulsive disorder; often involves fears of being unable to control impulses. 309

occipital lobe Part of the cerebral cortex of the brain which is involved in interpreting visual sensations. 85

occipital lobe Part of the cerebral cortex of the brain which is involved in interpreting visual sensations. 34

Oedipus complex The Freudian idea that the young boy has sexual feelings for his mother and is jealous of his father and must identify with his father to resolve the conflict. 261

off-the-job training Training often done by a professional away from the actual job site. 381

olfaction The smell sense. 99

olfactory bulbs Part of brain involved in sense of smell. 99

olfactory epithelium A sense receptor for smell that reacts chemically with odors to produce neural impulses. 99

on-the-job training Training of the current employee designed to increase job performance effectiveness; usually taught by the supervisor. 381

operant conditioning Learning in which behavior followed by reinforcement (satisfaction) increases in frequency. 138

opiates Narcotic analgesics; drugs whose effect on the body is similar to morphine, the analgesic ingredient derived from the opium poppy plant. 118

opponent-process theory Theory that when one emotion is experienced, the other is suppressed. 238

opponent-process theory of color vision Theory of color vision which postulated the existence of receptors sensitive to opposing pairs of colors. 86

optic chiasma Junction in the optic nerve which connects the nerve tracts from each eye carrying information from the same side of the visual field. 85

optic nerve Nerve which travels from the retina of the eye to the brain. 85

optimum level of arousal Motivation theory which states that the individual will seek a level of arousal that is comfortable. 214

oral stage First psychosexual stage, during which the baby receives pleasure from sucking. 59

order effects The possibility that the order of treatments in a within-subject design might have an effect on the dependent variable. 18

organ of Corti Sensory receptor for sound. 97

organic mental disorders Disorders which involve physical damage to the nervous system; can be caused by disease or by an accident. 317

organism In Rogers's humanistic personality theory, an individual person. 266

organizational psychology Area of industrial psychology that focuses on worker attitudes and motivation; derived primarily from personality and social psychology. 382

orgasm The climax of intense sexual excitement during which the release from building sexual tension occurs. 248

orientation training Training in an organization which is designed to develop job skills and give knowledge of the organization to the new employee. 381

osmoreceptors Cells in the anterior hypothalamus which are sensitive to the relative amount of water in the blood. 221

outer ear Outer part of the ear, which collects sound waves and directs them into the auditory canal. 96

ovaries Female reproductive glands. 41

overlearning Continuing to rehearse information after the initial learning is accomplished. 170

P

pain Skin sense which detects strong pressure. 101

paired-associate learning A verbal learning procedure in which the subject is presented with a series of pairs of items which must be remembered. 167

panic attack In the panic disorder, a specific period of intense anxiety, characterized by shortness of breath, dizziness, faintness, trembling, and nausea. 307

panic disorder Disorder characterized by the occurrence of panic attacks, specific periods of intense anxiety. 307

papillae Small bumps on the surface of the tongue that contain the taste buds. 100

paradoxical cold A phenomenon in which a person sometimes senses warm stimuli of 45° C (112° F) as cold. 103

paranoid schizophrenia A type of schizophrenia in which the individual often has delusions of grandeur and persecution, thinking that someone is out to get him. 315

paraphilia Sexual deviation characterized by the need for unusual behaviors for sexual arousal which interfere with normal sexual activities. 320

parasomnia Sleep disorder in which the chief symptom is an unusual event that disturbs sleep; they include sleep terror disorder, bedwetting, and sleep walking. 114

parasympathetic nervous system The branch of the autonomic nervous system that is more active under normal circumstances; it decreases breathing and heart rate. 39

parietal lobes The section of the cerebral cortex of the brain in which sensations such as touch are interpreted. 34

partial reinforcement Any schedule of reinforcement in which reinforcement follows only some of the correct responses. 142

partial reinforcement extinction effect The finding that partial reinforcement produces a response that takes longer to extinguish than continuous reinforcement. 142

passionate love An intense emotional experience that includes sexual desire, elation, anxiety, ecstasy, and tenderness; also called romantic love. 241

pattern recognition Memory process in which information attended to is compared with information already permanently stored in memory. 159

pedophilia A paraphilia in which an individual is sexually attracted to young children. 320

pegword A mnemonic technique which starts with a rhyme or series in which the key words serve as anchors to associate with other items to be remembered. 171

penis envy The Freudian idea that the young girl envies boys who have penises; she resolves this by suppressing her feelings toward her father and identifying with her mother. 261

perception The active process in which the sensory information that is carried through the nervous system to the brain is organized and interpreted; the interpretation of sensation. 78

perceptual constancy The tendency to perceive objects in a consistent manner despite the changing sensations received by sense organs; constancy plays an important role in helping us to adapt to the environment successfully. 87

perceptual expectancy The accumulation of life experiences that directs each individual to perceive the world from his or her own perspective. 78

performance The actual observed behavior of an individual. We often infer learning from observing performance. 130

periaqueductal gray (PAG) In a theory of pain, the area of the brainstem that produces endorphins that then inhibit the neurons in the spinal cord from transmitting pain. 102

peripheral nervous system The part of the human nervous system which receives messages from the sense organs and carries them to the muscles and glands; everything outside of the brain and spinal cord. 31

persecutory delusion A distortion of reality; the belief that other people are out to get one. 315

person perception The process of using the information we gather in forming impressions of people to make evaluations of others. 347

personal dispositions In Allport's personality theory, the individual traits of a person. 263

personal distance One of Hall's interpersonal distance categories, 1.5 to 4 feet. 387

personal space Space around a person which he or she claims as his or her own. 387

personal unconscious Jung's representation of the individual's repressed thoughts and memories. 261

personality The distinctive and enduring patterns of behavior that characterize a person's adaptation to life. 258

personality and social development Changes in an individual's personality, social functioning, and emotions over time. 50

personality disorders Problems in the basic personality structure of the individual. 319

personality theorists Psychologists who develop theories to explain behavior and personality. 258

person-centered approach Rogers's personality theory in which the emphasis is on the individual. 266

person-centered therapy Founded by Carl Rogers. The therapist provides a nonthreatening atmosphere of warmth and acceptance; also called client-centered therapy. 327

personnel psychology Area of industrial psychology that includes selection, training, and evaluation of new applicants and current employees. 380

perspective Changes in the appearance of objects or surfaces as the distance from the perceiving increases; monocular depth cues help us perceive correctly. 91

PET scan (Positron Emission Tomography) Examining brain-cell activity by recording utilization of radioactive glucose. 38

petting Sexual contact with the opposite sex excluding intercourse. 249

phallic stage Psychosexual stage beginning around the age of four, when the child starts to find pleasure in stimulating the genitals. 59

phantom-limb pain Phenomenon in which people who have lost an arm or leg still feel pain in the missing limb. 102

phencyclidine hydrochloride (PCP) Animal anesthetic that functions as a hallucinogen. 121

phenomenal field In Rogers's personality theory, the sum total of an individual's experiences. 266

phenotype The complete set of observable characteristics of an individual. 42

phenylketonuria (PKU) Form of mental retardation caused by a single gene; the body cannot metabolize the substance phenylalanine. 44

pheromones Chemicals secreted by the body used to communicate with other members of the same species. 99, 222, 243

phi phenomenon Perception of movement between two lights which are alternately going on and off; *see* stroboscopic motion. 93

phobias Acute excessive fears of specific situations or objects which have no convincing basis in reality. 308

phoneme Basic speech sound in a language. 179

phrenology Method developed by Franz Gall to describe behavioral characteristics by measuring bumps on the head. 36

physical dependence A condition in which the habitual user's body becomes biochemically dependent upon the drugs; addiction. 116

physical development Changes in an individual's bodily features, motor behavior, and physiological processes. 50

physiological Refers to biological responses that occur inside the body. 6

physiological needs First level of motives in Maslow's hierarchy; includes hunger, thirst, sex, exercise, and rest. 216

physiological psychology (also called biological psychology or psychobiology) The subfield of experimental psychology that is concerned with the influence of the biological response systems on animal behavior. 14, 28

pinna Large flap of outer ear. 96

pituitary gland Endocrine gland that is called the master gland; it secretes hormones that cause other endocrine glands to function. 40

PKU (phenylketonuria) Form of mental retardation caused by a single gene; the body cannot metabolize the substance phenylalanine. 202

place theory of hearing Emphasizes the place on the basilar membrane that produces pitch differences. 97

placebo An inert or inactive substance given to control subjects to test for bias effects. 19

plateau phase Second phase in the human sexual response cycle, during which the physiological arousal becomes more intense. 248

pleasure principle In Freudian theory, the idea that the instinctual drives of the id unconsciously and impulsively seek immediate pleasure. 260

Poggendorff illusion Illusion in which a straight line looks distorted. 95

polarization Normal electrical charge of a passive neuron in which there are more negative ions (such as chloride) inside the neuron and more positive ions (such as sodium and potassium) outside. 29

polygraph Instrument that records a variety of physiological responses, such as heart rate, respiration rate, blood pressure, and GSR. 234

pons The part of the hindbrain which is involved in breathing, feeding, and facial movement. 33

Ponzo illusion An illusion in which linear perspective makes us believe a line that looks larger is actually closer. 95

population Includes all of the individuals from the large group that the subjects were selected from. 24

positive reinforcement Giving a subject something good to increase the probability that the preceding behavior will be repeated. 144

positivity bias In forming impressions, the tendency to evaluate others positively. 347

post-traumatic stress disorder Condition that can occur when a person experiences a severely distressing event; characterized by constant memories of the event, avoidance of anything associated with it, and general arousal. 284

postconventional morality Level III in Kohlberg's theory, in which moral reasoning is based on personal standards and beliefs; highest level of moral thinking. 63

practicality Situation that occurs when a test is administered and scored in a reasonable amount of time. 193

preconscious mind In Freud's psychoanalytic theory of personality, the part of personality which contains information that we have learned but that we are not thinking about at the present time. 108

preconventional morality Level I of Kohlberg's theory, in which moral reasoning is largely due to the expectation of rewards and punishments. 63

prediction A goal of psychology; making educated guesses about future behavior. 7

prefrontal lobotomy Severing frontal lobes of the brain. 37

prejudice An unjustified attitude involving a fixed, usually negative, way of thinking about a person or object. 354

Premack principle Principle that states that, of any two re-

sponses, the one that is more likely to occur can be used to reinforce the response that is less likely to occur. 148

premature ejaculation Sexual dysfunction in which the male is not able to delay ejaculation until he wishes to have it. 251

prenatal development The growth of an individual from conception until birth. 50

preoperational thought period Period in cognitive development; from two to seven years, during which the child learns to represent the environment with objects and symbols. 61

presbyacusia Type of nerve deafness which normally occurs with increasing age. 98

pressure In sensation, the skin sense which detects contact on the skin. Also, what we experience when we strive to meet the social and psychological demands placed upon us; internal pressure results from self-demands, while external pressure results from demands from others. 100, 282

pretest Measure used to make sure the experimental and control groups in an experiment both contain similar subjects. 18

primary degenerative dementia of the Alzheimer type A progressive and deteriorating disorder in which cognitive abilities and personality functioning are severely disrupted. 317

primary effect A phenomenon in which items are remembered because they come at the beginning of a list. 167

primary narcissism A Freudian term which refers to the oral phase before the ego has developed; the individual constantly seeks pleasure. 316

primary reinforcement Reinforcement that is effective without having been associated with other reinforcers; sometimes called unconditioned reinforcement. 143

prisoner's dilemma Social simulation developed to measure competition and cooperation in a social situation (confessing to a crime to avoid heavy punishment). 365

proactive interference Interference caused by information learned before the material of interest. 168

probability (p) In inferential statistics, the likelihood that the difference between the experimental and control groups is due to the independent variable. 24

procedural memory The most basic type of long-term memory; involves the formation of associations between stimuli and responses. 162

profound retardation Lowest level of mental retardation; it includes individuals with IQs below 20. 202

programmed learning Form of instruction in which the student is guided by reinforcement and feedback through a series of small steps toward some goal; similar to personalized system of instruction (PSI). 146

progressive relaxation The individual learns to alternately tense and relax various parts of the body. 332

projection Defense mechanism in which a person attributes his unacceptable characteristics or motives to others rather than himself or herself. 294

projective personality test A personality test which presents ambiguous stimuli to which subjects are expected to respond with projections of their own personality. 273

proprioceptive senses The body sense of kinesthesis (bodily movement) and the vestibular sense (body balance). 100

prosocial behavior Behavior which is directed toward helping others. 371

proxemics The study of the interpersonal distance between people. 387

proximity Closeness in time and space. In perception, it is the Gestalt perceptual principle in which stimuli next to one another are included together. In punishment, it refers to the fact that punishment is most effective if it immediately follows the undesired behavior. 90, 146

psyche According to Jung, the thoughts and feelings (conscious and unconscious) of an individual. 261

psychedelic drugs Drugs which produce changes in emotional feelings and perceptions of the external world; also called hallucinogens. 119

psychiatric social worker A social worker who has had special training in counseling people and families. 324

psychiatrist A physician who specializes in treatment of abnormal behavior. 13, 324

psychic energy Another term for libido. 212, 260

psychoactive drug A drug that produces changes in behavior and cognition by modifying conscious awareness. 116

psychoactive substance-induced organic mental disorders Organic mental disorders caused by exposure to harmful environmental substances. 317

psychoanalysis In history, the school of thought founded by Sigmund Freud that stressed unconscious motivation. In abnormal psychology, an insight therapy in which the patient's unconscious motivation is intensively explored in order to bring repressed conflicts up to consciousness; psychoanalysis usually takes a long time to accomplish. 11, 325

psychoanalytic model Freud's approach to abnormal psychology which suggests that abnormal behavior is the result of a person's conflicts. 304

psychobiology (also called biological psychology or physiological psychology) The subfield of experimental psychology that is concerned with the influence of heredity and the biological response systems on behavior. 28

psychobiology The subfield in which psychologists study biological processes in animals; includes physiological psychology and comparative psychology. 14

psychogenic amnesia A dissociative disorder in which an individual loses his sense of identity. 319

psychogenic fugue A dissociative disorder in which an individual loses his or her sense of identity and goes to a new geographic location, forgetting all of the unpleasant emotions connected with the old life. 319

psycholinguistics The psychological study of how people convert the sounds of a language into meaningful symbols that can be used to communicate with others. 178

psychological dependence Situation in which a person craves a drug even though it is not biologically needed by the body. 116

psychological factors affecting physical condition Psychological influences that contribute to the initiation or aggravation of a physical condition, such as migraine headache, asthma, or ulcer; previously called psychosomatic illness or psychophysiological disorder. 291

psychological situation In Rotter's personality theory, the condition that results when an individual interacts with the environment. 270

psychological types Jung's term for different personality profiles; Jung combined two attitudes and four functions to produce eight psychological types. 261

psychology Science of behavior and cognition. 6

psychopharmacology Study of effects of psychoactive drugs on behavior. 116

psychophysics Researchers compare the physical energy of a stimulus with the sensation reported. 81

psychophysiological disorders Real physical problems (such as ulcers, migraine headaches, and high blood pressure) that are caused or aggravated by emotional stress; formerly called psychosomatic disorders. 291

psychosexual stages Freud's theoretical stages in personality development. 59

psychosomatic illness Formerly psychophysiological disorder; physical problem caused by emotional stress. 291

psychosurgery Surgery on the brain for treatment of psychological problems. 38, 339

psychotherapy Treatment of behavior disorders through psychological techniques; major psychotherapies include insight therapy, behavior therapy, and group therapy. 324

psychotic disorders The more severe categories of abnormal behavior. 310

puberty Sexual maturation; the time at which the individual is able to perform sexually and reproduce. 64

public distance Hall's widest interpersonal distance category, more than 12 feet. 387

pupil Part of the eye which adjusts to light intensities; when the pupil constricts, less light is permitted into the eye. 84

Q

quality of work life (QWL) Concept in which the individual's work experience is improved; includes financial security, sense of self-worth, and actual working conditions. 384

quasi-experiment Research design in which a true experiment cannot be conducted because naturally occurring events prevent it; natural events used to design the experiment. 19

R

random assignment In an experiment, the subjects are placed in either the experimental or control group, without regard to background or experience. 18

range In statistics, a measure of variability; the highest score minus the lowest score. 23

raphe nucleus Area in the back of the brain; this area appears to be involved in NREM sleep. 112

rating scale A pencil-and-paper form that observers fill out in their assessment of a subject; standardized form for recording personal evaluations of an employee. 272, 381

rational-emotive therapy A cognitive behavior modification technique in which a person is taught to identify irrational, self-defeating beliefs and then to overcome them. 333

rationalization Defense mechanism in which a person makes up logical excuses to justify his or her behavior rather than exposing the true motives. 295

reaction formation Defense mechanism in which a person masks an unconsciously distressing or unacceptable trait by assuming an opposite attitude or behavior pattern. 295

readiness to learn Children cannot learn until they are mature enough to be able to use their muscles properly. 54

real motion In perception, a situation in which we correctly perceive an object as moving. 93

realistic love Knox's theory that this type of love is characterized by a practical, calm, solid emotion. 241

reality principle In Freudian theory, the idea that the drives of the ego try to find socially acceptable ways to gratify the id. 260

recall (reconstruction) In memory, a measure of retention in which the subject is required to retrieve learned information from memory. 167

receiver operating characteristic (ROC) In perception, a curve which results from plotting graphically a subject's responses in signal detection procedure. 83

recency effect A phenomenon in which items are remembered because they come at the end of a list. 167

recessive Form of a gene reflected in the phenotype when both genes at a particular location are identical. 42

reciprocal inhibition Concept of Wolpe that states that it is possible to break the bond between anxiety-provoking stimuli and responses manifesting anxiety by facing those stimuli in a state antagonistic to anxiety. 331

recitation Repeating learned information from memory. 170

recognition A measure of retention in which the subject identifies items which were previously learned. 167

reconstructive memory Procedure in which an individual combines actual details of an event with other available information to fill in the gaps. 164

reference groups Group from which a person derives his or her values, attitudes, and identity. 361

reflex An automatic movement that occurs in direct response to a stimulus. 32

refractory period In physiology, a brief period of time after a neuron has fired during which it cannot fire again. 30

regression Defense mechanism in which a person retreats to an earlier, more immature form of behavior. 295

reinforcement Any event that increases the probability that the behavior which precedes it will be repeated; also called a reinforcer; similar to a reward. 142

reinforcement therapy A behavior therapy in which reinforcement is used to modify behavior. Techniques in reinforcement therapy include shaping, extinction, and token economy. 329

reinforcement value In Rotter's personality theory, the importance a person attaches to a particular reinforcement. 270

reinforcer Synonym for reinforcement. 139

releaser (sign stimulus) Specific environmental cues which stimulate a stereotyped behavior to occur; releasers cause fixed action patterns. 211

reliability The degree of consistency in the results of measurements taken at various times. 22, 193

REM (rapid eye movement) Type of sleep in which the eyes are rapidly moving around; dreaming occurs in REM sleep. 109

renin Hormone secreted by the kidneys that causes water retention and thirst. 221

replication In a research study, the duplicating of the research method to help test reliability. 17

repressed conflicts In psychoanalysis, these are conflicts and anxieties which the patient experienced early in life and has since forgotten (in order to reduce anxiety). 326

repression Defense mechanism in which painful memories and unacceptable thoughts and motives are conveniently forgotten so that they will not have to be dealt with. 294

reproductive glands Endocrine glands involved in sexual motivation and secondary sexual characteristics; testes and ovaries. 40

residual schizophrenia Type of schizophrenia in which the individual currently does not have major psychotic symptoms but has had a schizophrenic episode in the past. 315

resistance Psychoanalytic term used when a patient avoids a painful area of conflict. 326

resolution phase The last phase in the human sexual response cycle; the time after orgasm that the body gradually returns to the unaroused state. 248

response Specific actions taken by an individual in reaction to something in the environment. 130

resting potential The normal electrical charge of a passive (resting) neuron. 29

retention The amount of information that is accurately stored after learning has occurred. 156

reticular formation Network of neurons extending from the medulla to the forebrain centers of incoming information; sometimes the reticular formation is referred to as the reticular activating system (RAS). 33

retina A patch of tissue in which lie the rods and cones of the eye; the "film" of the eye. 84

retinal disparity Binocular cue in which each eye receives slightly different sensory information which must be combined for normal vision. 92

retrieval The process of pulling information out of the memory system. 157

retroactive interference Interference caused by information learned after the material of interest. 168

retrograde amnesia Forgetting information recently learned because of disruptive stimulus such as electric shock. 173

reversal The ability to work a problem backwards. 62

reversible figure In perception, a situation in which the figure and ground seem to reverse themselves; an illusion in which objects alternate as the main figure. 89

review Going over material to make sure you know it. 170

rhodopsin Photosensitive pigment that breaks down into chemicals which stimulate neurons sending visual messages to the brain. 84

risky-shift The tendency for groups to make riskier decisions than individuals. 364

rods One type of vision receptor; rods respond to differences in brightness but not to color variations. 84

romantic love Knox's theory that this type of love is characterized by excitement, arousal, and urgency. 241

rooting reflex Reflex that occurs when you touch a baby's cheek and he turns his head toward the source. 53

Rorschach Inkblot Test A projective personality test in which subjects are asked to discuss what they see in cards containing blots of ink. 273

rules In concept formation, what tells us how the features must be combined for a particular concept. 183

S

saccule Receptor located inside the inner ear that is involved in the vestibular sense of balance. 103

sadistic personality disorder Proposed DSM diagnostic category in which a person shows continual cruel, demeaning, aggressive behavior toward other people. 306

safety needs Second level of motives in Maslow's hierarchy; includes security, stability, dependency, protection, freedom from fear and anxiety and the need for structure and order. 216

sample Actual subjects that are used in a study. 24

sample size The size of the group of subjects used in a research study. 18

sampling technique In research, a method of selecting subjects that meet some criterion. A random sampling technique assures that each individual in a population has an equal chance of being selected. 16

saturation The purity of a hue; a hue from one wavelength is high in saturation. 83

savings (relearning) Measure of retention in which the subject first learns a task and then is required to relearn it; if it takes less time to relearn, savings has occurred. 168

scalloping effect When FI (fixed interval) responses are graphed, a pattern emerges in which the subject does not respond immediately after the reinforcement but increases frequency of responding as the interval continues; this produces a scalloping. 142

Schachter-Singer theory of emotion Theory of emotion which states that we interpret our arousal according to our environment and label our emotions accordingly. 237

scheme A unit of knowledge that the person possess; used in Piaget's cognitive development theory. 60

schizophrenia Severe psychotic disorder which is characterized by disruptions in thinking, perception, and emotion. 314

school of thought An approach to a discipline containing certain beliefs and methods. 9

school psychologists Give psychological tests to students, consult with students, teachers, and parents, and try to help students adjust to academic requirements. 392

school psychology Subfield in which psychologists are responsible for administering and interpreting tests for students, and consulting with teachers about student academic needs. 13

scientific method An attitude and procedure which scientists use to conduct research. The steps include: stating the problem, forming the hypothesis, collecting the information, evaluating the information, and drawing conclusions. 15

secondary reinforcement Reinforcement that is effective only after it has been associated with a primary reinforcer; also called conditioned reinforcement. 143

secondary traits In Allport's personality theory, the less important situation-specific traits that help round out personality; include attitudes, skills, and behavior patterns. 263

secure attachment Type of infant-parent attachment in which the infant actively seeks contact with the parent. 57

selective attention The perceptual process of screening out irrelevant information while focusing on significant stimuli in the environment. 78, 159

selective breeding (artificial selection) Procedure used in genetics in which similar animals are mated for many generations. 44

self In Rogers's humanistic personality theory, the individual's perception of "I" or "me" in relation to others. 266

self-actualization A humanistic term describing the state in which all of an individual's capacities are developed fully. Fifth and highest level of motives in Maslow's hierarchy; this level, the realization of one's potential, is rarely reached. 217, 266

self-actualized person A humanistic term describing the person who has met the demands placed upon him or her. 267

self-concept An individual's knowledge of who he or she is. 59

self-defeating personality disorder Proposed DSM diagnostic category in which a person shows a pattern of self-defeating behavior. 306

self-determination Part of Deci's intrinsic motivation theory which states rewards that help people believe they have competency can increase intrinsic motivation. 225

self-efficacy An individual's sense of self-worth and success in adjusting to the world. 269

self-perception theory Attitude theory which states that attitudes are based on an individual's perceptions of his or her own behavior. 354

self-regard In Rogers's humanistic personality theory, the image and perceived worth of one's self. 266

semantic differential Testing procedure in which a subject is required to evaluate a person by selecting which of a pair of traits is more descriptive. 347

semantic memory Type of long-term memory that can use cognitive activities, such as everyday knowledge; a subsystem of procedural memory. 163

semantics The meaning of language. 179

semicircular canals Canals in the inner ear which are receptors for the vestibular sense. 103

sensation The passive process in which stimuli are received by sense receptors and transformed into neural impulses that can be carried through the nervous system; first stage in becoming aware of environment. 78

sensation seeking Theory which states that people will seek stimulation until they reach their optimum, after which they will avoid it. 215

sense organs Specialized groups of cells that function to receive information from the environment; include eyes, nose, ears, and tongue. 28

sense receptors Structures at the end of neurons directly affected by environmental stimuli. 78

sensitivity training group (T-group) Therapy group that has the goal of making participants more aware of themselves and their ideas. 336

sensorimotor period Period in cognitive development; first two years, during which the infant learns to coordinate sensory experiences with motor activities. 60

sensory adaptation Tendency of the sense organs to adjust to continuous stimulation by reducing their functioning; a stimulus that once caused sensation and no longer does. 81

sensory deprivation Situation in which the norms of environmental sensory stimuli available to an individual are drastically reduced. 76, 223

sensory division A part of the somatic nervous system that carries messages from the sense organs to the central nervous system. 38

sensory memory The memory store that sensory information first enters in the memory system. 158

sensory neuron (also called afferent neuron) A neuron that carries messages from the sense organs toward the central nervous system. 29

separate-storage model Memory model of information processing in which distinct systems are believed to be responsible for memory; usually includes sensory register, short-term store, and long-term store. 158

septal area Brain structure in the limbic system that is involved in fear, aggression, and other social behaviors. 34

serial learning A verbal learning procedure in which the stimuli are always presented in the same order, and the subject has to learn them in the order in which they are presented. 166

serial position effect Finding of Ebbinghaus that people remember words at the beginning and end of a list better than those in the middle. 167

serotonin Neurotransmitter involved in sleep, motivation, and perception. 30

set-point theory Theory of obesity which suggests that obese people have a hypothalamus which maintains their weight at a point higher than normal. 219

severe retardation Level of retardation which includes individuals with IQs of between 20 and 35. 202

sex chromosomes Chromosomes that carry genes that determine the genetic sex of the individual. 42

sex roles The behaviors and attitudes that are determined to be appropriate for one sex or the other. 56, 247

sex stereotypes A prejudiced rigid mental image of what males and females are like. 356

sexual arousal disorder Sexual dysfunction in which the male is unable to attain or maintain erection or the female is unable to attain or maintain lubrication. 251

sexual differentiation Process in which the embryo becomes a male or female. If XY chromosomes are present, testosterone produces a male; otherwise a female is produced. 52

sexual dysfunctions Problems in normal sexual behavior, usually characterized by inhibitions in sexual arousal or problems in the sexual response cycle. 251

sexual masochism A paraphilia in which an individual receives sexual gratification by receiving pain. 320

sexual sadism A paraphilia in which an individual receives sexual gratification by inflicting pain on the partner. 320

shape constancy The tendency to perceive familiar objects as having a permanent shape, even if we look at the objects from different angles. 87

shaping In operant conditioning, the gradual process of reinforcing behaviors that get closer to some final desired behavior. Shaping is also called successive approximation. 139

short-term memory The memory store, with a capacity of about 7 items and enduring for up to 30 seconds, which handles current information. 159

shyness An uncomfortable feeling in the presence of other people; when we are shy, we lack confidence in our ability to act appropriately in social situations. 290

signal detection Theory and method in which the subject's behavior in detecting threshold is treated as a form of decision making. 82

similarity Gestalt principle in which similar stimuli are perceived as a unit. 90

simple phobias Excessive irrational fears that do not fall into other specific categories; fear of dogs, insects, snakes, or closed-in places, for example. 308

simultaneous conditioning A procedure in classical conditioning in which the CS and US are presented at exactly the same time. 133

situation anxiety Anxiety which is associated with a particular situation or event. 285

situational factors The external factors in determining causes of behavior. 348

Sixteen Personality Factor Questionnaire (16PF) Cattell's personality test designed to measure source traits. 273

size constancy Tendency to perceive objects as the same size even though the retinal size changes. 88

size perspective Monocular depth cue in which we normally interpret distance by the relative size of an object; the smaller an object, the farther away it seems. 91

skewed A distribution in which there are more scores at the high or low end. 24

skin senses Senses with receptors in or under the body's skin; include pressure, pain, cold, and warmth. 100

Skinner box Animal cage developed by B. F. Skinner which has a lever that triggers reinforcement for a subject. 140

sleep apnea A sleep disorder in which the person stops breathing and wakes up immediately after falling asleep. 114

sleep disorders Problems that involve sleeping activity. 115

sleep terror disorder (pavor nocturnus) NREM sleep disorder in which the person (usually a child) wakes up screaming and terrified, but cannot recall why. 115

sleepwalking (somnambulism) NREM sleep disorder in which the person walks in his or her sleep. 115

Snellen eye chart A popular eye test which measures visual acuity. 85

social cognition The process of understanding other people and ourselves by forming and utilizing information about the social world. 346

social comparison Theory proposed by Festinger which states that we have a tendency to compare our behavior to others to ensure that we are conforming. 357

social demands Demands made on a person by others. 56

social distance One of Hall's interpersonal distance categories—4 to 12 feet. 387

social exchange theory Theory of interpersonal relationships which states that people evaluate the costs and rewards of their relationships and act accordingly. 239

social facilitation Phenomenon in which the presence of others increases dominant behavior patterns in an individual; Zajonc's theory states that the presence of others enhances the emission of the dominant response of the individual. 364

social influence Influence designed to change the attitudes or behavior of other people; include conformity, compliance, and obedience. 356

social leader The one who tries to keep the people in a group happy with one another; the group maintenance leader. 367

social learning theory Social psychology theory which states that reinforcement is involved in motivation rather than learning; proposes that aggression is a form of learned behavior. 370

social loafing Each individual in a group puts in less effort than if he or she were acting alone. 364

social phobia Excessive irrational fear and embarrassment when interacting with other people. Social phobias may include fear of assertive behavior, fear of making mistakes, or fear of public speaking. 308

social psychology The study of how an individual's behavior, thoughts, and feelings are influenced by other people. 13, 346

sociobiology Study of the genetic basis of social behavior. 214

sociological role theory Theory of hypnosis that states that hypnotized subjects are in a normal state of consciousness and are trying to meet role expectations set up by the hypnotist and society. 122

soluble Ability of chemicals to dissolve in liquid solution. 100

soma The central portion of a body cell; includes the nucleus and genes. 29

somatic nervous system The part of the peripheral nervous system that carries messages from the sense organs and relays information that directs the voluntary movements of the skeletal muscles. 38

somatization disorder Somatoform disorder in which a person has medical complaints for which no physical cause is evident; sometimes called Briquet's syndrome. 318

somatoform disorders Disorders characterized by physical symptoms for which there are no obvious physical causes. 318

somatoform pain disorder Disorder in which the individual complains of severe, long-lasting pain for which there is no organic cause. 318

sound waves Rapid changes in air pressure caused by vibrating object in contact with the air. 96

source traits In Cattell's personality theory, the traits which are basic to the core of an individual's personality. 265

species-specific Behavior or trait shown by all members of a given species. 211

specific attachment phase Stage at about six months, in which the baby becomes attached to a specific person. 57

spinal cord Bundles of nerves that form a communication link between the brain and the peripheral nervous system; housed in the spinal backbone. 32

spinal nerves The peripheral nerves that connect with the central nervous system through the spinal cord. 32

split-brain research Popular name for Sperry's research on the syndrome of hemisphere deconnection; research on individuals with the corpus callosum severed. Normal functioning breaks down in split-brain subjects when different information is presented to each hemisphere. 35

spontaneous recovery In conditioning, the reappearance of a behavior that had disappeared during extinction. 134

sports psychology The field in which principles of psychology are applied to sports activities. 391

SQ3R A technique to improve learning and memory. Components include survey, question, read, recite, and review. 173

Stage 1 NREM sleep stage during which a person makes transition from relaxation to sleep; EEG characterized by theta activity with a frequency of 4–6 Hz. 109

Stage 2 NREM sleep stage characterized by EEG theta activity and sleep spindles, which are brief bursts of 12–14 Hz waves; people spend 50% of sleep time in Stage 2. 109

Stage 3 NREM sleep stage characterized by sleep spindles and delta activity of 1–3 Hz. 109

Stage 4 Deepest NREM sleep stage characterized by over 50% delta activity of 1–3 Hz. 109

stage of exhaustion Third stage in Selye's general adaptation syndrome. As the body continues to resist stress, it depletes its energy resources and the person becomes exhausted. 286

stage of resistance Second stage in Selye's general adaptation syndrome. When stress is prolonged, the body builds some resistance to the effects of stress. 286

standard deviation Measure of variability that describes how scores are distributed around the distribution mean. 23

standardization The process of obtaining a representative sample of scores in the population so that a particular score can be interpreted correctly. 193, 271

Stanford-Binet Intelligence Scale An intelligence test first revised by Lewis Terman at Stanford University in 1916; still a popular test used today. 194

state-dependent learning Situation in which what is learned in one state can only be remembered when the person is in that state. 172

statistical model The approach to abnormal psychology which views behavior whose frequency is vastly different from the normal population as abnormal. 306

statistically significant In inferential statistics, a finding that the independent variable did influence greatly the outcome of the experimental and control group. 24

stereochemical theory Theory of olfactory coding which states that the odor receptors have holes the same shape as the odor molecules. 99

stereotype An exaggerated and rigid mental image of a particular class of persons or objects. 355

stimulants Drugs that have an arousing effect on the central nervous system and the body. 118

stimulus A unit of the environment which causes a response in an individual; more specifically, a physical or chemical agent acting on an appropriate sense receptor. 130

stimulus discrimination Responding to relevant stimuli. 135

stimulus generalization Responding to stimuli similar to the stimulus that had caused the response. 134

stimulus motives Motivating factors that are internal and unlearned, but do not appear to have a physiological basis; stimulus motives cause an individual to seek out sensory stimulation through interaction with the environment. 223

stimulus trace The perceptual persistence of a stimulus after it is no longer present. 158

storage The process that keeps information in the memory system. 157

stranger anxiety Infants about eight or nine months of age begin to show a fear of strangers by crying when an unfamiliar person is present. 57

strategies Plans for attacking problems. 187

stress Anything that produces demands on us to adjust; the demands tax our capacity and threaten our well-being. 280

stress innoculation Technique for dealing with stress through education, rehearsal, and implementation. 297

stroboscopic motion Perception of movement when a series of still pictures are seen rapidly; each successive one is slightly different from the earlier one; the basis of movies. 93

Strong-Campbell Interest Inventory (SCII) An objective personality test which compares people's personalities to groups which achieve success in certain occupations. 272

structural family therapy Family therapy in which the emphasis is on modifying the organizational structure of the family so members can relate to one another more positively. 336

structuralism First school of thought in psychology; studied conscious experience to discover the structure of the mind. 8

structured interview An interview in which a standard set of questions is asked. 271

subject bias Source of potential error in an experiment from the action or expectancy of a subject; a subject might influence the experimental results in ways that masks the true outcome. 19

subjective organization Long-term memory procedures in which the individual provides a personal method of organizing information to be memorized. 163

sublimation Defense mechanism; socially undesirable urges redirected into socially acceptable behavior. 295

substantia-gelatinosa Area of the spinal cord which acts as a gate for pain. 101

successive approximation Synonym for shaping; in operant conditioning, the gradual process of reinforcing behaviors that get closer to some final desired behavior. 139

sucking reflex Reflex that occurs when something touches the baby's lips and he attempts sucking motions. 53

sudden infant death syndrome Situation in which a seemingly healthy infant dies suddenly in its sleep; also called crib death or SIDS. 115

superego Freud's representation of conscience. 260

superiority complex Adler's personality concept which states that when people try to compensate for their weaknesses, they sometimes overcompensate and exaggerate their abilities and characteristics. 262

suppression Defense mechanism by which the individual consciously avoids thinking about something as a way of dealing with stressful situations. 294

surface structure The sequence of morphemes we hear or see in a sentence. 179

surface traits In Cattell's personality theory, the observable characteristics of a person's behavior and personality. 265

survey Research method in which written questions are given to people for their responses. 16

swallowing reflex Reflex that occurs when something is in a baby's mouth and he or she forces it down his or her throat. 53

symbolization In Freud's dream theory, the process of converting the latent content of a dream into manifest symbols. 113

sympathetic nervous system The branch of the autonomic nervous system that is more active in emergencies; it causes a general arousal and increased breathing, heart rate, and blood pressure. 39

synapse The space between the axon of one neuron and the dendrites of the next. 30

syndrome of hemisphere deconnection Research of Roger Sperry on patients whose cerebral hemispheres act independently because the corpus callosum has been severed; also called split-brain research. 35

syntax A subset of rules of grammar that governs the order of words in sentences. 179

systematic desensitization Application of counterconditioning, in which the individual overcomes anxiety by learning to relax in the presence of stimuli that had once made him or her unbearably nervous. 331

T

task leader Leadership orientation in which the leader tries to get the work accomplished by directing members to carry out their tasks efficiently. 367

task-motivation theory Theory of hypnosis that states that hypnotism is not an altered state of consciousness but rather is a normal state in which the subject is motivated to attend to the suggestions of the hypnotist. 122

task-oriented coping Adjustment responses in which the person evaluates a stressful situation objectively, and then formulates a plan with which to solve the problem. 296

taste buds Receptors for sense of taste; taste buds are located on top and sides of the tongue. 100

tectorial membrane Organ in the ear above the organ of Corti. When basilar membrane hair cells brush against it, neural impulses are formed in the auditory nerve endings. 97

telegraphic speech Speech of children in which they use two-word sentences. 180

temperament Emotional part of personality; ways of responding to the environment that begin in infancy. 55

temporal lobes The section of the cerebral cortex of the brain in which auditory sensations are interpreted. 34, 97

test Research method of assessing a person's interests, personality, abilities, or intelligence in a standard form. 17

test of significance An inferential statistical technique used to determine whether the difference in scores between the experimental and control groups is really due to the effects of the independent variable or to random chance. If the probability of an outcome is low, we say that outcome is significant. 24

testes Male reproductive glands. 41

texture gradient Monocular depth cue in which small objects close to us show more detail than objects farther away. 92

thalamus The part of the forebrain involved in relay of sensory information. 34

thanatos Freud's term for a destructive instinct such as aggression; also called death instinct. 212, 260

THC delta-9-tetrahydrocannabinol The active ingredient of the cannabis marijuana plant. 121

Thematic Apperception Test (TAT) Projective personality test in which subjects are shown pictures of people in everyday settings; subjects must make up a story about the people portrayed. 225, 275

theory of social impact Latané's theory of social behavior; it states that each member of a group shares the responsibility equally. 364

Theory X Theory of McGregor stating the worker dislikes work and must be forced to do it. 383

Theory Y The humanistic approach to human motivation in a work environment; theory of McGregor. 383

therapy In psychology, the treatment of behavior problems; two major types of therapy include psychotherapy and biological therapy. 324

thinking The mental activity of manipulating symbols. 182

threshold The minimum strength of a stimulus required for a neuron to fire. 30

thyroid gland Gland that secretes thyroxin, a hormone that helps determine the rate of metabolism in the body. 40

thyroxin A hormone secreted by the thyroid gland that influences the rate of metabolism. 40

timbre Complexity of the mixture of sound waves. 96

time and motion studies In engineering psychology, studies which analyze the time it takes to perform an action and the movements which go into the action. 384

tip-of-the-tongue phenomenon A phenomenon in which the closer a person comes to recalling something, the more accurately he or she can remember details, such as the number of syllables or letters. 164

TM (transcendental meditation) A form of yoga in which the person repeats a specific sound over a period of time while trying to block out all other stimuli. 123

token economy A behavior therapy in which desired behaviors are reinforced immediately with tokens that can be exchanged at a later time for desired rewards, such as food or recreational privileges. 147, 331

tolerance When greater doses of drugs are necessary to produce same effects. 117

top-down processing The psycholinguistic process of communicating by beginning with a meaningful thought, selecting phrases to express the idea, and producing speech sounds that make up the words and phrases of our sentences. 179

trace conditioning A procedure in classical conditioning in which the CS is a discrete event that is presented and terminated before the US is presented. 133

trait A distinctive and stable attribute found in people. 263

trait anxiety Anxiety which is long-lasting; a relatively stable personality characteristic. 285

trance theory A theory of hypnosis that indicates that it involves an altered state of consciousness. 122

transduction The process of changing the stimulus energy from the environment into neural impulses that travel through the nervous system. 79

transference Psychoanalytic term used when a patient projects his feelings onto the therapist. 326

transformational grammar rules The rules that allow us to take ideas (deep structures) and convert them into meaningful sentences (surface structures). 179

transsexualism A condition in which a person feels trapped in the body of the wrong sex. 251

transvestic fetishism Paraphilia that involves sexual gratification from cross-dressing; usually exhibited in a heterosexual man who wears women's clothes when alone. 320

traveling wave principle Concept that sound waves traveling through the cochlea move the basilar membrane at a location that corresponds to the particular pitch. 98

trial and error learning Trying various behaviors in a situation until the solution is hit upon; past experiences lead us to try different responses until we are successful. 138

triangular theory of love Sternberg's theory that love consists of intimacy, passion, and decision/commitment. 242

triarchic theory Robert Sternberg's theory of intelligence which states that it consists of three parts: componential, experiential, and contextual subtheories. 191

trichromat A person with normal color vision. 86

trichromatic theory Young-Helmholtz idea of color vision. 86

trucking game Social simulation developed to measure bargaining of individuals in a social situation (delivering goods by truck). 365

Type A behavior Behavior shown by a particular type of individual; a personality pattern of behavior which can lead to stress and heart disease. 292

Type B behavior Behavior shown by an individual who is able to relax. 292

U

ulcer   A hole in the lining of the stomach or duodenum; can be caused or aggravated by stress. 291

ultrasound   Testing procedure in which extremely high-pitched sound waves are bounced off the embryo or fetus to produce a picture. 52

unconditional positive regard   Part of Rogers's personality theory; in person-centered therapy, total acceptance of the patient by the therapist. 267, 327

unconditioned response (UR)   An automatic reaction elicited by a stimulus. 132

unconditioned stimulus (US)   Any stimulus that elicits an automatic or reflexive reaction in an individual; it does not have to be learned in the present situation. 132

unconscious mind   In Freud's psychoanalytic theory of personality, the part of personality that is unavailable to us; Freud suggests that instincts and unpleasant memories are stored in the unconscious mind. 108

undifferentiated schizophrenia   Type of schizophrenia which does not fit into any particular category, or fits into more than one category. 315

unstructured interview   An interview in which there is no specific list of questions that must be followed. 271

utricle   Receptor for vestibular sense in the inner ear. 103

V

validity   The degree to which you actually measure what you intend to measure. 21, 193

variability   In statistics, variability measures the range of the scores. 23

variable interval (VI) schedule   Schedule of reinforcement in which the subject is reinforced for the first response given after a certain time interval, with the interval being different for each trial. 142

variable ratio (VR) schedule   Schedule of reinforcement in which the subject is given reinforcement after a varying number of responses; the number of responses required for reinforcement is different for every trial. 143

ventromedial hypothalamus (VMH)   Part of the hypothalamus involved in stopping eating behavior. 218

verbal learning   Learning that involves responses to words or symbols. 166

vestibular sense   Sense that helps us to keep our balance. 103

vicarious reinforcement   In the modeling theory of personality, the pleasureable effects of observing someone similar to oneself perform successfully. 269

visual acuity   Ability of a person to discriminate fine details when looking at something. 85

visual capture   The tendency for vision to dominate the other senses. 83

visual cliff   Apparatus used to test depth perception. 92

volley principle   Theory of hearing that states that individual neurons fire in sequence, thus increasing the total frequency of impulses possible to send to the brain. 97

voyeurism   A paraphilia in which an individual receives sexual satisfaction from looking at naked people without their knowledge or consent. 320

vulnerability-stress model   Theory of schizophrenia which states that some people have a biological tendency to develop schizophrenia if they are stressed enough by their environment. 317

W

waking consciousness   The awareness of sensations and thoughts while the person is awake and alert; also called conscious awareness. 108

wave amplitude   The height of a light wave amplitude determines the experience of brightness. 83

wavelength   The wavelength of light waves is the distance between any point on a wave and the corresponding point of the wave in the next cycle; wavelength determines experience of hue. 83

Weber's Law   Law that states that the difference threshold depends on the ratio of the intensity of one stimulus to another rather than on an absolute difference. 82

Wechsler Adult Intelligence Scale (WAIS)   An intelligence test for adults, first published by David Wechsler in 1955; it contains verbal and performance subscales. 195

well-being   A subjective positive emotional state characterized by general life satisfaction. 294

Wernicke's area   Area of the brain important in speech perception. 99

Whorfian hypothesis   Linguistic relativity hypothesis of Benjamin Whorf; language influences thought. 183

withdrawal   Unpleasant physical reactions a drug user experiences when he or she stops taking the drug. 117

within-subject experiment   An experimental design in which each subject is given all treatments, including the control condition; subjects serve in both experimental and control groups. 18

Y

Yerkes-Dodson Law   Popular idea that performance is best when arousal is at a medium level. 215

yoga   A form of meditation in which the individual modifies autonomic processes and focuses on a visual object. 123

Z

Zen   A form of meditation in which the individual focuses on breathing. 123

zygote   A fertilized egg; at conception a sperm fertilizes an egg to produce the zygote. 42

zygote stage   First stage in prenatal development; the zygote divides and travels down the fallopian tube to become attached to the wall of the uterus. 50

References

A

Abel, E. (1984). Opiates and sex. *Journal of Psychoactive Drugs, 16*, 205-216.

Abram, S.R., & Taylor, M. (1983). The genetics of schizophrenia: A reassessment using modern criteria. *American Journal of Psychiatry, 140*, 171-175.

Abramson, L., Seligman, M.E.P., & Teasdale, J. (1978). Learned helplessness in humans: Critique and reformulation. *Journal of Abnormal Psychology, 87*, 49-74.

Adams, J. (1980). *Learning and memory: An introduction.* Homewood, IL: Dorsey.

Adler, A. (1939). *Social interest.* New York: Putnam.

Adorno, T.W., Frankel-Brunswick, E., Levinson, D.S., & Sanford, R.N. (1950). *The authoritarian personality.* New York: Harper & Row.

Agnew, J.W., Jr., Webb, W.B., & Williams, R.L. (1964). The effects of stage four sleep deprivation. *Electroencephalography and Clinical Neurophysiology, 17*, 68-70.

Ainsworth, M.D.S. (1979). Infant-mother attachment. *American Psychologist, 34*, 932-937.

Ainsworth, M., Blechar, M., Waters, E., & Wall, S. (1978). *Patterns of attachment: A psychological study of the strange situation.* Hillsdale, NJ: Erlbaum.

Alcock, J. (1984). *Animal behavior: An evolutionary approach* (3rd ed.). Sunderland, MA: Sinauer.

Alderman, R.B. (1980). Strategies for motivating young athletes. In W. Straub (Ed.), *Sports psychology: An analysis of athletes' behavior.* Ithaca, NY: Mouvement.

Alexander, A.B. (1981). Asthma. In S. Haynes & L. Gannon (Eds.), *Psychosomatic disorders.* New York: Praeger.

Allport, G.W. (1937). *Personality: A psychological interpretation.* New York: Holt, Rinehart & Winston.

Allport, G.W. (1954). *The nature of prejudice.* Garden City, NY: Doubleday.

Allport, G.W. (1961). *Patterns and growth in personality.* New York: Holt, Rinehart & Winston.

Allport, G.W. (1985). The historical background of social psychology. In G. Lindzey & E. Aronson (Eds.), *Handbook of social psychology* (Vol. 1) (3rd ed.). New York: Random House.

Altman, I. (1975). *The environment and social behavior: Privacy, personal space, territory and crowding.* Monterey, CA: Brooks-Cole.

Amabile, T.M. (1983). *The social psychology of creativity.* New York: Springer-Verlag.

Amato, P. (1985). An investigation of planned helping behavior. *Journal of Research in Personality, 19*, 232-252.

Amelang, M., & Borkenau, P. (1982). On the factor structure and external validity of some questionnaire scales measuring dimensions of extraversion and neuroticism. *Zeitschrift fur Differentielle und Diagnostische Psychologie, 3*, 119-146.

American Heart Association (1984). *Heart facts, 1984.* Dallas: American Heart Association.

American Psychiatric Association (1987). *Diagnostic and statistical manual of mental disorders* (3rd ed., rev.). Washington, DC: American Psychiatric Association.

American Psychiatric Association. (1980). *Diagnostic and statistical manual of mental disorders* (3rd ed.). Washington, DC: Author.

American Psychological Association. (1986). *Careers in psychology.* Washington, DC: Author.

Amoore, J.E. (1970). *Molecular basis of odor.* Springfield, IL: Thomas.

Amoore, J.E., Johnston, J.W., Jr., & Rubin, M. (1964). The stereochemical theory of odor. *Scientific American, 210*, 42-49.

Anastasi, A. (1988). *Psychological testing.* (6th ed.). New York: Macmillan.

Anderson, J.R. (1985). *Cognitive psychology and its implications.* New York: Freeman.

Angrist, B. (1983). Psychoses induced by central nervous system stimulants and related drugs. In I. Creese (Ed.), *Stimulants: Neurochemical, behavioral and clinical perspectives.* New York: Raven.

Aronson, E. (1988). *The social animal* (5th ed.). New York: Freeman.

Asch, S. (1946). Forming impressions of personality. *Journal of Abnormal and Social Psychology, 41*, 258-290.

Asch, S. (1955). Opinions and social pressure. *Scientific American, 193*(5), 31-35.

Aserinsky, E., & Kleitman, N. (1953). Regularly occurring periods of eye motility and concomitant phenomena during sleep. *Science, 118*, 273-274.

Ashton, N., Shaw, M., & Worsham, A. (1980). Affective reactions to interpersonal distances by friends and strangers. *Bulletin of the Psychonomic Society, 15*, 306-308.

Astin, G., Barber, H. (1982). *Rhe rise and fall of national test scores.* New York: Academic Press.

Atchley, R.C. (1985). *Social forces and aging: An introduction to social gerontology.* Belmont, CA: Wadsworth.

Atkinson, J.W. (1981). Studying personality in the context of an advanced motivational psychology. *American Psychologist, 36*, 117-128.

Atkinson, J.W., & Birch, D. (1978). *Introduction to motivation* (2nd ed.). New York: Van Nostrand.

Atkinson, J.W., & Litwin, G. (1960). Achievement motive and test anxiety conceived as motive to approach success and motive to avoid failure. *Journal of Abnormal and Social Psychology, 60*, 52-63.

Atkinson, J.W., & Raynor, J.O. (1978). *Personality, motivation, and achievement.* New York: Halsted Press.

Atkinson, R.C., & Shiffrin, R.M. (1971). The control of short-term memory. *Scientific American, 225*, 82-90.

Averill, J.R. (1969). Autonomic response patterns during sadness and mirth. *Psychophysiology, 5*, 399-414.

Averill, J.R. (1983). Studies on anger and aggression: Implications for theories of emotion. *American Psychologist, 38*, 1145-1160.

Ax, A.F. (1953). The physiological differentiation between fear and anger in humans. *Psychosomatic Medicine, 15*, 433-442.

Axsom, D., & Cooper, J. (1985). Cognitive dissonance and psychotherapy: The role of effort justification in inducing weight loss. *Journal of Experimental Social Psychology, 21*, 149-160.

Ayllon, T., & Azrin, N.H. (1968). *The token economy: A motivational system for therapy and rehabilitation.* East Norwalk, CT: Appleton-Century-Crofts.

Azarin, N. (1959). Some notes on punishment and avoidance. *Journal of the Experimental Analysis of Behavior, 2*, 260.

B

Bachrach, W.H. (1982). Psychological elements of gastrointestinal disorders. In W. Fann, I. Karacan, A. Pokorny, & R. Williams (Eds.), *Phenomenology and treatment of psychophysiological disorders.* New York: Spectrum.

Baddeley, A. (1986). *Working memory.* New York: Oxford University Press.

Bahrick, H.P., Bahrick, P.O., & Wittinger, R.P. (1975). Fifty years of memory for names and faces: A cross-sectional approach. *Journal of Experimental Psychology: General, 104*, 54-75.

Bandura, A. (1973). *Aggression: A social learning analysis.* Englewood Cliffs, NJ: Prentice-Hall.

Bandura, A. (1977). *Social learning theory.* Englewood Cliffs, NJ: Prentice-Hall.

Bandura, A. (1982). Self-efficacy mechanism in human agency. *American Psychologist, 37* 122-147.

Bandura, A. (1986). *Social foundations of thought and action: A social cognitive theory.* Englewood Cliffs, NJ: Prentice-Hall.

Bandura, A., Ross, D., & Ross, S.A. (1961). Transmission of aggression through imitation of aggressive models. *Journal of Abnormal and Social Psychology, 63*, 575-582.

Bandura, A., Ross, D., & Ross, S.A. (1963). Imitation of film-mediated aggressive models. *Journal of Abnormal and Social Psychology, 66*, 3-11.

Banks, M., & Salapatek, P. (1983). Infant visual perception. In M. Haith & J. Campos (Eds.). *Handbook of child psychology* (Vol. 2). New York: Wiley.

Barash, D.P. (1982). *Sociobiology and behavior* (2nd ed.). New York: Elsevier.

Barber, T. (1976). *Advance in altered states of consciousness and human potentialities* (Vol. 1). New York: Psychological Dimensions.

Barber, T.X. (1969). *Hypnosis: A scientific approach.* Princeton, NJ: Van Nostrand.

Bard, P. (1928). A diencephalic mechanism for the expression of rage with special reference to the sympathetic nervous system. *American Journal of Physiology, 84*, 490-515.

Barkley, R.A. (1987). The assessment of attention deficit- hyperactivity disorder. *Behavioral Assessment, 9*, 207-233.

Barlow, D.H., Vermilyea, J., Blanchard, E., Vermilyea, B., & DiNardo, P. (1985). The phenomenon of panic. *Journal of Abnormal Psychology, 94*, 320-328.

Baron, R.A. (1981). Olfaction and human behavior: Effects of a pleasant scent on attraction and social perception. *Personality and Social Psychology Bulletin, 7*, 611-616.

Baron, R.A. (1983). *Behavior in organizations.* Newton, MA: Allyn & Bacon.

Baron, R.A. (1983). The control of human aggression: An optimistic perspective. *Journal of Social and Clinical Psychology, 1*, 97-119.

Baron, R.A. (1983). *Human aggression.* New York: Plenum.

Baron, R.A., & Byrne, D. (1987). *Social psychology: Understanding human interaction* (5th ed.). Newton, MA: Allyn & Bacon.

Baron, R.S. (1986). Distraction-conflict theory: Progress and problems. In L. Berkowitz (Ed.), *Advances in experimental social psychology* (Vol. 20). New York: Academic Press.

Bartol, C. (1983). *Psychology and American law.* Belmont, CA: Wadsworth.

Bartus, R., Dean, R. III, Beer, B., & Lippa, A. (1982). The cholinergic hypothesis of geriatric memory dysfunction. *Science, 217*, 408-417.

Baum, A., Fisher, J., & Solomon, S. (1981). Type of information, familiarity, and the reduction of crowding stress. *Journal of Personality and Social Psychology, 40*, 11-23.

Baumeister, R.F., & Covington, M.V. (1985). Self-esteem persuasion and retrospective distortion of initial attitudes. *Electronic Social Psychology, 1*, 1-22.

Baumrind, D. (1967). Child care practices anteceding three patterns of preschool behavior. *Genetic Psychology Monographs, 75*, 43-88.

Baxter, J.C. (1970). Interpersonal spacing in natural setting. *Sociometry, 33*, 444-456.

Beatty, W., Butters, N., & Janowsky, D. (1986). Patterns of memory failure after scopolamine treatment: Implications for cholinergic hypothesis of dementia. *Behavioral and Neural Biology, 45*, 196-211.

Beck, A.T. (1967). *Depression: Clinical, experimental, and theoretical aspects.* New York: Harper & Row.

Beck, A.T. (1976). *Cognitive therapy and emotional disorders.* New York: International Universities Press.

Beck, A.T. (1985). Theoretical perspectives on clinical anxiety. In A. Tuma & J. Maser (Eds.), *Anxiety and the anxiety disorders.* Hillsdale, NJ: Erlbaum.

Beck, A.T., & Emery, G. (1985). *Anxiety disorders and phobias: A cognitive perspective.* New York: Basic.

Beck, A.T., Hollon, S., Young, J., Bedrosian, R., & Budenz, D. (1985). Treatment of depression with cognitive therapy and amitriplyline. *Archives of General Psychiatry, 42*, 142-148.

Bee, H. (1985). *The developing child* (4th ed.). New York: Harper & Row.

Bekesy, G. von (1960). *Experiments in hearing.* New York: McGraw-Hill.

Bell, A., & Weinberg, M. (1978). *Homosexuality: A study of diversity among men and women.* New York: Simon & Schuster.

Bell, A., Weinberg, M., & Hammersmith, S. (1981). *Sexual preference: A study of human diversity.* New York: Simon & Schuster.

Bellezza, F.S. (1981). Mnemonic devices: Classification, characteristics and criteria. *Review of Educational Research, 51*, 247-275.

Bem, D.J. (1967). Self-perception: An alternative interpretation of cognitive dissonance phenomena. *Psychological Review, 74*, 183-200.

Bem, S.L. (1974). The measurement of psychological androgyny. *Journal of Consulting and Clinical Psychology, 42*, 155-162.

Bem, S.L. (1975). Sex-role adaptability: One consequence of psychological androgyny. *Journal of Personality and Social Psychology, 31*, 634-643.

Bem, S.L. (1987). Masculinity and feminity exist only in the mind of the perceiver. In J. Reinisch, L. Rosenblum, & S. Sanders (Eds.), *Masculinity/feminity: Basic perspectives*. New York: Oxford University Press.

Benjamin, L.T., Jr. (1988). *A history of psychology*. New York: McGraw-Hill.

Bennett, T.L. (1982). *Introduction to physiological psychology*. Monterey, CA: Brooks-Cole.

Benson, A. (1982). The vestibular sensory system. In H. Barlow & J. Mollon (Eds.), *The senses*. London: Cambridge University Press.

Berko, J. (1958). The child's learning of English morphology. *Word, 14*, 150-177.

Berkowitz, L. (1984). Some effects of thoughts on anti- and pro-social influences of media events: A cognitive neo-association analysis. *Psychological Bulletin, 95*, 410-427.

Berlyne, D.E. (1960). *Conflict, arousal, and curiosity*. New York: McGraw-Hill.

Berlyne, D.E. (1966). Curiosity and exploration. *Science, 153*, 25-33.

Bernstein, I. (1978). Learned taste aversions in children receiving chemotherapy. *Science, 200*, 1302-1303.

Bernstein, I.L. (1985). Learned food aversions in the progression of cancer and its treatment. In N. Braverman & P. Bernstein (Eds.), Experimental assessments and clinical application of conditioned food aversions. *Annals of the New York Academy of Sciences* (Vol. 443).

Berscheid, E. (1983). Emotion. In H. Kelley, E. Berscheid, A. Christensen, J. Harvey, T. Huston, G. Levinger, E. McClintock, L. Peplau, & D. Peterson (Eds.), *Close relationships*. New York: Freeman.

Berscheid, E., & Walster, E.H. (1978). *Interpersonal attraction* (2nd ed.). Reading, MA: Addison-Wesley.

Berscheid, E., Dion, K., Walster, E., & Walster, G.W. (1971). Physical attractiveness and dating choice: A test of the matching hypothesis. *Journal of Experimental Social Psychology, 7*, 173-189.

Bettman, J. (1986). Consumer psychology. *Annual Review of Psychology, 37*, 257-289.

Blasi, A. (1980). Bridging moral cognition and moral action: A critical review of the literature. *Psychological Bulletin, 88*, 1-45.

Block, J. (1983). Differential premises arising from differential socialization of the sexes: Some conjecture. *Child Development, 54*, 1335-1354.

Bloom, F.E. (1983). The endorphins: A growing family of pharmacologically pertinent peptides. *Annual Review of Pharmacology and Toxicology, 23*, 151-170.

Bolles, R., & Faneslow, M. (1982). Endorphins and behavior. *Annual Review of Psychology, 33*, 87-101.

Bolles, R.C. (1970). Species-specific defense reactions and avoidance learning. *Psychological Review, 77*, 32-48.

Bolles, R.C. (1975). *Theory of motivation* (2nd ed.). New York: Harper & Row.

Bouchard, T.J. (1981). The study of mental ability using twin and adoption designs. In *Twin research 3: Intelligence, personality, and development*. New York: Liss.

Bouchard, T.J. (1984). Twins reared apart: What they tell us about human diversity. In S. Fox (Ed.), *Individuality and determinism: Clinical and biological basis*. New York: Plenum Press.

Bouchard, T.J., & McGue, M. (1981). Familial studies of intelligence: A review. *Science, 212*, 1055-1059.

Bourne, L., Dominowski, R., Loftus, E., & Healy, A. (1986). *Cognitive processes*. Englewood Cliffs, NJ: Prentice-Hall.

Bower, B. (1985). The infection connection: The controversial role of viruses in schizophrenia is being examined from new angles. *Science News, 128*, 346-347.

Bower, G.H. (1981). Mood and memory. *American Psychologist, 36*, 129-148.

Bowlby, J. (1961). Childhood mourning and its implications for psychiatry. *American Journal of Psychiatry, 118*, 481-498.

Bowlby, J. (1980). *Attachment: Volume 1, Attachment and loss*. New York: Basic Books.

Bradley, R., & Caldwell, B. (1984). The relation of infants' home environments to achievement test performance in first grade: A follow- up study. *Child Development, 55*, 803-809.

Bransford, J.D., & Stein, B.S. (1984). *The IDEAL problem solver: A guide for improving thinking, learning, and creativity*. New York: Freeman.

Braveman, N.S., & Bronstein, P. (Eds.). (1985). Experimental assessments and clinical applications of conditioned food aversions. *Annals of the New York Academy of Sciences* (Vol. 443).

Brecher, E.M. (1972). *Licit and illicit drugs*. Boston: Little, Brown.

Breckler, S.J. (1984). Empirical validation of affect, behavior, and cognition as distinct components of attitude. *Journal of Personality and Social Psychology, 47*, 1191-1205.

Bregman, E. (1934). An attempt to modify the emotional attitudes of infants by the conditioned response technique. *Journal of Genetic Psychology, 45*, 169-198.

Breland, K., & Breland, M. (1961). The misbehavior of organisms. *American Psychologist, 16*, 681-684.

Brennan, J.H., & Hemsley, D.R. (1984). Illusory correlations in paranoid and nonparanoid schizophrenia. *British Journal of Clinical Psychology, 23*, 225-226.

Brewer, M. (1986). The role of ethnocentrism in intergroup conflict: In S. Worchel & W. Austin (Eds.), *Psychology of intergroup relations* (2nd ed.). Chicago: Nelson-Hall.

Brewer, M., & Kramer, R. (1985). The psychology of intergroup attitudes and behavior. *Annual Review of Psychology, 36*, 219-243.

Brewer, M., & Miller, N. (1984). Beyond the contact hypothesis: Theoretical perspectives on desegregation. In N. Miller & M. Brewer (Eds.), *Groups in contact: The psychology of desegregation*. New York: Academic Press.

Brewer, W., & Pani, J. (1983). The structure of human memory. In G.H. Bower (Ed.), *The psychology of learning and motivation: Advances in research and theory* (Vol. 17). New York: Academic Press.

Briddell, D.W., & Wilson, G.T. (1976). Effects of alcohol and expectancy set on male sexual arousal. *Journal of Abnormal Psychology, 85*, 225-234.

Bridges, K.M.B. (1932). Emotional development in early infancy. *Child Development, 3*, 324-341.

Bridges, L.J., Connell, J.P., & Belsky, J. (1988). Similarities and differences in infant-mother and infant-father interaction in the strange situation: A component process analysis. *Developmental Psychology, 24*, 92-100.

Brodsky, S.L. (1988). *The psychology of adjustment and well-being*. New York: Holt, Rinehart & Winston.

Brooks-Gunn, J., & Peterson, A.C. (1983). *Girls at puberty: Biological and psychosocial perspectives*. New York: Plenum Press.

Brown, J. (1958). Some tests of the decay theory of immediate memory. *Quarterly Journal of Experimental Psychology, 10*, 12-21.

Brown, R., & Kulik, J. (1977). Flashbulb memories. *Cognition, 5*, 73-79.

Brown, R.W., & McNeill, D. (1966). The "tip-of-the-tongue" phenomenon. *Journal of Verbal Learning and Verbal Behavior, 5*, 325-337.

Browne, M., & Mahoney, M. (1984). Sport psychology. *Annual Review of Psychology, 35*, 605-626.

Bruner, J., Goodnow, J., & Austin, G. (1956). *A study of thinking*. New York: Wiley.

Buckhout, R. (1980). Nearly 2,000 witnesses can be wrong. *Bulletin of the Psychonomic Society, 16*, 307-310.

Burgess, A. (1963). *A clockwork orange*. New York: Norton.

Burt, C. (1966). The genetic determination of differences in intelligence: A study of monozygotic twins reared together and apart. *British Journal of Psychology, 57*, 137-153.

Busemeyer, J., & Myung, E.J. (1988). A new method for investigating prototype learning. *Journal of Experimental Psychology: Learning, Memory and Cognition, 14*, 3-11.

Bushman, B.J. (1984). Perceived symbols of authority and their influence on compliance. *Journal of Applied Social Psychology, 14*, 501-508.

Butler, R.A., & Harlow, H.F. (1954). Persistence of visual exploration in monkeys. *Journal of Comparative and Physiological Psychology, 47*, 258-263.

Byrne, D., & Kelley, K. (1981). *An introduction to personality* (3rd ed.). Englewood Cliffs, NJ: Prentice-Hall.

Byrne, D., Baskett, G., & Hodges, L. (1971). Behavioral indicators of interpersonal attraction. *Journal of Applied Social Psychology, 1*, 137-149.

C

Cacioppo, J.T., Petty, R.E., Losch, M., & Kim, H.S. (1986). Electromyographic activity over facial muscle regions can differentiate the valence and intensity of affective reactions. *Journal of Personality and Social Psychology, 50*, 260-268.

Cairns, R. (1966). Attachment behavior of mammals. *Psychological Review, 73*, 409-426.

Calhoun, J.B. (1962). Population density and social pathology. *Scientific American, 206*, 139-148.

Cameron, P., Frank, R., Lifter, M., & Morrissey, P. (1968). Cognitive functionings of college students in a general psychology class. Paper presented at the American Psychological Association, San Francisco.

Campbell, D.P. (1974). *Manual for the Strong-Campbell interest inventory*. Stanford, CA: Stanford University Press.

Cannon, W.B. (1927). The James-Lange theory of emotions: A critical examination and an alternative theory. *American Journal of Psychology, 39*, 106-124.

Cannon, W.B. (1932). *The wisdom of the body*. New York: Norton.

Cannon, W.B. (1957). Voodoo death. *Psychosomatic Medicine, 19*, 182-190.

Cannon, W.B., & Washburn, A.L. (1912). An explanation of hunger. *American Journal of Physiology, 29*, 441-454.

Carlson, N.R. (1986). *Physiology of behavior* (3rd ed.). Newton, MA: Allyn & Bacon.

Carson, R.C., Butcher, J.N., & Coleman, J.C. (1988). *Abnormal psychology and modern life* (8th ed.). Glenview, IL: Scott, Foresman.

Carter, R. (1978). Sleep and dreams, part II. *Annual Review of Psychology, 29*, 223-252.

Cattell, R.B. (1965). *The scientific analysis of personality*. Baltimore: Penguin.

Cattell, R.B. (1971). *Abilities: Their structure, growth and action*. Boston: Houghton Mifflin.

Cattell, R.B., Eber, H.W., & Tatsuoka, M.M. (1970). *Handbook for the 16PF questionnaire*. Champaign, IL: Institute for Personality and Ability Testing.

Cermak, L. (1975). *Improving your memory*. New York: Norton.

Cernoch, J., & Porter, R. (1985). Recognition of maternal axillary odors by infants. *Child Development, 56*, 1593-1598.

Charlesworth, E., & Nathan, R. (1982). *Stress management: A comprehensive guide to wellness*. Houston: Biobehavioral Press.

Chase, M. (1986). Overview of sleep research, circa 1985. *Sleep, 9*, 452-457.

Chase, M., & Morales, F. (1983). Subthreshold excitatory activity and motorneuron discharge during REM periods of active sleep. *Science, 221*, 1195-1198.

Chesney, M.A., Eagleston, J.R., & Rosenman, R.H. (1981). Type A behavior: Assessment and intervention. In C. Prokop & L. Bradley (Eds.), *Medical psychology: Contributions to behavioral medicine*. New York: Academic Press.

Childers, T., & Houston, M. (1984). Conditions for a picture superiority effect on consumer memory. *Journal of Consumer Research, 11*, 643-654.

Chomsky, N. (1965). *Aspects of the theory of syntax*. Cambridge, MA: MIT Press.

Chomsky, N. (1968). *Language and mind*. New York: Harcourt Brace Jovanovich.

Chorover, S., & Schiller, P. (1965). Short-term retrograde amnesia in rats. *Journal of Comparative and Physiological Psychology, 59*, 73-78.

Christie, R. (1976). Probability vs. precedence: The social psychology of jury selection. In G. Bermant, C. Nemeth, & N. Vidmar (Eds.), *Psychology and the law: Research frontiers*. Lexington, MA: Lexington Books.

Cialdini, R. (1988). *Influence: Science and practice* (2nd ed.). Glenview, IL: Scott, Foresman.

Cialdini, R., & Schroeder, D. (1976). Compliance by legitimizing paltry contributions: When even a penny helps. *Journal of Personality and Social Psychology, 34*, 599-604.

Cialdini, R., Cacioppo, J., Bassett, R., & Miller, J. (1978). Low-ball procedure for producing compliance: Commitment then cost. *Journal of Personality and Social Psychology, 36*, 463-476.

Cialdini, R., Vincent, J., Lewis, S., Catalan, J., Wheeler, D., & Darby, B. (1975). Reciprocal concessions procedure for inducing compliance: The door-in-the-face technique. *Journal of Personality and Social Psychology, 31*, 206-215.

Clark, K.B., & Clark, M.P. (1947). Racial identificiation and preference in Negro children. In T. Newcomb & E. Hartley (Eds.), *Readings in Social Psychology*. New York: Holt.

Clark, K.J., & Horch, K.W. (1986). Kinesthesia. In K. Boff, L. Kaufman, & J.P. Thomas (Eds.), *Handbook of perception and human performance* (Vol. 1). New York: Wiley.

Claxton, C., & Murrell, P. (1987). *Learning styles: Implications for improving educational practices.* ASHE-ERIC Higher Education Report No. 4. Washington, DC: Association for the Study of Higher Education.

Cohen, S., & Hoberman, H. (1983). Positive events and social supports as buffers of life change stress. *Journal of Applied Social Psychology, 13,* 99-125.

Cohen, S., & Wills, T. (1985). Stress, social support, and the buffering hypothesis. *Psychological Bulletin, 98,* 310-357.

Cohen, S., Evans, G., Stokols, D., & Krantz, D. (1986). *Behavior, health and environmental stress.* New York: Plenum.

Cohen, S., Glass, D.C., & Singer, J.E. (1986). Apartment noise, auditory discrimination, and reading ability in children. *Journal of Experimental Social Psychology, 9,* 407-422.

Colangelo, N., Kelly, K., & Schrepfer, R. (1987). A comparison of gifted, general, and special learning needs students on academic and social self-concept. *Journal of Counseling and Development, 66,* 73-77.

Coles, C., Smith, I., Lancaster, J., & Falek, A. (1987). Persistence over the first month of neurobehavioral differences in infants exposed to alcohol prenatally. *Infant Behavior and Development, 10,* 23-37.

Collings, V. (1974). Human taste response as a function of locus on the tongue and soft palate. *Perception and Psychophysics, 16,* 169-174.

Colt, C.H. (1983, September/October). The enigma of suicide in America. *Harvard Magazine,* pp. 46-66.

Constantian, C.A. (1981). Attitudes, beliefs, and behavior in regard to spending time alone. Unpublished doctoral dissertation, Harvard University.

Coltheart, V., & Evans, J. (1981). An investigation of semantic memory in individuals. *Memory and Cognition, 9,* 524-532.

Conger, J., & Peterson, A. (1984). *Adolescence and youth* (3rd ed.). New York: Harper & Row.

Cook, S. (1984). Cooperative interaction in multiethnic contexts. In N. Miller & M. Brewer (Eds.), *Groups in conflict: The psychology of desegregation.* New York: Academic Press.

Cookerly, J.R. (1980). Does marital therapy do any lasting good? *Journal of Marital and Family Therapy, 6,* 393-397.

Cooper, J., & Fazio, R. (1984). A new look at dissonance theory. *Advances in Experimental Social Psychology, 17,* 229-266.

Cooper, J., Bloom, F., & Roth, R. (1986). *The biochemical basis of neuropharmacology* (5th ed.). New York: Oxford University Press.

Cooper, R., & Zubek, J. (1958). Effects of enriched and restricted early environments on the learning ability of bright and dull rats. *Canadian Journal of Psychology, 12,* 159-164.

Coppen, A., Metcalfe, M., & Wood, K. (1982). Lithium. In E. Pakel (Ed.), *Handbook of affective disorders.* New York: Guilford.

Coren, S., & Girgus, J.S. (1978). *Seeing is deceiving.* Hillsdale, NJ: Erlbaum.

Costa, P.T., Jr., & McCrae, R.R. (1980). Still stable after all these years: Personality as a key to some issues in adulthood and old age. In P. Baltes & O. Brim (Eds.), *Life span development and behavior* (Vol. 3). New York: Academic Press.

Costa, P.T., Jr., Zonderman, A.B., McCrae, R.R., & Williams, R.B., Jr. (1985). Content and comprehensiveness in the MMPI: An item factor analysis in a normal adult sample. *Journal of Personality and Social Psychology, 48,* 925-933.

Couch, J.V. (1987). *Fundamentals of statistics for the behavioral sciences* (2nd. ed.). St. Paul, MN: West.

Cowart, B.J. (1981). Development of taste perception in humans: Sensitivity and preference throughout the life span. *Psychological Bulletin, 90,* 43-73.

Cox, H. (1984). *Later life: The realities of aging.* Englewood Cliffs, NJ: Prentice-Hall.

Craik, F., & Lockhart, R. (1972). Levels of processing: A framework for memory research. *Journal of Verbal Learning and Verbal Behavior, 11,* 671-684.

Craik, F., & Watkins, M. (1973). The role of rehearsal in short-term memory. *Journal of Verbal Learning and Verbal Behavior, 12,* 599-607.

Crick, F., & Mitchison, G. (1983). The function of dream sleep. *Nature, 304,* 111-114.

Critelli, J.W. (1987). *Personal growth and effective behavior: The challenge of everyday life.* New York: Holt, Rinehart & Winston.

Crockenburg, S.B. (1972). Creativity tests: A boon or boondoggle for education? *Review of Educational Research, 42,* 27-45.

Crogle, R., & Cooper, J. (1983). Dissonance arousal: Physiological evidence. *Journal of Personality and Social Psychology, 45,* 782-791.

Crusco, A.H., & Wetzel, C.G. (1984). The Midas touch: The effects of interpersonal touch on restaurant tipping. *Personality and Social Psychology Bulletin, 10,* 512-517.

Cunningham, M.R. (1986). Measuring the physical in physical attractiveness: Quasi-experiments on the sociobiology of female facial beauty. *Journal of Personality and Social Psychology, 50,* 925-935.

Curry, J., & Haerer, D. (1981). The positive impact of flextime on employee relations. *The Personnel Administrator, 26,* 62-66.

Curtis, D., & Detert, L. (1981). *How to relax: A holistic approach to stress management.* New York: Mayfield.

Cutler, W.B., Preti, G., Krieger, A., Huggins, G.R., Garcia, C., & Lawley, H.J. (1986). Human axillary secretions influence women's menstrual cycles: The role of donor extract from men. *Hormones and Behavior, 20,* 463-473.

D

Darwin, C. (1859). *The origin of species by means of natural selection.* London: Murray.

Darwin, C. (1965). *The expression of the emotions in man and animals.* Chicago: University of Chicago Press. (Original work published London: Murray, 1872).

Darwin, C.J., Turvey, M.T., & Crowder, R.G. (1972). An auditory analog of the Sperling partial report procedure: Evidence for brief auditory storage. *Cognitive Psychology, 3,* 255-267.

Davies, P. (1985). A critical review of the role of the cholinergic system in human memory and cognition. *Annals of the New York Academy of Sciences, 444,* 212-217.

Davis, J., Laughlin, P., & Lomorita, S. (1976). The social psychology of small groups: Cooperative and mixed-motive interaction. *Annual Review of Psychology, 27,* 502-516.

Davis, R., Freeman, R., & Garner, D. (1988). A naturalistic investigation of eating behavior in bulimia nervosa. *Journal of Consulting and Clinical Psychology, 56*, 273-279.

Davison, G.C., & Neale, J.M. (1986). *Abnormal psychology: An experimental clinical approach* (4th ed.). New York: Wiley.

Dawkins, R. (1976). *The selfish gene.* New York: Oxford University Press.

DeCasper, A., & Fifer, W. (1980). Of human bonding: Newborns prefer their mothers' voices. *Science, 208*, 1174-1176.

Deci, E.L. (1975). *Intrinsic motivation.* New York: Plenum.

Deci, E.L. (1980). *The psychology of self-determination.* Lexington, MA: Lexington Books.

Deci, E.L., & Ryan, R.M. (1985). *Intrinsic motivation and self-determination in human behavior.* New York: Plenum Press.

Decker, P. (1982). The enhancement of behavior modeling training of supervisory skills by the inclusion of retention processes. *Personnel Psychology, 35*, 323-332.

Delack, J.B. (1976). Aspects of infant speech development in the first year of life. *Canadian Journal of Linguistics, 21*, 17-37.

Delgado, J.M.R. (1969). *Physical control of the mind: Toward a psychocivilized society.* New York: Harper & Row.

DeLuce, J., & Wilder, H.T. (Eds.). (1983). *Language in primates: Perspectives and implications.* New York: Springer-Verlag.

Dembroski, T.M., MacDougall, J., Williams, B., & Haney, T. (1985). Components of Type A, hostility, and anger-in: Relationship to angiographic findings. *Psychosomatic Medicine, 47*, 219-233.

Dement, W.C. (1960). The effect of dream deprivation. *Science, 131*, 1705-1707.

Dement, W.C. (1976). *Some must watch while some must sleep.* New York: Norton.

Dement, W.C., Carskadon, M., & Ley, R. (1973). The prevalence of narcolepsy. *Sleep Research, 2*, 147.

Denes, P.B., & Pinson, E.N. (1963). *The speech chain.* Murray Hill, NJ: Bell Laboratories.

Dennis, W., & Dennis, M.G. (1940). The effect of cradling practices upon the onset of walking in Hopi children. *Journal of Genetic Psychology, 56*, 77-86.

Depue, R., & Monroe, S. (1986). Conceptualization and measurement of human disorder in life stress research: The problem of chronic disturbances. *Psychological Bulletin, 99*, 36-51.

Deutsch, J.A. (1983). Dietary control and the stomach. *Progress in Neurobiology, 20*, 313-332.

Deutsch, J.A., & Hardy, W.T. (1977). Cholecystokinin produces bait shyness in rats. *Nature, 266*, 196.

Deutsch, M., & Krauss, R. (1960). The effect of threat on interpersonal bargaining. *Journal of Abnormal and Social Psychology, 61*, 181-189.

Dewey, J. (1896). The reflex arc concept in psychology. *Psychological Review, 3*, 357-370.

Diamond, M. (1980). Environment, air ions and brain chemistry. *Psychology Today, 14*, 19-26.

DiCaprio, N. (1983). *Personality theories: A guide to human nature* (2nd ed.). New York: Holt, Rinehart & Winston.

Dichter, E. (1975). *Packaging: The sixth sense.* Boston: Cahners.

Diener, E. (1984). Subjective well-being. *Psychological Bulletin, 95*, 542-575.

Digman, J.M., & Takemoto-Chock, N.K. (1981). Factors in the natural language of personality: Re-analysis, comparison, and interpretation of six major studies. *Mutlivariate Behavioral Research, 16*, 149-170.

Dion, K.K. (1972). Physical attractiveness and evaluations of children's transgressions. *Journal of Personality and Social Psychology, 24*, 207-213.

Dion, K.K. (1980). Physical attractiveness, sex roles, and heterosexual attraction. In M. Cook (Ed.), *The bases of sexual attraction.* New York: Academic Press.

Dion, K.K., Berscheid, E., & Walster, E. (1972). What is beautiful is good. *Journal of Personality and Social Psychology, 24*, 285-290.

Dion, K.L., & Dion, K.K. (1987). Belief in a just world and physical attractiveness stereotyping. *Journal of Personality and Social Psychology, 52*, 775-780.

Doane, J., West, M., Goldstein, M., & Rodnick, E. (1981). Parental communication deviance and affective style: Predictions of subsequent schizophrenia spectrum disorders in vulnerable adolescents. *Archives of General Psychiatry, 38*, 679-685.

Dodge, K.A. (1983). Behavioral antecedents of peer social status. *Child Development, 54*, 1386-1399.

Doherty, W.J., & Baldwin, C. (1985). Shifts and stability in locus of control during the 1970s: Divergence of the sexes. *Journal of Personality and Social Psychology, 48*, 1048-1053.

Dollard, J., & Miller, N.E. (1950). *Personality and psychotherapy.* New York: McGraw-Hill.

Dollard, J., Doob, L.W., Miller, N.E., Mowrer, O.H., & Sears, R.R. (1939). *Frustration and aggression.* New Haven: Yale University Press.

Doty, R.L., Green, P.A., Ram, C., & Uankell, S.L. (1982). Communication of gender from human breath odors: Relationship to perceived intensity and pleasantness. *Hormones and Behavior, 16*, 13-22.

Dovidio, J., & Gaertner, S. (Eds.). (1986). *Prejudice, discrimination, and racism.* New York: Academic Press.

Dowling, J., & Dubin, M. (1984). The vertebrate retina. In I. Darian-Smith (Ed.), *Handbook of physiology: Section I. The nervous system.* Baltimore: Waverly Press.

Dripke, D., & Gillin, J. (1985). Sleep disorders. In G. Klerman, M. Weissman, P. Applebaum, & L. Roth (Eds.). *Psychiatry* (Vol. 3). Philadelphia: Lippincott.

Dunn, J., Plomin, R., & Daniels, D. (1986). Consistency and change in mothers' behavior toward young siblings. *Child Development, 57*, 348-356.

Duquin, M. (1980). The dynamics of athletic persistence. In W. Straub (Ed.), *Sports psychology: An analysis of athletes' behavior.* Ithaca, NY: Mouvement.

Dutton, D., & Aron, A. (1974). Some evidence for heightened sexual attraction under conditions of high anxiety. *Journal of Personality and Social Psychology, 30*, 510-517.

E

Eagly, A.H. (1974). Comprehensibility of persuasive arguments as a determinant of opinion change. *Journal of Personality and Social Psychology, 29*, 758-773.

Eagly, A.H., & Carli, L.L. (1981). Sex of researchers and sex-typed communications as determinants of sex differences in influencability: A meta-analysis of social influence studies. *Psychological Bulletin, 90*, 1-20.

Eagly, A.H., & Crowley, M. (1986). Gender and helping behavior: A meta-analysis of the social psychological literature. *Psychological Bulletin, 100*, 283-308.

Eagly, A.H., & Himmelfarb, S. (1978). Attitudes and opinions. *Annual Review of Psychology*, 29, 517-554.

Eagly, A.H., & Steffen, V.J. (1986). Gender and aggressive behavior: A meta-analysis of the social psychological literature. *Psychological Bulletin*, 100, 309-330.

Eagly, A.H., Wood, W., & Chaiken, S. (1978). Causal inferences about communicators and their effect on opinion change. *Journal of Personality and Social Psychology*, 36, 424-435.

Ebbinghaus, H. (1913). *Memory*. (H.A. Ruger and C.E. Bussenius, Trans.). New York: Columbia University Press. (Original work published 1885).

Eibl-Eibesfeldt, I. (1972). *Love and hate: The natural history of behavior patterns*. New York: Holt, Rinehart & Winston.

Eisen, S. (1979). Actor-observer differences in information inferences and causal attribution. *Journal of Personality and Social Psychology*, 37, 261-272.

Eisenberg, N., Shell, R., Pasternack, J., Lennon, R., Beller, R., & Mathy, R. (1987). Prosocial development in middle childhood: A longitudinal study. *Developmental Psychology*, 23, 712-718.

Ekman, P. (1975). Face muscles talk every language. *Psychology Today*, 9, 35-39.

Ekman, P. (1980). *The face of man: Expressions of universal emotions in a New Guinea village*. New York: Garland STPM Press.

Ekman, P. (1982). *Emotion and the human face* (2nd ed.). New York: Cambridge University Press.

Ekman, P. (1985). *Telling lies: Clues to deceit in the marketplace, politics, and marriage*. New York: Norton.

Ekman, P., & Friesen, W.V. (1981). Measuring facial movement with the facial action coding system. In P. Ekman (Ed.), *Emotion in the human face* (2nd ed.). Cambridge: Cambridge University Press.

Ekman, P., & Friesen, W.V. (1986). A new pan-cultural facial expression of emotion. *Motivation and Emotion*, 10, 159-168.

Ekman, P., Friesen, W., O'Sullivan, M., Chan, H., Diacoyanni-Tarlatzis, I., Heider, K., Krause, R., LeCompte, W., Pitcairn, T., Ricci-Bitti, P., Scherer, K., Tomita, M., & Tzauaras, A. (1987). Universals and cultural differences in the judgments of facial expressions of emotion. *Journal of Personality and Social Psychology*, 53, 712-717.

Ekman, P., Levinson, R.W., & Friesen, W. (1983). Autonomic nervous system activity distinguishes among emotions. *Science*, 1208-1210.

Ellis, A. (1984). Rational-emotive therapy. In R.J. Corsini (Ed.), *Current psychotherapies* (3rd ed.). Itasca, IL: Peacock.

Ellis, H. (1978). *Fundamentals of human learning, memory, and cognition* (2nd ed.). Dubuque, IA: Brown.

Ellis, H. (1987). Recent developments in human memory. In V.P. Makowsky (Ed.), *The G. Stanley Hall Lecture Series* (Vol. 7). Washington, DC: American Psychological Association.

Epstein, A. (1982). The physiology of thirst. In D. Pfaff (Ed.), *The physiological mechanisms of motivation*. New York: Springer-Verlag.

Epstein, R., Kirshnit, C., Lanza, R., & Rubin, L. (1984). "Insight" in the pigeon: Antecedents and determinants of an intelligent performance. *Nature*, 308, 61-62.

Erikson, E.H. (1963). *Childhood and society* (2nd ed.). New York: Norton.

Erikson, R.P. (1984). On the neural bases of behavior. *American Scientist*, 72, 233-241.

Erlenmeyer-Kimling, L., & Jarvik, L.F. (1963). Genetics and intelligence: A review. *Science*, 142, 1477-1479.

Erlich, S., & Itabashi, H. (1986). Narcolepsy: A neuropathologic study. *Sleep*, 9, 126-132.

Eron, L.D. (1982). Parent-child interaction, television violence, and aggression of children. *American Psychologist*, 37, 197-211.

Evans, R., Rozelle, R., Lasater, T., Dembroski, T., & Allen, B. (1970). Fear arousal, persuasion, and actual versus implied behavioral change: New perspective utilizing a real-life dental hygiene program. *Journal of Personality and Social Psychology*, 16, 220-227.

Eysenck, H.J. (1952). *The scientific study of personality*. London: Routledge & Kegan Paul.

Eysenck, H.J. (1967). *The biological basis of personality*. Springfield, IL: Thomas.

Eysenck, H.J. (1970). *The structure of human personality*. London: Methuen.

Eysenck, H.J. (1982). *Personality, genetics, and behavior*. New York: Springer-Verlag.

F

Fantz, R.L. (1961). The origin of form perception. *Scientific American*, 204, 66-72.

Fantz, R.L. (1963). Pattern vision in newborn infants. *Science*, 140, 296-297.

Fechner, G.T. (1966). *Elements of psychophysics*, edited by D.H. Howes & E.G. Boring, (H.E. Adler Trans.). New York: Holt, Rinehart & Winston, (Original work published 1860).

Fehr, L. (1983). *Introduction to personality*. New York: Macmillan.

Feldman, S., Nash, S., & Aschenbrenner, B. (1983). Antecedents of fathering. *Child Development*, 54, 1628-1636.

Ferster, C., & Skinner, B.F. (1957). *Schedules of reinforcement*. East Norwalk, CT: Appleton-Century-Crofts.

Feshbach, S., & Weiner, B. (1986). *Personality* (2nd ed.). Lexington, MA: Heath.

Festinger, L. (1953). Group attraction and membership. In D. Cartwright and A. Zander (Eds.), *Group dynamics: Research and theory*. New York: Harper & Row.

Festinger, L. (1954). A theory of social comparison processes. *Human Relations*, 7, 117-140.

Festinger, L. (1957). *A theory of cognitive dissonance*. Stanford, CA: Stanford University Press.

Festinger, L., & Carlsmith, J.M. (1959). Cognitive consequences of forced compliance. *Journal of Abnormal and Social Psychology*, 58, 203-210.

Festinger, L., Schachter, S., & Back, K. (1950). *Social pressures in informal groups: A study of human factors in housing*. New York: Harper & Row.

Feuerstein, R. (1980). *Instrumental enrichment: An intervention program for cognitive modifiability*. Baltimore: University Park Press.

Fibiger, H.C. (1984). The neurobiological substrates of depression in Parkinson's disease. *Canadian Journal of Neurological Sciences*, 11, 105-107.

Fiedler, F. (1981). Leadership effectiveness. *American Behavioral Scientist*, 24, 619-632.

Field, T. (1987). Interaction and attachment in normal and atypical infants. *Journal of Consulting and Clinical Psychology*, 55, 853-859.

Fisher, D., & Byrne, D. (1975). Too close for comfort: Sex differences in response to invasions of personal space. *Journal of Personality and Social Psychology, 32*, 15-20.

Fisher, J.D., Rytting, M., & Heslin, R. (1976). Hands touching hands: Affective and evaluative effects of an interpersonal touch. *Sociometry, 39*, 416-421.

Fishman, J. (1985, September). Mapping the mind. *Psychology Today*, 18-19.

Fiske, S.T., & Taylor, S.E. (1984). *Social cognition*. New York: Random House.

Fitzpatrick, V., Pasnak, R., & Tyer, Z. (1982). The effect of familiar size at familiar distances. *Perception, 11*, 89-91.

Flaherty, C.F. (1985). *Animal learning and cognition*. New York: Knopf.

Flavel, J.H. (1982). Structures, stages, and sequences in cognitive development. In W. Collins (Ed.). *The concept of development: The Minnesota symposia on child psychology* (Vol. 15). Hillsdale, NJ: Erlbaum.

Flavel, J.H. (1985). *Cognitive development*. Englwood Cliffs, NJ: Prentice-Hall.

Fleming, J. (1983). *The impact of college environments on black students*. San Francisco: Jossey-Bass.

Foa, E., Steketee, G., & Young, M. (1984). Agoraphobia: Phenomenological aspects, associated characteristics, and theoretical considerations. *Clinical Psychology Review, 4*, 431-457.

Foegen, J., & Curry, T. (1980). Flextime: The way of the future? *Administrative Management, 41*, 26-29, 55-56.

Fosson, A., Knibbs, J., Bryant-Waugh, R., & Lask, B. (1987). Early onset anorexia nervosa. *Archives of Disease in Children, 62*, 114-118.

Fouts, R.S., Fouts, D.H., & Schoenfeld, D.J. (1984). Sign language conversational interaction between chimpanzees. *Sign Language Studies, 42*, 1-12.

Frankenburg, W.K., & Dodds, J.B. (1967). The Denver developmental screening test. *Journal of Pediatrics, 71*, 181-191.

Franks, C.M. (1984). Behavior therapy with children and adolescents. In G.T. Wilson, C.M. Franks, K.D. Brownell, & P.C. Kendall (Eds.), *Annual review of behavior therapy: Theory and practice*. New York: Guilford Press.

Fraser, C., & Foster, D. (1984). Social groups, nonsense groups and group polarization. In H. Tajfel (Ed.), *The social dimension: European developments in social psychology* (Vol. 2). London: Cambridge University Press.

Frederickson, R.C., & Geary, L.E. (1982). Endogenous opiod peptides: Review of physiological pharmacological and clinical aspects. *Progress in Neurobiology, 19*, 19-69.

Freedman, J.L. (1975). *Crowding and behavior*. San Francisco: Freeman.

Freedman, J.L. (1984). Effect of television violence on aggressiveness. *Psychological Bulletin, 96* 227-246.

Freedman, J.L., & Fraser, S.C. (1966). Compliance without pressure: The foot-in-the-door technique. *Journal of Personality and Social Psychology, 4*, 195-202.

Freedman, J.L., Levy, A.S., Buchanan, R.W., & Price, J. (1972). Crowding and human aggressiveness. *Journal of Experimental Social Psychology, 8*, 528-548.

Freud, S. (1894). The neuro-psychoses of defense. In J. Strachey (Ed.), *The standard edition of the complete psychological works of Sigmund Freud* (Vol. 3). London: Hogarth, 1952.

Freud, S. (1915). Instincts and their vicissitudes. In J. Riviere (Trans.), *Collected papers of Sigmund Freud* (Vol. 4). London: Hogarth.

Freud, S. (1915). The unconscious. In S. Freud, *Collected papers*, Vol. IV. London: Hogarth Press, 1949.

Freud, S. (1930). *Civilization and its discontent*. London: Hogarth.

Freud, S. (1933). *New introductory lectures on psychoanalysis*. New York: Norton.

Freud, S. (1949). *An outline of psychoanalysis*. New York: Norton.

Freud, S. (1950). The interpretation of dreams. In J. Strachey (Ed. and Trans.), *The standard edition of the complete psychological works*. London: Hogarth. (Original work published 1900).

Freudenberger, H.J. (1980). *Burnout: How to beat the high cost of success*. New York: Bantam.

Fridlund, A., Fowler, S., & Pritchard, D. (1980). Striate muscle tension patterning in frontalis EMG biofeedback. *Psychophysiology, 17*, 47-55.

Friedlund, A.J., Ekman, P., & Oster, H. (1987). Facial expressions of emotion. In A. Siegman & S. Feldstern (Eds.), *Nonverbal communication and behavior* (2nd ed.). Hillsdale, NJ: Erlbaum.

Friedman, A.P. (1982). Psychophysiological aspects of headache. In W. Fann, I. Kareacan, A. Pokorny, & R. Williams (Eds.), *Phenomenology and treatment of psychophysiological disorders*. New York: Spectrum.

Friedman, M., & Rosenman, R. (1974). *Type A behavior and your heart*. New York: Knopf.

Fries, J. & Crapo, L. (1981). *Vitality and ageing*. San Francisco: Freeman.

Frijda, N.H. (1988). The laws of emotion. *American Psychologist, 43*, 349-358.

Fromm, E. (1956). *The art of loving*. New York: Harper & Row.

Fusilier, M.R., Ganster, D.C., & Mayes, B.T. (1987). Effects of social support, role stress and locus of control on health. *Journal of Management, 13*, 517-528.

G

Gage, N.L., & Berliner, D.C. (1988). *Educational Psychology* (4th ed.). Boston: Houghton Mifflin.

Galanter, E. (1962). Contemporary psychophysics. In R. Brown, E. Galanter, E. Hess, & G. Mandler (Eds.), *New directions in psychology* (Vol. 1). New York: Holt, Rinehart & Winston.

Galinsky, E. (1981). *Between generations: The six stages of parenthood*. New York: Berkley.

Ganchrow, J., Steiner, J., & Daher, M. (1983). Neonatal facial expressions in response to different qualities and intensities of gustatory stimuli. *Infant Behavior and Development, 6*, 189-200.

Garcia, J., & Koelling, R. (1966). Relation of cue to consequence in avoidance learning. *Psychonomic Science, 4*, 123-124.

Garcia, J., Ervin, F., & Koelling, R. (1966). Learning with prolonged delay of reinforcement. *Psychonomic Science, 5*, 121-122.

Gardner, H. (1983). Prodigies' progress. *Psychology Today*, May, 75-79.

Gardner, R.A., & Gardner, B.T. (1969). Teaching sign language to a chimpanzee. *Science, 165*, 664-672.

Gazzaniga, M.S. (1983). Right hemisphere language following brain bisection: A 20 year perspective. *American Psychologist, 38*, 525-537.

Gelfand, D.M., & Hartmann, D.P. (1980). The development of prosocial behavior and moral judgement. In R.L. Ault (Ed.), *Developmental perspectives*. Santa Monica, CA: Goodyear.

Gelman, R., & Gallistel, C.R. (1978). *The young child's understanding of number: A window on early cognitive devleopment*. Cambridge, MA: Harvard University Press.

Gibson, E.J., & Walk, R.D. (1960). The visual cliff. *Scientific American, 202*, 64-71.

Gibson, J.J. (1968). What gives rise to the perception of motion? *Psychological Review, 75*, 335-346.

Ginsburg, N., & Pringle, L. (1988). Haptic numerosity perception: Effect of item arrangment. *American Journal of Psychology, 101*, 131-133.

Glass, D.C., & Singer, J.E. (1972). Behavioral aftereffects of unpredictable and uncontrollable aversive events. *American Scientist, 60*, 457-465.

Glick, P. (1984). Marriage, divorce, and living arrangements. *Journal of Family Issues, 5*, 7-26.

Gmelch, W. (1982). *Beyond stress to effective management*. New York: Wiley.

Godfrey, D., Jones, E., & Lord, C. (1986). Self-promotion is not ingratiating. *Journal of Personality and Social Psychology, 50*, 106-115.

Goebel, B.L., & Brown, D.R. (1981). Age differences in motivation related to Maslow's need hierarchy. *Developmental Psychology, 17*, 809-815.

Goldberger, L. (1982). Sensory deprivation and overload. In L. Goldberger & S. Bresnitz (Eds.), *Handbook of Stress: Theoretical and Clinical Aspects*. New York: Free Press.

Goldsmith, H.H. (1983). Genetic influences on personality from infancy to adulthood. *Child Development, 54*, 331-335.

Goldstein, A.P., & Krasner, L. (1987). *Modern applied psychology*. New York: Pergamon.

Goldstein, I. (1980). Training in work organizations. *Annual Review of Psychology, 31*, 229-272.

Goleman, D. (1980). 1,528 little geniuses and how they grew. *Psychology Today, 14*, 28-53.

Goleman, D.J. (1977). *The varieties of meditative experience*. New York: Dutton.

Gottesman, I.I., & Shields, J. (1972). *Schizophrenia and genetics: A twin study vantage point*. New York: Academic Press.

Gough, H.G. (1969). *Manual for the California psychological inventory* (rev. ed.). Palo Alto, CA: Consulting Psychologists Press.

Gould, R. (1978). *Transformations: Growth and changes in adult life*. New York: Simon & Schuster.

Graham, W., & Balloun, J. (1973). An empirical test of Maslow's need hierarchy theory. *Journal of Humanistic Psychology, 13*, 97-108.

Grasha, A. (1987). *Practical applications of psychology* (3rd ed.). Boston: Little, Brown.

Grasha, A.F., & Kirschenbaum, D.S. (1986). *Adjustment and competence: Concepts and applications*. St. Paul, MN: West.

Gravetter, F.J., & Wallnau, L.B. (1988). *Statistics for the behavioral sciences* (2nd ed.). St. Paul, MN: West.

Green, B.F. (1981). A primer of testing. *American Psychologist, 36*, 1001-1011.

Green, D.M., & Swets, J.A. (1966). *Signal detection theory and psychophysics*. New York: Wiley.

Green, E.J. (1976). *Psychology for law enforcement*. New York: Wiley.

Greenbaum, P., & Rosenfeld, H. (1978). Patterns of avoidance in response to interpersonal staring and proximity: Effects of bystanders on drivers at a traffic intersection. *Journal of Personality and Social Psychology, 36*, 575-587.

Greenberg, J. (1977). The brain and emotions: Crossing a new frontier. *Science News, 112*, 74-75.

Greene, R.L. (1987). Effects of maintenance rehearsal on human memory. *Psychological Bulletin, 102*, 403-413.

Gregorc, A.F. (1986). *An adult's guide to style*. New York, NY: Gabriel Systems.

Gregory, R. (1978). *Eye and brain: The psychology of seeing* (3rd ed.). New York: McGraw-Hill.

Greiser, C., Greenberg, R., & Harrison, R.H. (1972). The adaptive function of sleep: The differential effects of sleep and dreaming on recall. *Journal of Abnormal Psychology, 80*, 280-286.

Griffith, R.M., Miyagi, O., & Tago, A. (1958). The universality of typical dreams: Japanese vs. Americans. *American Anthropologist, 60*, 1173-1179.

Grinker, J. (1982). Physiological and behavioral basis of human obesity. In D. Pfaff (Ed.), *The physiological mechanisms of motivation*. New York: Springer-Verlag.

Grossman, Pollack, & Golding (1988). Fathers' role in parenting. *Developmental Psychology*.

Groves, P.M. & Rebec, G.V. (1988). *Introduction to biological psychology* (3rd ed.). Dubuque, IA: W.C. Brown.

Guerin, B. (1986). Mere presence effects in humans: A review. *Journal of Experimental Social Psychology, 22*, 38-77.

Guilford, J.P. (1967). *The nature of human intelligence*. New York: McGraw-Hill.

Guilford, J.P. (1981). Cognitive psychology's ambiguities: Some suggested remedies. *Psychological Review, 89*, 48-59.

Gurman, A., Kniskern, D. & Pinsof, W. (1986). Research on marital and family therapies. In S.L. Garfield & A. Bergin (Eds.), *Handbook of psychotherapy and behavior change*. New York: Wiley.

Gustavson, C.R., & Gustavson, J.C. (1985). Predation control using conditioned food aversion methodology: Theory, practice, and implications. In N. Braverman & P. Bernstein (Eds.), Experimental assessments and clinical application of conditioned food aversions. *Annals of the New York Academy of Sciences*, Vol. 443.

H

Haas, R., & Linder, D. (1972). Counter-argument availability and the effects of message structure on persuasion. *Journal of Personality and Social Psychology, 23*, 219-233.

Haber, R.N. (1980). Eidetic images are not just imaginary. *Psychology Today, 14*, 72-82.

Hager, J., & Ekman, P. (1979). Long-distance transmission of facial affect signals. *Ethology and Sociobiology, 1*, 77-82.

Hakel, N.D. (1982). Employment interviewing. In K. Rowland & C. Ferris (Eds.), *Personal management*. Boston: Allyn & Bacon.

Hales, P. (1980). *The complete book of sleep*. Reading, MA: Addison-Wesley.

Hall, C., & Lindzey, G. (1985). *Introduction to theories of personality*. New York: Wiley.

Hall, C.S. (1966). *The meaning of dreams*. New York: McGraw-Hill.

Hall, C.S. (1984). "Ubiquitous sex difference in dreams" revisited. *Journal of Personality and Social Psychology, 46,* 1109-1117.

Hall, C.S., Dornhoff, W., Blick, K.A., & Weesner, K.E. (1982). The dreams of college men and women in 1950 and 1980: A comparison of dream contents and sex differences. *Sleep, 5,* 188-194.

Hall, E.T. (1966). *The hidden dimension.* New York: Doubleday.

Hall, G.S. (1916). *Adolescence.* New York: Appleton.

Hall, J. (1986). The cardiopulmonary failure of sleep disordered breathing. *Journal of the American Medical Association, 255,* 930-933.

Hall, V.C., & Kaye, D.B. (1980). Early patterns of cognitive development. Monograph of the Society for Research in Child Development, 45, Whole Number 184.

Hallahan, D., Kauffman, J., & Lloyd, J. (1985). *Introduction to learning disabilities* (2nd ed.). Englewood Cliffs, NJ: Prentice-Hall.

Halmi, K., Falk, J., & Schwartz, E. (1981). Binge-eating and vomiting: A survey of a college population. *Psychological Medicine, 11,* 697-706.

Halpin, A.W. (1966). *Theory and research in administration.* New York: Macmillan.

Han, J.S., & Ternius, L. (1982). Neurochemical basis of acupuncture analgesia. *Annual Review of Pharmacological Toxicology, 22,* 193-220.

Hancock, P.A. (1986). The effect of skill on performance under an environment stressor. *Aviation, space, and environmental medicine. 57,* 59-64.

Hanewitz, W. (1978). Police personality: A Jungian perspective. *Crime and Delinquency, 24,* 152-172.

Haney, C., Banks, C., & Zimbardo, P.G. (1973). Interpersonal dynamics in a simulated prison. *International Journal of Crime and Penology, 1,* 69-97.

Hansen, J.C., & Campbell, D.P. (1985). *Manual for the SVIB-SCII* (4th ed.). Stanford, CA: Stanford University Press.

Harlow, H.F. (1949). The formation of learning sets. *Psychological Review, 56,* 51-65.

Harlow, H.F. (1958). The nature of love. *American Psychologist, 13,* 673-685.

Harlow, H.F. (1971). *Learning to love.* San Francisco: Albion.

Hartmann, E.L. (1973). *The functions of sleep.* New Haven: Yale University Press.

Hassett, J. (1978). *A primer of psychophysiology.* San Francisco: Freeman.

Hathaway, S.R., & McKinley, J.C. (1940). A multiphasic personality schedule (Minnesota): I. Construction of the schedule. *Journal of Psychology, 10,* 249-254.

Hayflick, L. (1980). The cell biology of human aging. *Scientific American, 242*(1), 58-65.

Hays, R.B. (1985). A longitudinal study of friendship development. *Journal of Personality and Social Psychology, 48,* 909-924.

Hearnshaw, L.S. (1979). *Cyril Burt: Psychologist.* Ithaca, NY: Cornell University Press.

Hebb, D.O. (1949). *The organization of behavior.* New York: Wiley.

Hebb, D.O. (1955). Drives and the C.N.S. (conceptual nervous system). *Psychological Review, 62,* 243-253.

Hecht, S., & Shlaer, S. (1938). An adaptometer for measuring human dark adaptation. *Journal of the Optical Society of America, 28,* 269-275.

Heiby, E.M. (1983). Depression as a function of the interaction of self- and environmentally-controlled reinforcement. *Behavior Therapy, 14,* 430-433.

Heider, E.R. (1972). Universals in color naming and memory. *Journal of Experimental Psychology, 93,* 10-21.

Heider, E.R., & Oliver, D.C. (1972). The structure of the color space in naming and memory in two languages. *Cognitive Psychology, 3,* 337-354.

Heider, F. (1958). *The psychology of interpersonal relations.* New York: Wiley.

Heimstra, N.W., & McFarling, L.H. (1974). *Environmental psychology.* Monterey, CA: Brooks-Cole.

Helmholtz, H.L.F. von (1863). *Die lehre von den tonemp findug en als physiologische Grundlage fur die theorie der Musik.* Braunschweig: Viewig V. Sohn.

Henderson, N. (1982). Human behavior genetics. *Annual Review of Psychology, 33,* 403-440.

Hendin, H. (1985). Suicide among the young: Psychodynamics and demography. In M. Peck, N. Farberow, & R. Litman (Eds.), *Youth Suicide.* New York: Springer.

Hensel, H. (1982). *Thermal sensations and thermoreceptors in man.* Springfield, IL: Thomas.

Herbert, W. (1983). Remembrance of things partly. *Science News, 124,* 378-381.

Heron, W. (1957). The pathology of boredom. *Scientific American, 196,* 52-56.

Herzberg, F. (1966). *Work and the nature of man.* New York: Crowell.

Hess, E.H. (1959). Imprinting. *Science, 130,* 133-141.

Hilgard, E.R. (1975). Hypnosis. *Annual Review of Psychology, 26,* 19-44.

Hilgard, E.R. (1979). Divided consciousness in hypnosis: The implications of the hidden observer. In E. Froom & R. Shor (Eds.), *Hypnosis: Developments in research and new perspectives.* New York: Aldine.

Hilgard, E.R., & Hilgard, J.R. (1983). *Hypnosis in the relief of pain.* Los Altos, CA: Kaufmann.

Hill, G.W. (1982). Group versus individual performance: Are N + 1 heads better than one? *Psychological Bulletin, 91,* 517-539.

Hinde, R.A. (1970). *Animal behavior: A synthesis of ethology and comparative psychology* (2nd ed.). New York: McGraw-Hill.

Hinz, L., & Williamson, D. (1987). Bulimia and depression: A review of the affective variant hypothesis. *Psychological Bulletin, 102,* 150-158.

Hirschman, E., & Mills, M. (1980). Sources shoppers use to pick stores. *Journal of Advertising Research, 20,* 47-51.

Hjelle, L. (1974). Transcendental meditation and psychological health. *Perceptual and Motor Skills, 39,* 623-628.

Hobson, J.A., & McCarley, R.W. (1977). The brain as a dream state generator: An activation-synthesis hypothesis of the dream process. *The American Journal of Psychiatry, 134,* 1335-1348.

Hoffman, L. (1977). Changes in family roles, socialization, and sex differences. *American Psychologist, 32,* 644-657.

Holahan, C.J. (1986). Environmental psychology. *Annual Review of Psychology, 37,* 381-407.

Holahan, C.J., & Moos, R.H. (1985). Life stress and health: Personality, coping, and family support in stress resistance. *Journal of Personality and Social Psychology, 49,* 739-747.

Holden, C. (1976). Hospices: For the dying, relief from pain and fear. *Science, 193,* 389-391.

Holden, C. (1980). The hospice movement and its implications. In R. Fox (Ed.), *The social meaning of death: Annals of the American academy of political and social psychology.*

Hollingshead, A.B., & Redlich, F.C. (1958). *Social class and mental illness: A community study.* New York: Wiley.

Holmes, D., Solomon, S., Cappo, B., & Greenberg, J. (1983). Effects of transcendental meditation versus resting on physiological and subjective arousal. *Journal of Personality and Social Psychology, 44,* 1244-1252.

Holmes, T.H., & Rahe, R.H. (1967). The social readjustment rating scale. *Journal of Psychosomatic Research, 11,* 213-218.

Holtzman, W.H., Thorpe, J.W., Swartz, J.D., & Herron, E.W. (1961). *Inkblot perception and personality: Holtzman Inkblot Technique.* Austin: University of Texas Press.

Homans, G.C. (1961). *Social behavior: Its elementary forms.* New York: Harcourt Brace Jovanovich.

Horn, J.M. (1983). The Texas adoption project. Adopted children and their intellectual resemblance to biological and adoptive parents. *Child Development, 54,* 268-275.

Horner, M.S. (1972). Toward an understanding of achievement-related conflicts in women. *Journal of Social Issues, 28,* 157-175.

Horner, M.S. (1978). The measurement and behavioral implications of fear of success in women. In J.W. Atkinson & J.O. Raynor (Eds.), *Personality, motivation and achievement.* New York: Halsted Press.

Horney, K. (1939). *New ways in psychoanalysis.* New York: Norton.

Horowitz, F.D., & O'Brien, M. (1986). Gifted and talented children: State of knowledge and directions for research. *American Psychologist, 41,* 1147-1152.

Horton, D., & Turnage, T. (1976). *Human learning.* Englewood Cliffs, NJ: Prentice-Hall.

Houston, J.P. (1985) *Motivation.* New York: Macmillan.

Houston, J.P. (1986). *Fundamentals of learning and memory* (3rd ed.). New York: Harcourt Brace Jovanovich.

Howard, K., Kopta, S., Krause, M., & Orlinski, D. (1986). The dose-effect relationship in psychotherapy. *American Psychologist, 41,* 159-164.

Howell, W.C., & Dipboye, R.L. (1982). *Essentials of industrial and organizational psychology* (rev ed.). Homewood, IL: Dorsey.

Hruska, S., & Grasha, A. (1982). The Grasha-Riechmann student learning style scales. In *Student styles and brain behavior.* Reston, VA: National Association of Secondary School Principals.

Hull, C.L. (1920). Quantitative aspects of the evolution of concepts. *Psychological Monographs,* Whole No. 123.

Hull, C.L. (1943). *Principles of behavior.* East Norwalk, CT: Appleton-Century-Crofts.

Hull, C.L. (1952). *A behavior system: An introduction to behavior theory concerning the individual organism.* New Haven, CT: Yale University Press.

Hunt, M. (1974). *Sexual behavior in the 1970s.* Chicago: Playboy Press.

Huston, A. (1983). Sex-typing. In P. Mussen (Ed.), *Handbook of child psychology* (Vol. 4) (4th ed.). New York: Wiley.

Hyde, J.S. (1986). *Understanding human sexuality* (3rd ed.). New York: McGraw-Hill.

Hyde, T., & Jenkins, J. (1969). Differential effects of incidental tasks on the organization of recall of a list of highly associated words. *Journal of Experimental Psychology, 82,* 472-481.

I

Intons-Peterson, M.J., & Fournier, J. (1986). External and internal memory aids: When and how often do we use them? *Journal of Experimental Psychology: General, 115,* 267-280.

Isenberg, D.J. (1986). Group polarization: A critical review and meta-analysis. *Journal of Personality and Social Psychology, 50,* 1141-1151.

Iversen, S.D., & Iversen, L.L. (1975). *Behavioral pharmacology.* New York: Oxford University Press.

Izard, C. (1972). *Patterns of emotions: A new analysis of anxiety and depression.* New York: Academic Press.

Izard, C. (1977). *Human emotions.* New York: Plenum.

Izard, C. (1982). The psychology of emotion comes of age on the coattails of Darwin. *Contemporary Psychology, 27,* 426-429.

Izard, C., Huebner, R., Risser, D., McGinnes, G., & Dougherty, L. (1980). The young infant's ability to produce discrete emotional expressions. *Developmental Psychology, 16,* 132-140.

J

Jackson, J.M., & Harkins, S.G. (1985). Equity in effort: An explanation of the social loafing effect. *Journal of Personality and Social Psychology, 49,* 1199-1206.

Jackson, J.M., & Williams, K.D. (1985). Social loafing on difficult tasks: Working collectively can improve performance. *Journal of Personality and Social Psychology, 49,* 937-942.

Jacobson, E. (1929). *Progressive relaxation.* Chicago: University of Chicago Press.

Jacoby, J. (1984). Perspectives on information overload. *Journal of Consumer Research, 10,* 432-435.

James, W. (1884). What is an emotion? *Mind, 9,* 188-205.

James, W. (1890). *Principles of psychology.* New York: Holt.

James, W. (1904). Does consciousness exist? *Journal of Philosophy, Psychology, and Scientific Methods, 1,* 447-491.

Janis, I.L. (1982). *Groupthink: Psychological studies of policy decision and fiascoes* (2nd ed.). Boston: Houghton Mifflin.

Janis, I.L. (1982). *Victims of groupthink: A psychological study of foreign-policy decisions and fiascos.* Boston: Houghton Mifflin.

Janowsky, D., & Risch, S. (1984). Adrenergic and cholinergic balance and affective disorders. *The Psychiatric Hospital, 15,* 163-171.

Jensen, A.R. (1969). How much can we boost IQ and scholastic achievement? *Harvard Educational Review, 39,* 1-123.

Jessor, R., Casta, F., Jessor, L., & Donovan, J. (1983). Time of first intercourse: A prospective study. *Journal of Personality and Social Psychology, 44,* 608-626.

Johnson, C., & Larson, R. (1982). Bulimia: An analysis of moods and behavior. *Psychosomatic Medicine, 44,* 341-351.

Johnson, R.N. (1972). *Aggression in man and animals.* Philadelphia: Saunders.

Johnson-Laird, P.N., & Wason, P.C. (1977). Introduction to conceptual thinking. In P.N. Johnson-Laird & P.C. Wason (Eds.), *Thinking: Readings in cognitive science.* Cambridge: Cambridge University Press.

Jones, B.E., Harper, S.T., & Halaris, A.E. (1977). Effects of coeruleus lesions upon cerebral meonamine content, sleep wakefulness states and the response to amphetamine in the cat. *Brain Research, 124,* 473-496.

Jones, E.E., & Davis, K. (1965). From acts to dispositions: The attribution process in person perception. In L. Berkowitz (Ed.), *Advances in experimental social psychology* (Vol. 2). New York: Academic Press.

Jones, E.E., & Nisbett, R.E. (1972). The actor and the observer: Divergent perceptions of the causes of behavior. In E.E. Jones, *Attribution: Perceiving the causes of behavior.* Morristown, NJ: General Learning Press.

Jones, M. (1965). Psychological correlates of somatic development. *Child Development, 36,* 899-911.

Jones, M.C. (1924). A laboratory study of fear: The case of Peter. *Pedagogical Seminary, 31,* 308-315.

Jones, N., Kearins, J., & Watson, J. (1987). The human tongue show and observers' willingness to interact: Replication and extensions. *Psychological Reports, 60,* 759-764.

Jones, W., & Carpenter, B. (1986). Shyness, social behavior, and relationships. In W. Jones, J. Cheek, & S. Briggs (Eds.), *Shyness: Perspectives on research and treatment.* New York: Plenum.

Jouvet, M. (1967). Neurophysiology of the states of sleep. *Physiological Reviews, 47,* 117-177.

Julien, R.M. (1985). *A primer of drug action* (4th ed.). New York: Freeman.

Jung, C.G. (1923). *Psychological types.* London: Rutledge and Kagan Paul.

Jung, C.G. (1939). *The integration of the personality.* New York: Farrar & Rinehart.

K

Kagan, J. (1982). Canalization of early psychological development. *Pediatrics, 70*(3), 474-483.

Kahn, J.P., Kornfield, P., Frank, L., Heller, S., & Hoar, P. (1980). Type A behavior and blood pressure during coronary artery bypass surgery. *Psychosomatic Medicine, 42,* 407-414.

Kaitz, M., Good, A., Rokem, A., & Eidelman, A. (1987). Mothers' recognition of their newborns by olfactory cues. *Developmental Psychology, 206,* 587-591.

Kamin, L.J. (1974). *The Science and Politics of IQ.* Hillsdale, NJ: Erlbaum.

Kaplan, E., & Kaplan, G. (1971). The prelinguistic child. In J. Elliot (Ed.), *Human development and cognitive processes.* New York: Holt, Rinehart & Winston.

Karabenick, S. (1977). Fear of success, achievement and affiliation dispositions, and the performance of men and women under individual competitive conditions. *Journal of Personality, 45,* 117-149.

Katchadourian, H. (1985). *Fundamentals of human sexuality* (4th ed.). New York: Holt, Rinehart & Winston.

Kaufman, L., & Rock, I. (1962). The moon illusion, I. *Science, 136,* 953-961.

Kazkin, A.E. (1980). *Behavior modification in applied settings* (2nd ed.). Homewood, IL: Dorsey.

Kelley, H. (1950). The warm-cold variable in first impressions. *Journal of Personality, 18,* 431-439.

Kelley, H.H. (1973). The processes of causal attribution. *American Psychologist, 28,* 107-128.

Kellman, P.J., Gleitman, H., & Spelke, E.S. (1987). Object and observer motion in the perception of objects by infants. *Journal of Experimental Psychology: Human Perception and Performance. 13,* 586-593.

Kelly, D.D. (1981). Disorders of sleep and consciousness. In E.R. Kandel & J.H. Schwartz (Eds.), *Principles of neural science.* New York: Elsevier.

Kelly, G.F. (1988). *Sexuality Today: The Human Perspective.* Guilford, CT: Dushkin.

Kessler, R., Price, P., & Worthman, C. (1985). Social factors in psychopathology: Stress, social support, and coping processes. *Annual Review of Psychology, 36,* 531-572.

Kety, S. (1983). Mental illness in the biological and adoptive relatives of schizophrenic adoptees: Findings relevant to genetic and environmental factors in etiology. *American Journal of Psychiatry, 140* 720-727.

Kiester, E., Jr. (1980). Images of the night. *Science 80, 1,* 36-43.

Kihlstrom, J.F. (1984). Conscious, subconscious, unconscious: A cognitive view. In K. Bowers & D. Meichenbaum, (Eds.), *The unconscious: Reconsidered.* New York: Wiley.

Kimble, G.A. (1961). *Hilgard and Marquis' conditioning and learning.* East Norwalk, CT: Appleton-Century-Crofts.

Kinsey, A.C., Pomeroy, W.B., & Martin, C.E. (1948). *Sexual behavior in the human male.* Philadelphia: Saunders.

Kinsey, A.C., Pomeroy, W.B., Martin, C.E., & Gebhard, P.H. (1953). *Sexual behavior in the human female.* Philadelphia: Saunders.

Kirk, S.A., & Gallagher, J.J. (1986). *Education's exceptional children* (5th ed.). Boston: Houghton Mifflin.

Klatzky, R.L. (1984). *Memory and awareness: An information processing perspective.* New York: Freeman.

Klein, S.B. (1987). *Learning.* New York: McGraw-Hill.

Kleiner, K.A., & Banks, M.S. (1987). Stimulus energy does not account for 2-month-olds' face preference. *Journal of Experimental Psychology: Human Perception and Performance, 13,* 594-600.

Kleinke, C.L. (1986). Gaze and eye contact: A research review. *Psychological Bulletin, 100,* 78-200.

Kleinke, C.L., & Walton, J.H. (1982). Influence of reinforced smiling on affective responses in an interview. *Journal of Personality and Social Psychology, 42,* 557-565.

Kleinke, C.L., Meeker, F., & LaFong, C. (1974). Effects of gaze, touch and use of name on evaluation of "engaged" couples. *Journal of Research in Personality, 7,* 368-373.

Klineberg, O. (1938). Emotional expression in Chinese literature. *Journal of Abnormal and Social Psychology, 33,* 517-520.

Kluegel, J., & Smith, E. (1986). *Beliefs about inequality.* New York: Aldine.

Knox, D. (1985). *Choices in relationships.* St. Paul: West.

Knox, D.H., Jr. (1970a). Attitudes toward love of high school seniors. *Adolescence, 5,* 89-100.

Knox, D.H., Jr. (1970b). Conceptions of love at three developmental levels. *The Family Coordinator, 19,* 151-157.

Kobasa, S.C. (1982). The hardy personality: Toward a social psychology of stress and health. In G. Snaders & J. Suls (Eds.), *Social psychology of health and illness.* Hillsdale, NJ: Erlbaum.

Kobasa, S.C., Maddi, S., & Kahn, S. (1982). Hardiness and health: A prospective study. *Journal of Personality and Social Psychology, 42,* 168-177.

Koffka, K. (1935). *Principles of Gestalt psychology.* New York: Harcourt Brace.

Kohlberg, L. (1966). A cognitive-developmental model analysis of children's sex-role concepts and attitudes. In E. Maccoby (Ed.), *The development of sex differences*. Stanford: Stanford University Press.

Kohlberg, L. (1968). The child as a moral philosopher. *Psychology Today, 1*, 25-30.

Kohlberg, L. (1969). *Stages in the development of moral thought and action*. New York: Holt, Rinehart & Winston.

Kohlberg, L. (1985). *Essays on moral development. Volume 1: The philosophy of moral development*. New York: Harper & Row.

Kohlberg, L. (1985). *The psychology of moral development*. San Francisco: Harper and Row.

Köhler, W. (1927). The mentality of apes. E. Winter (Trans.). 1st Eng ed., 1925. 2nd Eng. ed. New York: Harcourt, Brace.

Kolata, G. (1983). First trimester prenatal diagnosis. *Science, 22*, 1031-1032.

Kolb, B., & Whishaw, I. (1985). *Human neuropsychology*. New York: Freeman.

Komorita, S., & Lapworth, C. (1982). Cooperative choice among individuals versus groups in an N-person dilemma situation. *Journal of Personality and Social Psychology, 42*, 487-496.

Kondrasuk, J.N. (1981). Studies in MBO effectiveness. *Academy of Management Review, 6*, 419-430.

Korner, A., Zeanach, C., Linden, J., Berkowitz, R., Kraener, H., & Agras, W. (1985). Relation between neonatal and later activity and temperament. *Child Development, 56*, 38-42.

Kübler-Ross, E. (1969). *On death and dying*. New York: Macmillan.

Kübler-Ross, E. (1981). *Living with death and dying*. New York: Macmillan.

Kulik, J.A., Kulik, C.C., & Gangert-Drowns, R.L. (1985). Effectiveness of computer-based education in elementary schools. *Computers in Human Behavior, 1*, 59-74.

Kuo, Z.Y. (1921). Giving up instincts in psychology. *Journal of Philosophy, 17*, 645-664.

Kutash, I., & Wolf, A. (Eds.). (1986). *Psychotherapists' casebook*. San Francisco: Josey-Bass.

L

Laing, R.D. (1964). Is schizophrenia a disease? *International Journal of Social Psychiatry, 10*, 184-193.

Lakein, A. (1973). *How to get control of your time and your life*. New York: Signet.

Lamaze, F. (1970). *Painless childbirth: The Lamaze method*. Chicago: Regnery.

Lambert, M., Shapiro, D., & Bergin, A. (1986). The effectiveness of psychotherapy. In S. Garfield & A. Bergin (Eds.), *Handbook of psychotherapy and behavior change* (3rd ed.). New York: Wiley.

Lamm, H., & Trommsdorf, G. (1973). Group versus individual performance on tasks requiring ideational proficiency (brainstorming): A review. *European Journal of Social Psychology, 3*, 361-388.

Landers, D. (1982). Arousal, attention, and skilled performance: Further considerations. *Quest, 33*, 271-283.

Landers, S. (1988). Skinner joins aversive debate. *APA Monitor, 19*, 22-23.

Landy, F.J. (1989). *Psychology of work behavior* (2nd ed.). Homewood, IL: Dorsey.

Laner, M. (1983). Courtship abuse and aggression: Contextual aspects. *Sociological Spectrum, 3*, 69-83.

Lange, C.G. (1922). *The emotions*. Baltimore: Williams & Wilkins.

Langer, E., & Saegert, S. (1977). Crowding and cognitive control. *Journal of Personality and Social Psychology, 35*, 175-182.

Lanyon, R.I. (1984). Personality assessment. *Annual Review of Psychology, 35*, 667-701.

Lashley, K. (1950). In search of the engram. *Symposia of the Society of Experimental Biology, 4*, 454-482.

Latané, B. (1981). The psychology of social impact. *American Psychologist, 36*, 343-356.

Latané, B., & Darley, J.M. (1968). Group inhibition of bystander intervention in emergencies. *Journal of Personality and Social Psychology, 10*, 215-221.

Latané, B., & Darley, J.M. (1970). *The unresponsive bystander: Why doesn't he help?* New York: Appleton-Century-Crofts.

Lavidge, R., & Steiner, G. (1961). A model for predictive measurements of advertising effectiveness. *Journal of Marketing, 25*, 59-62.

Lawler, E.E. (1982). Strategies for improving the quality of work life. *American Psychologist, 37*, 486-493.

Lazar, I., & Darlington, R. (1982). Lasting effects of early education: A report from the Consortium of Longitudinal Studies. *Monographs of the Society for Research in Child Development, 47*, Whole Number 195.

Lazarus, R.S. (1980). The stress and coping paradigm. In L. Bond & J. Rosen (Eds.), *Competence and coping during adulthood*. Hanover, NH: University Press of New England.

Lazarus, R.S. (1981). Little hassles can be hazardous to health. *Psychology Today, 15*, 58-62.

Lazarus, R.S. (1984). On the primacy of cognition. *American Psychologist, 39*, 124-129.

Lazarus, R.S., DeLongis, A., Folkman, S., & Gruen, R. (1985). Stress and adaptational outcomes. *American Psychologist, 40*, 770-779.

Leal, L. (1987). Investigation of the relation between metamemory and university students' examination performance. *Journal of Educational Psychology, 79*, 35-40.

Lebow, M., Goldberg, P., & Collins, A. (1977). Eating behavior of overweight and nonoverweight persons in the natural environment. *Journal of Consulting and Clinical Psychology, 45*, 1204-1205.

Leeming, F., & Little, G. (1977). Escape learning in houseflies. *Journal of Comparative and Physiological Psychology, 91*, 260-269.

Lefrancois, G. (1976). *Adolescents*. Belmont, CA: Wadsworth.

Lemere, F., & Voegtlin, W. (1950). An evaluation of the aversive treatment of alcoholism. *Quarterly Journal of Studies on Alcohol, 11*, 199-204.

Leonard, C.V. (1974). Depression and suicidality. *Journal of Consulting and Clinical Psychology, 42*, 98-104.

Leonard, C.V. (1977). The MMPI as a suicide predictor. *Journal of Consulting and Clinical Psychology, 45*, 367-377.

Lepper, M.R., Greene, D., & Nisbett, R.E. (1973). Undermining children's intrinsic interest with extrinsic rewards: A test of the "overjustification" hypothesis. *Journal of Personality and Social Psychology, 28*, 129-137.

Lerner, M.J. (1980). *The belief in a just world: A fundamental delusion*. New York: Plenum.

Leventhal, H., & Tomarken, A. (1986). Emotion: Today's problems. *Annual Review of Psychology, 37,* 565-610.

Leventhal, H., Singer, R., & Jones, S. (1965). The effects of fear and specificity of recommendation upon attitudes and behavior. *Journal of Personality and Social Psychology, 2,* 20-29.

Levinson, D. (1978). *The seasons of a man's life.* New York: Ballantine.

Levitt, E., & Klassen, A. (1974). Public attitudes toward homosexuality: Part of the 1970 national survey by the Institute for Sex Research. *Journal of Homosexuality, 1,* 29-43.

Levy, J. (1985). Right brain, left brain: Fact and fiction. *Psychology Today, 19,* 38-44.

Lewin, K. (1935). *A dynamic theory of personality.* New York: McGraw-Hill.

Linberg, K.A., & Fisher, S.K. (1986). An ultrastructural study of interplexiform cell synapses in the human retina. *The Journal of Comparative Neurology, 243,* 561-576.

Loehlin, J.C., & Nichols, R.C. (1976). *Heredity, environment, and personality.* Austin: University of Texas Press.

Loftus, E.F. (1974). Reconstructing memory: The incredible eyewitness. *Psychology Today, 8,* 116-119.

Loftus, E.F. (1979). *Eyewitness testimony.* Cambridge, MA: Harvard University Press.

Loftus, E.F. (1980). *Memory.* Reading, MA: Addison-Wesley.

Loftus, E.F. (1983). Misfortunes of memory. *Philosophical transactions of the Royal Society, London, 302,* 413-421.

Loftus, E.F. (1984). Eyewitness: Essential but unreliable. *Psychology Today,* February, 22-27.

Loftus, E.F. & Loftus, G.R. (1980). On the permanence of stored information in the human brain. *American Psychologist, 35,* 409-420.

London, P. (1964). *The modes and morals of psychotherapy.* New York: Holt, Rinehart & Winston.

Lorenz, K. (1937). The companion in the bird's world. *Auk, 54,* 245-273.

Lorenz, K. (1965). *Evolution and modification of behavior.* Chicago: University of Chicago Press.

Lorenz, K. (1966). *On aggression.* New York: Harcourt Brace & World.

Lovaas, O.I. (1977). *The autistic child: Language development through behavior modification.* New York: Irvington.

Lubin, B. (1983). Group therapy. In I.B. Weiner (Ed.), *Clinical methods in psychology* (2nd ed.). New York: Wiley.

Lubin, B., Larsen, R., Matarazzo, J., & Seever, M. (1985). Psychological test usage patterns in five professional settings. *American Psychologist, 40,* 857-861.

Lucero, M.A. (1970). Lengthening of REM sleep duration consecutive to learning in the rat. *Brain Research, 20,* 319-322.

Luh, C. (1922). The conditions of retention. *Psychological Monographs.* No. 142.

M

Maas, A. & Clark, R. (1984). Hidden impact of minorities: Fifteen years of minority influence research. *Psychological Bulletin, 95,* 428-450.

Maccoby, E. (1980). *Social development: Psychological growth and the parent-child relationship.* New York: Harcourt Brace Jovanovich.

MacDonald, A., Jr. (1970). Internal-external locus of control and the practice of birth control. *Psychological Reports, 27,* 206.

MacFarlane, J.A. (1977). *The psychology of childbirth.* Cambridge, MA: Harvard University Press.

Macht, J. (1975). *Teaching our children.* New York: Wiley.

MacLean, P.D. (1949). Psychosomatic disease and the "visceral brain": Recent developments bearing on the Papez theory of emotion. *Psychosomatic Medicine, 11,* 338-353.

MacLean, P.D. (1970). The limbic brain in relation to the psychoses. In P. Black (Ed.), *Physiological correlates of emotion.* New York: Academic Press.

MacNichol, E.F., Jr. (1964). Three-pigment color vision. *Scientific American, 211,* 48-56.

Makens, J. (1965). Effect of brand preference upon consumer's perceived taste of turkey meat. *Journal of Applied Psychology, 49,* 261-263.

Marcel, A.J. (1983). Conscious and unconscious perception: An approach to the relation between phenomenal experience and perceptual processes. *Cognitive Psychology, 15,* 238-300.

Marcia, J.E. (1980). Identity in adolescence. In J. Adelson (Ed.), *Handbook of adolescent psychology.* New York: Wiley.

Martin, P. (1987). Psychology and the immune system. *New Scientist,* April 9, 46-50.

Maslach, C. (1978). Emotional consequences of arousal without reason. In C. Izard (Ed.), *Emotions and psychopathology.* New York: Plenum.

Maslach, C. (1979). Negative emotional biasing of unexplained arousal. *Journal of Personality and Social Psychology, 37,* 953-969.

Maslach, C. (1982). *Burnout: The cost of caring.* Englewood Cliffs, NJ: Prentice-Hall.

Maslach, C., & Jackson, S. (1981). The measurement of experienced burnout. *Journal of Occupational Behavior, 2,* 99-113.

Maslow, A.H. (1968). *Toward a psychology of being* (2nd ed.). New York: Van Nostrand.

Maslow, A.H. (1970). *Motivation and personality* (2nd ed.). New York: Harper & Row.

Maslow, A.H. (1987). *Motivation and personality* (3rd Ed.). New York: Harper & Row. (Revised by R. Frager, J. Fadiman, C. McReynolds, & R. Cox)

Masters, W.H., & Johnson, V.E. (1966). *Human sexual response.* Boston: Little, Brown.

Masters, W.H., Johnson, V.E., & Kolodny, R.C. (1985). *Human sexuality* (2nd ed.). Boston: Little, Brown.

Masters, W.H., Johnson, V.E., & Kolodny, R.C. (1988). *Human sexuality* (3rd ed.). Glenview, IL: Scott, Foresman.

Matarazzo, J.D. (1972). *Wechsler's measurement and appraisal of adult intelligence* (5th ed.). Baltimore: Williams & Wilkins.

Matheny, A.P. Jr., Riese, M.L., & Wilson, R.S. (1985). Rudiments of infant temperament: Newborn to 9 months. *Developmental Psychology, 213,* 486-494.

Mathews, K.E., & Canon, L.K. (1975). Environmental noise level as a determinant of helping behavior. *Journal of Personality and Social Psychology, 32,* 571-577.

Matlin, M. (1983). *Cognition.* New York: Holt, Rinehart & Winston.

Matlin, M.N. (1987). *The psychology of women.* New York: Holt, Rinehart & Winston.

Matlin, M.N. (1989). *Cognition* (2nd ed.). New York: Holt, Rinehart & Winston.

Matlin, M.W. (1988). *Sensation and perception* (2nd ed.). Boston: Allyn-Bacon.

Matthews, K.A. (1982). Psychological perspectives on the Type A behavior pattern. *Psychological Bulletin, 91,* 293-323.

Mayer, J. (1953). Glucostatic mechanism of regulation of food intake. *New England Journal of Medicine, 249,* 13-16.

Mayer, J. (1955). Regulation of energy intake and the body weight: The glucostatic theory and the lipostatic hypothesis. *Annals of the New York Academy of Science, 63,* 15-43.

McBurney, D., & Collings, V. (1984). *Introduction to sensation and perception.* Englewood Cliffs, NJ: Prentice-Hall.

McCanne, T.R., & Anderson, J.A. (1987). Emotional responding following experimental manipulation of facial electromyographic activity. *Journal of Personality and Social Psychology, 52,* 759-768.

McCarley, R.W., & Hoffman, E. (1981). REM sleep dreams and the activation-synthesis hypothesis. *American Journal of Psychiatry, 138,* 904-912.

McClelland, D.C. (1958). Methods of measuring human motivation. In J.W. Atkinson (Ed.), *Motives in fantasy, action and society.* Princeton, NJ: Van Nostrand.

McClelland, D.C. (1965). N achievement and entrepreneurship: A longitudinal study. *Journal of Personality and Social Psychology, 1,* 389-392.

McClelland, D.C. (1978). Managing motivation to expand human freedom. *American Psychologist, 33,* 201-210.

McClelland, D.C. (1985a). *Human motivation.* Glenview, IL: Scott, Foresman.

McClelland, D.C. (1985b). How motives, skills, and values determine what people do. *American Psychologist, 40,* 812-825.

McClelland, D.C., Atkinson, J.W., Clark, R.A., & Lowell, E.L. (1953). *The achievement motive.* East Norwalk, CT: Appleton-Century-Crofts.

McClelland, L. (1976). Interaction level and acquaintance as mediators of density effects. *Personality and Social Psychology Bulletin, 2,* 175-178.

McCloskey, M., Wible, C., & Cohen, N. (1988). Is there a special flashbulb memory mechanism? *Journal of Experimental Psychology: General, 117,* 171-181.

McConkey, K., & Kinoshita, S. (1988). The influence of hypnosis on memory after one day and one week. *Journal of Abnormal Psychology, 97,* 48-53.

McCrae, R.R., & Costa, P.T., Jr. (1985). Updating Norman's "Adequate Taxonomy": Intelligence and personality dimensions in natural language and in questionnaires. *Journal of Personality and Social Psychology, 49,* 710-721.

McCrae, R.R., & Costa, P.T., Jr. (1986). Clinical assessment can benefit from recent advances in personality psychology. *American Psychologist, 41,* 1001-1003.

McCrae, R.R., & Costa, P.T., Jr. (1987). Validation of the five-factor model of personality across instruments and observers. *Journal of Personality and Social Psychology, 52,* 81-90.

McDougall, W. (1908). *Social psychology.* New York: G.P. Putnam's Sons.

McDougall, W. (1921). *An introduction to social psychology.* Boston: Luce.

McGaugh, J.L. (1983). Preserving the presence of the past: Hormonal influences on memory storage. *American Psychologist, 38,* 161-174.

McGeer, P., & McGeer, E. (1980). Chemistry of mood and emotion. *Annual Review of Psychology, 31,* 273-307.

McGrath, J.E. (1984). *Groups: Interaction and performance.* Englewood Cliffs, NJ: Prentice-Hall.

McGregor, D. (1960). *The human side of enterprise.* New York: McGraw-Hill.

McGuigan, F. (1984). Progressive relaxation: Origins, principles, and clinical applications. In R. Woolfolk & P. Lehrer (Eds.), *Principles and practice of stress management.* New York: Guilford.

McGuire, W.J. (1985). Attitudes and attitude change. In G. Lindzey & E. Aronson (Eds.), *Handbook of social psychology* (Vol. 2) (3rd ed.). New York: Random House.

McHugh, P.R., & Moran, T.H. (1985). The stomach: A conception of its dynamic role in satiety. *Progress in Psychobiology and Psychology, 11,* 197-232.

McKean, K. (1985, April). Of two minds: Selling the right brain. *Discover,* pg 30-41, 60.

McKenzie, S. (1980). *Aging and old age.* Glenview, IL: Scott, Foresman.

McLean, P. (1968). The paranoid streak in man. In A. Koestler and J.T. Smythies (Eds.), *Beyond reductionism.* Princeton, NJ: Princeton University Press.

McMinn, M. (1984). Mechanisms of energy balance in obesity. *Behavioral Neuroscience, 98,* 375-393.

McNeal, E.T. & Cimbolic, P. (1986). Antidepressants and biochemical theories of depression. *Psychological Bulletin, 99,* 361-374.

Megargee, E. (1972). *The California psychological inventory handbook.* San Francisco: Jossey-Bass.

Mehrabian, A. (1969). Significance of posture and position in the communication of attitude and status relationships. *Psychological Bulletin, 71,* 359-372.

Meichenbaum, D. (1985). *Stress in oculation training.* New York: Pergamon.

Melzack, R. (1973). *The puzzle of pain.* New York: Basic Books.

Mendlewicz, J. (1985). Genetic research in depressive disorders. In E. Beckham & W. Leber (Eds.), *Handbook of depression: Treatment, assessment, and research.* Homewood, IL: Dorsey.

Meredith, N. (1984). The gay dilemma. *Psychology Today, 18,* 56-62.

Messing, R., & Sparber, S. (1985). Greater taste difficulty amplifies the facilitatory effect of des-glycinamide arginine vasopressin on appetitively motivated learning. *Behavioral Neuroscience, 99,* 1114-1119.

Meyers, F.H., Jawetz, E., & Goldfien, A. (1978). *Review of medical pharmacology* (6th ed.). Los Altos, CA: Lange Medical Publications.

Mikhail, A. (1981). Stress: A psychophysiological conception. *Journal of Human Stress, 7,* 9-15.

Milgram, S. (1963). Behavioral study of obedience. *Journal of Abnormal and Social Psychology, 67,* 371-378.

Milgram, S. (1965). Some conditions of obedience and disobedience to authority. *Human Relations, 18,* 57-76.

Milgram, S. (1974). *Obedience to authority.* New York: Harper & Row.

Miller, A.G. (1986). *The obedience experiments: A case study of controversy in social science.* New York: Praeger.

Miller, G.A. (1956). The magical number seven, plus or minus two: Some limits on our capacity for processing information. *Psychological Review, 63,* 81-97.

Miller, L., & Branconnier, R. (1983). Cannabis: Effects on memory and the cholinergic limbic system. *Psychological Bulletin, 93,* 441-456.

Miller, N. (1973). *Biofeedback and self-control.* Chicago: Aldine.

Miller, N. (1978). Biofeedback and visceral learning. *Annual Review of Psychology, 29,* 421-452.

Miller, N., & Banuazizi, A. (1968). Instrumental learning by curarized rats of a specific visceral response, intestinal or cardiac. *Journal of Comparative and Physiological Psychology, 65,* 1-17.

Milner, B. (1972). Disorders of learning and memory after temporal lobe lesions in man. *Clinical Neurosurgery, 19,* 421-446.

Mineka, S., & Henderson, R. (1985). Controllability and predictability in acquired motivation. *Annual Review of Psychology, 36,* 495-529.

Miner, J.B. (1984). The validity and usefulness of theories in an emerging organizational science. *Academy of Management Review, 9,* 296-306.

Mirsky, A.F., & Duncan, C.C. (1986). Etiology and expression of schizophrenia: Neurobiological and psychosocial factors. *Annual Review of Psychology, 37,* 291-319.

Mischel, W. (1986). *Introduction to personality* (4th ed.). New York: Holt, Rinehart & Winston.

Mishkin, M. (1982). A memory system in the monkey. *Philosophical Transactions of the Royal Society of London, 298,* 85-95.

Mitchell, T.R., & Larson, J.R., Jr. (1987). *People in organizations: An introduction to organizational behavior.* New York: McGraw-Hill.

Moates, D., & Schumacher, G. (1980). *An introduction to cognitive psychology.* Belmont, CA: Wadsworth.

Moerk, E.L. (1980). Relationships between parental input frequencies and children's language acquisition: A reanalysis of Brown's data. *Journal of Child Language, 7,* 105-118.

Moldofsky, H., & Scarisbrick. P. (1976). Induction of neurasthenic musculoskeletal pain syndrome by selective sleep stage deprivation. *Psychosomatic Medicine, 38,* 35-44.

Monahan, J., & Loftus, E.F. (1982). The psychology of law. *Annual Review of Psychology, 33,* 441-475.

Money, J. (1977). Determinants of human gender identity/role. In J. Money & H. Musaph (Eds.), *Handbook of sexology.* New York: Exerpta Medica.

Money, J. (1987). Propaedeutics of diecious G-I/R: Theoretical foundations for understanding dimorphic gender-identity/role. In J. Reinisch, L. Rosenblum, & S. Sanders (Eds.), *Masculinity/feminity: Basic perspectives.* New York: Oxford University Press.

Money, J., & Ehrhardt, A. (1972). *Man and woman, boy and girl.* Baltimore: Johns Hopkins University Press.

Monroe, L.J. (1967). Psychological and physiological differences between good and poor sleepers. *Journal of Abnormal Psychology, 72,* 255-264.

Monroe, S.M. (1982). Life events and disorder: Event-symptom associations and the course of disorder. *Journal of Abnormal Psychology, 91,* 14-24.

Mook, D.G. (1987). *Motivation: The organization of action.* New York: Norton.

Moran, G., & Comfort, J. (1982). Scientific juror selection: Sex as a moderator of demographic and personality predictors of impaneled felony juror behavior. *Journal of Personality and Social Psychology, 43,* 1052-1063.

Moreland, R., & Zajonc, R. (1982). Exposure effects in person perception: Familiarity, similarity, and attraction. *Journal of Experimental and Social Psychology, 18,* 395-415.

Morley, J., Bartness, T., Gosnell, B., & Levine, A. (1985). Peptidergic regulation of feeding. *International Review of Neurobiology, 27,* 207-298.

Morosko, T., & Baer, P. (1970). Avoidance conditioning of alcoholics. In R. Ulrich, T. Stachnik, & J. Mabry (Eds.),

Control of human behavior (Vol. 2). Glenview, IL: Scott, Foresman.

Morris, N., & Udry, J. (1978). Pheromonal influences on human sexual behavior: An experimental search. *Journal of Biosocial Science, 10,* 147-157.

Moscovici, S. (1985). Social influence and conformity. In G. Lindzey & W. Aronson (Eds.), *Handbook of social psychology* (Vol. 2) (3rd ed.). New York: Random House.

Moushon, J., & Lennie, P. (1979). Pattern-selective adaptation in visual cortical neurons. *Nature, 278,* 850-852.

Mowrer, O.H., & Mowrer, W.M. (1938). Enuresis—a method for its study and treatment. *American Journal of Orthopsychiatry, 8,* 436-459.

Mudd, E., & Taubin, S. (1982). Success in family living: Does it last? A twenty-year follow-up. *Journal of Family Therapy, 10,* 59-67.

Murdock, B.B. (1974). *Human memory: Theory and data.* New York: Wiley.

Murray, C.L., & Fibiger, H.C. (1986). Pilocarpine and physostigmine attenuate spatial memory impairments produced by lesions of the nucleus basalis magnocellularis. *Behavioral Neuroscience, 100,* 23-32.

Murray, H.A. (1938). *Exploration in personality.* New York: Oxford University Press.

Murray, H.A. (1943). *Thematic apperception test manual.* Cambridge, MA: Harvard University Press.

Muuss, R. (1985). Adolescent eating disorder: Anorexia nervosa. *Adolescence, 79,* 525-536.

Myers, I.B. (1962). *Manual: The Myers-Briggs Type Indicator.* Princeton: Educational Testing Service.

N

Nachman, M., & Jones, D. (1974). Learned taste aversions over long delay in rats: The role of learned safety. *Journal of Comparative and Physiological Psychology, 86,* 949-956.

Napoli, V., Kilbride, J., & Tebbs, D. (1982). *Adjustment and growth in a changing world.* St. Paul, MN: West.

Nelson, G., & Cone, J. (1979). Multiple-baseline analysis of a token economy for psychiatric inpatients. *Journal of Applied Behavior Analysis, 12,* 255-271.

Nemeth, C. (1981). Jury trials: Psychology and law. *Advances in Experimental Social Psychology, 14,* 309-367.

Nemeth, C. (1986). Differential contributions of majority and minority influence. *Psychological Review, 93,* 23-32.

Neuchterlein, K., & Dawson, M.E. (1984). A heuristic vulnerability/stress model of schizophrenic episodes. *Schizophrenic Bulletin, 10,* 300-311.

Nickerson, R.S., & Adams, M.J. (1979). Long-term memory for a common object. *Cognition Psychology, 11,* 287-307.

Nisbett, R.E. (1972). Hunger, obesity, and the ventromedial hypothalamus. *Psychological Review, 79,* 433-453.

Nisbett, R.E., & Wilson, T. (1977). The halo effect: Evidence for the unconscious alteration of judgments. *Journal of Personality and Social Psychology, 35,* 450-456.

Norman, W.T. (1963). Toward an adequate taxonomy of personality attributes: Replicated factor structure in peer nomination personality ratings. *Journal of Abnormal and Social Psychology, 66,* 574-583.

Noyes, R., Jr., Crowe, R., Harris, E., Hamra, B., & McChesney, C. (1986). Relationship between panic disorder and agoraphobia: A family study. *Archives of General Psychiatry, 43,* 227-232.

O

O'Leary, K.D. (1984). The image of behavior therapy: It is time to take a stand. *Behavior Therapy*, *15*, 219-233.

O'Leary, K.D., & Wilson, G.T. (1987). *Behavior therapy: Application and outcome* (2nd ed.). Englewood Cliffs, NJ: Prentice-Hall.

Olds, J., & Milner, P. (1954). Positive reinforcement produced by electrical stimulation of septal area and other regions of rat brain. *Journal of Comparative and Physiological Psychology*, *47*, 419-427.

Onyehalu, A. (1981). Identity crisis in adolescence. *Adolescence*, *16*, 629-632.

Ornstein, R.E. (1986). *The psychology of consciousness* (rev. ed.). New York: Penguin Books.

Osgood, C., Suci, G., & Tannenbaum, P. (1957). *The measurement of meaning*. Urbana, IL: University of Illinois Press.

Ouchi, W.G. (1981). *Theory Z: How American business can meet the Japanese challenge*. Reading, MA: Addison-Wesley.

Overton, D.A. (1972). State-dependent learning produced by alcohol and its relevance to alcoholism. In B. Kissin and H. Begleiter (Eds.), *Physiology and behavior: The biology of alcoholism* (Vol. 2). New York: Plenum.

P

Palmer, R. (1981). (Ed.). *Electroconvulsive therapy: An appraisal*. New York: Oxford University Press.

Palumbo, S.R. (1978). *Dreaming and memory: A new information-processing model*. New York: Basic Books.

Pam, A., Plutchik, R., & Conte, H. (1975). Love: A psychometric approach. *Psychological Reports*, *37*, 83-88.

Panksepp, J. (1986). The neurochemistry of behavior. *Annual Review of Psychology*, *37*, 77-107.

Papez, J.W. (1937). A proposed mechanism of emotion. *Archives of Neurology and Psychiatry*, *38* 725-743.

Parke, R., & Sawin, D. (1980). The family in early infancy: Social interactional and attitudinal analyses. In F. Pedersen (Ed.), *The father-infant relationship: Observational studies in the family setting*. New York: Praeger.

Parker, J.G. & Asher, S.R. (1987). Peer relations and later personal adjustment: Are low-accepted children at risk? *Psychological Bulletin*, *102*, 357-389.

Parloff, M., Waskow, I., & Wolfe, B. (1978). Research on therapist variables in relation to process and outcome. In S. Garfield & A. Bergin (Eds.), *Handbook of psychotherapy and behavior change: An empirical analysis* (2nd ed.). New York: Wiley.

Paterson, C.E. (1984). The effects of a program of muscle relaxation, cue control relaxation, and image training program on the batting and pitching performance of college baseball players. Unpublished master's thesis, The Ohio State University.

Paterson, C.E., & Pettijohn, T.F. (1982). Age and human mate selection. *Psychological Reports*, *51*, 70.

Patterson, F.G. (1978). The gestures of a gorilla: Language acquisition in another pongid. *Brain and Language*, *5*, 72-97.

Pattison, E.M. (1977). The experience of dying. In E.M. Pattison (Ed.), *The experience of dying*. Englewood Cliffs, NJ: Prentice-Hall.

Paulus, P. (1980). Crowding: In P. Paulus (Ed.), *Psychology of group influence*. Hillsdale, NJ: Erlbaum.

Pavlov, I. (1927). *Conditioned reflexes*. London: Clarendon Press.

Paykel, E. (Ed.). (1982). *Handbook of affective disorders*. New York: Guilford Press.

Peabody, D. (1984). Personality dimensions through trait inferences. *Journal of Personality and Social Psychology*, *46*, 384-403.

Peck, J., & Novin, D. (1971). Evidence that osmoreceptors mediating drinking in rabbits are in the lateral preoptic area. *Journal of Comparative and Physiological Psychology*, *74*, 134-147.

Peck, M., Farberow, N., & Litman, R. (Eds.). (1985). *Youth suicide*. New York: Springer.

Penfield, W. (1975). *The mystery of the mind*. Princeton, NJ: Princeton University Press.

Penfield, W., & Jasper, H. (1954). *Epilepsy and the functional anatomy of the human brain*. Boston: Little, Brown.

Penfield, W., & Rasmussen, T. (1950). *The cerebral cortex of man: A clinical study of localization*. New York: Macmillan.

Penrod, S. (1986). *Social Psychology* (2nd ed.). Englewood Cliffs, NJ: Prentice-Hall.

Perkins, D. (1982). The assessment of stress using life events scales. In L. Goldberger & S. Breznitz (Eds.), *Handbook of stress: Theoretical and clinical aspects*. New York: Free Press.

Perley, M., & Guze, S. (1962). Hysteria: The stability and usefulness of clinical criteria. *New England Journal of Medicine*, *266*, 421-426.

Perls, F.S. (1969). *Gestalt therapy verbatim*. Moab, UT: Real People Press.

Perris, C. (1982). The distinction between bipolar and unipolar affective disorders. In E. Paykel (Ed.), *Handbook of affective disorders*. New York: Guilford Press.

Pervin, L. (1984). *Personality: Theory and research* (4th ed.). New York: Wiley.

Peters, T., & Waterman, R., Jr. (1982). *In search of excellence: Lessons from America's best-run companies*. New York: Harper & Row.

Peterson, C., & Seligman, M.E.P. (1985). The learned helplessness model of depression: Current status of theory and research. In E. Beckham & W. Leber (Eds.), *Handbook of depression*. Homewood, IL: Dorsey.

Peterson, L., & Peterson, M. (1959). Short-term retention of individual items. *Journal of Experimental Psychology*, *58*, 193-198.

Petri, H.L. (1986). *Motivation: Theory and research* (2nd ed.). Belmont, CA: Wadsworth.

Pettijohn, T.F. (1977). Social desirability among male prisoners and college students. *Psychological Reports*, *41*, 110.

Pettijohn, T.F. (1979). Effects of alcohol on agonistic behavior in the Telomian dog. *Psychopharmacology*, *60*, 295-301.

Pettijohn, T.F. (1981). Conditioned social aversion in the male Mongolian gerbil. *Journal of Comparative and Physiological Psychology*, *95*, 228-239.

Pettijohn, T.F. (1985). Development of a computer tutoring and testing program for the general psychology course. *Teaching of Psychology*, *12*(2), 103-104.

Pettijohn, T.F. (1988) Content of dreams in college students. Unpublished manuscript.

Pettijohn, T.F., Davis, K., & Scott, J.P. (1980). Influence of living space on agonistic interaction in Telomian dogs. *Behavioral and Neural Biology*, *28*, 343-349.

Petty, R.E., & Cacioppo, J.T. (1981). *Attitudes and persuasion: Classic and contemporary approaches*. Dubuque, IA: W.C. Brown.

Petty, R.E., & Cacioppo, J.T. (1985). The elaboration likelihood model of persuasion. In L. Berkowitz (Eds.), *Advances in experimental social psychology* (Vol. 19). New York: Academic Press.

Pfau, H.D., & Murphy, M.D. (1988). Role of verbal knowledge in chess skill. *American Journal of Psychology, 101*, 73-86.

Phares, E.J. (1986). *Introduction to personality* (2nd ed.). Glenview, IL: Scott, Foresman.

Phillips, D.P. (1983). The impact of mass media violence on U.S. homicides. *American Sociological Review, 48*, 560-568.

Phillips, E.L. (1988). Length of psychotherapy and outcome: Observations stimulated by Howard, Kopta, Krause, and Orlinsky. *American Psychologist, 43*, 669-670.

Phillips, G.M. (1981). *Help for shy people*. Englewood Cliffs, NJ: Prentice-Hall.

Phillips, J.L. (1981). *Piaget's theory: A primer*. San Francisco: Freeman.

Piaget, J. (1960). *The child's conception of the world*. London: Routledge.

Piaget, J. (1967). *Six psychological studies*. New York: Vintage Books.

Pittenger, D.J., & Pavlik, W.B. (1988). Analysis of the partial reinforcement extinction effect in humans using absolute and relative comparisons of schedules. *American Journal of Psychology, 101*, 1-14.

Pittner, M., Houston, B., & Spiridigliozzi, G. (1983). Control over stress, type A behavior pattern, and response to stress. *Journal of Personality and Social Psychology, 44*, 627-637.

Plomin, R., & DeFries, J.C. (1980). Genetics and intelligence: Recent data. *Intelligence, 4*, 15-24.

Plomin, R., DeFries, J., & McClearn, G. (1980). *Behavioral genetics: A primer*. San Francisco: Freeman.

Plutchik, R. (1962). *The emotions: Facts, theories, and a new model*. New York: Random House.

Plutchik, R. (1980). *Emotion: A psychoevolutionary synthesis*. New York: Harper & Row.

Plutchik, R. (1983). *Foundations of experimental psychology* (3rd ed.). New York: Harper & Row.

Pomeroy, W. (1972). *Dr. Kinsey and the Institute for Sex Research*. New York: Harper & Row.

Premack, D. (1965). Reinforcement theory. *Nebraska Symposium on motivation*. Lincoln: University of Nebraska Press.

Premack, D. (1971). Language in chimpanzees? *Science, 172*, 808-822.

Price, R.H., & Lynn, S.J. (1986). *Abnormal psychology* (2nd ed.). Chicago: Dorsey.

Prince, J.S. (1980). Environments that work for people. *Adminstrative Management, 41*, 36-41.

Provost, J. (1984). *A casebook: Applications of the Myers-Briggs type indicator in counseling*. Gainesville, FL: Center for Applications of Psychological Type.

Q

Quintanaar, L., Crowell, C., & Pryor, J. (1982). Human-computer interaction: A preliminary social psychological analysis. *Behavior Research Methods and Instrumentation, 14*(2), 210-220.

R

Rahe, T., Romo, M., Bennett, L., & Siltanen, P. (1974). Recent life changes, myocardial infarction, and abrupt coronary death: Studies in Helsinki. *Archives of Internal Medicine, 133*, 221-228.

Raichle, M. (1983). Positron emission tomography. *Annual Review of Neuroscience, 6*, 249-267.

Ray, W.J., & Ravizza, R. (1988). *Methods: Toward a science of behavior and experience*. Belmont, CA: Wadsworth.

Raymond, C. (1986). Popular, yes, but jury still out on apnea surgery. *Journal of the American Medical Association, 256*, 439-441.

Reisberg, B. (Ed.). (1983). *Alzheimer's disease: The standard reference*. New York: Free Press.

Reiser, R.A. (1984). Reducing student procrastination in a personalized system of instruction course. *Educational Communication and Technology: A Journal of Theory, Research, and Development, 32*, 41-49.

Reynolds, R.I., & Takooshian, H. (1988). Where were you on August 8, 1985? *Bulletin of the Psychonomic Society, 26*, 23-25.

Rice, P.L. (1987). *Stress and health: Principles and practice for coping and wellness*. Monterrey, CA: Brooks/Cole.

Richardson, J. (1983). Mental imagery in thinking and problem solving. In J. Evans (Ed.), *Thinking and reasoning: Psychological approaches*. London: Routledge & Kegan Paul.

Ridgeway, C. (1983). *The dynamics of small groups*. New York: St. Martin's Press.

Ringler, N., Trause, M., Klaus, M., & Kennel, J. (1978). The effects of post partum contact and maternal speech patterns on children's IQs, speech, and language comprehension at five. *Child Development, 49*, 862-865.

Roberts, A.H. (1985). Biofeedback: Research, training, and clinical roles. *American Psychologist, 40*, 938-941.

Roberts, D., & Maccoby, N. (1985). Effects of mass communication. In G. Lindzey & E. Aronson (Eds.), *Handbook of social psychology* (Vol. 2) (3rd ed.). New York: Random House.

Roberts, E. (1986). GABA: The road to neurotransmitter status. In *Benzodiazepine/GABA receptors and chloride channels: Structural and functional properties*. New York: Alan Liss.

Robins, L., & Helzer, J. (1986). Diagnosis and clinical assessment: The current state of psychiatric diagnosis. *Annual Review of Psychology, 37*, 409-432.

Robins, L., Helzer, J., Weissman, M., Oruaschel, H., Gruenberg, E., Burke, J., & Regier, D. (1984). Lifetime prevalence of specific psychiatric disorders in three sites. *Archives of General Psychiatry, 41*, 949-958.

Rodin, J. (1981). Current status of the internal-external hypothesis for obesity. *American Psychologist, 36*, 361-371.

Rodin, J. (1985). The application of social psychology. In G. Lindzey & E. Aronson (Eds.), *Handbook of Social Psychology* (Vol. 2) (3rd ed.). New York: Random House.

Roethlisberger, F.J., & Dickson, W.J. (1939). *Management and the worker: An account of a research program conducted by Western Electric Company*. Cambridge, MA: Harvard University Press.

Roff, J.D., & Knight, R. (1981). Family characteristics, childhood symptoms, and adult outcome in schizophrenia. *Journal of Abnormal Psychology, 90*, 510-520.

Roffwarg, H.P., Muzio, J.N., & Dement, W.C. (1966). Ontogenetic development of the human sleep-dream cycle. *Science, 152,* 604-619.

Rogers, C.R. (1951). *Client-centered therapy.* Boston: Houghton Mifflin.

Rogers, C.R. (1970). *Carl Rogers on encounter groups.* New York: Harper & Row.

Rogers, C.R. (1971). A theory of personality. In S. Maddi (Ed.), *Perspectives on personality.* Boston: Little, Brown.

Rogers, C.R. (1980). *A way of being.* Boston: Houghton Mifflin.

Rogers, D. (1980). *The adult years: An introduction to aging.* Englewood Cliffs, NJ: Prentice-Hall.

Rorschach, H. (1921). *Psychodiagnostics.* Berne: Hans Huber.

Rosch, E. (1978). Principles of categorization. In E. Rosch & B. Lloyd (Eds.), *Cognition and categorization.* Hillsdale, NJ: Erlbaum.

Rosenhan, D.L. (1973). On being sane in insane places. *Science, 179,* 250-258.

Rosenman, R.H., Friedman, M., Straus, R., Wurm, M., Kositichek, R., Hahn, W., & Werthessen, N. (1964). A predictive study of coronary heart disease. *Journal of the American Medical Association, 189,* 103-110.

Rosenthal, R., & Jacobson, L. (1968). *Pygmalion in the classroom.* New York: Holt, Rinehart & Winston.

Ross, L. (1977). The intuitive psychologist and his shortcomings: Distortions in the attribution process. In L. Berkowitz (Ed.), *Advances in experimental social psychology* (Vol. 10). New York: Academic Press.

Rotter, J.B. (1954). *Social learning and clinical psychology.* Englewood Cliffs, NJ: Prentice-Hall.

Rotter, J.B. (1966). Generalized expectancies for internal versus external control of reinforcement. *Psychological Monographs, 80,* (Whole No. 609), 1-28.

Rotter, J.B. (1971). External control and internal control. *Psychology Today, 5*(1), 37-42, 58-59.

Roy, A. (1985). Early parental separation and adult depression. *Archives of General Psychiatry, 42,* 987-991.

Rubenstein, C. (1983). The modern art of courtly love. *Psychology Today,* June, 39-49.

Rubin, Z. (1970). Measurement of romantic love. *Journal of Personality and Social Psychology, 16,* 265-273.

Rubin, Z. (1973). *Liking and loving.* New York: Holt, Rinehart & Winston.

Ruch, L.O., & Holmes, T.H. (1971). Scaling of life change: Comparison of direct and indirect methods. *Journal of Psychosomatic Research, 15,* 221-227.

Rumbaugh, D.M. (Ed.). (1977). *Language learning by a chimpanzee: The Lana project.* New York: Academic Press.

Russek, M. Lora-Vilchis, M., & Islas-Chaires, M. (1980). Food intake inhibition elicited by intraportal glucose and adrenaline in dogs on a 22-hour fasting 2-hour feeding schedule. *Physiology and Behavior, 24,* 157-161.

Russell, J.A. (1980). A circumplex model of affect. *Journal of Personality and Social Psychology, 39,* 1161-1178.

Russell, J.A., & Bullock, M. (1985). Multidimensional scaling of emotional facial features: Similarity from preschoolers to adults. *Journal of Personality and Social Psychology, 48,* 1290-1298.

Russell, J.A., & Bullock, M. (1986). Fuzzy concepts and the perception of emotion in facial expressions. *Social Cognition, 4,* 309-341.

Russell, J.A., & Fehr, B. (1987). Relativity in the perception of emotion in facial expressions. *Journal of Experimental Psychology: General, 116,* 223-237.

Russell, M.J., Switz, G.M., & Thompson, K. (1980). Olfactory influences on the human menstrual cycle. *Pharmacology, Biochemistry, and Behavior, 13,* 737-738.

Rutherford, W.A. (1886). A new theory of hearing. *Journal of Anatomy and Physiology, 21,* 166-168.

S

Samuel, W. (1981). *Personality: Searching for the sources of human behavior.* New York: McGraw-Hill.

Sarason, I.G., & Sarason, B.R. (1980). *Abnormal psychology: The problem of maladaptive behavior* (3rd ed.). Englewood Cliffs, NJ: Prentice-Hall.

Sarbin, T., & Coe, W. (1979). Hypnosis and psychopathology: Replacing old myths with fresh metaphors. *Journal of Abnormal Psychology, 88,* 506-526.

Sassin, J.F., Parker, D.C., Mace, J.W., Gotlin, R.W., Johnson, L.C., & Rossman, L.G. (1969). Human growth hormone release: Relation to slow-wave sleep and sleepwalking cycles. *Science, 165,* 513-515.

Satinoff, E. (1974). Neural integration of thermoregulatory responses. In L. DiCara (Ed.), *Limbic and autonomic nervous system: Advances in research.* New York: Plenum.

Sattler, J.M. (1982). *Assessment of children's intelligence and special abilities* (2nd ed.). Boston: Allyn & Bacon.

Savage-Rumbaugh, E.S., Rumbaugh, D.M., & Boysen, S. (1980). Do apes use language? *American Scientist, 68,* 49-61.

Savage-Rumbaugh, E.S., Sevcik, R.A., Rumbaugh, D.M., & Rubert, E. (1985). The capacity of animals to acquire language: Do species differences have anything to say to us? *Philosophical Transactions,* Royal Society of London, *B308,* 177-185.

Saxe, L., Doughterty, D., & Cross, T. (1985). The validity of polygraph testing: Scientific analysis and public controversy. *American Psychologist, 40,* 355-366.

Scarr, S., & Weinberg, R.A. (1976). IQ test performance of black children adopted by white families. *American Psychologist, 31,* 726-739.

Scarr, S., & Weinberg, R.A. (1983). The Minnesota adoption studies: Genetic differences and malleability. *Child Development, 54,* 260-267.

Schacht, T., & Nathan, P. (1977). But is it good for psychologists? Appraisal and status of DSM-III. *American Psychologist, 32,* 1017-1925.

Schachter, S. (1959). *The psychology of affiliation: Experimental studies of the sources of gregariousness.* Stanford, CA: Stanford University Press.

Schachter, S. (1971a). *Emotion, obesity and crime.* New York: Academic Press.

Schachter, S. (1971b). Some extraordinary facts about obese humans and rats. *American Psychologist, 26,* 129-144.

Schachter, S., & Gross, L. (1968). Manipulated time and eating behavior. *Journal of Personality and Social Psychology, 10,* 98-106.

Schachter, S., & Singer, J. (1962). Cognitive, social, and physiological determinants of emotional state. *Psychological Review, 69,* 379-399.

Schaffer, H.R., & Emerson, P.E. (1964). The development of social attachments in infancy. *Monographs of the Society for Research in Child Development, 29,* (Whole No. 94).

Schaie, K.W. (1983). Age changes in adult intelligence. In D. Woodruff & J. Birren (Eds.), *Again: Scientific perspectives and social issues* (2nd ed.). Monterrey, CA: Brooks-Cole.

Schaie, K.W., & LaBouvie-Vief, G. (1974). Generational versus ontogenetic components of change in adult cognitive behavior: A 14-year cross-sequential study. *Developmental Psychology, 10,* 305-320.

Scheerer, M. (1963). Problem-solving. *Scientific American, 208*(4), 118-128.

Schiffman, S.S. (1983). Taste and smell in disease. *New England Journal of Medicine, 308,* 1275-1279, 1337-1343.

Schiffman, S.S., Reynolds, M.L., & Young, F.L. (1981). *Introduction to multidimensional scaling.* New York: Academic Press.

Schildkraut, J.J., & Kety, S.S. (1967). Biogenic amines and emotion. *Science, 156,* 21-30.

Schmitt, R.C. (1966). Density, health and social disorganization. *Journal of the American Institute of Planners, 32,* 38-40.

Schrank, J. (1977). *Snap, crackle and popular taste: The illusion of free choice in America.* New York: Dell.

Schwartz, B. (1984). *Psychology of learning and behavior.* New York: Norton.

Scott, J.P. (1968). *Early experience and the organization of behavior.* Belmont, CA: Brooks-Cole.

Scott, J.P. (1971). Attachment and separation in dog and man. In H.R. Schaffer (Ed.). *The origin of human social relations.* New York: Academic Press.

Scott, J.P. (1972). *Animal behavior* (2nd ed.). Chicago: University of Chicago Press.

Scott, J.P. (1975). *Aggression* (2nd ed.). Chicago: University of Chicago Press.

Scott, J.P., & Fuller, J. (1965). *Genetics and the social behavior of the dog.* Chicago: University of Chicago Press.

Sears, D.O. (1983). The person-positivity bias. *Journal of Personality and Social Psychology, 44,* 233-250.

Sears, D.O., Peplau, L.A., Freedman, J.L., & Taylor, S.E. (1988). *Social psychology* (6th ed.). Englewood Cliffs, NJ: Prentice-Hall.

Seligman, M.E.P. (1970). On the generality of the laws of learning. *Psychological Review, 77,* 406-418.

Seligman, M.E.P. (1971). Phobias and preparedness. *Behavior Therapy, 2,* 307-320.

Seligman, M.E.P. (1972). Phobias and preparedness. In M.E.P. Seligman & J.L. Hagen (Eds.), *Biological boundaries of learning.* Englewood Cliffs, NJ: Prentice-Hall.

Seligman, M.E.P. (1974). Depression and learned helplessness. In R.J. Friedman & M.M. Katz (Eds.), *The psychology of depression: Contemporary theory and research.* Washington, DC: Winston-Wiley.

Seligman, M.E.P. (1975). *Helplessness: On depression, development and death.* San Francisco: Freeman.

Seligman, M.E.P., & Maier, S.F. (1967). Failure to escape traumatic shock. *Journal of Experimental Psychology, 74,* 1-9.

Selye, H. (1976). *The stress of life* (rev. ed.). New York: McGraw-Hill.

Selye, H. (1980). The stress concept today. In E. Kutash & L. Schlesinger (Eds.), *Handbook on stress and anxiety.* San Francisco: Jossey-Bass.

Shapiro, C., Bortz, R., Mitchell, D., Bartel, P., & Jooste, P. (1981). Slow-wave sleep: A recovery period after exercise. *Science, 214,* 1253-1254.

Shapiro, D. (1985). Clinical use of meditation as a self-regulation strategy. Comments on Holmes' conclusions and implications. *American Psychologist, 40,* 719-722.

Sheehan, P., & Tilden, J. (1983). Effects of suggestibility and hypnosis on accurate and distorted retrieval from memory. *Journal of Experimental Psychology: Learning, Memory and Cognition, 9,* 283-293.

Sheldon, W.H. (1954). *Atlas of men: A guide for somatotyping the adult male at all ages.* New York: Harper & Row.

Sherif, M. (1936). *The psychology of social norms.* New York: Harper & Row.

Sherman, J.E. (1978). U.S. inflation with trace and simultaneous fear conditioning. *Animal Learning and Behavior, 6,* 463-468.

Sherrick, C., & Cholewiak, R. (1986). Cutaneous sensitivity. In K. Boff, L. Kaufman, & J.P. Thomas (Eds.), *Handbook of perception and human performance* (Vol. 1). New York: Wiley.

Shinn, M., Rosario, M., Morch, H., & Chestnut, D. (1984). Coping with job stress and burn-out in the human services. *Journal of Personality and Social Psychology, 46,* 854-876.

Shostrom, E. (1964). An inventory for measurement of self-actualization. *Educational and Psychological Measurement, 24,* 207-218.

Simpson, J.B., & Routtenberg, A. (1973). Subfornical organ: Site of drinking elicitation by angiotensin II. *Science, 181,* 1172-1174.

Singer, J. (1984). *The human personality.* San Diego: Harcourt Brace Jovanovich.

Skalka, P. (1984). *The American Medical Association guide to health and well-being after fifty.* New York: Random House.

Skeels, H.M. (1942). A study of the effects of differential stimulation on mentally retarded children: A follow-up report. *American Journal of Mental Deficiency, 46,* 340-350.

Skeels, H.M. (1966). Adult status of children with contrasting early life experiences. *Monographs of the Society for Research in Child Development,* (Whole No. 31), 1-65.

Skinner, B.F. (1938). *The behavior of organisms: An experimental analysis.* East Norwalk, CT: Appleton-Century-Crofts.

Skinner, B.F. (1948). *Walden two.* New York: Macmillan.

Skinner, B.F. (1953). *Science and human behavior.* New York: Free Press.

Skinner, B.F. (1957). *Verbal behavior.* Englewood Cliffs, NJ: Prentice-Hall.

Skinner, B.F. (1958). Teaching machines. *Science, 128,* 969-977.

Skinner, B.F. (1961). Teaching machines. *Scientific American, 205,* 90-102.

Skinner, B.F. (1962). Two "synthetic social relations." *Journal of the Experimental Analysis of Behavior, 5,* 531-533.

Skinner, B.F. (1971). *Beyond freedom and dignity.* New York: Knopf.

Skinner, B.F. (1987). *Upon further reflection.* Englewood Cliffs, NJ: Prentice-Hall.

Skinner, B.F. (1987). What ever happened to psychology as the science of behavior? *American Psychologist, 42,* 780-786.

Skinner, B.F. (1988). *Personal communication.*

Skoklnick, P., & Heslin, R. (1971). Approval dependence and reactions to bad arguments and low credibility sources. *Journal of Experimental Research in Personality, 5,* 199-207.

Sleight, R.B. (1948). The effect of instrument dial shape on legibility. *Journal of Applied Psychology, 32,* 170-188.

Smith, A., & Stansfeld, S. (1986). Aircraft noise exposure, noise sensitivity, and everyday errors. *Environment and Behavior, 18*, 214-226.

Smith, D. (1982). Trends in counseling and psychotherapy. *American Psychologist, 37*, 802-809.

Smith, G., & Gibbs, J. (1976). Cholecystokinin and satiety: Theoretic and therapeutic implications. In D. Novin, W. Wihyrwicka, and G. Bray (Eds.), *Hunger: Basic mechanisms and clinical implications.* New York: Raven.

Smith, M.E. (1926). An investigation of the development of the sentence and the extent of vocabulary in young children. *University of Iowa Studies in Child Welfare, 3*(5), 1-92.

Smith, M.L., & Glass, G.V. (1977). Meta-analysis of psychotherapy outcome studies. *American Psychologist, 32*, 752-760.

Smith, M.L., Glass, G.V., & Miller, T.I. (1980). *The benefits of psychotherapy.* Baltimore: Johns Hopkins University Press.

Solomon, R.L. (1980). The opponent-process theory of acquired motivation: The costs of pleasure and the benefits of pain. *American Psychologist, 35*, 691-712.

Solomon, R.L., & Corbit, J.D. (1974). An opponent-process theory of motivation. I. Temporal dynamics of affect. *Psychological Review, 81*, 119-145.

Solomon, R.L., & Wynne, L.C. (1953). Traumatic avoidance learning: Acquisition in normal dogs. *Psychological Monographs, 67* (Whole No. 354).

Sommer, R. (1966). *Personal space.* Englewood Cliffs, NJ: Prentice-Hall.

Sommer, R., & Sommer, B. (1986). *A practical guide to behavioral research: Tools and techniques.* New York: Oxford University Press.

Sorce, J.F., Emde, R.N., Campos, J., & Klinnert, M.D. (1985). Maternal emotional signaling: Its effect on the visual cliff behavior of 1-year-olds. *Developmental Psychology, 21*, 195-200.

Spearman, C. (1904). General intelligence objectively determined and measured. *American Journal of Psychology, 15*, 201-293.

Speer, D.C. (1971). Rate of caller re-use of a telephone crisis service. *Crisis Intervention, 3*, 83-86.

Speilberger, C.D., & London, P. (1982). Rage boomerangs. *American Health, 1*, 52-56.

Sperling, G. (1960). The information available in brief visual presentations. *Psychological Monographs, 74*, (Whole No. 498), 1-29.

Sperry, R. (1968). Hemisphere deconnection and unity in conscious awareness. *American Psychologist, 23*, 723-733.

Spielberger, C.D., Johnson, E., Russell, S., Crane, R., Jacobs, G., & Worden, T. (1985). The experience and expression of anger. In M. Chesney, S. Goldston, & R. Rosenman (Eds.), *Anger and hostility in cardiovascular and behavioral disorders.* New York: Hemisphere.

Squire, L. (1982). The neuropsychology of human memory. *Annual Review of Neuroscience, 5*, 241-273.

Squire, L. (1987). *Memory and the brain.* New York: Oxford University Press.

Staats, S. (1983). Perceived sources of stress and happiness in married and single college students. *Psychological Reports, 52*, 179-184.

Stapp, J., Tucker, A., & VanderBos, G. (1985). Census of psychological personnel: 1983. *American Psychologist, 40*, 1317-1351.

Stassen, M., & Staats, S. (1988). Hope and happiness: A comparison of some discrepancies. *Social Indicators Research, 20*, 45-58.

Stechler, G., & Halton, A. (1982). Prenatal influences on human development. In B. Wolman (Ed.), *Handbook of developmental psychology.* Englewood Cliffs, NJ: Prentice-Hall.

Steinberg, L. (1988). Reciprocal relation between parent-child distance and pubertal maturation. *Developmental Psychology, 24*, 122-128.

Steiner, I.D. (1972). *Group processes and productivity.* New York: Academic Press.

Steiner, J. (1979). Facial expressions in response to taste and smell discrimination. In H. Reese & L. Lipsitt (Eds.), *Advances in child development and behavior* (Vol. 13). New York: Academic Press.

Sterling, P. (1983). Retinal microcircuitry. *Annual Review of Neuroscience*, 149-185.

Sternberg, R.J. (1982). Who's intelligent? *Psychology Today, 16*, 30-39.

Sternberg, R.J. (1984). Toward a triarchic theory of human intelligence. *The Behavioral and Brain Science, 7*, 269-315.

Sternberg, R.J. (1985). *Beyond IQ: A triarchic theory of human intelligence.* New York: Cambridge University Press.

Sternberg, R.J. (1986). *Intelligence applied: Understanding and increasing your intellectual skills.* San Diego: Harcourt Brace Jovanovich.

Sternberg, R.J. (1986). A triangular theory of love. *Psychological Review, 93*, 119-135.

Sternberg, R.J. (1987). Liking versus loving: A comparative evaluation of theories. *Psychological Bulletin, 102*, 331-345.

Sternberg, R.J., & Davidson, J. (1982). The mind of the puzzler. *Psychology Today, 16*, 37-44.

Sternberg, R.J., & Davidson, J.E. (1985). Cognitive development in the gifted and talented. In F.D. Horowitz & M. O'Brien (Eds.), *The gifted and talented: Developmental perspectives.* Washington, DC: American Psychological Association.

Sternberg, S. (1966). High-speed scanning in human memory. *Science, 153*, 652-654.

Sternberg, S. (1969). Memory-scanning: Mental processes revealed by reaction-time experiments. *American Scientist, 57*, 421-457.

Stevens, D., & Truss, C. (1985). Stability and change in adult personality over 12 and 20 years. *Developmental Psychology, 21*, 568- 584.

Stevens, J.C. (1979). Variation of cold sensitivity over the body surface. *Sensory Processes, 3*, 317-326.

Stevens, J.C., Marks, L.E., & Simonson, D.C. (1974). Regional sensitivity and spatial summation in the warmth sense. *Physiology and Behavior, 13*, 825-836.

Stier, D.S., & Hall, J.A. (1984). Gender differences in touch: An empirical and theoretical review. *Journal of Personality and Social Psychology, 47*, 440-459.

Stinnett, N., Walters, J., & Kaye, E. (1984). *Relationships in marriage and the family.* New York: Macmillan.

Stock, M.B., & Smythe, P.M. (1963). Does undernutrition during infancy inhibit brain growth and subsequent intellectual development? *Archives of Disorders in Childhood, 38*, 546-552.

Stokols, D. (1972). On the distinction between density and crowding: Some implications for future research. *Psychological Review, 79*, 275-277.

Stoner, J. (1961). A comparison of individual and group decisions involving risk. Unpublished master's thesis. Massachusetts Institute of Technology, School of Industrial Management.

Stotland, E., & Berberich, J. (1979). The psychology of the police. In H. Touch (Ed.), *Psychology of crime and criminal justice*. New York: Holt, Rinehart & Winston.

Straus, M., Gelles, R., & Steinmetz, S. (1980). *Behind closed doors: Violence in the American family*. Garden City, NJ: Anchor Books.

Striegel-Moore, R., Silberstein, L., & Rodin, J. (1986). Toward an understanding of risk factors for bulimia. *American Psychologist, 41*, 246-263.

Stroebe, M.S., & Stroebe, W. (1983). Who suffers more? Sex differences in health risks of the widowed. *Psychological Bulletin, 93*, 279-301.

Strongman, K.T. (1978). *The psychology of emotion* (2nd ed.). New York: Wiley.

Strupp, H., & Hadley, S. (1977). A tripartite model of mental health and therapeutic outcomes. *American Psychologist, 32*, 187-196.

Sue, D. (1979). Erotic fantasies of college students during coitus. *Journal of Sex Research, 15*, 299-309.

Sue, D., Sue, D., & Sue, S. (1986). *Understanding abnormal behavior* (2nd ed.). Boston: Houghton Mifflin.

Szasz, T.S. (1960). *The myth of mental illness*. New York: Harper & Row.

T

Tart, C. (1969). *Altered states of consciousness*. New York: Wiley.

Tavris, C., & Wade, C. (1984). *The longest war: Sex differences in perspective* (2nd ed.). San Diego: Harcourt Brace Jovanovich.

Taylor, J.A. (1953). A personality scale of manifest anxiety. *Journal of Abnormal and Social Psychology, 48*, 285-290.

Taylor, J.A., Gatchel, R., & Korman, M. (1982). Psychophysiological and cognitive characteristics of ulcer and rheumatoid arthritis patients. *Journal of Behavioral Medicine, 5*, 173-188.

Taylor, S.E. (1986). *Health psychology*. New York: Random House.

Terman, L.M. (1925). *Genetic studies of genius*. Stanford, CA: Stanford University Press.

Termine, N.T., & Izard, C.E. (1988). Infants' responses to their mothers' expressions of joy and sadness. *Developmental Psychology, 24*(2), 223-229.

Terrace, H.S. (1979). *Nim: A chimpanzee who learned sign language*. New York: Knopf.

Terrace, H.S. (1985). In the beginning was the "name." *American Psychologist, 40*, 1011-1028.

Thase, M., Frank, E., & Kupfer, D.J. (1985). Biological processes in major depression. In E. Beckham & W. Leber (Eds.), *Handbook of depression: Treatment, assessment, and research*. Homewood, IL: Dorsey.

Thayer, P.W. (1983). Industrial/organizational psychology: Science and application. In C.J. Scheirer & A.M. Rogers (Eds.), *The G. Stanley Hall lecture series* (Vol. 3). Washington, DC: American Psychological Association.

Thoits, P.A. (1983). Dimensions of life events as influences upon the genesis of psychological distress and associated conditions: An evaluation and synthesis of the literature. In H.B. Kaplan (Ed.), *Psychosocial stress: Trends in theory and research*. New York: Academic Press.

Thomas, A. & Chess, S. (1977). *Temperament and development*. New York: Brunner/Mazel.

Thomas, M.H. (1982). Physiological arousal, exposure to a relatively lengthy aggressive film, and aggressive behavior. *Journal of Research in Personality, 16*, 72-81.

Thompson, R. (1985). *The brain*. San Francisco: Freeman.

Thompson, R. (1986). The neurobiology of learning and memory. *Science, 233*, 941-947.

Thornburg, H. (1984). *Introduction to educational psychology*. St. Paul, MN: West.

Thorndike, E.L. (1911). *Animal intelligence*. New York: Macmillan.

Thorndike, E.L. (1932). *The fundamentals of learning*. New York: Teachers College Press.

Thurstone, L.L. (1938). Primary mental abilities. *Psychometric Monographs, 1*. Chicago: University of Chicago Press.

Tinbergen, N. (1952). The curious behavior of the stickleback. *Scientific American, 182*, 22-26.

Tolman, E.C. (1923). The nature of instinct. *Psychological Bulletin, 20*, 200-218.

Tolman, E.C. (1948). Cognitive maps in rats and men. *Psychological Review, 55*, 189-208.

Tolman, E.C., & Honzik, C.H. (1930). Introduction and removal of reward, and maze performance in rats. *University of California Publications in Psychology, 4*, 257-275.

Tomkins, S.S. (1962). *Affect imagery consciousness. Vol. 1, The positive affects*. New York: Springer.

Tomkins, S.S. (1981). The quest for primary motives: Biography and autobiography of an idea. *Journal of Personality and Social Psychology, 41*, 306-329.

Tomkins, S.S., & McCarter, R. (1964). What and where are the primary affects? Some evidence for a theory. *Perceptual and Motor Skills, 18*, 119-158.

Tracy, R., & Ainsworth, M.D.S. (1981). Maternal affectionate behavior and infant-mother attachment patterns. *Child Development, 52*, 1341-1343.

Tryon, , R.C. (1940). Genetic differences in maze-learning ability in rats. *Yearbook of the National Society for the Study of Education, 1*, 111-119.

Tulving, E. (1962). Subjective organization in free recall of unrelated words. *Psychological Review, 69*, 344-354.

Tulving, E. (1972). Episodic and semantic memory. In E. Tulving & W. Donaldson (Eds.), *Organization and memory*. New York: Academic Press.

Tulving, E. (1983). *Elements of episodic memory*. New York: Oxford University Press.

Tulving, E. (1985). How many memory systems are there? *American Psychologist, 40*, 385-398.

Tupes, E.C., & Christal, R.E. (1961). Recurrent personality factors based on trait ratings. *USAF ASD Technical Report* (No. 61-97).

Turing, A.M. (1950). Computing machinery and intelligence. *Mind, 59*, 433-460.

Turnbull, C.M. (1961). Some observations regarding the experience and behavior of Ba Mbuti Pygmies. *American Journal of Psychology, 74*, 304-308.

Turner, S.M., Beidel, D.C., & Nathan, R.S. (1985). Biological factors in obsessive compulsive disorders. *Psychological Bulletin, 97* 430-450.

Tybout, A., & Scott, C. (1983). Availability of well-defined internal knowledge and the attitude formation process: Information aggregation versus self-perception. *Journal of Personality and Social Psychology, 44*, 474-491.

U

Underwood, B.J. (1983). *Attributes of memory*. Glenview, IL: Scott, Foresman.

U.S. Bureau of the Census. (1982). Current population reports, Series P-20, No. 371. Washington, DC: U.S. Government Printing Office.

U.S. Department of Health, Education, and Welfare. (1980). *The health consequences of smoking for women: A report of the Surgeon General*. Washington, DC.

V

Valenstein, E.S. (1973). *Brain control*. New York: Wiley.

Valenstein, E.S. (1986). *Great and desperate cures*. New York: Basic Books.

Van Lawick-Goodall, J. (1971). *In the shadow of man*. New York: Dell.

Veninga, R.L., & Spradley, J.P. (1981). *The work stress connection*. Boston: Little, Brown.

Vernon, P.E. (1979). *Intelligence: Heredity and environment*. San Francisco: Freeman.

Veroff, J. (1957). Development and validation of a projective measure of power motivation. *Journal of Abnormal and Social Psychology*. 54, 1-8.

Veroff, J. (1982). Assertive motivations: Achievement versus power. In D. Winter & A.J. Stewart (Eds.). *Motivation and Society*. San Francisco: Jossey-Bass.

Von Békésy, G. (1957). The ear. *Scientific American*, 196, 66-78.

Von Frisch, K. (1967). *The dance language and orientation of bees* (L. Chadwick, Trans.). Cambridge, MA: Harvard University Press.

W

Wachtel, S. (1983). *H-Y antigen and the biology of sex determination*. New York: Grune & Stratton.

Wade, N. (1976). IQ and heredity: Suspicion of fraud beclouds classic experiment. *Science*, 194, 916-919.

Wadsworth, T. (1984). *Piaget's theory of cognitive and affective development*. New York: Longman.

Wagner, H.L., MacDonald, C.J., & Manstead, A.S.R. (1986). Communication of individual emotions by spontaneous facial expressions. *Journal of Personality and Social Psychology*, 50, 737-743.

Wallace, B., & Fisher, L. (1987). *Consciousness and behavior*, (2nd ed.). Boston: Allyn & Bacon.

Wallace, R., & Benson, H. (1972). The physiology of meditation. *Scientific American*, 226, 84-90.

Wallas, G. (1926). *The art of thought*. New York: Harcourt, Brace.

Walster, E., & Walster, G.W. (1978). *A new look at love*. Reading, MA: Addison-Wesley.

Walster, E., Walster, G.W., & Berscheid, E. (1978). *Equity theory and research*. Boston: Allyn & Bacon.

Warner, C. (1988). Understanding your learning disability. Unpublished manuscript. The Ohio State University.

Warren, D. (1982). The development of haptic perception. In

W. Schiff & E. Foulke (Eds.), *Tactual perception: A sourcebook*. Cambridge: Cambridge University Press.

Wason, P. (1968). On the failure to eliminate hypotheses—a second look. In P. Wason & P. Johnson-Laird (Eds.), *Thinking and reasoning*. Baltimore: Penguin.

Watson, J.B., & Rayner, R. (1920). Conditioned emotional reactions. *Journal of Experimental Psychology*, 3, 1-14.

Watson, J.D., & Crick, F. (1953). Genetical implications of the structure of deoxyribonucleic acid. *Nature*, 171, 964-967.

Webb, W.B. (1974). Sleep as an adaptive response. *Perceptual and Motor Skills*, 38, 1023-1027.

Webb, W.B. (1975). *Sleep: The gentle tyrant*. Englewood Cliffs, NJ: Prentice-Hall.

Webb, W.B. (1981). The return of consciousness. In L.T. Benjamin, Jr. (Ed.), *The G. Stanley Hall lecture series* (Vol. 1). Washington, DC: American Psychological Association.

Webb, W.B., & Campbell, S. (1983). Relationships in sleep characteristics of identical and fraternal twins. *Archives of General Psychiatry*, 40, 1093-1095.

Wechsler, D. (1975). Intelligence defined and undefined. *American Psychologist*, 30, 135-139.

Weil, A.T. (1973). *The natural mind*. Boston: Houghton Mifflin.

Weiner, B. (1985). *Human motivation*. New York: Springer-Verlag.

Weiner, B. (1986). *An attributional theory of motivation and emotion*. New York: Springer-Verlag.

Weiner, B., Freize, I., Kukla, A., Reed, L., Rest, S., & Rosenbaum, R. (1972). Perceiving the causes of success and failure. In E. Jones, D. Kanouse, H. Kelley, R. Nisbett, S. Valins, & B. Weiner (Eds.), *Attribution: Perceiving the causes of behavior*. Morristown, NJ: General Learning Press.

Weinstein, S. (1968). Intensive and extensive aspects of tactile sensitivity as a function of body part, sex, and laterality. In D. Kenshato (Ed.), *The skin senses*. Springfield, IL: Thomas.

Weisberg, R. (1986). *Creativity: Genius and other myths*. New York: Freeman.

Weiss, R. (1987). How dare we? *Science News*, 132, 57-59.

Weiten, W. (1983). *Psychology applied to modern life: Adjustment in the 1980s*. Monterey, CA: Brooks-Cole.

Weizenbaum, J. (1966). ELIZA—A computer program for the study of natural language communication between man and machine. *Communications of the Association for Computing Machinery*, 9, 36-43.

Weld, H., & Roff, M. (1938). A study of the formation of opinion based upon legal evidence. *American Journal of Psychology*, 51 609-628.

Wells, G.L., & Murray, D.M. (1983). What can psychology say about the Neil vs. Biggers criteria for judging eyewitness accuracy? *Journal of Applied Psychology*, 68, 347-362.

Wells, G.L., Wrightsman, L.S., & Miene, P.K. (1985). The timing of the defense opening statement: Don't wait until the evidence is in. *Journal of Applied Social Psychology*, 68, 347-362.

Wenzel, B.M. (1973). Chemoreception. In E.C. Carterette & M.P. Friedman (Eds.), *Handbook of perception (Vol. 3): Biology of perceptual systems*. New York: Academic Press.

Werner, E. (1979). *Cross-cultural child development*. Monterrey, CA: Brooks-Cole.

Wetzel, C., & Insko, C. (1982). The similarity-attraction relationship: Is there an ideal one? *Journal of Experimental Social Psychology*, 18, 253-276.

Wever, E.G. (1949). *Theory of hearing*. New York: Wiley.

Wever, E.G., & Bray, C. (1937). The perception of low tones and the resonance-volley theory. *Journal of Physiology, 3*, 101-114.

White, R.W. (1959). Motivation reconsidered: The concept of competence. *Psychological Review, 66*, 297-333.

Whitten, W.B., & Leonard, J. (1981). Directed search through autobiographical memory. *Memory and Cognition, 9*, 566-579.

Whorf, B.L. (1956). Language, thought and reality. In J.B. Carroll (Ed.), *Selected writings of Benjamin Lee Whorf*. New York: Wiley.

Wichman, H. (1970). Effects of isolation and communication on cooperation in a two-person game. *Journal of Personality and Social Psychology, 16*, 114-120.

Williams, R., & Long, J. (1983). *Toward a self-managed life style* (3rd ed.). Boston: Houghton Mifflin.

Williams, R.B., Barefoot, J., & Shekelle, R. (1984). The health consequences of hostility. In M. Chesney, S. Goldston, & R. Rosenman (Eds.), *Anger: Hostility in behavior medicine*. Washington, DC: Hemisphere.

Wilson, E.O. (1968). Chemical Systems. In T.A. Sebeok (Ed.), *Animal communication*. Bloomington, IN: Indiana University Press.

Wilson, E.O. (1975). *Sociobiology: The new synthesis*. Cambridge, MA: Harvard University Press.

Wilson, G.T., & O'Leary, K.D. (1980). *Principles of behavior therapy*. Englewood Cliffs, NJ: Prentice-Hall.

Wilson, R.S. (1983). The Louisville twin study: Developmental synchronies in behavior. *Child Development, 54*, 298-316.

Wilson, T.D., Goldin, J.C., & Charbonneau-Powis, M. (1983). Comparative efficacy of behavioral and cognitive treatments of depression. *Cognitive Therapy and Research, 7*, 111-124.

Wingfield, A., & Byrnes, D.L. (1981). *The psychology of human memory*. New York: Academic Press.

Winokur, G. (1985). The validity of neurotic-reactive depression: New data and reappraisal. *Archives of General Psychiatry, 42*, 1116-1122.

Winter, D.G. (1973). *The power motive*. New York: Free Press.

Winter, D.G. (1982). *The power motive in women*. Unpublished manuscript.

Wise, C.D., & Stein, L. (1973). Dopamine-beta-hydroxylase deficits in the brain of schizophrenic patients. *Science, 181*, 344-347.

Wise, R., & Bozarth, M. (1984). Brain reward circuitry: Four circuit elements "wired" in apparent series. *Brain Research Bulletin, 12*, 203-208.

Witkin, H.A. (1976). Cognitive style in academic performance and in teacher-student relations. In S. Messick (Ed.), *Individuality in learning*. San Francisco: Jossey-Bass.

Wolpe, J. (1958). *Psychotherapy by reciprocal inhibition*. Stanford, CA: Stanford University Press.

Woodworth, R.S. (1918). *Dynamic psychology*. New York: Columbia University Press.

Wright, L. (1988). The Type A behavior pattern and coronary artery disease: Quest for the active ingredients and the elusive mechanism. *American Psychologist, 43*, 2-14.

Y

Yinon, Y., Sharon, I., Gonen, Y., & Adam, R. (1982). Escape from responsibility and help in emergencies among persons alone or within groups. *European Journal of Social Psychology, 12*, 301-305.

Yonas, A. (1984). Reaching as a measure of infant spatial perception. In G. Gottlieb & N. Krasnegor (Eds.), *Measurement of audition and vision in the first year of postnatal life: A methodological review*. Norwood, NJ: Ablex.

Z

Zajonc, R.B. (1965). Social facilitation. *Science, 149*, 269-274.

Zajonc, R.B. (1984). On the primacy of affect. *American Psychologist, 39*, 117-123.

Zajonc, R.B. (1986). The decline and rise of scholastic aptitude scores: A prediction derived from the confluence model. *American Psychologist, 41*, 862-867.

Zajonc, R.B., & Markus, G.B. (1975). Birth order and intellectual development. *Psychological Review, 82*, 74-88.

Zeigler, H.P., & Leibowitz, H. (1957). Apparent visual size as a function of distance for children and adults. *American Journal of Psychology, 70*, 106-109.

Zerbin-Rubin, E. (1972). Genetic research and the theory of schizophrenia. *International Journal of Mental Health, 1*, 42-62.

Zhang, G., & Simon, H.A. (1985). STM capacity for Chinese words and idioms: Chunking and acoustical loop hypotheses. *Memory and Cognition, 13*, 193-201.

Zigler, E., & Berman, W. (1983). Discerning the future of early childhood intervention. *American Psychologist, 38*, 894-906.

Zigler, E., & Finn-Stevenson, M. (1987). *Children: Development and social issues*. Lexington, MA: Heath.

Zimbardo, P.G. (1977). *Shyness: What it is and what to do about it*. Reading, MA: Addison-Wesley.

Zimbardo, P.G. (1986). The Stanford Shyness Project. In W. Jones, J. Cheek, & S. Briggs (Eds.), *Shyness: Perspectives on research and treatment*. New York: Plenum.

Zimbardo, P.G., Andersen, S., & Kabat, L. (1981). Induced hearing deficit generates experimental paranoia. *Science, 212*, 1529-1531.

Zinkhan, G., & Syoiadin, L. (1984). Impact of sex role stereotypes on service priority in department stores. *Journal of Applied Psychology, 69*, 691-693.

Zubin, J., & Ludwig, A. (1983). What is schizophrenia? *Schizophrenic Bulletin, 9*, 331-334.

Zuckerman, M. (1979). *Sensation seeking: Beyond the optimal level of arousal*. Hillsdale, NJ: Erlbaum.

Zuckerman, M. (1980). Sensation seeking. In H. London and J. Exner (Eds.), *Dimensions of personality*. New York: Wiley.

Zuckerman, M. (1984). Experience and desire: A new format for sensation seeking scales. *Journal of Behavioral Assessment, 6*, 101-114.

Zuckerman, M., & Como, P. (1983). Sensation seeking and arousal systems. *Personality and Individual Differences, 4*, 381-386.

Zuckerman, M., & Wheeler, L. (1975). To dispel fantasies about the fantasy-based measure of fear of success. *Psychological Bulletin, 82*, 932-946.

Index

Page references in *italics* indicate figures, tables or other illustrative material.
Page references in **bold** indicate glossary terms.

A

Credits & Acknowledgments

continued from page iv

McAvoy, *Life* magazine, (c) 1955, Time Inc.   p. 156 The Bettmann Archive.   p. 162 "Long-Term Memory for a Common Object," by R. S. Nickerson and M. J. Adams, 1979, *Cognitive Psychology*, *11*, 287–307.   p. 164 UPI/Bettmann Newsphotos.   p. 165 UN photo by D. Siegel.   p. 166 Courtesy Elizabeth Loftus.   p. 177 UN photo by Jane Hanckel.   p. 179 *Speech Chain: The Physics & Biology of Spoken Language*, by P. B. Denes and E. N. Pinson, 1963, 1973, Murray Hill, NJ: AT&T Bell Laboratories.   p. 180 *Aspects of the Theory of Syntax* by N. Chomsky, 1966, Cambridge: MIT; "The Acquisition of Language," by B. A. Moskowitz, Nov. 1978, *Scientific American*, *239*(5), 92–108.   p. 181 Les Films du Carrosse, Paris, France.   p. 182 Black Star.   p. 185 "Problem Solving," by M. Scheerer, April 1963, *Scientific American*, *208*(4), 119; Yerkes Regional Primate Research Center, Emory University, Atlanta, GA.   p. 193 The Bettmann Archive.   p. 197 Mr. & Mrs. Langenderfer; "Familiar Studies of Intelligence," by Bouchard & McGue, 1981, *Science*, *212*, 1055–1059.   p. 200 UN photo by John Isaac; David S. Stricker—Monkmeyer Press Photo Service.   p. 201 UN photo by Y. Nagata.   p. 202 UN photo by L. Solmssen.   p. 203 Frank Lodge—NYT Pictures.   p. 209 Courtesy Peter M. Milner, McGill University.   p. 211 Ron Garrison (c) Zoological Society of San Diego; Laurence E. Perkins—Photo Researchers.   p. 214 Pamela Carley Petersen—DPG.   p. 215 UN photo by Gasten Guarda.   p. 216 Photo by William Carter, courtesy of Bertha Maslow.   p. 218 Cary Wolinsky—Stock, Boston.   p. 220 Courtesy Dr. Neal E. Miller.   p. 222 F. D. Schmidt (c) Zoological Society of San Diego.   p. 223 UN photo by John Isaac; University of Wisconsin Primate Laboratory.   p. 224 University of Wisconsin Primate Laboratory.   p. 225 Courtesy Lily K. Lai.   p. 227 UN photo by Margo Granitsas.   p. 232 Elaine Ward.   p. 233 Harry Wilks—Stock, Boston.   p. 234 Los Angeles Police Department.   p. 235 UN photo by John Isaac.   p. 236 *Emotion: A Psychoevolutionary Synthesis* by R. Plutchik, 1980, New York: Harper & Row; Daniel Brody—Stock, Boston.   p. 237 The Bettmann Archive.   p. 241 M. Marcuss Oslander; Cheryl Kinne—DPG.   p. 244 Gardner, Department of Psychology, University of Nevada; Courtesy Yerkes Primate Research Center, Emory University, Atlanta, GA.   p. 245 Ekman & Friesen Human Interaction Laboratory.   p. 246 UN photo by Michael Tzovaras.   p. 247 Courtesy Sean Connolly.   p. 250 Robert V. Eckert—EKM-Nepenthe.   p. 251 AP/Wide World Photos; Rick Brownie—Picture Group.   p. 257 "External Control and Internal Control," by J. Rotter, 1971, *Psychology Today*.   p. 260 Pictorial Parade.   p. 262 Culver Pictures.   p. 263 UPI/Bettmann Newsphotos.   p. 264 Institute for Personality and Ability Testing.   p. 267 *Motivation and Personality* by A. Maslow, 1970, New York: Harper & Row.   p. 268 UN photo; (c) Southern Christian Leadership Conference; The Bettmann Archive.   p. 269 Apple Computers.   p. 271 (c) Freda Leinwand—Monkmeyer Press Photo Service.   p. 272 Mimi Forsyth—Monkmeyer Press Photo Service.   p. 274 *Minnesota Multiphasic Personality Inventory Profile*, 1948, New York: The Psychological Corporation.   p. 275

Card 12F Thematic Apperception Test Manual, by H. Murray & staff of Harvard University Press, 1934, Cambridge, MA; Harvard University Press.   p. 279 UN photo by P. S. Sudhakaran.   p. 281 "Social Readjustment Rating Scale," by T. H. Holmes and R. H. Ruch, 1971, *The Journal of Psychosomatic Research*, *15*, 221–227.   p. 282 Melanie Kaestner Carr—Zephyr Picture Agency.   p. 284 M. Marcuss Oslander.   p. 285 (c) Edith G. Haun—Stock, Boston.   p. 286 *The Stress of Life*, by H. Selye, 1976, New York: McGraw-Hill.   p. 287 The Bettmann Archive.   p. 288 Paul S. Conklin—Monkmeyer Press Photo Service.   p. 289 Cheryl Kinne—DPG.   p. 293 (c) Dion Ogust—The Image Works.   p. 295 Photo by Augie Bevill, Magnolia, TX, Courtesy Scholastic Kodak Photography Awards.   p. 296 AP/Wide World.   p. 303 Zalesky/Clemmer—Black Star.   p. 305 UPI/Bettmann Newsphotos.   p. 307 American Psychiatric Association: *Diagnostic and Statistical Manual of Mental Disorders, 3rd ed.*, 1980, Washington, DC: American Psychiatric Association.   p. 308 UN photo by John Isaac.   p. 309 Cheryl Kinne—DPG.   p. 310 (c) W. Marc Bernsau—The Image Works.   p. 311 UPI/Bettmann Newsphotos.   p. 313 Derek Bayes—*Life* magazine, (c) Time Inc.   p. 315 Grunnitus—Monkmeyer Press Photo Service.   p. 319 AP/Wide World.   p. 323 New Castle State Developmental Center.   p. 325 Culver Pictures.   p. 326 Judith D. Sedwick—The Picture Cube.   p. 327 Tim Koors—NYT Pictures.   p. 328 Michael Rougler—*Life* magazine, (c) Time Inc.   p. 329 Photo by Allan Grant, courtesy Dr. Ivar Lovars.   p. 332 Albert Bandura, Stanford University.   p. 333 Curt Gunther—Camera 5.   p. 334 Mark Antman—The Image Works.   p. 336 Bohdan Hrynewych—Stock, Boston.   p. 340 Will McIntyre—Photo Researchers.   p. 345 (c) 1965 by Stanley Milgram, film *Obedience*, courtesy Alexandra Milgram.   347 Robert Kalman—The Image Works.   p. 348 Robert Kalman—The Image Works.   p. 351 Robert Kalman—The Image Works.   p. 352 UPI/Bettmann Newsphotos.   p. 353 American Cancer Society.   p. 354 Photo by Karen Zebulon, courtesy Leon Festinger.   p. 355 UN photo by John Isaac.   p. 356 UN photo by Faust.   p. 358 Cheryl Kinne—DPG.   p. 361 Photo by Erik Kroll, courtesy Alexandra Milgram.   p. 362 UN photo by Bedrich Grunzweig.   p. 363 WHO photo by L. Almsay/E. Mandelmann.   p. 365 Daniel S. Brody—Stock, Boston.   p. 366 Robert V. Eckert, Jr.—EKM-Nepenthe; (c) Bohdan Hrynewych—Stock, Boston.   p. 367 (c) Elizabeth Crews—Stock, Boston.   p. 368 Albert Bandura, Stanford University.   p. 369 Peter Menzei—Stock, Boston.   p. 370 (c) ABC-TV News, 1982/AP/Wide World.   p. 371 "The Unresponsive Bystander: Why Doesn't He Help?" by B. Latané and J. Darley, 1970, adapted by permission of Prentice-Hall.   p. 375 Philip Zimbardo, Stanford University.   p. 376 Courtesy Philip Zimbardo.   p. 377 UN photo.   p. 380 National Archives.   p. 381 Jim Pickerell—Chick/Chicago.   p. 382 Courtesy Anne Anastasi.   p. 383 Alan Carey—The Image Works.   p. 385 (c) Revlon, Inc.   p. 386 Pamela Carley Petersen—DPG.   p. 387 UN photo by David Burnett.   p. 388 Pamela Carley Petersen—DPG.   p. 389 New York Convention & Visitors Bureau.   p. 390 Robert V. Eckert, Jr.—Stock, Boston.   p. 391 M. Marcuss Oslander.   p. 393 Harriet Gans—The Image Works.

Staff

Editor M. Marcuss Oslander
Production Manager Brenda S. Filley
Designer Charles Vitelli
Photo Editor Pamela Carley Petersen
Typesetting Coordinator Libra Ann Cusack
Typesetter Juliana Arbo
Systems Coordinator Richard Tietjen
Production Assistant Lynn Shannon
Proofreader Diane Barker

The body of the text was set in Times Roman, captions were set in Omega and glossary entries were set in Triumvirate.

Charts and graphs were rendered by Charles Vitelli.

Anatomical figures were drawn by Mel Erikson.

The text was printed in narrow web offset lithography and bound by the Banta Company, Inc., at Harrisonburg, VA. The text paper is 50 lb. Butte des Morts.

The cover material is 10 pt. Carolina coated one-side (softbound) and an impregnated Latex Type II (Alcolite S11), non-woven stock manufactured by Appleton Papers, Inc., Appleton, WI (casebound).

Cover design by Charles Vitelli. Illustration is *Future Therapies*, collage by Frederick Otnes.